Author of:

Mystery & History in Georgia, Volumes I & II (2022 & 2023)
Some Genealogy Keys to Some Georgia Family Trees (2023)
Memories of Army Life and MPs of the 529th (2023)
John Henry "Doc" Holliday: A Simple Matter of Survival (2023)
After All That We've Been Through (2024)

Table of Contents

Foreword

In the pioneer days of what today is the state of Georgia, intrepid explorers, desperadoes, and opportunists of all types and description emigrated to the state, many of them ultimately continuing westward in search of a new life. It was a great movement documented in the concept of "Manifest Destiny" which helped to shape the modern nation known today as the United States.

These travelers invariably were characterized by three main types of individuals: <u>gunmen</u> who were either intent upon self-defense or upon the taking of whatever they wanted from whomever they wished whenever they wished; <u>lawmen</u> who were either simply honest men intent upon obeying the laws of that day or men serving as genuine law enforcement officers. And then there was the third type who were just plain "<u>wild men</u>" by nature. They weren't necessarily criminal in nature, but many times were individuals who were just as unpredictable, and loathe to tolerate any nonsense from anyone attempting to take advantage of or harm them.

It is difficult for many in today's "civilized" society to imagine the harsh realities of those days in the wilderness of early America, where confrontations with Native Americans could quickly become inflamed to violence, and daily hazards of travel across an uncharted wilderness were a constant threat to life. And if that wasn't bad enough, there were thieves and highwaymen aplenty who were fully prepared to rape, rob, and pillage whomever and whatever might be alone and vulnerable in this wilderness.

To be certain, the exploration and settlement of early Georgia – just like the nation as a whole – was an endeavor in which usually only the strong survived. There were no corner drug stores from which an influenza vaccine or an antibiotic might be purchased; nor reliable automobiles in which safe, comfortable and quick travel might be obtained, nor AAA "Horse" Service which might provide emergency assistance if one's mount pulled up lame.

There also were no emergency hospitals for serious injuries, nor convenient Howard Johnson Motor Inns in which one might sleep the night away, comfortable and safe. If the traveler encountered an emergency and was unable to manage it him or herself, that injured or ill individual many times simply died. It was just as simple as that. There was no "9-1-1" emergency rescue option.

The only mode of transportation for most of these pioneers was that provided by one's own feet and the occasional horse or mule if one was lucky enough to have such. One traveled in the freezing cold and numbing rains of winter and in a blazing hot tick, chigger, scorpion, poison ivy and venomous snake-infested wilderness in summer. At every turn, one had to guard against the numerous grizzly bears, mountain lions, immense wolves and other dangerous wildlife which were ever-present and constantly confronted.

At night, if one even hoped to awaken in the morning, one or more individuals not only "volunteered," but were required to stand guard and remain awake while the others struggled for sleep, shivering on the cold hard earth around a bleak campfire. It was an ultra-miserable existence at best, and at worst, even the natural elements were life-threatening.

Worse yet, this uncharted region had no roads which one might use in these dangerous travels, and certainly no signage to suggest the proper route. To the contrary, there was a vast ocean of virgin almost-impenetrable forests and thick undergrowth through which one many times was forced to hack and cut his way; the soaring Blue Ridge Mountains which one had to scale; unpredictable wildlife at every turn; and rushing un-bridged and dangerous rivers and streams which one had to somehow ford to continue westward – always westward.

This type of existence required extremely-determined and unbelievably-hardened individuals – both male and female – to successfully complete such a trek and ultimately establish a new home in this wild land. Those who were weak-willed, poorly-constituted, and not of sufficient physical strength and skills, died out quickly. Many of their graves still litter the remaining forests and exist anonymously beneath the present-day asphalt jungles and homes of modern man, totally unbeknownst to present-day citizens.

Within this mass of travelers could be found those accustomed to obeying the laws of man and honoring the precepts of Biblical training. They usually made excellent dependable citizens, friends and neighbors.

Also included, however, were those of evil and greedy intent who cared little about their fellow man, and had no compunction whatsoever about the commission of the worst crimes known to man in the pursuit of their ill-gotten gains. They observed few if any laws of society, making up their rules as they went along, instilling terror and despair into those they encountered along the way.

And then there were those possessed of that nature implicit in honest and dependable individuals who simply sought an existence where no civilized man or woman had previously trod. They desired only free land – which was abundant in America in those days – and a peaceful co-existence with nature, free from the constraints of or abuse by their fellow man. Sometimes wild in nature, these individuals also were many times possessed of unusual physical strength and determination, both of which allowed them to persevere where others feared to tread.

Most all of the individuals described on the pages within this book fall into one or more of these categories. Many of them were courageous, strong and independent almost to the extreme, and are often remembered for their admirable qualities in the folklore of Americana. Their stories have been passed down by word-of-mouth and in written accounts and histories simply because they warranted remembrance.

Those in the other extremes are recalled for the abuses – and sometimes even the horrible crimes – they perpetrated upon their fellow man, leaving damaged and destroyed humanity in their wake.

This, then, is the story of some of these individuals.

The Birthplace and Grim Life Of Gangster "Pretty Boy" Floyd

Though little-known today, one of America's most infamous criminals was born and lived his formative years in the town of Adairsville, Georgia.

Most Georgians and historians alike, are unaware that one of the most notorious criminals in U.S. history was born in the sleepy north Georgia town of Adairsville. Charles Arthur "Pretty Boy" Floyd lived most of his life in Oklahoma but was nevertheless Georgian by birth. He also was ultimately listed on the Federal Bureau of Investigation's (FBI) "Ten Most Wanted Criminals" list and died in a hail of gunfire in Ohio.

The house in which Floyd was born still stands (as of this writing) at 102 Railroad Street[1] in Adairsville. The Floyd, Murphey, Pinson, Echols, Gaines, and other families – many members of which still reside in the area – are related to this outlaw. These families came to Cass (now Bartow) County from South Carolina shortly after the removal of the Cherokees in 1838.[2]

Family Roots

Charles Floyd's great-great-great-grandfather, Roger Murphey, Jr., migrated to Cass from Laurens County, South Carolina in the early days of the settlement of America. He and his father had both held property in Laurens, giving them a financial base from which to ultimately acquire land in the Georgia counties of Forsyth, DeKalb, and Cass.[3]

The two men apparently entertained the prospect of becoming part of the "planter elite" class just beginning to take hold in the South. This becomes even more obvious when considering their real estate investments, and their known desire to acquire slaves and engage in large-scale agricultural endeavors.

Though their professional intentions were steadfast, the Murpheys never quite achieved the status they desired. They were able to purchase a number of slaves to help in their farming efforts, but they ultimately wound up laboring right along beside their workers just to be able to claim a profit at the end of each growing season. Such was the unfortunate lot of many yeoman farmers in the pre-Civil War South.

In 1854 when Roger passed away, his estate was divided among his children. His home and property were purchased by his son, John, who used a portion of the slaves to continue farming.[4]

John Murphey's wife, Frances, has been described by relatives as a hearty individual. She also undoubtedly was

The Echols family lived in the Towes Chapel area of Bartow County, near Cassville. Charles Arthur Floyd (front row, 1st from left) was photographed here with his Echols relatives circa 1909. (Photo courtesy of Father Phillip Paul Scott)

quite brave and out-going. According to accounts of her life, it was not uncommon for her to saddle-up her horse and ride the many miles back to South Carolina to visit relatives and friends. This was no easy trek, particularly for a woman in the mid-19th century, and the fact that she accomplished it alone makes it even more compelling.[5]

When John and Frances Murphey died, their farm was purchased by a daughter and son-in-law – Redding and Katherine Murphey Floyd. Redding was the son of Samuel and Patience Pinson Floyd. The Pinsons were of the "Particular Baptist" faith. A number of Pinson family members worked as millwrights in South Carolina and continued their tradition in Cass County, Georgia, constructing a number of water-powered mills in the area.[6]

Hard Times

Charles Arthur "Pretty Boy" Floyd's great-grandfather, Redding Floyd, had two brothers – Newport and Jasper. Floyd family members, for various and sundry reasons, had begun moving away from Cass County prior to the U.S. Civil War. Newport and Jasper followed this

trend, migrating to Arkansas circa late 1850s.

According to family lore, the pair had gotten as far as Arkansas when they stopped at a cabin to inquire about directions to Fort Smith, which at that time was one of the few sites representing "law & order" west of the Arkansas River. An elderly gentleman who lived in the cabin provided the requested information, then, apparently in the process of the conversation, he learned that the two men with whom he was conversing were from Georgia. When, in the midst of his conversation, he learned that the men were Floyds from "Cass County," Georgia, he was stunned, suddenly exclaiming that he was their father – Samuel Floyd.

It seems that in years prior, Samuel and Patience Pinson Floyd had split up, as was sometimes the case in those days, just as today. Samuel had moved away and the family had never heard from him again.

Apparently determined never to lose his "family" again, the old gentleman seems to have accompanied Newport and Jasper to their new home, because the *1860 Census of Arkansas* indicates that he was living in Newport's household at that time.[7]

Meanwhile, back in Georgia, the boys' other brother – Redding – had decided to remain behind, farming the old Murphey place. At the time of the Civil War, he owned three slaves and the farm, which apparently produced a reasonable living for his family.

In November of 1862, Redding enlisted in Company F of the 12th Georgia Cavalry in Kingston, Georgia. His brother-in-law, Matthias Murphey, wrote a letter to Redding on January 18, 1863, not knowing that Redding had already enlisted. His letter, in part, indicates that even at that early date, morale was a definite problem within the Confederate ranks:

".... I understand that you have a couple of heirs (referring to Redding's recently born twins) at your house and I wish you great sicess (sic) in raising of them... Red, between me and you and the gait post we have got the meanest Colonel in the confederate service. I never shall like Abda Johnson (later mayor of Cartersville, Georgia) *any more as long as I live. ... Red the Soldiers are all getting very tired of this war and if it is not stopt shortly they will stop it themselves by throwing down their muskets and going home. I am going to stay til July and if they don't let me come home on fair terms I am coming on fowl terms. This is the worst place we have been camped at yet - bad water, bad beef and bad weather."*[8]

Starting Anew In The West

The advent of the U.S. Civil War, understandably, had a progressively-ly-damaging impact upon general farming in the South. Slaves became more and more difficult to manage; necessary products became more and more difficult to obtain as naval blockades eliminated access to the coastal ports; and the Confederate dollars purchased less and less as the war progressed.

And as if this were not bad enough, in 1863, President Abraham Lincoln issued his now-famous dictum, the "Emancipation Proclamation" setting most of the slaves in the South free. Lincoln, however, made no effort to hide the fact that he was using emancipation not in a noble endeavor to free an enslaved people, but rather in a concerted strategic effort to cripple the commerce of the South after it had become painfully clear in the early years of the war that the North might actually be defeated by the

The house in which Charles Arthur Floyd was born and lived the early part of his life still stands as of this writing (2024) at 102 Railroad Street in Adairsville, GA.

South. *(Northern armies – though four times the size of Southern armies in this war – lost battle after battle and engagement after engagement almost continuously until 1863. Check the record.)* Lincoln was desperate for victory.

As a result, with the eventual culmination of the war and the utter devastation it had wrought upon the South, many Southerners – the Floyds and Murpheys included – yearned for a new beginning and struck out for the West, abandoning their Georgia property to whomever wished to take it. From Anderson County, Texas in 1870, C.M. Murphey wrote to his brother-in-law, Redding Floyd, about the great promise of post-war Texas:

"Texas looks like a world of cotton. People kill all their meat out of the woods as fat as they are in georgia when we feed them 10 Bushels of corn apiece. use cast plows never sharpen them. cheaper than iron plows on Georgia. Water better than I expected to find."[9]

Redding Floyd received the same kind of mail extolling the virtues of Pike County, Arkansas from his brother, Jasper. This love affair with the West continued in the Floyd and Murphey families, but Redding, strangely, was never enticed to leave his native Bartow County farm, despite the devastation and poverty all around him beginning in 1864.

One reason Redding never departed was his elderly mother for whom he tenderly cared. He reportedly simply did not want to uproot her and take her on the long, dangerous journey westward.[10]

Though Redding chose to remain behind, a second wave of migratory Floyds and their allied kin followed the final land rush which began in 1895 and continued until around 1915. The *Land Rush of 1895* was the smallest and last land run in Oklahoma, and occurred as the result of a relocation agreement between the Kickapoo tribe and the U.S. federal government.

The opening of the former Indian territory and the opportunity it offered to acquire fertile agricultural lands at limited or no cost was simply too much for many intrepid pioneers – including the Floyds – to resist. It was particularly tempting for those young enough and eager to start anew in a more productive location. Redding Floyd, however, was unmoved.

Formative Years Of "Pretty Boy"

One of the families that went West during this second exodus (around 1912) was that of Redding's grandson, Walter Floyd, whose son was a young Charles Arthur Floyd, called "Charlie" by the family.[11] Charlie had been born in Adairsville on February 3, 1904, living most of his formative years in that community.

Walter Floyd had married Mamie Echols in 1897 in Bartow County. Mamie's mother - Emily Elizabeth Gaines Echols – wife of Elmer Echols – hailed from one of the South's most illustrious families – the Gaines – of Culpepper County, Virginia.[12]

Charles Arthur "Pretty Boy" Floyd is remembered primarily as a bank robber in the annals of U.S. criminal history. From time to time, however, he is also anointed with the mantle of a folk hero. He was occasionally described as *"the Robin Hood of the Cookson Hills."*

While robbing banks in that area, Floyd reportedly tore up first mortgages, hoping they had not yet been recorded. This act, if true, freed many of the destitute Depression-era families from loan obligations when hard cash was almost nonexistent.[13]

Today, the official FBI file on the career of Charles Floyd is in excess of 15,000 pages. Books, magazine articles, and movies have chronicled his life and times, often substituting fiction for fact to embellish circumstances.

Though his personality turned criminal almost from his adolescence forward, Charlie actually came from a very law-abiding family. His brother, E.W. Floyd, served many terms as sheriff of Sequoyah County, Oklahoma, and was highly respected in the law enforcement community. A cousin, Duff Floyd, was a famed revenue officer of north Georgia. On one occasion when he was asked what he would have done had Charles Floyd crossed his path, Duff reportedly replied "I would have arrested him like any other criminal."[14]

Today, it is unknown for certain whether or not Charles "Pretty Boy" Floyd ever returned to Georgia to the land of his youth. According to folklore, however, he did once hide out in a house on Montgomery Street in Cartersville, Georgia.

Beginning A Life Of Crime

Floyd's first run-in with law enforcement personnel occurred in Akin, Oklahoma, in 1922, when he was 18

4

years of age. According to accounts of the incident, he took $350.00 in pennies from the post office there. This might seem like a somewhat modest sum today, but in 1922, it was the equivalent of approximately $6,595.00 in 2024 dollars. Though he was convicted of the theft, Charles was sentenced only to probation.

For a short period of time, Charles seemed to follow "the straight and narrow," moving to Sallisaw, Oklahoma, where he found work as a plumber and baker. Two years later (1924), at the age of 20, he married 16-year-old Wilma Ruby Hardgrave. Marriage and the grind of a daily job however apparently proved to be a lifestyle to which Charles simply could never adjust.

It wasn't long before he was back up to his old tricks. In 1925, he and an accomplice robbed a St. Louis, Missouri, Kroger store of $11,984.00 (equivalent to approximately $222,240.00 in 2024 dollars). In that day and time, this obviously was an extremely profitable robbery – more than enough to retire upon in 1925 – but Floyd seemingly was like "a moth to flame" when it came to crime. He simply couldn't resist it.

For the St. Louis robbery, Floyd was ultimately arrested at his home in Sallisaw. He was again convicted of the crime, and this time he was sent to the Missouri State Penitentiary at Jefferson City for five years.

While Charles was in prison, Ruby gave birth to their only son, Jack Dempsey Floyd. Though she loved their son, Ruby apparently had given up on Charles, and divorced him shortly after Jack's birth. Later, the couple reconciled for a short period of time – without "benefit of clergy" – but then separated permanently.

After he was released from the state

The home of Redding Floyd, great-grandfather of Charles Arthur Floyd, still stands as of this writing (2024) in Folsom, GA. Redding and his wife, Katheryn, are buried nearby in Macland Cemetery. (Photo courtesy of Father Phillip Paul Scott)

penitentiary, Charles was unrepentant, and resumed his criminal lifestyle almost immediately. He and a friend, Bert Walker, stole a car and robbed a bank in Sylvania, Ohio.

By coincidence, while making a raid on a Kenmore Boulevard home, Officer Sherman Gandee of the Akron Police encountered Floyd and Walker. During an ensuing gun battle, Officer Harland F. Manes was shot dead by Walker.

A phone number discovered among the duo's items in the Kenmore Boulevard house led to another house on Lodi Street in Akron where Floyd and Walker were subsequently captured. Walker eventually earned an appointment with the electric chair for his deeds. Meanwhile, Floyd, on his way to the Ohio State Penitentiary, amazingly jumped out of a train window and successfully escaped.

First Murders

Charles eventually found his way to Toledo, Ohio, where two brothers, William and Wallace Ash, befriended him. It was a friendship, however, that apparently was not reciprocated by Floyd,

Charles Arthur "Pretty Boy" Floyd was photographed following an arrest in Colorado. (Photo courtesy of Western History Collection, University of Oklahoma Library)

who, by this point, had assumed a murderous personality. The Ash brothers were later discovered dead from gunshot wounds to the head. Their wives and Floyd had left town and later turned up in Kentucky.

Bowling Green, Kentucky, was the scene of Charles' next crime spree. He, William "Baby Face Billy" Miller, and the Ash women were at a Bowling Green hardware store when Officer Ralph Castner reportedly approached their car. Witnesses, who later identified Floyd, stated he opened fire on the policeman who was killed in the fray along with Miller. A ballistics analysis later matched the bullets in the policeman with those from the heads of the Ash brothers.

By this time, Floyd was now a suspect in three murders. In his career, he ultimately stood accused of killing twelve men, ten of whom were officers

of the law. Floyd now was long past the point of no return.

From May through December of 1931, Charles allegedly committed some fifteen bank robberies in Missouri, Kansas, and Oklahoma. When the governor of Oklahoma posted a $1,000.00 reward for Floyd's capture, the daring criminal promptly sent the good governor a letter.

"You either withdraw that $1,000 at once or suffer the consequences," Floyd penned. *"No kidding, I have robbed no one but moneyed men. Floyd."*

Despite the reward (which was not withdrawn), Floyd was not caught. From June through December of 1932, he continued his odyssey, staging robberies in some 40 additional banks, establishing himself as one of the top criminals in the nation.

On June 16, 1933, Floyd, Adam "Eddy" Richetti, and Vern Miller, allegedly made an unsuccessful attempt to free their friend, Frank Nash, who was being transferred to a federal prison. The effort, which was made at Union Station in Kansas City, resulted in a shoot-out between federal officers and Floyd and his accomplices. Agent Raymond J. Caffrey of the Federal Bureau of Investigation lived just long enough to identify his attackers as a group led by "Pretty Boy" Floyd.

Kansas City Massacre

Following the "Kansas City Massacre," as it came to be known, the Kansas City Police received a postcard from the ever-colorful Floyd.

"Dear Sirs:

"I, Charles Floyd, want it made known that I did not participate in the masacree (sic) of officers at Kansas City. Charles Floyd."

The postcard had been mailed in Oklahoma which prompted Gov.

Murray to send the National Guard into Floyd's old lair in the Cookson Hills again. They did indeed flush the criminal out, but the ever-wily Floyd escaped once again.

Charles turned up next in Cresco, Ohio. The police in Cresco also cornered Charles, but he miraculously shot his way out to freedom once again. Accompanied by two women, he and Adam Richetti reunited and made their way to Wellsville, Ohio, where their car developed mechanical problems.

While the two women took the car to be repaired, Floyd and Richetti hid out in the nearby hills. A suspicious local resident spotted the two men and reported them to the Wellsville Police Department.

Chief John Fultz, along with his deputy, Grover Potts, went to investigate the reported strange men. A gun battle ensued. Richetti was captured, but Floyd escaped yet again. He had lost his machine gun, but he still had his two .45 caliber pistols.

His Last Day

On Monday, October 22, 1934, Mrs. Ellen Conkle was scrubbing her floors when she noticed a man in her driveway. She did not know it at the time, but she was face-to-face with one of the most notorious criminals of all time.

Floyd said he needed a ride into Youngstown, and Mrs. Conkle replied that her brother could oblige. Floyd was already seated in the car with Mrs. Conkle's brother when two other cars drove up the driveway.

Realizing that the cars contained police officers, Floyd jumped out and ran for cover behind the Conkles' corn crib. East Liverpool officer, Chester Smith, saw Charles and advanced on the corn crib. Floyd ran again, and Smith fired

A "Wanted" poster for outlaw Charles Arthur Floyd. The Federal Bureau of Investigation and its director – J. Edgar Hoover – named Floyd "Public Enemy No. 1" on July 23, 1934, following the death of notorious bank robber John Dillinger who had previously held the dubious #1 honor. Local police and FBI agents led by Agent Melvin Purvis shot Floyd on October 22, 1934, in a cornfield in East Liverpool, Ohio. Accounts differ on who actually shot him and the manner in which he was actually killed.

two shots at the elusive outlaw. One of the rounds hit Floyd in the back and knocked him off his feet.

The account of what next transpired depends upon what one wishes to believe. According to one respected account, at the very least, FBI agent Melvin Purvis closed in on Floyd – who was lying on the ground, seriously wounded in the shoulder, and disarmed him.

The circumstances of what next transpired are, at best, sketchy today. It has, however, been reported that rather than risk a hung jury and/or the lives of further law enforcement personnel, Purvis left it to an agent named Hawless to deal finally with Floyd. Whatever actually occurred, Charles "Pretty Boy" Floyd – in addition to the round he had taken through his shoulder – ended up

Pictured is the death mask taken of Charles Arthur Floyd following his embalming. His last words reportedly were "You got me twice," which he reportedly uttered to FBI agent Melvin Purvis as he was being questioned. Though fatally wounded in a cornfield a number of times as he fled his final capture, Floyd believed he had only been hit twice.

with a bullet hole through the heart, and "DRT" ("Dead Right There").

The life and bloody career of Charles "Pretty Boy" Floyd thus ended on a lonely Ohio farm, a long way from the criminal's north Georgia roots. In an ironic twist of fate, most modern-day references to Floyd list his hometown as Akin, Oklahoma, and it was to that locale that his body was conveyed for burial.

Today, as of this writing, no historic marker identifies the house (which still stands) in which Floyd was born and in which he lived during his early years in Adairsville, Georgia. Also as of this writing, however, an effort is underway to identify the site at which Floyd died in Ohio.

Endnotes

1/ Interview with Mrs. Bessie Darby, March, 1995. Also, telephone interview with city clerk, city of Adairsville, Georgia, March, 1995.

2/ Early deed books in the office of the Clerk of the Superior Court of Bartow County indicate many titles recorded to these families in the 1830s and '40s. See also the 1840 U.S. Census Population Schedule for Cass County, Georgia.

3/ See land title records, Laurens County, South Carolina and Forsyth, DeKalb and Cass counties, Georgia. The Murphey farming operation in DeKalb County seems to have been conducted by Roger's son, Charles, while the farm in Cass County was managed primarily by Roger and John. Little is known about the Forsyth County Land.

4/ Letters of Administration, Administration Returns, and Inventories for 1855-56, Office of the Probate Judge, Bartow County, Georgia.

5/ Fannie Mae Floyd Moss interview, 1983. Fannie Mae Floyd Moss owned the old Redding Floyd farm until her death. She was the custodian of the old farm, and also was an unofficial repository of a wealth of folklore and stories involving the family line of Charles Arthur Floyd.

6/ Pinson genealogical data in the files of the author.

7/ Pike County, Arkansas population schedule for the 1860 and 1870 Censuses of the United States.

8/ Fannie Mae Floyd Moss papers. Photo copy in the collection of the author.

9/ Fannie Mae Floyd Moss papers in the custody of Katheryn Floyd, Ed.D.

10/ Fannie Mae Floyd Moss interview, 1983.

11/ Dale Floyd interview (Walter Floyd's grandson), 1992. As of this writing, Mr. Floyd resides in Oklahoma and is the nephew of Charles Arthur Floyd.

12/ Mary Kathryn Gaines Korstian, "History Of The Gaines Family," Rome, Georgia: Brazelton-Wallis, 1973.

13/ Sandy Lesberg. "A Picture History Of Crime," New York: Haddington House, 1976, pp 109-110. Most of the material concerning Charles Arthur Floyd's career after he left Georgia was drawn from an extensive feature in the Sunday Magazine of the "Akron Beacon Journal," Akron, Ohio, October 20, 1974.

14/ Telephone interview with Katheryn Floyd, Ed. D., daughter of Duff Floyd. The author personally recalls hearing Mr. Floyd recount this statement once at a family reunion..

Wild & Wooley Robberies Of Old Taylorsville Bank

Taylorsville Bank has been a mainstay in the farming community of southeastern Bartow County almost since the days of the pioneers. The immensely-rich loam in these alluvial soils attracted farmers who in turn needed banking facilities to carry on their profession. Due to its locale, the small bank founded here has enjoyed almost no competition over the years, but its isolated nature also caused it to become a target of bandits, many of whom, surprisingly, proved to be comically inept.

It was during the desperate years of the 1930s and '40s, when gangsters first came into vogue as a result of the Great Depression that the small banking facility in tiny Taylorsville, Georgia, rose to fame as a target of bandits. It, amazingly, was robbed time and again, but due to the Federal Depositors Insurance Corporation (FDIC) and other assurances, coupled with its status as a bank with very limited competition, the Bank of Taylorsville not only weathered the storms, but thrived. And in 1976, the last bandits discovered the little bank isn't such an easy hit anymore.

Interestingly, the events which often transpired during the various robberies at this bank many times resembled a comic opera rather than vicious and violent acts, and many area residents still chuckle in remembrance of some of the circumstances of one or more of these occasions. With its isolated location and former limited law enforcement personnel, the Bank of Taylorsville was a natural target of bandits.

The little bank, however, "rolled with the punches" and continued doing business in the hard times until progress and better finances allowed it to upgrade its defenses to a quality exceeding many larger banks now. Today, intensive security precautions and beefed up law enforcement have eliminated many of the bank's former vulnerabilities, making it a much less enticing target for criminals.

Tiny Taylorsville remains a very rural and slow-paced community. It also is quite historic, although little focus is made upon this aspect of the community. Though native aboriginals had villages on and near this spot in prehistoric times and Union Army troops during the U.S. Civil War passed through and camped in the vicinity, locals pay scant heed to these historic trivialities today. Farming is the business at hand, and Taylorsville Bank plays a major role in this commerce.

It therefore can only be viewed as paradoxical that this community is still known today not for its history, but as a repeated target for bank robbers.

Early Bandits

One manager – Mr. M.A. Perry – who came to the Taylorsville bank in the

Bartow County Sheriff Jim Wheeler (l) confers with several FBI agents following a robbery at the Peoples Bank of Bartow in Taylorsville in 1976. (Photo reprinted with permission courtesy of Golden Memory Photos, Cartersville, GA)

early 1930s, was forced to endure two such robberies under his watch. His son, W.J. "Bill" Perry, was six or eight years of age at the time, and despite his young age, recalled the incident quite clearly.

"The first robbery Dad experienced at Taylorsville was about 1933," the younger Perry explained. "The gunman locked Dad in the vault and he was lucky to have survived it with the lack of oxygen in there. Dad was the only person in the bank in those days, so he was all alone.

"Fortunately, an individual named Mr. Bob Taylor (perhaps from the namesake family of "Taylorsville"), who was a bank director, made it his business to check on the bank every day," Perry continued. "He was the only other person in town who knew the combination to the vault, and he just happened to stop by shortly after the robbery. He heard Dad banging on the inside of the vault, and he hurriedly opened the large door.

"The second robbery during Dad's time in Taylorsville occurred sometime around 1936 or '37," Perry added. "Dad had a .38 caliber 'Police Special' that he had begun carrying to defend the bank. One day, a man drove up in a 1934 or '35 Chevy. He walked in and quickly pulled a gun on Dad and ordered him back inside the vault yet again, only this time, Dad wasn't locked inside. The gunman took all the money and put it into a washtub, then told Dad 'You get on the floor. If you come out, I'll kill you.'

"Well. . . Dad laid on the floor until he heard the motor start in that old Chevy. He then grabbed his gun and ran outside and emptied all six rounds at the fleeing car. The car never slowed up though.

"A few days later, that thief was brazen enough to phone in and cackle about how Dad 'couldn't hit the side of a barn.' It sure wasn't from a lack of trying though."

A Run On The Bank

The 1930s in the United States during the height of the Great Depression were indeed very desperate times. Bread lines were long and "soup kitchens" were constant reminders of the desperate circumstances afoot in the U.S. The nature of this desperation gave rise to outlaw "celebrities" such as Charles "Pretty Boy" Floyd, John Dillinger, Bonnie Parker and Clyde Barrow, "Baby Face" Nelson, and many others.

"Pretty Boy" Floyd, who died October 22, 1934, in a hail of bullets in Wellsville, Ohio, ironically was born and grew up just a few miles down the road from Taylorsville in Adairsville, Georgia. His family home still stands there on Railroad Street.

Aside from having to deal with the outlaws of that day, banking institutions had to be concerned with "a run on the bank" as well. The Taylorsville Bank was no different. In 1932, it also suffered a "run" on its funds, where depositors, suddenly fearful that the bank was about to fail, lined up at the door demanding the facility "cough up" their money.

Few were the banks who successfully weathered such a threat to survival. Once depositors begin collecting en masse at a bank to withdraw their funds, very few such institutions had enough cash reserves on hand to survive those circumstances. When this situation arose at the Taylorsville Bank, however, a simple clever strategy allowed it to survive the storm.

"Many of the farmers in the area got the idea the bank was about to fail," Perry continued. "When people started lining up to withdraw their money, Dad called Mr. W. D. Tripp, who was a stockholder and on the board of directors.

"Tripp was a seasoned financial expert, and though he no doubt was highly concerned after receiving the phone call from Mr. Perry, he did not panic. He didn't hesitate a moment in applying a quick remedy to the situation.

"Mr. Tripp told Dad to stall as long as possible and pay out just as slowly as possible until he (Mr. Tripp) had a chance to get there," Perry added. He (Mr. Tripp) then went quickly to another bank with which he was associated in Bartow County and borrowed $2,000 – all in one-dollar bills – and put it all in a big bag. He then reportedly rushed down to the Taylorsville Bank, walked calmly inside, dumped the $2,000 in bills out on a counter and announced 'I understand some people want their money.'

"Well, in 1932, that $2,000 looked like a million bucks today," Perry smiled. [In reality, at that time (1932), $2,000.00 was in fact a great deal of money, being the equivalent of approximately $46,232.00 in 2024 dollars.] "A large number of the accounts in the Taylorsville Bank were only eight and ten-dollar accounts. Before you knew it, people just began walking away, and that was the end of the crisis."

Comedic Robberies

Crises at a little bank, however, were not the foundation upon which Mr. Perry wished to build his career. After all, he had worked long and hard to become a banker in order to obtain a steady and lucrative income, so that he could avoid the stresses of life. After he had experienced a second bank robbery in Taylorsville, he began looking around for an employment opportunity at a less risky bank.

The 1976 robbery of the Taylorsville bank was planned with a diversion in mind. An explosive charge with a detonator timed to activate during the bank robbery had been set in the crawl-space beneath historic Euharlee Presbyterian Church. The explosives' detonator fortunately proved to be defective, rendering the device harmless.

M.A. Perry soon moved to what he considered to be a much more secure situation in nearby Rockmart in Polk County. The Rockmart Bank was a very secure facility and was located right across the street from the Rockmart Police Department.

A person today can only imagine Perry's shock and dismay when, two years later (about 1939), the Rockmart Bank itself was robbed. Even worse, it was the only robbery ever experienced by the Rockmart Bank. Luckily, however, the elder Perry had gone home for lunch that day, and thankfully missed all the excitement of the hold-up.

Interestingly, in a scene right out of the major motion picture *The Pink Panther*, the Rockmart robbery involved a somewhat comic element. After the robbery, the bandits leapt into their getaway car and were prepared to race away from town, when, to their shock and dismay, they discovered their car would not crank. Just as they were about to flee the scene on foot, one of the friendly Rockmart citizens – completely unaware of the circumstances into which he had stepped – actually assisted the criminals in starting the troublesome vehicle and kindly waved as the bandits – now smiling broadly – drove eagerly away. It was a scene almost identical to the role played by the late Peter Sellers as "Inspector Clouseau."

Yet another episode of comedy also survives – undoubtedly with some embellishment – from a 1940 Taylorsville Bank robbery. The bank manager at that time, William Dorsey, was victimized one morning just as the bank opened for business. The bandits unceremoniously tied Dorsey to an old pot-bellied stove, an act to which the banker strangely took great umbrage, considering it a tremendous humiliation for reasons still unknown.

Even years later, Dorsey continued to react angrily – to the amusement of anyone around him – whenever reminded of the event. "There wasn't no need for that," he would quickly growl. "They had no business tying me to that stove." (Just why the bandits decided to tie him to the stove is unknown today. And no, the stove wasn't hot.)

Today, bank robberies which went awry and in which no one was injured can be subjects of considerable amusement, but the situation is anything but funny for a bank teller gazing down the business end of a loaded revolver or shotgun. Long after one particularly disturbing robbery, one bank official expressed his feelings thusly: "I was always thankful that they did get away, especially after I found out who they were."

Planning A Robbery

It is the last robbery – in 1976 – inflicted upon the little bank in Taylorsville that is remembered most vividly by many area residents today, mainly because it was one of the most unusual – and potentially the deadliest. It was also the first robbery of that facility which emphasized the fact that the Taylorsville Bank was no longer "an easy mark."

The two "masterminds" of the '76 hold-up reportedly were experienced professionals despite their ineptitude. According to later courtroom testimony, they arrived in the Cartersville area from their home base in Indianapolis, Indiana, and settled into a multi-purpose truck-stop/pool hall/boarding house on U.S. Highway 41.

One of the men, Leon Johnson, walked with a distinctive limp. The other, Donald Anderson, had "rotten teeth." These characteristics of these men made them easy marks for later identification. The bank employees at Taylorsville would remember these "tells" years after the crime.

The duo became a trio when they met up with Marvina Satterfield, described as an individual who was exceptionally masculine in appearance, more nearly resembling a man with long hair than a female – a not altogether flattering identity. Those three still later were joined by a fourth accomplice – an attractive blonde named Charmaine Garrett – who witnesses would also easily recall and later identify.

The four partners in crime all had one thing in common: They all needed money and intended to obtain it illicitly – violently if necessary.

It wasn't long before the quartet began forging a plan to accomplish their ill deed. They no doubt took

their time, observing the rural countryside, plotting which bank would surrender the most loot with the least risk.

Clayton J. Harris, bank manager at the Taylorsville Bank in 1976, says the initial plan of the gang was to rob the First National Bank of Cartersville. Their scheme involved kidnapping bank manager Russell Archer, taking his family hostage, then threatening harm to them unless Archer opened the bank vault. This plan was squelched, however, when Marvina Satterfield objected, explaining that she might be recognized by the Archer family.

The crooks therefore had to cast about for a new target bank.

Taylorsville, with its isolated location soon drew their attention. Its well-known history of robbery and burglary may even have been a contributing factor in their choice.

Despite an obvious lack of security and law enforcement personnel in the vicinity of the bank, the bandits decided a diversion would increase their margin of safety. Their plan called for the creation of an emergency situation – such as a bombing – a short distance away, to draw away any police in the area.

The conspirators located a church several miles away in the little community of Euharlee in Bartow County. They decided to blow it up with dynamite, using a delayed fuse.

"Fortunately for the church and the community, their plan failed," recalled church member Bill Thomason

The conspirators located a church several miles away in the little community of Euharlee in Bartow County.

13

thankfully. "The fuse wasn't attached properly and had actually fallen out. As a result, the dynamite did not detonate."

The newspapers of that day reported many details of the robbery, as well as the subsequent manhunt, but there was not a single word describing the deadly explosives at Euharlee. Bank manager Clayton Harris, however, does recall the FBI informing him of the discovery of the dynamite three or four weeks later.

One can only imagine the somber congregation singing and praying in the little church on Sunday, completely unaware of the deadly explosives right beneath their feet, underneath the church floor. Harris says he was infuriated when he learned of the proposed wanton destruction of the historic religious structure. "I really didn't get mad about that robbery – you know, angry, angry mad – until I found out about that church deal. The money they stole from the bank was unimportant compared to the (possible loss of life) in the church."

To make their plan as effective as possible, the conspirators reportedly scouted the back-roads and made practice driving runs for a number of days prior to the crime. They had to time the driving routes; select a discreet rendezvous point where they could abandon their "hot" car; and select a drop-off point where the men could hide out with the money overnight while the two women evaded roadblocks.

The criminals decided to steal a car for their getaway vehicle which they would abandon as soon as possible following the robbery. This tactic ultimately proved successful in temporarily delaying police who were hot on their trail in pursuit.

The stolen car – a 12-year-old Ford Galaxie – was snatched in Marietta.

The criminals "hot-wired" the ignition to start the car. Before traveling back to Taylorsville, they stopped in Kennesaw where they stole a Michigan license plate, using it to replace the Georgia plate on the Galaxie.

Now the group had two vehicles: the Galaxie for the actual robbery, and a 1970 or '71 "dirty-brown" Ford or Chevrolet, owned by one of the members and which would be used for an escape after abandoning the Galaxie.

The Hold-Up Day

Thursday, March 11, 1976, was the appointed day for the crime. The thieves' first act was to set the explosives beneath the Presbyterian Church at Euharlee and then return to the bank.

At approximately 10:00 a.m., the thieves arrived in Taylorsville, and parked the stolen car directly in front of the bank. Charmaine Garrett remained at the wheel with the engine running, while the others quickly prepared themselves for the robbery.

The two men – Johnson and Anderson – were packing revolvers, and had pulled ski masks over their faces to obscure their features. They had taken pillow cases to use in the collection of the bank notes.

The men burst through the front door of the bank anticipating a quick "score," when to their unmitigated surprise they discovered themselves facing tellers who were protected behind bullet-proof glass (since the bank management had obviously begun taking precautionary measures after the numerous previous robberies). Ironically, despite the protective glass, the door leading to the interior of the "teller cage" was quickly and easily penetrated by the gunmen due to a flaw in the protective system, according to Clayton Harris.

The Ford Galaxie used as an escape vehicle in the 1976 robbery is pictured. The right front tire was flattened by .22 rounds fired by Charles Ford, a bystander at the bank during the robbery. (Photo reprinted with permission courtesy of Golden Memory Photos, Cartersville, GA)

Harris explained he was escorting two Boy Scout executives out after a meeting in his office. "I was still chatting with them as I opened the door, when these robbers came bouncing in the front door and got the drop on us." It was a lucky break for the bandits – one that the bank personnel would make certain never happened again in the future.

Harris said Johnson pushed him back inside the secure area, then went from one teller to the next with his pillow cases in a villainous sort of "trick-or-treat." Tellers Glenn Williams and Shelva Campbell scooped up the greenbacks and dumped them into the bags.

Johnson reached one flustered teller and reportedly yelled "Big money!" She dropped a handful of hundred-dollar bills into the bag then froze in fear. Johnson promptly prodded her for more with his gun.

Meanwhile, the other bandit, Donald Anderson, stationed himself next to the security door. Assistant Vice President Jackie Smith was sitting at her desk beneath Anderson's gaze, desperately trying to think of what she could do to save the diamond earrings she was wearing. She stealthily slipped them into the garbage can at her desk. The robbers, however, were not bothering with jewelry or coins that day. They were too busy bagging what turned out to be little more than $22,000.

Harris remembered that one customer in the bank, Marron Haas, began to edge slowly towards the front door. Anderson turned his gun on him and stated matter-of-factly that if he took one more step, he would blow him in half.

"That got me right back up to the counter and got both my hands on the counter just like they were supposed to be," Haas later recounted. "I didn't make another move."

Calling The Cavalry

It was about this time that the gunmen's luck began to fade. Ray Hughes, a repairman, was working on a faulty air conditioner next to the bank's side door. He had been making frequent trips in and out of the bank, and had wedged a small screwdriver in the side door to keep it from locking.

It was on one of his trips from the air conditioner back into the bank that he suddenly noticed the masked men with guns, and he quickly and quietly backed out the door, unseen. He ran across the street to Wolfe's convenience store, instructing them to call the police and report the robbery.

Next in the fast-moving sequence of events, a bank customer drove up and parked around the corner from the front door. He was near Ray Hughes who had run back to the side of the bank. Either Hughes or a bystander reportedly shouted, "They're robbing the bank!"

When he learned the circumstances unfolding around him, the newly-arrived customer – Charles Ford – ran to his pickup truck and grabbed a .22 caliber, two-shot derringer. He looked around quickly and thought he recognized the getaway car in which Charmaine Garrett sat. He started toward the getaway car, intending to confront the driver with his derringer, but thought better of it (which may have been wise, since Garrett had a sawed-off shotgun in the car with her).

Just as Ford returned to his pickup, the masked bandits dashed from the bank and jumped into their car. Garrett gunned the stolen Galaxie around the corner past Ford and his derringer, past Ray Hughes, the air conditioner repairman, and down the road leading to a rendezvous site three miles east of town.

As the vehicle roared past Charles Ford, he fired two shots at the front tire of the getaway car. The fleeing bandits fired back as they sped away, but the shots were poorly aimed and no one was hit. When the car was found later, the right front tire was flat with two bullet holes.

Meanwhile, the planned diversion – the detonation of the explosives beneath Euharlee Presbyterian Church – never happened. And with no diversion, the forces of law and order were able to collectively focus upon the bank theft. More bad luck for the bandits.

The charming 1853 Presbyterian Church, unchanged in more than a century, was spared. It was weeks, however, before anyone even knew of the existence of the hidden dynamite. All this time, church members were lifted spiritually as they sat in their lovely old sanctuary each Sunday morning. Little did they know at that time how close they had come to being lifted "physically" by the dynamite into eternity. Prayers in this house of worship undoubtedly took on a new dimension following discovery of the explosives.

Hot Pursuit

Meanwhile, the alarm had gone out to law enforcement contingents in a three or four county area following the report from the convenience store. Police forces quickly mobilized and concentrated on the shaken little community as well as on every back road in the county. Within ten minutes, Georgia State Patrol aircraft, including a helicopter, were overhead scouring the area.

According to press reports of that day, *"Every available road leading out of Bartow County was covered. Shortly after the robbery, nearby Georgia State Patrol officers from Cartersville, Canton, Rome, Cedartown and Polk County, plus the Cedartown and Cartersville police departments, assisted in the investigation."*

In a race with destiny, the stolen getaway car careened down the road from town, crossing GA Highway 113 and ignoring the stop sign. The bank robbers headed along Davistown Road for their appointed rendezvous.

R.C. Free was traveling in the opposite direction on Davistown toward Taylorsville. He noticed the reckless driving of the bandits and he was able to get a good look at the occupants of the car. He later assisted in their identification.

The bandits eventually reached their pre-planned rendezvous spot where they awaited the second car driven by Marvina Satterfield. During all the excitement, Satterfield had been constantly circling the back roads.

A nearby resident noticed that Satterfield stopped beside the getaway car, picked up its occupants, then drove off. The bandits' carefully laid plans did not take into consideration the attentive eyes of curious bystanders.

An hour later, area police discovered the abandoned getaway car, its engine still running. They took fingerprints and searched for other incriminating evidence.

The bandits meanwhile had continued to follow their plan, with the two men hiding out in the woods overnight, and the two women driving on alone to pass through the roadblocks. That night, weather forecasters had predicted scattered showers by morning and a low in the mid to upper 40s.

As a result of the inclement weather, both Anderson and Johnson, no doubt, were soggy and suffering from severe exposure by the time the women returned in the wee hours of Friday morning to the little creaking bridge over Floyd Creek to pick them up. Despite

According to later court testimony, it was at the rusted bridge (above) that Leon Johnson and Donald Anderson were picked up by their accomplices after hiding out overnight during a cold winter rainfall.

the suffering they had done overnight, the criminals undoubtedly were feeling a little better about their odds for success after being picked up. They headed south on GA Highway 61, and reportedly stopped to hide in an American Legion building for the remainder of the night.

Upon arrival in Paulding County, Donald Anderson, amazingly, focused not upon furthering his escape from a capital crime, but rather upon vanity – getting his decayed teeth repaired by a local dentist. He even mindlessly used a portion of the stolen money to pay this bill, because the bank notes were soon traced by the FBI, and Anderson was the first of the gang arrested.

In a continuing comedy of errors, the remaining bandits apparently boldly traveled back to Bartow County and Cartersville where they – also mindlessly – purchased a brand-new Lincoln Continental at City Motors. According to Clayton Harris, Johnson, Satterfield, and Garrett brazenly made a down payment on that expense with some of the stolen money as well, then had the audacity to visit the First National Bank of

Cartersville (their original robbery target) where they sought a loan to finance the car.

The bandits' movements in Georgia after that point are unknown, but several weeks later, Charmaine Garrett was located and arrested by FBI agents. Following an intensive interrogation, she confessed to her part in the crimes. A few weeks later, Johnson also was caught, as was Marvina Satterfield. All, except Johnson, were quick to plea-bargain in exchange for lighter sentences.

The Trial

At this time, a federal trial for armed bank robbery in Cartersville, Georgia, would have taken place in Rome, but the defendants were considered too dangerous for the Rome jail. Also, Leon Johnson's brother, Morris, who was in the custody of federal agents in New Orleans at the time, was subpoenaed by the defense to testify on his brother's behalf.

Both of the Johnson brothers had previously escaped from jail. Morris Johnson, amazingly, had twice escaped from the Atlanta Federal Penitentiary, a feat which remains a record to this day.

Morris Johnson also was the proud owner of yet another milestone for criminals – that of making the FBI's *"10 Most Wanted"* list. Atlanta, therefore, with its more secure incarceration facilities, was chosen as the site for the trial.

Five months after the bank robbery, Leon Johnson was tried for his part in the crimes. He was the only defendant to plead *"Not Guilty."* Morris Johnson and five witnesses testified that Leon was home in Indiana at the time of the holdup.

Interestingly, Morris claimed it was he, not Leon, who had masterminded the Taylorsville job. His comments were carried in an article in the ***Atlanta Constitution***:

"When the prosecutor asked Johnson if he committed the robbery, he answered, 'I pulled it. Yes.'"

The jury in the trial, however, was unmoved by the subterfuge. The trial lasted only a few days. On August 6, 1976, the jury took just 33 minutes to return a verdict of *"Guilty"* for Leon Johnson.

In September when the bandits were sentenced, Johnson drew a total of 50 years, Satterfield six years, Garrett ten years, and Anderson 15 years.

Bank robberies in recent years have increased at a pace not seen since the 1970s. One FBI official offered a surprising explanation for the increase:

"Lots of bank robbers convicted in the late 1970s and early 1980s are now back on the streets (because of liberal parole policies put into place by liberal politicians)."

If Leon Johnson was paroled after serving a third of his sentence, the entire Taylorsville Bank robbery gang may all be freely circulating again someplace in Georgia.

Meanwhile, back at the Taylorsville Bank, the window tellers in the tiny facility say they still keep a nervous eye on the front door as each customer enters today. . . . and nobody – nobody – dares to leave the door to the teller cage ajar anymore.

*[Copyright, 1996, 1999, **A North Georgia Journal of History, Volume III** by R. Olin Jackson (Legacy Communications, Inc., 1987-2005) and Daniel M. Roper, Legacy Communications, Inc., Rome, GA. All rights reserved. Reprinted with permission.]*

(Period photographs courtesy of Golden Memory Photos, Cartersville, GA. Reprinted with permission)

(Grateful appreciation is expressed herewith in memory of the late Gordon Sargent for the accumulation of information necessary for this article.)

The Strange & Horrific
Woolfolk Family Murders

It was one of the most terrible crimes in Georgia history, and it almost certainly occurred as a result of mental derangement. In a modern trial for such a crime, Tom Woolfolk quite possibly would have been judged criminally insane. In 1889, however, he received a "Guilty" verdict in a few minutes, then was hung for eighteen minutes until dead. Today, serious questions about this trial and the actual perpetrator of this crime remain unanswered.

As of the date of this writing (2024), it has now been almost 140 years since the horror which occurred on August 6, 1887, in Bibb County, Georgia, yet distant members of the family carrying the name of the perpetrator of the crime still cannot escape association with this tragedy. It remains as one of the most heinous and horrible crimes in Georgia history.

Though the crime occurred in Bibb approximately 12 miles west of Macon, its roots lie at 247 Pulaski Street, just off Prince Avenue, in Athens, Georgia, not far from the sprawling campus of present-day University of Georgia. Though few are aware of it today, this impressive Athens neighborhood became the spawning ground for this terrible crime.

It was in this Pulaski Street home that a youngster – raised in a privileged realm – found security and hope. It was here that he became accustomed to a life which eventually was harshly taken from him as a child, casting him into another world which was alien and foreign, and which resigned him to a life over which he had no control and in which he could not bear to live. In his family life, he went from being an only child and the center of attention, to being a virtual outcast in a very large family of half-brothers and half-sisters.

Tom Woolfolk's (pronounced "Wool-fork") father – Richard Franklin Woolfolk[1] – was graduated from the University of Georgia in 1854, and soon thereafter was married to a Miss Susan Moore, daughter of Mr. Thomas Moore in Athens. Susan and Richard moved to Bibb County, Georgia, where the Woolfolk family owned a plantation, and it was here that they settled to live their lives and raise their family. It was a short-lived dream, however.

Richard's father – Thomas Woolfolk – hailed from a prominent North Carolina family. He (Thomas) had ambitiously migrated to the Macon area to seek his fortune when much of that area was still a virgin wilderness inhabited by the native Creek Indians.

Why Thomas chose Bibb County in south Georgia for his home is a mystery today. Perhaps he recognized the possibilities for growth in the area coupled with the extremely inexpensive nature of the real estate there at that time.

Whatever the circumstances, Thomas purchased a one hundred-acre tract of land which he ultimately developed into a substantial enterprise, allowing him the latitude to play a major role in the early growth of Macon.

Following his marriage to Susan, Richard returned to his father's plantation to take up the reins of the family enterprises. All went well initially, but there were dark clouds on the horizon.

Early Life

From the union of Susan and Richard came three children – two little girls and a darkly quiet little boy. The two females were named Floride and Lillie. The little boy – Thomas G. Woolfolk – was born on June 18, 1860, just prior to the U.S. Civil War.

Susan, sadly, died soon after her son's entry into this world. The circumstances in rural Bibb County in the 1860s were primitive, so Susan's death is understandable. Childbirth often resulted in the death of the mother in pioneer days prior to hospital births.

There was not even a nearby cemetery in which to bury Susan, so she was interred in the yard of the Woolfolk home, where a holly bush was planted to mark the site for posterity.

Shortly thereafter, Richard answered the call to service in the Confederate Army. With no direct parental supervision remaining on the plantation north of Macon, young Tom was sent to Athens to be raised by his mother's sister, Fannie Moore Crane, who was married to John Ross Crane, a builder of some renown in that city prior to the war.[2]

Tom spent the first seven years of his life in the Pulaski Street neighborhood in a substantial house that John Crane had built in 1842. This structure still stands as of this writing (2024), and

has been occupied for many years by the University of Georgia chapter of Sigma Alpha Epsilon (SAE) fraternity.[3]

As the fighting raged in the far off confines of Virginia and Maryland as the U.S. Civil War progressed, Aunt Fannie fed, bathed, and clothed young Tom in an all-encompassing security in Athens, Georgia. She quite likely pushed him in an infant carriage down Prince Avenue on some days, past the magnificent Taylor-Grady mansion (which also still stands as of this writing) and other well-known Athens edifices during the early 1860s.

Though they escaped most of the destructive circumstances of the war – since Athens was not a priority target of the Gen. William Tecumseh Sherman and the Federal Army – there nevertheless were sacrifices to be made until the South recovered. A somewhat limited amount of these, however, touched the Cranes and young Tom.

A few years later, during Georgia's "Reconstruction" days, Tom no doubt continued playing happily, without any hint of the dark evil possibly lurking within his psyche. The Cranes had chickens and other farm produce upon which to survive, and as a center of higher education, Athens was not a poverty-stricken area like much of the rest of the state.

At war's end, Richard Woolfolk returned to Georgia and remarried. At that point in his life, there were many more females living in Georgia than males as a result of the decimation of the male population by the casualties of war, and returning soldiers often could take their pick among the most eligible females. Richard's new bride was Mattie E. Howard, a graduate of the Forsyth Female Collegiate Institute in nearby Monroe County.

Richard and Mattie began a new family which, by 1887, included six more children – two boys and four little girls.[4]

At age seven, young Tom was suddenly returned to his father back at the Woolfolk family plantation twelve miles north of Macon, where his life began anew with his father and step-mother. It no doubt was a harsh adjustment, since by that point, there were a total of nine children in the Woolfolk household, and instead of being the sole focus of Aunt Fannie's attentions, young Tom was relegated instead to a home filled with large strangers, and in which he received scant attention from his new step-mother. One can only imagine today the fears and misgivings he must have harbored all those years of early youth when he was isolated and ostracized.

The "cracks" in the façade of what he now called "home" were obvious too. Almost immediately, there were problems. He reportedly never warmed to his step-mother Mattie, and no doubt missed his Aunt Fannie terribly since she had served as his center of stability and safety since his earliest days.

In an early display of his response to his rejection by his mother and half-siblings, Tom openly rebelled against Mattie, becoming the epitome of "a problem child." Richard and Mattie often gave up in exasperation with young Tom, returning him periodically to the care of Aunt Fannie in Athens where Tom's life once again became "normal." But then, just as soon as he had re-adapted to that secure environment, Tom's father and Mattie returned to take him back to the farm in the wilderness.

First Failures

Despite the on-going problems with young Tom, the Woolfolk family adapted to the circumstances as best they could with nine children to clothe and feed. Richard's successes on the plantation and in his other business and civic endeavors however, coupled with his family responsibilities, continued to absorb more and more of his time, causing Tom to receive less and less loving attention.

The years passed by steadily, with Tom growing progressively more introspective and withdrawn. Upon reaching maturity, he sought a profession of his own in order to establish a semblance of independence. He attempted numerous business endeavors, almost all with the financial support of his father in the early going. He, nevertheless, ultimately was a miserable failure in each one, including stints at running a separate plantation, managing a store, driving a streetcar in Macon, and owning a grocery store. His social skills were practically nonexistent, and his introversion progressed daily.

Nothing seemed to work for Tom Woolfolk; everywhere he turned failure loomed. Was it a continuous intentional rebellion on his part? Was it, in his mind, a way to punish his father for the loss of his mother and/or Aunt Fannie and the ostracizing inattention he had received? Or was he simply psychologically incapable of a life of independence and therefore living in a fantasy-world? We'll never know.

Despite his many failures, money and property nevertheless continued to be an obsession with Tom as he matured – no doubt in a constant quest for the security he had never received at home. He told his "friends" (who more often than not were merely acquaintances or "hangers-on") that he hoped to get his father's estate. However, as more children were born to his father and Mattie, it became increasingly obvious this dream would never be fulfilled.

As a result of this frustrating obsession, Tom became more and more embittered toward not only his step-mother, but his father as well, as he matured and time passed. His step-mother increasingly became a target for his unpleasantness, and the object of blame for his deprivation of an inheritance.

When he was 27, Tom married Georgia Bird, the daughter of a well-to-do farmer. In what could only be described as a rather strange ceremony, Tom and Georgia boarded a train at the Holton, Georgia, depot in Jones County where Georgia's family lived. The train was a south-bound passenger headed to Macon, and Tom and Georgia were married in the aisle as the train proceeded full-speed ahead.

Following the wedding, Tom promised his new bride that he would take her "to a fine mansion in Macon." In reality, however, he had nowhere to take her except to the home of his older sister. Unsurprisingly, his new bride was not impressed, and his marriage, just as all his business endeavors, was very short-lived, lasting all of three weeks.

Strange behavior, however, had become the norm for Tom. Prior to his wedding, he had already attracted considerable attention to himself for highly questionable activity. He had begun openly carrying a sidearm – even when visiting the safe confines of Aunt Fannie in Athens – which was yet another indication of his growing insecurity and mental instability.

Following his failed attempt at marriage, Tom told one acquaintance that everybody was "against him," and that he had no friends – yet another indication of his growing mental illness. He also said that he was a fool for marrying Georgia, because she was "no good," and that he might have had "to frail her out"

(beat her) – yet another indicator of destabilization.

The Murders

After his professional and marital failures, Tom dejectedly returned to the Woolfolk plantation, since he had no other home or form of support. He, however, was far too old for his father to just "take him back" as a family member to be raised with his brothers and sisters, so his father "put him on wages" at $9.00 per month (the equivalent of approximately $260.00 per month or roughly $60 per week in 2024 dollars) in order to "earn his keep." His labors in this capacity undoubtedly were a rude awakening – far from the privileged life he had envisioned and craved.

It is unknown for certain today, but at some point shortly after beginning work for his father on the farm, Tom's anger, jealousy and resentment finally boiled over. The life to which he had been relegated was just more than he could bear mentally, and he finally lashed out in insanity early one fateful morning, sending his life careening into a dark void from which he would never recover.

On Saturday, August 6, 1887, between 2 and 4 a.m., Tom reportedly knocked on the door of a local cabin where he awoke Green Locket, a black man who worked for the family. He told Green that something awful had happened. "Someone got into the house and killed my family," he reportedly blurted.

Upon their arrival at the Woolfolk plantation, Tom tried to persuade Locket to enter the house to investigate. Locket's mother, however, had not raised a fool. Instead of entering the crime scene, Green Locket chose instead to immediately seek out neighbors for help.

When the neighbors of Hazzard District in Bibb County arrived, Tom repeated his claim that "someone entered the house and murdered the family." He said he had luckily escaped by jumping through a window.

In what may have been a tragic twist of fate, later testimony indicates one of the neighbors who had gathered on the scene that night had remarked that he heard a noise in the house. Tom, reportedly, immediately reentered the house without hesitation to investigate. According to eyewitnesses, he remained inside for fully twenty to thirty minutes, and when he reemerged, he told those gathered outside that he could find no one alive. Tragically, this action quite possibly cost the life of one barely-surviving family member inside the house who might have been saved if those present had been aware of the true circumstances afoot.

The following is an account of the murder scene as published in the October 30, 1890 issue of the **Macon Telegraph** newspaper.[5] It undoubtedly was a reprint of the original news report of 1887. This account is provided in an abbreviated format, since the full account is far too graphic to be included in this article.

"Finally it was decided to make an investigation, and not until then was the whole horror of the butchery discovered.

"In the back room on the left of the hall the bodies of Capt. Woolfolk and his wife were found lying on the bed with their skulls crushed by fearful blows. Across the foot of the same bed was the body of the baby (eighteen months), also with its head crushed.

"Across the foot of the same bed and half on the floor was Miss Pearl (age 17). She had dreadful cuts on the back of the neck as well as on the hand, which showed that she had defended her life with desperate courage, and the position of the body showed that her murderer had killed her either in another room or in the hall and then dragged the body across the floor and thrown it where it was found.

"Just inside the door of the same room, the body of Charles H. Woolfolk, a small boy (age 5) was found. It was evident that he had entered the room and a single blow had crushed in his skull and his body had been left lying where it fell.

"A little further into the room was the body of Richard Woolfolk, Jr., a young man of 20, and it was evident that he, too, had made a struggle for life and had not been killed easily. His forehead and part of his face were disfigured with numerous small gashes, which gave rise to the theory that he had seized the axe in the hands of the murderer and had held to it until the sharp edge had pushed into his face so often that he became blinded with his own blood and could struggle no longer with his opponent. The coup de grace was delivered in the top of the head, crushing the skull....

"Across the hall was the body of Mrs. Temperance West,[6] an aged lady who was on a visit, and those of Rosebud, aged 7 years, and Annie, aged 10, were found (as well). Mrs. West had been struck while asleep and one hand still rested under the head which was horribly crushed.

"On the floor, little Rosebud was stretched, and near the window, half covered with a sheet, was Annie. It was evident that Annie had been the last victim, and that she had dragged the sheet from the bed in a wild effort to hide herself, and that while crawling to the open window to make her escape, she had been overtaken by the murderer and slaughtered like the rest of her family by blows from an axe."

Convincing Evidence

From the outset, most individuals immediately suspected Tom as the guilty party. According to the **Telegraph**, the neighbors, even before law enforcement authorities arrived, had gone to Tom and *"with hard-set faces and determined voices, told him that he was under arrest for murder, and if he attempted to escape he would be killed like a dog."*

As could be imagined, a heinous murder such as this brought out the "looky-looks" in droves. Word of the murder spread like wildfire, and hundreds of curious people reportedly arrived at the scene the following morning. Every clue in the investigation continued to point to Tom.

Bloody footprints were found in all of the rooms of the house. Surprisingly, Tom didn't even attempt to claim that they might have belonged to someone else. He no doubt was clearly aware of this condemning evidence from the outset, and possibly had initially hoped to lure Green Locket into entering the premises in order to thereby explain away the presence of his own footprints. . . or perhaps to frame Locket for the crime.

In the room that Tom shared with his brothers, it was discovered that the floor had been scrubbed with soap and water within a few hours of those murders. Tom attempted to explain this away to investigators by saying he had washed his feet because they were bloody and that he had then, for inexplicable reasons, *"wiped up the floor."* Despite all the circumstances it remained abundantly clear to all who investigated the scene of the crime that had anyone other than Tom been the perpetrator of the crime, that individual could not have avoided leaving bloody footprints in the house as well, yet Tom's easily-identifiable tracks were the only such prints in the premises.

The gathering crowd also noticed that Tom had on a dirty shirt and trousers which were much too large for him. Later, the clothes were proven to be the property of his murdered brother. Tom,

again obviously guilty, neither could nor would explain what had become of his own clothes.

Remarkably, despite the heinous nature of the crime, Tom had displayed – from the outset – an unusually calm demeanor. As news of the terrible crime spread and more and more people began arriving, Tom, reportedly, sat beneath a tree outside, totally emotionless. No tears were shed and *"not a muscle quivered in agitation"* in his body. It was almost as if he had slain a monster, and his world was secure once again.

In another strange turn of events during the initial investigation, Tom, apparently dehydrated from his immense activities in the previous hours, requested that a china cup be filled with water from the well and brought to him. When the water arrived, however, Tom reportedly looked at the cup for a moment, touched it to his lips, and then strangely dumped the water on the ground.

Local tradition maintains that it was this clue which caused Sheriff Cooper to discover the critical evidence which was used against Tom. Another version of this story maintains that Cooper went to the well and drew a bucket of water, offering Tom a drink. When he became visibly repulsed at the offer, it aroused Cooper's suspicions. He reportedly sent a man down into the well where Tom's blood-stained clothes were soon discovered.

Newspaper accounts of the incidents that day, however, offered a slightly different version of the story. In these reports, a Sheriff Westcot is credited with the discovery of the bloody clothing:

"A bundle of clothes, soaked in blood, was brought up, and they were identified beyond the peradventure of a doubt as having belonged to Tom. There was a shirt, an undershirt, a pair of trousers,

and a pair of drawers. *They were all dyed a deep red, except the drawers and even they were terribly stained. They had been rolled up in such a way that the water had not been able to soak it (the blood) out and on the leg of the drawers, just above the knee, on the inside, was the imprint of a hand, with the fingers pointing up, just as they would have been if a struggling person had grasped the murderer by the leg."*

The bloody footprints inside the house, the bloody hand-print on the leg of his clothing, Tom's revulsion at the thought of drinking the water from the well, and his otherwise unusually calm demeanor following such a shattering event, collectively became the damning primary evidence used at his later trial. Even worse, Tom made virtually no effort to deny any of the damning evidence at all.

Following the discovery of the bloody clothing, Sheriff Westcot immediately arrested Tom and removed him to the Macon jail, because the incensed crowd at that point was threatening to lynch him on the spot.

Upon arrival at the jail, Tom was stripped of all his clothing and searched. According to reports, on the inside of his bare leg, in exactly the same spot corresponding with the hand-mark upon his underclothing, a similar hand-mark was even imprinted upon his leg – dyed into his flesh with blood. Tom argued that he had rested his hand when it was wet with his own blood on his leg. It soon became obvious, however, that in order for him to have successfully accomplished that feat, he would have been *"obliged to assume an acrobatic posture, as the fingers pointed up instead of down."*

Coroner Hodnet conducted an inquest that same day. Tom was stripped yet again to reveal the bloody handprint to the coroner's jury. They, as a result, became convinced there was enough evidence to try Tom for capital murder. He was moved shortly thereafter from Macon to Atlanta to prevent mob violence.

Questionable Journalism

The *Atlanta Constitution* newspaper reporter(s) immediately began coverage of the Woolfolk murders and the story eventually was carried in papers as far away as the *Cincinnati Enquirer* and even on the front page of the *New York Times*. The *Times* called it *"the bloodiest, blackest chapter in Georgia criminal history."* Other papers called it a crime *"without parallel in the criminal history of the South if not the world,"* and *"the bloodiest tragedy in the annals of crime."* It was the press which first labeled the accused murderer as *"Bloody Tom."*

It, however, was a Macon photographer who captured the true grisliness of the crime. Traveling to the Woolfolk home the morning following the crime, before even any part of the scene had been disturbed, he photographed the mangled corpses and blood-stained walls and furniture. The photos sadly were sold on the streets as collectables, and mailed out for a price to various newspapers.

Thankfully, none of the photos taken in 1887 are known to still be in existence today. A copy of the October 29, 1890 issue of the *Macon Evening News* however, offered a glimpse of the carnage in the terrible crime scene, with sketches likely drawn from the grisly photographs. The illustrations show not only a bloody murder scene, but also a vivid reminder that Annie, the child of ten, had tried desperately to escape. The sketch shows how she made it to the window, but no farther, as the terrible blows from the axe rendered her unconscious, her hands still clutching the open window sill.

The *Evening News* also detailed the layout of the home. It was described as a one-story four-room structure with a porch of six columns. It had a central hallway with three bedrooms and a parlor.

The boys slept in the front bedroom on the left, across the hallway from the parlor which was on the right. Captain and Mrs. Woolfolk occupied the back bedroom on the left. The baby's cradle was in their room too. The girls and the guest, Mrs. West, slept in the third bedroom in the right rear portion of the house. Six of the victims were found in one room and three in another.

According to reports, a Macon undertaker was the individual responsible for going to the scene of the tragedy and preparing the bodies for burial. The task took longer than expected, and it reportedly was Sunday morning around 6:00 a.m. when the funeral procession left the plantation and headed to Rose Hill Cemetery.

The nine murdered Woolfolk family members were laid to rest in two rows at Rose Hill Cemetery in Macon under an ancient tree on a hill just above Macon's Civil War veterans. This is the same cemetery in Macon which today contains the remains of a number of famous individuals, including guitarist Duane Allman, keyboardist and vocalist Gregg Allman, drummer Butch Trucks and bassist Berry Oakley all of the famed *Allman Brothers Band.*

The Woolfolk graves are topped by rectangular brick and are unmarked. The only identity is the name *Woolfolk* engraved upon the steps that lead down to the graves.

According to reports, the five adults were buried in black coffins and lie in one row. The only indication of who rests beneath each of the brick coverings is the slight difference in the length of the last two brick overlays. The slightly shorter overlays obviously indicate where Richard Jr. and Pearl were placed.

These rectangles also suggest the order of the first row (from left to right): Richard F. Woolfolk, Mattie H., Temperance West, Richard Jr., and Pearl. The four small children undoubtedly lay in the second row, probably also in order of age: Annie, Rosebud, Charles, and the baby, Mattie.

Tom (understandably) and his two older full-sisters were not buried with the family.

The Trials

Interestingly, Aunt Fannie Crane and Tom's two older sisters, Floride Woolfolk Edwards Shackelford and Lillie Woolfolk Cowan, stood by him throughout the desperate trial – despite the overwhelming evidence against him.

The sisters reportedly greeted Tom with a kiss upon their arrival in court each day. When someone in the audience shouted "Hang him! Hang him!" during the closing arguments of the first trial, Tom's sisters threw their arms around him as if to protect him from the mob in the courtroom.

Despite their show of support, Tom was quickly (understandably) found *"Guilty"* by a Bibb County jury which rendered a verdict in only twelve minutes. John C. Rutherford, Tom's lawyer, immediately requested a new trial.

And Aunt Fannie, as devoted as the sisters, was there to pin a bouquet of violets on Tom in 1889 when he was granted the new trial. The three stood by Tom without hesitation during the proceedings of the first trial in Bibb County, the second in Houston County, and during hearings in the Georgia Supreme Court for a third trial. The three always arrived with flowers, fruit and a kiss, and all three testified to Tom's affection for the whole family.

As for Tom, he strangely continued to exhibit the total disinterest he had demonstrated the night the bodies were discovered – again, as if a huge burden had simply been lifted from his back. During the second trial, he resorted to outright disrespect by spending most of his time reading Joel Tyler Headley's *Napoleon and His Marshals*.

Tom had hired John C. Rutherford of Athens as his lawyer. The Rutherfords were prominent Athenians as were the Cranes. John C.'s father had been a professor at the University of Georgia. John's sister, Mildred, was principal of The Lucy Cobb Institute, a historic education facility which still stands today on Milledge Avenue in Athens.

During his defense of Tom in the Bibb County trial in December of 1887, Rutherford was understandably unable to blame the slaughter on anyone else, and though the evidence in law terms was "circumstantial," it was also considered very strong. There simply was no one else at which to direct the vehemence of those wishing to convict Tom, and he did make a very convincing target.

Many clearly understood Green Locket, in refusing to enter the premises that night, had foiled Tom's original plan for an alibi. Most believed it was Tom's intention to get Locket inside the house that night, then either kill him, and accuse him of committing the heinous butchery, or to simply get Locket's footprints imprinted on the bloody floor with his (Tom's) own, in order to provide an alibi for his own footprints, or in order to frame Locket in the crime.

And then there was the question of what Tom had been doing when, after noises were heard inside the home, he inexplicably reentered and remained

inside for some 20 or 30 minutes. In the account of the murders in the *Macon Evening News*, it was speculated that Pearl had actually revived early that morning after the neighbors arrived. She quite likely made the noise that unfortunately drew Tom (instead of friendly forces) so quickly back inside the house.

Many believed that Pearl received the initial blows from the axe in the hallway, but since her body was found lying across the foot of the bed on which her father and mother lay, she possibly had revived from the early blows and had made it to the bed, and was struggling there when Tom returned inside the home to finish her.

Tom reportedly showed no nervousness or anxiety whatsoever during the first trial. His calmness was recorded over and over in news accounts.

The Georgia Supreme Court ordered a new trial in February of 1889. Tom was to be re-tried for the murder of his father, but the presiding judge warned him that even if he were found *"Not Guilty,"* there were still eight other indictments on which he could be tried.

The new trial took place in Perry, Georgia, in May of 1889. Once again, in less than an hour, the Houston County jury quickly brought back the verdict of *"Guilty."*

Some ladies in Macon strangely sent Tom flowers, fruits, and "delicacies" after the second *"Guilty"* verdict. His ex-wife, however, openly rejected him. She had successfully sued him for divorce, and had taken back her maiden name – Bird. She had no intention of being associated with the name "Woolfolk" ever again, and wanted everyone to know it.

Undeterred in the first two losses, Rutherford filed for a third trial. It was denied. Rutherford then appealed to the Georgia Supreme Court. Some said Rutherford was a determined lawyer and would take the case all the way to the United States Supreme Court if he lost the appeal. Unfortunately, his only hope for a legal absolution for Tom would have been a plea of "Insanity," but for unknown reasons it was not even considered.

The Georgia Supreme Court heard arguments in June of 1890. In July of 1890, the Court upheld the second conviction of Tom Woolfolk and refused to order another trial.

Rutherford became ill soon thereafter, and was unable to handle Tom's case any further. Tom was finally sentenced, and his date of execution was set for October 29, 1890.

Execution

In a valley where Big Indian Creek joins Fanny Gresham Branch beneath the Dr. A.C. Hendrick Memorial Bridge, a gallows was built for the disposition of the death sentence of Tom Woolfolk. On the day of the execution, a reporter from the *Macon Telegraph* wrote that a *"noticeable feature of the day is the immense number of ladies and children in attendance."* Local folklore maintains some of the onlookers even munched on 'possum sandwiches as they eagerly awaited the fateful event.

The *Telegraph* report continued by explaining that *"the Perry Rifles, who had recently won a prize at a state drill in Atlanta, were marched to the jail under the command of Capt. W.C. Davis, and formed a line"* in front to maintain order.

"Soon, Sheriff Cooper and Deputy Sheriff Riley escorted Tom Woolfolk to a carriage waiting in front. Under the escort of the Rifles, the carriage moved to the scene of execution, moving past the red brick courthouse. The crowd, estimated at from 7,000 to 10,000, followed."

The *Telegraph* reporter also described the appearance of the execution site. *"Meanwhile, as the hour of noon came near, the multitude began to gather about the gallows, which had been erected in a little valley half a mile from the courthouse and on the Central road. A small stream flowed through the depression which was surrounded by hills almost shutting it in on all sides and forming a natural coliseum. On the one side was the railroad crossing the brook on a low trestle. On the other was the town cemetery. It was on a hill top, looking down upon the scene with its white monuments confronting the victim as he stood upon the scaffold. Three Negro churches crowned the hill tops around. The white gallows stood in the middle of the little valley.*

"A circular space of 150 feet had been roped off at the scaffold for those who had tickets, around 200 people. The military marched inside the enclosure and with fixed bayonets assisted the deputies in keeping the mass of people from pressing upon the reserved space. Tom Woolfolk declared his innocence from the scaffold and prayed with his head upraised toward heaven. A few seconds before the drop fell, Tom said 'God bless you all.'"

According to reports, the fall through the scaffold trap-door unfortunately did not break Tom Woolfolk's neck, even though the noose positioning and the rate of fall are designed specifically to accomplish that task and bring about almost instantaneous death. The noose did not do its job because it had slipped from its proper position under Tom's right ear.

The wrenching rope partially tore the black death shroud from Tom's head, revealing his stretched neck. Seven minutes later, Woolfolk's pulse reportedly was amazingly still beating. Every ten or twenty seconds, his breast would heave and his shoulders would draw up. Eleven minutes later, however, his body had given up the ghost and his pulse had ceased. He was pronounced dead at 1:58 p.m.

The body was cut down, placed in a coffin, and sent by hearse to Hawkinsville.

Final Resting Place

Tom Woolfolk was buried in Orange Hill Cemetery in Hawkinsville, and his older sister, Floride Shackelford, was later buried beside him. The tombstone – undoubtedly provided by his Aunt Fannie, or his elder sisters, or even all three – appears to have been vandalized at some point in time, and then repaired. The name engraved upon it, "Thomas G. Woolfolk," is barely discernable as of this writing.

Prior to his death, Tom had been concerned about his place of burial. It was he (not another family member) who requested that he not be buried in Macon with his murdered family. He had also requested that no one view the body except his brother-in-law, Mr. Cowan, husband of Lillie Cowan. His grave was dug in Orange Hill Cemetery, the body placed therein, and walled with brick and cemented.

Tom never admitted to the murders. However, even Aunt Fannie and one sister stated that he had exhibited strange behavior just prior to the murders.

In an interview in the *Athens Weekly Banner-Watchman* shortly after the crime, Floride and Aunt Fannie said they had discussed Tom and had agreed that he must be losing his mind. Floride said she had told her father of their conclusion but that Captain Woolfolk had not agreed.

Curiously, evidence revealed years after Tom's execution, placed a modicum of doubt upon his guilt. Unexpected confessions to murders for which others have paid the penalty, while not unusual, almost always are fabrications, but in Tom Woolfolk's case, at least two of them gave pause to the confidence of those who convicted him so readily.

In 1893, a letter appeared in the *Pittsburgh Dispatch* which stated that the writer of the letter had met a tramp who killed not only the Borden family of Massachusetts in that highly publicized crime, but a farm family near Macon, Georgia. The tramp confessed that he and some friends were in Macon a few years earlier where they had trouble with a farmer. He said they went into his house and killed all but one son that had escaped. They said they took some of his clothes and threw them, with blood on them, into the well.

A reprint of the article appeared in the *Macon Telegraph* on August 28, 1893. It identified the similarities of the two crimes. Both Tom and Lizzie were at odds with their parents over money. Both had step-mothers. Both exhibited extraordinary self-control during the subsequent investigations and trials. Both murders included an axe, and both occurred in early August. The Bordens were murdered on a Thursday, August 4.

There is also one other similarity: the massive sensationalistic publicity which occurred as a result of both crimes which quite possibly contributed to the outcome of both trials. However, in the case of Lizzie Borden, positive newspaper coverage quite possibly contributed not to a *"Guilty"* verdict, but instead to a *"Not Guilty"* verdict.

Tom Woolfolk, by comparison, received considerable negative publicity well in advance of his two trials, and quickly received *"Guilty"* verdicts in both instances. He was in fact virtually convicted in newspapers all over the state.

Articles in the August 6, 1987 issue of the *Telegraph* and in the August

7, 1987 issue of the Anderson (SC) *Independent-Mail* revealed that ten years after Tom's execution, a criminal named Simon Cooper had been lynched in South Carolina and a note found in his diary stated ominously: *"Tom Woolfolk was mighty slick, but I fixed him. I would have killed him with the rest of the damn family, but he was not at home."*

Sometime after the hanging, the Woolfolk plantation land in Bibb County was divided between the two sisters and then sold. The old house where the violent murders took place stood vacant for many years.

In 1909, the home, interestingly, became, for a short while, the headquarters of the Macon Auto Club. Then it stood vacant again for more years.

In 1964, Merton E. Coulter, history professor at the University of Georgia, visited the site when writing an article for the *Georgia Historical Quarterly*. In his article, he described how *"nothing was left except two large piles of brick and stones marking the chimney places, a depression, appearing to have been the cellar, a well nearly filled up near a cedar tree, some shrubbery, and a large holly tree, undoubtedly marking the spot where Susan M. Woolfolk, Tom's mother, had been buried all those years ago."*

Today, individuals visiting the notorious site – unless they are archaeologists or skilled researchers familiar with such investigations – will find absolutely nothing at all. The terrible crime scene, which no one wished to purchase or live upon since that terrible day, has disappeared appropriately from the landscape.

Endnotes:

1/ Richard F. Woolfolk was one of four sons born (1832) to Thomas Woolfolk.

2/ John Ross Crane was responsible for the construction of the University Chapel (1832) and New College (1832) on the old campus of the University of Georgia, the First Presbyterian Church, and a number of very prominent homes, including the Ferdinand Phinizy house (1857) in Athens.

3/ Several previous articles have stated that Tom Woolfolk grew up on Prince Avenue. The home supposedly was located at 716 Prince, and was described as having been demolished. However, following research on the work of John Ross Crane in Athens, it was discovered that his home was still in existence. Crane built a home for himself in 1842 on Pulaski (an extension of Prince). In 1924, the house was sold out of private ownership to the Athens Lodge and then again in 1929 to Sigma Alpha Epsilon (SAE) fraternity. As of this writing, it continues to serve as the fraternity house. Crane died in 1866, leaving the home to Fannie Moore Crane. In Longstreet's *Annals of Athens*, there is a reference to a Mrs. Ross Crane. She was living on Prince in the home of a Col. Billups. This house, destroyed by fire, was not the fine home built by John Ross Crane (as previous articles have erroneously indicated). Research indicates Fannie Crane sold her large home on Pulaski Street following her husband's death in 1866, moving into the Billups home shortly thereafter. Former writers undoubtedly were confused by the recorded fact that Mrs. Ross Crane's last known residence (which was quite near the 1842 home built by her husband), was destroyed by fire, deducing they were one and the same. It is therefore quite likely that Tom Woolfolk was raised for seven years in the fine structure which today houses SAE fraternity in Athens. It was shortly after John Ross Crane's death in 1866, that young Tom was sent back to Macon. Therefore, when he visited Athens from that point forward, he may indeed have stayed with Aunt Fannie Crane at her home (the old Billups house) on Prince Avenue, but it and the 1842 house on Pulaski Street were not one and the same.

4/ In 1887, the day of the murders, Richard F., Jr. was age 20; and Charles age 5. The girls included Pearl, age 17, a student at Wesleyan Female College; Anne, age 10; Rosebud, age 7; and Mattie, eighteen months.

5/ The account was republished in the Wednesday, October 29 1890 issue of the *Macon Telegraph* following the hanging.

6/ Temperance West was Mattie Howard's aunt.

(Grateful appreciation is acknowledged herewith to Kathryn Gray-White who provided most of the information contained in this article.)

The Shocking Assassination of Chief William McIntosh

The Treaty of Indian Spring marked the beginning of the end for the once-great Creek Indian Nation in what today is the southeastern United States. On a spring night in 1825, Creek warriors stole silently to the home of one of their most prominent leaders who had signed the Treaty. They set his home ablaze, then slowly and methodically assassinated Chief William McIntosh in retribution for his actions.

Not even the faintest clue foretold the terrible events about to unfold in the early morning hours of Saturday, April 25, 1825, as the fatal day dawned at the home of Creek Indian Chief William McIntosh at his reservation in what today is known as Carroll County, Georgia. Though he had no inkling of the situation unfolding around him since his Creek brethren had been keenly diligent in silently stealing to his home, he was only moments away from a terrible death.

At that time, other Creek Indian leaders and the tribe which existed mainly in Alabama and Georgia had organized to exact retribution against McIntosh who had committed the fatal deed of ceding the tribe's native lands in Georgia. Depending upon which side one takes in the issue, the Creeks were about to either murder or legally execute one of their major headmen for signing of the *Treaty of Indian Spring.* That document sold to the state of Georgia most of the former homeland of the Creeks in what today is the southeastern United States, dispossessing the Creeks in that area forever. Two other Creek leaders who had also participated in the treaty would

shortly receive a similar punishment.

The response of the Creeks would later be mirrored in similar retaliations by the neighboring Cherokees in 1839 when they meted out equally brutal deaths to Major Ridge, Elias Boudinot, and other tribal leaders for signing the *Treaty of New Echota* in 1835 which sold away the Cherokee lands. Just as the Creeks, the Cherokees would also be enraged that their brethren had engaged in actions which betrayed the trust of their people.

Despite this fact, Boudinot, Ridge, Stand Watie and other Cherokees were agreeing to what they accurately perceived was the absolute best option for their people. Those that opposed the *Treaty* simply could not seem to grasp the fact that regardless of the circumstances, they were going to be removed from their land by the White government one way or the other, and the options for them were limited to either a peaceful relocation after being paid an exceptionally fair price for their properties, or a forced and painful relocation and perhaps limited payment for their properties, depending upon the circumstances.

Final Visage – In the spring of 1825 just prior to his murder that year, a dramatic painting was rendered of Chief William McIntosh in full regalia – including a checkered shirt possibly in homage to his Scottish heritage. It is not known if this work was commissioned by McIntosh himself, or undertaken solely by an artist of that day. As a major chief of the Creek Indians of the Southeast, he was a man of dignity, intellect and great respect, as is portrayed in the painting. He was assassinated by his Creek brethren after signing away his tribe's lands in the Treaty of Indian Spring in what he viewed as the only reasonable solution for his tribe's preservation. He mistook their capacity for complacency with his forfeiture of their homeland. (Reproduction from the McKenney-Hall Portrait of American Indians)

The Cherokees, however, who were much more highly advanced and who had made great strides in a desperate attempt to assimilate into the White culture, differed greatly in that respect from their Creek brothers. The Cherokees had evolved to actual independent "ownership" of individual plots of land and the improvements upon those lands, so that an evaluation and appraisal was easily effected by property value assessors, and a fair value easily attached to each Cherokee's plot of land so that equitable payment could be made. A large percentage of the individual Cherokees, at least would therefore be granted a handsome reimbursement for their properties by the U.S. federal government.

In contrast, the Creeks' personal association with their lands were entirely different. They had no concept of the "ownership" of land. No Creek, in fact, actually owned any individual property. They merely were entitled collectively to live in the realm as a member of the tribe. Even the crude mud huts and other structures in their settlements were not controlled by the male population, but rather by the females in a matriarchal society of clans. The men controlled nothing, and could even be legally "divorced" and banished from their homes by their spouses.

So when the Creeks were dispossessed of their lands, none of them received any type of "payment" whatsoever in return for the loss of their homeland. They simply no longer had a home and were to be removed to a strange reservation out West in Oklahoma to begin anew. They, however, did know that their leader, McIntosh, was supposedly being paid a great sum of "money," and being allotted a handsome personal reservation of property in Georgia for himself and his family in return for his signature on the *Treaty*. His fellow Creeks, therefore, just as would be many Cherokees in later years, were enraged, and understandably so.

Negotiations for ratification of the *Treaty of Indian Spring* had been on-going for a number of years, because Georgia had been pressing for more land to enable the expansion of her frontiers westward, but a large portion of the Creek Nation – which, again, would later mirror the circumstances of the Cherokees – simply did not wish to part with their land. The Creeks, in fact, viewed with alarm their diminishing homeland, and were highly reluctant to lose yet another large portion of it to land-hungry Whites, and they certainly did not want to be relocated to a strange land out West.

William McIntosh, however, a mixed-blood Creek Indian chieftain, had seen the handwriting on the wall. He was well aware that there was an endless stream of Europeans traveling across the ocean to the fledgling United States, and that if his people hoped to remain in existence at all as an organized tribe, they had no choice but to leverage the best opportunity available to them regarding their lands in Georgia, and move peacefully to a reservation out West.

Caught in the vortex of these negotiations for the Creek lands not only was McIntosh, but also Georgia Governor George Troup. McIntosh, interestingly, was Troup's cousin. The two were related through the governor's mother who was a sister of McIntosh's father, making the two leaders first cousins.

Both men were astute politicians in their own domains, and both essentially conspired to cede the Creeks' last vestige of lands in today's Georgia to the encroaching Whites in return for the provision of a substantial payment and Georgia domicile reservation for McIntosh. Nevertheless, had the payment even been made directly to each member of the Creek Nation instead of solely to McIntosh, the reaction of the tribe almost certainly would have been the same. "Money" in the White culture traditional sense (gold or silver, etc.) held no value whatsoever to the Creeks.

Their culture, essentially, was not based upon items of material value.

In the 1820s, despite the constant immigration of White colonists into the region, most of Georgia was still a dense frontier; and the indigenous natives, by and large, still lived by their own code of ethics, morals and commerce. Warnings had been sounded through the years by other headmen of the Creek Nation, extolling to all who would listen, the punishment which would be meted out according to Creek law to any member of the Nation involved with any further diminishment of the tribe's land.

McIntosh, however, assumed erroneously that he was not susceptible to these threats. He was of the opinion that his power and lofty status as a Creek "headman" would exempt him from such punishment. He also believed erroneously that in addition to his own powers as a top leader of the Creeks, his relationship as a cousin to the head of the rapidly growing White government in Georgia would further protect him from any retribution by his people. It was a fatal mistake.

On February 12, 1825, McIntosh, along with a contingent of lower chiefs, had signed the now infamous *Treaty of Indian Spring*, so-called because the signing was conducted at the site of McIntosh's fine home (which still stands as of this writing in 2024) in present-day Butts County, Georgia. This impressive structure, though totally unprotected in the years after McIntosh's assassination, somehow managed to survive intact into the 21st Century, and is today preserved and maintained at Indian Spring by the Butts County Historic Society.

In payment for signing the treaty, the U.S. Government agreed to pay the Creek Nation (actually McIntosh) the sum of $200,000.00 *"as soon as is practicable after ratification of this treaty."* The Creek chieftain also received other considerations as well, including his large reservation of property and another home on the Chattahoochee River in present-day western Georgia.

For years, a pervading myth has maintained that McIntosh was paid the $200,000.00 in person and in gold. One tale even relates how many wagons were necessary to transport the gold to McIntosh's Chattahoochee River plantation. No evidence, however, has ever surfaced to substantiate these stories, and no mention of gold was made in the language of the *Treaty*. Despite this fact, rumors persist to this day, and searches continue for "McIntosh's gold" all along the road from Indian Spring in Butts County to the site of McIntosh's Chattahoochee River home in present-day Carroll County.

The present-day fascination with the prospect of this gold is understandable. In 1820, one Troy ounce of gold was valued at approximately $20.00, so the $200,000.00 payment would translate to approximately 10,000 ounces of gold if payment was made in that precious metal. In 2024, the value of gold is approximately $2,300.00 per ounce (and rising), so the payment to McIntosh just in the value of the gold itself, would be worth approximately $23,000,000.00 today if discovered. And if the payment to McIntosh was paid in gold coins of that day, the value would be almost incalculable. It is small wonder that so much interest has been focused upon this presumed "treasure" over the years.

Immediately after the *Treaty* was signed, the Creek chiefs who had opposed the signing met in secret at several Creek towns of east-central Alabama, where they began discussions of retaliation against those individuals who had

signed away the tribal lands. It was decided that at the very least, William McIntosh would die, as would his son-in-law, Samuel Hawkins. Hawkins lived on the Tallapoosa River near the Creek towns which once existed in today's central Alabama.

Within the secret meetings, detailed and careful instructions were provided to a special group of the tribe's warriors on how they were to meet and advance upon McIntosh at his plantation on the Chattahoochee and how he was to be executed. The exact number of Creeks involved in this execution is unknown today; best estimates range from 170 to 400 warriors, according to several different sources through which events of that day were recorded. The mere number of warriors assigned to this task is an indication of the respect they yet held for McIntosh and his power.

The group, principally from Ocfuskee and Tookabatchie, both of which were large Indian towns in east-central Alabama, met and advanced on foot in single file toward Georgia. They traveled so silently and efficiently that they were completely undetected on their journey, reaching the neighborhood of McIntosh's Chattahoochee plantation on the evening of the second day.

The warriors reportedly stationed themselves on both sides of an intersection about one mile northwest of McIntosh's home, and awaited the wee hours of early morning to carry out the assassination. It was at this intersection that an ironic event occurred. On the evening of the warriors' arrival and concealment in the undergrowth at this site, McIntosh and his son-in-law Samuel Hawkins – both of whom were slated for execution by the Creeks – met on horseback at this very spot. The Creek warriors were so well-concealed and noiseless that

Horror in the Making – Shouting "McIntosh we have come for you!" warriors from the Creek tribe no doubt horrified this one-time respected chief as they demonstrated their anger before exacting their revenge upon him for signing the *Treaty of Indian Spring* relinquishing the Creek lands in what today is Georgia. McIntosh's solitary grave has existed undisturbed a few feet from the site of his assassination for almost 200 years as of this writing (2024) in what today is a Carroll County, Georgia park approximately four miles south of Whitesburg. A reproduction of the home which the Creek warriors burned in 1825 was later reconstructed on the original site of his home (rear). (Photo courtesy of Marion Hemperley)

McIntosh and Hawkins were completely unaware of the presence of the natives.

McIntosh and Hawkins remained upon their mounts as they conversed at length. The assassination warriors reportedly were so near to the pair that they could almost have reached out and touched the two unsuspecting men. The warriors could easily have killed the two there on that spot had they chosen to do so, but they had been specifically instructed that for maximum effect, McIntosh was to be executed *"in his own yard, in the presence of his family, and to let his blood run upon the soil of that reservation which the Georgians had secured to him in the treaty which he had made with them."*

It was that important to them to send that type of message to the remainder of the tribe.

After concluding his meeting with McIntosh, Hawkins reportedly turned and started for home, with McIntosh riding a short distance beside him. Turning back toward his own home shortly thereafter, McIntosh again passed right through the hidden Indians, and again they had an opportunity to kill him on the spot, but did not.

As Hawkins continued westward to return to his farm on the Tallapoosa River (near present-day Talladega, Alabama), a chosen few of the warriors separated from the main group and silently followed him, intent upon an equally bloody execution for him. The Creek numbers had already been decimated approximately ten years earlier in 1814 by Gen. Andrew Jackson at nearby Horseshoe Bend in Alabama, where upwards of 800 of the 1,000-warrior-strong Creek Nation were destroyed. These depleted numbers no doubt lent further confidence to McIntosh in his *Treaty* actions. The warriors, notably, were desperate for some measure of vengeance for being so overwhelmed by the White settlers.

The main body of the Creek warriors reportedly remained in the woods at McIntosh's reservation until about 3:00 a.m. of the fateful morning, at which time, they gathered "fat lighter" (the highly-flammable resinous heartwood of aged pine trees) to use to burn McIntosh's log house. They quietly surrounded the home, and at daybreak, set the structure ablaze to force the headman and his family outside.

For a number of years, McIntosh (as did several other prominent Indian chiefs during this period in Georgia history) had operated an inn as well as a ferry near this home on the Chattahoochee River. The inn provided accommodations for travelers using a branch of the "Alabama Road" to travel westward. The portion of the road which led to McIntosh's home and Inn was known in that day as "the McIntosh Trail." Vestiges of this historic trail near the former site of the famed chieftain's home may still be seen even today.

Inside McIntosh's inn on the night of the fatal attack, five persons were sleeping, including Chilly McIntosh, son of the doomed William. As he was also one of the signers of the hated *Treaty*, and undoubtedly knew his life was also in grave danger, Chilly quite likely quickly sized up the situation upon

hearing the commotion outside in the yard. He no doubt decided that discretion was the better part of valor, and leapt from a rear window of the inn and then plunged into what could only have been icy cold April waters in the Chattahoochee to swim to the opposite shore and safety. Better alive, cold, wet and in danger of hypothermia on the opposite shore of the Chattahoochee than temporarily warm in the inn and soon to be stone-cold from death.

The Creek warriors, meanwhile, had had the presence of mind to bring a White man (named Hudman or Hutton; records differ on the spelling of the name) with them, in order to certify that no harm had come to any Whites in the inn. There were Whites sleeping there, including one peddler. Accounts of the day maintain that the peddler *"became a most wretched man"* after the commotion began, until Hutton assured him that no harm would come his way. The Indians, true to their word, left the peddler unharmed, but destroyed his wares, along with everything else in sight.

Yet another of the signers of the *Treaty of Indian Spring*, a minor Creek headman named Toma Tustinugee who was also sleeping in the inn, was not so lucky. The warriors, totally unexpecting this additional prize, removed Toma to the yard, where, in the light of McIntosh's burning home, they summarily executed him within McIntosh's view, firing some fifty bullets into his body. The site of his burial is unknown today.

McIntosh, in the meantime, was having problems of his own. The flames from his home threw a bright light over the yard, giving his horrified family a clear view of the terrifying painted warriors surrounding the house. To the warriors' credit, they allowed McIntosh's two wives and his children to remove themselves from the burning house; no harm befell them. They, however, did not allow the women or children to remove any articles with them from the burning structure. Consequently, the women were wearing only their sparse night clothing, and the children were naked in the chill early morning April air.

After the women and children were removed, McIntosh reportedly barricaded the front door and stood near it until it was forced open. He then retreated to the second floor, guns in his hands, returning the fire from the warriors. According to later reports, his attackers stood in his yard mockingly and eerily shouting "McIntosh! We have come! We have come! We told you, if you sold the land to the Georgians, we would come!" The Creek assassins continued to discharge their weapons into the burning house.

McIntosh's wives, meanwhile, were imploring the assailants to spare their husband, or at the very least to remove him from the burning house before shooting him. They screamed to the Creeks that McIntosh was an Indian like themselves, and, as a brave man, did not deserve to die a horrible death in the flames.

The burning house soon became a conflagration, forcing McIntosh to return to the first floor where he reportedly was met by a hail of bullets. He fell to the floor severely wounded, where he was seized by the legs and dragged into the yard outside by the warriors before the flaming house cooked him any further. While lying in the yard, and with blood coursing from numerous wounds, McIntosh reportedly raised himself on one arm and surveyed his murderers with a look of defiance. At that moment, an Ocfuskee Indian plunged a long knife to the hilt into McIntosh's breast. It is

recorded that he took one long gasping breath before collapsing and dying.

The Indians, however, were far from finished. Their appetites had only been whetted and their wrath was yet to be depleted. They proceeded to plunder the out-houses and to kill every domesticated animal in sight. Anything they could not carry with them, they destroyed with a vengeance. Hogs were shot and left lying in the yard beside the dead men. All the peddler's goods were removed from the inn and destroyed.

One of McIntosh's wives went to the warriors and requested that they give her a white suit in which to bury her husband. This request was quickly refused. McIntosh, to the further horror of the females, was subsequently scalped and left lying in the yard where he had died. Later, after the warriors had departed, McIntosh's body was buried a short distance away, not far from where he had fallen and died.

After looting and destroying the plantation, the Indians returned to their Alabama homes, carrying McIntosh's scalp with them. It was later ceremoniously exhibited in the public square at Ocfuskee. The scalp was a further warning to others who might be tempted to take similar measures with the remaining Creek lands.

Samuel Hawkins suffered a similar fate. After following Hawkins home to Alabama, the Creek warriors assigned to him quietly surrounded his farmhouse where they remained until daybreak. Following instructions, Hawkins was not killed out-right, but was taken prisoner until the fate of McIntosh could be certified. About 3:00 p.m., after word had been received of McIntosh's death, Hawkins also was killed and scalped. The latter trophy was displayed with that of McIntosh's in Ocfuskee Town.

Ancient Native American Trail – An abandoned portion of the original McIntosh Road in the former "McIntosh Reserve" of present-day Carroll County, Georgia, is still clearly visible through the forest. This ancient former Indian trail, identified by the late Marion Hemperley, deputy surveyor-general of Georgia prior to his death, is just north of and parallel to the Chattahoochee River in the Reserve. It was used in pre-history by the Native Americans of this area, and later by pioneer settlers as one of the trails westward to Alabama and beyond. The McIntosh Reserve was included as a portion of the pay-off to McIntosh in return for his signature on the *Treaty of Indian Spring*. It and the monetary pay-off he supposedly received eventually became his death warrant. (Photo courtesy of Marion Hemperley)

The resulting repercussions of these killings were felt all the way to the halls of Congress. Called *"murder"* by the Whites, and *"a legal execution"* by the Indians, the incident was actually an act of desperation by a nation of people quickly being displaced from their homeland by an on-rushing tide of White settlers. It would only be a short ten years before the state and federal governments would remove the Indians completely from their remaining lands in Alabama, shipping them west to present-day Oklahoma.

Today, one can visit the site of the McIntosh killing in a Carroll County park located about four miles southwest of Whitesburg. It holds no hint of the horrors perpetrated here in April of 1825. It is a beautiful, quiet and secluded spot overlooking the very scenic Chattahoochee River. It is small wonder that McIntosh chose this for his final home.

The remains of a later house built on or near the site of McIntosh's burned home actually stood until the late 20th century. The later structure, however, eventually was almost completely destroyed by greedy "treasure hunters" and vandals, many of whom were voraciously searching for McIntosh's mythical gold. As of this writing, a replica of McIntosh's burned home has been reconstructed yet again at the site, and is preserved there today.

If one visits the intersection of the park road with GA Highway 5 just north of the old home-place, he or she will be in the exact spot where McIntosh and Hawkins conversed on that fateful night so long ago. For those who desire to re-trace the original McIntosh Road west-ward from Indian Spring, the following directions are provided:

Leaving Indian Spring in a south-westwardly direction, the old road passed just north of present-day Mt. Ver-non Church and by Elgin and Liberty Churches, before going through an area once known as "Sandy Plains."

The road next passed through the old ghost town of Waltham, be-fore reaching Spalding County on to-day's GA Highway 16. It continued by Union and Ringgold Churches to the in-tersection of GA Highways 16 and 156. At that crossing there was once a well-known stagecoach stop known as "Dou-ble Cabins" (the Militia District today retains the name: "Cabin District").

Double Cabins was due north of present-day Griffin and the McIntosh Road in running through the former town, missed Griffin completely. Along that stretch, the old road was once known as the "Old Madison Alabama Stage Road," and also as "Upper Cabin Road."

Passing on through the upper fringes of Experiment, the McIntosh Road took the left fork at McIntosh School, be-fore going through Rio and Vaughn and crossing the Flint Riv-er into Fayette Coun-ty. It ran on westward through Brooks and Senoia, passing just north of Turin to go through Sharpsburg and Raymond, close on GA Highway 16, before reaching Newnan on McIntosh Street, a name obviously retained from the original McIntosh Road.

From Newnan, the old thorough-fare turned northwest to cross the Chat-tahoochee River near the mouth of Pearsons Creek. At that stream, the McIntosh Road crossed over McIntosh's Ferry into present-day Carroll County where it reached the settlement of Wil-liam McIntosh.

As of this writing, there is an area on McIntosh's old reservation just west of the Chattahoochee River where an aban-doned remnant of the old original McIn-tosh Trail is still discernible. Turning up the hill from the river, the road passes the site at which McIntosh's home and inn, the site of his murder, once existed.

Continuing northward for a short distance, the old road reached an inter-section just west of today's Rotherwood. This, again, is the intersection at which William McIntosh and Samuel Hawkins conversed while the silent Indians sur-rounding them awaited the moment to assassinate them.

From this point, the McIntosh Road turned directly west-ward to run on GA Highway 5 all the way into Alabama, pass-ing through Low-ell, Roopville, and Tyrus along the way. It was along the latter stretch that Sam Haw-kins made the final trip to his home in Ala-bama before dying at the hands of his Creek brethren.

Continuing northward for a short distance, the old road reached an intersection just west of today's Rotherwood.

Today, there is a great interest in the McIntosh saga. In Peachtree City, just north of the actual route of the road, there is a McIntosh Opry as well as a McIntosh High School. In fact, all along the way from Indian Spring in present-day Butts County westward, remnants of the name are retained, and many persons living today along the old route are familiar with details concerning the McIntosh legend.

Though he has departed this earth, and though the worldly possessions of Chief William McIntosh have been scattered and lost, the historic milestones of this once-prominent member of the Creek Indian Nation live on . . . as does McIntosh's legend.

Today, archived at the University of Georgia Libraries are two letters, one written by two of the three wives of Chief William McIntosh, and another written by the daughter of the third wife. The letters were written immediately following McIntosh's murder.

The letters were sent to White leaders of that day in 1825. They represented the McIntosh family's desperate pleas for help. These sad plaintive documents vividly describe the horror and anguish suffered by Peggy and Susannah McIntosh (two of the wives), and of Jane Hawkins (a daughter of the third wife). The letters also provide a clear indication of the oftentimes harsh and unforgiving circumstances encountered by 19th Century American Indian

leaders (and, subsequently, their families) who dared to negotiate with and bargain away tribal lands to the U.S. government. These letters are maintained in the Telamon Cuyler Collection at UGA Libraries, and are provided in their entirety below.

May 3, 1825. Line Creek, Fayette Co.

To Col. Duncan G. Campbell and Major James Meriwether U.S. Commss

Gentlemen,

When you see this letter stained with the blood of my husband the last drop of which is now spilt for the friendship he has shown for your people, I know you will remember your pledge to us in behalf of your nation, that in the worst of events you would assist and protect us. And when I tell you that at day light on Saturday morning last, hundreds of the Hostiles surrounded our house, and instantly murdered Genl McIntosh & Tom Tustunnuge, by shooting near one hundred balls into them (Chilly and Moody Kennard making their escape thro' a Window) they then Commenced burning and plundering in the most unprincipled way, so that here I am driven from the ashes of my smoking dwelling, left with nothing but my poor little naked hungry children, who need some immediate aid from our white friends, and we lean upon you white, you lean upon your government.

About the same time of the morning that they committed the horrid act on the

> *These sad plaintive documents vividly describe the horror and anguish suffered by Peggy and Susannah McIntosh.*

General, another party caught Col Saml Hawkins, and kept him tied until about 3 o'clock when the chiefs returned from our house and gave orders for his execution in the same way, and refused to leave his impliments to cover his body up with, so that it was left exposed to the Fowls of the Air and the beasts of the Forest, and Jinny and her child are here, in the same condition as we are - this party consisted principally of Oakfuskies, Talledegers & Muckfaws, tho' there were others with them - The Chiefs that appeared to head the party were Intockunge of Muckfaw, Thloc-co-cos-co mico of Arpachoochee, Munnawho, but I know not where he was from, who said they were ordered to do it by the Little prince and Hopoeth Yoholo, and that they were supported and encouraged in it by the Agent and the chiefs that were left after the Big Warriors Death in a council at Broken Arrow where they decreed that they would murder all the Chiefs who had any hand in selling the Land, and burn & destroy and take away all they had, and then send on to the President that he should not have the Land - I have not heard of the murder of any others but expect all are dead that could be catchd.

But by reason of a great freshet in the Chattahochee they could not get Col Miller nor Hogey McIntosh nor the Darisaws, and they and Chilly are gone to the Governor. Our country is in a most ruined State so far as I have heard (tho' by reason of the high waters word has not circulated fast) all have fled from their homes in our parts and taken refuge among their white friends, and I learn there are now at Genl Wares (near this place) from 150 to 200 of them who are afraid to go to their homes to get a grain of what little corn they have to eat, much more to try to make any more, and if You and Your people do not assist us, God help us - we must die either by the Sword or the famin.

This moment Genl. Ware has come in and will in a few minutes start with a few men and a few friendly Indians to try to get a little something for us to eat. I hope so soon as you read this, You will lay it before the Governor and the President that they may know our miserable condition, & afford us relief as soon as possible, I followed them to their camp about one and one-half miles to try to beg of them something to cover the dead with, but it was denied me. I tryed also to get a Horse to take my little children and some provisions to last us to the White Settlements which was given up to me and then taken Back - and had it not have been for some White men who assisted in burying the Dead and getting us to the White Settlements, we should have been worse off then we were if possible - before I close I must remark that the whole of the party so far as I knew them were hostile during the War.

Peggy & Susannah McIntosh
Fayett County, 3rd May, 1825

Colo Campbell and Major Meriwether,

My dear friends, I send you this paper, which will not tell you a lie, but if it had ten tongues it could not tell you all the truth. On the Morning of the 30th of April at break of day, my Fathers house was surrounded by a party of Hostile Indians, to the number of several hundred, who instantly fired his dwelling, and Murdered him, and Thomas Tustunnuggee by shooting more than one hundred balls into them, and took away the whole of Fathers money and property which they coud carry off, and destroyed the rest leaving the family no clothes (some not one rag) nor provision. - Brother Chilly was at Fathers and made his escape through a Window under cover of a Travelling white man who obtained leave for them to come out that way, It being not yet light, he was not discovered.

While those hostiles were Murdering my beloved Father, they were tying my Husband (Colo Saml. Hawkins) with Cords, to wait the arrival of Itockchunga, Thloccocoscomicco and Munnawwa, who were the commanders at Fathers, to give orders for the Colos execution also, which took place about 3 oclock the same day. And these barbarous men, not content with spilling the blood of both my Husband and Father to attone for their constant friendship to both your Nation and our own; refused my hands the painful previledge of covering his body up in the very ground which he lately defended, against those Hostile Murderers, and drove me from my home, stript of my two best friends in one day, Stript of all my property my provision, and my clothing, with a more painful reflection than all these, that the body of my poor murdered husband should remain unburied, to be devoured by the birds, and the beasts. (Was ever poor woman worse off than I?).

I have this moment arrived among our white friends, who altho they are very kind, have but little to bestow on me, and my poor helpless infant, who must suffer befor any aid can reach us from you, but I can live a great while on very little, besides the confidence I have on you, and your government. For I know by your promise, you will aid and defend us, as soon as you hear from our situation.

These Murderers are the very same Hostiles who treated the whites 10 years ago as they have now treated my husband and Father, who say they are determined to kill all who had any hand in selling the land, and when they have completed the work, of Murdering, Burning, plundering and destruction, they will send the President word that they have saved their Land, and taken it back and that he and the white people never shall have it again. Which is the order of the heads of the Nation, by the advice of the Agent.

We expect that many of our best friends are already Killed, but have not heard, by reason of the waters being too high for word to go quick, which is the only reason Colo Miller and others on his side of the River were not Killed. We are in a dreadful Condition, & I dont think there will be one ear of corn made in this part of the Nation, for the whole of the friendly party have fled to Dekalb and Fayett Counties two much alarmed to return to their houses to get a little grain of what corn they left, for themselves and their families to subsist on, much more to stay at home to make more, and we fear every day that what little provision left will be destroyed.

I am afraid you will think I make it worse, but how can that be, for it is worse of its self than any pen can write, my condition admits of no equal, & mocks me when I try to speak of it. After I was stript of my last Frock but one, humanty and duty called on me to pull it off and spread it over the body of my dead Husband, (which was allowed no other covering) which I did, as a Farewell witness of my Affection, I was 25 miles from any friend (but sister Catharine, who was with me) and had to stay all night in the woods, surrounded by a thousand hostile Indians, who were constantly insulting and affrighting us. And now I am here with only one old coat to my back, and not a Morsel of Bread to save us from perishing, or a rag of Blanket to cover my poor little boy from the sun at noon or the due at night, & I am a poor distracted orphan and Widow.

Jane Hawkins

(Grateful appreciation is expressed herewith in memory of the late Marion Hemperley, former deputy surveyor-general of the state of Georgia, for some of the details included in this article.)

Mob Maven From Marietta:
The Virginia Hill Story

Though gentle and kind to friends and family, life was less rewarding to the attractive young lady from Cobb County, Georgia, who grew up to become the kept woman of Chicago mobsters. She ultimately died a lonely death far from home, and later was immortalized upon the silver screen in her life of crime with Benjamin "Bugsy" Siegel.

Down through the years of its storied history, north Georgia's Cobb County, has produced any number of individuals who have gone on to achieve national – if not international – fame and fortune. Who could forget, for instance, Academy Award-winning actresses Joann Woodward (Mrs. Paul Newman) and Julia Roberts, or country music singer, songwriter, actor, and hit-maker Travis Tritt, just to name a few. There is, however, another "celebrity" from Cobb who, perhaps, is even more famous than these individuals, but her name unfortunately must first also be qualified with the adjective "notorious." Her name was Virginia Hill.

Virginia was actually born a few miles away in Lipscomb, Alabama, on August 26, 1916, to Margaret and Mack Hill, spending her earliest years in Bessemer, Alabama. Mack was an itinerant blacksmith and horse-trader back when horses were still a marginal form of public transportation. When Virginia was 8 years of age, Mack moved his growing family to what then were the rural confines of Acworth, Georgia, just north of Marietta, possibly as a result of the multitudes of horses and mules

being regularly marketed in that vicinity. At some point the family moved down to Marietta.

Virginia was one of nine or ten children fathered by Mack. According to later stories, Virginia's father was anything but a model parent, often beating her during her childhood . . . that is . . . until the day she threw a hot skillet at him following her latest abusive treatment. That got his attention, and sent the message that Virginia was not one with whom to be trifled.

An early "bloomer," young Virginia reportedly was sexually active with boys at age 12, and doubtless contributed more than her share to the acrimonious relationship with her father by regularly publicly flaunting her sexuality. As she reached her higher teenage years, Virginia came to the attention of growing numbers of the male population in the nearby Marietta environs. "Miss Virginia," you see, was quite the "looker," and she knew it and used it to every advantage.

The late Bill Kinney, a long-time Cobb resident and former reporter and editor of the ***Marietta Daily Journal*** apparently knew Virginia quite well, and once described her as "a

Testy Testimony – Virginia Hill sits uncomfortably, possibly in advance of the U.S. Senate Hearings on Organized Crime in which she was called to testify.

saucy, curvaceous, red-headed bombshell, who burst upon Marietta's serenity during the hard times of the Great Depression.

"In those days, women were just getting around to wearing one-piece bathing suits," Kinney recalled, "but Virginia (routinely) wore a halter-top and 'short' short-shorts." Dressed provocatively as such and barefooted, she, according to Kinney, would ride her horse down Church Street into Marietta and around the town square, and then back up Cherokee Street to her house. She was the talk of the town among the adolescents, and apparently was everything just short of "Lady Godiva" riding naked, and the young men absolutely loved it.

On Her Own

Virginia attended the public schools in Marietta until she was 14, when, in order to escape her abusive father, she married (or at least ran off with) a mysterious man named "George." In 1933, at the height of the Great Depression and at the tender age of 17, Virginia moved with George to Chicago, where she promptly ditched him and set out on her own. Back in Georgia, Mack Hill abandoned the remainder of the family, leaving Margaret and the children to fend for themselves.

Ever resourceful in the use of her sexuality to gain the things she needed – or wanted – Virginia shortly found employment as a "shimmy dancer" at the *1933 World's Fair* in Chicago, and it was there that she made the acquaintance of an individual by the name of Joe Epstein, who was to figure prominently in her life for the remainder of her days. Epstein was employed as the bookkeeper and close associate of notorious Chicago mobster Alphonse "Al" Capone.

Virginia Hill may have had little in the way of a formal academic education, but when it came to "street smarts," she was *Phi Beta Kappa*. In short order, she had leveraged her beauty and beguiling personality into an apprenticeship to Epstein who, accordingly, facilitated her move up the ladder within the Mob hierarchy and became her constant source of income.

Through Epstein, Virginia tapped into a tutelage for a lifestyle of crime and graft which gave her easy access to huge sums of Mob-related money. After demonstrating that she could be a loyal and reliable courier for laundered funds and narcotics to and from Mob-controlled income centers like Havana, Cuba, New York, St. Louis, and

Chicago, she graduated to Mob maven, and never looked back.

Always well-dressed and bejeweled, Virginia – though certainly not included within inner circles of the Mob – was eventually considered to be a very valuable employee, since she not only was trustworthy, but also far less-likely than the typical male Mob foot-soldier to become a target of searches (and loser of the Mob money-laundered funds). And, as a result of Epstein's loyalty and endless financial support, she became a devoted follower, willing to do virtually anything.

Virginia was a fast-study in graft too. She was often given thousands of dollars to bet on pre-arranged horses at the race tracks. She followed Epstein's precise instructions, brought back the winning tickets and got a 10 percent share of the proceeds. Epstein also showed her how to lure unsuspecting men into "sucker" bets – pure profit for bookies – such as for fixed boxing matches. She was a natural for these illicit activities.

"Joe Epstein ran the gambling business around Chicago," Kinney added. "Of course, things like the races at the tracks were fixed, and Joe Adonis and the other racketeers at those locales not only made a lot of money placing bets there, but so also did Epstein and Virginia."

With incredible ease, using her intoxicating beauty, sexual liaisons and talents for laundering money and stolen merchandise, Virginia rose higher than any other woman in the nation's underworld, associating with the most infamous male racketeers of that era, including Meyer Lansky, Charles "Lucky" Luciano, Joe Adonis, Frank Costello, Johnny Rosselli, Charles and Joe Fischetti, Tony Accardo, Frank Nitti, William "Ice Pick Willie" Alderman, Jack Dragna

Pursuing a Dream – A publicity print of Virginia Hill during her days as a Hollywood starlet. (**Associated Press** photo courtesy of Bill Kinney, **Marietta Daily Journal**)

and, most famously, Benjamin "Bugsy" Siegel.

Despite her growing notoriety in Mob activities, few people back home in Marietta were even vaguely aware of Virginia's involvement with the underworld in Chicago. She often returned home to Marietta during the early 1930s, but when she did, she always had enough money to bankroll Elvis, and no one could figure out where she got it. Her Marietta followers just knew she was very attractive, had "lots" of money, and freely shared whatever she had with her friends.

"When Virginia came back to town to visit," Kinney smiled in remembrance, "all the women would warn their husbands and boyfriends 'You stay away from that hussy!' But all of we young fellows stood there on the (Marietta town) square at the corner of Hodge's Drug Store anyway, just waiting on her. . . We were all on 'Virginia watch.'

"We just thought by that time that she was an actress, or rich heiress, or that she had married very well into money," Kinney continued. "Nobody asked many questions, because she was so good to us."

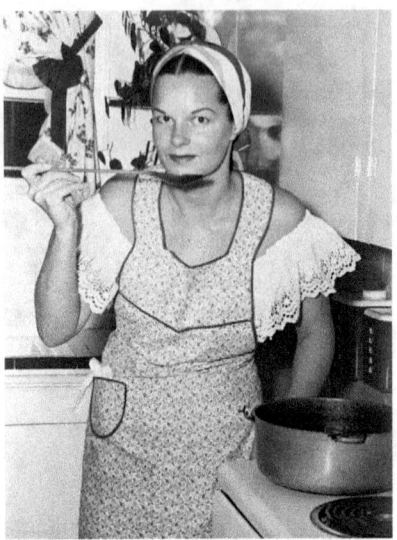

Dependable Deliveries – Joe Epstein, a prominent bookkeeper and associate of Alphonse Capone, became acquainted with Virginia during her days in Chicago. She made it clear that she was trustworthy and dependable, and was soon tapped by the mob to transport large sums of illicit cash between Miami, Florida, and Chicago. Epstein made regular mob payments to Hill for her loyalty. Virginia reportedly was quite fond of cooking for her friends, and is pictured here in a home purchased for her in Miami by mobster Benjamin "Bugsy" Siegel. (**Associated Press** photo courtesy of Bill Kinney, **Marietta Daily Journal**)

Benjamin "Bugsy" Siegel

It was Virginia's association and brief relationship with hitman, hustler and racketeer Benjamin "Bugsy" Siegel which earned her the greatest measure of notoriety and renown within the annals of Mob history. The two began seeing each other as early as 1937, and despite his reputation as a heartless killer, Siegel was drawn to Virginia like a moth to flame – completely infatuated and overwhelmed by her womanly charms.

Siegel was one of Mob boss Joe Adonis' main earners in the 1930s, and with his equal charm, handsome good looks and blue eyes, he was just as attractive to Virginia as was she to him. The two reportedly began a sexual relationship almost immediately upon meeting each other, an action which both hurt and enraged Adonis who was equally smitten with Virginia.

As a result of this jealousy, Adonis made his anger known to the Chicago Outfit. Since Siegel was virtually untouchable and uncontrollable, it fell to Virginia to suffer the punishment for her perceived amorous transgression, and her financial stream via Joe Epstein was cut dramatically to send her a message. Unfazed, Virginia merely moved back to Georgia for a brief spell to allow her Mob friends time "to find another courier as trustworthy as she" – if that was possible. She also wished simply to visit with her mother in Marietta, so she took some time off.

This period of separation from Siegel, however, was anything but long-term, and they both knew it. It wasn't long before they were an item yet again. Despite the heat they generated together, Virginia's overall relationship with Siegel was nevertheless known to be "stormy" at best. Beneath her sweet exterior veneer and earthy female attraction, Virginia was very independent-minded, and didn't hesitate to speak her mind to Siegel, nor did she allow herself to be controlled, a scenario which often resulted in fierce fighting between the two.

To the already-married Siegel, Hill was his ideal woman in many respects. Their intense pairing and Mob business eventually led them to the West Coast and actor George Raft's Hollywood home in 1939. Raft and Siegel had known each other as kids and remained closely associated throughout their lives.

It no doubt was through Raft that

Early Arrest – In one of his police mug-shots – this one following an arrest in 1928 – Benjamin Siegel offers a hostile gaze to the camera. It was during the period in which she lived in Chicago that Virginia Hill began her association with mobsters such as Siegel, and her role as a courier of large sums of illicit cash from mob-controlled casinos in Havana, Cuba, sent northward to Chicago and New York.

Virginia learned how to acquire an agent and to work her way into the acting world as a starlet. Her beauty and smoldering sexuality were undeniable, and she no doubt made frequent use of the "casting couch" in her efforts to gain admission to Hollywood.

The years 1939 and 1940 would be busy ones for the actress-wannabe.

Other Conquests

While Siegel was cooling his heels in prison from August to November of 1940 after being charged with murder, Virginia, surprisingly, took up with a Mexican nightclub dancer named Miguelito Valdez. She even married Valdez during this period in order that he might gain readmission to the United States so that he could resume his lucrative performing career.

Virginia returned with Valdez to Chicago, then shortly departed for Georgia, where she met a 19-year-old college football player at a bar, then married him on the spur of the moment, just as she had done with Valdez. But barely six months later, she had the marriage

Favored Outfit – Benjamin Siegel is pictured here circa 1946 in a sports jacket of which he apparently was quite fond since it appears in a number of his photographs. He has assumed his usual posture with his patented hostile glare.

with her athletic conquest annulled and returned to Valdez. To say the least, Virginia Hill got around.

According to speculation, Virginia may also have taken Louis Dragna's top associate, Johnny Rosselli, as a lover as well. With her credibility within the Mob in high gear, she invested Outfit cash into a nightclub called "The Hurricane" in New York, and appeared at the opening, dancing the rumba in her bare feet with Valdez before news cameras.

After the opening at the nightclub, Virginia tricked the hapless Valdez into signing a contractual agreement which he foolishly thought was a booking for The Hurricane. In reality, it was an uncontested divorce agreement. Virginia was moving on again.

Fluent in Spanish by that point, Hill had also become involved in drug trafficking – specifically heroin – out of

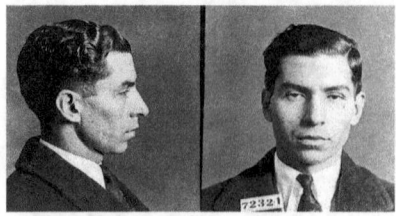

Mob Boss – Charles "Lucky" Luciano was a close associate of Virginia Hill's love-interest, Benjamin Siegel. Luciano is pictured here in a mug-shot from one of his arrests. If Siegel's death was in fact a mob-hit, it almost certainly would have been Luciano - in association with mob leader Meyer Lansky - who signed off on Siegel's termination. Other potential perpetrators of the crime, however, have also been suggested over the years.

Mexico for her Chicago patrons. To curry favor and obtain important information for the Outfit south of the border, she reportedly had affairs with the son of a Mexican finance minister and a connected politician.

Meanwhile, since the day he had first helped her obtain work inside the Outfit, Joe Epstein was still regularly funneling cash through the mail to Virginia – virtually whenever she requested it. It was an income stream which would continue well into the mid-1960s.

Both Luciano and Meyer Lansky used Hill to distribute Mob cash, likely realizing her double attraction as a Mob money courier who not only made financial deliveries, but also provided sexual favors to the recipient on the opposite end. In addition to her other services, the seductress was a spy for and confidant to Mob bosses, exchanging verbal communications with underlings and then reporting back to Epstein, Lansky, Luciano, and others on whatever might have been transpiring "under the table." Virginia received steady income from these pursuits as well.

Show Biz Dreams

By the early 1940s, Virginia was pursuing a career in Hollywood in earnest. She and brother Chick took acting lessons, and she yearned for a serious opportunity in the acting world, not necessarily for the money – for she had plenty of that – but for the glitz, glamour, and public adulation which it would afford. She reportedly spent thousands of dollars on her appearance, buying furs and jewelry, renting suites of rooms at the Beverly Hills Hotel, and hosting lavish parties, and even dropping $7,500 on one celebrity event which was a small fortune in those days. In the end, however, it was all for naught, as all her work resulted basically in a tiny bit part in 1941's *Manpower*, a film noir directed by Raoul Walsh and starring Edward G. Robinson, Marlene Dietrich, and George Raft. Virginia appeared momentarily in the film as a hat-check girl. The movie did quite well at the box office, but it did nothing for Virginia's Hollywood career.

Ironically, Virginia would soon find great fame on television – but of an undesirable type – during the U.S. Senate investigation into organized crime which was broadcast into homes around the nation. She had the misfortune to be subpoenaed for her testimony on what she knew about the organized crime figures with whom she associated. In pressure situations, Virginia could quickly become testy, and she was never at a loss for clever responses when pressed on issues she found distasteful.

When Ben Siegel was acquitted – for lack of evidence – of the murder for which he had been charged, he renewed his underworld crime activities in the horse-racing and gambling rackets on the west coast of which New York Mob boss Luciano wished to gain control. He also renewed his relationship with Virginia at that time. Her association with the Chicago Outfit's Charles Fischetti and Fischetti's Los Angeles boss, Jack Dragna, allowed them to use her to keep tabs on the always independent-minded Siegel.

Meanwhile, during her trips back down to Marietta, Georgia, even though she knew that her activities were nefarious at best and highly illegal at worst, Virginia eventually ceased trying to conceal her involvement with the Mob from her friends at home. She often returned to Marietta was to visit and aid her poverty-stricken mother and family, but she remained highly invested in her illicit activities as a courier to Miami and Havana, Cuba, for the Mob.

"Virginia was sort of our economy back in those days," Kinney smiled again. "She was our roving branch bank. She carried a roll of hundred dollar bills at a time when you could throw down a twenty dollar bill and ring every cash register on the square in Marietta."

As a result of her meager circumstances as a child, Virginia had grown up being snubbed in her early life. She therefore didn't hesitate to throw her support to her poorer friends when they needed it. "One time Virginia decided to carry us all night-clubbing in Atlanta," Kinney recounted. "We drove down the four-lane (old U.S. Highway 41) stopping at roadside inns along the way. We would just drop in, pay a little visit, and then leave.

"We ended up at the Paradise Room at the Henry Grady Hotel in downtown Atlanta. There we were," Kinney smiled again in remembrance, "just a bunch of rag-tag country boys from Marietta. The maître de refused to seat us, but Virginia just heaved her hefty bosoms and showed him a roll of hundred dollar

Hill House – The Beverly Hills, California mansion rented by Virginia Hill in the mid-1940s is pictured. It was here that mobster Benjamin Siegel was assassinated, ostensibly by a mob hitman, on June 20, 1947. Days prior to his murder, Siegel and Hill reportedly had argued and fought, and she had departed for Europe on more mob courier business. After learning of Siegel's assassination, she, understandably, never returned to this home.

bills. It wasn't long before we were sitting down 'in front.' And to top it off, while we were there, Virginia introduced us to the performer – Red Skelton. She knew him because he had previously appeared at her club in New York."

Flamingo Folly

Though she loved to visit and party with her Marietta friends and admirers, Virginia never dallied long. Her forays back to Georgia rarely extended beyond a few days before it was quickly back to work for the Mob for her. Her involvement with Siegel also had not cooled at all, despite their continued frequent arguments and fights.

In 1945, Siegel became a partner with Hollywood nightclub owner and publisher Billy Wilkerson, whose planned resort project in then-tiny desert-stranded Las Vegas had run out of money after he had gambled away his cash.

Siegel, sensing an opportunity, obtained about $1.5 million in financing from, among others, Meyer Lansky and Chicago's Fischetti brothers and Murray Humphreys, then took over Wilkerson's project, expanding upon it greatly. Ben Siegel didn't believe in doing things in a small way.

Though the desert casino idea – which Siegel dubbed *The Pink Flamingo,* reportedly after Virginia's long legs – ultimately made millions of dollars for the Mob, it was initially viewed by Mob bosses as a "white elephant" after construction costs began skyrocketing. Despite the unique idea on which he had sold his Mob boss investors with glowing descriptions of the income possibilities, Siegel had no experience whatsoever in the development business, and was soon being buried by unimaginable expenses, and huge cost over-runs. He was spending far more of the Mob's money than he had originally stated would be necessary in the idea he had pitched to them.

Even worse, by 1947, though there was no proof, rumors had begun swirling that Siegel had skimmed $2 million off the top of the funds intended for the Flamingo's building expenses and given it to his inveterate cash-carrying girlfriend to hide in a Swiss bank account.

Slow Start of a Dynamo – At a cost in excess of $6 million (originally estimated to cost $3 million) the 105-room Pink Flamingo Hotel & Casino finally opened on Boxing Day 1946. The rainy premier was an absolute disaster and the Flamingo suffered huge losses requiring it to close for several months before re-opening. It was discovered that the brain-trust for the huge development in the Nevada desert - Benjamin Siegel - had considerably underestimated the building costs of the Flamingo. He also reportedly had the temerity to "skim" several million dollars for himself from the construction funds provided by his mob bosses. As can be seen from this photo, at the time of its construction, the Flamingo was virtually the only resort in what then was the tiny town of Las Vegas. Ironically, Siegel's concept of a gambling resort in the Nevada desert ultimately proved to be successful beyond anyone's wildest dreams, culminating in what today is the largest city in Nevada.

Just to provide an idea of the import of this "rumored" graft by Siegel, in 1947, $2 million was the equivalent (in buying power) of approximately $28,402,000.00 in 2024 dollars – a breath-taking amount of money, both then and now. And the fact that the building expenses for the Flamingo had already topped $6 million with the end still nowhere in sight certainly didn't help matters.

And if that wasn't bad enough, by 1947, Ben Siegel's luck apparently had just flat run out. Aside from the fact that his expenditures had far exceeded the original estimates, the huge complex finally opened during a rare summer deluge of rain, severely curtailing attendance by patrons. With dwindling operation funds, Siegel was forced to close the casino, then re-open it months later, then endure months of losses before it actually began making a little money.

It was also at about this same time that it unfortunately was discovered that Siegel had indeed been skimming from the construction funds, taking $600,000.00 in cash which he had instructed his buddy "Fat Irish" Green to hold for him (Green later wisely returned the money to Lansky). By that point, Benjamin Siegel was a marked man in severely-terminal health.

Bugsy's Final Hours

According to later revelations by Mob insiders, in early June of 1947, after the above-described problems had reached a fever pitch, Virginia was

And if that wasn't bad enough, by 1947, Ben Siegel's luck apparently had just flat run out.

ordered to leave Las Vegas, and to tell Siegel that she was going to Europe to buy exclusive wines for the Flamingo. Still spending money that was not his to spend, Siegel reportedly chartered a plane to fly her solo back to Los Angeles.

A few days later, Siegel also flew back to Los Angeles, returning to Virginia's Beverly Hills home at 810 North Linden Drive which she had rented (with Siegel's money) from her friend, Juan Romero, her former Hollywood movie agent. Siegel was so confident of his importance to the Mob and the clout that he believed he carried, that he took absolutely no precautions for his personal safety. He drew no drapes on the windows at night as he sat in the lighted room reading, and he didn't bother with hiring any security personnel for his protection. Under the circumstances, it is surprising that he actually lived as long as he did.

According to the Los Angeles Police Department's report on the incident, while relaxing and reading the newspaper inside Virginia's Hollywood mansion late in the evening on the warm night of June 21, 1947, Siegel was suddenly struck by four rounds (a total of seven were fired) fired through the window from a .30 caliber M-1 carbine. Two of the rounds hit him in the head, and two hit him in the torso, killing him instantly.

The identity of his executioner has never been discovered – or at least not ever publicly-revealed. The final report by the Homicide Division indicated one of the .30-caliber

Death Scene – At then-Hollywood starlet Virginia Hill's 810 North Linden Drive residence in Beverly Hills, mobster Benjamin Siegel was assassinated at 10:45 pm on the warm summer evening of June 21, 1947. His executioner, who many presume was mob-connected, fired seven rounds through the window of Hill's rented mansion. According to the Los Angeles Police Coroner's Report, two of the rounds struck Siegel in the head and two in the torso, killing him instantly. The police homicide report indicated one of the .30-caliber projectiles passed through Siegel's skull striking the bridge of his nose as it exited his head, ejecting his left eyeball out of its socket and 14 feet across the room where it was later discovered intact by investigating officers. No one was ever charged with the crime.

projectiles had struck the bridge of Siegel's nose, ejecting his left eyeball out of its socket and sending it 14 feet across the room where it was later discovered intact by investigating officers.

Virginia reportedly learned of Siegel's death from a fellow reveler during a party on a boat in Paris. In the coming

weeks in Europe she apparently descended into a deep depression and attempted to commit suicide on three separate occasions. Even after returning to the States, she tried to kill herself a fourth time in Miami where Siegel had purchased her a home.

As if she didn't already have enough problems, by this point federal authorities were investigating Hill for income tax evasion. Virginia had long since ceased laundering the illicit funds she received, and therefore had no means to explain their source to government officials. From that point forward, it was easy pickings for the Internal Revenue Service. After all, how could a person with no employment nor any visible legitimate source of income have so much cash to spend on a regular basis?

Virginia's New Man

Virginia inevitably began searching for a place to hide. In early 1950, records indicate she traveled to the popular ski resort of Sun Valley, Idaho, where she met and fell in love with a ski instructor named Hans Hauser, a former world champion downhill racer from Austria. By that point in her life, Virginia was still only 33 years of age, but her hard living had robbed her of her former charm and beauty. Hauser's friend and fellow ski teacher Otto Lang described Hill as *"far from pretty, a bit short and dumpy"* who strangely and compulsively pulled out her eyelashes *"hair by hair."*

Lang also couldn't avoid noting the questionable associates with whom Virginia still involved herself, penning *"some shady and ominous characters began to drift in and call on Virginia, then leave again without skiing."* Despite her by-then virtually nonexistent role in the Chicago Outfit's "business," Virginia reportedly still regularly received

A Los Angeles Police Homicide Division close-up photograph of the deceased Benjamin Siegel.

Another Los Angeles Police Department photo of the 1947 death scene with Benjamin Siegel in Virginia Hill's home in Beverly Hills, California.

deliveries of cash on which she subsisted from the ever-reliable Joe Epstein. With the Kefauver Hearings already focusing intensely upon the Mob, they no doubt wished merely to keep Virginia quietly satisfied by this point – even though she was nevertheless fast becoming a problem – in order to avoid drawing any more attention to themselves and their nefarious activities.

When the FBI began investigating her at the lodge in Sun Valley, the resort's management abruptly asked her to leave. Despite her background and reduced beauty, Hauser sprang a surprise on family and acquaintances by suddenly asking Virginia to marry him. Lang reportedly immediately advised his friend against such a rash action, but Hauser ignored him and eloped with Virginia the next morning.

Not only did the marriage last, Virginia and Hans, to the surprise of many more, soon became the proud parents of a son, Peter, on November 20, 1950, in Brighton, Massachusetts. By this point, Virginia, however, had begun experiencing severe bouts of depression which haunted her constantly.

In 1951, the Kefauver Committee ultimately subpoenaed Virginia, now 34, to appear in New York to testify regarding her mob-related activities and associations, and the proceedings were nationally televised. She arrived on March 16, 1951, several months after giving birth. She entered the Foley Courthouse in a $5,000 mink cape, broadbrimmed hat and silk gloves, and though she was crippled emotionally, she somehow summoned an inner strength. Her ability for clever repartee returned with a flourish, and she didn't pull any punches as the committee members peppered her with questions in an attempt to get her to incriminate various members of the Mob.

Though some hoped and believed that her testimony would open the door for mass-arrests of organized crime

On To The Morgue – The body of Benjamin Siegel is removed by the county coroner from the Beverly Hills home of Virginia Hill where he had been assassinated.

figures, Virginia Hill artfully evaded every question from committee counsel Halley about her organized crime associations. She "denied," "denied," "denied," and gave nothing but vague responses to the very pointed questions.

When asked to explain the source of the hundreds of thousands of dollars she had spent – and continued to spend – Virginia merely responded that all her money came from her winnings on race track bets. She explained her expensive home and possessions by saying they were simply gifts which had been provided for her by Siegel and others.

"Bought me everything I wanted, when I was with Ben. He paid for everything. And he gave me some money, too; bought me a house in Florida," she stated matter-of-factly. She also admitted recently receiving $10,000 in cash from friends in Mexico. What did they expect her to do? Return it???

As far as her long-time association with known criminals was concerned, Virginia merely stated, "I never knew anything about their business. They didn't tell me about their business. Why would they tell me? I didn't care

anything about that business in the first place. I don't even understand it."

In the end, little Virginia Hill from Marietta, Georgia, gave the all-powerful Kefauver Committee members absolutely nothing they could use against her organized crime friends. That, obviously, was just the way the Mob wanted it too, and it probably lengthened her life by a number of years.

Unbearable Circumstances

Virginia Hill's later life nevertheless, was just as mentally-distressing as had been the 1950s. As a result, her mental status spiraled steadily into a destructive oblivion.

Virginia and Hans did not remain in the United States very long. He flew to Chile to teach skiing and took their son, Peter, with him. The IRS continued its incessant pursuit of Virginia, indicting her for tax evasion, serving her with liens, and seizing her possessions wherever possible such as automobiles, homes, jewelry and furs, and auctioning them off to the highest bidder.

Though Virginia still had some funds squirreled away with Joe Epstein, they were fast being expended. She had never been much of a money-manager, because for most of her life up to that point, she had thrived on more money than she could spend.

Virginia ultimately moved with Hans and Peter to his native Austria, but her residence there was just as unhappy. She eventually wished desperately to return home to America and just be left alone. By the mid-1960s, she wearily began to openly express a wish to simply die.

In 1965, Hans discovered her comatose once again after an overdose of sedatives. He rushed her to the hospital where her stomach was pumped yet again to save her life. From all appearances, Hans Hauser was a remarkably devoted husband in extremely-trying circumstances.

After she had recovered, Virginia flew next to Cuba to attempt residence there, but her identity and reputation had preceded her and she was denied entry. The locus of Hans at this point is unknown.

Finally, in 1966, with her funds completely depleted, Virginia became dangerously distraught. Even her old faithful friend, Joe Epstein had finally turned his back on her when she was no longer of use to the Mob. Whether she at that point threatened to reveal what she knew about the Mob if they did not provide her with a continued source of income is unknown today. It is known, however, that she spoke via telephone on March 20 of that year to Joe Adonis, who was then living in Italy.

Barely four days later, on March 24, 1966, passersby walking on a footpath beside a small brook near Salzburg, Austria, discovered a body beside a tree that was later identified as Virginia. Her coat reportedly was neatly folded on the ground beside her. Also discovered was a note which stated simply that she was *"tired of life."*

An Austrian official concluded the 49-year-old Virginia had died of a self-administered overdose of sedatives, which did not come as a surprise, since she had made numerous previous attempts at suicide. One also obviously cannot dismiss the possibility of a Mob-related death either.

Sadly, Virginia's husband, Hans Hauser had also suffered from severe depression. He also died from an apparent suicide eight years later in Austria in 1974. His brother, Peter Hauser, a decorated U.S. Army veteran of the Vietnam

Gravesite of a Georgian – On March 24, 1966, passersby walking on a footpath beside a small brook near Salzburg, Austria, discovered a body beside a tree that was later identified as Virginia Hill. Also discovered was a note which stated simply, "tired of life." Following her mysterious death which ultimately was attributed to a drug overdose, Virginia was buried in Salzburg, in the family plot of her Austrian husband. A portion of her name is faintly visible in the extreme lower portion of the headstone in this photo.

War, died in a car accident in Toulouse, France in 1994. All three are buried together in a cemetery in Salzburg, Austria.

In the end, the kind but flamboyant temptress not only lost everything, she was denied the ability to return to the one place she had truly called "home" – Marietta, Georgia – where the carefree and happy days of her early life had been spent all those years ago. In a strange sort of way, Virginia Hill had finally won the acclaim – albeit notoriously – for which she had so grievously hungered in her days of youth.

Champion Racers and "Moonshine" Makers of Old Dawson County, GA

From its earliest days, right up to the 1970s, Dawson County was known as a "moonshine" mecca. And as a result of the driving skills necessary to evade law enforcement while transporting the illicit liquor to buyers, Dawson also produced some of the fastest racecar drivers alive.

From the 1970s, right up to the 1990s, Dawsonville native Bill Elliott reigned as the most celebrated racing champion from Georgia (and indeed, the nation), but he's not the only famous competitor to emerge from north Georgia – not by a long shot.

Out of necessity, moonshiners learned early-on how to rebuild their automobile engines with immense horsepower and to reconfigure the vehicle suspensions to carry extra weight yet still be fast and agile enough to maintain an advantage over their law enforcement pursuers. The county's legacy lives on today in its annual *"Moonshine Festival."*

The life of a moonshiner is/was replete with danger and death at every turn. If one didn't die trying to out-run law enforcement personnel, he quite often faced animosities at home from competing moonshiners.

In a lonely graveyard overlooking downtown Dawsonville today, the stark tombstone of Lloyd Seay stands in mute testimony to that fact. He is just one of these racing legends for which the county has gained fame and fortune but he also met an early death.

"Awesome Bill"

Of course, not every early racing champion in the South evolved from outrunning state or federal revenue agents, "but a good many of them did," explained Dawsonville businessman and racing historian Gordon Pirkle. "Bill Elliott and his progeny are the 'latest and greatest' in the county's stock-car racing profession, but they never dealt with the dangers of moonshining in their off-hours."

Pirkle founded the "Dawsonville Poolroom," the management of which has been turned over to his son, Gordon Pirkle, Jr. The Poolroom has become renowned for its Dawsonville racing memorabilia, and whatever doesn't exist there can be found a mile or so away in the town's *Georgia Racing Hall of Fame* – a museum filled with NASCAR racing memorabilia generated over the years by the county's favorite sons.

The moment one walks inside the Dawsonville Poolroom, he or she

"Awesome Bill from Dawsonville" – Many of the racecars guided to victory lane by NASCAR champion and Dawsonville native Bill Elliott are displayed in the Bill Elliott Museum today near Dawsonville, GA. (Photo by Judy Bates)

Dawsonville Poolroom – This now-famous Dawsonville establishment enjoys a long association with racing history and memorabilia, thanks to long-time owner Gordon Pirkle.

instantly realizes that it isn't just another pool hall in yet another slow-paced Georgia town. To the contrary, Mr. Pirkle's place is quite literally a museum and a shrine in its own right.

Located at 9 *Bill Elliott Street*, just a short block from the central traffic circle around the historic county courthouse, the Poolroom displays a plethora of memorabilia of Elliott's glory days – along with that of the county's other legends as well. Elliot's racing collectibles, however, are by far the dominant focus of the Poolroom, simply because his credentials are almost too numerous to mention.

"Awesome Bill from Dawsonville" won the *1988 Winston Cup* Championship, ultimately racking up 44 wins in that series, including two *Daytona 500* victories in 1985 and 1987, three *Southern 500* victories in 1985, 1988, and 1994, one *Winston 500* victory in 1985, one *Brickyard 400* victory in 2002, and a record four consecutive wins at Michigan International Speedway in the 1980s.

Bill is the owner of many other records as well. He holds the track record for fastest qualifying speed at *Talladega* at 212.809 miles per hour (342.483 km/h) and *Daytona International Speedway* at 210.364 miles per hour (338.548 km/h), both of which were set in 1987 (the mark at *Talladega* is the fastest qualifying speed for any NASCAR race ever). With the current usage of restrictor plates at Daytona and Talladega beginning since 1988, it is highly unlikely that these two qualifying speed records will ever be topped again.

In 1985, Elliott also made racing history by winning the first ever *"Winston Million,"* a million dollar bonus to any driver that could win three out of the four crown jewel races of NASCAR: The *Daytona 500* at Daytona, the *Winston 500* at Talladega, the *World 600* at Charlotte, and the *Southern 500* at Darlington. In a year dominated by Elliott, he went on to win 11 races (with 4 "season sweeps": *Atlanta, Pocono, Michigan,* and *Darlington*) and 11 pole positions, with three of those 11 wins being the *Daytona 500*, the *Winston 500*, and the *Southern 500*, earning Bill the vaunted *"Winston Million Dollar Bonus"* and the nickname *"Million Dollar Bill."*

Elliott also won *NASCAR's Most Popular Driver Award* a record 16 times

Gober Sosebee – Dawsonville native Sosebee poses beside his 1939 Ford coupe which he raced to victory lane in the 1950 and '51 Daytona 500s. "I came in first in '49 too," he lamented, "but they disqualified me."

(1984-1988, 1991–2000, 2002). He withdrew his name from the ballot for that award after winning it in 2002.

In 2005, the Georgia State Legislature declared October 8 as *Bill Elliott Day* in the state of Georgia. He was inducted into the *Motorsports Hall of Fame of America* on August 15, 2007 and into the 2015 class of the *NASCAR Hall of Fame*. Elliott has also been honored by the state legislature with a stretch of roadway (the entirety of Georgia State Route 183) in his native Dawson County renamed *Elliott Family Parkway*.

Dawsonville Poolroom

Though not being honored with as lengthy a list of awards as Elliott, others in the county were nonetheless champions of their day as well, in the days when moonshine was also king in the county. Just east of the Poolroom, *Gober Sosebee*

Street crosses *Main*. To the west, the names of long-ago trailblazers *Raymond Parks, Roy Hall* and *Lloyd Seay* adorn additional signs.

Interestingly, in an earlier day at the Dawsonville Poolroom, the game of billiards was really all it offered. It was a local hang-out for individuals with "idle time" on their hands. Racing legends and moonshine weren't really the focus.

But that was then. Today, "this place ain't about pool," Pirkle, Sr. once intoned about his establishment since Elliott's emergence in the racing world. "It's about racing."

And indeed, every wall in the building is covered with information about the sport. Newspaper clippings and pictures stretch from ceiling to floor, attesting to the fame of not only local and national hero, Elliott, but to many of the other Dawson County notables from yesteryear as well, including Gober Sosebee, Lloyd Seay, and Roy Hall, to mention a few.

"Lloyd and Roy were both known to run liquor," said Pirkle with a smile. "I don't know if Gober ran any or not, but man, he burned those backroads and racetracks plumb up."

The races of choice of yesteryear, according to Pirkle, most often were those that were run half on low-tide beach sand and half on the paved surface of Atlantic Avenue in Daytona Beach, Florida, during the early years of the famed *Daytona 500*.

Agent Charley Weems

One never knows just who will be stopping by the Poolroom on a given day for a visit either – whether a racer from yesteryear, or a "revenoor" from yesteryear. Charley Weems, a former ATF (*Alcohol Tobacco & Firearms*) agent for the U.S. Treasury Department in the 1950s and '60s, was active during the same time that many of the racing legends were in their heydays in Dawson County. When he has visited the Poolroom, the stories of his adventures have filled hours of time, just as they fill the pages of his two books: *A Breed Apart* and *Agents That Fly*.

"I was alone one night," Weems explained as he described one incident from his colorful career, "and I came up behind a vehicle I recognized. You know the man that was in it," he says to Pirkle with a smile, whispering the name to him. "He was from around here.

"I ran him down and he jumped out of the passenger side and tumbled down a kudzu-covered bank in the dark. I didn't want him to get away, so I just jumped out into the night and landed smack on top of him. I knew the minute I landed that I had a'hold of a big, strong man, and that I was in trouble.

A Race with Destiny – With a devil-may-care grin and square-jawed determination, Dawsonville native Lloyd Seay grins for the camera following one of his races. His hot racing streak, however, turned out to be brief.

"Well, I weighed about 165 pounds in those days," Weems continued. "I knew I either needed a real good plan, or I was about to get one heck of a beating. I hollered out, 'It's okay Coppe! I've got him,' to suggest to the fellow I'd just landed on that I wasn't alone," Weems added with a smile. "Every violator in the state at that time knew Carl Coppe. You might say he was a very 'dedicated' officer, and most of the liquor law violators not only respected him, they feared him.

"When we got back up the bank, my prisoner asked 'Where's your partner?' I just told him that he was over at the car and behind the lights. It wasn't until I got him cuffed and secured in the car that he finally figured out that I was alone," Weems smiled.

From the 1930s through the 1950s, moonshiners many times were so prolific in north Georgia that the difference between them and the celebrity racecar drivers was almost indistinguishable. As often as not, the racecar driver and day-tripper transporting the illegal liquor were one and the same.

"There's plenty of folks around here try to separate the racing from the

Against the Wind – Lloyd Seay's tombstone is a bleak reminder of this former racing great from Dawsonville and the fragility of life. Though he was a well-known and successful short-track racer from the late 1930s to the early 1940s, Lloyd Seay was murdered on September 2, 1941, just a short distance outside Dawsonville in a simple dispute over moonshine supplies. The day prior to his death, he had won the Lakewood 100 at the old Lakewood Speedway in Atlanta

whiskey-makin' and transportin',"" Pirkle grinned again. "To me, that's just so much wishful thinkin'."

The production of illegal or untaxed liquor of course evolved in north Georgia generations before the days of stockcar racing. Immigrants from the Ulster region of what today is Northern Ireland brought their liquor distilling skills to America, spreading the craft throughout the Appalachians as they settled in the region.

Pirkle credits two incidents in the history of our nation for the evolution of "moonshining" as a big-time illegal money-making enterprise.

"It was the *Depression* and *Prohibition* that done it," he explains without hesitation. "The poultry industry and tourism were (still far away) in the future; the forests were long gone, having been cut for lumber production (eliminating the timber industry); the ground wouldn't grow good crops; and there just wasn't many other ways to make a livin'."

"Moonshining" became the sole source of income for many poor north Georgians, and from the production and distribution of illicit liquor sprang the race car drivers.

Lloyd Seay Murder

Perhaps one of the most charismatic of the early Dawson County racers was a handsome and lead-footed devil-may-care driver known as Lloyd Seay.

"Lloyd could drive," Pirkle agreed. "The law couldn't catch him at all. There's no tellin' how far he could have gone as a race driver if he had 'a-lived."

Unfortunately, Seay didn't live beyond his 21st birthday, and the manner of his death both shocked and disgusted the world of racing in the 1940s. The circumstances surrounding the tragedy were so insignificant, they verged upon the pathetic, and yet so tragic, they were breath-taking.

The whole incident amazingly involved a simple disagreement about "sugar." Seay reportedly had purchased a large amount of the sweetener for the family's whiskey-making enterprise. He apparently had used a cousin's line of credit – without obtaining the obligatory prior permission from that cousin – to buy the sugar. In the process, he exhausted his cousin's quota of available sugar for that month. That type behavior just wasn't allowed in the world of illicit liquor production in the Appalachian Mountains where money was extremely tight.

In the "moonshine bidness," one's ability to produce a product depended upon one's ability to obtain sugar, which was – and continues to be – important in the distilling process. When Lloyd Seay maxed-out his cousin's sugar quota, that shut down his cousin's moonshining operations – and that was a serious

Caught? – A typical north Georgia moonshine operation was captured on film here circa 1930s. Judging from the downcast countenances of those pictured, this photograph quite possibly was taken after discovery of the site (and just prior to its destruction) by law enforcement officials. Since the perpetrators in this crime would have had no photography equipment nor known how to use it, this likely is a photograph taken for evidentiary purposes. Those pictured quite likely were the operators of this illicit liquor production site. (Photo courtesy of the GA Dept. of Archives & History, Atlanta, GA)

infraction of the social mores of the area. As a result, Woodrow Anderson, Lloyd's cousin, who was already "hot-headed," was fit to be tied.

The previous day, Seay had won the then-prestigious *Lakewood 100* race in Atlanta on the old Lakewood Speedway. It was Labor Day, 1941, and Seay had won in his newly-numbered open-top '39 Ford roadster. He had always run with lucky #7 painted on the side of his racer, but on the day of the *Lakewood 100*, for unknown reasons, Seay strangely painted #13 on his doors – an unlucky omen of the events which would transpire in less than 24 hours.

According to reports of the tragedy, after the race, Seay had gone to the tiny hamlet of Burtsboro, between Dawsonville and Dahlonega, to spend the night at the house of his brother Garnett Seay.

Early the next morning, Woodrow Anderson appeared at the home, insisting that Seay "go with him to settle up."

Anderson said they would go to the house of another family member – an aunt to all three of them – who was respected by all and who would settle the dispute. Lloyd Seay, his brother Garnett, and Anderson, left together, but they never reached "Aunt Monnie's" house.

After stopping briefly at his own house, Anderson drove to the house of his father, Grover Anderson, reportedly "to put water in the car radiator." At this point, Woodrow invited Garnett Seay to get out of the car "if you don't want to get mixed up in somethin.'"

According to court records, Garnett's account of the incident sent Woodrow Anderson to prison for life. He (Garnett) testified that when he re-

Dejecting Circumstances – Yet another north Georgia "moonshine" operation photographed undoubtedly just prior to its destruction. Some of these pictured individuals appear distinctly gloomy, while others sport impish grins. The elderly gentleman in the center appears particularly morose. He either is a law enforcement official or the primary moonshiner about to be forced to destroy his entire livelihood. (Photo courtesy of the GA Dept. of Archives & History, Atlanta, GA)

fused to get out of the vehicle, Anderson jumped on Lloyd and began striking him with his fists.

"Then he pulled a gun out of the bib of his overalls and shot me in the neck," Garnett explained in his court testimony. "He shot Lloyd right through the heart and told me he would finish me off if I ever said anything about it."

To say the least, Woodrow Anderson's gunfire was "dead-on." Lloyd Seay was "DRT" (Dead Right There).

When word got out that local favorite son Lloyd Seay had been killed, the people in Dawson County were simply stunned, particularly since Seay had just won the *Lakewood 100* and was a big local celebrity. It was tantamount to super-stardom in Dawson County at that time.

Lloyd Seay's funeral drew friends, relatives, and fans in numbers never previously witnessed in the little town of Dawsonville. Seay's tombstone in Dawsonville City Cemetery was purchased by Raymond Parks who owned the cars that Seay raced. Parks also was one of Seay's biggest fans, and the flamboyance of the tombstone clearly reflects this admiration.

Carved into the stone is the requisite image of a racecar of the 1940s. It has a large #7 (not #13) on the door. At the wheel of the vehicle sits Lloyd Grayson Seay, his photograph frozen forever in a block of crystal embedded in the granite headstone, smiling his best winning smile back to his fans for eternity.

Gober Sosebee

Yet another Dawson County winner of the Daytona Beach Race was Gober Sosebee who was tragically killed in an agricultural accident at his home in 1996. He had been a popular fixture in Dawsonville lore for generations. Sosebee won two *Grand National Series* races, one in 1952 and one in 1954. He also was a three-time winner of the *Daytona Beach* race in 1949, 1950, and 1951, and had 33 "Top Ten" finishes in NASCAR races.

A drive to Sosebee's home only a short distance from the Poolroom rekindled a lot of memories for both Weems and Pirkle as they pointed out first a former "moonshine still" location and then the home of a former moonshiner.

"That's old Snuffy's place," says Pirkle.

"I remember him," Weems replied. "We just passed over the place back there where his son, Clifton, had a head-on collision with Doug Denney and James Stratigos (former ATF agents). Three people died from that, counting the boy riding with Clifton. James was nearly killed too, but he managed to survive."

"I wonder why Gober never made it into the *Racing Hall Of Fame*?" Weems muttered matter-of-factly. "There's plenty of men in there who can't hold a candle to him and who never won *Daytona* – not even once."

"It sure don't seem right," agrees Pirkle. "I'm sure that for many years, it was because of hard feelings on (Bill) France's (NASCAR founder) part, and now, so many years have gone by."

In the early days of moonshine production in Georgia, Highway 9 was famous as a lifeline for the whiskey trippers transporting their outlawed goods to market. It was one of the original "Thunder Road" routes. The black-top snakes from the foot of the Southern Appalachians all the way to Atlanta. The cars of Awesome Bill and son, Chase, have both been emblazoned with the #9 identity since they began racing.

"Visitors will ask me if Bill is the first Dawson County driver to win at Daytona, or they'll ask if he was the only winner from around here," Pirkle says, "and I'll tell them 'Neither. He's the latest, but about the sixth to win it.'

"All those others preceded him. There was Lloyd Seay and Roy Hall, Bernard G. Long, Gober Sosebee, and a lady (believe it or not) by the name of Carleen Rouse," Pirkle added. "All in all, Dawson County drivers have won at Daytona more than ten times.

"Of course we're talking about the '40s and '50s, when it was the *Daytona Beach Race*, and it was run at low tide, half on the beach and half on Atlantic Avenue," Pirkle smiled again. "It was some race in them days.

It was at this point that Pirkle enjoyed explaining an amusing peculiarity of big city sports reporting involving Dawson County racers. "It's interesting," he smiled . . . "Whenever one of our drivers won a race anywhere, the Atlanta papers used to always declare 'Atlanta driver wins at so and so.' But just let that same driver get caught runnin' likker (in Atlanta) the next week, and those same papers would all say 'Dawson County violator arrested.'"

The memories came easily to the two aged icons from Dawson County's moonshining past, but they're fading fast. Most of the old moonshiners are long gone now, and the individuals with any memories associated with those events of yesteryear are swiftly disappearing as well.

"Reverend Devil" of the Covered Bridges:

Notorious Bandit John A. Murrell

Great efforts have been taken to preserve and protect North Georgia's treasured covered bridges. Though their history is extensive, these fabled structures were also once the realm of a very nasty band of outlaws with an even nastier leader.

Some early bandits of America grew contagiously from folklore and tales of yesteryear. Many of them, however, actually existed – to one degree or another. One particular bunch operated over a wide region and were led by a very resourceful bandit who used a religious frock to conceal his illicit activities. His name was John A. Murrell, and the outlaws he organized and led were known in history as "the Murrell Gang."

Some sources maintain the Murrells were a loosely-organized group of outlaws; others have indicated they were highly organized and efficient, taking hundreds of thousands of dollars in valuables. No one disputes the fact, however, that they were a very nasty group of outlaws responsible for a long list of unpardonable crimes.

The Murrells once terrorized a realm all the way from north Georgia westward to Arkansas in the early 1800s, but their leader came from a pious background. The earlier sedate and truly-religious Murrell family was headed up by the Reverend William Murrell. On the surface, Rev. Murrell maintained an honest and admirable reputation in the sanctuary, but the church pulpit was as far as that sanctimony extended. At home and elsewhere, "the old lady" who was wild and loose ruled the roost, and her children were just as hedonistic.

A son, John, was born about 1800. The exact site of his birth is not known today, but the family originally lived about 25 miles south of Nashville, Tennessee, near the village of Bethesda, a serene and peaceful community surrounded and half-hidden by the Cumberland Mountains.

If young John was charmed by this picturesque setting, he never spoke of it. From his earliest days, the youngster was more interested in what was known in that day and time as "speculations." He watched the constant ox and wagon traffic passing over the Natchez Trace and talked with travelers who roomed at a tavern operated by his lawlessly-oriented mother.

According to family tradition, John never had aspirations to become a "man of God" like his father who he considered basically to be boring. Instead, he

listened to breath-taking stories of robberies and looting and adventures on the
trail from highwaymen overnighting at
his mother's boisterous tavern, dreaming
of the day when he too could become an
outlaw, casting off the rules and baggage
of society, and seeking fame, ill-gotten
gains, and adventure on the road.

Later and down through the years,
John A. Murrell would repeatedly maintain that it was his mother who initiated his life of crime. "My mother was the
one with true grit; she learned me and
all her children to steal as soon as we
could walk," he reportedly once claimed.
"Whatever we stole, she hid for us, and
dared my father to touch it. She made
us hate the proud ones and go after those
who had more than we did." Spoken like
a true criminal in training.

It was at age 16, John stated years
later, that he committed his first petty crime, swindling a storekeeper. Petty crime came easy to the youngster.
Neighbors and acquaintances however,
became suspicious and began watching
him just a bit too closely.

John eventually decided his close-
knit rural neighborhood offered a less-
than-ideal site for illicit operations.
He ultimately abandoned his Tennessee home to take up the life of a highwayman, pursuing his "speculations" on
a grander scale in new places. It is unknown today how young John made the
first money to expedite his advanced life
of crime, but it must have come from
some form of petty theft or perhaps even
an initial armed robbery.

Though he despised his father,
John eventually learned to hide his illicit activities by posing as a minister of
the Gospel. He often related to his cronies that as a child, he had been amused
at the blind confidence a "man of God"
could inspire, even a sorry minister like

"Reverend Devil" – Bandit John Andrews
Murrell pictured shortly before his death.

his father. John subsequently adopted
the device of preaching as a side-line profession, undoubtedly dipping into untold sums of money contributed to the
church along the way.

His preoccupation with crime and
a subsequent heated pursuit by law enforcement authorities no doubt eventually forced John's migration down into
Georgia. Men of unsavory reputations
from all walks of life began joining his
band.

In that day and time, long coats and
high-top hats were symbols of authority,
superiority, honor and intelligence. The
arrival of an itinerant preacher dressed
in this garb was a virtual announcement
that a "Revival" event was about to take
place. It would attract settlers – and
their funds – from miles around.

Revival and camp meetings became regular devices for illicit income
for John. His gang members, needless to
say, were very busy at these events as well.

Bolding Covered Bridge – This early covered bridge spanning the Chestatee River once linked Hall and Forsyth counties on the Old Dawsonville Road. In the 1800s, it gained a reputation as a dangerous spot for travelers and was the site of numerous robberies conducted by bandits such as John Murrell and his underlings who would hide in the rafters of the bridge then drop down upon and rob unsuspecting travelers. Mr. W.R. Bolding who owned it later sold this bridge to Hall County. Following the construction of Lake Lanier in 1956, Bolding Bridge was deemed unworthy of demolition, and was simply abandoned to be submerged beneath the rising waters of the new lake. (Photo courtesy of Chestatee Regional Library, Gainesville, GA)

"Reverend" Murrell found that these revivals in particular were fertile ground for "opportunities." During the campaigns, Murrell was quietly directing his lieutenants in horse-stealing, as well as various and sundry other criminal pursuits as he became aware of the assets of his revival service attendees.

Aside from his routine of posing as a religious minister, another of the specialties in which John eventually became quite adept was the assault of travelers by dropping down from the interior rafters of the roofs over the dark covered bridges which proliferated in pioneer America. Initially, all he needed was a threatening knife which he would use to cow his victims once he had surprised them from the bridge rafters.

Once his quarry – usually individuals traveling in wagons – had been cornered, it was a simple matter to hold the sharp knife – and later a firearm – on the victims while he and his men emptied their pockets into his hat. When all the valuables had been taken, a swift escape either directly into a thick forest or by his own fast horse provided a safe getaway.

John also knew instinctively that "the money was in the numbers." He knew that if he recruited others into his life of crime, he could double, triple and quadruple his "earnings," and he wouldn't even have to do any of the work. He maintained his top lieutenants as "enforcers," then, as he trained others in his covered bridge rafter assaults and other illicit activities, he would require regular "percentages" of their takings. If they didn't immediately come forth with his portion of their ill-gotten gains, he would use his lieutenants to punish the disloyal follower.

North Georgia became a site of intense activity by the bandits due to the multitude of covered bridges in that territory. It is a region which once was dotted with these structures. Unsuspecting travelers, businessmen, gold miners, stagecoaches, et cetera, offered a growing number of larcenous opportunities in which seasoned travelers and even former victims never knew when to anticipate an attack from the unlit rafters of the covered bridges.

One particular hideout of the men was noted in Hall County, Georgia history as *"the notorious Bolding house."* It once existed near the Chestatee River on the Hall County, Georgia, side of the river, and was a minor "headquarters" of sorts for the Murrells shortly after the discovery of gold in the area. And just beyond the Bolding home, Bolding Covered Bridge likewise became a frequent site at which gang members pillaged travelers.

Law enforcement officials of this era were well aware that these outlaws frequented this site, but they struggled in vain to capture them. The Bolding family whose members were rewarded for their assistances in support of the Murrell Gang activities, used a sophisticated "early warning system" to alert the outlaw and his men at their camp on a hillside just above Bolding Bridge. When they became aware of advancing law enforcement officials on the narrow Dawsonville Road, they would signal their fellow outlaws with special lanterns and candles.

The men, understandably, didn't always focus their robbery activities solely on Bolding Bridge either. They functioned throughout northeast Georgia and, as noted above, even as far west as Arkansas in their criminal operations.

In the early days in north Georgia, there were few roads. Travelers rode on horseback, or walked over rough trails which had originated with migratory

Bolding Homestead – Located on the Hall County side of the Chestatee River on the old Dawsonville Highway, this home was demolished in 1956 during the construction of Lake Lanier. It reportedly was frequented by John A. Murrell and his bandit associates circa 1830s. Murrell often posed as an itinerant preacher, stealing proceeds from the church service tithing plates on Sundays, and unsuspecting travelers the remainder of the week, earning him the nickname of "Reverend Devil." According to folklore, an opening at the edge of the ceiling above the porch of the Bolding home (circled in white) was used to send signals to outlaws at a hideout on a nearby hill when law enforcement officers or travelers were enroute. (Photo courtesy of Chestatee Regional Library, Gainesville)

animals and Native Americans. These trails eventually began to widen, as ox-drawn carts and mule-drawn wagons began to proliferate with increasingly more pioneers moving westward.

In the early pioneer days, there were no bridges in the Southeast, and the task of crossing a stream with a loaded cart or wagon was often not only difficult but decidedly treacherous. Good river and

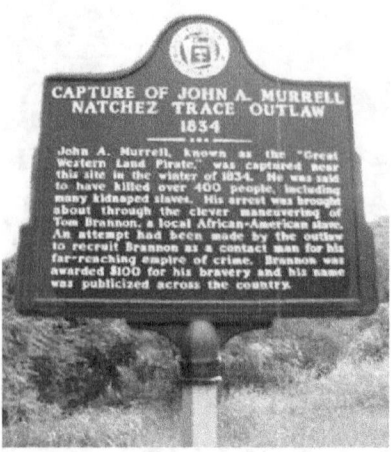

Captured & Incarcerated - This historic marker at Florence, Alabama, was erected near the spot at which notorious outlaw John A. Murrell - to whom reference was often made as "Reverend Devil" - was captured in 1834. He ultimately was convicted and sent to prison, and considered fortunate to have escaped the hangman's noose.

creek fords usually were only available at the few shoals and low spots in the streams, during the dry season, requiring travelers to search out these shallow fords. Virtually all of the stream crossings were particularly dangerous during rainy weather and wet seasons until the advent of wooden bridges.

Sturdy wooden bridges across the deeper rivers and streams in early America offered a highly-improved method of travel – at least to the degree of the stability of the bridges. The bodies of water could then be safely and easily crossed year-round, and travel routes were much more direct when ferries and bridges allowed travelers to ford even the deepest rivers. It also soon became a common practice to cover these bridges with roofs and sides in order to preserve them as long as possible, since they were expensive and difficult to construct, and this is

where the Murrell Gang entered the picture.

Murrell and his accomplices not only were adept at assault and theft from the vantage of the rafters of the covered bridges, they also dealt in other illicit activities as well, including horse-theft. Murrell's network of thieves eventually made him a rich man, and after one particularly productive period, he returned to his former home in Tennessee for a period of bragging, free-spending, and general carousing, but he, amazingly, had soon spent all his ill-gotten gains.

To recoup his fortune, John set out to steal several horses which he had noticed were pastured nearby. This time, however, he was caught in the act. After a speedy trial, the court's sentence stated: *"John A. Murrell shall receive on his bare back at the public whipping post in Davidson County thirty lashes, set in the pillory two hours on Monday, two hours on Thursday, and two hours on Wednesday, next, that he be branded on the left thumb with the letters H.T. (horse thief) in the presence of the court; that he be imprisoned twelve months from this day and be rendered infamous."*

From that terrible day forward, John Murrell was an embittered and unrepentant man with a passion for violence and revenge. He constantly plotted methods in which he might advance his thievery while despoiling anything and everything around him.

While in his prison cell John uncharacteristically maintained a stack of old books – a Bible and numerous law books – which he had requested in an attempt to appear contrite for his sins, but they were all a "smoke screen." He pored over these books day after day, week after week, learning each and every nuance he might use from the knowledge in the books if he should ever need it later from a legal perspective or in one of his many ideas of thievery. John Murrell later ironically stated that his study of criminal law and fundamental theology made him prepared for anything he might encounter in life.

John's brother, William Jr., met his sibling when he stepped out the prison door as a free man twelve months later, and another life of criminal activity began immediately. The two men rode off on two fine, freshly-stolen horses. John didn't intend to allow his incarceration to affect his approach to life one iota.

Despite the realm into which Murrell's operations eventually spread, his intended goal in fact was much larger in scope. The hatred and bitterness in him was welling more to the surface with each passing day. His vendetta was against the whole of established society in the South, and he was intent upon the destruction of as much of it as possible. Had he been alive in the 21st Century he quite likely could easily have been inclined toward terrorism.

One of John's many other-worldly plots, later uncovered and thwarted, was fabricated around the idea of a slave uprising. According to Murrell's plan, all White people would be killed in the uprising with the exception of some of the beautiful White women. Murrell promised the slaves (which he had been stealing now for many months and hiding away) their freedom, their own homes and money from the plantations they would plunder.

John Murrell's boldness, ruthlessness and lavish distribution of spoils eventually attracted scores of followers and his band was amazingly reputed to have numbered around 1,000 members. His operations, which extended over a number of states, eventually escalated to the robbery of mails, banks, and stores;

the piracy of river boats; and slave-kidnapping. Legend also attributes hundreds of murders to Murrell and his unholy crew.

Murrell's lawlessness reportedly continued until 1834, when he encountered an individual named Virgil Stewart. Stewart eventually gained Murrell's trust, luring him to a spot where he could be captured by law enforcement authorities.

Taken to Nashville, Tennessee, Murrell stood trial for his crimes. He somehow escaped the gallows, being sentenced instead to only ten years in the Tennessee State Penitentiary. His sentence, no doubt was aided by the fact that he had confessed to every crime he had committed – except murder, which he knew was a "hanging offense."

While in prison, Murrell was required to learn a new trade. He took up blacksmithing. After he had served his sentence and was freed, Murrell went to Pikeville, Tennessee, where he opened a blacksmith shop. He only lived nine months after his release, however, passing away on November 21, 1844 at the age of 38, from tuberculosis.

Today, most of the covered bridges from which John Murrell began his career of crime, have vanished from north Georgia, Alabama, Arkansas and Tennessee - victims of "progress." The outlaw's reputed hideouts have been decimated in a search for the remains of the treasure he took during his life of crime – almost all of which was in silver or gold and believed to have been buried in the vicinity of his various hideouts.

The romantic aura and historic significance of the covered bridges – what few still exist today – live on, but memories of John A. Murrell – the "Reverend Devil of the Covered Bridges" – has faded into history.

Murder In The Mail:

Postman James Langston's Last Delivery

If a complete tally of the number of deaths associated with the illicit production and sale of un-taxed whiskey in the United States could be obtained, the number would understandably be astronomical. Worse, many of the deaths were completely needless. They could easily have been avoided. A gruesome murder on a backroad just south of Atlanta on a crisp autumn morning in 1922 is one such example. On that day, a completely-innocent U.S. postman was brutally murdered for an act with which he had no involvement whatsoever – and his murderers knew it. In the end, the perpetrators – all "moonshiners" – received what could only be described as light sentences, and no rational explanation was ever provided for this heinous crime.

James C. Langston was a simple postman who worked for the Fairburn, Georgia branch of the U.S. Postal Service just south of Atlanta. He was a tall, popular individual known for his big feet and easy-going style. Delivery of the mail was all he had ever done and all he had ever wished to do. His career, however, was cut short by murder.

Langston worked a rural route and usually stopped mid-route on Kite Bridge Road almost every day to eat his lunch beside a peaceful little stream which passed beneath a wooden bridge at that site. The stream was fed by a sweet-tasting fresh-water spring at which many travelers paused for refreshment. On October 28, 1922, as he approached this quiet spot to partake of his lunch, death awaited James Langston.

The jocular postman was a very likeable and well-known individual. His friends all teased and joked about his large feet, and, indeed, his feet were so expansive that the foot pedals on his Model-T Ford had to be specially-rebuilt by a local blacksmith in order for James to be able to actually drive the vehicle.

Langston knew nothing of the fate awaiting him as he left the Fairburn Post Office on his rural mail route that autumn day. He stepped into his Ford, adjusted the clutch with his special peddle, and drove off to begin his route as usual.

Just as do many today, Langston no doubt loved his sunny autumn days. Every year about this time, his state's football teams – the Georgia Tech "Yellow Jackets" and the University of Georgia "Bulldogs" would be competing against other Southeastern Conference teams with SEC Championship hopes. It is unknown today if James Langston even followed football, but he treasured his Saturdays nonetheless. He certainly didn't want them to be ended forever.

Deadly Chain Of Events

It was at this same general time that Fayette County Sheriff Tom Kerlin and U.S. Revenue Agents Milam and T. B. Harris had raided an illegal liquor ("moonshine") distillery ("still") just off Kite Bridge Road in upper Fayette. They were accompanied on their mission that night by at least one other person – Abner (Ab) Davis – a peddler who lived in the nearby Kenwood community about two miles east of the still site. Davis no doubt was an informer, who, as a civic duty perhaps, was leading the law enforcement officers to the still.

The moonshine distillery itself (remnants of which still amazingly existed as recently as the 1990s) had a 50-gallon capacity, and was located on the property of John Waller just off Kenwood on Kite. John and his brother – Charlie – were well-known moonshiners and bootleggers in the illicit trade.

And for those unaware of the trade parlance, a "moonshiner" is one who distills liquor – usually from corn – illicitly on the sly, and then sells the product without obtaining the proper license nor paying the required tax imposed by the U.S. federal government. A "bootlegger," is one who actually transports the illicit corn liquor to a market – usually in the form of secret purchasers – where he sells it for a profit.

John and Charlie Waller enjoyed a steady business in the countryside south of Atlanta. They were shrewd criminals who had been moonshiners for many years, and knew all the "dos" and "don'ts" necessary to avoid capture by law enforcement authorities.

When buyers approached them for moonshine, they (the Wallers) would take payment, then instruct these clients to "walk back into the garden and look under (a certain) cabbage plant." If everything went according to plan, a bottle of "shine" would be waiting there for the buyer.

All went well for the Waller brothers until an informant eventually alerted law-enforcement officials to the presence of their operations. That information led to the night raid by Sheriff Kerlin. Ab Davis, as stated, was with the officers and assisted in the destruction of the still.

Ora Whittle, who also was a moonshiner and who lived nearby, silently watched from a hiding spot as Sheriff Kerlin, his men, and Ab Davis destroyed the still site and then departed. Ora, in particular, noted Ab Davis's presence in the group. Davis was well-known in the area because he often peddled his products along the road.

The moonshiner community is a close-knit organization by necessity. They are well aware that if one of them "goes down" to law enforcement, there is a very good chance that individual will, in order to avoid being prosecuted himself, "rat-out" any other moonshiners of which he is aware. Word of Ab Davis' involvement in the site destruction therefore spread quickly.

On the Sunday morning following the destruction of the Waller brothers' still, with church attendance not even a faint consideration, a group of the moonshiners consisting of Ora Whittle, John and Charlie Waller, and Rainey Cauthen, met at the home of John Waller. Ora filled the men in on Ab Davis's involvement and the angry men then plotted ways to appropriately "punish" Davis for his actions. Needless to say, Davis no doubt would have been horrified had he been aware of their plans.

According to later courtroom testimony, John Waller initially wanted to "whip Davis," but Charlie Waller and Ora Whittle opted for a more severe punishment which would serve as a better "teaching tool" in the moonshine community. "We should make an example of him and kill him," they admonished.

The men reportedly argued back and forth until an agreement was finally reached whereby they would pay Cauthen approximately $125.00 to "whip Davis, but not kill him." Though that may seem like a paltry sum today, $125.00 in 1922 was the equivalent of just over $2,356.00 in 2024 dollars, so it would have been a really nice payday for Cauthen had it actually occurred. . . but would it send the right message?

The more the men pondered this punishment, the more they felt it was simply inadequate and too weak a response to Ab Davis's disloyalty, particularly in view of the huge amount of money it had cost the Waller brothers. The construction and erection of a liquor distillery alone – made mostly from lead and copper – was very expensive.

Since they couldn't arrive at a decision that day – probably as a result of a bottle of their "shine" which they passed around – another meeting eventually was scheduled at John Waller's house the following Wednesday, and at this session, the plans reportedly were altered from merely "whipping" Davis to "killing" him.

The deed was set to be accomplished the following Saturday morning, since Davis was known to travel down Kite Road each Saturday to sell his wares. The men originally planned to use a firearm of some sort to murder

Davis, but then decided another weapon would be more appropriate. A gun would make a racket which someone might overhear. An axe (and, for reasons unknown today, a maul) – were selected instead. They would not only be silent, but also just as deadly if used appropriately.

By this time, a total of eight moonshiners had been recruited into the group conspiring to kill Davis. Why the men chose to bring in so many additional individuals who would make the task of secrecy so much more difficult is unknown today as well. One has to conclude, however, that the brain trust in this affair was not going to be making any scientific calculations anytime soon.

According to later news accounts and courtroom testimony, the murderous group was ultimately enlarged even further to include Arthur Alexander, Melvin Brown, Oscar Dutton, and Melvin Windham. Perhaps the intention of the Wallers, Cauthen and Whittle was to recruit as many of their fellow moonshiners as possible in order to spread around the message of what one might expect to receive for such disloyalty in the future. In the final analysis, the matter of "logic" seems to have completely escaped these criminals.

Murder Site

Kite Bridge Road, Kite Lake Road, or South Kite Road as the route has been variously known in recent years, turns northward from Kenwood Road and immediately begins a gentle downhill descent to a small tributary of Morning Creek before continuing up the hill on the opposite side. A bridge at the bottom of the hill was to be the site of the killing, and an ambush was carefully planned for that spot. Today, this site is well-developed with numerous homes, but in 1922, it was a very secluded and isolated locale, with no residences near the bridge or the creek.

John Waller's home, located approximately 150 yards up the hill, was the nearest residence to the creek. Today, in retrospect, the selection of an ambush and murder site so near to the headquarters of the perpetrators was an even more infantile decision. It was one of many aspects of this gruesome crime which defied logic, and which remain unexplained today.

A few long-time Fayette residents still remember the very good spring at the bottom of the hill. Travelers often stopped at the spot for a cool drink in the early 1900s, and as stated above, postman Langston also regularly stopped at the spring for a drink and usually ate his lunch there. This, however, somewhat contradicts the murderers' testimony.

According to courtroom testimony in the later murder trial, just before 11:00 a.m. on the appointed day of October 28, 1922, Postman Jim Langston crested the hill in his Ford automobile, his bag of mail in the seat beside him. He drove on down the slope and was suddenly surprised when Rainey Cauthen stepped out of the bushes along the roadside and flagged him to a stop.

Langston immediately informed Cauthen that he was unable to provide him with transportation, saying, "I'm a government man and can't give you a ride." James was accustomed to the necessity of this action, since in 1922, as

the nation approached the years eventually identified as "the Great Depression" (1929-1939), there were very few individuals with automobiles, and foot travelers constantly appealed to Langston for a ride.

It was at this point that Langston's heart must have jumped into his throat, because Melvin Brown suddenly jumped out into the road as well, and covered the by-now dumbfounded Langston with his shotgun.

"What are you fellows up to?? What do you want? I have nothing but the mail," Langston reportedly exclaimed.

"We're going to teach you how to report stills," Cauthen reportedly responded, as Ora Whittle, an axe in his hands, and Oscar Dutton, hefting a large wooden maul, jumped menacingly from their hiding spots nearby.

Now at this point, one might ask why these men had suddenly substituted James Langston – a federal official – for Ab Davis. He didn't look like Ab Davis. He had identified himself as "a government man," and he was carrying a mail bag. How could they have confused him with Ab Davis?

No one at the trial, nor anyone since that time has been able to provide a logical explanation. As stated above, logic eventually does not enter the equation with moonshiners who many times partake of their product liberally to the detriment of their senses.

Despite the fact that Langston

> *"What are you fellows up to?? What do you want? I have nothing but the mail,"*

obviously was not the intended victim (Ab Davis), the men nevertheless proceeded with their grisly plans as if it would somehow satisfy their anger with Ab Davis. Were they simply so eager for revenge that they were willing to exact retribution from Langston despite the fact that he had had absolutely nothing whatsoever to do with the still site destruction? Or were they simply too eager, mistakenly stopping Langston, and then fearing he would later implicate them if they released him and then subsequently committed the ill deed on Davis? The true circumstances likely will never be known.

The Murder

By this point, Rainey Cauthen must have begun having second thoughts, because he reportedly instructed the group to "Let the man go. We were going to whip him, not kill him." (With this comment, Cauthen does indeed seem to somehow be confusing James Langston with Ab Davis.)

"Alright," Whittle replied deceivingly. At that point, Whittle and Dutton reached in and somehow literally yanked the by-now horrified lanky Langston through the driver-side window and out of the vehicle to dump him unceremoniously upon the hard ground. They clearly had no intention of halting their murderous intentions, and appear to almost have been insane with an irrepressible urge for bloody revenge.

"You're not going to kill me for nothing?" the by-now terror-stricken Langston reportedly croaked, realizing the bloodthirsty gleam in the eyes of the men standing around him. These words, reportedly, were the last ever uttered by Jim Langston.

Again, the more sensible and merciful Cauthen repeated "We weren't going to hurt anyone, but whip Ab Davis." It was at this point that Windham, also apparently desiring mercy, said to Dutton and Whittle "Turn him loose."

Langston, apparently thinking he might somehow actually escape this terrible nightmare, went around to the front of his car to re-crank it. It was the last move he ever made. According to further courtroom testimony – and for reasons still unexplained today – Whittle suddenly struck Langston viciously in the back of the head with his axe.

With that blow, James Langston collapsed on the spot, falling to his knees. Dutton, his own thirst for violence now peaking, then struck Langston again with his heavy maul, crushing the entire top of Langston's head. The mailman fell immediately upon his face, flat on ground, instantly dead.

It must have been about this time (if at all) that reality began to dawn upon the murderers. If they had not previously noticed the mail bag, and if for some unknown reason they still somehow believed that Langston was Davis, the existence of the mail could not have failed to have tipped them off to their mistake.

Accounts differ somewhat as to the next actions of the men. Newspapers of that day state that all the men literally ran in different directions and later met at Kite's Lake, trying all the while to disguise their trails with a turpentine and camphor mixture which they spread liberally behind them to confuse the bloodhounds they knew would eventually be brought in to track the perpetrators.

It would almost seem like a comical Chinese fire-drill today, had not the crime been so heinous. Before departing the murder scene, Whittle hid the axe in nearby woods. No mention of the disposition of the maul was ever made in courtroom testimony.

All the murderers (again defying logic) met at approximately 12:00 or 12:30 p.m. at John Waller's house (again, at the top of the hill, just a very short inexplicable distance from the murder site).

At this point, according to later testimony, John Waller stated matter-of-factly "Well, we got the wrong man," to which Whittle replied "Yes, but it's too late to pray after the devil's done got you."

Murder Investigation

Meanwhile, Rosa Porch, sometimes known as "Lizzie," was a black lady who lived on the corner of Kenwood and Kite Roads, just above John Whittle. It was she who informed Fayette County Sheriff Tom Kerlin of the murder.

Kerlin immediately contacted U.S Department of Revenue Officer T. B. Harris before speeding to the crime scene. When he (Kerlin) arrived, he noted Langston's car on the bridge in the center of the road with Langston stretched out on the ground in front of the automobile, his skull crushed and the U.S. Mail bag and its contents strewn in the road along the side of the car.

By 3:00 p.m., Revenue Agent Harris had arrived from his office in Newnan, Georgia, and began assisting in the investigation. U.S. Postal Inspector J.W. Cole also aided. He was replaced sometime later by Inspector Frank Ellis, who in turn was assisted from time to time by Inspectors J.R. Smith and W.W. Hodge.

The authorities instantly suspected the Waller brothers. After all, they were known bootleggers.

Strangely, despite all this investigation, no records of the federal government investigation of the murder remain today, and none of the men involved in the murder were ever charged with any federal crimes. U.S. Postal Service officials apparently were content to allow local law enforcement to investigate, arrest and prosecute the perpetrators solely for the crime of murder, which is a state, not a federal offence.

The authorities instantly suspected the Waller brothers. After all, they were known bootleggers and John lived almost within sight of the murder scene, and had not bothered to report anything out of the ordinary despite the fact that James Langston was clearly stretched out bloody and motionless in front of his vehicle and was clearly visible from the Waller home.

Following an initial investigation, John and Charles Waller, as well as George B. Samuels, were all arrested the following week on suspicion of murder. Samuels was *"a Spaniard who had been in the World War"* and who lived with Lula Waller, daughter of John. All these men denied any knowledge of the crime and were released.

Over the span of the next two years, Ora Whittle and John Waller were both arrested, but were only charged with possession of intoxicants. They were both subsequently found *"Not guilty"* and amazingly released.

Despite the difficulties involved in solving this case, the local authorities did not give up. Three years after the fact in May of 1925, Oscar Dutton and Ora Whittle were finally arrested as suspects in the case. Dutton was sent to the Coweta County Jail in Newnan and Whittle was held in Atlanta, both probably for safe-keeping.

Both men, initially, had flatly denied any connection with the murder and openly proclaimed their innocence. While in jail, however, Dutton eventually confessed and implicated some of the others, including John Waller who was promptly re-arrested.

The Trial & Sentences

A special June session of Fayette County Superior Court was called in 1925 to try Whittle and Dutton for the murder of James Langston, and also to try John Waller as *"an accessory before the fact"* of the murder. The **Fayette County News** reported that despite a June heat wave, large crowds attended the trial and the Fayette County Courthouse was completely filled. Overflow spectators surrounded the building, hoping to hear some of the trial through the open windows.

All three men ultimately were found *"Guilty"* of the horrible crime on July 3, 1925. Though sentenced to *"Life"* in prison, they interestingly received recommendations for *"Mercy."* Existing records are not clear as to how the other perpetrators were implicated in this case, but by December, eight men involved in the crime had been tried and found *"Guilty."* Melvin Brown, Rainey Cauthen, Charlie Waller, Arthur Alexander and Melvin Windham were also given *"Life"* sentences with recommendations for *"Mercy."*

One would normally think that for such a brutal crime, these men would have received harsher sentences, but for

reasons unknown, they did not. Perhaps the jury felt that due to the lack of forensics – with DNA evidence and fingerprinting still in the future – *"Life"* imprisonment would be a suitable penalty. That sentence might in fact have been sufficient if the men had actually served it, but their terms of actual imprisonment were relatively brief – amounting to approximately ten years or less each before they were paroled.

All eight men were sent to different prison camps to serve out their sentences. Some long-time Fayette County residents today can still remember Dutton and Whittle serving on the local "chain gang," once located just east of Fayetteville.

As stated, most of the men inexplicably served relatively short sentences. Charlie Waller was paroled in July of 1932, and his brother, John, in November of 1935. Melvin Windham received a parole in September of 1933, and Oscar Dutton was granted parole in January of 1935. No record has been located for the release date of Ora Whittle, Melvin Brown, Arthur Alexander or Rainey Cauthen.

Meanwhile, Ab Davis, the original object of all the hatred and vicious blood-letting on an October morning in 1922, continued to prosper peacefully in the produce business and in later years ran a store in Kenwood. He lived out his life without incident.

(Author's Note: Information on the murder of Jim Langston is a matter of public record in the Fayette and Spalding County courthouses, the Georgia Department of Archives and History, and the archives of the local newspapers.)

(Grateful appreciation is expressed herewith in memory of the late Marion Hemperley, former deputy surveyor-general of Georgia, for the research and details provided in this article. Special thanks is also extended to U.S. Postman Jon Wolleat for additional details involving this murder.)

The Calhoun – Williamson Duel And The CR&C Railroad

A well documented formal duel between two angered men degenerated into comic adventure before becoming the last such event in Georgia – and possibly Alabama – history.

On August 8, 1889, two men in Atlanta, Georgia, exchanged words that threatened to change their lives forever. The events that led to a challenge to a duel between Pat Calhoun and Captain John D. Williamson are virtually forgotten today, but they caused quite a stir at the time in north Georgia.

Captain Williamson was the president of the Chattanooga, Rome and Columbus Railroad Company (CR&C). Pat Calhoun was general counsel and a director of the Central Railroad and Banking Company (CR&B) of Georgia. Young Pat enjoyed the added distinction of being the grandson of famed fiery South Carolina statesman and former vice-president of the United States John C. Calhoun. Both men were highly respected in their professions.

At the time of the incident, Captain Williamson resided part-time in Rome at the Armstrong Hotel located on Howard Street (present-day Second Avenue) in Rome. Pat Calhoun was from the Atlanta area.

The trouble between the two men began at a legislative committee hearing at the Georgia state capitol in Atlanta.

Williamson was in favor of a bill that would prevent the consolidation of competing railroad companies. He assured the committee that his Chattanooga, Rome & Columbus Railroad was and would remain an "independent line."

Pat Calhoun, however, representing a company that was actively consolidating railroads in the South, strongly opposed the bill. At some point in the discussions of the new bill, Calhoun, referring to Captain Williamson, reportedly remarked, "The gentleman knows that the first project he had in the building of this road was to unload it on the Central. That would have been done had I not stood in the way."

Captain Williamson took umbrage at the remark, bounding to his feet and countering, "When Mr. Calhoun states that it was my purpose to unload on the Central, he states what is unqualifiedly false…I never had any talk with Mr. Calhoun on the subject, and never made any proposition of the kind he indicates."

With this dangerous charge of falsehood, a deafening silence fell over the committee room. In times past, it had not been uncommon for words of this nature to be followed with the challenge of a duel, and this day would prove to be no exception. Without any further exchange and in an attempt to stem the anger between the two men, the committee meeting was immediately terminated, but the fateful words had already been spoken.

After leaving the meeting, neither man hesitated to obtain a representative – known as "a second" – to handle any correspondence between them. Mr. Calhoun sent for his friend Captain Henry Jackson, while Captain Williamson telegraphed Jack King of Rome, Georgia, to represent him.

If there had been any hope that this confrontation between the two men could be halted, it was soon shattered. On the evening of August 8th, Pat Calhoun sent a letter to Captain Williamson which read as follows:

Dear Sir:

Before the railroad commission of the House of Representatives this afternoon, in the discussion of the Olive bill, you characterized certain statements which had been made by me as false. I request an unqualified retraction of this charge.

This communication will be handed to you by my friend, Mr. Henry Jackson, who is authorized to receive the reply, which you may see proper to make.

Respectfully,
Pat Calhoun

That same evening, Williamson responded to Calhoun's letter as follows:

Dear Sir:

Your note of this evening has been delivered to me by Mr. Henry Jackson. You stated before the committee that I had solicited you to act as a general counsel of the Chattanooga, Rome and Columbus Railroad Company, and that my purpose

was to unload that road upon the Central Railroad Company of Georgia through your influence.

This statement carried with it a reflection upon myself. It was without foundation, and I promptly pronounced it false. So long as this language, used by you, is not withdrawn, I must decline to make any retraction, which you request.

This will be handed to you by my friend, Hon. J. Lindsay Johnson.

Respectfully,
J.D. Williamson

After several additional communications, the last written correspondence between the two men names the time and place for the duel.

Dear Sir:

My friend, Mr. J. King of Rome, Georgia, has arrived and has been put in possession of contents of the correspondence between us. In conformity with your request in your last note delivered at 1:05 p.m. today, I will meet you in Alabama, at Cedar Bluff, on the Rome and Decatur Railroad, tomorrow (Saturday) afternoon at 5 o'clock. Unless I hear to the contrary, I shall expect to find you there at that hour.

My friend, Mr. King, will deliver this note.

Respectfully,
J.D. Williamson

Word had gotten out that there was to be a duel, and a substantial attempt was made by government officials to intercept the principals to avoid bloodshed. Governor John B. Gordon of Georgia, sent telegrams to the governors of Tennessee and Alabama asking them to stop the duel and arrest the principals. The same request was sent out to law officers at Rome and Cedartown, as well as to Anniston, Alabama. Alabama's Governor Tom Seay did the same for likely points in his state.

The *Atlanta Constitution* as well as the *Atlanta Journal* (separate newspapers at that time) eventually learned of the details of the duel. From the *Constitution*, E.W. Barrett was assigned to the Williamson party and Edward C. Bruffey was assigned to the Calhoun group. Gordon N. Hurtel from the *Journal* was given orders to stick with Williamson and his party until a resolution was reached or until the duel had occurred.

As a result of the publicity surrounding the scheduled duel, the task of actually reaching the appointed meeting place was no easy chore for either party. Friday night, August 9, Captain Jackson met Pat Calhoun and both departed on a sleeping car from Union Station in downtown Atlanta. They overnighted at the Anniston Inn in Anniston, Alabama. The next morning, they slipped out the rear door of the inn.

According to Bruffey's newspaper account of the incident, while Williamson and his party were making their way to the duel site, Jackson had taken Pat Calhoun out for some target practice. Jackson reportedly tossed a coin in the air and instructed Calhoun to hit it. After five shots had been fired, the results showed three of the rounds had hit the mark – a somewhat amazing feat.

After witnessing Calhoun's accuracy with the pistol, Jackson reportedly

> *The next morning, they slipped out the rear door of the inn.*

remarked, "That's good Pat. Now, if we can't have peace and must have war, and you can do that – well, you will come home alive."

Calhoun spent the next couple of hours napping at a friend's house. The two men had sent for their luggage at the hotel, but reportedly were forced to abandon the property when they saw lawmen following the carriage conveying the luggage.

When they went to catch the 11:00 o'clock train, Jackson recognized the Anniston city police chief at the depot, so a quick decision was made to backtrack through the woods to nearby Leathertown to board the train there. After having lunch in Gadsden, the men boarded a Rome and Decatur train to be on their way to the site of the duel.

Meanwhile, Captain Williamson's trip to the meeting place was turning out to be quite an adventure as well. Gordon Hurtel, the *Journal* reporter, was able to give a detailed account because he faithfully followed the Williamson party.

Hurtel left Union Station in Atlanta at 8:00 a.m. He boarded a westbound Western & Atlantic train to find that Williamson and his party were occupying the parlor car. His party consisted of Mr. Jack King, Williamson's second; Judge H.B. Tompkins; and Major C.B. Lowe. Dr. Henry Battey boarded the train in Rome.

The men then set out for Kingston, Georgia, where Williamson's private car was waiting. The private car was coupled to the engine and the train set out for Rome.

Hurtel was a determined news correspondent, but he suspected that his ride would be short-lived because he had been spotted. He believed that Rome would be his place of departure from the group and he was not far off the mark.

"As I expected," Hurtel explained in his article, *"the special car was uncoupled* [from the other cars behind it] *and run through town at the rate of twenty miles an hour. Two miles the other side of Rome, Mr. Jack King discovered me hiding on the steps* [of the car]. *The train was stopped and I was put off like a tramp, and had to count the cross-ties for two miles through the hot sun* [back to Rome]."

Little did Williamson and Hurtel know, however, that fate would bring them together again where they would become allies. With the help of E.W. Barrett, who had been put off the train along with Hurtel, the two men were able to get an engine and engineer (W.T. Dozier) to drive a locomotive for them.

After procuring the locomotive *"Daniel S. Printup"* from the Forrestville Station in north Rome, the men set out in hot pursuit of Williamson and his party. They encountered them sooner than expected.

Roughly two or three miles down the track, Captain Williamson's train had been sidetracked at the Rome & Decatur junction for lack of an engineer who knew the route. Seizing the

The men all scrambled to get back on the private car.

opportunity, Hurtel offered the men his engineer in exchange for the privilege of riding along with them. Williamson took Hurtel up on the offer and the men were welcomed into his private car.

While in the private car, Barrett and Hurtel were given a fine lunch, cigars and champagne. Hurtel later noted, *"This was the same car from which I had been fired like a tramp an hour earlier."*

While Williamson was awaiting the departure of his party, the men went into the nearby woods in order to allow the captain an opportunity to practice with his revolver. The target practice was short-lived, however, because a runner alerted the men that a sheriff from Floyd County, with a deputy, was coming down the tracks. In order to elude the sheriff, Captain Williamson and Jack King ran through the woods to a point a couple of miles down the track where they re-boarded the private car.

After picking the two men up, the train was once again on its way to Cedar Bluff, Alabama. It reached its destination about 4:00 p.m. in the afternoon. At Cedar Bluff, the train was side-tracked for an east-bound passenger train, and no sooner had the cars come to a halt when someone called out, "Here comes the sheriff!" The men all scrambled to get back on the private car.

According to a vivid description provided by journalist Hurtel, *"We were in Cherokee County, Alabama, and the sheriff was one of those bushy, black-whiskered fellows with a broad-brimmed hat who meant business."*

Hurtel went on to explain that Williamson's private car did not get far before it was caught and returned to the sheriff. Williamson, however, was nowhere to be found.

Meanwhile, Pat Calhoun and Henry Jackson had been on the regular passenger train coming from Atlanta by way of Anniston. The train stopped and Calhoun got off and was promptly arrested by the sheriff who said "Mr. Williamson, consider yourself under arrest."

If not for Captain Seay – who was known by the sheriff and attested that Mr. Calhoun was not Captain Williamson – the situation might have become even more confusing. Calhoun, however, was released and the Chinese fire-drill continued.

The sheriff would not give up easily, however. He swore he would find Williamson, never realizing he had just released the other principal, Mr. Calhoun. Both trains were searched, but the men were not found. Pat Calhoun and Captain Jackson were locked up in a closet in the private car. Captain Williamson and Jack King were hidden in a closet on the regular passenger train. These two men were determined to end the day with a duel, come hell or high water.

When the passenger train was finally released, it carried Captain Williamson, Mr. King, Dr. Battey, Captain Williamson's private secretary, Captain Seay and Gordon Hurtel. The train

The engineer ducked down in the cab and pulled the throttle wide open.

continued down the tracks to Raynes' Station, five miles closer to Rome. Calhoun's train also arrived at Rayne's Station and it seemed the two duelists might be about to effect their stated mission.

The bushy-bearded sheriff, however, was a determined man, and also proceeded to Raynes' Station. He was then led to believe that both of the dueling parties were on the train and that apologies had been made and everything was settled.

After the sheriff – being convinced that everything was alright – had departed, the men all got off the train. The seconds were arranging preliminaries and Hurtel was wiring the **Journal**. About that time, four men, believed to be deputies, riding mules and brandishing shotguns, came clamoring up and one of them shouted, "If anybody moves, I'll shoot." One has to wonder at this point if the lawmen were going to kill someone to avoid a killing.

Taking their chances, the men scrambled for the train. The engineer ducked down in the cab and pulled the throttle wide open. The previously somber preparations for a duel were quickly taking on the appearance of comical hijinks.

The train sped away from the lawmen. Three miles down the tracks, the men once again disembarked and the seconds began conferring. It was already beginning to get dark. As Jackson and King were talking someone yelled, "Look out! Everybody on the train!"

The warning had come just in time.

The four men with the shotguns seemed to be just as determined as the black-whiskered sheriff. Once again, everyone jumped aboard the train which again headed down the tracks. About four or five miles nearer to Rome, the men stopped again to prepare for the duel.

The final destination for the duel was Farill, Alabama, on the Farill Plantation (about three miles east of the location where General Nathan Bedford Forrest captured Col. Streight's men in the battle of 1863). A small natural clearing in an oak grove was selected for the duel.

Captain Seay made one last futile attempt to stop the affair, but the men had come too far to abandon the fight now. Captain Williamson, having the choice of weapons, chose the hammerless Smith & Wesson five shooter. By this time, it was well into dusk, and the light was fading as the moon rose over the treetops in the east.

The two seconds, Mr. King and Captain Jackson, were attempting to load the pistols for their principals. Captain Jackson, being unfamiliar with this pistol, was having trouble loading his. Mr. Bruffey, with the *Constitution*, spoke up, "I can help Cap."

Within seconds, an explosion broke the silence in the dark woods. "There, my finger's gone!" Mr. Bruffey suddenly shouted, walking off and holding up a bloody hand. A part of the third finger

"There, my finger's gone!" Mr. Bruffey suddenly shouted, walking off and holding up a bloody hand.

of his right hand had been torn away by the ball.

"Let me dress it," said Dr. Cooper who was standing by. "Oh, go on with the fight," Bruffey huffed as he wrapped a handkerchief about his wounded finger. "A finger don't amount to anything."

Captain Jackson then loaded Mr. Calhoun's pistol and handed it to him. As the two men were preparing to face off with each other, Captain Seay made one last desperate attempt to put a stop to the duel. "As a citizen of Georgia and in the name of the Governor of Alabama" cried out Seay, "I call upon you to stop!" Seay obviously didn't know which state he was in, so he was covering all the bases.

His pleas, however, fell upon deaf ears once again.

"Gentlemen, are you ready?" called out Mr. King. The men acknowledged their readiness. The paces were counted off and the command to "Fire!" was given.

Six rapid shots followed the command. The deed was done. All the men held their breath, waiting to see which duelist crumpled to the ground. Both seconds ran to their principals to see if they were injured and discovered they were not.

There had been some confusion as to the procedure that was to be used. Captain Williamson had thought that all shots were to be fired in succession, so he had fired all five of his shots at once. Pat Calhoun, however, had fired only once, thus leaving four balls remaining in his weapon. What would Calhoun do with those remaining shots?

"Mr. Williamson," Calhoun intoned, "I have four remaining balls which I have the right to fire at you. I now ask if you will withdraw the statement you made before the legislative committee."

"I will," Williamson responded, "provided you will say that you meant no personal reflection upon me."

It quickly became apparent that despite the circumstances, Captain Williamson was still refusing to unequivocally retract his statement. And even though he had braved the hail of bullets from Captain Williamson, Pat Calhoun, to his credit, had no further desire to fire at his opponent.

After a short additional verbal exchange between the two men, Pat Calhoun spoke these words: "Mr. Williamson, in my remarks before the legislative committee you personally did not enter my mind." Calhoun then raised his pistol in the air and fired his remaining four balls into the air.

"Since you have stated you meant nothing personal in your remarks," Williamson said, "I now withdraw the statement I made before the committee." The two men shook hands and ended the matter.

The party retired to the train and celebrated with cigars and champagne. They arrived in Rome a few minutes after 9 p.m. News of the results was telegraphed to Atlanta.

According to records, this duel was the last such formal incident associated with Georgia, and since it actually occurred in Alabama, it may have been the final such occurrence there as well. If so,

it was a dramatic final curtain for an old custom, despite the somewhat comical circumstances under which this incident took place.

Several of the sites mentioned in this incident still exist today. Captain Williamson's residence – the *Armstrong Hotel* – burned in 1932, but was rebuilt as the *Greystone Hotel*. The Greystone, which still exists today, boasts some of the original stonework from the Armstrong, and is listed on the **National Register of Historic Places**.

Much of downtown Rome remains the same as it was in 1889, with many of the buildings being from that era. Howard Street, known today as Second Avenue, does not have a trolley track down the center any longer, but it is just as busy as it was a hundred years ago.

The Forrestville Station no longer exists, but the Rome & Decatur junction where Williamson's car was side-tracked is still in use today.

A trip to Farill, Alabama, to the former dueling site can be an adventure. Judy Smith and her husband live next to the old Farill homeplace. Judy once lived in the Farill house and can still point out the old roadbed where the railroad once existed beside the house. Even though the exact location of the duel is unknown today, it was quite near to this vicinity.

It is unknown today if Captain Williamson and Pat Calhoun lived long fruitful lives, but it is known that on a hot August night in 1889, their lives were spared that day, and happiness reigned supreme once again – at least for the moment.

Endnotes

1/ Battey, George Magruder; *A History of Rome and Floyd County*; Cherokee Publishing Company, Marietta, Georgia, (1922).

Jacob Pettyjohn's Odyssey After a Conviction for Murder

Though he sought a normal, law-abiding life, Jacob Pettyjohn's life became nightmarish in 1859, when events quite nearly conspired to end his life. At the somewhat young age of 42, he was convicted of murder for failure to render assistance to a victim in need. After winning a "Stay of Execution" in his case, he did not wait around hoping for a reversed judgment. Jacob Pettyjohn had "seen the handwriting on the wall," and struck out for Texas, departing the state of Georgia forever.

The Pettyjohn family from Virginia – just as most families – is not without its unusual twists and turns, even to the point of being implicated in a documented murder. Though the Pettyjohn lineage reportedly hails from early royalty in France, this stature was anything but obvious in the Georgia branch of this family.

James D. Pettyjohn (b. 1790 in VA) married **Temperance Rogers** (b. 1800 or 1806 in Jackson Co., GA) in 1815 or 1818. This group of Pettyjohns – either through the Pettyjohns themselves or through relations with the Rogers family – reportedly was part Native American.

The children of James and Temperance, all of whom were born in Jackson Co., Georgia, were: Nancy (b. 1816); **Jacob** (b. 11/01/1817 in Jackson Co., GA); Sarah Ann (b. 1819); Oliver Perry (b. 1821); John Rodgers (b. 1824); Elizabeth (b. 1827); Mary Evaline (b. 1828); Adaline Permilia and Addison Bainbridge (b. 1832); **Arabella (Arabel Ellen) (b.**

1834); James Decatur (b. 1836); William Franklin (b. 1837); Thomas Jefferson (b. 1840); and Marion Gates (b. 1843).

Jacob Pettyjohn was destined to live a most unusual life, and he is central to the topic of this story. It begins in Forsyth County, Georgia, to which Jacob had moved sometime between 1840 and 1845, with his wife **Mary Mariah Whitmire** and their five children. Jacob, reportedly, had previously served as a deputy sheriff, and was well-acquainted with law enforcement and its procedures.

On the afternoon of August 7, 1858, Jacob, along with **Isaac Freeland, Levi Q.C. McGinnis, William R. Brannon, James McGinnis, Abraham Buice, William Buice, Claiborn Vaughan and his brother** were involved in a violent incident which ultimately resulted in Claiborn Vaughan's murder.

According to most accounts, **Jacob was not directly involved with the murder**, but by the simple fact that he was in the vicinity, aware of the situation, and did not render aid nor come to the defense of the victim, he also was surprisingly charged with and ultimately convicted of the crime of *"Second Degree Murder"* of Vaughan.

According to Forsyth County records, **Isaac Freeland was charged with the actual slaying of Vaughan**, using a knife with a one by four-inch blade – essentially a hunting knife – to cut a large gash on the left side of the victim's neck, severing the jugular vein. The other four defendants – Pettyjohn, Levi McGinnis, James McGinnis and William R. Brannon – were accused of *"feloniously, willfully, unlawfully, and of their malice aforethought. . . . aiding, helping, abetting, comforting, assisting, and maintaining the said Isaac Freeland"* in the commission of a violent crime.

The problems all began when court was held by the Justices of the Peace of Forsyth County for the Wildcat District on the first Saturday of August, 1858. The McGinnises, Vaughans, Buices, and several of their companions were in attendance at the courthouse. Like church camp meetings, "Court Week" was a very popular opportunity to meet and socialize with friends, relatives and neighbors, as well as a venue for the observance of any punishments which might be handed out to convicted felons.

By noon that day, several others had congregated at the court ground: Isaac Freeland, Jacob Pettyjohn, Pinkney Lindsey, Ransom Barnes, Freeland's older sons, and others to watch the proceedings. Court week not only was a big event, it literally was the entertainment medium of that day, especially when serious trials were being heard in court. Little did these men know that they would themselves become the focus of intense attention in a Court Week of the not-too-distant future.

One of the standard "side attractions" during Court Week was a "liquor wagon" where corn and rye whiskeys were dispensed by the pint or quart for sale to the public. It was, in fact, a time-honored tradition which invariably – and ironically – led to trouble for the participants, and even though liquor consumption at these events was questionable legally, that circumstance was far out-weighed by the custom and popularity of the practice of "imbibing."

Out of the social aspect of alcohol consumption during Court Week grew other "sideline events" – such as competitive shooting matches – and the first Saturday in August, 1858, was no exception, with Abraham Buice and Archibald Martin competing against each other in one of the initial matches, and William Buice and Clayborn Vaughan placing side-bets against Jacob Pettyjohn and John Brannon, Jr.'s bets on the Buice-Martin match.

> *Court week not only was a big event, it literally was the entertainment medium of that day*

In order to find a place for the marksmanship contest, the group walked about a quarter of a mile southwest from the court grounds to a roadside clearing halfway between Wildcat Courthouse and Freeland's home. These events served as lead-ups to the later popular observation of whatever punishments might be meted out at the courthouse for the county's convicted criminals.

Though Abe Buice won the first match fairly, Martin was declared the initial winner of the second match before a loud argument from Buice declared that he had actually won that match also. With the outcome of the second match in question and a quarrel quickly in the making, the men decided to just return to the Wildcat Court ground, but that didn't help matters – not by a long shot. The ubiquitous whiskey which was readily available at the courthouse, along with several individuals who were particularly argumentative that day, served only to fan the flames of a quickly-building major quarrel.

Buice continued to insist he had won both shooting matches, and demanded that Pettyjohn and Brannon turn over their illegitimate winnings to him. According to reports, Pettyjohn ultimately complied, stating *"If I didn't win the money, I don't want it,"* and took the money out of his pocket and handed it to Buice.

According to the late Don Shadburn's **Pioneer History of Forsyth County**, *"Billy Buice, Jim McGinnis, Levi McGinnis, and Thomas Stone were standing nearby listening and watching. Several of the men soon fell into an argument, instigated by Jim McGinnis who sidled up to Pettyjohn and told him to knock Buice down. McGinnis then began walking around swearing under his breath.*

"Overhearing the remarks, Billy Buice started cursing McGinnis and Pettyjohn, and Levi McGinnis quickly stepped forward and offered his support. 'Jim (McGinnis), say what you please (to Buice),' he stated emphatically, rolling up his sleeves. 'If you can't whip him, I can.'

"At this point, cooler heads attempted to take control. Jacob Pettyjohn (to his credit) attempted to calm the men and ease their tempers before serious trouble erupted, but his efforts were in vain.

"Sometime later, not long before sundown, Levi McGinnis suggested they 'go get something to drink and make friends.' Several of the men walked down to Ransom Barnes' wagon, tied up 'a little piece below the courthouse, and got a quart of liquor.' – each man contributing a few cents toward the purchase. The quart jar was passed quickly from hand to hand among the few who were eager to take it. The whiskey, however, only aggravated the still unresolved quarrel.

"Levi McGinnis, finding courage from the bottle, grew louder and bolder with his remarks about 'the South Carolinians.' Suddenly, he jerked Abe Buice's gun from his hand and hit him in the head with the breach, making Buice stagger."

According to later testimony, a general scuffling reportedly quickly ensued, with McGinnis grabbing Buice by the hair of his head and racing down the hill screaming *"G__ damn you! I'll jerk you as bald-headed as I did Pink Lindsey!"* The two soon fell to the ground panting and cursing, clawing, and ripping at each other like animals. After being broken up, Buice said he was leaving, and gathered his gun and hat.

About 15 minutes after the fight ended, as nightfall approached, the Buices and Vaughan departed. At this point, Levi McGinnis, weaving about with a bottle in his hand, loudly told the Buices and Vaughans to leave, otherwise he would *"kill every last damned South Carolinian of them."*

Witnesses said that Billy Buice, in his drunken state, made the mistake of bragging that he had been the bully in North Carolina and South Carolina, and that he would be the bully in Georgia too. He apparently intended to clearly indicate he was not intimidated in the least by McGinnis.

Claiborn Vaughan had managed to remain clear of the fighting which seemed to have no logical genesis or intent. The Vaughans and Buices headed in the direction of Billy Buice's house. Buice, McGinnis and Freeland were all still fighting among themselves, with none of them really knowing or understanding what they were fighting about, or why. They were just mad as hornets in a drunken state, and nothing short of a state of unconsciousness was going to alter their lust for conflict.

By this point, still headed down the trail, Abraham Buice – no doubt was still stunned from the blow to his head – was not only confused, but also fearful of the way the situation was so quickly getting out of control. He was particularly frightened of another confrontation with the drunken Freeland whose actions could easily have been interpreted as being just short of insane.

According to later court testimony,

> *Claiborn Vaughan had managed to remain clear of the fighting which seemed to have no logical genesis or intent.*

in order to collect himself and avoid further conflict with Freeland, Abraham Buice said he *"ran off about forty yards from the place where Claiborne Vaughan later would be killed and sat down upon a log to hide."* As he sat in his hideaway, Buice later testified that he *"saw three men race down the darkened hill and hollow, toward the second branch across the old Mill Road."* Buice said it was much too dark for him to be able to make out the identity of the three phantom figures, and that soon, yet another individual gave a brief chase before suddenly stopping just short of the creek and turning back in the direction of the court ground.

According to further court testimony, after even more confusion and fighting and cursing and unfounded accusations, Levi McGinnis, Freeland, and Brannon, in the presence of Pettyjohn, confronted the unfortunate Claiborne Vaughan who was mounted upon a mare. This, no doubt, was precipitated solely by the fact that Vaughan had been identified and associated with the Buices as a "South Carolinian." Brandishing pocket knives, one or more of the men began dragging Vaughan off the mare, and, as evidence would later indicate, one or more of them also assaulted Vaughan with a knife – in a deadly manner.

Abe Buice further testified that while he was hiding nearby in the undergrowth and brush, he heard more scuffling sounds, shouting and cursing involving his friend, Vaughan. He stated that he distinctly recognized Vaughan's voice when the victim called out to his attackers *"I surrender! I surrender!"* Then, Buice testified that, in a louder voice, he next heard Vaughan scream *"Murder! Murder!"*

Vaughan, after falling from his horse, continued to kick and struggle in vain, as his wails of anguish and pain grew weaker. Jeremiah Freeland who had been following the group saw the silhouetted figure of Vaughan lying in the road. He witnessed Vaughan raise himself on his hands and slowly crawl to the edge of the road moaning *"I'm a dead man . . . . dead man."* Pettyjohn, Jim McGinnis and Bill Brannon reportedly stood nearby, possibly in shock at what had occurred. They, however, had made the tragic mistake of failing to render assistance to a victim in dire need.

Later, after being identified as a suspect and being arrested and placed on trial, Jacob Pettyjohn testified that he had gone along with the crowd merely as an "idle spectator," to watch Freeland and Buice fight. He stated under oath that *"while following the Buices* (who took to concealment) *to the creek, he had heard the fighting and returned to the place where he earlier had passed Claib Vaughan."*

Pettyjohn added that he saw William Brannon again at that spot and that Brannon had staggered over to Vaughan, kicked him a few times, and demanded, *"Are you dead G___ damn you, old man? If Freeland has not whipped you, I can."*

The east-headed old Blackstock Mill Road on which the murder occurred was intersected north-south with what today would be old U.S. 19, an ancient Indian and game trail in pre-history. The Mill Road passed through three north-south flowing streams – which combine south of the road to form the main tributary of Dick's Creek.

Levi McGinnis and Isaac Freeland who had also been arrested and placed on trial for Vaughan's murder were both ultimately convicted of murder and sentenced to *"Death."* They were later hung on a gallows at the Forsyth County Jail. Freeland had the distinction of being the first person in recorded history to be hanged in Forsyth County.

William Brannon and Jim McGinnis were likewise found *"Guilty,"* but drew the lesser penalty of *"Involuntary Manslaughter,"* and sentenced to three years of hard labor at the state penitentiary in Milledgeville. By comparison, they "got off easy."

Meanwhile, a by-now totally crestfallen Jacob Pettyjohn who had heretofore been accustomed to being on the opposite end (law enforcement) of the legal spectrum, was, on April 16, 1859, being tried for the capital crime of *"Murder"* of Claiborn Vaughan as a result of his presence and failure to intercede in the matter. To Pettyjohn's shock, on the 23rd day of April, a jury found him *"Guilty"* of *"Second Degree Murder"* and, even more shockingly, sentenced him to be *"publicly hanged by the neck on a gallows until he is dead."* The reason for his being charged with and ultimately convicted of Second Degree Murder instead of Involuntary Manslaughter is unknown today.

To his great fortune, however, Pettyjohn – no doubt at least partially as a result of his previous unblemished record – won a *"Stay of Execution"* written by Judge Rice on May 21, 1859. The case was bound over to the State Supreme Court of Georgia, and, also as a result of his otherwise sterling record and professional experience as a former law enforcement officer, Pettyjohn was released on bail to await his new trial.

By this point, however, the thunderstruck Jacob Pettyjohn had "seen the handwriting on the wall." He had no idea why he had been convicted of such a heinous crime for which he held no responsibility, and he had no intention of waiting around for yet another verdict to be rendered on the matter. Very quickly and quietly, he departed Georgia forever, traveling secretly to Texas, where he began life anew, ultimately joining the Confederate Army where he reportedly *"served his country heroically during the war years as a high-ranking Confederate officer."*

According to the Confederate Army records at the Texas State Archives, *"Jacob C. Pettijohn enlisted in the Confederate Army on April 20, 1861, for a period of 12 months."* He was *"a private in Company A, 1st Regiment, Texas Mounted Riflemen,"* commanded by Henry E. McCulloch.

Interestingly, according to his final mustering out information, *"Private Jacob Pettijohn left Ft. Pemberton April 11; arrived at Snyder's Bluff April 13, camped until the 19th when they reached Camp Timmins; due 1 muster & payroll combined dated December 31, 1862 to February 28, 1863; 1 muster roll dated*

By this point, however, the thunderstruck Jacob Pettyjohn had "seen the handwriting on the wall."

February 28, 1863 to April 30, 1863; Absent, left sick in hospital at Vicksburg February 18. Last paid August 31, 1862; bounty due him of $50.00; due him for clothing $33.83; and service 6 months at $11.00 per month = $66.00 plus $50.00 bounty, plus $33.83 commu. due him for 6 months & clothing. Total: $149.84."

In 1863, $149.84 was the equivalent of slightly more than 8 months of average income, since the average male salary was approximately $18.00 per month. It was also the equivalent of approximately $3,655.00 in 2024 dollars, and represented a modest windfall, since a horse could be purchased for as little as $10.00.

It is unknown today if Pettyjohn ever collected any of the mustering out pay which was owed to him. Even if he did collect payment, it would have been virtually valueless by 1864 if it was paid in Confederate paper money (instead of silver or gold). Since there are no further records on him in Texas, any details concerning the disposition of his life from that point forward are unknown as well.

The ultimate resolution of the life of Jacob Pettyjohn (even his burial site) is also unknown today. The one "known" final aspect of his life is that it appears he was fruitful and multiplied in his residence in Texas, since many Pettyjohn descendants reside there today.

The Mysterious Murder and Burial Of Cherokee Chief James Vann II

On a frigid winter night in 1809, at an isolated inn located on the Federal Road at what today would be the county line between Forsyth and Cherokee counties, an important chief of the Cherokee Nation was brutally murdered in cold blood. Though he was buried and his grave clearly marked a short distance away in Blackburn Cemetery, the specific location of his interment has been strangely lost through time. Today, no one knows for certain where the last mortal remains of Chief Vann now lie, nor even the exact site at which he was murdered.

Most historians today who are familiar with the Cherokee Indians in north Georgia are aware of the story and legacy of James Vann II. Descriptions of his stately mansion at Spring Place (near present-day Chatsworth, Georgia), stories of his wealth and wide-spread business affairs, and finally, his murder at Buffington's Tavern near the present-day Forsyth/Cherokee County line in Georgia, have been handed down from generation to generation. But how many people really know the actual site of Vann's murder or his final resting place? I'll tell you how many. . . . . Not a single person.

Much of the controversial issue of the location of Vann's grave stems from a tendency of the general public – and even of some respected historians – to perpetuate myths and false stories created in the absence of factual information. Vann's grave no doubt exists in the general vicinity of the site suspected by researchers. It, however, has been totally confused with other graves and other landmarks over the years.

Vann was a prominent and wealthy leader of the Cherokees in the Southeast in the late 18th century, and the owner of impressive plantations, complete with slaves, and extensive business enterprises.

The Federal Road – along which most all of Vann's properties existed – created tremendous commercial opportunities for the Native American culture, and Vann was quick to take advantage of the circumstances, achieving enormous wealth for that day. The route grew out of an ancient Native American trading path, and was the first navigable wagon-trail, as well as the earliest postal route, across what today is northwest Georgia. It began on the southeastern boundary of the native Cherokee Indian Territory not far from present-day Athens, Georgia, and linked Georgia and Tennessee across the Indian Country. Rights to open the thoroughfare were granted informally by the Cherokees in

1803 and confirmed in the 1805 *Treaty of Tellico*, Tennessee.

In addition to his previously-mentioned plantations, Vann also operated a stagecoach stop ("stand"), a trading post and tavern on the Federal Road near Eton, Georgia, as well as a ferry and inn where the Federal Road crossed the Chattahoochee River in present-day Forsyth County, and a second plantation near that same location along the fertile river bottomlands.

At the site where the Federal Road crossed the Conasauga River just west of his home at *Spring Place* Vann owned yet another ferry, as well as a mill on Vann's Mill Creek, a tributary of the Conasauga. *(Note: The Federal Road crossed the Conasauga on Lot #149, District 9, Section 3, according to the 1832 surveys of old Cherokee County by David Duke, D.S., June, 1832).*

Though described as having occurred at several different sites throughout most of the more than two centuries since it transpired, Vann's murder is believed by most researchers to have taken place at an early inn by the name of Buffington's Tavern (the original site of which, not surprisingly, is also a controversy). The physical remnants of Buffington's Tavern disappeared long ago, and its assumed site has become confused with Blackburn's Public House in present-day Forsyth.

Many individuals for many years identified an old log structure which once existed across the road from the former site of the Sherrill home on the Old Federal Road in Forsyth County as the remains of Buffington's Tavern, but nothing could be further from the truth, according to the late Forsyth County Historian Don L. Shadburn who did considerable research on the topic, and who has written extensively

Vann Rendering – Born at Spring Place in February of 1766, in what today is Murray County, Georgia, when few White men existed on the North American continent, James Clement Vann II grew into a very imposing figure of a man. He was unusually tall, and filled a room with his presence. He died at the age of either 42 or 43 by murder (or assassination) at Buffington's Tavern in what today quite likely would be Cherokee County, Georgia. Some researchers also claim the site of his murder was nearby Blackburn's Public House near what then was known as "Hightower," in what today is Forsyth County, Georgia. He is believed to have been buried in Blackburn Cemetery in Forsyth, though no conclusive proof to that effect has yet been discovered.

on the Cherokees of Georgia in his seminal *"Cherokee Planters, 1832-1838"* (1989).

"That's true," Shadburn confirmed in an interview prior to his death. "Vann was killed at Buffington's Tavern, and Buffington's Tavern was on the old Federal Road not far from the Sherrill Place, but it (Buffington's) isn't the old structure (which existed) across the road from Sherrill's. That structure is part of

Spring Place Mansion – The impressive former home constructed by James Vann II at Spring Place circa 1804, near Chatsworth, Georgia, has been preserved as a state historic site. (Photo courtesy of GA Dept. of Natural Resources)

what used to be Lewis Blackburn's Public House built around 1820. It (Blackburn's Public House) is very historic in its own right, but it is not Buffington's Tavern."

The structure which once existed across from the old Sherrill home to which Shadburn refers has recently been removed from that site to the Cumming, Georgia, fairgrounds where it has been put on public exposition. According to reports, the relocation committee (*Forsyth County Historic Society*) has declared this structure to have been the actual site of Vann's murder. Unfortunately, there is no definitive evidence to support this claim.

Constructed of heavy log timbers 20" x 6" x 32', Blackburn's Public House is immensely sturdy, accounting for its endurance. It is awe-inspiring to stand in the doorway of this building and understand the history that has passed across its threshold over the past 200+ years.

"Part of the confusion between Buffington's Tavern and Blackburn's

Public House centers around the fact that Lewis Blackburn married Tom Buffington's widow after Tom died," Shadburn added. "Lewis and the former Mrs. Buffington lived at Buffington's Tavern for a short while before moving to Blackburn's Public House at the site of the present-day Sherrill home-place. (In contrast) Buffington's Tavern actually existed on up the old Federal Road from the Sherrill Place (back toward Canton), and was on the right, just across the Forsyth County line in Cherokee County."

This specification by Shadburn that Buffington's Tavern existed on the "right" side of the road is a critical detail. It is known for a fact that the public house formerly existing on the Sherrill property and later removed to the Cumming Fairgrounds was originally built on the "left" side of the road as one proceeds toward Canton, not on the right.

The information in *Ebenezer Newton's* (who was an eye-witness to the site in October of 1818) *Diary* adds credence to this claim. In his journal describing his trip, Newton details how his travels led him to Vann's Tavern on the Chattahoochee River and how, the following morning, he continued on up the road toward Tennessee. *"Soon after we passed the 'High tower' by the Indians called 'Ittowah' (Etowah River), and came to the top of the hill, we observed by the roadside on an eminence, a tomb, paled in and painted black, with an inscription at the head on a board: 'Here lies the body of James Vann who departed this life Feb. 1809, aged 43.'"* This description almost perfectly describes present-day Blackburn Cemetery.

The Sherrill family stated categorically that they moved the historic public house (rolling it upon greased logs) on their property from the left side of the Old Federal Road (as one travels toward

Canton) to the right, in order that they might build their home on that desirable site many years ago. The former Sherrill property public house (now on exposition in Cumming) therefore almost certainly was Lewis Blackburn's Public House, and therefore NOT the site of Vann's murder.

Shadburn said another myth involving Vann and his death included Vann's sister – Nancy Falling/Fawling – who supposedly lived across the road from Buffington's Tavern. "That's just another case in which the facts have been embellished and twisted," he explained. "Nancy lived south of Spring Place at Vann's home near present-day Chatsworth."

For years, local folklore has maintained that Nancy's supposed residence across the road from Buffington's Tavern in some way connected her with Vann's death. Vann was, in fact, responsible for the death of Nancy's husband – John Fawling – but no definite connection between her and Vann's death has ever been established. Nevertheless, many historians today do agree that it quite probably was Falling's family which was in fact responsible for Vann's death, as was the Cherokee custom at that time.

Despite his enterprising and peaceful nature when sober, James Vann II was characterized by Moravian missionaries (who lived at Vann's Spring Place plantation) and, subsequently by historians, as a very violent, arrogant, and abusive person when under the influence of alcoholic beverages which he reportedly consumed in ever-increasing quantities during his later years in life. It was during one of his fits of anger, that Vann reportedly was responsible for the death of Fawling.

It is ironic that history has chosen to characterize Vann as violent and abusive. An argument could be made for the

Blackburn's or Buffington's? – Constructed very similarly to Buffington's Tavern, Blackburn's Public House was one of the first such structures on the Georgia frontier in the early 1800s when this area was still controlled by the native Indians. Whether this historic structure (pictured) on the Federal Road near the Etowah River was actually Blackburn's or Buffington's has not ever been conclusively determined. It is, however, documentable that this structure originally existed on the south side of the Old Federal Road at a site later occupied by the Sherrill home in present-day Forsyth County. Photographed inside the structure in the 1990s is the late Clifford Ruddell who points out the ancient stairs leading to the upper level where travelers from yesteryear once slept overnight. (Photo by Olin Jackson)

fact that he was a victim of circumstances beyond his control in a quest to best portray his section of the Cherokee Nation as law-abiding and socially acceptable in the face of an advancing tide of white settlers who were by this time openly seeking reasons to displace the natives.

It is well documented that Vann ordered the use of such devices as painful whippings, etc., for the punishment of criminals, a practice which no doubt enhanced his reputation as a man of

Ebenezer Newton's Diary – In the early 1980s, Rev. Charles O. Walker, a noted and respected historian and illustrator recreated this historically accurate depiction of Vann's grave on the Federal Road, based upon a description recorded in Ebenezer Newton's diary of 1818 and other documentation. The Federal Road was the first navigable wagon-trail, as well as the earliest postal route across what today is north Georgia. It began near the southeastern boundary of the land once claimed by the native Cherokees not far from present-day Flowery Branch, Georgia, and linked Georgia and Tennessee across the Cherokee Indian Territory. Rights to open the thoroughfare were granted informally to the U.S. federal government by the Cherokees in 1803 and confirmed in the 1805 Treaty of Tellico, in what today is Tennessee. It is worth noting that the public house in this depiction is accurately placed on the "left" or "south" side of the Federal Road as one travels toward Canton, as was the original case with the historic public house removed from the old Sherrill home-place in 2004 on that road. Conversely, the site at which Vann was murdered – "Buffington's Tavern" – was on the "right" or "north" side of the road, a critical detail which has left modern researchers perplexed as to the determination of the actual site of his murder. (Illustration courtesy of Rev. Charles O. Walker)

cruelty. The fact that is not so well documented, is that in doing so, Vann was actually carrying out Cherokee law as decided by the entire Cherokee Nation. He also undoubtedly was helping to diminish lawlessness among his people in a desperate attempt to enhance their assimilation into the White culture.

Indeed, in the *Laws of the Cherokees*, published in the *Cherokee Advocate* at Tahlequah, Oklahoma in 1852, a glimpse into Indian life on the frontier is provided. One of the laws (in an order from the chiefs and warriors in *National Council* at "Broom's Town" on

September 11, 1808, the year prior to Vann's murder) provided for the formation of *"regulating companies"* of one captain, one lieutenant and four privates each, for the purpose of arresting horse thieves and protecting property.

The penalty in the Cherokee Nation for stealing a horse was 100 lashes on the bare back of the thief, be it male or female, and fewer lashes for things of less value, and if a thief resisted the regulators with gun, axe, spear or knife, he or she could be killed on the spot. This law was signed by Black Fox, principal chief; Charles Hicks, secretary to the Council;

Path Killer; and Toochalar, all of whom formed the inner circle of Cherokee leadership at the time.

Even more interesting, this same National Council barely a year and a half later on April 10, 1810 (a year after Vann's death) passed the following law: *"Be it known that this day the various clans and tribes which compose the Cherokee Nation have agreed that should it happen that a brother, forgetting his natural affection, should use his hand in anger and kill his brother, he shall be accounted guilty of murder and suffer accordingly; and if a man has a horse stolen, and overtakes the thief, and should his anger be so great as to cause him to kill him, let his blood remain on his own conscience, but no satisfaction shall be demanded for his life from his relatives or the clan to which he may belong."*

One of the more enlightened and enduring achievements of Vann was his association and support of Moravian missionaries whom he allowed to establish a mission near his home at Spring Place. It is from the diaries kept by the Moravians that one of the most reliable accounts of Vann's murder is described. On February 21, 1809, the following entry was made:

"We received the startling news of the murder of Mr. Vann. Here and there, he and his had punished Indians for stealing. When one of them refused to surrender, Vann ordered him to be shot.

"For a few days thereafter, Vann stopped at the tavern of a half-breed, Tom Buffington, about 56 miles from here. While there, he drank heavily and became involved in altercations with some of his friends for whom he had taken a violent dislike. He feuded with them, was most abusive, and made violent threats.

"Toward midnight, Vann stepped out of the tavern and stood before the open door, when suddenly, a shot was fired from

Vann's Grave? – The late Clifford Ruddell was one of the workers who exhumed the remains which were assumed to have been those of James Vann II from Blackburn Cemetery in 1962. He points to the site at which the exhumation was made at that time. (Photo by Olin Jackson)

without which pierced his heart. He fell lifeless to the floor without his perpetrator being seen.

"After hearing the shot, Joseph, his son, and a Negro rapidly gathered up the belongings of father and son, including Vann's 'pocketbook' with a considerable amount of cash and bank notes. Wrapped in a blanket, Joseph with the Negro fled to his father's plantation on the Chattahoochee River, 13 miles from Buffington's Tavern.

"At the crack of dawn, Mrs. Vann and other members of the family fled to Buffington's but before they arrived, Vann's body had been buried in the woods not far from the road."

It was this and similar descriptions which have led historians and residents to believe that Vann's grave was located

Vann's Tavern – James Vann II was traveling to his (Vann's) public house (pictured) which once existed on the Chattahoochee River near the present-day Forsyth – Hall county line, when he was assassinated while pausing at Buffington's Tavern, quite likely near the present-day Cherokee-Forsyth County line. Built around 1800, Vann's Tavern survived the ravages of time, but was about to be inundated by the rising waters of then-newly-constructed Lake Lanier when, in 1956, it was rescued, dismantled and removed to the state historic site, New Echota, near Calhoun, Georgia, where it was reconstructed for permanent display. New Echota was the last capital of the Cherokee Nation in the southeast prior to relocation of the tribe to the West.

in present-day Blackburn Cemetery, situated not far from the old tavern site.

"That's right," Shadburn continued. "There's no doubt that Blackburn Cemetery or its general vicinity is the burial site. In October of 1818, an individual by the name of Ebenezer Newton was traveling on the Federal Road from Athens, Georgia to Tennessee. In a journal describing his trip, he details how his travels led him to Vann's Tavern on the Chattahoochee River. The following morning, he describes how he continued on up the road toward Tennessee, crossing the Hightower (Etowah) River, and suddenly encountering a grave on the right *'on an eminence, paled in* (to keep out livestock)*, and painted, with a headboard and inscription which read: "Here Lies The Body Of James Vann Who Departed This Life February, 1809, Aged 40."'* Newton's description of the location

of Vann's grave almost perfectly fits the description of present-day Blackburn Cemetery," Shadburn added.

But, the story doesn't end there. In the 1960s, when a team of what has been described as "amateur archaeologists" and a descendant of Vann – J. Raymond Vann of Mt. Vernon, New York – exhumed what they and many others assumed to be the remains of Vann, they received a surprise. According to an associated article in the **Atlanta Journal**, of August 29, 1962:

"Dalton archaeologist Wayne Yeager has confirmed that he removed the skeleton of Chief Vann from his grave near Ball Ground, Georgia, and brought the remains to a local funeral home which he declined to name.

"The local archaeologist said it took seven hours to exhume the remains from the old Blackburn family cemetery on the Etowah River between Ball Ground and

Cumming. Mr. Yeager said the skeleton is in good condition considering that it has been 153 years since Chief Vann's death.

"Mr. Yeager said he is positive that he has the right skeleton because of several factors:

"No. 1 is that local residents pin-pointed the grave from local common knowledge, although it was not marked.

"No. 2, the upper right arm bone had been fractured as if by a bullet. Mr. Yeager said Chief Vann fought a political duel from horseback with his brother-in-law, John Fawling, shortly before his death, and accounts of the duel say that Fawling was killed and Chief Vann was hit in the right arm by a bullet.

"No. 3, Mr. Yeager has compared the shirt buttons found in the grave and the buttons of a shirt of the same era, and found them to be the same. The shirt used for comparison belonged to Tarleton Lewis, an ancestor of Mr. B.J. Bundy, (a Dalton historian).

"Mr. Yeager said the grave was located on property owned by Mr. and Mrs. Ernest Sherrill, and that Mr. Sherrill's 94-year-old aunt, known only as 'Becky,' stated that she could remember when the grave was marked with a wooden slab.

"In fact, after the Georgia Historical Commission established the location of the grave, Mr. Sherrill piled brush over it and refused to tell curious historians where it was located in fear that they might dig into the grave.

"However, Mr. Sherrill did show the grave to Raymond Vann and Mr. Vann secured an order from Forsyth County Ordinary A.B. Tollison to exhume his ancestor. Mr. Tollison acted as an official witness during the excavation.

"Found in the grave were seven glass buttons, approximately 50 nails from the coffin, and a belt buckle. Mr. Yeager said

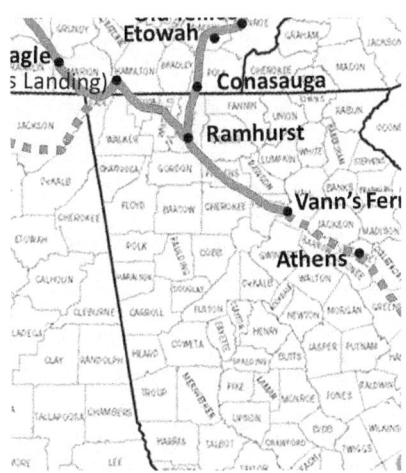

Federal Road – The route of the old Federal Road is depicted. It was along much of this route that James Vann and other prominent Cherokees owned and operated public houses, ferries, and plantations in the accumulation of great wealth for that day and time.

the bottom of the grave was in the exact shape of the old-time wooden coffins.

"Mr. Yeager (also) said two gold rings were discovered on the hands of the skeleton, *and these rings are now being cleaned by Jack Zbar, another Dalton archaeologist and chemist. The rings appear to be inscribed, but the cleaning process has not been finished."*

On the surface, the exhumation described in the **Atlanta Journal** article sounded very conclusive, and seemed to convincingly identify Vann's grave, but was it accurate? Perhaps. Perhaps not.

In the early 1990s, Clifford Ruddell had lived in the vicinity of Blackburn Cemetery most of his life, and he well remembered the day the remains were removed from the grave site. He was one of the diggers hired to perform the labor.

"We dug for a good long while, and then all of a sudden, we were into the bones," he explained. "They told us to

A Vast Wilderness – As is obvious from this early map of Georgia, very little existed within the interior of the state during pioneer days except thick, deep forests and wild streams and rivers through which the Native Indians had cut trading paths over hundreds of years.

get out of the hole, and they jumped in with all these little tools and brushes.

"Eventually, when they had collected all they wanted from the grave; they put it in bags and then left," he continued. "I don't remember exactly how long it was, but later on, they came back, and I think they put the bones or something back into the grave, and then they covered it all back over. That always struck me as kinda strange."

Strange indeed. For far from ending a controversy, the exhumation of this grave actually began spawning additional ones.

In the *Dalton Daily News* of August 29, 1962, a bold headline proclaimed *"Vann Excavation Stirs Controversy."* The article went on to describe how state and local officials were casting considerable doubt on the findings of Yeager and Zbar as well as their credentials. The article stated:

"...Dalton amateur archaeologist Wayne Yeager has stirred a controversy among historians and archaeologists

throughout the state. Doubt has been expressed on the part of at least one archaeologist, Clemens deBaillou, as to whether the remains of Chief Vann have actually been found.

"However, on the other hand, the Rev. Mr. Yeager, a Baptist minister, said today that an inscription uncovered on one of the gold rings found on the hands of the skeleton (leaves no) doubt in his mind that he found Chief Vann.

"Rev. Yeager said one of the plain, gold rings was inscribed with a 'V', and he doubts very much that anyone else buried in the Blackburn Cemetery in Forsyth County near Ball ground would have had a name starting with the letter 'V.'"

Ironically, the proclaimed discovery of the ring with the "V" inscribed in it greatly complicated (rather than simplified) the issue of identification of the remains. In the April 25, 1971 issue of the ***Chattanooga News-Free Press***, **Dalton Historian Mrs. B.J. Bandy said that her investigation of the census records of the early 1800s time-period indicated no one in that area had a name starting with a "V" except the Vanns. Therefore, the likelihood of anyone but James Vann being in possession of, not one, but two gold rings, particularly a ring inscribed with a "V," would have been extremely remote.**

Imagine the surprise and disappointment then of all involved, when the analysis of the remains – which were supposed to have been James Vann's bones – reportedly indicated that the bones were "Negroid."

"...the man appointed by the Georgia Historical Commission had been against the whole thing from the start," Mrs. Bandy continued. *"He was determined that it wasn't Vann. He insisted it was a slave, although I never heard of a slave with a gold*

ring. He turned in a documentary report against it, so there was nothing we could do.

"I was just sick," Bandy added, "but when you have done all you can, you can't do anything else. I took the bones back and re-buried them where we got them (in Blackburn Cemetery)."

Where then rest the remains of Cherokee Chief James Vann? Do they lie moldering still in some unmarked grave in or around Blackburn Cemetery? Or were those actually James Vann's bones unearthed on a hot summer in August of 1962?

Could James Vann II have been part Negro, thus accounting for the bone analysis? Or could there have been a misinterpretation as Negroid instead of Mongoloid? More serious mistakes than that have certainly been previously made.

"At the very least, I'm convinced those were not the bones of Vann exhumed in 1962," explained historian Don Shadburn. "There were just too many conclusive facts to the contrary. Even the nails used in the coffin apparently were of a type not in existence in 1809. I've seen that report, (by the Georgia Historic Commission done in 1962) and their conclusions were very thorough."

Archaeologists Yeager and Zbar and Historian Bandy later returned to Forsyth County seeking another court order from County Ordinary A.B. Tollison for the exhumation of yet another grave believed to be Vann's, but by that time, Mr. Tollison had endured all he was going to allow. He denied their request.

The exact location of Vann's grave now may never be known, other than the fact that it is somewhere in or near Blackburn Cemetery in Forsyth County.

Despite all of the above, just as some individuals have irresponsibly claimed to have "identified" a historic structure (which may actually be Blackburn's Public House) as Buffington's Tavern, these same individuals have also placed a grave-marker in Blackburn Cemetery "identifying the grave of James Vann II."

Today, the positive identification of the actual sites of Buffington's Tavern and Blackburn's Public House would, in all likelihood, be extremely difficult to ascertain. And as for the positive identification of Vann's actual remains and grave site, the only way that will occur now is if bodies are continuously exhumed in the vicinity of the supposed gravesite until remains which can be proven to be Vann's can be found, and that is highly unlikely to occur.

One important sidebar to this whole affair is the fact that at the time the 1962 exhumation, it is painfully unfortunate that a DNA comparison of Mr. Raymond Vann and his ancestor, James Vann II, could not have been effected to ascertain identity. Under that type of examination, the entire mystery of Vann's grave could have been quickly and positively solved, but unfortunately, such an option simply did not exist at that time.

It's probably just as well, that Vann simply be remembered for his remarkable achievements, such as the home at Spring Place, and the nurturing of the Moravian Mission there which provided the diaries revealing the style and substance of pioneer life in north Georgia in the early 1800s. At this point, as far as the grave site and the delineation between Buffington's Tavern and Blackburn's Public House are concerned to "responsible" historians, these items undoubtedly will simply have to remain almost totally as speculation.

The Life and Legend of Captain Whit Anderson

He was a folk hero to those who knew him. Twice-wounded in action in the Civil War, he defended the "little man," was loyal to his friends, loved no one more than his family and the old South, and had the courage to stand toe to toe with an enemy on a city street, dueling in a shoot-out reminiscent of the Old West.

There are no monuments in Atlanta today for Captain "Whit" Anderson. The only memorial whatsoever is a crude tombstone in an Auraria, Georgia cemetery outside Dahlonega, Georgia, where he was buried. The lettering on the stone is unprofessional and the spelling imperfect. There is no date of birth and no date of death. But according to the late – and famed – former Atlanta historian Franklin Garrett, he was in fact *"one of Atlanta's most colorful characters."*

His full name was George Whitfield Anderson and he was born around 1822 in the Pendleton District of South Carolina, the son of Rueben Anderson and Susannah Welch Anderson. The exact year in which the family moved to Georgia is uncertain, but they almost certainly were part of the gold rush mania which hit the upper realm of the state in 1828.

Early Life

Dahlonega's Col. William P. Price, a close friend of Whit's, was being interviewed in 1894 for a news article about early Dahlonega. When describing Whit within that story, he told *Atlanta Constitution* reporter, P.J. Moran: *"His father, Rueben Anderson, brought him from South Carolina when a boy."*

Rueben's name appears in the *1830 Habersham County Census*. Was he just another migrant traveling down the eastern seaboard to circumvent the immense obstacle of the Appalachian Mountains, or had he traveled to Georgia as a result of the Georgia gold rush? There are few clues today, but there were equally few motivations for him to have chanced the dangerous travel to such a wilderness environment still occupied by the native Cherokee Indians if not in answer to the lure of the gold discovered there.

A disabled veteran of the War of 1812, Reuben was an officer in the Georgia Militia. In 1840, he served as an Inferior Court judge in Lumpkin County. And in the *1850 Lumpkin County Census*, Reuben is listed as a miner living in the Auraria District of Georgia that year.

Muhlenbrink's Saloon – This historic site from the late 1800s – though forgotten for half a century or more – still existed beneath the blocks-long concrete viaduct which was paved over "railroad gulch" in old downtown Atlanta in 1906, allowing city streets to pass unobstructed over the gulch. The historic building storefronts beneath the viaducts were "rediscovered" and converted into the attraction "Underground Atlanta" in 1969. A portion of the concrete and steel viaduct can be seen in the upper section of this photo. Old Whitehall Street which passed in front of Muhlenbrink's and intersected with Alabama Street is pictured. It was at this very site that Capt. Whit Anderson met Deputy Sheriff Tom Shivers for a pitched gun battle in the middle of Whitehall outside the saloon. When the gunsmoke had cleared, Shivers had departed this earth and Whit Anderson had entered the ranks of legend. (Photo by Jimmy Anderson)

In addition to Whit who was the oldest child, and William Martin who was the youngest, Rueben and Susannah had four other children – David, John, Mary, and Nancy.

According to Colonel Price, Whit grew up in what was known as "Nuckollsville," the original unofficial name of Auraria. Although the name seems to have accurately described the frontier atmosphere of the place – since street fights and brawls were quite common there – the town actually took its name from an early settler by the name of Nathaniel Nuckolls.

When U.S. Senator John C. Calhoun learned that the town near his gold mine was named Nuckollsville, he refused to allow the post office in the town to be identified by what he regarded as a name too vulgar, and used his position and influence to have it changed to Auraria. Regardless of the official post office name, the town remained a wide open settlement, and in at least one of the many fights that took place there,

V.A. Higgins Store (circa 1910) – Pictured is the business of V.A. Higgins which once existed in Auraria, GA. It was in operation from 1833 to 1937, and was used as the first post office in Lumpkin County. It was located 2 to 3 lots below what was known more recently as "Woody Store" near the intersection of the town's main street (Gold Diggers' Road) and Castleberry Bridge Road. Capt. Whit Anderson would have frequented this store in his travels to and from Auraria. (Photo courtesy of the GA Dept. of Archives & History, Atlanta)

Colonel Price maintained that Whit took a leading role.

The flashpoint for this early fisticuffs was an insult hurled by the manager of a circus which reportedly had set up at Nuckollsville. According to the tale, Whit and his younger brothers had taken umbrage at the manager's comments, and undertook to thrash the whole circus company in a wild free-for-all.

The Anderson brothers reportedly were acquitting themselves quite well, until the circus-men called in reinforcements. At that point, the Andersons apparently decided that discretion was the better part of valor, for they beat a hasty retreat. As it turned out, it was a fortunate withdrawal, as they soon discovered they would have been facing a large band of men, some armed with axe handles.

In 1846 as the Mexican War broke out, Whit helped to organize a company of Lumpkin County Volunteers. His obituary notes that he remained in Mexico until the war was over, adding, *"It was in the battles then fought that he first evinced that great bravery for which he was famous."*

Whit's official Mexican War records show that he was a lieutenant in Captain Nelson's Company, Calhoun's Mounted Battalion, Georgia Volunteers and that he was involved in the battles leading to the capture of Mexico City.

Early Gold Miner

After the war Whit returned to Auraria, but he apparently didn't remain there long. News of the discovery of gold in California prompted many young men of Lumpkin County to leave for the California gold fields, and Whit was among them.

He appears in the *1850 Census of Sutter County, California*. His occupation: *"miner."* Of this time in California, his obituary states that he remained *"for quite awhile and it was said by those who knew him intimately, (he was) the discoverer of the celebrated gold hills which have given up many fortunes."* The obituary, however, adds somewhat ominously, *"On account of a personal difficulty, however, he was compelled to leave California in 1856."*

Since the exact circumstances of that "personal difficulty" are unclear today, one can only speculate, but Colonel Price, in his 1894 newspaper reminiscence, provides a clue. *"He was a firm believer in the rights of man: that the humblest man that lived had rights which should be accorded to him even at the cost of human life. That way of thinking made him at times wrangle about technical rights in a manner that frequently led to personal difficulties. In those affrays more than one man was killed."*

As if to soften any adverse reflection on his friend's character that such

"Downtown" Auraria, GA (circa 1908) – This once burgeoning gold rush community was photographed in the center of town on main street (Gold Diggers' Road). In the mid- to late-1800s, Auraria reportedly was still a substantial town. From one mile north of the site pictured here to a half mile south, it was one continuous "thick settlement" according to Professor Andrew Cain's **History of Lumpkin County 1832-1932.** By the early 1900s, with the exception of one or two stalwart businesses, virtually the entire town had disappeared. (Photo courtesy of the GA Dept. of Archives & History, Atlanta)

an observation might assign, the Colonel adds: *"He always befriended the friendless."* Price does not elaborate on the point specifically, but goes on to say that Whit was *"popular with the poor, as well as private soldiers, prisoners, and colored people."*

In 1859, according to an early Atlanta history published in 1902 by an organization called the *"Pioneers of Atlanta,"* Whit was elected as a deputy marshal in Georgia's capital, a position he held until the outbreak of the U.S. Civil War. Helping to corroborate that bit of information is the fact that he appears in the *1860 Census of Fulton County, Georgia*. His age is given as 38 and his

occupation as *"deputy marshal."* His residence is the *"Atlanta Hotel."*

U.S. Civil War

As war erupted in 1861, Whit was commissioned a lieutenant in the First Georgia Regulars. He missed *First Manassas*, but was serving in the Confederate army during its victory on the same battlefield a year later. One has no idea of the terrors one might face, until service in hand-to-hand combat upon a battlefield becomes a requirement for survival, and Whit undoubtedly faced these circumstances on more than one occasion. It is a brutal and terrifying affair.

Old Graham Hotel – By 1983, one of the last-remaining structures in Auraria – the Graham Hotel – was almost beyond repair, and by 1993, it, unfortunately, had disappeared completely from the landscape. Built in the 1830s, this historic hostelry once hosted such famous dignitaries as South Carolina Senator and former Vice President of the United States John C. Calhoun who owned a nearby gold mine. Capt. Whit Anderson also quite likely once patronized this former inn. (Photo by Olin Jackson)

In the official records of the *War of the Rebellion*, the First Georgia Regulars' activities at *Second Manassas* are described this way: *"From the nature of the ground and the impenetrable thickets of laurel and brush, none of the regiments except the First Georgia Regulars obtained a favorable position, but the Regulars succeeded in getting a good position and inflicted a very severe chastisement on the superior force of the enemy. The Regulars in this affair (officers and men) behaved with distinguished gallantry, and I only regret that our whole army is not composed of just such men."*

Whit was severely wounded in this battle and was returned to an Atlanta hospital to recuperate. While he was recovering, he was drawn into an episode that would stamp his name indelibly in Atlanta's history.

In February, 1863, while still on *"wounded furlough,"* Whit became a candidate for his old job of deputy marshal against the incumbent, Tom Shivers. In those days, deputy marshals were elected by the Atlanta City Council, but on this occasion, the balloting resulted in a tie. Mayor James M. Calhoun broke the deadlock by casting his vote for Shivers, but the matter did not end there.

Fabled Shoot-Out

According to an account in the *Atlanta Journal Magazine* of April 29, 1923, Shivers and Anderson met accidentally the next day in a saloon on Whitehall Street. They played a game of cards, and eventually became engaged in a quarrel. Shivers unfortunately became violent, striking Whit on the head with a pistol and then throwing a bottle at him.

When the fight was finally broken up, Shivers said, *"I suppose I'll see you again, Anderson."* Pointing a finger, which, according to the *Journal* article was *"dripping with blood,"* Whit, who was unarmed, replied, *"Just as sure as I live, I'll see you tomorrow"* . . . and he meant it. It was anything but idle bravado.

The next day (February 2, 1863) Whit and Shivers met in front of Muhlenbrink's Saloon on Whitehall Street. *(Author's Note: Muhlenbrink's Saloon was among several blocks-worth of old Atlanta storefronts which had been forgotten for over half a century when the huge concrete viaduct was paved over "railroad gulch" and the lower portions of these early-Atlanta structures in the old downtown portion of the city in 1906 to facilitate traffic and commercial activity across* the gulch. In 1969, the old storefronts and structures below the viaduct were "rediscovered" and converted into the entertainment complex "Underground Atlanta" which flourished from the 1970s to the turn of the century. In their early Atlanta life, the old store-fronts had existed at "street level" along the railroad in the gulch. Those structures – including the old original stretch of Whitehall Street in front of Muhlenbrink's Saloon, still exist as of this writing in 2024.) According to Franklin Garrett in his *Atlanta & Environs* Whit said to Shivers, "*I am now fixed up. Are you ready?*"

No other word was spoken. The two men reportedly quickly drew their revolvers and began firing at each other with abandon. Whit Anderson must have been a dead-shot, because Shivers was struck not once, but twice, mortally, and died within the hour. Whit was untouched.

Atlanta City Council minutes for its first meeting in February, 1863, note the death of Deputy Marshal Shivers, but provide no details, possibly in an effort to avoid any comments which might influence a jury. A resolution offered by Councilman James E. Williams and adopted by the council simply states: "*Resolved that the Mayor and Council do deeply regret the late and sad occurrence that deprived our Deputy Marshal Thomas Shivers of his life, and this City of an efficient officer, and that his wife and children have our sympathies in this, their great bereavement.*"

Interestingly, despite only defending himself in the street shooting, Whit ultimately was indicted for murder by a Fulton County Grand Jury in April of 1863. He plead "*Self Defense.*" The April 11, 1863 edition of *The Southern Confederacy*, an Atlanta daily which did not survive the war, carries a terse account of the trial: "*Captain G.W. Anderson, charged with the killing of Thomas Shivers, late Marshal of the City in February last, was tried and acquitted by the Superior Court of this county now in session. The verdict which was rendered in a few moments after the case was submitted, justified the homicide.*"

More Military Duty

Patriotic as ever, Whit apparently returned to military duty at some point in the summer of 1863, but the record of his service is unclear during at least a portion of that period. A letter in his service file to Confederate General P.G.T. Beauregard from an officer whose signature unfortunately is undecipherable, shows that Whit, still too weak for infantry duty, was seeking to raise a company of cavalry.

"*General,*" the letter reads, "*Captain G.W. Anderson, a brave and chivalric officer who was among the very first to respond to the call of arms in defense of our country – and our inherent right – after serving through many severe conflicts was wounded at Manassas on the 30th of August, last, so badly that he is now unfit for active infantry service, desires – in conjunction with W.C. Humphrey – a gallant soldier who fought bravely at the First Battle of Manassas and was taken prisoner – to raise a cavalry company for active service and desires to obtain your approval of the same. I take leave to recommend these gentlemen to your consideration and hope that you will give your respect to their enterprise.*"

There is no record in Whit's service file as to whether General Beauregard ever responded or whether Whit, in fact, ever even raised a cavalry company. But he evidently did return to the war. His obituary states that he was again wounded "*in the battles before Richmond in*

1864," and his service record places him in the General Hospital at Atlanta on December 22 of the same year.

If Whit was in fact in a hospital in Atlanta at that time – and there is no reason to believe he was not – it undoubtedly was a very crowded facility, since General William T. Sherman had burned and destroyed much of the city months earlier in the *Battle of Atlanta*. How Whit Anderson even arrived in Atlanta at that time is a mystery today, since all of the rail lines into the city had been cut by the Union Army.

Post-War Life

The able soldier and former lawman, however, was perhaps not too seriously incapacitated, to be interviewed for an article by a reporter for the *Augusta* Georgia *Chronicle and Sentinel* which appeared in December, 1864. It reported on the resurgence of the city of Atlanta after Sherman's army had burned it to the ground. Among other news items in the paper, the following appeared: *"Many of the old citizens are returning, and the general watch-word is repair and re-build. Whit Anderson has opened a bar-room on Decatur Street where he serves his customers with dignity and grace..."*

The next published record of Whit's life appears in the 1866 edition of the *Journal of the Georgia Senate* (then meeting in the state capital at Milledgeville) which notes that Whit had been elected the Senate's "Sergeant at Arms," but he held this position for only a short time. In Atlanta it was time again for the election of city officers, and the City Council – apparently forgiving and forgetting Whit's volatile encounter with the ill-fated Tom Shivers – sent word of its desire to name him marshal of the city. Whit returned to Atlanta to take the job and he continued to hold law enforcement positions there for the next decade and a half.

For several years after the war Whit's life – as was the case with many Confederate veterans – seems to have been spent in clandestine resistance to the "carpetbagger" rule and Reconstruction government in the state. It was an exceedingly difficult period in the state's – and indeed in the South's – history, when undue punishments were routinely handed out by occupying federal officials to White Southerners.

Colonel Price states that Whit was the leader of an Atlanta secret organization – presumably the Ku Klux Klan – and in August, 1870, was prepared to lead a band of some 200 armed men into the State Legislature to prevent the enactment of a bill which would have extended the legislators' terms without the necessity of holding a popular referendum on the issue. The scheme apparently had been organized by a group of what then were termed "Radical Republicans" (read "carpet-baggers") who sought every means, both legal and illegal, to maintain federal control of the governments in Southern states.

Colonel Price, a Democrat, discouraged Whit from taking such a desperate step in such a dangerous time. On a dramatic roll-call vote, with Whit and his unarmed friends seated in the gallery, the measure was lawfully defeated by a slim margin of ten.

It is interesting that Whit could maintain such an active role in political affairs of that day, since he was employed as a deputy-marshal in Atlanta, and the Georgia state capitol at that time was located in Milledgeville, Georgia, a distance of approximately 100 miles. Even if he was traveling back and forth by rail (which is unlikely), that is a significant amount of ground to cover.

Despite the accounts in the newspapers, Whit's post-war years apparently were not all spent with the tribulations of Reconstruction in Georgia. He had been an accomplished fiddler since his youth in the north Georgia mountains, and Atlanta historian Franklin Garrett wrote that *"he had been known as the best fiddler in Nuckollsville."*

At an October, 1870 fair in Fulton County, Whit competed his way into the finals in a contest to decide the best fiddler in Georgia. His last opponent was Thomas F. "Uncle Tommy" Lowe. The two men fiddled back and forth with renditions of *Arkansas Traveler* which were so stirring that, according to Garrett, they created *"a veritable sensation."*

When Lowe finally was declared the winner, Garrett writes, *"Whit went up to him and said: 'Mr. Lowe, I want to say that having found somebody who can beat me playing Arkansas Traveler as bad as you can, I will never draw another bow.'"* Adds Garrett, *"And they say he never did."*

The death of Whit's mother, Susannah, was a blow from which the now somewhat elderly lawman never fully recovered. A life-long bachelor, he was attached to his mother with a kind of Old South devotion that is endearing.

Liquor Prohibition

Colonel Price recalled visiting Whit once when he was sick and sleeping in a bunk at the Fulton County Jail. *"His mind was as changeful as a kaleidoscope,"* Price said. *"He talked of friends we both knew and sorrowfully of those who had bravely fallen in battle. Then he would speak tenderly of his mother and of the Democratic Party as the hope of the country.*

"His mother always came first. The

The Big Sleep – Auraria Church, founded at least as early as the 1840s, was photographed here in 1983. This facility, which still exists today, is well over 175 years old as of 2024. Capt. Whit Anderson – along with numerous other Lumpkin County notables – is buried in the historic cemetery to the rear of this church on an unusual rise. (Photo by Olin Jackson)

Democratic Party next – sometimes," Price continued, *"his turbulent feelings could be subdivided by the mere mention of her name...*

While a member of the Legislature of 1877, I was requested by a majority of the population of Nuckollsville, to have an act passed to prohibit the sale of whiskey in that place...It escaped the watchful eye of Captain Anderson, who was not aware of the fact until he visited his hometown in the summer following and found that he had to send elsewhere for his whiskey. The next time he saw me in Atlanta, he expressed himself in no soft language about the matter. He said, 'Nuckollsville belongs to me and I should have been consulted before you dared to pass such a law. Prohibition may do for Dahlonega and other towns, but Nuckollsville should always be left free to have whiskey.'

"I assured him that the act was passed

at the request of many Nuckollsville people, some of whom had used liquor intemperately. He asked me to name some of the signers. I gave him the name of his brother, Dave.

"He scouted the idea of his brother's name as worth anything in such a case. He demanded other names. I added several old friends of his who were hard drinkers, but were sober when they signed the petition.

'Then,' said Whit, 'if they were sober, they were not in their right minds, and they should not be considered.'

"He wanted still more names, which I gave him, and, lowering my voice, I gave him the name of his mother, Susannah Anderson. Tears came at once into the eyes of this strong man, who, putting his arm around my shoulders said: 'Whatever my mother does is right. We will say nothing more about this matter now.'"

Last Days

In January, 1881, Whit supported a rival candidate against Angus Perkerson in the campaign for sheriff of Fulton County. He apparently did so with the expectation of being named a deputy.

Perkerson, however, was nevertheless elected and the loss was a bitter blow to Whit. Susannah had died only a few years earlier. With Atlanta law enforcement no longer an option after almost two decades of service, Whit was left "swinging in the wind."

It wasn't long after this time that he became ill and in October, at age 59, went back home to Nuckollsville.

"He sent for me in his last illness," Colonel Price wrote. "He had come home to die. The message came too late for me to look on his face again in this life. More than twelve years ago it was, they buried him among the trees on this steep hill

overlooking the little village which in life he had called his own."

Whit's solemn tombstone, crafted obviously by one untrained in proper spelling, reads: "Captin Whit Anderson at Rest." No other information follows on the lonely marker in this lonely graveyard behind the old Auraria church.

On page 1 of the Nov. 22, 1881 edition of the **Atlanta Constitution**, a story headlined "Captain Whit Anderson's Death" concludes with these lines: "When Sherman captured Atlanta he issued a proclamation outlawing Captain Anderson on account of his part in the capture of some Federal soldiers and this fact has handed his name to posterity in history. Since last January he has been gradually sinking and his death ended the life of as good and pure a man as ever breathed."

So who, in truth, was Whit Anderson? In answering that, it may be easier to first say what he was not. He was not a pillar of Atlanta's emerging "New South" society. He cared not a "whit" for the errant philosophy of Henry W. Grady. He was not a leader in business, trade or commerce. He was not a spell-binding orator, lawyer, or minister of the gospel.

Henry W. Grady's **Atlanta Constitution** – though often reflecting somewhat overstated sentiments of the times, and sometimes even given to what could only be described as flights of fantasy – nevertheless was right on the money with its assessment of Whit. "He was a genuine folk hero to those who knew him, and a friend among friends, brave, loyal, and honest right to the end."

Perhaps even old Henry was fearful of angering Capt. Whit though he was laid low in a grave.

(Grateful appreciation is expressed herewith to Robert E. Anderson who provided much factual information necessary for this article.)

Gunfight at Doublehead Gap

The "frontier" in America is often deemed synonymous with what today is known as "the old West." In reality, the frontier actually began on the eastern seaboard of what today is the United States, and moved westward as the lands became settled and areas were "civilized." Accordingly, there not only were "shoot-outs" and gunfights in the old West, but in the "old East" as well. One such event occurred in 1884 in Gilmer County, Georgia.

From the onset of the U.S. Civil War up through the period known as "Reconstruction" in the South, ill feelings – and yes, sometimes even downright hate – persisted as a result of the devastation the war had wrought upon that region and the elimination of the former ways of life held so dear. One major participant within the vortex of this climate of hate in north Georgia was a famed lawman by the name of Walter Webster "Web" Findley of Pickens (and later Fannin) County.

Findley was born on May 20, 1841, the son of James R. and Catherine Findley. The Findley family members were ardent secessionists, with many political connections within the area's Democrat Party. In those days, "Republicans" were not the conservative element of the national political spectrum, but rather the radical extremists.

Though many of the weapons owned by Southerners had been confiscated by Union authorities at war's end, many weapons also still existed, due to the lawless and hostile climate in the South at war's end. From the 1860s through to the 1890s, the social climate remained so dangerous and unpredictable and outlaws so numerous, that many residents routinely carried firearms, just as they did in the old West.

Throughout the war, some north Georgia residents had remained loyal to the Union, fully supporting the Northern cause. Everyone knew who they were, and they were generally despised and often ostracized by those supporting the Confederacy.

The Findley family members made no bones about their often-hostile attitude regarding these "Unionists" (Southern residents who had sympathized with and remained loyal to the Union following secession). Web Findley's brother was Col. James Jefferson Findley, a Dahlonega, Georgia resident well-known for his still-strong pro-Confederate attitude after the war. Web had served as a second lieutenant in the Gilmer County militia during the war, and had gained a reputation as a pugnacious adversary of his pro-Union neighbors in the mountainous portions of north Georgia.

A sometime lawman, Web later won fame and fortune by tracking down and bringing to justice Jackson County murderer Sanford Pirkle in 1875, Fannin County killer Ayers Jones in 1876, and Pickens County murderess Kate

Southern in 1877. Ironically, despite his strong sentiments in favor of the Southern cause, Findley's home was frequently used as a headquarters by federal revenue agents, including Web, during raids on illegal untaxed liquor ("moonshine") distilleries in north Georgia. His career as a lawman might have been even more extensive had he learned to read and write.

Interestingly, Findley – as did many mountaineers during this period – sometimes worked the other side of "the straight and narrow" as well, when it suited his sense of "right" and "wrong." Kinship and friendship, rather than the U.S. legal system or the Southern cause, often determined the actions and allegiances of area residents such as Web. This apparently was a motivating factor for Findley's actions which ultimately resulted in the shoot-out at Doublehead Gap.

The production and sale of home-produced untaxed corn liquor and tobacco were considered "God-given" rights by most mountaineers, particularly those of Scots-Irish descendancy, and the income derived from such products was important to the very limited incomes of these hardy early pioneers. Any tampering with these rights – especially by the U.S. government authorities – was very serious business.

John A. Stuart, who had the misfortune of being a north Georgia Unionist during the war, was the Deputy

His career as a lawman might have been even more extensive had he learned to read and write.

Collector of Internal Revenue following the war, and the law enforcement branch of the department. His quick but effective methods earned him a reputation as an able lawman who was respected despite his political stance.

In one massive raid in north Georgia during this time, Stuart led posses which destroyed fourteen illegal liquor distilleries in Fannin, Towns, and Union counties. To Stuart, this action was merely an enforcement of the laws which were on the books, but actions such as this could easily get a man maimed or killed, no matter what his position of authority might be.

As with most of the rest of the highlands of the Appalachian and Blue Ridge Mountains, much of north Georgia was settled by independent-minded Scots-Irish immigrants from Europe in the 16th and 17th centuries who were accustomed to mountain living. One of the numerous aspects of their culture which came with their relocation to these areas was the production of corn liquor and tobacco. These were among the very few products which could be produced in these harsh upland environments and sold for modest income. As long as their rights to these products weren't threatened, things went reasonably well. . . but tamper with them, and things went bad in a hurry.

The "moonshiners," against whom Stuart led his posses in this instance were headed up by none other than Walter

Webster Findley, who retaliated against Stuart by attacking his farm in the early morning hours of April 6, 1880, burning his storehouse and slightly wounding Stuart's son when the attackers fired upon the revenue lawman's home.

Twenty men – who, interestingly, included both former Unionists and former Confederate soldiers – were later indicted for, but were not necessarily responsible for, the attack. Those arrested were: Benjamin M. Tilly, John D. Fricks, S.J. Simmons, Cub Newberry, J.W. Vandergriff, Bud Hill, J.F. Bingham, William Crisp, James Findley, Samuel White, Jasper Long, Charles Smith, Walter W. Findley, Jackson Bearden, R.V. Hughes, Bud Roberts, William Teague, Milton Dill, Wilson Bryant, and George Sparks.

The two Findleys, Bearden and Sparks were the first of the group to be tried. All but Sparks were found "Guilty" in federal court in Atlanta on October 14, 1882. Many of the cases made by the revenue officials were hollow and without merit, and their pursuit and arrest tactics were often illicit and abusive during this period, so the issue of untaxed alcohol and tobacco in the Appalachian highlands was further exacerbated by these circumstances.

Amazingly, following the reading of the verdict, the Findleys (who, incidentally, were father and son) and Bearden brandished pistols and fled. Bearden was quickly subdued, but James Findley escaped (later to be recaptured in Gilmer County in 1886). Walter Findley had an injured hip,

The two Findleys, Bearden and Sparks were the first of the group to be tried.

and, not being able to run, quietly surrendered.

Walter was sentenced on February 10, 1883. For the crime of producing untaxed corn liquor in order to survive in his home in the mountains, he received two years in the terrible Erie County Penitentiary in Buffalo, New York, far from home.

After he had served six months in the horrendous circumstances of the Erie Pen, Findley made application to the President of the United States (a Democrat) for a pardon. To strengthen his plea, a petition campaign calling for his release came from Lumpkin, Fannin, Gilmer, Hall, Pickens, White, and Forsyth counties, as well as, surprisingly, from the prison authorities themselves. Both of Georgia's U.S. senators and a congressman also wrote letters of endorsement, and several members of the Georgia State Legislature signed a pro-Findley petition as well.

At the same time, however, another petition signed by a group of pious church members, ministers, and the Fannin County sheriff, requested the President NOT grant Findley a pardon, a request which was seconded by the United States Attorney General, all of which Walter Webster Findley duly noted. The anti-pardon campaign interestingly was led by Robert P. Woody (1838-1901), a native north Georgian, ardent Unionist, and a Union Army officer during the Civil War.[1]

Woody had supposedly been injured during the war, and was receiving a federal pension as a disabled veteran. Despite his residence so near to Findley in north Georgia, he had nevertheless assisted the prosecution in its conviction of Findley. Although the two men held opposing political views, they, ironically, had once been friends. Following Findley's conviction and sentence, they became vicious enemies.

To the surprise of the anti-pardon contingent, the President ultimately granted Findley a pardon over the loud objections of his attorney general and the others of the group. The trial judge and the U.S. Pardon Attorney had recommended the leniency, pointing out that when the time Findley had spent confined in Atlanta awaiting trial was added to the time he had served in New York, his sentence had nearly expired anyway. The U.S. Attorney for North Georgia consented because of reports of Findley's poor health, and also no doubt in view of his past law enforcement record.[2]

Following Findley's release, he and Woody, though residing in the same locale, refused to greet or even acknowledge each other in passing. As time passed, their hatred of each other grew more pronounced with each succeeding week.

Finally, on Sunday, September 28, 1884, the animosity between the two men "came to a head," when they chanced to meet at Mt. Pleasant Church, Doublehead Gap, near the Gilmer-Fannin County Line. Woody had traveled to the site with his wife for a church meeting which Findley was also attending.

When the two surprised men caught sight of each other, night had already fallen, but a full moon provided reasonably-good visibility. Woody was bringing up his ox-drawn wagon when he was greeted by several friends who later stated they knew trouble was brewing when they smelled liquor on Woody's breath.

According to Woody's version of the events which transpired that night, he was helping his wife out of the wagon when Findley loudly remarked: "By God, roll her out Woody." Mrs. Woody's excessive weight had often caused her difficulty mounting and dismounting carriages and wagons.

Woody, who very nearly was deaf, could easily have mistaken Findley's comments. Findley later claimed that his remarks in fact were not directed toward Mrs. Woody, but rather to Jesse Bailey and a saddle blanket, and had no application to Woody's spouse whatsoever. There, therefore was room for mistaken circumstances on both sides.

Woody, in response to Findley's remarks, angrily replied, "By God, I'll roll you down," and then cursed Findley as a thief, a house-burner, and a jailbird. Findley responded in kind, calling Woody a "lie swearer."

The two men – who both were carrying arms as was customary in that day – suddenly drew their side-arms in anger and began firing at each other at the murderous range of only fifteen to thirty feet. Several shots were exchanged as the two men drew even nearer, and both attackers, in their rage, ignored the several individuals between them who were attempting to flee or stop the fight.

Woody was wounded in the hand on the initial exchange, but he, nevertheless, managed to get off a second shot. Findley's second shot surprisingly passed harmlessly through Woody's vest and Woody's third shot nicked Findley's shirt. Despite the close range, the men were firing many rounds but doing little harm. They quite likely were armed with

inexpensive ten to fif-
teen-dollar weapons
from Southern facto-
ries which were crude
affairs, offering very
limited accuracy and
dependability.

Woody's pistol
eventually began mis-
firing, and Findley
wounded him again
– this time seriously –
in the stomach. Both
men fell to the ground.
Findley apparently fell
simply because some-
one had hit him in the
head with a rock in or-
der to stop the fight.

Meanwhile, in
the midst of all the gunfire, a bystander
– William Kimsey – had been mortally wounded before he had been able to
dash out of the line of fire. He lay dying
on the ground with the two combatants.

That neither Findley nor Woody
was killed in the exchange is not nearly as
amazing as the fact that more of the other bystanders had not been hit. Though
the hand-guns of that day manufactured
in the South were often inaccurate weapons, they also could understandably
be quite deadly when they found their
mark.

When order was finally restored,
Woody was arrested. He subsequently
was found *"Guilty"* of assaulting Findley and served one year in the Georgia
State Penitentiary. He and Findley were
both charged with *"Murder"* for Kimsey's death, but were acquitted.[3]

Findley later successfully gathered
information which caused Woody's disability pension to be revoked as fraudulent. An appointment as U.S. Postmaster at the community of Dial, however,

> *The feud between
> the two men,
> surprisingly, ended
> without further
> blood-shed.*

not only replaced the
disability income loss,
but added still more to
Woody's coffers.

The feud between
the two men, surpris-
ingly, ended without
further blood-shed.
According to a Woody
relative – Willis Rack-
ley – Woody eventu-
ally tired of Findley's
public insults (mainly
in the form of public
snubs). On one such
occasion shortly after
the gunfight at Dou-
blehead Gap, he de-
manded that Findley
either have the courte-
sy to speak to him in public and treat
him civilly, or the two of them would
end the matter once and for all in yet
another shoot-out to the death. From
that day forward, the feud ceased to exist.[4]

Famed former lawman Walter
Webster Findley died peacefully in Fannin County on June 9, 1910.

Endnotes

*1/ A transcript of a pro-Woody official report of the
events leading to the gunfight is available in Lawrence L. Stanley's* **A Little History Of Gilmer
County,** *(1975), and in the Robert Barker Collection, Knoxville Public Library.*

*2/ Findley's pardon papers are on record in the Na-
tional Archives, Washington, D.C., in Record Group
204.*

*3/ A transcript of the Woody trial (The State versus
Robert Woody) is available in the Gilmer County
Court Case Papers, Record Group 161-12-11, Box 24,
Georgia Department of Archives and History.*

*4/ Information on Robert P. Woody came from Wil-
lis Rackley and an article by William C. Farmer in*
**Facets Of Fannin: A History Of Fannin County,
Georgia,** *(1989)*

The 1876-1877 Federal War on North Georgia "Moonshine"

The north Georgia mountains have long been a refuge and home for descendants of those hardy early pioneers who chose that environment, and who, as a result, were continuously dependent upon the production of untaxed liquor ("moonshine") as a cash crop and as a way of life. When the federal government "outlawed" the production of untaxed liquor, it was essentially a declaration of war.

As with most of the rest of the highlands of the Appalachian and Blue Ridge Mountains, much of these lofty realms were settled by independent-minded Scots-Irish immigrants from Europe in the 16th and 17th centuries who were accustomed to mountain living. One of the numerous aspects of their culture which came with their relocation to these areas was the production of corn liquor and tobacco. These were among the very few products which could be produced in these harsh upland environments and sold for modest income. As long as their rights to these products weren't threatened, things went reasonably well. . . but tamper with them, and things went bad in a hurry.

Excise taxes on alcoholic beverages began with the 1791 tax, a short lived imposition designed to help meet the costs of the Revolutionary War debt. This hated tax which robbed the residents of the mountains of virtually all of their pitiful income, was resurrected briefly during the War of 1812 to help pay for that war

then discontinued. Taxes on both alcohol and tobacco were imposed to finance the cost of the U.S. Civil War, and taxation of alcohol has continued on and off. From the 1791 tax to the present day, the mountaineers of north Georgia, Tennessee, the Carolinas and other scattered spots have been driven into the criminal activity of the illicit production of corn liquor.

No one enjoys paying taxes, but they are a simple fact of life in modern society. Nevertheless, when the imposition of a tax on a commodity – which is readily and easily produced and vital for the survival of a group such as the upland Scots-Irish residents – essentially denies that once legal and very vital product to the group, the issue could quickly reach a flash-point, just as it did in 1876.

In contrast to many other countries of the world, the United States, by and large, has historically been very reluctant to use regular army troops against its own civilian population for the enforcement of its laws. There have, however, been some rare exceptions, and considering the very negative results of even these few incidents, a strong argument could be made for the strict confinement of the U.S. Army's duties solely to the defense of the nation from "external" enemies. Modern 21st century American government leaders would be well-served to take particular note of this issue.

A good example of one of these failures was the misuse of the Army in an abortive attempt by U.S. agents to enforce taxation laws involving alcohol and tobacco in the north Georgia mountains in the 1870s. Taxation on the production of alcohol and tobacco through the requirement of licenses imposed a tremendous hardship disproportionately upon Appalachian families, many of whom depended upon their production of spirituous liquors as their main cash crop.

Many of these Scots-Irish Americans interpreted this form of taxation as abusive and designed solely to punish the poor uplanders, particularly in the South. Ironically many of these same mountain families took their lives and livelihoods in their hands to defy the Confederacy during the U.S. Civil War as they adamantly supported the federal government. In the 1870s, they began paying a stiff price for that loyal support.

Due to their isolated highland homes where extensive productive farmland and commercial endeavors were practically nonexistent, mountain families turned to the production of whiskey and tobacco, since these items were virtually the only producible and marketable cash commodities in the area in which they lived. Their ancestors had long been producing home-made liquor for hundreds of years in Scotland and Ireland, prior to their immigration to the American colonies, and these hardy

upland residents continued this tradition freely and legally in their adopted American homeland.

Further exacerbating the already volatile situation was the fact that the federal revenue laws did not distinguish between alcohol and tobacco used for home needs (such as medicinal remedies) and that used for illegal sale (untaxed) on the public market. So even if the isolated Scots-Irish produced a very limited quantity of alcohol strictly for medicinal use where medicines were almost nonexistent, they nevertheless were still required to pay the oppressive tax, which basically negated legal corn liquor production.

Brutal Laws & Enforcement

The taxation was levied in the form of liquor "licenses," which were required of anyone producing any "liquor" of any type. These licenses required for the "legal" production and sale of this commodity invariably simply cost more than the average mountaineer could afford to pay, and thousands of otherwise honest citizens therefore were driven, much to their distaste, into criminal activity. By 1876, cases involving prosecutions for "moonshining" (production and sale of untaxed spirituous liquor) virtually monopolized the docket of the Federal District Court in Atlanta, Georgia.

Due to the difficulty of enforcement of the federal liquor tax laws, the law enforcement efforts quickly became overzealous and abusive. Revenue agents and deputy U.S. marshals, unlike the more highly regarded (at least at that time) Justice Department officials, were paid based upon the number of liquor "stills" (illegal distilleries) they captured and the number of moonshiner arrests they made. The agents often made fraudulent arrests to pad their fees, and their incomes reportedly were also supplemented by bribes, blackmail, and profiteering from the illegal sale of captured stills.

Making the matter even worse in the early 1870s, it was discovered that many of the revenue agents charging and arresting violators of the revenue laws – though working for Republican administrations who initially created and enacted the untaxed liquor laws – were in actuality Southern Democrats who were using the law to persecute the mountaineers because so many of them had turned their backs on the Confederacy only a few years earlier in the 1860s. The memories of those disloyalties, coupled with the pain and suffering still being experienced in the South under Reconstruction was fuel on the fire of punishment for that lack of support.

And matters went from bad to worse when the situation began to feed upon itself. Residents in the areas under surveillance for liquor law offenses were often hired to spy upon and testify against their neighbors, pitting neighbor against neighbor and fueling constant retributory activities which snowballed as the months passed.

As if that weren't bad enough, once federal law enforcement authorities had been sent into the upland areas – again, particularly in north Georgia – the revenue agents carried a reputation for being brutal, profane and heartless. When an individual was arrested for violating the revenue laws, there was no "probation" or "grace period" to make good on unpaid taxes and/or unpurchased licenses. No. . Those violators were immediately taken to Atlanta where they were confined in prisons to await their trials.

Innocent mountain families could – and often did – lose everything they owned, including their homes and property, in order to obtain a viable legal defense for their "offense," even if they were, in fact, ultimately confirmed to be innocent, which they many times were. These families would then have no choice but to return by foot to the mountains, with no home, no food, no warmth in the cold winters, and very little in the way of clothing or the other necessities of life awaiting them when they arrived back "home." These victims often couldn't even turn to relatives for charity either, because their poor relatives often had been charged as well.

Warrantless Arrests

As federal efforts to eliminate the production and sale of untaxed liquor increased and became more violent, many of the mountain men decided they had no choice but to organize and fight back. As a result, the north Georgia counties of the late 1870s were the most violent of the Southern Appalachian mountain region, with more than twice the number of alleged revenue agent casualties as those reported in second-place Tennessee. North Georgia literally became a battle ground.

In order to conduct this war on moonshiners, the U.S. government began using federal troops to protect its agents during raids as early as 1872. In what may have been a signature incident that year, U.S. Deputy Marshal Charles B. Blacker, accompanied by a Lieutenant Wolf of the 2nd U.S. Infantry, was fired upon in the Fightingtown (Boardtown) area of Fannin County, Georgia. When that occurred, President Ulysses S. Grant immediately authorized the use of U.S. Army troops for the support and protection of his revenue agents, with instructions to fire if necessary. "U.S." Grant had no problem punishing the South.

One of the favored techniques of

this "punishment" was "arrests without warrants." This highly-illegal technique was specifically addressed in the U.S. Constitution, but when those who the Founding Fathers had envisioned as the defenders of the Constitutional rights of Americans began to be the ones actually making the violations, there were no remaining options for the protection of those rights. That horse had already left the barn.

One such incident involved a patrol led by Deputy Marshal Blacker at Santa Luca in Gilmer County. Blacker visited the home of the elderly John Emory (formerly of Pickens County) on the night of January 14, 1876, and arrested – without warrants – four men who were waiting for daylight at Emory's still-house (illicit liquor distillery).

When Emory emerged from his house that evening to investigate the cause of the commotion outside, he was unceremoniously shot in the face (almost exactly between the eyes) and killed instantly without warning or provocation by Private William O'Grady, a federal soldier. With two other soldiers – Edward P. Wells and Frederick E. Newman – Private O'Grady concealed Emory's corpse in a nearby creek where Emory's grief-stricken widow discovered it the following morning.

On February 13, United States Deputy Marshal James A. Findley and his men fired upon Lafayette

They captured two of Southern's stills, a wagon and a team, and 120 gallons of untaxed illegal whiskey.

Southern seven times on a raid in the nearby Cartecay District. They captured two of Southern's stills, a wagon and a team, and 120 gallons of untaxed illegal whiskey. Findley and his crew then arrested – again without a warrant – James Sitton, who was in bed in ill health, for no other reason other than the fact that he resided nearby.

Outraged Gilmer Countians immediately organized a written protest to the Governor of Georgia. The Georgia State Legislature was in session at that time and William Robert Rankin of Gordon County introduced resolutions in the Georgia House which culminated in a demand that Governor Smith authorize a full investigation of what could only be considered as crimes committed by revenue agents in north Georgia.

A warrant was issued almost immediately by Gilmer County Justice of the Peace M.A. Berry for the soldiers responsible for John Emory's death. O'Grady – the triggerman in the John Emory shooting – and his colleagues were arrested in Atlanta for Emory's death, but before they could be tried in Gilmer County, a *Writ of Habeas Corpus* from no less than the President of the United States himself – old U.S. Grant – authorized a transferal of the trial to the then-highly-favorable U.S. Federal Circuit Court in Atlanta. These early instances of a U.S. President and a Justice Department (which he considers his own army of enforcement), are emblematic of the exact same evils pervasive in the United States and its government from 2021 to 2024. Literally a carbon copy – and they just keep getting away with an unjust manipulation of the system in incident after incident.

The federal government attempted to hire Blue Ridge District Solicitor General Charles D. Phillips to defend O'Grady and his fellow offenders. Phillips, however, declined the opportunity, choosing instead to be the prosecutor, and even taking as his fee no income other than "Mrs. Emory's tears." Nevertheless, a largely Black, and obviously politically-motivated jury in those post-Civil War days of "Pay-Back" subsequently found O'Grady and the other two soldiers *"Not Guilty."*

U.S. Army Troops

Adding still more fuel to the growing inferno was the fact that revenue agents in the area used this incident to reinforce their calls for still more federal troops to wage still more irresponsible violence upon the north Georgians, contending that Emory's death had encouraged organized resistance and even revenge against federal officials. Surprisingly, had the agents known just how well-founded their fears had been, they may have been even more vocal, for the events leading up to the night of February 10, 1877, had already been set in motion.

Federal revenue agents, supported by federal troops from McPherson Barracks in Atlanta, left Cartersville, Georgia, on February 1, 1877. They made camp at Ellijay, Georgia, the county seat of Gilmer County. From there, they dispatched detachments with instructions to raid moonshiners and illegal tobacco manufacturers in Gilmer, Pickens, and Fannin counties.

Deputy Marshal Blacker, with a party of revenue agents and soldiers, left Ellijay at noon on February 9. They arrived at the home of a Mr. Ayers Jones at 2:45 A.M. the next morning. They were actually in the Frog Mountain region of western Fannin County (although they were close enough to the county line to believe they were in Gilmer County) on the headwaters of Conasauga Creek.

Having seen the light from Jones' cabin, the men initially suspected that they had chanced upon a moonshine distillery. Upon closer inspection however, they discovered the cabin contained only Mrs. Jones and seven little children, all huddled around a fire, trying desperately to stay warm in the un-chinked, un-insulated freezing cabin.

According to Mrs. Jones' later deposition, the men burst into the cabin unannounced, again with no warrant and with weapons drawn. They questioned her at length, and when she could not, or would not tell them where her husband was or the location of his still-house, Blacker became very outraged and profane.

According to her further later testimony, Mrs. Jones repeatedly asked the men to leave her cabin, and one of the soldiers, apparently taking pity on the poor family, even supported her, urging that he and his fellow troops withdraw. But Blacker, continuing with his swearing and abusive behavior, announced that he (and his men) would stay as long as he pleased. Mrs. Jones and the children, some of whom were sick, remained in the cabin with Blacker, a Corporal Calloway, two guides, and Lieutenant Augustine McIntyre, while the remainder of the party began searching the area for the still-house.

Mountaineer Attack

According to later reports of the incident, approximately fifteen minutes had passed since Blacker and his men had arrived, when footsteps were heard outside by the men inside the cabin. It was assumed by the men inside that the sounds they were hearing were from the return of their compatriot soldiers and agents dispatched to search for the still-house.

Imagine the surprise of those soldiers inside the cabin who opened the front door to what they thought were their own friendly men outside, when they suddenly were confronted instead by a fearsome group of very angry and revenge-minded mountaineers. A stout, dark-haired man with whiskers, nearly six feet tall, stood in the doorway with a large pistol.

Shouting "Stand, God damn you... You're in the wrong place tonight!" The stranger then fired his pistol, sending the soldiers and Blacker scurrying for cover.

Corporal Callaway, standing by the cabin hearth, fired his carbine and then put out the lamp on the hearth. A pine knot still burned in the fireplace, but reportedly did not shed enough illumination to give the attackers any view of the inside of the cabin.

Shortly thereafter, Ralston and Anglin who had served as guides for the soldiers, fled in terror out the back of the cabin, slamming the door behind them, leaving Callaway, Blacker, and McIntyre to face the music alone. The mountain men stormed the house four times, firing shotguns, pistols, and rifles. Both sides emptied their weapons through the doorway. Blacker reportedly told McIntyre repeatedly to take cover behind the bedstead, but he refused, fearing that the children might be hit by a stray bullet.

On the fourth volley from the attackers outside, Lt. McIntyre was wounded. He reportedly cried out: "Blacker, I'm shot through the heart."

With their ammunition running out, the lieutenant, corporal, and Blacker fled out the rear door as well. McIntyre, now weak from his wound, stumbled and fell off the rear steps of the cabin. When Blacker attempted to help him, the lieutenant, apparently realizing his wound was mortal, urged the deputy marshal to save himself.

Shortly thereafter, Blacker retreated, leaving McIntyre behind. Shouts in the distance were soon heard to the effect of: "Oh yes, we've got one of the damned sons of bitches," and ".... We'll fix you!"

The next morning, Blacker, amazingly reinforced with only five men, returned to the cabin. McIntyre's body still lay grotesquely where he had fallen earlier that morning. Blacker found Mrs. Jones and her children still huddled in the cabin in bed, still attempting desperately to avoid the cold and hypothermia.

When the men questioned Mrs. Jones about the attackers, she pleaded ignorance. The men began cursing her. Blacker reportedly warned her that they were out for revenge, and would in three weeks burn all the cabins in the area.

Mountaineer Mercy

During Blacker's tirade, one of the men suddenly exclaimed "Look out!" Stepping outside, Blacker saw before his eyes a forest filled with armed men, some behind rocks no more than 300 feet away. He ordered his men to once again withdraw immediately, surprisingly leaving McIntyre's body behind once again. Under the circumstances, the mountaineers exercised amazing restraint in allowing Blacker to retreat without harm.

At 3:00 P.M. that afternoon, the troops returned, but this time they were twenty-two in number. Led by Lieutenant James Ulio, they finally recovered McIntyre's corpse, carrying it out on a horse, since the terrain was far too rugged for a wheeled wagon or cart.

As the men departed with McIntyre's body, they were fired upon by a party of attackers from a ravine 200 yards away. According to an article entitled *"Gilmer's Guerrillas,"* published in the February 13, 1877 issue of *The Atlanta Constitution*, three of the mountaineers were killed in this skirmish. McIntyre's corpse had been robbed, and a hob-nail boot print was found on his forehead.

Despite their lack of losses but due nevertheless to the attack upon the federal troops, retaliation was swift and highly abusive once again. On February 23, revenue agents, accompanied by soldiers, arrested seventy to eighty individuals, both men and women, simply because they lived or were apprehended within fifteen to twenty miles of Frog Mountain. Using old arrest warrants or no warrants at all, they took the trussed arrestees to Cartersville. Many of the persons arrested were seized in the middle of the night while asleep in bed, and subsequently subjected to conditions of hunger and exposure from which some were not expected to recover.

Some of the prisoners for whom no charges could ultimately be conjured, eventually were set free after having been transported to Atlanta. They were forced to make their way back home on foot in the dead of winter, a distance of more than 130 miles.

On March 13, 1877, the *Atlanta Constitution* reported that on March 12, sixty-nine of those arrested for revenue violations were released in Atlanta after pleading *"Guilty,"* and receiving suspended sentences. And in the week just prior, 247 prisoners had been similarly sent home. With other arrests, the total number eventually exceeded 500 persons.

Due to the fact that it had become a target for federal revenue enforcement officers, the Frog Mountain area was gradually abandoned by its families, as men who had escaped the dragnet hid out or fled to neighboring states.

Some residents remained however. The *Atlanta Constitution* reported that the local people were stockpiling powder and shot for self defense against another raid.

More Illegal Arrests

The quest for injustice involving the murder of Lt. McIntyre did not die easily either. Rewards were offered by the Governor of Georgia as well as by the federal government for the killers. Despite their avoidance of violence, the residents of Frog Mountain and surrounding areas were labeled as extremists and radicals.

James Holt and his three sons were eventually arrested in Nashville, Tennessee, for McIntyre's death, but were released when it was revealed that the only evidence against them was the fact that they were former Frog Mountain residents preparing to move to Texas. It was a scene very reminiscent of the dark days immediately preceding and after the U.S. Civil War, when residents, with their homes and way of life completely destroyed, simply packed what little possessions they had retained, and departed the South in search of a better life elsewhere. It was the epitome of government run amok.

Embarrassed by this mistake, federal authorities quietly and cautiously spirited their next group of suspects

– John Davenport and five of his neighbors – into Atlanta. The only evidence against these individuals was reported to have been the testimony of a lone female. Following a hearing, Davenport and his friends were also released. Much of the harassment at this time was occurring in vengeance of the death of Lt. McIntyre whose commanding officer had proceeded with a very ill-advised mission, placing all his men in highly-unnecessary danger.

The U.S. Army believed that the man who had appeared in the doorway of the Jones cabin had been Ayers Jones himself, and even claimed that the whole incident, including the light from the cabin and the women and children, had all been an elaborate plot to lure McIntyre and his party into an ambush. In order to "explain away" the disaster, the army claimed that the Jones family members were part Indian and had moved to Frog Mountain after fleeing the mountains of western North Carolina during the Cherokee relocation of 1838, the implication now being that they were radical Cherokees who had illegally departed the reservation.

Ayers Jones' wife and son were later arrested, but subsequently also released. Try as it might, the U.S. Justice Department and prosecuting officials simply could not find enough evidentiary material to successfully make a case against any of the Frog Mountain residents, and things just kept going from bad to worse for them.

Ayers Jones himself, and his brother Tom, were not caught until 1879. They were not tried for murder, but were indicted – of all things – for *"a conspiracy to avoid the service of a warrant"* by Blacker, the man with no warrant in the first place. Jones and his brother were eventually tried, only to join the other innocents in a verdict of *"Not Guilty,"* which was again handed down due to a lack of evidence and witnesses.

Papers in the case file involving Jones and his brother may be reviewed in the National Archives, Atlanta Branch, and shed some very interesting sidelights on the death of McIntyre and details of the incident. Informants in the incident apparently claimed that an Elijah Johnson had been in the Army's camp, and, acting as a spy, Johnson had sent three men to Frog Mountain to warn the mountaineers of the impending raid.

As matters were sorted out, it became apparent that the Jones family and their neighbors had subsequently armed themselves and banded together. Prior to the raid by the agents and soldiers on Jones' cabin, it was determined that the mountaineers were actually attempting to avoid confrontation, but decided instead to storm the cabin after becoming enraged and concerned over the abuse being heaped upon Mrs. Jones by Blacker.

The National Archives papers further indicate that one witness testified that a W.H. Green who was related to the Jones family, was in possession of McIntyre's pistol and knew where his watch could be found. And later, during a daring rescue of a fellow moonshiner, Ayers Jones allegedly boasted that his pistol had killed McIntyre.

Ayers Jones however, was also described as being *"as pure a specimen of a child of nature as can be imagined,"* so illiterate and backward that he had never even seen a railroad. He was however, a substantial landowner, with some 700 acres in the 980th District of Fannin County. He, ironically, was later murdered by his son – John – in nearby Chattooga County on September 11, 1893.

Investigation of the Feds

In 1877, mass meetings were being held in Gilmer and Fannin counties (more than 100 persons attended the Fannin meeting) where declarations were signed and sent to newly-elected Governor Alfred Colquitt. The resolutions condemned the killing of Lt. McIntyre and the persons violating the revenue laws, but they also charged that the revenue agents were, in actuality, the root of the current crisis. The declaration called the agents *"men without any social standing, without honor, or integrity, and who themselves have been, up to the present time, without a single exception, the most persistent violators of the law in our midst."*

The *Atlanta Constitution* also blamed McIntyre's death on the revenue agents themselves, describing them as *"a hungry pack of remorseless and heartless spies and vampires."*

When the Georgia State Legislature was again in session, Rep. B.C. Duggar of Gilmer County and Lemuel J. Allred of Pickens introduced new resolutions which were passed, requesting that Governor Colquitt investigate the situation in north Georgia. The House also passed resolutions condemning the revenue laws on alcohol production and the system designed to enforce those laws.

Colonel Samuel C. Williams was sent to north Georgia by Governor Colquitt to conduct the investigation. He arrived in Ellijay on February 28. Traveling through Pickens, Gilmer, and Fannin counties, he collected more than 130 depositions, many of which were later published in the *Atlanta Constitution* of May 8, 1877.

Not satisfied with only "looking into the matter at hand," Williams recorded information on the events and persons going back to 1872. He personally visited the sites involved, including Frog Mountain and the Jones cabin. Everywhere, he received "not only a willingness, but a desire to help," as men even left their work to aid him in his investigation.

Williams' report was a lengthy condemnation of the entire revenue enforcement system in north Georgia, and of the men who ran it. He collected dozens of depositions of people arrested without warrants who were compelled to hire lawyers at considerable expense to clear themselves of nonexistent offenses, and of brutal revenue agents who extorted blackmail, took bribes, and sold liquor distilleries captured in raids. Army officers interviewed were no less negative about the revenue agents, and expressed their regrets in being forced to be involved in helping these men.

Col. Williams' investigation of the death of Lt. McIntyre was no less positive. He discovered that had the "guerrillas" actually wished to wipe out the entire party of agents and soldiers, a successful ambush could have been easily carried out by two men at any of several places on the narrow trail to the cabin. The mountaineers, however, had wisely restrained themselves.

And the Jones' cabin itself, could also have been a tremendous kill site had the mountaineers wished to truly exact revenge. It was described as *"an oak log pen, 12 by 14 feet in size, neither chinked nor daubed."* The attackers would have needed to do little more than to fire through the three to five-inch cracks between the logs to have killed Blacker and his entire party as they stood in the cabin.

Clearly, Williams concluded, the attackers had not intended to massacre the raiding party or to harm the soldiers.

As for the mass arrests, Williams reported that McIntyre's commander believed that the attackers were not thirty men, but only four or five.

In the interim following this incident, Deputy Marshals Blacker and Findley, accompanied by federal troops and with the full support of U.S. Grant, continued to actively incite ill will with their tactics in north Georgia. Starting from Dawson County, they and a posse arrested a Harrison Barker of Forsyth County at his home in March, 1877. In their account of the daring and dangerous capture, Blacker and Findley described Harrison Barker as a legendary north Georgia moonshining "Jesse James" of many a daring escape and blazing gun battle.

Barker, who was subsequently captured and tried, turned out to be little more than a wiry man of average height who claimed never to have been convicted of moonshining or charged with any "mean thing." He speculated that his notoriety as a legitimate tavern keeper in Cumming may have led to his being singled out by Blacker and Findley.

Whatever the circumstances, Barker nevertheless took flight after wounding Blacker in the arrest attempt. Blacker and Findley later pursued him to Kentucky where they re-captured him, bringing him back to Atlanta for trial.

Barker eventually lived up to his previously-assigned "notorious" reputation, escaping from the prison in which he was being held. He, however, remained peacefully at home, until dragged out of his bed by Findley early one morning in 1877.

Barker eventually plead "Guilty" to selling moonshine, in order to obtain a suspended sentence, the implication being that Findley and Blacker were inter-ested only in being able to confirm that violations actually existed in order to justify their actions. Had Barker not plead "Guilty" and proceeded to trial, the evidence would once again have been extremely skimpy. Barker had also been indicted for shooting Blacker in 1873, but was never even tried on this charge.

On April 10, 1877, the U.S. Army finally left Ellijay and Gilmer County. In 1879, an act of Congress finally prohibited the use of troops to aid civilian authorities in making such arrests.

So ended what came to be known as "the North Georgia Moonshine War of 1876-1877." The official score stood at one civilian and one officer killed, with an untold number of other unnecessary casualties among the moonshiners and revenue agents. The United States Justice Department and the office of the Presidency also received "black eyes" in the process.

Contrary to the hopes of the mountain people, the revenue laws, the revenue law enforcement agents, and the local resistance all continued through to the days of the "whitecaps," also known as "the night riders," and on to the more recent moonshining days of "Thunder Road."

Some headway was made against moonshiners by such federal agents as Commissioner of Internal Revenue Green B. Raum, who, in the 1880s, used what Dr. Wilbur R. Miller has called "a systematic strategy combining force and restraint," built both upon persistence, honest and effective legal techniques, and on winning local support. That moonshining has been greatly reduced in north Georgia, however, is due not to law enforcement, but simply to the rising cost of sugar, new economic opportunities in north Georgia, and more affordable, "taxed" liquor.

Courage in the Face of Certain Death:

The Astounding Story of Stand Watie

*This brave Native American knew he almost certainly would suffer a brutal death at the hands of his Cherokee brethren – just as did his brother, cousin and uncle – for signing the **Treaty of New Echota** in 1835. Stand Watie, however, also was convinced it was the best choice for the survival of his race and he was willing to make that sacrifice. Amazingly, Stand Watie was a "warrior extraordinaire." He not only survived the Cherokee death squads, but later rose to the rank of brigadier general in the Confederate Army. Though his sacrifices were legion, he has been virtually forgotten by the modern-day residents of his former homeland.*

He was born on December 12, 1806[1], in the village of Oothcaloga south of New Echota in the Cherokee Nation in what today is the southeastern United States. He was originally named *Ta-ker-taw-ker* which, when translated into English meant "to stand firm," and the rest of the Cherokee Nation would soon learn just how firm a stance he could actually take when necessary. It would not be long before Stand Watie would earn both fame and fortune[2] as a result of his strength of character, so he was well-named.

He later was formally named according to tribal custom as *De-gado-ga*, which meant *"he stands on two feet."* Somewhat later still, his preferred name evolved to a combination of a shortened form of the English translation of his Cherokee name – *"to stand firm"* – and a contraction of his father's name – *Oo-Wa-tie* – which led to the name by which he earned lasting fame – *Stand Watie*.[3]

He spent his boyhood years along the creek that flowed gently through the pleasant valley[4] of what today is Gordon County, Georgia, and was later baptized into the Christian religion in the nearby Moravian Church and given the Christian name *Isaac*.

In his youth, Stand Watie lived in a comfortable home built in the 1790s by his father, David Watie *(the double Oo, as in "Oo-Wa-tie" was, at some point, dropped from his name)*. In addition to the income earned by the fruits of his plantation, David operated a ferry on the Hightower (Etowah) River from 1825 to 1831.

Futile Assimilation

By this point in time, the Cherokees had adopted many of the ways of the White settlers in the area in a desperate attempt to assimilate into White culture. Many of their leaders had come to realize that, due to the vast numbers of White settlers pouring into their homeland, assimilation and peaceful co-existence were their only hope for the survival of their race.

No matter the efforts made by the Cherokees, however, White settlers pressed unceasingly for ownership of more land, and that meant that the Cherokees were pushed farther and farther to the West out of their native homeland. It also didn't help that gold had been discovered in Georgia at about this same time, and the mad rush to grab land and seek fortunes from the precious yellow metal had seized the White race, and became the death knell of the Cherokees' existence in the East.

Interestingly, the assumption of the customs of the White man by the Native Americans included by default the custom of owning Black slaves to work the plantations of the wealthy upper-crust Cherokees. They had no way of knowing this practice would soon become abhorrent and unacceptable in the young American nation.

Even more interestingly, a youthful Stand Watie was nevertheless raised by his father to work alongside the slaves in the fields. After his chores for the day had been completed, he often went hunting in the forest to bring in fresh meat for the family.[5]

The Native Cherokees were so intent upon assimilation into the White culture that they also readily took up arms to defend the issues of the Whites, including the submission of the *Red Stick* Creek Indians in what today is southern Alabama, who were violently opposing White settlers, contrary to the peaceful assimilation being practiced by the Cherokees.

National Recognition – On June 29, 1995, the U.S. Post Office issued a set of 20 commemorative stamps showing 16 individuals and 4 battles of the U.S. Civil War. Despite the fact that he represented the Confederacy in the Civil War, Brigadier General (CSA) Stand Watie (1806-1871) was one of the individuals selected to appear on these stamps. He is pictured here, in a dramatic horseback pose, following a raid on a Union river boat. (Image courtesy of Joe Griffith and the U.S. Postal Service)

When Stand Watie was only six or seven years of age, his father, David, was appointed as a captain in a regiment of 600 Cherokee volunteers – mostly mixed-bloods – commanded by his brother, Major Ridge. Under the overall command of Andrew Jackson, the regiment was a portion of a larger force sent to fight the *Red Stick* Creek faction in present-day Alabama.

In March of 1814 at the *Battle of Horseshoe Bend* on the Tallapoosa River, the Andrew Jackson forces crushed the *Red Stick* uprising, quite nearly killing all of this violent branch of the Creeks in the process. It was during that campaign

Marked For Death – Stand Watie (1806-1871), a Cherokee Native American is pictured. He was the brother of Buck Watie (Elias Boudinot), and the nephew of Major Ridge, all prominent Cherokee leaders of that era. He was a plantation owner in what today is Gordon County and also a member of the Treaty Party who advocated relinquishment of the Cherokee lands in what today are northern Alabama, southern Tennessee, western Carolina and northwest Georgia, in return for reimbursement and relocation to new lands in the West in Oklahoma and Arkansas territories. As a result of their support of the treaty, Ridge, Boudinot, Stand Watie and other leaders became targets for assassination by their own people. Stand Watie – who survived the Cherokee Death Squads – later became the highest ranking Indian officer in the U.S. Civil War, rising to brigadier general in the Confederate Army. (Image courtesy of Western History Collection, University of Oklahoma Library)

that "Major" Ridge acquired what later evolved into his first name when he was commissioned as a major in the United States Army by Andrew Jackson.[6]

It can only be considered bitterly ironic today, that it would soon be

"President" Andrew Jackson who was the driving force in denying the Cherokees the retention of their ownership of their Georgia homeland, even though the U.S. Supreme Court had ruled in favor of the tribe's retention. Despite all of this, Stand Watie, his father, Major Ridge, and the rest of the *Treaty Faction* remained firm in their pursuit of a peaceful and orderly assimilation into and coexistence with the White culture.

White Education

Stand Watie, who spoke only his native tongue until he was twelve years of age, learned to speak, read, and write English at the Moravian Mission Schools, attending classes at both the school at Spring Place and another at Brainerd, Tennessee. It is amazing today to understand the lengths to which the Cherokees were willing to go to attempt assimilation, and despite almost endless earnest efforts, they still ultimately were denied and rejected.

When not pursuing his studies at the Moravian Mission Schools, young Watie was especially interested in sports. He was small in stature, but reportedly was an outstanding athlete as well as an excellent rider. He was considered one of the best players in the games of ball in the "challenge" competitions in the Cherokee Nation.[7]

Stand Watie had a brother who was four years older than he named Kilakeena, meaning "stag" or "male deer." He eventually gained the nickname of "Buck" Watie. In time, the two boys were joined by other siblings for a total of eight children – four boys and four girls.

Buck Watie and his cousin, John Ridge (the son of Major Ridge), were sent to complete their education at the

American Board of Commissioners for Foreign Mission Schools at Cornwall, Connecticut. While there, in addition to a higher education, Buck gained a new name, and both Buck and John gained New England girls as their wives. One can only imagine today the culture shock these two young Cherokees must have experienced in this determined continued – and noble – effort at assimilation.

By comparison, 21st Century immigrants being accepted into the United States make virtually no effort whatsoever toward assimilation. These immigrants often violently oppose American culture, and see their American citizenship as an opportunity to gain a foothold for their nation within the United States in order to weaken the United States. In reality, they seek solely a "nation within a nation" relationship, violating and altering American principles, laws and social mores wherever possible, while taking full advantage nevertheless of all the wonderful benefits of American citizenship. It is a circumstance which has been the downfall of countless great cultures over the ages, and currently seriously threatens the United States as well. The Cherokees of modern society no doubt smile knowingly when they observe this situation today.

According to a common practice in the 1830s, Cherokees who had been assisted in life toward American citizenship by a benefactor took that benefactor's name as his or her own in tribute to the individual. Buck Watie accordingly adopted the name of his White benefactor – Elias Boudinot – who was a Philadelphia philanthropist. In 1827, Buck (now also called Elias Boudinot) married Harriet Gold – a White New Englander – and brought her home to live at New Echota.[8]

Buck Watie, also known as "Elias Boudinot" (1802-1839), was editor of the **Cherokee Phoenix** newspaper. His courage and support for the **Removal Treaty** caused him to be replaced as editor of the paper, and later, to be brutally assassinated by a Cherokee Death Squad at his new home in Park Hill, Arkansas. (Image courtesy of Western History Collection, University of Oklahoma Library)

Eastern Cherokees

In 1819, the sprawling Cherokee settlement of "New Town" was established on the south bank of the Oostanaula River just below the confluence of the Coosawattee and Connasauga rivers. In 1820, at *New Town*, a law was passed by the tribal council dividing the Cherokee country in what today are Georgia, Alabama and Tennessee into eight territorial and judicial districts. Although Stand Watie and Major Ridge lived 30 miles apart, they both lived within the *Coosawattee District*.[9]

In 1825, New Town was designated as the new Cherokee National Capital and renamed *New Echota* (*Echota* being the Cherokee term for "town"). *New*

Courageous Leader – The stern visage of Major Ridge reveals the seriousness of the circumstances in the Cherokee Nation of the 1830s. He was speaker of the lower house in the Cherokee Council. He also was chief of the Cherokee Police, a close advisor to Chief John Ross, and yet a strong supporter of the treaty being urged by the United States government which would cede the Cherokee lands to the Whites. His support for this treaty eventually cost him his life. (Photo courtesy of GA Dept. of Archives & History, Atlanta)

Echota was (and the historic remnants still are) located east of present-day Calhoun, Georgia, in Gordon County, off GA Highway 225 at the present-day locus of *New Echota State Historic Site*.[10]

About eight miles south of *New Echota*, the Indian town of *Oothcaloga* once stood in the Oothcaloga Valley. Christianity was strongly held in the community as witnessed by a large number of converts made during the revivals held there in 1819-20. Soon thereafter, a prominent group of Cherokee leaders requested that a Moravian Mission be established in their neighborhood to conduct regular church services.

Many of the Cherokees – and not only those of higher education – were strong advocates of Christianity, and held firm to their beliefs regardless of the circumstances. They also had realized the positive benefits of learning all facets of White culture from the Moravians as well, their objective being to take every opportunity to assimilate into the White culture, rather than live as a small island of the Cherokee culture in a sea of White culture. They knew they would lose a portion of their own identity, but it was their hope that in doing so, they would retain possession of their beloved properties in the Southeast.

Major Ridge, his wife, Susanna, and their son, John, were among the first to invite the Moravians to come to the valley. In addition, David Watie and his wife, Susannah, and their sons, Elias Boudinot and Stand Watie, encouraged the establishment of both a church and a school. Thus, from 1822 to 1833, the *Oothcaloga Mission Station* was operated by the Moravian Church in the valley.[11]

According to the **Cherokee Constitution** adopted on July 26, 1827, the *Cherokee Supreme Court* was authorized to appoint a clerk to a term of four years. Stand Watie was appointed to this capacity in 1828, and at age 22, began a long career in legal work that eventually gained him a license to practice law in the Cherokee Nation[12] – which was no small achievement.

The Watie Family

During the time of his residence in the East, Stand Watie married three of the four wives with whom he was associated during his lifetime. These wives all had Christian names and there were no children from any of these marriages in the East.

His first wife was Elizabeth "Betsy" Fields, who sadly died in childbirth, as did the child in late March of 1836.

His second marriage – in September of 1836 – was to the former wife of a deceased Cherokee neighbor Eli Hicks. Her name was Isabella Hicks, and she had a son by the previous marriage.

Watie's third marriage was to Eleanor Looney. No details of this marriage are known today.

Stand Watie married his fourth wife – Sarah ("Sallie") Carolina Bell – after he was a resident in the *Western Indian Territory* in 1843. With Sarah, Stand Watie had five children – three sons and two daughters.[13]

When they reached maturity, the three cousins – Stand Watie, Elias Boudinot and John Ridge, along with the older Major Ridge, came to be not only a tightly-knitted family group, but, in 1832, the leadership core of a pro-treaty party favoring the removal of the tribe to the West. They had ultimately realized that assimilation into the White culture of the East was a futile effort. There simply were too many European settlers arriving in successive overpowering waves. The tide seemed endless, as were the White demands for land.

Therefore, resettlement in the West – after obtaining fair reimbursement in the sale of their properties in the East – seemed to the pro-treaty party to be the only logical option, particularly in view of the fact that they also understood that if they did not take this step, their lands and properties in the East would simply be taken from them by the Whites – quite likely with limited reimbursement. It was a tragedy almost beyond comparison, since they had struggled so tirelessly for so many

Cherokee Chieftain – John Ross (1790-1866), principal chief of the Cherokee Nation from 1828 until his death, appeared to have much more White blood than he did Cherokee blood, and, in fact, he did. He was but an eighth-blood Cherokee, yet was still selected as the leader of the Cherokees. He also was unflinchingly opposed to the treaty which would cede the Cherokee lands to the Whites, and led the punishment of those who signed the *Treaty of New Echota*. (Photo courtesy of Western History Collection, University of Oklahoma Library)

years simply to be accepted into White culture.

In order to achieve these objectives, the pro-treaty group (Stand Watie, Elias Boudinot, John Ridge, Major Ridge, etc.) found it necessary to gain control in the Cherokee Nation over the anti-treaty faction, which opposed the tribe's removal. The anti-treaty faction was led by the principal chief of the Cherokees, John Ross, and, collectively, they represented not just opposition, but violent opposition.[14]

After Andrew Jackson, the U.S. Congress, and the state of Georgia rec-

Site of Nativity – This historic structure exists on the Bray Farm near Calhoun, Georgia, in Gordon County. Local lore maintains that the core of this home is an early log cabin built by David Watie who fathered both Stand Watie and Buck Watie ("Elias Boudinot") in the 1790s. Many historians believe both Stand and Buck Watie were born in this cabin. (Photo by Joe Griffith)

ognized the pro-treaty faction as the legitimate representatives of the Cherokee Nation, they (the pro-treaty faction) took the lead in negotiating the *Treaty of New Echota* in 1835, surrendering the Cherokees' ancestral homes in the Southeast for new lands in the West.[15]

On December 29, 1835, at Elias Boudinot's house at New Echota, the Watie-Ridge-Boudinot-led faction signed the *Treaty of New Echota*. They gave up all claims to their lands in the East in return for new land west of the Mississippi River and just compensation for any improvements departing Cherokees had made upon their land in the East.

Conversely, many of the Cherokees – led by the anti-treaty party leader John Ross – were not present for the signing of the *Treaty of New Echota*, and bitterly opposed it and the removal of the tribe. In order to exact revenge for what they considered to be not only disloyalty but an unpardonable sin, the anti-treaty group vowed to exact retribution from the Watie-Boudinot-Ridge pro-treaty faction.

The United States Senate, nevertheless, quickly ratified the treaty after it was executed by the pro-treaty faction, and three years later, the United States Army enforced the removal of any remaining Cherokees in the East in what came to be known as *The Trail of Tears*.[16]

Western Cherokees

In the spring of 1837 – prior to the forced removal of those Cherokees who refused to leave the Southeast – the Stand Watie, Elias Boudinot and Ridge families began their voluntary migratory journey to the Indian Territory in the West. Upon arrival, they joined forces with the "Old Settlers" – those earlier Cherokees who had also voluntarily relocated to the Indian Territory in 1817 long before the Treaty of New Echota had even been conceived.

Contrary to their expectations, the Watie-Boudinot-Ridge families and their allies among the Old Settlers were unable to gain leadership over the Cherokee Nation in the West. Their old treaty opponent – John Ross, who had arrived in the West in mid-March of 1839 in the wake of the forced removal – still retained the allegiance of the majority of the Cherokees, who, if anything, were loyal to their elected government.[17]

On June 21, 1839, at Double Springs in the Indian Territory, a secret meeting of the Cherokees who had opposed the removal treaty was held to judge those who had violated the "blood law," and, without authorization, sold the Cherokee lands in the East. A verdict of death was passed against all the signers and endorsers of the *Treaty of New Echota*.

On the next day on June 22, the sentences were carried out by surprise execution squads and three of the most prominent signers – Major Ridge, who was Stand Watie's uncle; John Ridge, who was Stand Watie's cousin; and Elias Boudinot, who was Stand Watie's brother – were all brutally and horribly murdered.

Elias Boudinot was hacked to death with a war axe on the morning of June 22, 1839, outside his home at Park Hill, Oklahoma, as his family watched in horror nearby. His skull was crushed with the terrible blows from the heavy weapon.

Stand Watie, however, who was working in his store, received advance news of the triple murders of Boudinot, Major Ridge, and his son, John. Though also marked for execution, Stand Watie managed to escape the assassins.[18]

For his protection, Stand Watie organized a band of warriors at Old Fort Wayne as his personal bodyguards. The next few years were a time of murderous internal feuding between the two treaty factions. Relations between the factions bordered on civil war, with many acts of vengeance and retaliation being carried out by both sides.

Eventually, a restless calm emerged in the Indian Territory, and Stand Watie, who had attained prominent social and political stature in the territory by that point, amazingly, openly joined the *Tribal Council* where he served from 1845 to 1861. Such a manifestation of courage is rarely seen today outside the theaters of modern warfare. Despite the many threats the anti-treaty party members had made upon his life during that time, Stand Watie participated nonetheless in active leadership of the Cherokee Nation until the beginning of the U.S. Civil War.[19]

Winds of War

In the spring of 1861, the Union abandoned all of its military posts in

Historic Cabin – Major Ridge, the uncle of Stand Watie, departed for the West in 1837. The structure in this photograph has a documented Indian log cabin at its core which was Ridge's home in Cherokee Indian Territory in what today is northwest Georgia. Ridge also operated a ferry and several other business endeavors at this site in the 1820s and '30s. Today, this structure is called Chieftains Museum, and is a National Historic Landmark dedicated to the preservation of the heritage of the Cherokees. (Photo by Joe Griffith)

the Indian Territory. The Confederates quickly took advantage of this situation and occupied these forts.

As a prosperous planter and slave owner, Stand Watie was sympathetic to the Southern cause, but his dedication undoubtedly had little to do with his loyalty to the Southern states. In all likelihood, he actually envisioned his involvement in the White's war as an opportunity to get rid of his old treaty party enemies – the John Ross regime – which, being pro-Union, fully supported the U.S. federal government.

When Confederate emissaries approached Stand Watie for his support, he readily agreed to organize a cavalry unit. With the outbreak of the war, he, due to his leadership capabilities, was made a colonel in the Confederate army and he raised a regiment of mostly mixed-blood soldiers known as the *Cherokee Mounted Volunteers*.[20]

As a military unit, the *Cherokee Mounted Volunteers* fought as a band of

Last Remains – Following the removal of the Cherokees in 1838, New Echota – the final capital of the Cherokees in their original homeland in what today is the southeastern United States – fell into ruin and was forgotten, and the land reverted to agricultural usage. In the foreground in this photo, the last remnants – a few foundation stones and the outline of the original hand-dug well – of the Buck Watie (Elias Boudinot) home are visible. Buck was the older brother of Stand Watie and served as the first editor of the *Cherokee Phoenix* newspaper. He constructed a large two-story home on this site in 1827, and, following relocation to the West, was among those assassinated at the Cherokee reservation in Park Hill, Oklahoma, for his support of the *Treaty of New Echota*. (Photo by Joe Griffith)

very irregular cavalry. They wore oddly-colored shirts and pants, moccasins, and hats with feathers protruding from the sides. Despite their support of the Southern cause, they were not supplied by any normal Confederate unit. As such, they had no reliable source of arms, munitions, clothing or food, and therefore were dependent upon captured Union supplies and equipment for their logistical support. Interestingly, the Union weapons were the most advanced of that day and time, so in some instances, the Cherokees were better equipped than the line Confederate units.

In cold weather, the Cherokee Mounted Volunteers were known to wear captured pieces of Yankee blue uniforms and overcoats. Watie and his men – armed mostly with shotguns, knives and war axes – preferred to fight on horseback, conducting slashing raids on unsuspecting enemies in the tradition of the guerrilla tactics of Francis Marion, the "Swamp Fox," in South Carolina during the American Revolution. Watie and his men operated with the same dash and daring as they ambushed wagon supply trains, steamboats, and military escorts during the war, gaining renown and generating fear in their opponents.[21]

It is a matter of record, however, that Watie and his men did participate in one traditional infantry battle. On March 7-8, 1862, his unit was part of Confederate Major General Earl Van Dorn's 16,000-man army in the vicinity of Fayetteville, Arkansas. Van Dorn was trying to encircle the right flank of Major General Samuel R. Curtis's Union Army of 12,000 men.

Curtis was defending "good ground" about 30 miles to the northeast of Fayetteville at a place called Pea Ridge. He apparently was well-prepared and provisioned for an attack and managed to fight off the Confederates in two days of fierce battle, forcing Van Dorn's forces to retreat in complete disarray.[22]

Ironically, in that defeat, Stand Watie's reputation as a fierce fighter and capable combat leader was displayed "front and center," earning him a revered place in the combat lore of American forces. In a driving snow storm, Colonel Stand Watie's men, who were for the first time being employed on foot as regular infantry, were aligned with other units on the left flank of the attacking force.

During the attack, Watie's men charged a Union artillery battery of three guns protected by dismounted Union cavalry. As they ran across the open field screaming a blood-curdling Rebel yell and brandishing the cold steel of their weapons, Watie's men caused the startled Yankees to break from their positions and flee in terror.

In the process of this terrified disorganized retreat, three Union Army cannons were captured – an accomplishment which was considered a great victory at that time. As a result of this courage in the face of terrific fire, Watie and his men were cheered and honored by the other units in this engagement.[23]

Interestingly, despite the great victory in the capture of the cannons, Watie had no horses or harnesses to move the cannons to the rear. He therefore directed his men – still under heavy hostile fire from other Union artillery units – to drag the captured pieces into the woods where they were secured. Unfortunately, Watie's advanced position became untenable as other Confederate forces in the line began retreating, and he was forced to withdraw with them.

Watie and his men, nevertheless, had successfully fought in their one and only battle deployed as traditional infantrymen, despite the engagement's classification as a Confederate loss. Unfortunately, by the end of the day, the battle had become not just a loss, but a crushing defeat for the Confederates.[24]

Following the defeat at Pea Ridge, John Ross – who had initially supported the Confederacy – became a turn-coat and suddenly switched sides. Sensing the eventual outcome of the war, Ross realigned his Cherokee supporters with the Union army and cause, deciding that instead of bravely fighting on in loyalty to his original cause, he would simply "join the winning side."

If that action by Ross wasn't enough to re-divide the Cherokees back into "pro-treaty" and "anti-treaty" factions, another action by Ross left no doubt. A short time after the bloody Pea Ridge engagement, a Union force – with the co-operation of Ross and his people – invaded the Western Cherokee Indian Territory, setting into motion once again the bitter inter-Cherokee bloodbath.

As a result, pro-Union Cherokees battled pro-Confederate Cherokees, with the Ross faction once again bitterly engaging the Watie faction. Following four years of violence based almost entirely upon tribal animosity rather than U.S. Civil War conflicts, the Cherokee homeland in the West was generally laid to waste.

Many of the Cherokees began leaving their resettlement homes to resettle once again, but this time they traveled south into Texas below the Red River. It is for this reason that a Cherokee population ultimately took root in this vicinity.

It took more than four long years for the well-equipped and well-fed Union armies to defeat the starving weaponless Confederacy but it eventually occurred. This culmination of the war returned John Ross to his position of control over the Cherokee Nation. Factional violence within the Nation essentially ended at the conclusion of the U.S. Civil War, but bitterness and hatred endured well into the next century.[25]

Honored Leader

Prior to war's end on May 6, 1864, Stand Watie had been promoted to the rank of brigadier general, becoming the highest-ranking Indian to fight in the U.S. Civil War. In 1995, the United States Post Office issued a set of commemorative stamps featuring distinguished individuals and battles of the United States Civil War. In the foreground on one of those stamps, the image of a Cherokee Indian who also was a brigadier general in the Confederate Army, is prominently displayed riding on horseback. It is not difficult to discern the identity of this Indian.

In the distant background on this same commemorative postage stamp, smoke can be seen rising from the burning hulk of the Federal steam-driven ferryboat – the J.R. Williams – on the Arkansas River. Watie and his men ambushed this vessel during the U.S. Civil War on June 15, 1864.

While the J.R. Williams was steaming upriver on its way to Fort Gibson in the western Indian Territory, the vessel was fired upon and disabled by Watie's artillery. The Indians made their assault "Indian-style" from behind bushes on a bluff overlooking the river – almost invisible to the boat crew. Blasted out of control, the boat ran aground on a sandbar on the north side of the river.

The outnumbered Federal soldiers aboard the boat were taken completely by surprise. Those who survived the ambush fled on foot southward back toward Fort Smith from whence they had come. The boat's crew deserted to the Confederates.

Watie's men swarmed over the captured vessel, looting the boat of its cargo of commissary stores, quartermaster supplies and subtler goods intended for Fort Gibson. After they had gathered up what booty they could carry, most of the Indians fled the scene to rejoin their destitute families who were living along the Red River in Texas where they had taken refuge from the invading Union Army.

Watie loaded up as much of the supplies as he and his remaining Cherokee soldiers could carry away with them, then set fire to the boat. He then departed for his camp on the Limestone Prairie in the Cherokee Nation, because he knew a strong Federal reaction force would be arriving at the site of the burned ferryboat in short order.[27]

The Stand Watie stamp commemorates this amazing leader's many years of perseverance and devotion to both the Cherokee Indian and Confederate American lost causes. Despite being cast as a fighter for two major losing causes, his loyalty never wavered – contrary to that of his opponent, John Ross. In the realities of this world, few things are more important than loyalty.

As a three-quarter-blood Cherokee aristocrat, prosperous planter, and leader of his mixed-blood allies, Stand Watie somehow survived the many years of bloody tribal feuding in both the East and the West. As a Confederate Army Brigadier General, Watie also survived this conflict despite regular service in combat situations.

Stand Watie was also the highest-ranking Native American to fight in the Civil War – on either side.[26] On June 23, 1865, over two months after General Lee's surrender, Stand Watie became the last Confederate general to surrender his forces, fighting to the bitter end.

Following the war, Watie tried unsuccessfully to rebuild his fortune, but the constant combat – both in the Civil War and against the anti-treaty faction – had taken a heavy toll upon his normally strong constitution. With his body weakened and ill, he died on September 9, 1871, at his home on Honey Creek in Delaware County, Oklahoma, near the northwest corner of Arkansas.[27]

**Vestiges of Stand Watie
In Georgia Today**

Back at Stand Watie's old home-site in what today is northwest Georgia, there is no commemorative marker of any type at the birth-site of this amazing Cherokee. The only public recognition whatsoever is found in the form of the *Sons of Confederate Veterans, General Stand Watie Camp #915* in Calhoun, Georgia, which honors his name. If one knows where to look, however, vestiges of Watie's former existence can still be seen in the area.[28]

The first site of interest undoubtedly would be the spot where Stand Watie was born in 1806. The actual location of this site, however, may be in question.

The ***Calhoun Times and Gordon County News*** reported on March 11, 1998, that *"The site* [the Bray farm] *includes a historic home-place historians estimate was built around 1796 by Oo-Watie* [David Watie], *'The Ancient One,' brother of Major Ridge.* [David Watie's sons] *Elias Boudinot and Stand Watie, a leading family of the Cherokee Nation, were both born on the site."*[29]

Others claim the old home place at Bray Farm (also known as "Daffodil Farm"), was built by a Methodist minister, Bannister Bray in 1837. For example, Jewell B. Reeve in her book ***Climb***

Sacred Ground – Pictured here is a Georgia Historic Commission reproduction of the structure in which the **Cherokee Phoenix** was published in the 1830s on the grounds of New Echota in what formerly was Cherokee Indian Territory and today is Gordon County, Georgia. Elias Boudinot, the brother of Stand Watie, was the editor of the **Phoenix** and an important cog in the wheels of progress for the Cherokee Nation, spending many hours at this site. Stand Watie assisted his brother with the paper from time to time, and was acting editor in 1832 during his brother's absence. (Photo by Joe Griffith)

the Hills of Gordon writes, *"There, near a grove of oak and cedar trees surrounding three springs, he built a house of logs covered with white clapboard and faced with a row of six majestic white columns."*[30] Reeve makes no mention of anything connected to Stand Watie.

Regardless of the circumstances, a historic farmhouse is located on Land Lot 119, District 15, Section 3, about five miles south of downtown Calhoun, Georgia, in Gordon County. The farm on which this structure exists was purchased by Dr. J. Brent Box in the year 2000.

According to Dr. Box, he investigated the claim that Stand Watie was born in the house on his property, but to date, no evidence has been found to confirm this claim. Conversely, no evidence has been found to deny it either.

Interestingly, Dr. Box also maintains that he has researched the construction of the house, and has been informed that the current structure actually has *an earlier log structure at its core,* very similar in style in fact, to that of the Cherokee dwellings of the early 19th century.[31]

Another historic house of interest is the large two-story home of Stand Watie's uncle – Major Ridge. This documented structure is well-preserved in Rome, Georgia, beside the Oostanaula River, approximately 30 miles south of New Echota.

"The Ridge," as he was called, reportedly migrated to the Oothcaloga Valley in what today is north Georgia as a young man. He was one of the first Cherokees to adopt the farming and herding methods of the White man. He acquired Black slaves and established an efficient plantation.

As a *National Historic Landmark,* his former home presently houses the *Chieftains Museum,* an interesting repository of memorabilia and artifacts relating to the Cherokee Indian culture of the 18th and 19th centuries. At the core of this house – which has been renovated numerous times – is the original four-room "dog-trot style" log structure which was built by Ridge after 1794. In the museum is a small wall exhibit with a photograph and information about the life of Ridge's famous nephew, Stand Watie.[32]

The site of the home of Stand Watie's older brother – Elias Boudinot – is located at the northwest corner of the *New Echota* town square on the *New Echota State Historic Site* near Calhoun, Georgia. Boudinot served as the first editor of the ***Cherokee Phoenix*** newspaper, and a short distance from the printing shop where he published the paper, he built a two-story frame house in 1827.

It was at Boudinot's house that, on December 29, 1835, the ***Treaty of New Echota*** was signed by twenty Cherokees, including Major Ridge and Elias Boudinot. Stand Watie and John Ridge later signed the treaty in Washington City (D.C.) on March 1, 1836.

Sadly, today, only corner stones and an abandoned well remain to mark this historic site. The *New Echota State Historic Site* has a visitors center and a museum, and is open daily for a self-guided tour of the historic buildings and archaeological sites.[33]

According to James F. Smith in his book *The Cherokee Land Lottery,* Stand Watie's personal property as an adult was located in the 14th District, 3rd Section in present-day Gordon County, Georgia. Specifically, the property was located in and adjacent to the town of *New Echota* near the confluence of the Coosawattee and Connasauga rivers.

Survey notes indicate that most of Watie's improvements (e.g. buildings, outbuildings and orchards) were located astride the convergence of Land Lots 92, 93, 124 and 125. In addition, some improvements were scattered along a line between Land Lots 93 and 94.[34]

To date, the actual site upon which Stand Watie's home (during his adult years in the Southeast) once stood has not been located or identified. He may possibly have lived near his brother, Elias Boudinot, at *New Echota.* Land Lottery records indicate Stand Watie owned 95 additional acres of improved land in the Oothcaloga Valley as a part of Land Lot 156 in the 15th District and 3rd Section of present-day Gordon County, Georgia. This property might also possibly have been the site of his home in his adult years in the Southeast.

Land Lot 156 is located approximately six miles south of downtown Calhoun, Georgia. Oothcaloga Creek runs north through this tract of land which is just west of the present-day intersection of Highway 41 and Taylor Bridge Road about a mile north of the lower Gordon County line. On November 15, 1836, his improvements were appraised at $2,392.00 by the land lottery surveyors.[35]

Interestingly, Isabella Watie, Stand Watie's third wife, did not migrate with him to the West, and claimed separate improvements on Oothcaloga Creek. These improvements included 80 acres of improved land, buildings, and orchards for which she was paid $3,095. This property quite possibly was owned by Isabella's first husband - Eli Hicks – and willed to her following his death.[36]

As previously mentioned, the site at which *Oothcaloga Mission Station* once stood may be viewed today approximately three miles to the northeast of the Stand Watie property. The mission was located on Land Lot 209. The Ridge and Watie families attended church there from 1822 to 1833.

To visit the *Oothcaloga Mission Station* site, start at the intersection of present-day Highway 41 and Taylor Bridge Road. Proceed north on Highway 41 approximately 1.8 miles to Union Grove Road. Turn right and proceed eastward one mile to Belwood Road and turn left. Proceed north for approximately two-tenths of a mile to a site overgrown with trees and brush on the left side of the road.

The structures at historic *Oothcaloga Mission Station* no longer exist. Sadly, the two-story frame main building fell into ruin in recent years and has virtually disappeared.

At this same location, but on the opposite side of the road, is a dirt road. Approximately 100 yards up that road to the east is old Morrow Cemetery. John Gambold, the first Moravian missionary at *Oothcaloga Mission Station* in 1822, was buried in this cemetery in 1827. Gambold not only was a missionary, but also the only known Revolutionary War veteran buried in Gordon County.[37]

Stand Watie Vestiges In The West

In the former Indian Territory in the West, historic monuments, markers and national historical sites honor Stand Watie in present-day Oklahoma, Arkansas, Missouri and Texas.

The courageous Cherokee's grave may be visited in old Ridge Cemetery (later known as Polson Cemetery) in present-day Delaware County, Oklahoma. Outside the cemetery, a historical marker provides details of his life for travelers.

There are additional markers and monuments at Honey Creek, Old Fort Wayne, Park Hill, Cabin Creek and Doaksville. Three miles east of present-day Gore, Oklahoma, at the original capital of the Cherokee Nation in the West, there is an exhibit honoring the Watie, Boudinot and Ridge families at Tahlonteskee Museum. At Sequoyah's home in Sequoyah County, Oklahoma, there is an exhibit honoring Stand Watie and his cousin John Ridge.

At the Pea Ridge Civil War Battleground in Arkansas, there is an exhibit commemorating Stand Watie's participation in that famous battle.

Endnotes

1/ Don L. Shadburn, **Cherokee Planters In Georgia, 1832-1838** (Roswell, GA: W.H. Wolfe Associates, 1990) 25.

2/ Frank Cunningham, **General Stand Watie's**

Confederate Indians (Norman, OK: University of Oklahoma Press, 1998), 2-4.

3/ Frank Cunningham, *General Stand Watie's Confederate Indians* (Norman, OK: University of Oklahoma Press, 1998), 2-4.

4/ Franks, *Stand Watie*, 2-3.

5/ Franks, *Stand Watie*, 2-3.

6/ Don L. Shadburn, *Cherokee Planters In Georgia, 1832-1838* (Roswell, GA: W.H. Wolfe Associates, 1990) 25.

7/ Roger Aycock, "Stand Watie Strong Leader In Times Of War And Peace," *Rome* (Georgia) *News-Tribune*, 10 October 1971, 8-B.

8/ Franks, *Stand Watie*, 4.

9/ George Magruder Battey, Jr., *A History Of Rome and Floyd County* (Atlanta, GA: Cherokee Publishing Company, 1979) 27,51.

10/ Ibid, 27.

11/ William G. McLoughlin, *Cherokees and Missionaries, 1788-1839* (New Haven, CN: Yale University Press, 1984), 146.

12/ Battey, *A History Of Rome*, 26-28; Franks, *Stand Watie*, 10-12; James F. Smith, *The Cherokee Land Lottery*, "Field Notes" (Atlanta, GA: Records of the Georgia Surveyor-General Department, nd), 256-263.

13/ Battey, *A History Of Rome*, 211-212; Cunningham, *Confederate Indians*, 16; Franks, *Stand Watie*, 8, 37, 9-41; Gary E. Moulton, ed., *The Papers Of Chief John Ross, Volume II, 1840-1866* (Norman, OK: University of Oklahoma Press, 1984), 738.

14/ Franks, *Stand Watie*, 2-3.

15/ Ibid, 13, 14-36.

16/ Franks, *Stand Watie*, 26-27; Shadburn, *Cherokee Planters*, 17-19.

17/ Franks, *Stand Watie*, 8.

18/ Battey, *A History Of Rome*, 89-90.

19/ Franks, *Stand Watie*, 96-97.

20/ Ibid, 114-118.

21/ Cunningham, *Confederate Indians*, 1-3.

22/ Franks, *Stand Watie*, 124-125.

23/ Ibid.

24/ Ibid.

25/ Ibid, 126-212 passim.

26/ George Magruder Battey, Jr., *A History of Rome and Floyd County* (Atlanta, GA: Cherokee Publishing Co., 1979) 47.

27/ Kenny A. Franks, *Stand Watie and the Agony of the Cherokee Nation* (Memphis, TN: Memphis State University Press, 1979), 160-164.

28/ The Sons of Confederate Veterans, General Stand Watie Camp #915 of Calhoun, GA.

29/ "Bray Farm To Hold Annual Open House," *The Calhoun Times and Gordon County News*, 11 March 1998.

30/ Gordon County Bicentennial Committee, *A Historical Tour of Gordon County Celebrating 1976, American's Bicentennial Year* (Calhoun, GA: Published by GCBC, 1976), 1-3; Jewell B. Reeve, *Climb The Hills Of Gordon* (Easley, SC: Southern Historical Press, 1979, c 1962), 218-225.

31/ Telephone conversation between Joe Griffith, the author, and Dr. J. Brent Box, the current owner of the Bray farm, 26 January 2002.

32/ Battey, *A History Of Rome*, 37, 50; Sesquicentennial Committee of the City of Rome, *Rome and Floyd County: An Illustrated History* (Charlotte, NC: The Delmar Company, 1986), 14-15; McLoughlin, *Cherokees and Missionaries*, 1788-1839, 85.

33/ New Echota State Historic Site, *New Echota Self-Guiding Trail Guide*, Calhoun, Georgia.

34/ Franks, *Stand Watie*, 10-12; Shadburn, *Cherokee Planters*, 34; Gary E. Moulton, ed., *The Papers Of Chief John Ross, Volume II, 1840-1866* (Norman, OK: University of Oklahoma Press, 1984), 738.

35/ Franks, *Stand Watie*, 39; Shadburn, *Cherokee Planters*, 34, 38.

36/ Franks, *Stand Watie*, 39-41; Shadburn, *Cherokee Planters*, 13, 34.

37/ Kenneth W. Boyd, *The Historical Markers of North Georgia* (Atlanta, GA: Cherokee Publishing Company, 1993), 84-87, 89-90; John M. Brown, ed., *Yesterdays 1830-1977* (Calhoun, GA: Gordon County Historical Society, Inc., 1977), 8.

(Grateful appreciation is expressed herewith to Joe Griffith who provided the extremely-detailed factual information necessary to complete this article.)

Old West Bandit Bill Miner's Capture in North Georgia

He haunted the stagecoach and train routes throughout the old West and as far as northeast Canada, robbing and pillaging at will, but always with a polite manner. Though captured and imprisoned numerous times, he always escaped to continue his high crimes... that is, until advanced age and infirmity down South in Georgia combined to bring his highwayman days to a close forever.

George Anderson of Jackson County, Kentucky, was born in 1843. Instead of the normal law-abiding life of most citizens, George apparently decided early-on that he was better suited for a life of crime. In fairness, as the son of a sometime school teacher mother and a fly-by-night father who abandoned his family before George was even ten years of age, the youngster was "running against the wind" before he ever reached manhood. Though no one knew it at the time, he would eventually become one of the most notorious criminals in American history.

Without proper supervision, young George quickly earned a reputation as a daredevil and irresponsible youth – traits by which he would live for the rest of his "devil-may-care" life. Throughout his existence, in order to maintain a measure of anonymity, he used a variety of names, including George Morgan, California Billy, George Edwards, George Bud, and Louis Colquhoun, among many others, but he was known most notoriously as "Bill Miner."

Shortly before the U.S. Civil War,

Miner (Anderson) left home for the gold fields of California where he landed a job as a pony express rider. He, however, either quickly tired of this job, or else it tired of him. Whatever the circumstances, instead of "delivering" the mail, Miner flipped the script to "robbing" the mail. He began with stagecoach robberies early in his career, and with the advent of "the iron horse," he graduated to train robberies which were much more lucrative.

The nation watched in earnest, as young Billy-the-Kid, Jesse James, Black Bart, Cole Younger, the Daltons, Butch Cassidy and the Sundance Kid, and many other notorious outlaws of the old West rose to prominence and then faded into the mists of time. Miner was cut from the same cloth and was considered by many to have been even more notorious than most of his counterparts. To be certain, he was one of the last surviving members of this fraternity, and was still robbing trains well into the 20th century.

Despite the criminal nature of his "profession," Miner, for reasons unknown, was oft-times very polite and gentlemanly as he robbed his victims.

Captured – Now middle-aged, Miner is beginning to show some wear and tear in this photo which no doubt was taken following one of his numerous captures for his crimes. The date and place of this photo is unknown, but it is unmistakably Anderson / Miner.

Young & Feisty – With his hat at a jaunty angle, a lit cigar in his mouth, and wearing a nice suit of clothing, a youthful George Anderson, a.k.a. "Bill Miner," had already established himself in a life of crime when he sat (and, quite possibly actually paid) for this photo to be taken. (Photo courtesy of Robert G. McCubbin Collection)

Over time, this manner in which he operated earned him the moniker *"the gentleman bandit."*

Railroad Evangelist

On the cold morning of February 18, 1911, the by-then "elderly" Miner planned to rob Southern Railway's Train No. 36 near White Sulphur Station north of Gainesville, Georgia. The reasoning behind his selection of this train at this site is unknown today. The reason for his travel all the way from Canada down to Georgia is equaling mystifying.

By the time Train No. 36 had steamed out of Atlanta at 12:15 AM earlier that morning, Engineer David J. Fant – who also carried a distinct nickname of *"Evangelist of the Rails"* – was already late due to circumstances beyond

his control. Nevertheless, he was well aware that it would be he who would be held accountable for the lost time, and in the railroad business, "time literally was money." The U.S. Mails and other shippers paid "by the minute," and the faster the railroad was able to make these deliveries to distant destinations, the more money it earned. . . and in some instances, such as with the mail, we're talking big money too.

As Fant steamed steadily toward Gainesville, Georgia, trying his best to make up some of the lost time, he suddenly caught sight of a signalman up ahead in the rails, waving a red lantern back and forth side to side, indicating that the train should halt. This delay near White Sulphur Station was completely unexpected, and had he not been a devout Christian, Fant might have issued a curse under his breath, such was his frustration.

As he slowed No. 36 to a complete halt and the steam chuffed from the engine's idling pistons, Fant not only was exasperated, he was infuriated. On this, of all days, H.E. Hudgens, general superintendent of the railroad was on board in a private car at the rear of No. 36, and now someone was delaying the train's schedule even further.

Fant assumed a lineman or a farmer had discovered a broken rail and was trying to save the train from wrecking. If that proved to be the case, he at least would be extremely thankful.

As he slid down from the engine cab, Fant called out to the signalman, inquiring if the track was being repaired. Out of the darkness, two other men suddenly appeared, and to Fant's shock, he realized they were brandishing revolvers. To the trainman's further shock, they announced the obvious. Southern Railway No. 36 was being robbed!

The three bandits, all wearing masks and calling each other "captain," "number four" and "number five," first ordered Fant's black fireman Rufus Johnson to "disappear," a command to which the normally affable fireman, the whites of his terrified eyes now clearly visible in the darkness, quickly complied.

While the bandit with the lantern – who clearly was the leader of the group – trained his revolver on Fant, the other two robbers walked down to the express car with the intention of releasing the train from that point rearward, so that the robbery could be completed farther up the track, without having to contend with a lot of panicky, confused passengers.

At this point, flagman C.H. Shirley and conductor Walter T. Mooney, both of Atlanta, began walking up to the engine to find out why the train had been halted. Seeing the man with the lantern, Mooney called out but the suspicious-looking signalman merely ignored him. Unaccustomed to such treatment, the conductor, who later recalled that he had assumed he was simply dealing with "a block-head," grabbed the man's

Canada Capture – This photo is believed to have been taken of Anderson / Miner, following a robbery attempt in Ottawa, Canada, and shows an almost elderly bandit. Just as described by countless lawmen and victims alike, Miner often "appeared" to be a friendly grandfatherly-type individual, rather than the dangerous outlaw who was involved in numerous robberies from California to Georgia, and was reportedly responsible for more than one murder. According to a reward posted for him in 1907, he had escaped from New Westminster, British Columbia, Canada in August of that year at the age of 65. He escaped from a Milledgeville, Georgia prison in 1912, so he was criminally-active at least into his 70s. (Photo courtesy of Canadian Marshals Service)

arm and gave him a shove, demanding to know why the train had been stopped.

Even though he was an outlaw, Miner, as explained above, normally was a calm and polite individual – almost respectful. Nevertheless, his tolerance for abusive behavior was nonexistent. He quickly responded to the conductor by sticking a revolver in Mooney's face, and rasped at him that he was being robbed.

Thinking this was all just a bad joke, the conductor exclaimed "Cut out this foolishness. I've got to look after my

$500 Reward

The above reward will be paid for the arrest and detention of WILLIAM (Bill) MINER, alias Edwards, who escaped from the New Westminster Penitentiary, at New Westminster, British Columbia, on the 8th August, 1907, where he was serving a life sentence for train robbery.

DESCRIPTION:

Age 65 years; 138 pounds; 5 feet 8½ inches; dark complexion; brown eyes; grey hair; slight build; face spotted; tattoo base of left thumb, star and ballet girl right forearm; wrist joint-bones large; moles centre of breast, 1 under left breast, 1 on right shoulder, 1 on left shoulder-blade; discoloration left buttock; scars on left shin, right leg, inside, at knee, 2 on neck.

Communicate with

LT.-COL. A. P. SHERWOOD,
Commissioner Dominion Police.
Ottawa, Canada.

Escape Artist – In 1907, the amount of $500.00 was equivalent in value to $16,315.00 in 2024 dollars, so though it was not a huge reward, it was an indication nevertheless that the Canadian Marshal's Service did not take lightly to Miner's escape from their prison. The notorious bandit, however, had become so adept at slipping the shackles of confinement that he eventually earned the moniker "The Grey Fox." At 5 feet 8 and one-half inches and 138 pounds, Miner was anything but imposing, but it is believed his slight build may have aided him in his numerous prison escapes. He felt that no prison of that day and time could confine him indefinitely, and he was correct more often than not. He escaped from the prison in Georgia not once, but twice!

train." Only then when the masked man responded with a string of obscenities and was on the verge of pistol-whipping him, did Mooney realize the full implication of the situation, and that he had just courted disaster.

Loot from the Train

Mooney, if anything, was clearly aware of the time to retreat, and he slowly walked back toward the rear of the train. Once he was beyond Miner's view, however, he quickly and demonstrably – but quietly – instructed Shirley to try to slip past the rear of the train and go get help at White Sulphur. The flagman did just that, running to the little station which was a small flag-stop about a mile away.

Meanwhile, Walter B. Miller, in the express car, had learned of the robbery-in-progress, and was desperately attempting to quickly lock all of the doors to thwart the bandits' efforts, but despite his best intentions, the men entered through a door he had overlooked, and demanded the keys to the two safes. Luckily, the keys were not kept on the train, so the bandits realized they would have to use more powerful measures if any theft of valuables was to occur.

Disappointed but undeterred, Miner, amazingly, had come prepared for this possibility. He brought Fant and a shovel from the engine. With dirt from the outside, the bandits packed dynamite under the safes, lit the fuses, fled the vicinity of the car, and were lucky to have done so. The resulting explosion was so immense, it tore holes through the roof and sides of the car, shattered all the windows, and the concussion was even great enough to extinguish the train's lights. To the bandits' abject disappointment, when the smoke had cleared, only the smaller of the two safes had been blown open. The larger one still stood, firmly locked.

With time running out, "the captain" filled a bag with what little "loot" was available, and then he and his two accomplices semi-panicked, running into the woods. They nevertheless made good on their escape, *"disappearing as if the earth had swallowed them up,"* according to a subsequent newspaper report.

Once the men had departed, Fant,

still with live steam in his damaged engine and rolling stock which was still operational, chuffed his way to the nearby community of Lula where he telegraphed a report of the robbery to railroad officials. Ten minutes prior to his report, flagman Shirley had reached the White Sulphur Station, where he had hurriedly also reported news of the robbery to local law enforcement authorities.

As could be expected under the circumstances, initial reports of the robbery became twisted and distorted as the news was passed from person to person. Two mythical additional bandits were included in early reports as having been passengers on the train. The gang's escape was described in various accounts as involving an automobile, a buggy, and even as involving a ride hitched on the underside of the very train they had robbed.

Though no complete accounting of the stolen items/money was ever officially made, railroad authorities estimated that at the very least, approximately $800.00 in U.S. currency, $770.00 in Mexican pesos, an unknown amount in several other foreign currencies, a pair of pearl ear screws, and a watch were taken by the thieves.

Interestingly, had the bandits known what they had left behind in the larger safe which their detonation had failed to open, they undoubtedly would have been thunderstruck. Still intact within the confines of that container, $65,000 in gold and cash had been left untouched, an amount equivalent to $2,166,000.00 in 2024 dollars. It would have ranked among the most valuable robberies in U.S. history, and in that day and time that amount was a king's ransom.

Nevertheless, even the $800.00 in U.S. currency in Miner's loot was a

Hall Robbery Site – The late Ray Shaw, former U.S. Postman in Gainesville, Georgia, was photographed in 1987 at the site at which Southern Railway's Train #36 was flagged down and robbed by Miner and his accomplices near White Sulphur, Georgia, on a cold February morning in 1911. (Photo by Olin Jackson)

considerable pay-day for the bandits. It was the approximate equivalent of $26,660.00 in 2024 which certainly was not a small amount in that day, particularly for paupers such as "the gentleman bandit" and his accomplices.

Partners in Crime

Miner had recruited his two deputies in the Gainesville robbery – Charlie Hunter and James Handford – in Pennsylvania and Virginia respectively, in 1910. Hunter, a thirty-year-old Irishman from Michigan agreed, after some persuasion, to accompany the old bandit to a locale in the South, "to try holding up a Southern train." The pair worked for two months in a Virginia sawmill where they completed their group by recruiting 33-year-old Handford from Nebraska.

The trio had moved on to Georgia to prepare for what was almost unthinkable at that time – a Wild West-style train holdup in the East. The week before they finally struck Southern Railway's No. 36, Hunter had pawned Miner's watch in Atlanta, using the money

White Sulphur Depot – White Sulphur Road at the intersection with the old Southern Railroad in Hall County was photographed in 1987. In 1911, the train depot at White Sulphur stood at the approximate location of the warning signal pictured here. It was to this point that flagman C.H. Shirley ran to report the robbery of Southern Railway's Train #36. (Photo by Olin Jackson)

to buy whiskey and the lantern they had used in the robbery.

When the site was later investigated by law enforcement and Southern Railway authorities, they discovered a "track wrench" at Miner's camp in the woods, clearly indicating that he and his men had at least considered the terrible option of a derailment in order to halt Train No. 36. Had that occurred, the results obviously would have been devastating, with the loss of many lives instead of merely stolen valuables.

The first reports of the incident were met with incredulity by a disbelieving Gainesville populace. According to newspaper accounts of that day, most of the townspeople dismissed the news of the robbery, thinking it was a joke. Most were dumbfounded when they learned the robbery had in fact actually occurred.

"The truth dawned at last," the local newspaper intoned, *"and they were confronted with the fact that here in a free, civilized, God-fearing, and law-abiding community, a train robbery was committed* that would abash the most God-forsaken Wild West country to be found. That such a daring hold-up could take place right at our doors was inconceivable."

The Atlanta newspapers had a field day with the event. The ***Atlanta Journal*** filled the first two pages of the February 18 issue with the news. The train crew, all of whom were Atlanta residents, were interviewed and their photographs published.

Pursued by Lawmen

When the report of the robbery reached the Hall County Police Office in the early morning hours of February 18, Sheriff W.A. Crow was home sick with the mumps. He arose from his sick bed to organize a posse by telephone.

Assembling his deputies, Crow gave them a pep talk: "I want you to go out into the country and mountains now, and don't come back here until you bag these train robbers," he instructed. "Bring them back alive if you can.... but if not, just bring them along anyway."

To their surprise, the initial efforts to locate the bandits proved absolutely futile. Deputy Sheriff Little, with the help of county officials and railroad detectives, began a search of Gainesville, to see if the robbers might have come into town to try to mix with the populace.

Though bloodhounds were to be used with the posse to track the men, the matter was delayed considerably awaiting the hounds which had to be brought in from Gwinnett County. By the time the dogs arrived, the rain and pepper and snuff reportedly scattered by Miner and his two accomplices had effectively obscured the trail.

To Sheriff Crow's posse were added the Pinkertons, a deputy U.S. marshal, and detectives of the Southern Railway and Express. All local law enforcement officials also went into the field, using the promise of a $1,500 reward (almost more than the bandits actually took) offered by the State of Georgia and Southern Railway, to enlist men and boys for an intensive search. Despite all these efforts, the ultimate capture of the train robbers was accomplished not by this mass of investigators, hounds and posses as the editor of the 1911 *Dahlonega Nugget* would later explain, but rather "*by mountaineers skilled in tracking.*"

Only a few days after the robbery, the search efforts were losing steam. Officials conducting the man-hunt were sitting around the main room of the old Dixie Hunt Hotel – their headquarters in Gainesville – so despondent, that they hardly noticed when the telephone began ringing. When one of the lawmen finally picked up the receiver, the caller turned out to be ex-Lumpkin County Sheriff Jim Davis calling from Dahlonega to announce that he believed he had found the train robbers in an abandoned house nearby. How the bandits had made it through the rough north Georgia mountains toward Dahlonega in such a short time is unknown today. Both their mounts and their maps must have been exceptional, because they had to have been making really good travel time through some really rough country where roads were almost nonexistent. The bandits almost certainly would have avoided the few actual roads that were available because they would

How the bandits had made it through the rough north Georgia mountains toward Dahlonega in such a short time is unknown today.

have anticipated watchmen along these routes.

Davis had learned of the men earlier, and both he and Lumpkin County Sheriff John Sergeant detected suspicious circumstances almost immediately. The men claimed to be prospectors and had overnighted at Sergeant's hotel in downtown Dahlonega. However, between them, the three strangers had no prospecting tools other than one broken and split shovel.

When Lumpkin County resident Pete Carmichael later reported the three men near his farm, Sergeant became even more suspicious. He set out for the Carmichael place where he picked up two sets of tracks. At that point, Miner apparently decided to separate from his accomplices, feeling his best opportunity for escape lay in solitary flight. Sergeant, nevertheless decided to follow Minor's single set of tracks.

Before setting out in pursuit, Sergeant assembled a posse which included the aforementioned Jim Davis and Davis' two sons – Rufus and Joe. The trail at length led the group to the Elbert Kendall farm some 17 miles northwest of Dahlonega in the present-day Nimberwill community. When the posse arrived, the Kendalls reported that they did indeed have a male boarder who was sleeping on a cot upstairs in a loft.

Davis and his sons reportedly mounted the stairs where they found a person who appeared to be asleep.

Taking On Supplies – The home of Merritt M. London which formerly existed at the intersection of Long Branch Road and Highway 60 in Lumpkin County, is pictured in this primitive print. While fleeing lawmen in February of 1911 following the robbery of Southern Railway's Train #36, George Anderson (alias Bill Miner) and his accomplices reportedly paused at the country grocery in front of this home to purchase supplies. Pictured in this photo are: Merritt M. London (with white beard and hat in center). His wife, Mary Neisler London stands beside the tree. Sons Frank (in the wagon) and Bob (2nd from left) also appear. The identity of the individual in overalls is unknown. (Photo courtesy of Annie Lou Dobbs of Toccoa, GA, daughter of Frank and Annie Kemp London)

The historic Merritt M. London home-place which once stood at the intersection of Long Branch Road and GA Highway 60 in Lumpkin County was photographed here in 1993 just a few years prior to its unfortunate demolition. (Photo by Olin Jackson)

As Davis pulled the blanket away, however, the stranger quickly trained a .45 revolver on him. Davis's salvation was found in his two sons who had a shotgun and a .22 rifle directed at the old man who in fact turned out to be George Anderson, alias Bill Miner, though at the time, the lawmen had no idea of the notorious nature of the man.

Rufus Davis was still alive in 1987, and lived in Cartersville, Georgia. Though in his nineties at the time, Rufus still remembered details of this day. He also still possessed the set of handcuffs used to restrain Miner after his capture.

Jim Davis eventually collected the reward offered for the capture of the train robbers *(Miner's accomplices in the robbery had been arrested earlier in the day prior to Miner's arrest.)* Sheriff Sergeant unsuccessfully sued Davis for part of the reward, claiming the last capture was really his work.

Bandit Celebrity

Despite all the clamor of the event, the detectives, sheriffs, and other officials in the manhunt still had no idea who they had actually captured even after Miner had been clapped into chains. Though the old bandit had identified himself by his real name – George Anderson – and all the official Georgia police and criminal records relating to him identified him by that name, they still had no idea who they had actually captured.

It was probably the first time in many years that Miner/Anderson had used his actual name for identification purposes. Interestingly, when the name by which he was commonly known – "Bill Miner" – was finally discovered by the authorities, it was assumed that was his actual name, and that the moniker "George Anderson" was an alias.

While waiting in the Lumpkin

Dixie Hunt Man-Hunt – The posse created to search for the bandits who robbed Southern Railway's Train #36 was headquartered at the Dixie Hunt Hotel in Gainesville, Georgia. This structure, built in 1882 on the corner of Main and Spring streets, was photographed here in 1900 just a few years prior to the robbery. A portion of this building still exists as of this writing (2024) in downtown Gainesville. (Photo courtesy of GA Dept. of Archives & History, Atlanta)

County jail, Anderson (Miner) talked of the great potential of Dahlonega's inactive gold mines in such a way that the *Dahlonega Nugget* published his remarks as if he were a prominent geologist, stroking local civic pride. It is ironic to note that Miner began his life of crime at the site of the second great gold rush in California and ended it at the site of the first major U.S. gold rush in Dahlonega, Georgia.

After his capture in Dahlonega, Miner was transported to Gainesville for trial. His arrival by automobile in that town was greeted by crowds of hundreds of people, gathered as if to see a street parade, and caused Miner to remark "They must think I am a bear." *(Amusingly, the citizens gawking at Miner were doing so only because he was a train robber; they as yet were still unaware that he was a notorious outlaw.)*

A special session of the Hall Coun-ty Superior Court was held on March 3, 1911, to try the train robbers. Charlie Hunter confessed his role in the robbery and became the state's chief witness against Miner. Hunter received a sentence of fifteen years, but escaped within a year, and surprisingly, no effort was ever made to recapture him. James Handford also pleaded guilty, received the same sentence, and was granted a parole in 1918.

Miner however, differed from his henchmen in that he demanded, for unknown reasons, a jury trial. Despite the fact that witness after witness testified against him, Miner sat impassively. Some observers maintained that *"the gentleman bandit"* believed his almost flawlessly polite manners might carry the day in the trial and somehow set him free, but at the trial's conclusion, the Hall County jury steadfastly returned a verdict of *"Guilty."*

Miner's only show of emotion in the verdict came when Howard Thompson, special attorney for the express company, spoke of the dynamite used in the express car potentially *"blowing into eternity sleeping women and children on the train."* A reporter witnessed Miner answer that charge *"with a most vengeful, glaring, and hateful glance."*

When Judge Sims sentenced Miner to twenty years in prison, the old outlaw reportedly thanked him, stood up and turned to a group of college girls and ladies and proceeded to provide a moral for the story they had witnessed unfolding before them: *"When one breaks the law, one must expect to pay the penalty. I am old, but during all my life, I have found the golden rule the best guide to man in this world,"* he said. He then smiled and sat down.

Though one of the most cold-blooded and notorious thugs in the colorful history of train robberies in the U.S., Miner is routinely described as *"looking more 'grandfatherly' than criminal."* Yet, this kindly-looking old man reportedly had methodically gunned down virtually all of a group of posse-men pursuing him from the scene of a stagecoach robbery in 1881 in California. He also was identified as associated with numerous other capital crimes throughout his life.

Books and even modern feature-length movies have been made about Bill Miner, some of them actually portraying him as somehow justified for some or all of his crimes. Though this final event in Georgia ended forever

> *A reporter witnessed Miner answer that charge "with a most vengeful, glaring, and hateful glance."*

Miner's stagecoach/train robbing days, it did not bring to a close his ability to continue to cause mayhem and galvanize public attention.

Escape Artist

Above and beyond his notoriety as a train robber, Miner was also literally a legend as an escape artist. Prior to his crimes in Georgia, he had escaped from numerous prisons in Canada and elsewhere and often boasted that no prison could hold him indefinitely. He had been so successful that he had earned a second moniker of *"The Grey Fox"* from the news media.

William Pinkerton, head of the well-known detective agency of the same name, was a spectator at the Gainesville trial, and warned the press that he doubted that any Georgia prison could hold Miner very long. The Pinkerton Detective Agency is a private security guard and detective agency established around 1850 in the United States by Scottish-born American Allan Pinkerton and Chicago attorney Edward Rucker. It became famous when its men claimed to have foiled the *Baltimore Plot* to assassinate President-elect Abraham Lincoln in 1861. Lincoln subsequently hired Pinkerton agents to act as his personal security during the U.S. Civil War.

William Pinkerton's comments proved prophetic. Miner escaped not once, but twice from prison in Milledgeville, Georgia, after his incarceration there. Had it not been for his aging

Sheriff's Posse – Photographed in front of the old Lumpkin County Jail (which still stands in Dahlonega as of this writing in 2024) are: (L to R) Sheriff James M. "Jim" Davis, Gordon Davis, Joe Davis, William S. "Bill" Davis, Charles C. Davis, and Rufus Tilman "R.T." Davis. George Anderson (alias Bill Miner) was captured by newly-elected Sheriff John Sergeant, former Sheriff Jim Davis, and Davis's two sons – Rufus and Joe – in Lumpkin County's Nimblewill community. Following this capture, Miner was incarcerated in this jail. (Photo courtesy of C.C. Davis, Jr.)

condition and lack of resistance to exposure and the elements after his escapes, he might not have been recaptured. If anything, the man was just short of amazing.

Following the trial in Gainesville, the convicted trio was sent to Georgia's huge prison camp in Newton County. Life in the camp, however, did not suit Miner. A personal appeal to Robert E. Davison, then chairman of the State Prison Board, finally earned him a transfer to the state prison farm for the infirm in Milledgeville.

While at the farm, Miner recruited the efforts of convicted murderers John B. Watts and Tom H. Moore for an escape. Late one night, Watts somehow managed to remove the peep-hole apparatus out of the door of his cell, and squeeze through the opening. He took the keys and a pistol from a sleeping guard, and released Miner and Moore. The trio made a clean getaway.

Following his escape, Miner was even brazen enough to mail a letter to Robert Davison, thanking him for giving him his opportunity for escape. *"My dear sir,"* he wrote, *"I want to thank you for your kindness in putting me at Milledgeville. My dear sir, don't trust a prisoner, don't matter how sick he is or makes out he is. Yours truly, B. Miner"*

The chairman's embarrassment was also the embarrassment of the state of Georgia and the newspapers and citizens as well who had urged that the *"sick old man be allowed to die in peace"* at the lightly-guarded prison farm. The *Atlanta Journal* proclaimed that *"wherever Bill Miner is, he is probably grinning and the joke is on Georgia."*

It wasn't long however, before Miner was recaptured. He and Moore had headed for Augusta, Georgia. At a tiny community nearby called Keysville, a J.W. Whittle overheard a railroad brakeman talking to two "bums" in

Old Jail Today – The old Lumpkin County Jail in Dahlonega, Georgia, in which Miner was incarcerated was photographed in 1993. (Photo by Olin Jackson)

a boxcar. When it was realized that the two matched a description of escaped convicts, Whittle summoned help.

The boxcar was shortly thereafter surrounded by a posse, and Miner recaptured yet again. Moore, however, chose not to return – at least not alive. He reportedly fired a single shot in the vicinity of the posse, and then in turn was killed by a single shot to the face. Inside the boxcar, members of the posse found dynamite and fuses which Miner explained *"were good for catching fish."* Old Bill had been a breath away from yet another train robbery, and this time, it appeared that he actually intended to follow through with the derailment idea.

Returned to his prison cell in Milledgeville, Miner boasted that he would escape again at the first opportunity. His guards, understandably, took no chances against any future embarrassment. One can only imagine their total humiliation when, on the morning of June 27, 1912, they found *The Grey Fox* gone yet again, his ankle and arm bracelets locked to his bunk, the window bars sawed out, and the bedding made into a rope which he had used to climb to the ground. It was literally the

stuff of legends, and one of the reasons for the notoriety associated with Miner.

Accompanied by convicts W.J. Windencamp and W.M. Wiggins this time, Miner was once again making good his escape. The trio took a boat into the Oconee River, with the plan of reaching a port where they could ship out as deck hands. However, the boat reportedly capsized, drowning Windencamp. It is not known today for certain if that was the actual circumstance.

For three days afterwards, Miner and Wiggins were lost in an almost endless boggy swamp near Oconee, Georgia, living on blackberries and unable to find safe drinking water. When they finally came out near Toombsboro, they offered no resistance to a posse which found them at a home begging for breakfast. Miner's escape this time had lasted only five days, and his age and failing constitution were fast catching up with him.

Last Days

The reception the old outlaw received upon his return to Milledgeville this time even exceeded Bill's wildest imaginings. Driven in an open, heavily-guarded automobile and shackled securely, Bill was met in the downtown area by an extremely large crowd of admiring townspeople who reportedly literally applauded him and passed him money and cigars.

Always gracious, Miner stood up in the car and waved his hat to his fans. The ***Union Recorder*** claimed that *"for a short time, it looked like a hero had come to the city instead of a man who had wrecked and robbed trains."* This, however, was the last adventure for the grizzled old *Grey Fox* who had been involved in thievery from coast to coast.

Today, the exact circumstances of Miner's last days are unknown, but it is believed the hunger, exposure to the weather, and contaminated water he consumed during his escape, apparently took their toll on him, causing him to lapse into illness.

The *Atlanta Journal*, learning that Miner was near death in September of 1913, interviewed him one last time. Before they could get the story printed, however, the *Angel of Death* visited the cell of the *Grey Fox*, and spirited him away, granting him permanent freedom at last.

Though accounts of his actual burial site vary today, the final resting place of Bill Miner is in the old city cemetery known as *Memory Hill* in Milledgeville. Miner's grave is marked with a simple headstone, and is found on the southeast side of *Memory Hill* where the cemetery slopes toward Fishing Creek, a place where many convicts were buried when the penitentiary was located at Milledgeville. His headstone bears his pseudonym *Bill Miner*, since no one at the time was certain of his true name.

Treasure-hunters still ply the railroads and other sites suspected of holding portions of the loot Miner supposedly left behind somewhere in Hall or Lumpkin counties in north Georgia. Though almost all of the money and valuables stolen by Miner and his henchmen in the robbery in Gainesville supposedly were recovered, there is no absolute certainty of this having occurred. In order to rebuild and maintain the public's confidence in their services following a robbery, purveyors of valuables quite often will report a full recovery of stolen items when no such recovery actually occurred.

Bill Miner and his two accomplices had also gone their separate ways when they were captured in Lumpkin County,

Escape-Proof Prison – The grave of notorious outlaw Bill Miner in the convicts burial section of Memory Hill Cemetery in Milledgeville, Georgia is pictured. His grave was one prison from which Miner's mortal remains finally could not escape.

and the report of their capture did not include any description of any recovered valuables. Miner supposedly later provided Sheriff Crow (of Hall County) with directions to two caches of loot, but one would have to question the authenticity of this action as well, since there was virtually nothing to be gained by him in such a revelation. There were reports of the discovery of several caches the men had left which were later supposedly revealed.

Bill Miner was the subject of a major motion picture in 1983 entitled *"The Grey Fox,"* starring Richard Farnsworth – who is a dead ringer in appearance for Miner – in the title role.

Today, the site of the famed train robbery in north Georgia is still a quiet peaceful area of limited inhabitation. It bears mute testimony to the events of February 18, 1911 with the crossing at White Sulphur being named *"Bill Miner Crossing."*

(Grateful appreciation is expressed herewith to Robert S. Davis, Jr. for most of the research and details necessary for this article.)

The Gun-Fights and Mysterious Life Of Lumpkin Pioneer Harrison Riley

In the tumultuous days of the 19th Century, one of the early pioneers to the gold fields of Lumpkin County, Georgia, became renowned as a wealthy plantation owner and businessman, and even more so as an aggressive fighter who wasn't averse to a shoot-out on the town square if necessary.

Harrison W. Riley was a name which invoked a measure of admiration and respect, but also fear and trepidation in the hearts and minds of some of his contemporaries. He possibly was born dirt poor, but when he died, he quite likely was one of the richest men in all of north Georgia. Upon his final breath in 1874 at the age of 70, those with whom he had done battle in his lifetime undoubtedly felt not remorse, but relief, and possibly even a measure of vengeance.

Riley was the kind of person who evoked strong emotions from almost anyone who knew him, whether it be respect from the electorate, love from the women he squired, or hatred from his political adversaries and challengers in general. No one was neutral about Harrison Riley.

At least a portion of any ill feelings was based upon simple jealousy. Riley was never one to "rest upon his laurels." He was a man of constant action. As such, he was successful in his pursuit of public office as well as in the accumulation of wealth during his lifetime. These qualities singled him out for acclaim, but also made him a target for animosity as well.

Several details and characteristics of Harrison W. Riley's life – even if taken singly – would make him considerably noteworthy in the history of north Georgia:

1/ If one considers both hard cash and real estate, Riley undoubtedly was the wealthiest man at least in the northeast Georgia region for a number of years.

2/ The full extent of all of his former real estate holdings possibly will never be known, due to the fact that a number of them were placed in the names of individuals he loved and cherished. It is known for certain, however, that he once owned several substantial plantations – including slaves – in Georgia, and at least one in Alabama.

3/ Throughout his early life, Riley had coveted a military position of high authority. Though he was never actually commissioned as an officer in either the U.S. military or the Confederate Army, he assumed the rank of – and was addressed as – "General" from the 1860s until his death. At one point in the 1860s, he assured Georgia authorities that he could raise a 1,000-man army for the Confederacy from the northeast region of the state.

4/ Riley was known far and wide as a "scrapper" who would fight with fists, dirks, or firearms and both challenge others and defend himself in the legal arena at the drop of a hat. He neither gave any "quarter" to his opponents, nor asked for any for himself. The court records of Lumpkin County are replete with accounts of his numerous battles – both legal and physical. He was fearless, and did not hesitate to engage even in pitched gunfights, several of which were waged on the Dahlonega, Georgia, town square with his enemies.

5/ When he died, Riley reportedly left a hidden treasure that, as of this writing, has never been found, or at least never *publicly acknowledged* if it was discovered. It could conceivably be worth millions of dollars today and is still sometimes sought by treasure hunters. The property around his former home in White County resembles a lunar landscape today as a result of years of excavations made by treasure hunters in search of that gold.

6/ Riley served in the Georgia General Assembly as a representative from the Lumpkin County area for a number of terms. In fact, for a period of 30 years, it was a rare event when he did not hold public office. He so competitively sought service in the political arena that one of his outraged opponents once attempted to assassinate him as he stooped to light his pipe from the coals of a hearth.

7/ And finally, the aspect of his life which created the most notoriety of all, involved the numerous females with whom he consorted throughout his life. He reportedly was the father of numerous children, by several different women, and not once was he ever legally married.

Early Life

The first thirty years of the life of Harrison W. Riley are a mystery which quite possibly will never be solved. It is known, however, that he was born in North Carolina circa 1804.

One early newspaper article states that Harrison Riley was *"a penniless orphan boy"* when he came to Dahlonega. This statement, however, cannot be completely accurate. Riley certainly was not penniless and he was not an orphan, although it is possible that his father pre-deceased him at an early age. His mother, Mrs. Susan Riley, was still living and she along with another son, Jesse L. Riley, moved to Dahlonega at the same time as did Harrison.

It is also possible that there was a third Riley brother in the group. They were joined a few years later (about 1837) by a sister and a brother-in-law, Mary P. and John M. Harris, and their children.

A portion of the inscription on Susan Riley's grave marker reads *"She was born in Person Co., N.C. about the year 1787"* (1787 - Aug. 3, 1856). A search of the public records in Person Co., N.C. reveals that a William Riley posted a marriage bond there on January 24, 1802 (actual records of marriages were not recorded until years later).

William Riley owned property and lived in the Deep Creek section of Person County, and the Riley name may still be found there today. Harrison Riley's family apparently followed the migratory trend of settlers moving from east to west in early pioneer days, traveling from North Carolina to Monroe

Co., Tennessee prior to the family's move down into north Georgia.

Riley's sister, Mary, whose husband John M. Harris had died July 2, 1848 on his way home from the Mexican War, stated in a widow's pension application that she and her late husband were married about November 20, 1833 in Monroe Co., Tennessee. Mary was only 18 years of age at the time of her marriage and it is highly unlikely that she would have moved from North Carolina to Tennessee without her family, so the entire Riley family – including Harrison – most probably lived in Tennessee in the early 1830s prior to moving to the gold fields of north Georgia.

Lumpkin County at the time of Harrison Riley's arrival was a frontier land. Andrew Cain's *History of Lumpkin County (1832-1932)* describes it as follows:

"The rush to the mines brought into the country thousands of men of great diversity and character, many of whom were of that reckless class who disregard the laws of God and man. . . .Gamblers and swindlers of all kinds thronged hither to cheat the miners out of their easily gotten gold. Drinking, gambling and fighting were rife and the laws were little known and less cared for."

Harrison Riley was one of the first settlers in Lumpkin, arriving shortly after the county was created on December 3, 1832, following the first land lottery from the Indian property confiscated by the state of Georgia. The state was insistent upon acquiring the land in order to enlarge its scope and gain access to the gold fields in the northern portion of the state. Riley no doubt had traveled to Lumpkin to seek his fortune either directly or indirectly via the gold fields.

According to period newspaper accounts, Riley arrived *"before a stick of* *timber was cut where the city of Dahlonega is situated today."* At that time, the area which ultimately grew into the city of Dahlonega was a deep and dark wilderness, exceedingly difficult to penetrate, particularly since there simply were no roads.

Commercial Investment

It was the perfect situation for an opportunist vagabond such as Riley. He apparently decided that instead of back-breaking labor for himself, he would let others do the dirty work of finding the gold, and he would provide a place for the miners to come to spend their newly-discovered riches. It was infinitely easier to find gold with a deck of cards or by the sale of price-inflated merchandise, than it was with a pick and shovel. Riley, if anything, was always clever and resourceful.

Interestingly, it wasn't long before he erected the first store in Dahlonega on the east side of the town square, and soon began to accumulate his vast fortune. The origin of the funds required for this early mercantile development is a matter of high suspicion today.

It has been speculated over the years that Riley's foundational funds which he used to initially begin his business endeavors in Dahlonega could have originated from a 1838 triple-murder in South Carolina. In a sale transaction involving slaves, three travelers were returning home from Dahlonega one day with their funds from the sale when they reportedly stopped to camp for the night at the Georgia border. Suddenly, out of the darkness two horsemen appeared (according to later courtroom testimony) and set upon the three campers, killing them horribly by hacking them to death with a hatchet and then stealing their funds which supposedly were in gold dust. (Since very little coinage – and certainly no paper money – existed in that locale at that day and time.)

Lawmen eventually tracked – to Dahlonega – a suspect to the crime who, interestingly, turned out to be one of Riley's slaves named Isaac. They charged him with the crime after they discovered him in possession of a quantity of the gold from the travelers. How that particular gold was determined to have belonged to the travelers is unknown today.

In a bid to save himself from the gallows, Isaac testified at his trial in South Carolina that no lesser a man than Harrison Riley had promised to grant him (the slave) his freedom, and to even share a portion of the stolen gold with him (which must have been fairly substantial) if he would commit the crime.

Whether a portion of the bargain Riley supposedly struck with his slave involved the murder of the victims, or merely the theft of their money, is unknown today. Regardless, Isaac ultimately was convicted of the crime, but his testimony against his owner was not believed to be credible – at least not by those jurors – and Riley was never charged with any crime.

It was only a very short time later, that Riley the businessman began construction of his gold rush-era expansive hotel on the south side of the Dahlonega public square and also the accumulation of acreage all around north Georgia, as well as in Alabama. The sudden origin of the funds for these investments is unknown today.

Illegitimate Family

As for Riley's prolific fatherhood, many of his children reportedly were born among 14 slaves which he owned.

Don't Tread on Me – Harrison Riley of Dahlonega, Georgia, carried the visage of a man which suggested very troubled times for any challengers. Though a fearful foe to his detractors and political opponents, he, nevertheless, reportedly was kind and strongly supportive of the women and children in his very extended family. (Photo courtesy of the GA Dept. of Archives & History, Atlanta, GA)

Some estimated he had as many as 100 children, both black and white, but the actual figure was more likely 25 to 30. Most of his life, he didn't live with any of his women, maintaining separate residences for them and taking good care of them and their children. In his will bequeathing property to various people, he didn't refer to any of the children as "his children," but rather as the children of whatever mother had birthed them.

The *1834 State Census of Lumpkin County* shows *#374 Harrison W. Riley, head of a household of 6*. The *1838 Census*, however, indicates that Riley's fortunes had improved considerably in the previous four years. He was listed as the head of a household of 18, 14 of whom were slaves.

Interestingly, there also was a "*Wm. H. Riley*" listed in the *1834 Census* as the head of household #379, a family of 3. The exact relationship between Harrison W. Riley and William H. Riley is unclear today, although there are indications that they were related – if not the same person. On June 1, 1835, William H. Riley purchased one-half of town lot #113 located at the present intersection of South Chestatee and West Main Streets and erected a tavern. Jesse L. Riley, Harrison's brother, purchased the same property on June 6, 1837 and Harrison W. Riley acquired it on March 4, 1841.

Riley had previously acquired a one-half interest in city lots #96 and #97 which were located on the corner of South Chestatee Street and the town square, lot #110 (*in front of the present-day Smith House*) and lots #111 and #115 (*the southwest corner of the town square up to West Main Street*). He and John M. McAfee bought them at a sheriff's sale on April 7, 1840 for $1,739.00, a substantial sum at that time equal to approximately $61,735.00 in 2024 dollars.

Riley's brother Jesse bought out McAfee's share on April 15, 1841 for $1,000.00, and he subsequently sold his interest in this property to Harrison at a later date. With full control of this town property, Riley then began construction of a substantial hotel on the courthouse square (city lots #96 and #97) which must have looked like a palace in the wilderness at that time in the 1840s.

As for Riley's prolific fatherhood, many of his children reportedly were born among 14 slaves which he owned.

Eagle Hotel

When completed, the Riley or "Eagle Hotel" was almost half a block long and had two elliptically arched doorways, six dormers with arched windows, and paneled rooms with hand-crafted mantels and heart-pine wainscoting.

His entrepreneurial skills growing by the day, the shrewd businessman no doubt realized that he could easily make back the cost of construction of the hotel in just a few short years with all the easy money floating around with the many miners and travelers who would frequent the Riley businesses as a result of their conveniently accessible location on the town square in the county seat of government.

According to Andrew Cain's *History of Lumpkin County, 1832-1932*, there once was even an upstairs bridge across the dusty road which provided easy access for Riley's hotel patrons to also patronize his tavern and gambling establishment (which once existed from the southwest corner of the town square up to West Main Street). The Eagle Hotel was such a fine structure that it was blue-printed through the federal government's *Historic Buildings Survey* for the *Library of Congress*.

Legal Battles

The land records of Lumpkin County offer an overview of Riley's rapid accumulation of property, but another section of the courthouse records – the *Writs and Bonds* – tell another side of the story.

Almost from the day he arrived in the gold fields, Riley was involved in legal scraps or physical altercations with a long line of competitors, swindlers, and just careless businessmen. As a result, he was required to regularly appear in court – either in response to a suit he had filed, or in answer to a suit filed against him by someone else – for the rest of his life.

Interestingly, most of the suits filed against Riley were for *Assault and Battery*. One man suing Riley for $5,000.00 on March 10, 1838, described the beating Riley gave him as follows:

"Harrison W. with force and arms, to wit with swords, knives, dirks, sticks, rocks, fists, hands, feet and teeth furiously and violently assaulted and beat your petitioner and... violently caught hold of your petitioner and threw him upon the ground and then and there struck your petitioner a great many violent blows on the head and diverse parts of the body with the rocks, fists, sticks and weapons aforesaid and shook and pulled about your petitioner and.... pulled a great quantity of hair from your petitioner's head by means of which said premise and ill treatment your petitioner was then and there greatly hurt, bruised and wounded and became and was sick, sore, lame and disordered so much that the life of your petitioner was then and there greatly despaired of...."

The man said that he had spent $50 on medical treatment and was unable to work for a month. The court ruled in favor of the plaintiff but awarded him only $100.00 in damages plus $14.31¼ in court costs, a fine Riley easily paid.

Another suit filed against him on March 8, 1853, stated that Riley had *".. with force and arms assaulted your petitioner. ... with his fists and a large stick with great violence struck your petitioner upon the head and upon divers parts of the body by means whereof your petitioner*

was then and there greatly hurt, beat and bruised and then and there became sick, sore and lame..."

This petitioner asked for the more substantial sum of $500.00 in damages. The most interesting part of this suit was the fact that the petitioner was a woman! Even more interesting, the court ruled in Riley's favor this time.

Harrison Riley was even sued May 29, 1856 by a slave owner named Daniel Weaver for alleged damages to *"a certain Negro man slave named Cesar (sic) of great value to wit of the value of one thousand dollars."* Weaver sued for $1,000.00 and swore that Riley *"...confined said negro man in the common jail of said county for a long space of time to wit twenty-four hours. ... petitioner was forced and obliged to and did necessary expend divers large sums of money. .... the sum of two hundred dollars in and amount recovering possession of said Negro man...."*

Once again the court ruled in Riley's favor. The voluminous court records indicate that Riley was indeed constantly in legal suits, waging battle with many and varied plaintiffs, but he won more suits than he lost. And in fairness to the man, it appears that many of the suits were brought against him simply because of his reputation and the fact that he was extremely wealthy, making him a good target.

Powerful Political Figure

Though it is clear from public records that Riley had many enemies, he also had a devoted group of friends and followers as well. He ran for and was elected to a number of different public offices. In fact, for a period of thirty years (1843-1873) he was seldom out of public office.

His first elected position in Lumpkin County was that of state

Political Headquarters – Riley's Eagle Hotel from which he once waged a gun battle with a foe served as his headquarters for many years, and was built by him at least as early as the 1840s. Renamed the Besser Hotel by a later owner, it was the site of many political campaigns and celebrations during his lifetime. (Photo courtesy of GA Dept. of Archives & History, Atlanta)

representative. He was first elected in 1843 and served until 1845. He was again elected and served 1849-1851 and 1853-1855.

In 1858 Riley ran for and was elected to the office of state senator. It appears that he was re-elected in 1860 since the next senator was Weir Boyd who took office in 1861 when Lumpkin, White and Dawson were combined to form the Thirty-Second Senatorial District.

It was about this time that Riley's political policies almost cost him his life. There are several versions of the assassination attempt made on his life after a particularly bitter campaign. Andrew Cain's *History of Lumpkin County* describes the incident as follows:

"During his long and stormy career, Riley received only one bullet; and that was planted in his shoulder by a political enemy. In that day and time everybody who smoked used a cob pipe or a clay pipe - the kind that was molded by Mrs. Rachel Medford and sold all over this section at a cent a piece. Now Riley was fully able to smoke the finest tobacco in a meerschaum, and to light his pipe with a match, even though matches were then rare and expensive. But he did not care to do things that way. He smoked one of Mrs. Medford's one-cent pipes, and dipped it into the embers to light it.

"One day, just as he stooped to light his pipe preparatory to celebrating one of his political victories, an enemy who is said to have sworn that Riley would never again go to the Legislature, shot him; but the wound was not serious."

A story written in 1960 by Andrew Sparks in the *Atlanta Journal & Constitution* Sunday Magazine quotes Joe Thomas Sr., an old-timer who was born soon after Riley's death and lived near the old Riley plantation in White County:

"From all accounts he was a pretty rough citizen. But he never killed anybody that I know of and he never got shot but once. That was after he was elected to the Georgia Senate. Him and Dan Davis run, and Riley beat. Davis said Riley never would serve and he came to the house when Riley was stooped over at the fireplace lighting his pipe and shot him in the arm from the back. Riley got up and got him a gun and shot a hole in Davis's hat as he ran away."

Daniel Davis (2/8/1785 – 6/9/1868) was a very wealthy planter who lived in the Davis District of Lumpkin County. He was a leading citizen and, just as Harrison Riley, he had moved to the area when it was still a part of the Cherokee Nation.

That being said, a letter donated to the Dahlonega Courthouse Gold Museum by a descendant of Daniel Davis indicates another possibility altogether in the shooting incident. In that scenario, it may have been one of Davis' sons who made the attempt upon Riley's life. The letter postmarked *Grand River, Cherokee Nation* and dated *17th December 1860*, was addressed to *L.D.* (Lorenzo Dow) *Davis* (Daniel's son), *Calhoun, Ga.*, and was written by a cousin, J.M. Lynch, at the request of Joseph C. Davis.

"Dear cousin,
I write you these lines to let you know that your brother Joe has arrived here safe and will remain with us until he hears from you - I have not yet seen Joe though he is at Les Thompson's about six miles from my house - he sent Les to my house on yesterday to get me to write this letter and send it to the post office, he wishes you to write to him everything in regard to his difficulty with Riley - whether Riley is dead or likely to recover and whether he has sent any one in pursuit of him or not....."

Riley did recover of course and Joseph Davis eventually returned to Lumpkin County of his own free will. Davis, just another in the long line of Riley's political enemies, died of natural causes Aug. 27, 1889 and is buried in the Davis Cemetery in Lumpkin County.

Riley & the Civil War

At the time that Riley was serving in the Georgia General Assembly, the capital of Georgia – and therefore the General Assembly – was located at Milledgeville, Georgia. This was quite a trip for anyone from Lumpkin County to be making on a regular basis on horseback or by horse and buggy. It is unknown today exactly how Riley in fact made the trip.

It is a matter of public record that Riley attended the *Secession Convention* in Milledgeville in January, 1861. Although his exact role is unclear, the unpublished **Diary Of Amory Dexter** notes: *"Jan. 20, 1861, Riley returned from Milledgeville and says Georgia out of the Union."*

At this juncture, Riley actively "campaigned" for his coveted military commission from the Confederacy. The following letters, written by him shortly after the beginning of the Civil War, are on file at the Georgia Department of Archives & History in Atlanta:

"Head Quarters
August 25th, 1861
Second Brigade Seventh Division
To the Executive Department

Dear Sir,
Your order of the 27th inst received calling on the Major General, Brigadier

Generals, Colonels and other officers for speedy organization of the militia of this state.

I not knowing whether the Major General of this brigade is living or not, I have assumed responsibility of responding to the call hoping that I have not done wrong in obedience to said order. I enclose to you a complete list of my staff. I also enclose my order for a thorough organization of the militia of my brigade.

I also state to you that I will with pleasure attend to and distribute any order that may come from your department. I am your most obedient servant.

H.W. Riley

Dahlonega
November the 12th 1861
General A. Hansell"
"Dear Sir,

After all due regard allow me to offer you some apology for troubling you at this time but circumstances are of such a pressing and urgent nature at this time that I am compelled to call on you as a special friend believing that you will do all you can to promote my interest.

I have just made the tour through my brigade. I have visited six counties and reviewed the troops in all those six counties. I find, on examining my Brigade Inspections Report of the strength of my brigade, that it is composed of three thousand one hundred and fifteen (3115) hale, hearty, stout warriors as ever breathed a pure mountain atmosphere all of them professed a perfect willingness to turn out in the defense of their native state for twelve months unless sooner discharged.

I took the companies, one at a time, in every county in the brigade and put the question in this way "that if the officers and men should be called on by the governor or his authority to go to the coast for twelve months unless sooner discharged

- if there was any that had any excuse why he should not go for such a one to step two paces to the front." [Strange] to say not one came to the front, all stood firm which with the exception of some forty sick men which were excused.

Now my dear friend, I want you to use your influence with his Excellency the governor to secure a permit for me to raise a regiment or a battalion to go to the coast to rendezvous at Dahlonega to be called the Dahlonega Regiment or Battalion. I ask this favor of you knowing that you are well appraised that if I go at all it must be on a horse as it is impossible for me to walk owing to my bodily afflictions.

There is in White, Habersham and Hall about some one thousand good men who possess a perfect willingness to go if I can get any positive assurance that I will be received and that the governor will allow me I will take hold of it and you know I am not slow when I take hold. I will be at all the expense and trouble of raising the regiment or battalion whichever his excellency will allow.

Please attend to this for me on the spot and let me hear from you at your earliest opportunity dear sir. I have the honor to remain your most obedient humble servant.

To General Andrew I Hansell
Harrison W. Riley"

Despite his obviously earnest and diligent efforts, Riley ultimately failed to get the commission he so desired. Weir Boyd, a local lawyer, was elected colonel of the unit that became the 52nd Georgia Infantry Regiment. Nevertheless, Harrison Riley from that day forward was always addressed as "General," both in person and in print. His grave marker even has this title preceding his name.

The actual origin of Riley's rank is unknown today. In all likelihood, it represents little more than a local or honorary title due to his command of the local militia unit. Interestingly, there is no record in either the state or national archives of any military service – either in the U.S. or Confederate forces – served by Harrison Riley.

It was also during this time that the legend of Riley's "hidden treasure" originated.

Final Battle

The Georgia House of Representatives in which Riley served several terms, honored him in 1873, near the end of his illustrious career, with the following resolution:

"Resolved that a seat upon the floor of this House be tendered to the 'unlearned' but stout old Champion of the People's Rights, and Representative, Man of the Mountains, General Harrison W. Riley of the County of Lumpkin."

This was the last year that Riley held public office and the year before he began his final battle in life. . . . one of the few battles that he did not win. The ravages of illness and time had finally caught up with him, and on November 1, 1874, in spite of the attention of four of the most prominent doctors in the area, he realized that his death was imminent.

On this day, three days before his death on November 4, he executed his *Last Will & Testament.* This remarkable document, (now on file in the office of the probate judge of Lumpkin County), is the most lasting evidence of the paradoxical nature of Riley's life.

It was also during this time that the legend of Riley's "hidden treasure" originated. According to the folklore, as well as various written accounts, Riley called two of his most trusted friends to his bedside and confided to them the location of $2,000.00 in gold that he had hidden.

Today, the ultimate disposition of this gold cache is unknown. Perhaps the treasure was quietly recovered years ago, or perhaps it has been lost forever. Regardless of the circumstances, the legend continues to this day. The following article, dated December 30, 1898, appeared in the **Mountain Signal** newspaper 24 years after Harrison Riley's death:

$2,000 Gold Buried

Judge Brittain is one of the few old landmarks that is left. He was a special friend to Harrison W. Riley who has long since passed away. Judge Brittain is one of two men to whom General Riley told where he hid about two thousand dollars in gold. The other old gentleman is still alive and lives out in the country. They are the only two persons that were told the whereabouts of the hidden treasure and will likely die without disclosing the secret. The Judge says that the money is not his and he is not going to tell it so as to create a lawsuit.

The name of the second person to which the above article refers, has been lost to history. If Riley's gold is still buried, how much would it be worth today?

In 1874, gold dust was selling for $20.76 per ounce. As of this writing

(2024), the price is slightly more than $2,000.00 per ounce, so if the buried gold was all dust, it would have been approximately 96.34 ounces in volume and would have had a flat gold value of approximately $192,678.00.

But what if the gold was coinage? In 1874, Dahlonega gold coins were quite common. Depending of course upon the year and denomination, $2,000 in Dahlonega gold coins could be worth millions today. If part of the gold included the extremely-rare "Templeton Reid" gold coins (minted in Gainesville), the current value could easily exceed tens of millions of dollars in value.

At the time of his death, Riley owned thousands of acres of land. However, most of the treasure hunting for his gold has occurred around his plantation in White County where Riley spent his final days. The ruins of this former home still existed in the 1990s, but the site was inaccessible except on foot, and difficult to reach. The rubble no doubt has disappeared entirely today.

During the last years of Riley's life and for several years thereafter, the house and plantation were the home of Elizabeth (Eliza) Wood and her son and daughter, reportedly two of Harrison Riley's many children.

Eliza Wood also raised a nephew, Sidney Dowdy. Sidney (1868-1944) was the son of Eliza's sister, Margaret, and her husband, Alfred J. Dowdy. Sidney was undoubtedly one of the last people who actually remembered Harrison Riley, the man, and not just the legend.

A grandson of Sidney Dowdy, Hoyt T. Booth of Bowman, Georgia, recalled many tales that his grandfather had handed down concerning Riley. According to Booth, Dowdy once described an incident during the Civil War revealed to him by his aunt Eliza.

According to the story, during the dark days of the war, the plantation was raided by outlaws. Whether they were deserters from the Union or Confederate armies, or simply thieves taking advantage of an area in which law enforcement was nonexistent in the 1860s, is unknown today. What is certain, is that they were looking for Harrison Riley's gold.

Even in the 1860s, Riley's gold was legendary, and highly coveted. The raiders reportedly tore the home apart in search of the coins – even to the point of ripping open the bedding. The only place they did not search was a pile of filthy-dirty stinking soiled clothing strewn beneath the home's staircase.

When the raiders rode away empty-handed, they had no idea that they had overlooked much of Riley's treasure reported to have been approximately $20,000 in gold which, according to the tale, had been hidden practically in plain view – beneath the pile of filthy clothes! Today (2024), at just over $2,000.00 per ounce, that cache of gold would have been worth slightly more than $1.9 million. And, again, if all or only a portion of this gold was in the coinage of that period, its value today would be incalculable.

Harrison Riley's obsession with gold was so well known that at the time of secession in January, 1861, it almost caused an incident of statewide proportions. When Georgia seceded from the Union, there was a U.S. Branch Mint in operation in Dahlonega. It continued to operate for about a month, and the problem of protecting the stocks of bullion and coin on hand at the Mint swiftly became a source of major concern.

Mint Spoils of War

The assayer of the Mint at that time – Capt. Isaac L. Todd – explained it as follows:

Burned to the Ground – By the 1940s, Harrison Riley's beloved mountain hotel on the Dahlonega Public Square had been relegated to use as a men's dormitory (called Moore Hall) for North Georgia College. Some of the students smoked and some studied by candlelight. On the night of January 9, 1943, Riley's signature creation was accidentally set afire and burned to the ground, but the gold rush entrepreneur and politician who had departed this earth in 1874, was blissfully unaware.

"There were some rough characters in the mountains in those early days, and when the state seceded, one of them by the name of Harrison W. Riley threatened to organize a crowd and make a raid on the mint, as he declared that the money belonged to nobody in particular, and that he was as much entitled to it as anybody.

"We hears of the threatened raid and armed ourselves, closing the vaults and putting the keys in a place of safety. Riley evidently thought better of the matter, for he never put in an appearance."

Capt. Todd's version, while accurate, does not tell the entire story. Gov. Joseph Emerson Brown had grown up in Union County, just north of Dahlonega, and later lived near Canton, Georgia. He was well acquainted with Harrison Riley and knew precisely how to deal with him.

When the report of Riley's threat to seize the Mint was telegraphed to Gov. Brown, several leading men of the state pressured the governor to send in state troops at once to secure the Mint by force and avoid allowing Riley or anyone else an opportunity to make an attempt of this nature.

Governor Brown reportedly suspected that a substantial portion of Riley's motivation for this threat was a desire to attract notoriety, and that he was too shrewd to actually participate in such an action which could be interpreted as a rebellion against the state and treasonous – unless advantage was given him.

The governor was also well aware however, that with so large a proportion of Union sentiment as there was in that section of the state, if any difficulty was raised with Riley about the Mint, the popular sympathy quite probably would have been with the man from Dahlonega, thus putting the state in a ticklish position.

A few days later, the governor wrote to several prominent citizens of Dahlonega, telling them that he had heard such a report in reference to Gen. Riley, but had known him too long and had too high an appreciation of his good sense and patriotism to believe he would attempt such a thing, and that as old personal friends, he and Riley must have no collision.

The governor did not think it best to write to Riley personally or directly, but wrote instead to friends who he knew would communicate the facts to Riley. This course of action apparently had a soothing effect upon Riley, and toned him down.

The governor also notified the superintendent of the Mint that the state now held and possessed it. The superintendent formally recognized the authority of Georgia over the Mint, and consented to act under the executive who gave him written orders.

Governor Brown was criticized by the newspapers for not making a demonstration upon the Mint, but considering

A great-granddaughter of Harrison Riley has reported that she grew up hearing that Riley fathered approximately 100 children.

Riley's influence and following, Brown's actions seem almost a stroke of enlightened genius. Harrison Riley remained a strong political supporter of Gov. Brown for the remainder of his life.

The Final Chapter

A great-granddaughter of Harrison Riley has reported that she grew up hearing that Riley fathered approximately 100 children. On the surface, this number seems somewhat exaggerated. Nevertheless, one thing is almost certain: Harrison Riley fathered several children by several different women – both black and white.

In the absence of birth and death records during Riley's lifetime, it is doubtful that it will ever be known, with any degree of certainty, just how many children Harrison actually fathered. In fact, it is doubtful that he knew exactly himself!

In 1838, Riley owned 14 slaves. It would not be realistic to assume he was the father of all the children born to the female slaves, but it is highly likely that he was the father of at least several.

Research is further complicated by the fact that some of his children used the last name Riley while others used their mothers' maiden names. It also appears that, except for the last few years of his life, Riley never actually lived for any period of time with any of his female consorts. He maintained a separate residence for each of them and never presented them socially.

In the days when a "shotgun wedding" involved a real shotgun, one might wonder just how Riley managed to survive while living such an unorthodox lifestyle. How did he manage to avoid being gunned down by an irate father?

The answer seems two-fold. First of all, Riley took exceptionally good care of his consorts – and their children: They lived in substantial households; the children received the best educations; and the lifestyle of the mothers and children was considerably better than that of the average family in what then was a rugged mining country of north Georgia.

Secondly, Harrison Riley had proven beyond a shadow of a doubt that any challengers – or even assassins – were taking their lives in their hands by attacking him in any manner whatsoever. If he couldn't shoot them dead in an open gunfight, he'd file suit against them to see how much damage he might cause in that manner. He also was wealthy enough to simply hire someone to eliminate anyone attacking him. The residents of Dahlonega were all aware of these things.

Additionally, there was always the matter of Riley's fabled fortune. Any woman and/or children to whom Riley could establish lineage quite possibly would be denied any financial support if Riley perished in an attack. They knew it and he knew it, and this provided yet another measure of protection.

Descendants

A paragraph of Harrison Riley's *Last Will & Testament* reads as follows:

"I hereby bequeath to Eliza Jefferson. . . . my farm known as Sprigg's Place in Dawson County. . . . at her death to Julia Rutherford and Susan Mathis and a little girl, the daughter of Lorena Witherow, deceased, now living with Susan Mathis, given name not recollected, also to Alice Pilgrim, and I further give to the said Susan Mathis, the farm she is now living on for and during her natural life. . . . at her death to her children."

Eliza Jefferson, born about 1819, was a former slave that Harrison Riley had purchased November 5, 1839, from R. A. Holt for the sum of $1,250.00. She was about 20 years of age and had four children: Henry, about 5 years old; Rial, a boy of about 3; June, a girl about 18 months old; and a female child about 6 months old.

Over the next 20 plus years, Eliza had seven more children, possibly more:

1) Goliath Riley, born 1841/43, was left $500.00 in Harrison Riley's will. He moved to Alabama.

2) Julia, born 1844/45, married (as Julia Riley) Franklin Rutherford on September 23, 1860. The marriage was performed by John C. Brittain, judge of the Inferior Court and one of the two men to whom Riley supposedly revealed the location of his buried gold. Franklin Rutherford was a white man who joined Co. C, 52nd Georgia Regiment, C.S.A. on March 4, 1862, and served until July 10, when he furnished a substitute. Julia is the same Julia Rutherford mentioned above in Harrison Riley's will.

3) Sarah Ann (known as Susan), born about 1847, married (as Susan Riley) Jasper Matthews on October 20, 1863. Susan is the same Susan Mathis mentioned above in Riley's will. The diversion in the last name is probably a spelling error or a transcription error at some point.

4) Jesse T., born August, 1850.

5) Charles, born about 1853.

6) Mary, born about 1855.

7) Son, born about 1858, was still not named at the time of the **1860 Census**. There were possibly other children born after the **1860 Federal Census**. Who were *"Lorena Witherow, deceased,"* and her *"little girl....given name not recollected?"*

On October 13, 1862, Harrison W. Riley sold to. . . . *"Alice Witherow, a female daughter of Alfred H. Witherow. . . . in consideration of the sum of four hundred seventy five dollars. . . . in the 1st Section, 13th District. . . . Land lot #44 (40 acres) a portion of Land lot 343 (35 acres), and Land lot 374 (40 acres). . . . if the said Alice Witherow dies before she becomes of proper age, the title to the above premises to remain to the said Alfred A. Witherow."*

A check of the census records in 1870 found the same family living in the Auraria section of Lumpkin County #3-3:

Alfred Witherow, age 60;

Nancy Witherow, age 30;

Alice Witherow, age 10;

John Witherow, age 5;

Kirby Witherow, age 3.

This undoubtedly means that when Harrison Riley sold 115 acres to Alice Witherow, Alice was only 2 years old!

Although Eliza Jefferson was purchased as a slave, her heritage must have included only a very small portion of Negro blood. Her children were light enough (even in pre-Civil War days) to be accepted as white children. Even before the war and emancipation of the slaves, Elizabeth Jefferson was living with her family in a house in town and working as a seamstress.

In another section of his **Will**, Riley bequeathed to: *"Eliza Wood (a white woman who lived at Riley's plantation in White County). . . . lot of land. . . . known as the Nix Place. . . . and bequeath to the said Eliza Wood. . . . lot of land. . . . known as the Gen. Field's place. . . . in her natural life and at her death to be equally divided between her children now in life, names as follows: David Sherman, about ten years of age, and Josephine, about nine years of age. I make the above bequeath as some compensation to the said Elizabeth Wood for waiting on me in my afflictions."*

Riley also bequeathed to Elizabeth Wood all his household and kitchen stock (except his old mare and mule) plus all present crops and provisions on same to be used for her support and the support and education of her children heretofore mentioned.

David Sherman Riley was born December, 1864, in White County, Georgia, and married Molly Margaret Hunt, May 11, 1884. They were the parents of six children, the first five were born in White County, Georgia and the sixth was born after they moved to Dallas, Texas:

1) Clarence Riley, born 1886.

2) Hattie Riley, born 1890.

3) Marley Riley, born 1892.

4) Lonnie Riley, born 1894, married Joe Monroe Epps, May 11, 1913, died 1938.

5) Roy Riley, born 1897.

6) Grace Riley, born 1907; still living as of the summer of 1986.

Josephine Callie Riley, (known as Callie) was born in White County in 1868. She married Frank Cleveland Hunt, brother of Molly Margaret Hunt. They were the parents of eight or more children. Callie died in 1915. Frank, born in 1861, died in 1939. Both are buried in Alta Vista Cemetery in Gainesville, Georgia (Hall County).

The last child mentioned in Harrison Riley's will was William Taylor Dowdy.

Taylor Dowdy's mother was Julia Ann Dowdy (1837-December 28, 1922) daughter of John M. Dowdy (1808-1892) and Anna Johnson Dowdy.

On March 4, 1862, when William T. Dowdy was just three years of age, Riley sold to Julia Ann Dowdy, for the sum of $50.00, 40 acres of land "*. . . . being the same lot whereon the Rev. John Dowdy, father of Julia Dowdy now lives. . . .*"

In his will, Riley stated:

"*I hereby give and bequeath to Taylor Dowdy, all other lands to me belonging in Georgia, not heretofore mentioned, to be sold by his grandfather John Dowdy and the proceeds turned over to Taylor Dowdy.*"

Later in this will, Riley added a stipulation to the sale of 900 acres of land that he owned in Alabama:

"*I hereby further direct that two hundred and fifty dollars be paid to Taylor Dowdy from the proceeds of said lands.*"

William T. (known as Taylor) was raised in the household of his grandfather, John M. Dowdy. John was a Baptist preacher and a school teacher. Taylor Dowdy grew up to become one of the best known and most beloved Baptist preachers in the Lumpkin County area.

Another missing piece of the Harrison Riley puzzle involves H.W. Riley, Jr., who enlisted in Company E, Phillips Legion, "Blue Ridge Rifles" C.S.A., on July 9, 1861. He gave his residence as Dahlonega, Georgia, and his age as 14.

H.W., Jr. apparently was wounded at Hanover Junction, Virginia, on May 27, 1864, and was received at General Hospital No. 9, Richmond, Virginia, on May 30. Records indicate that he had been shot in the left hip. He was given a 60 days medical furlough on July 11, 1864. On the final muster roll dated January 30, 1865, he is listed as being absent without leave (AWOL). No further records have ever been found of H.W. Riley, Jr. either before or after the Civil War.

Gen. Harrison W. Riley died on a cold Wednesday morning, November 4, 1874 at his plantation in White County and was buried two days later beside his mother in the Riley family plot in Mt. Hope Cemetery in Dahlonega. All the places of business in Dahlonega were closed respectfully for his funeral and the citizens of the town and the surrounding area turned out in mass to pay their final respects to this man who, during the forty-plus years since his arrival in the wilderness that was to become Dahlonega, had become the most famous (or infamous) character that north Georgia's gold rush produced.

There, no doubt, were others who came simply out of curiosity; maybe they sensed that they were witnessing the end of an era – the final passing from rough and tumble frontier to civilization. Still another group – possibly the larger – came just to see for their own satisfaction that Harrison Riley was really finally dead.

Today, the Dahlonega Courthouse Gold Museum receives numerous inquiries almost weekly, and certainly monthly, from family researchers all over the United States trying to prove a link to the infamous Riley. This man whose gravestone reads, "*Let his faults be buried with his bones,*" also inspired the lines: "*Harrison Riley... At the very mention of his name, Heaven blushes, Hell trembles, and the whole world shudders.*"

(Grateful appreciation is acknowledged herewith to Jimmy Anderson of Dahlonega who researched and provided most of the very detailed information used in this article.)

Grandpa Was Simply
An Outlaw

As was the case in most all of north Georgia during and after the U.S. Civil War, outlaws proliferated in the region, robbing, raping, murdering, and burning almost at will, and one of the worst of these was an individual by the name of Jeff Anderson. After being captured and imprisoned in Lumpkin County, he escaped, only to be re-captured and imprisoned in Atlanta where he escaped yet again. Following this second escape, however, Jeff fled and lived for short stretches in Polk, Whitfield and Walker counties before striking out for parts westward in 1901. Though it is believed he never again returned to Georgia, recently uncovered information has revealed the former outlaw quite probably lived his final years near Chattanooga, Tennessee, . . . and even more interestingly, that he had a wife and children there in addition to the wife and children he abandoned in Georgia.

William H. Anderson and his brother, John, migrated from Habersham County to Lumpkin County in time to be listed in the 1834 Federal Census of Lumpkin shortly after the county was formed. One of William's children was named Thomas Jefferson, and though his family was respectable, young "Jeff," for reasons unknown today, apparently decided early-on that outlawry was to be the life he would pursue, and he did so with a vengeance.

These Andersons settled in Crumby District, east of Dahlonega in the Philippi Community (present-day Cavender Creek vicinity).[1] In the early 1830s, Cherokee natives still resided in the vicinity.

"*John and William must have been prosperous due to the numerous records one may still find documenting their activities at the Dahlonega Clerk of Court's Office,*" wrote family researchers who provided information about the pioneer brothers for various publications.[2] Among other pursuits, the brothers farmed, bought and sold land, and owned stock in the Spring Place Mining Company in Fannin County.

William H. and Margaret Anderson were the parents of a total of seven sons and two daughters who eventually were strung out all across north Georgia. Thomas Jefferson was their sixth child, born in 1839. There is no way of knowing today whether Jeff showed violent tendencies in his earlier years or if his criminal inclinations were a product of family divisiveness created by the Civil War.

Census records reveal that William H. Anderson owned one slave. Military records show that Jeff's brothers – William M., Isaac, Henry, and Benjamin – fought for the Confederacy, but their sibling, Thomas Abraham, enlisted in the Union Army and despised slavery. Pockets of the mountaineers throughout north Georgia remained loyal to the Union and were distastefully known as "Unionists" by the Confederates.

Many will argue today that the U.S. Civil War was solely ignited by the slavery issue, but the documented history of our nation freely indicates that it was the politics of *"States' Rights"* which separated the northern states from the southern states as far back as the 1830s. Since the late 1700s, the agrarian South had been relegated to status as the site of production of raw materials for refinement in the factories and millineries of the North, at which time the finished products were sold back to the South at inflated prices. *The Tariff of 1828*, known derisively as *"the Tariff of Abominations"* by Southerners was enacted specifically to quell the sale of raw materials to European markets by the South, and helped in particular to ignite the *States' Rights* issue.

Jeff Anderson himself initially enlisted in the First Georgia Volunteer Infantry, perhaps in support of *States' Rights*, but, true to form, soon deserted. Was this perhaps due to the influence of his older brother Abraham's anti-slavery stance? It, more likely than anything was simply a budding example of his growing lawless nature.

Just as Jeff's early character development is hazy and obscure today, so also is any explanation as to why he ultimately morphed not only into outlawry, but also into the bloodthirsty leader of a band of outlaws known as *"the bridge burners."* These individuals terrorized not only the citizens, but the soldiers of north Georgia as well, using guerrilla tactics to constantly harass local Confederate units.

An uneasy Jeff Anderson was photographed here, probably in his late 20s or early 30s in a long frock coat. This may have been a prison photo, due to the position of the hands which is strangely reminiscent of the circumstances when one is wearing handcuffs and attempting to hide that fact. (Photo courtesy of George Anderson)

According to research conducted by the late Dahlonega historian Bill Kinsland, Jeff Anderson was arrested by Lumpkin County Sheriff John Early in February of 1862, and tried for *Assault and Battery*, *Assault and Battery with Intent to Rape*, and *Misdemeanor*. He was also arrested under an order from Captain William Martin and charged with desertion from the First Georgia Volunteer Infantry.

Dahlonega Escape

Considered a very dangerous man, Jeff was confined to the "common jail"

Mary "Mollie" Rebecca Dilbeck Anderson (1862-1952), wife of Civil War outlaw Jeff Anderson, lived many places with her itinerant husband, including Dahlonega and Rockmart, Georgia. She passed away in Tennessee, at the ripe old age of 90 years.

in Dahlonega with his legs securely fastened to the wall with a heavy logging chain. The sheriff no doubt was convinced that chain was all it took to lock down the criminal.

The Dahlonega "common jail" of those days was little more than a heavy, two-story log box joined by spikes, with a trap-door opening in the top floor through which prisoners could lower themselves into the lock-up by way of a ladder. This structure was very poorly weatherized, and to some degree was open to the elements and any and all vermin and other wildlife which might plague and torment the prisoners. There was no fresh water and no toilet, and the circumstances, to put it mildly, were filthy and extremely inhospitable.

Historians today believe this jail quite probably was the one referenced in early Lumpkin County documents as having existed on the east side of Ches-

tatee Street one block south of the old Baptist Church building in Dahlonega. This would have been an isolated site on the side of a dusty trail which was exposed to the cold northeast winds. No one ever wanted to be arrested and confined in "the Dahlonega box."

Early on March 9 of 1862, – the day that Jeff Anderson was due to be picked up by military authorities to be returned to his unit for punishment for desertion – his brothers Henry and Benjamin "Dock" Anderson, accompanied by a friend named Bart Edge, rode quietly and anonymously into town. The men nonchalantly tied their horses in front of the jail. The street on this cold morning no doubt was deserted.

Back in the 1860s in north Georgia, the good Lord simply made men "tough." They had to be, just to survive. The ambient temperature in that log calaboose in which Jeff was incarcerated undoubtedly was well below freezing that frigid March morning, and Jeff had survived in it all night long.

When jailer John McCoskey arrived to bring Anderson his breakfast, Bart Edge reportedly approached the lawman and asked to visit the prisoner. McCoskey – apparently unfamiliar with the men and sensing little if any danger in the request – obligingly led Edge and one of the Andersons into the jail where he opened the dungeon door.

Upon recognition of his brother, Jeff immediately complained that he was *"powerful sick"* and begged for "Doc" Howard to come attend to him. Caught completely off guard, McCoskey went to the front door to send someone for Dr. Howard, but before he could take a step back, Jeff Anderson was already *"halfway out of the dungeon, coat and boots off"* sprinting for freedom.

McCoskey later testified in court

that Anderson *"pitched through the jail door, I after him, and down the steps."* The jailer's nephew Walter McCoskey gave testimony that the escaped prisoner hit him in the head as he ran by and that he saw one of the men step in front of his uncle (McCoskey) to delay his pursuit of the jail-breaker.

Whatever the circumstances, by the time McCoskey could manoeuver around the obstructing relative, Jeff Anderson, reportedly, was already fading from sight up the street, ironically toward the county courthouse. According to an account of the incident, he *"ran across the square, past the Mustering Grounds and down Wimpy Mill Road,"* before disappearing.

Bart Edge, Dock and Henry Anderson were later arrested and charged with the crime of *"Rescue."* Sheriff Early testified that Jeff Anderson, amazingly, had used an old rusty rasp to cut himself loose from the heavy log chain. How his no-doubt numb fingers had been able to saw through a thick logging chain with what no doubt was at best a second-rate worn-out rasp is anybody's guess today. As previously stated, the outlaws of the 1860s were mighty tough hombres.

Edge and the Anderson brothers later testified that they had not helped Jeff to escape at all, and *"would have caught him if they could."* Despite the obvious prison-break and other charges, there is no record today of the case ever having come to trial.

Henry Anderson, who was two years younger than Jeff, was 21 at the time. He enlisted in Smith's Legion of the Georgia Volunteers two months later. He was transferred to Company C, 65th Regiment, Georgia Infantry a year later. He subsequently died in the Loudon, Tennessee hospital on March 29, 1863.

"Dock," whose real name was Benjamin F. Anderson, was Jeff's youngest brother and only 17 years of age at the time. He served in Company C of the 52nd Regiment of the Georgia Volunteers, Barton's Brigade. Bart Edge had enlisted in the same unit, and was captured at the Battle of Vicksburg in July of 1863.

Re-Captured & Re-Escaped

After his jail-break in Dahlonega, Jeff Anderson remained on the run for several months before finally being recaptured. An article in the October 4, 1862 *Atlanta Southern Confederacy* noted, *"Yesterday a mounted escort, detailed from Captain Tillet's Artillery Company, arrived here in charge of a large amount of Gold from the Mint at Dahlonega, belonging to the Confederate government. They also brought with them in chains a desperado named Anderson, whose outrages in Lumpkin County and the vicinity have been intolerable for some time. He is a deserter from the 1st Georgia Regulars, and has been hiding himself in the caves and dens of the mountains for the last five or six months, harboring runaway negroes, stealing, robbing widows and helpless women and children whose husbands and fathers are in the war, and had become a terror to the whole country. He will be properly cared for."*

It is difficult to imagine today how one could survive more than a week or two in a cave in the mountains above Dahlonega, Georgia – much of that time in the dead of winter – but somehow Jeff Anderson managed just such a feat for almost eight months.

In his Atlanta imprisonment, Anderson was lodged in the Atlanta jail along with *"fellow Bridge Burners, Yankee POWs, and some 'Engine Thieves' who were captured during the failed Andrews'*

and and foot. Had	The news from the Continent is unimpor-	them promptly. A
ed Maryland, they	tant. Garibaldi is worse.	for Subscribers ha
once recruited to the	The Opinion Nationale, of Paris, Prince Na-	for delivery. They
in arms. Let it not	poleon's organ, condemns the idea of an	Receipts, and we w
id is unwilling, cold,	emancipation proclamation for the negroes in	may direct. We ho
not so.	anticipation, and in very severe terms, while	owners.
still throwing up the	the Dublin Freeman's Journal (a Union paper)	The Cotton of Su
de of Washington.—	points out the inutility of such a measure for	the market price b
rom the Potomac to	the negroes themselves.	change for Bonds

Beneath the sub-headline "*Arrival of Gold - A Deserter*," an article in the **Columbus** (Georgia) **Sun** newspaper of October 6, 1862, documents in its second paragraph outlaw Jeff Anderson's transport from the Lumpkin County Jail to the Atlanta City Jail. Interestingly, he was incarcerated in Atlanta with a group of captured Union spies known in history as "Andrews Raiders" who had recently stolen a locomotive in Big Shanty, Georgia. Several of these men later managed to escape from the Atlanta Jail with Anderson to hide out in the north Georgia mountains. Several others – including leader James J. Andrews – were not so fortunate, being hung by the neck until dead in Atlanta. Those executed later were posthumously-awarded the **Congressional Medal of Honor** – the nation's highest award. They also won even more fame from a 20th Century major motion picture – **"The Great Locomotive Chase"** – filmed in 1957 in northeast Georgia and starring Fess Parker, Jeffrey Hunter, Slim Pickens and others. (Period news clipping courtesy of the Digital Library of Georgia Newspapers and Robert S. Davis, Jr.)

Raid."[3] The story of how Union spies stole a train and attempted to destroy the Confederate rail line between Atlanta and Chattanooga was portrayed in the Walt Disney major motion picture **The Great Locomotive Chase** filmed in northeast Georgia in the 1955.[4]

Some of the incarcerated *"Engine Thieves"* and *"Bridge Burners"* subsequently made a daring escape from the Atlanta prison.[5] Some of Andrews' men who escaped and survived to tell the tale

later described one of their party as a *"Rebel Deserter"* who stayed with their group for a few days before leaving them somewhere north of Atlanta. This may well have been Jeff Anderson, who was known to have returned to the mountains of north Georgia where he continued his guerilla war tactics.

After the war was over in 1865, Jeff, who was still a *"Wanted"* man, reportedly hid out on his older brother Abraham's farm in Whitfield County near

Dalton for a number of years. Abraham, the Union sympathizer, was described as *"religious and kindhearted"* and perhaps thought that his wayward brother could be reformed by providing him with a safe haven and kindness. Wrong again.

If these were Abraham's thoughts and hopes, they ultimately were vanquished. Jeff, though remaining with his brother for over two decades, ultimately could not shake the demons which apparently possessed him, and departed for parts unknown sometime in the mid-1880s, apparently as a result of a serious family rift.

The details of Jeff Anderson's life from the mid-1880s to the turn of the 20th century remained a mystery for approximately a century before a distant relative – Bill Smyth – appeared in Dahlonega searching for information about his unique forebear among the voluminous records of that town. In the midst of his inquiries, Mr. Smyth explained to Dahlonega historians that his notorious grandfather Jeff had married Mary "Mollie" Rebecca Dilbeck (1862-1952) from the Jack's River area in Fannin County in 1886 when he was 47 and she was 24. They had eight children – four boys and four girls.

Flight to Rockmart?

The first child was Bill Smyth's mother, Mary Georgia Ann Anderson, who reportedly was born in Rockmart, Georgia, on January 29, 1887. If this is accurate, Jeff and Mollie Rebecca

This may well have been Jeff Anderson, who was known to have returned to the mountains of north Georgia where he continued his guerilla war tactics.

must have been among the early settlers in Rockmart, since that town was incorporated in 1872.

Jeff and Mollie could also have been residents of what then was a tiny side-community of Rockmart – Vanwert – which had once been a thriving settlement and the original county seat of Paulding County. With its location on the edge of the western frontier in Georgia, Vanwert had become known as a hideout of sorts for all manner of riff-raff and outlawry.

Vanwert was in existence as a trading post as early as 1837, while native Cherokee Indians still resided in substantial numbers in the area. Documented Native American villages once existed in that vicinity near the confluences of Simpson and Thompson creeks, and Euharlee and Fish creeks. In the early days of its development, Vanwert was reported to be so filthy and degenerate that area residents and Native Americans alike referred to it derisively as "Clean Town."

After being named the county seat of Paulding, Vanwert soon had a population in excess of 100, a courthouse, a church, two hotels, several commercial shops and businesses, a county courthouse, a blacksmith shop, several saloons, an array of prostitutes, and even an academy. The nearby discovery of gold didn't hurt the growth trend.

In 1851, when a portion of Paulding (which included Vanwert) was taken to form adjacent Polk

Bill Smyth, grandson of Thomas Jefferson "Jeff" Anderson. (Photo courtesy of Anne Amerson)

County, Vanwert lost its county-seat status, and withered and died. Its outlaw locus, however, continued to persevere, due to its isolated location. Vanwert remained a "back-water" fiefdom for well over 20 years, until the founding of adjacent Rockmart.

Whether Jeff Anderson lived here with wife Mollie Rebecca for any length of time is unknown today. It is known only that "Rockmart" was the residence of his wife.

Though difficult to conceive today, there were few roads across or through western Georgia prior to the 1870s, and only very limited stagecoach roads from the state's east coast to its central locales. The lone exceptions were several rough trails, one group of which was known collectively as "the Alabama Roads." A branch of the Alabama Road passed through Dahlonega and continued

across Georgia, eventually passing between Rockmart and the pioneer community of Cedartown several miles away. Vanwert, with its location near this travel route had evolved out of pure necessity as a "stop-over" for a semblance of "civilization."

As a primary route westward, passing quite near Vanwert, the Alabama Road would have been a natural avenue for a criminal to use in flight. Rockmart (and/or Vanwert) was an area in which a *"Wanted"* criminal could easily enjoy anonymity, since law enforcement – particularly in pre- and post-Civil War north Georgia – was virtually nonexistent.

From Rockmart to The Cove

The other Anderson children sired by Jeff Anderson who lived in Rockmart were Maud Josephine (b. 1889); Mattie (b. 1891 and married Oscar Hunter, a policeman); Charles Martin (b. 1893); William Arthur (b. 1896, and known as "Clint"); Henry Franklin (b. 1899); Benjamin Harrison (born 1901) and Viola (born 1904). William, Henry and Benjamin bear the same names coincidentally as three of Jeff's brothers. It quite possibly was the arrival of the railroad, coupled with the increased growth of Vanwert – and subsequently Rockmart – which gave rise to Jeff's "itch to move on."

"Mama told me about moving to McLemore Cove between Pigeon Mountain and Lookout Mountain when she was six years old," Bill Smyth recounted. "They moved in three covered wagons, and Mama slept in the one that held the barrels of Grandpa's whiskey. When she woke up, she couldn't walk from breathing the fumes!

McLemore Cove in extreme northwest Georgia, was another secluded locale which offered refuge to those who wished to avoid law enforcement authorities, and was yet another natural hide-out for Jeff. Due to its inaccessibility caused by the high surrounding peaks of the Blue Ridge Mountains south of Chattanooga, "the cove" continues to be very lightly populated even today.

It was spots such as Rockmart and McLemore Cove which allowed Jeff to avoid recapture by law enforcement authorities for all the remaining years of his life. He lived a life generally of avoidance and disguise.

"Mama said they returned to Dahlonega one time when she was young," Bill continued. "She always wanted to come back (to Lumpkin County) too after that, but she said there was no good way to come because there simply were no bridges or even a real road back then."

Another reason Bill's mother may not have returned with her family to Dahlonega, was that her father not only was *persona non grata*, he quite likely was still a *"Wanted"* criminal in Lumpkin County. There is, however, evidence to indicate Jeff Anderson did return to Dahlonega in the 1880s when his mother died.

Smyth said his mother, Mary Georgia Ann, described the house in which she had grown up as being on stilts and having a metal roof. She remembered how frightened they were when they heard mountain panthers jump on the tin roof. When that happened, a hot fire reportedly would be built in the fireplace to keep the wild cats from

coming down the chimney. The home described by Bill's mother quite likely was the one in which they lived in McLemore Cove. It no doubt continued Jeff's pattern of a life of avoidance out in the wild countryside beyond the reach of law enforcement.

Mary Georgia Ann ultimately grew into womanhood and married Robert Henry Smyth in 1905. The couple raised six boys, one of whom died in childbirth. Lewis was born in 1906, Chester (known as "Chub") in 1908, Jack in 1916, Robert Lee ("Bud") in 1919, and William ("Bill") in 1927.

Jeff's wife, Mary Rebecca, reportedly lived in Tennessee until 1952 when she was 90. According to her grandson Bill, she was still working in her garden and cooking at that time, even though she weighed only 76 pounds. She also reportedly did not have a gray hair on her head, and was said to have been a full-blood Indian.

"Grandma was the sweetest person you'd ever meet," Bill said. "Mama was just like her too. She and her sisters were very hard-working and religious. You'd never suspect that their father was an outlaw. The boys were hard-working too, but I've heard tell they were about as rough as their father."

Bill remembers his mother describing her father as having red hair and pale blue eyes that "looked like they were looking right through you."

"I've been told Grandpa was quite a fiddle player too,"

It was spots such as Rockmart and McLemore Cove which allowed Jeff to avoid recapture by law enforcement authorities.

Bill smiled. "His son, William Arthur, whom I called 'Uncle Clint,' learned to play by watching Grandpa. When Grandpa would call the steps for people to dance, they said you could hear him a mile away."

A Secret Wife?

According to information about Jeff Anderson in *The Heritage of Lumpkin County 1832-1996*, he, for unknown reasons eventually migrated westward to Bonham, Texas (near Dallas) in the autumn of 1901. Anderson descendants of Thomas Abraham wrote, *"We are certain Jeff was in Texas during this period because his nephew, Henry, and his wife Cordelia, went to Texas to find Jeff. While they were there, their third son William was born on October 19, 1901.*

"Jeff later went to Oklahoma in order to avoid being captured because there was no law there. Oklahoma was Indian Territory at this time. . . . We are certain Jeff was in Durant, Oklahoma around April 1905, because Henry and Henry's wife Cordelia went on a second trip in a covered wagon to find Jeff.

"While they were there, their fourth son, Clint was born on April 29, 1905. Henry and Cordelia spotted Jeff at a distance, but he left with some men on horseback and they never caught him. The family received messages from Jeff on two occasions, once from Durant and another time from Hugo. Jeff never returned."

That information about the outlaw Jeff Anderson was submitted by George Anderson of Maryville, Tennessee, the grandson of Abraham's son, Henry Clay Anderson, and his wife Cordelia, who went to Texas and Oklahoma looking for Jeff. George was astonished to learn that Jeff had married and fathered a number of additional children.

"I'm not sure we're talking about the same man," George puzzled, even after speaking by phone with Bill Smyth, possibly a cousin of whom he had known nothing until recently. "There are lots of Andersons, and there may have been two Jeff Andersons. Some of the dates just don't seem to correspond."

Could there possibly have been two different "Jeff Andersons" who were both Civil War-era outlaws who originated from the same locale? Possible, but not likely.

Nevertheless, if Bill Smyth's grandfather was the same man as George Anderson's great-great uncle, why did he keep his marriage a secret from his family and why did he not inform them of his whereabouts? Why indeed did he leave his Georgia wife – Mary Rebecca – in the first place?

A possible explanation may lie in the fact that the alienation between the brothers at the time Jeff left Abraham's household may have been so bitter that Jeff simply chose to permanently cut all ties and disappear forever. Worse relationships have existed throughout history. The simple lure of a new life with a new wife could have provided all the motivation an individual like Jeff Anderson needed.

More GA Children?

If the man believed to be in Texas and Oklahoma for several years following the turn of the century was in fact Bill Smyth's grandfather, he must at least have traveled back to Georgia on occasion, because he reportedly sired additional children there in 1901 and 1904 with Mary Mollie Rebecca Dilbeck Anderson.

Interestingly, prior to his move to the West, Jeff Anderson had made his home near the Tennessee border (probably at or near the aforementioned Mc-

Lemore Cove), less than forty miles northwest of Abraham Anderson's farm near Dalton. Despite the nearness of their residences, they apparently never again encountered one another following their final separation, possibly due to innate animosities and the mountainous terrain separating them.

According to stories Bill described about his grandpa Jeff Anderson, the outlaw apparently mellowed at least to some extent with age and a family, but remained feisty even into his later years.

"(I've been told) Grandpa's (Jeff's) dog went missing one time," he laughed again. "When he heard a dog barking that sounded like his, he followed the sound until he came to a fenced-in yard. He opened the gate and walked in and started to untie his dog. When a man appeared and demanded to know what he was doing, Grandpa calmly ignored him.

"Don't you know you can get into trouble coming into a man's yard and stealing his dog?" the fellow demanded.

"Grandpa - according to the story - pulled out his gun and replied, 'Well, son, don't you know it works both ways?' He then turned around and walked back out the gate leading his dog."

Bill Smyth says he has information showing that his grandfather died in 1913, and remembers his mother showing him the outlaw's unmarked grave at Strawhill Cemetery, "down the Dalton pike" from Cleveland, Tennessee. Could it be possible that his body was returned there from Texas or Oklahoma for burial following his death? Or had he returned to live out his later years in that vicinity with Mollie?

In actuality, it is very unlikely that the body of a virtually penniless man would have been returned from Texas or Oklahoma to be buried in Tennessee

in 1913. That just didn't happen. Under those circumstances, the body – almost without exception – was quickly buried near to the site of death. If "the" Jeff Anderson was buried in Tennessee, that's where he undoubtedly had been living (or at least visiting) prior to his death.

Bill Smyth's grandmother, Mary "Mollie" Rebecca Anderson lived a number of years longer (until 1952) and was buried at Red Hill Cemetery just outside Cleveland, Tennessee. She did not want to be buried beside Jeff because she thought that cemetery was too far from her children.

Bill added that he has heard that his grandfather died from being "bled," which once was a popular medical treatment for numerous ailments. It seems ironic that in an age when maverick behavior was often blamed upon "bad blood," the notorious "black sheep" of the family should meet his end by a treatment thought to rid the body of "bad blood" even though he apparently "had gone straight" later in his life.

Endnotes

1/ *United States Federal Census, Lumpkin County, GA*, (1834)

2/ Lumpkin County Heritage Book Committee and Don Mills, Inc, Walsworth Publishing, *Heritage of Lumpkin County, 1832-1996* (1996)

3/ O'Kelley, Harold E., *Dahlonega's Blue Ridge Rangers in the Civil War*, Georgia Printing Co. (1992)

4/ Jackson, R. Olin, *Mystery & History in Georgia, Volume I*, Whippoorwill Publications, LLC (2023)

5/ O'Kelley, Harold E., *Dahlonega's Blue Ridge Rangers in the Civil War*, Georgia Printing Co. (1992)

(Grateful appreciation is expressed herewith to the late Anne Amerson, Dahlonega, Georgia, for the accumulation of information necessary for this article.)

Old West Bandit Visits the Old London Homestead

It was a landmark in the county for approximately 125 years before sadly succumbing to "progress" and demolition for new construction at the Georgia 400 – Georgia Highway 60 intersection in Lumpkin County. A famous old West outlaw – memorialized in best-selling books and at least one major motion picture – also once stopped by this historic house.

The intangible entity known as "progress" can be both a good thing, and a bad thing. When it comes to historic preservation, "progress" many times falls on the "bad" side of the spectrum. Such was the case with construction of the intersection of Georgia 400 Highway and Highway 60 south of Dahlonega, because it required the removal/demolition of one of the most historic homes in the county known as "the old London home-place."

It is unknown today exactly when the Merritt M. London homestead was built, but it quite possibly was constructed during the earlier gold mining days in the area. From the early 1920s until sometime around the year 2000, travelers driving on Highway 60 from Gainesville to Dahlonega caught a glimpse of the rear of a large imposing farmhouse on the right at the intersection of Long Branch Road.

To most, this home also seemed oddly situated, but that can be easily explained. You see, it was built so long ago, that it faced a road which no longer existed in more modern times. By the time Georgia Highway 60 from Gainesville was constructed past the old home,

it (the home) had already been in existence for many years, and was originally situated to face the ancient wagon road – Neisler Trail.

Merritt London Farm

Merritt London, the builder and original owner of the home, came to Dahlonega from Burke County, North Carolina. As the son of James Wadkins London and Elizabeth Conley London, Merritt prospered in his new north Georgia home, farming the rich bottom lands along the Chestatee River during the latter half of the 19th century.

London was twenty-eight years of age when he married 17-year-old Mary Neisler in Lumpkin County in 1859. Mary's father – Daniel Neisler – was one of the earliest settlers in the area.

Today, much of Georgia Highway 60 follows the old wagon trail once known as "Neisler's Road." Mary's sister – Frances "Fannie" Neisler – married William H. Early and lived in an equally-historic house which still stands on Long Branch Road a short distance from the former site of the London home.

Most of the present-day information about Merritt and Mary N. London

On The Run – The home of Merritt M. London stood near the intersection of Long Branch Road and GA Highway 60 in Lumpkin County for a century or more until construction and development at the terminus of modern-day Georgia Highway 400 with Long Branch Road required the historic home's demolition in the mid-1990s. Outlaw George Anderson (a.k.a. "Bill Miner") and his accomplices reportedly paused at London's Store in front of this home just long enough to stock up on a few supplies, before continuing their flight from justice after having robbed Southern Railway's Train #36 at White Sulphur in nearby Hall County.

Flight Food – The "M. M. London & Sons Cash Store," once operated by Merritt M. London in his later years, was photographed circa 1930s. It was at this store that outlaw Bill Miner reportedly paused to purchase a few supplies following his robbery of Southern Railway's Train #36 in Hall County. (Photo courtesy of Anne Amerson)

came from two of their descendants who, until recent times, lived in Gainesville, Georgia. Merritt and Mary had nine children – four boys and five girls. The late Mary Annie Hope, the daughter of Merritt and Mary's youngest daughter – Flossie – was 89 years of age in 1994 when she was interviewed about her family and the home.

"I could hardly wait for school to let out so I could go visit Grandpa and Grandma London's farm outside Dahlonega," Miss Hope reminisced. "Since we lived in Gainesville, I rode with Uncle Bob in his covered wagon pulled by a pair of mules.

"Grandpa raised cows, hogs, chickens, ducks, and geese," Miss Hope continued. "I remember helping to pluck the geese to make pillows. It has to be done at a certain time, or the feathers won't pull out easily and it hurts the

skin. It takes twenty pounds of feathers to make a feather mattress, and Grandma gave each of her girls a feather bed when they married.

"The hens always made their nests in the grass at the edge of the woods, and I loved to go hunting for their eggs," Mary Annie added. "Grandma was always anxious to get a hen to set so she could get some early fryers. It was such a pretty sight to see a gang of little chicks running around in the yard (even if they were soon destined for the frying pan).

"Grandpa farmed the bottomlands all the way to the river. He grew a lot of corn for his stock, but he didn't believe much in cotton – just enough to pay his taxes.

"I don't know how old the house was, but I do know that Grandpa had the timbers cut and the bricks burned for it," she explained. "Water was piped into the house from a spring, and there were two wooden troughs on the porch where the water flowed through. I used to love to wade in the branch in the summertime.

179

Last Image – M.M. London's Cash Store was photographed at the old London homestead in 1993, just prior to its demolition for new construction at the intersection of Georgia Highway 400 and Georgia Highway 60 south of Dahlonega, Georgia. (Photo courtesy of Anne Amerson)

Jim London Farm – Photographed circa 1890, members of the Long Branch community participate in a "corn-shucking" at the Jim London farm. The young lady (second from right in front) is Myrtle London (born 1891). (Photo courtesy of GA Dept. of Archives & History, Atlanta, GA)

"Some men who worked on the dredge boats that mined the Chestatee River for gold used to board with Grandma and Grandpa, and they always paid off in gold dust," Mary Annie continued. "Grandma used it to have gold rings made for Mama and her sister, Mollie.

"Mollie married George Moore, the son of Col. Robert Hughes Moore, who came to Dahlonega in 1839 to mine for gold. George and Mollie moved to Gainesville where he started the G.W. Moore Coal Company.

"I don't remember Grandpa London very well, since he died in 1908 when I was only five years old. The last time I visited the farm was in 1913, because Grandma moved to Gainesville after that.

"Mama (Flossie) married Charlie Hope, a mule trader like his father, 'Doc' Hope, who used to run a livery stable in Dahlonega in the 1880s. Before they moved to Gainesville, Grandpa and Grandma Hope lived in one of the oldest houses in town."

{Author's Note: Even though it passed through many other hands after

A.A. Hope sold it in 1891, the historic structure, built circa 1845, continued to be known as the "Hope House" through the years. It was built and for many years stood in front of the present-day Smith House Restaurant in Dahlonega, prior to being moved from that site (in 1985) to a spot known as "Mountain Music Park" on Highway 60 South where it may still exist today.}

Outlaw Bill Miner

Merritt and Mary's daughter – Alice – married James "Jimmy" Elrod, and their daughter, Mae, was the mother of Mrs. Clara Belle Eades, who lived for many years on Thompson Bridge Road outside Gainesville. She, too, remembered visiting the Merritt London farm when she was a small girl.

Mrs. Eades also recalls the tragic story of Merritt and Mary's son, Ben, who reportedly went out to tend the sheep one winter night. When his little dog returned without him, Grandma London burst out crying and said, "If some of you don't go see about Ben, I will!"

Following a search of the property,

Dredge Barge Workers – One of the large gold-dredging barges which once plied the gravels of the Chestatee River on the London property is pictured. Workers on the barges often boarded at the London home. (Photo courtesy of GA Dept. of Archives & History, Atlanta, GA)

members of the family found Ben leaning over a fence rail – dead of unknown causes. After that day, Grandma London never again enjoyed snowfall. She also lost another son – Willie – who had a twin sister named Mattie.

When Grandpa Merritt got too old to work in the fields, his surviving sons – Bob (who never married) and Frank (who married Annie Kemp) – reportedly built him a country store near the London home-place. A family legend and local folklore maintain that the infamous outlaw – Bill Miner – entered the store with his accomplices one day in 1911, to purchase supplies. Whoever was tending the store at the time – likely one of Grandpa Merritt's sons – remembered that the stranger was in an awfully big hurry, and thought it unusual, until the posse tracking him arrived the following day.

Miner was wanted in California

and numerous other spots for murder and train and stagecoach holdups, and had just robbed Southern Railway's Train Number 36 just north of Gainesville. *(Readers please see "Old West Bandit Bill Miner's Capture in North Georgia" in this book.)*

An article in an issue of the February, 1911 ***Dahlonega Nugget*** newspaper recorded the fact that one of Miner's accomplices in the robbery ate breakfast at the home of W.H. Early (brother-in-law of Merritt London) whose now-historic home still stands – as of this writing (2024) – on Long Branch Road just a short distance from the Georgia 400 – Highway 60 intersection. The article explains the outlaw had earlier purchased tobacco and candy at McGuire's soda fountain in Dahlonega, as well as six boxes of snuff at J.W. Moore's store.

The article goes on to explain that

W.H. Early home – Built at roughly the same time as the Merritt London homestead the historic Early home a short distance northeastward down Long Branch Road still exists as of this writing (2024). Merritt M. London married Mary Neisler of nearby Neisler's Ford. Mary's sister – Frances "Fannie" Neisler – married William H. Early who built and lived in the W.H. Early home which is strikingly similar to the London home in design.

Merritt M. London, the family patriarch, is pictured above as he appeared in his later years. (Photo courtesy of Annie Lou Dobbs)

it was determined the man put the snuff in his shoes later to keep tracking dogs from finding him. After the robbery of Southern's Train Number 36, Miner and his two accomplices reportedly traveled to Dahlonega where they then went separate ways. Miner was later captured in the Nimblewill community northwest of Dahlonega.

George W. Moore, Jr., the son of Mollie London and George W. Moore, operated the family coal business until 1980. He recalled attending a reunion at the old Merritt London home-place when he was about seven years old and playing with some of his cousins there. He says the house was unpainted in those days, and there was a fence around it to keep out the livestock, since that was in the days prior to stock laws.

"I'm not sure when the London farm was sold, but (later owners of the property) found the sign from Grandpa Merritt's store and gave it to my brother and me," George explained. "It's made of a single board twelve feet long and three feet wide. Even after nearly a century, the black lettering 'M. M. London & Sons Cash Store' is still very legible."

Neighbors & Relatives

Mrs. Hester Burns Rickman was born in 1897 and grew up just down the road from the Londons. "We could see the store from our house," she explained, "and Mama would send me to get things like sugar and coffee. Uncle Merritt had a long white beard that tickled when he hugged me. He wasn't really my uncle, but we called him that out of respect, because we were children and he was elderly."

Clara Belle Eades' daughter – Joyce Howard – of Stockbridge, still has an old ledger used to keep records in the London store in the late 1890s. It shows that bills were frequently not paid in cash but in other ways, such as "credit by 2 turkeys" (worth $1.35), "credit by 1 day's work killing hogs" (worth 40 cents), "credit by one day mowing" (worth 50 cents), and "credit by 8 gr gold" (worth 30 cents).

Jim London Home – The Jim London family members were photographed at their home near the Merritt London home circa 1897. (Seated L-R): Fannie Martin London and Jim London. (Standing L-R): Dave, Julia Martin, Myrtle, Floyd ("Doc"), (female beside him is unidentified), Clarence (with banjo), Eve, Emma, and Tom. Notice how a chimney had been removed (background) from the gable-end of the home. (Photo courtesy of GA Dept. of Archives & History, Atlanta, GA)

Merritt M. London Home – As is obvious from this circa 1897 photo, the Merritt London home had changed little prior to its demolition in 1995. Pictured are: Merritt (center, with white beard & hat); his wife Mary Neisler (beside tree); and his sons, Frank (in wagon) and Bob (second from left). (Photo courtesy of GA Dept. of Archives & History, Atlanta, GA)

James A. "Jim" London was Merritt's younger brother. He also was born in Burke County, North Carolina, and he has a number of known descendants in Lumpkin County today. There are other signs of his passing too.

Dahlonega's Doug Cain remembers the Jim London house well, because his family lived in it from 1917 until 1949. It once stood less than half a mile from the Chestatee River, and was on the opposite side of the river from the Merritt London home-place. It faced the old wagon road to Auraria, and was also tragically demolished when Georgia Highway 400 was built in the early 1980s.

Jim's first wife – Martha A. Nicely – died in 1876 at the age of forty, leaving him with several young children. A little over two months later, he married a 25-year-old widow named Fanny Martin, who had four small children from her first marriage.

Jim and Fanny ultimately had seven children of their own – Thomas Jefferson, Floyd, Emma, Eva, James Albert, Clarence, and Myrtle.

Although Jim was five years younger than Merritt, he preceded him in death by several years. His will was probated in 1901.

An item in the February 5, 1892 issue of *The Dahlonega Signal* noted that James A. London *"is anxious to sell his farm at Martin's Ford, on the Chestatee River, and move his family to the Indian Territory,"* but he apparently never did.

In Merritt London's obituary, he was described as *"among our oldest citizens."* The newspaper account noted that he *"came to Lumpkin County in 1858 or 1859, where he took up the occupation of farming"* and that he *"had been a member of the Methodist Church ever since he was sixteen years of age."* He and Mary Neisler London are both buried at St. Paul's Church near the Lumpkin-Hall County line.

Today, well over a century after Merritt London's death, the area around the intersection of Highways 60 and 400 is still referred to as "the old London farm."

Gunfight on the Square

The 1913 Bank of Lumpkin Co. Robbery

It is but a footnote in history today, but back in the early 1900s, a group of bandits attempted to rob Dahlonega's Bank of Lumpkin County, and met with a bit more resistance than they had anticipated. The ensuing blazing gun-battle rivaled a scene right out of the old West.

The impressive country-style home originally built by the Jones family still sits prominently on the west-northwest corner of the town square in Dahlonega, Georgia. As of this writing in 2024, it is occupied by commercial businesses, but back on the cold night of February 12, 1913, it housed the brood of Dr. and Mrs. C.H. Jones. Its residents didn't know it at the time, but they were about to witness a shocking attempted bank robbery.

Theodocia Jones – recently widowed by the death of her physician husband – had been awakened from her sleep by strangers milling about and muttering on the sidewalk outside her home and she instinctively suspected that something unusual was afoot. Little did she know that her intuition had sniffed out a major crime in the making.

Just as Theodocia was seriously considering the summoning of help, the men suddenly just disappeared. Though she was eventually able to get back to sleep, it was a troubled slumber. She was still uneasy enough the following morning to go to the little drugstore next door to their home to warn the "coffee-klatch" patrons warming themselves casually around the wood stove, telling them beseechingly that they needed to be concerned; that strangers were hanging about the town square in the middle of the night.

As men typically will do until directly confronted by a dangerous circumstance, they dismissed her concerns as neurotic alarmism. Everyone knew that Theodocia had lost her husband the previous year. The men in the drug store good-naturedly attempted to do little more than console her.

Frustrated and put-out with the men, Theodocia went back home next door and pursued her daily tasks – but with a still-growing feeling of fear. She was so concerned that she sent her daughter – Wanda – to fetch a friend to come spend the next night at their home.

"Boom!" in the Night

That evening, sure enough, shortly after midnight in the wee hours of the morning, a muffled explosion suddenly

"Meaders Corner" – Photographed circa 1950s, this early home/business (foreground) appears exactly as it did on the cold winter night of February 13, 1913, when owner Robert C. "Mista Bob" Meaders slipped out the rear door and then, with the assistance of Sheriff Tom Ray, blazed away with two different firearms to thwart an attempted robbery of the Bank of Lumpkin County on the north side of the town square. One of the large windows visible on the upstairs porch of the Meaders home was shattered by gunfire from one of the bandits when Robert's wife, Margaret, illuminated the room to call the sheriff. All of the structures visible in this photo are unchanged from the way they appeared on the night of the attempted robbery, and a number of them still exist today on the old town square, though the Meaders home has sadly disappeared. (Photo courtesy of Margaret Meaders)

broke the calm of their winter sleep. Theodocia was fully awake almost immediately. She tenderly but quickly scooped up her infant daughter, Frances, in her arms, then hustled the other children – Wanda and Charles Harry – into the dining room where they all hid behind the chimney.

In 1913, the tiny and rural mountain town of Dahlonega, Georgia, was composed of little more than 200 households. Many of them also had heard the substantial racket and some were concerned. This, after all, was barely 48 years after the close of the U.S. Civil War, and the more concerned men remembered those types of noises quite well. Nevertheless, it was also the dead of winter outside, and the noise they had detected

simply was not alarming enough to urge them out of their warm beds into the frigid winter weather for an investigation.

Mischievous cadets just up the street at North Georgia Agricultural College (NGAC) were notorious for firing off the college cannon at odd hours and waking the town residents. Most of the awakened sleepers therefore merely wrote off the commotion to more adolescent mischief and went back to sleep.

The explosion had occurred just below the Hall House on the north side of the Dahlonega town square where one NGAC student by the name of Cleveland Duncan was rooming on the second floor. When he stepped out of his

Hall House – Photographed circa 1900 at the site of the 1913 attempted robbery of the Bank of Lumpkin County, one of the upper rooms of the Hall House (pictured) was occupied by North Georgia Agricultural College (fore-runner of present-day University of North Georgia in Dahlonega) student Cleveland Duncan. After hearing the muffled explosion of the attempted break-in by bandits at the bank downstairs, Duncan peered over the railing of the upper level and was immediately fired upon by one of the bank robbers standing directly below. The small bank building (bricked with barred windows) is visible on the left. All of these structures still exist as of this writing (2024) on the Dahlonega town square. (Photo courtesy of GA Dept. of Archives & History, Atlanta)

room onto the Hall House's second floor porch to investigate the source of the noise, Cleveland was shocked to see a man with a revolver standing directly below him in front of the small Bank of Lumpkin County building. It did not require a super-intellect to deduce that something out of the ordinary was afoot, and the young college student was immediately suspicious.

Interestingly, at about this same time, the stranger with the revolver looked up and discovered young Cleveland witnessing his actions, and he immediately fired a round from his pistol at the young student, much to Cleveland's shock. Just as would anyone who didn't want their head perforated – Duncan jerked back inside his room.

With the pop of gunfire now joining the unusual noises outside, the boldness – or ignorance – of the bandits soon became responsible for the attraction of still more attention, but this time, it would be a much more serious confrontation.

"Mista Bob"

By 1913 there were over six million telephones in use in the United States, but only a precious few of them existed in what then was the very remotely-located backwoods mountain town of Dahlonega, Georgia. Fortunately, a phone did exist in the lobby of the Hall House, and Cleveland Duncan had the presence of mind to make use of it.

Across the town square at an angle from where Duncan stood was what was known in those days as "Meaders' Corner." It existed at the corner of Main and North Park streets, and was owned and occupied by Robert C. "Mista Bob" Meaders. The Meaders family lived in the downstairs portion of this structure and the local Dahlonega telephone exchange – which was owned and operated by Bob – was located in the upper level.

Aside from his communications responsibilities, Mista Bob was also the president of the Lumpkin County Bank. Cleveland Duncan knew that if he called the telephone exchange, a special buzzer downstairs used to summon "Central" (the person operating the telephone exchange at any given time) would awaken the Meaders and bring someone to the telephone. *(Author's Note: In the 21st Century, it is somewhat amusing to imagine the telephone operator being awakened from sleep in order to travel "upstairs" to answer "Central," in order to connect someone else with a distant caller, but those were the circumstances in 1913.)*

Unbeknownst to young Cleveland, no awakening was necessary at this point for Bob Meaders. We're talking serious consequences for anyone brazen enough to try to steal money from Mista Bob, and any "boom" immediately got his attention. The dedicated town leader was already on his way upstairs to the telephone switchboard when Cleveland's call set off the buzzer.

Cleveland, no doubt, was almost beside himself at this point. He had already been fired upon by the perpetrators on the town square. When he excitedly described the circumstances to Bob, the bank president quickly dressed, retrieved his revolver, and then set out to investigate. Before he left, he

"Mista Bob" – Robert C. Meaders was photographed here in his later years. When younger, he had no reservations about a shoot-out on the Dahlonega town square in order to thwart a bank robbery which was in progress early on a cold morning in February of 1913.

instructed his wife, Maggie, to "Call the sheriff and tell him the bank is being robbed."

Bob then didn't waste any time slipping quietly out the back door of his home into the mid-winter freezing weather and easing down behind Will Jones's store and then on up to the Sergeant Building at the northeast corner of the town square. After taking extreme caution to remain undetected by the thieves, Bob next moved through what at that time was a vacant lot to the east end of the Hall House. The bandits had not yet caught wind of Bob's actions as he reconnoitered the situation.

Two of the bandits had been posted as "look-outs" at the courthouse (present-day Dahlonega Gold Museum). The large picture window of the upstairs telephone exchange in the Meaders building had been dark up to this point. Having never previously dealt with a situation of this nature, Miss Maggie thought nothing of turning on the lights to reveal the switchboard in order to summon Sheriff Tom Ray.

However, when the room lit up and Maggie stepped in front of the picture window to initiate the call, the bandits immediately knew what she was doing and opened fire on her. A totally shocked Maggie Meaders dropped instantly to the floor as the window shattered and broken glass rained all around her as a result of the gunfire.

Though shaken, Maggie was unharmed, and reached up to plug in the appropriate connections on the telephone switchboard to call not only the sheriff, but everyone else of whom she could think to summon. Fingers had never moved so quickly on a telephone switchboard.

"High Noon"

Meanwhile, back down on the square, Mista Bob hadn't taken kindly to his bank being robbed, and when his wife was fired upon, that was the last straw as far as he was concerned. He opened up with a blaze of gunfire of his own at the bandits. He later explained that it was so dark, he couldn't actually see the thieves, but he knew where they were by the muzzle-flashes from their weapons, and he had concentrated his gunfire upon those locations.

It was about this point that Sheriff

It was now very clear that these outlaws thought nothing of killing someone to achieve their objective of robbery of the bank.

Ray hurriedly rounded the corner onto the square, having run the several blocks down Main Street from the Lumpkin County Jail (which also still exists today). Since he was unaware of the actual circumstances, Ray was incautious in his advance, and Bob shouted a quick warning to him to take cover.

It was at this point that a round fired by one of the bandits shattered a store window directly behind the sheriff, so he didn't require any further encouragement. It was now very clear that these outlaws thought nothing of killing someone to achieve their objective of robbery of the bank.

Still somewhat confused with the circumstances, Ray reportedly shouted to Bob inquiring about the identity of the men and the nature of their actions. Bob, losing patience with the lawman, reportedly shouted back "You idiot! They're robbing the bank and they've been shooting at you ever since you rounded the corner!"

When Ray finally realized the actual circumstances, he worked his way around the square to where Bob was crouched behind the Hall House. He handed Meaders another handgun. Bob reloaded his own revolver and the two of them then advanced steadily on the criminals, reportedly firing with weapons in both hands, in a scene reminiscent of *High Noon*.

Attempted Getaway

The duo's determined gunfire produced dividends almost immediately as one of the bandits went down with a wound. When the remaining thieves took stock of the situation, they apparently decided that discretion was the better part of valor and they took flight, running for an automobile parked just off the square on South Main Street. They then drove quickly off into the darkness, southward down old U.S. 19 Highway.

Though the thieves had departed, Mista Bob and the sheriff were unaware at this point of their whereabouts, and had taken cover to take stock and then advance upon them once again. A short time later, they were informed by other town residents that the perpetrators had left in a vehicle.

As daylight began breaking over the horizon onto the Dahlonega town square, the sheriff began organizing a posse. Though the thieves had quickly exited the area in a vehicle, the posse was composed of some two dozen men on horseback.

Surprisingly, though the thieves had enjoyed a sizeable advantage in their getaway in the vehicle, for reasons unknown today, they had later paused to grab some sleep – perhaps exhausted from their several continuous days and nights of canvassing the Dahlonega streets and businesses to plan the robbery.

According to accounts of the incident, the men, amazingly, were eventually discovered sleeping in a ditch. The arrests took place near Ellijay, Georgia. Though their getaway had seemed almost assured since they were speeding away in an automobile, it seems surprising today that men on horseback were able to overtake and capture the criminals seemingly so easily.

In those days, however, all the "streets" – bar none – were no more than dusty mountain trails, and a talented tracker on horseback was easily able to follow the tracks of an automobile on a dirt road little-traveled by other vehicles. By eight o'clock that evening, all the men were behind bars at the Lumpkin County Jail in Dahlonega, under the watchful eye of Sheriff Ray. (And they were lucky Mista Bob – still smarting from the attacks upon his wife – couldn't get to them too.)

Aftermath

Much to his financial relief, Mista Bob reportedly discovered that the only items the thieves had managed to actually steal from the bank were two pistols. In more recent times, Bob's son – Robert Meadors, Jr. of Camarillo, California, – stated "They apparently were unfamiliar with (and had been thwarted by) the type of safe used by the bank which had two (instead of only one) access doors.

"After drilling through the outer door, they had attempted to blast through the second door," Meaders added, "but the explosion had actually done more to deter than to help them. It had sealed the inner door into the safe to produce what amounted to an almost solid steel box. That safe later had to be placed on the sidewalk outside the bank and cut open with a blow torch."

In an article penned by writer (and Mista Bob's sister) Margaret Meaders which was later published in the June-July, 1970 issue of *Georgia Magazine*, she explained the outlaws *"gave assumed names throughout most of their trial, but eventually were identified as professional thieves on their way to Knoxville, Tennessee, from Atlanta. Hearing about the two little banks in Dahlonega, they had decided to 'knock off' one or both on their way north and pick up a little 'easy money.'"*

According to an article in the February 28, 1913 issue of the *Dahlonega Nugget* newspaper:

"The parties who gave their names

as Charles Miller, John M. Harris, William Thornton and W.M. Flynn, charged with entering the Bank of Lumpkin County and blowing open the outer door of its safe on the morning of the 14th inst., at about one o'clock were here last Monday before Justice of the Peace W.B. Townsend, and all bound over to the next term of Lumpkin Superior Court on the charge of burglary, bond of each being fixed at ten thousand dollars, who have been sent to Fulton County Jail by Judge Jones for safe-keeping.

The old "Will Jones Store," however, one of the oldest structures in Dahlonega, still stands and has housed a number of businesses over the years.

"The parties who entered the bank got nothing but a couple of pistols, but they seceeded (sic) in wrecking the front of the safe before they were run off by Sheriff T.M. Ray and R.C. Meaders, president of the bank. The insurance company had to replace the safe with a new one. Neither was there any positive or direct evidence that these men did enter this bank, but the circumstantial proof was strong against them, all of whom beyond a doubt were traveling under false colors by using assumed names.

"The quartette (sic) was convicted of burglary, by the Superior Court of Lumpkin County, and were sent to the penitentiary; but were soon pardoned out by the Governor." (Author's Note: Absolutely amazing. Some things never change.)

Yesteryear's Buildings

Interestingly, due to preservation-minded residents, much of the old town square has been preserved and still exists just as it did on the night of this attempted robbery in 1913.

One of the few exceptions is the old Meaders building on the corner once owned by Mista Bob and in which he and his family lived and operated Dahlonega's first telephone exchange for many years. It, unfortunately, was demolished years ago and a new structure was built upon that site.

The old "Will Jones Store," however, one of the oldest structures in Dahlonega, still stands and has housed a number of businesses over the years. It continues to be a popular business site today.

The "Sargent Building" also still stands and was an automobile dealership for many years. It also continues to be a popular locale for shops and businesses.

The "vacant lot" between the Sargent Building and the "Hall House" is no longer "vacant," having been occupied later by a building which still stands today.

The "Hall House," constructed in the early 1880s (and known as the "Robert M. Moore Building" for many years) was built by early Dahlonega businessman Frank W. Hall, and also still stands as of this writing. It is a popular site of shops, restaurants, and other businesses both upstairs and downstairs.

The focus of all the excitement in 1913 – the little one-story Lumpkin County Bank building – also still stands as of this writing. Built in 1881, it originally served as Frank W. Hall's business office. Hall was a mining and real estate entrepreneur who reportedly was the richest individual in Lumpkin County in his day. He also contracted for the construction of and owned "Hall's Block" on the northwestern corner of the square (behind the bank), the aforementioned "Hall House," the present-day eatery known as "The Smith House" restaurant, as well as a number of other edifices in the county.

Hall departed Dahlonega somewhat mysteriously in 1900. Over 100 years later in 2006, it was discovered that he apparently had, for a number of years, been illicitly mining gold ore from a substantial shaft beneath what today is the Smith House Restaurant (*Readers please see "The Secret Gold Mine Beneath the Smith House" in the Lumpkin County section of "Mystery & History in Georgia, Volume 2," also by author R. Olin Jackson*).

Captain Hall was also responsible for the construction of historic Lumpkin County Jail where the outlaws were imprisoned (and which still stands today) a short distance from the town square. Though it served as a lock-up for numerous figures down through the county's history, including notorious old West outlaw Bill Miner, captured outside Dahlonega in 1911, it has not served as a jail for many years. Today, it is a preserved historic site, serving as of this writing as the site of the Lumpkin County Historic Society.

In 1931, a few years after the 1913 robbery attempt, the Bank of Lumpkin County ceased to exist after it was merged with the Bank of Dahlonega. The combined banks were relocated to the southeast corner of the town square where the business existed for many years. That structure also still stands today, although used for purposes other than banking.

The historic Jones home – built circa 1885 – is known as "the Conner House" as of this writing and houses several gift shops today.

The historic Lumpkin County Courthouse – built in 1836 – also still exists and houses the Dahlonega Gold Museum today. Visitors from throughout the world come to view its pioneer-justice interior month after month, year after year, some seeking information about relatives and other aspects of the county's history among the many archives housed in this building. One of its upstairs display cases houses a Smith & Wesson revolver taken from one of the bandits arrested in the 1913 robbery attempt.

Also on display in the Gold Museum is a bullet discovered embedded in one of the columns that were an original part of the interior of the old courthouse. The source of the round is unknown today, and since the streets of the Dahlonega town square have experienced quite a bit of gunfire over the years – all the way back to the 1830s – the source of the round likely will never be known.

All of those involved with the attempted 1913 bank robbery – including Mista Bob and Miss Maggie Meaders, Sheriff Tom Ray and the others – all sleep the big sleep in area graveyards today.

Hall departed Dahlonega somewhat mysteriously in 1900.

The Life & Legend of "Boney Tank"

Any way one cuts it, "Boney Tank" was an extraordinary individual and a fearless opponent if one ever chanced to oppose him. He joins a list of unusual personalities from Lumpkin County, Georgia, in the mid- to late-19th Century who rose to fame and legendary status in the state's history.

Ever heard of a person by the name of "Boney Tank?" Neither have a lot of people, but if one is a student of Georgia history, his name almost certainly is a known entity. As one of the most colorful and legendary individuals in the state's history, he has been chronicled in books, magazine articles, and news stories during and after his lifetime.

The American West has spawned a long list of characters who have been celebrated in song, story and major motion picture productions for well over 100 years now. Who, for instance, has not heard of such notables as John Henry "Doc" Holliday or Meriwether Lewis or John C. Fremont?

These individuals are deeply ingrained in the folklore and history of America. Despite this fact, few people today are aware that these men were Georgians by birth before they were legends of the frontier West.

Many "legendary" characters, in fact, came from the state of Georgia in the 1800s. One of the most famous – and yet also obscure today – of these was a fellow with the exceedingly odd name of "Charles and Napoleon Bonaparte 'Boney Tank' Tankersley."

Frontier Existence

Known generally as simply "Boney Tank," this somewhat incredible Georgian was born August 20, 1840, and ultimately became an adventurer, gold miner, wounded Civil War veteran, outrageous businessman, and fearless fighter of great renown. "Boney" genuinely enjoyed his reputation as a captivating personality, and sought to add to his legend whenever possible.

At one time in the youthful years of America, the "western frontier" was what today is the state of Georgia. As "Manifest Destiny" and pioneer migration constantly pushed the American frontier farther and farther westward, Georgia gradually became more and more civilized, forcing out the Native Americans, and the adventurers who preferred a less restricted and uninhibited environment.

By the 1840s, Georgia's "frontier"

days – for the most part – were behind her, but there were exceptions. There were still pockets where vestiges of frontier life still existed. One such spot was what today is known as Lumpkin County where gold had been discovered in 1828. This was where the story of Boney Tank began.

Lumpkin remained a lawless territory until well into the 1870s – particularly during and after the U.S. Civil War. It was a place which just naturally attracted opportunists and adventurers – and cut-throats. Just as with legends such as Texas's Judge Roy Bean, Boney Tank undoubtedly enjoyed fame and notoriety which exceeded his actual accomplishments and life experiences, but so also did many of the other famous personalities from yesteryear. Boney, however, often lived up to his legend.

One Tankersley family remembrance maintains that Boney and his brother, "Tip," were twins born in a cave to a Cherokee woman who was hiding from the U.S. troops who were rounding up the Indians during the infamous "Trail Of Tears." The father of the two boys, as the legend goes, was a reporter and later editor of *The New York World* newspaper – forerunner of the later *New York Times*. Interestingly, when he died, Boney Tank was eulogized in *The New York World* as *"The Man Who Was Never Whipped"* with *"peace to his unconquered ashes,"* and other eloquent flatteries. How did they even know about him?

The family legend also maintains that the two brothers eventually had a bitter falling out after it was discovered that Boney had been involved in an affair with Tip's wife. Tip, according to the tale, abandoned Georgia and his wife and struck out for Oklahoma. The climactic conclusion to this story

Charles and Napoleon "Boney Tank" Tankersley was uniquely-named, to be certain. He was photographed here in the later years of his life. (Photo courtesy of GA Dept. of Archives & History, Atlanta)

maintains that Boney – on his deathbed – married Tip's wife upon learning of Tip's death (Tip supposedly had never divorced his wife).

The actual circumstances of the life and times of Boney Tankersley were in fact considerably different, though no less captivating. Reality has a way of diminishing the luster of the exploits of most folk heroes, but even in reality, Boney Tankersley remains a remarkable personality.

Boney in fact was abandoned by his mother and father at a young age. Following his orphaned adolescence in Lumpkin County, Georgia, he departed that locality for the newly-emerging city of Atlanta. The site was fast becoming a railroad crossroads with rapid growth, and Boney apparently was eager to seek his fortune there.

There is some indication that Tank-

"Gold Diggers' Road" – Looking south down the aptly-named byway (present-day Hwy 9E) in Lumpkin County's Auraria, Georgia, the one-time burgeoning community had withered and died by the time this photograph was taken in the early 1900s. To the right on the vacant lot once stood the Paschal Hotel operated by Agnes Paschal. The two-story Graham Hotel built in the 1830s is visible in the distance on the left. It managed to hang on with no preservation until the 1990s before succumbing to the elements and termites. When not staying at his mother's home in this community, Boney Tank quite likely used both of these hotel rooming opportunities when he returned to Auraria, and would have frequented any number of the saloons which once fronted this road. (Photo courtesy of GA Dept. of Archives & History, Atlanta)

ersley worked briefly as a policeman in Atlanta, but by 1859 at 19 years of age, he was employed as a laborer named Napoleon C. Tank in the Atlanta Rolling Mill, an enormous factory where railroad rails were manufactured and refurbished. It was extremely-hard work which could build a mountain of muscle upon a man.

Civil War Veteran

According to reports, two years later at the age of 21, Boney answered the call to duty, enlisting in Company K of the 7th Georgia Confederate Infantry Regiment. His unit fought at the Battle of First Manassas (also known as Bull Run) on July 21, 1861, the first major engagement of the U.S. Civil War.

In this hard-fought battle, Boney's leg was shattered by one of the huge .69 caliber minie balls fired from the large smooth-bore muskets so dominant early in the war. It was a miracle the leg did not require amputation. It was months before he could walk again, and thereafter, he was lame for the remainder of his life, with a painful wound which constantly festered and never completely healed. According to accounts, Boney also lost an eye in the battle, although no such injury is mentioned in his service records.

Shipped back to Atlanta, Boney had the honor of being among the first of thousands of wounded soldiers eventually sent to the Confederate hospitals of the city. As an early patient returning from the battlefield, Boney was treated to a hero's welcome, complaining years later that with all the parties and attention, he was nearly killed with kindness.

Wounds, however, could not keep Boney Tank out of action, and it was through handicaps such as these that his true mettle shined through. Discharged from the 7th Georgia Infantry as a result of his injury, he merely reenlisted in Company D of the 1st (Galt's) State Line Infantry Regiment and then in Cavalry Company G (the famous "Fulton Dragoons") of Cobb's Legion (the unit of the mythical Major Ashley Wilkes in the Academy Award-winning motion picture *Gone With The Wind*.). He always enlisted as Charles N. Tank, so it was fairly difficult for his name to become confused with that of anyone else.

Thrust back into combat yet again in Virginia, Boney continued his fearless combativeness. A comrade later commented in remembrance that *"no man took more chances in battle than Boney Tank."* He was again wounded – once again in his bad leg – when his horse was shot from beneath him. Medical leave and want of a horse brought him back home and gained him temporary duty in Georgia with the Nitre Bureau (where he helped with explosives) and at another rolling mill making critically-needed horseshoes for the Confederacy – yet another employment stint which continued adding to his mountain of bodily muscle.

Boney later returned from the war to Lumpkin County as a disabled veteran. Despite his courageous efforts in the war, he discovered to his immense disappointment that he had few prospects for a livelihood outside the military.

Professional Life

By 1870, however, Boney reappears as *"Napoleon Tankersley, liqour dealor of Auraria,"* living with Malissa "Eliza"

Lowe Tankersley and the couple's two children. Boney also apparently dabbled in the production of illegal whiskey ("moonshining") since he was tried in federal court in 1873, identified in the indictment as *"N.C. Tankersley."* However, since the practice of moonshining was virtually akin to an honorable profession at that time for mountain families, Tankersley's reputation undoubtedly was enhanced, rather than tarnished, by his encounter with the authorities.

Boney seems ultimately to have found his calling as an agent for the sales of cotton, whiskey and gold mines. The latter – usually sold to Northern interests – led to at least one charge of fraud for the sale of a "salted" mine, where the property in question had been doctored with a few gold nuggets and dust to make the mine appear more valuable. This practice of "salting a mine" was a time-honored profession among Southerners, and indeed was undoubtedly considered "just desserts for Yankee carpet-baggers."

Boney's success as an agent eventually earned him acclaim across the country. One family story maintains that he was even invited to work in a group of mines in Africa, a deal which fell through when Boney saw the ocean for the first time. No way was he getting out on that endless body of water.

Boney eventually was even successful as a financial agent – a feat later considered astounding, since he could neither read nor write. His professional endeavors, however, were not all graft and deception.

In time, he became a respected leader of his little "kingdom" centered around the old mining town of Auraria (originally known as "Nuckollsville") near Dahlonega in Lumpkin County. An editor in Gainesville described him in 1896 as *"cool, serene, and imperturbable. . . . He still wears his hat cocked to the left side, over his absent eye, chews his tobacco on the same side, and has the same fascinating presence. When you talk with him you feel you are with a genius of his kind – that there is only one of him in the wide universe and you have found him."*

Folk Hero

The *New York World* wrote that although Boney appeared in no *"Who's Who"* of local despotism, he was *"a giant, ruling his domain by his powerful fists, taking on any bully or any contender in Auraria."* The *World* called him *"the man who was never whipped"* and *"a Napoleon without a Waterloo."* Again, how did the *World* even know of Boney Tank? Such widely-spread fame is still a mystery today.

Despite his acclaim, and while acknowledging that there may be no rock in Auraria not thrown by Boney at someone at some point in time, his descendants also remember at least one incident in which Boney did taste defeat.

The circumstances involved one of the traveling salesmen who refused a time-honored tradition of a "treat" of a free shot of whiskey for a few regulars at a local gathering spot. Boney apparently attempted to persuade the fellow to honor the custom. The salesman, in return, reportedly unceremoniously dumped the disabled Boney into a meal barrel. Asked later about the incident, Boney merely replied honestly and good-naturedly that he *"had been taken to the mill for a good grinding."*

These types of incidents, however, apparently were few and far between, because aside from his tenacity as a fighter, Boney Tank also enjoyed an army of friends, and few if any enemies. His opinions carried great weight locally and the candidates he backed inevitably won in local elections.

It was in the years after the U.S. Civil War that Boney Tank truly emerged as a folk hero. His reputation was based upon real incidents reported in the contemporary issues of the Atlanta, Dahlonega and Gainesville, Georgia newspapers. The fact that Boney always made "good copy" didn't hurt either.

For example, in 1883, he made news as the defendant in *"the great mule case,"* wherein he was sued by another one-eyed man over a mule that had somehow had its tongue removed. Also in 1883, Boney fought his battle with a monster beaver that, when killed, proved to weigh sixty-nine pounds after being fully dressed – a huge specimen to say the least.

Despite his popularity, extreme charisma, and extraordinary feats of accomplishment which sometimes are just naturally exaggerated, it goes without saying that one must closely examine the details of any incident involving an individual such as Boney Tank. As a result, he usually was closely monitored, but again, he rarely disappointed his fans.

Family Legend

Nevertheless, in regard to the legend about Boney and his brother, Augustus Henry "Tip" Tankersley, the latter was not dead nor was Boney Tankersley on his death-bed when Boney married Eliza Lowe (on April 1, 1895) – who was already the mother of his seven children. It is also unlikely (though not impossible) that Boney Tank was born in a cave during the "Trail of Tears," nor is it certain that his father – Jim Tankersley – worked for *The New York World* (but that substantial news leader in the far-off reaches of New York amazingly seemed to remain routinely-appraised

V.A. Higgins Store – Pictured is the business of V.A. Higgins in Auraria, GA, circa 1910. It was in operation from 1833 to 1937, and was used as the first post office in Lumpkin County. It was located 2 to 3 lots below what was known more recently as "Woody's Store" near the intersection of the town's Main Street and Castleberry Bridge Road. Boney Tank almost certainly would have frequented this store for supplies during his travels to and from Auraria. (Photo courtesy of GA Dept. of Archives & History, Atlanta)

of many of the activities of the legendary Boney Tank).

Boney and his brother appear in the **1850 Federal Census of Lumpkin County** as *"Napoleon"* (age 11, born in Alabama) and *"Henry"* (age 8, born in North Carolina) *"Taonk"* respectively, living with *"Sally Taonk"* (age 27, born North Carolina) and a gold miner named *"James W. Lawrence"* (who was not the father of the boys). That age, interestingly, places his birth quite near the same time as the relocation of the Cherokees to a reservation in 1838.

Interestingly, "Henry Taonk," living years later in Oklahoma as Augustus Henry "Tip Tank" Tankersley, actually filed a claim as a Cherokee Indian against the United States. He listed his mother as *Sarah Mahala "Mary" Narcissa*

Satterfield, the daughter of half-Cherokee Indian Lucy Ward (Mrs. John Satterfield). He stated that his parents had split up after he was born and that his mother eventually married Rubin Moss. (As *Mary Moss*, the boys' mother appears in the **1884 Federal Census of the Eastern Cherokees** as living in Dawson County, Georgia.)

Tip also claimed his mother died in 1885 and that his father was Jim Tankersley, born in Georgia and dead by 1851. Testimony provided by Augustus Henry "Tip" Tankersley on other occasions, however, conflicts with information known about the family. In separate places, he is on record for having stated that he had no brothers or sisters, alive or dead, and that he was the only child of his mother.

197

Boney Tank, interestingly, also filed a claim as a Cherokee Indian. He even cited the claims of Tip's application for Cherokee citizenship in his (Boney's) application for Cherokee funds. In his testimony, Boney added that while he and his brother were young, his mother had married James Lawrence, and had left the two boys on their own *"without home or friends."* He stated that their own father, born in Georgia or North Carolina, had died around 1841.

Tip must have kept better tabs on his mother than did Boney, since Boney had reported her as having died in 1863. As for their Indian heritage, Boney claimed that his grandfather (sic? great-grandfather?) was James Mohannee (also called Ward), a full Cherokee who migrated west on the "Trail of Tears." He also stated that James's wife abandoned him and "went into hiding with the couple's children in the area known today as Lumpkin County."

Boney Tankersley's last living daughter remembered him as a good father, but the Gainesville, Georgia newspaper reported in 1883 of the troubles Boney was experiencing in raising his son Charley, Jr. The son apparently was a genuine "chip off the old block." In separate incidents, he nearly cut off his foot, broke his arm, had his throat cut in a knife-fight, and then shot himself in the thigh. Boney, however, wanted everyone to know that his son and namesake was still a "mighty good boy."

Final Days

Never professing any religion, *"the man who never was whipped,"* required ten days of the ministrations of Baptist preacher Joe Bell, before finally converting just prior to his death on April 23, 1908. He is buried in the Baptist Church cemetery in Auraria, Georgia, among many other legends of Lumpkin County's wild history, including such notables as Capt. Whit Anderson *(Readers please reference "The Amazing Life & Legend of Capt. Whit Anderson" article also in this publication.)* and "Grandma" Agnes Paschal, the "Angel of Mercy."

Because of his impact upon the social fabric of life in numerous communities in north Georgia, Boney Tank enjoys acclaim in a number of county histories. Today (2024), over 115 years after his death, it is sometimes difficult to separate fanciful legend from factual legacy.

During the pioneer days when the western portion of our nation was still being settled, legendary characters inevitably emerged from the battle-tested and danger-experienced migrants who sought a new and better life. All too often, when the truth is uncovered, the persona of these folk heroes is diminished. Charles and Napoleon Bonaparte "Boney Tank" Tankersley, however, just seems to become more extraordinary with each passing year.

Endnotes

Aside from the records of the National Archives and the Georgia Department of Archives and History, information in this article came from James E. Dorsey's **The History Of Hall County, Georgia** *(1991); Andrew W. Cain's* **History Of Lumpkin County – 1832-1932** *(1934); and Andrew Sparks's "Bony Tank Was A Fighting Man,"* **Atlanta Journal Constitution** *Magazine, July 31, 1966, pp. 8-11. Grateful appreciation is extended herewith to Robert S. Davis, Jr. for provision of many factual details used within this article. The author would also like to acknowledge the kind assistance provided by the late Madeline Anthony, Lumpkin County historian; by the late Franklin M. Garrett, Atlanta historian; by Indian genealogists Sarron Ashton and Weldon Hudson; and by Tim Lawson of Gainesville, Georgia.*

The Strange Crime of Corn Tassels and Its Impact On Cherokee Sovereignty

The epic trial and subsequent execution of this Cherokee in Gainesville, Georgia, in 1830, unerringly set the stage for the heart-breaking "Trail of Tears" debacle, and one of the darkest chapters in U.S. history. All details of the Corn Tassels incident have, unsurprisingly, disappeared from the official public record.

One of the most enduring, and indeed compelling criminal incidents in the history of the United States is today essentially a matter of mystery and controversy, and undoubtedly will remain that way forever. At a Cherokee Indian town in what today is north Georgia – the specific site of which, ironically, is also a mystery today – a native Cherokee named George Corn Tassels murdered another Cherokee. Tassels' precedent-setting trial and execution for this crime by the state of Georgia had civil rights and legal implications which still resound today through the U.S. halls of injustice.

The specific criminal proceedings involving Tassels – as serious as they were and which ultimately rose all the way to the Supreme Court of the United States for a decisive verdict – pale to insignificance within the outrageous politics surrounding his case. From a strict legal perspective, Tassels' trial should have been conducted solely within the court system of the Cherokee Nation, since the murder physically occurred in what then was still legally Cherokee Indian Territory. However, in order to establish its dominance and jurisdiction for the ultimate removal of the Cherokees from the Southeast, the state of Georgia chose to ignore the U.S. Supreme Court's mandate regarding the Cherokees' jurisdictional precedence, in essence "hijacking" what had evolved as an admirable Native American criminal justice system.

Aside from its immense lust for the gold recently discovered in the Cherokee Nation in 1828, the state of Georgia also coveted the new geographic boundaries it wished to establish which would usurp those lands currently controlled by the Cherokee Nation. In order to illicitly achieve those objectives, Georgia officials knew they first must require the Cherokee Nation to submit to the laws of the state of Georgia, so that

Voted Down – Georgia Governor George R. Gilmer actively pursued the removal of the Cherokees from what today is the southeastern United States in order to gain legal access to the newly-discovered gold in north Georgia. He ultimately lost his political support (and his elective office) for promoting state (instead of private citizen) ownership of the gold mines as a means of reducing property taxes for wealthy Georgia planters. (From Annals of Gilmer)

the indigenous peoples could ultimately be legally removed to reservations in the West.

George Corn Tassels' amazing and confounding involvement in this incident actually is originally rooted in the American Revolution where the Cherokee Indians unfortunately threw their support and loyalty to the British government who the Cherokees had hoped would remove the invading colonists from the New World. This strategy of course failed miserably when the colonists' vengeful retaliations forced the Native Americans to move south-westward from their homelands in the Carolinas to escape the decimation being inflicted upon them.

As a result, the remnants of the Cherokees now facing extinction mi-grated downward into what today is north Georgia, particularly northwest Georgia, in a quest for survival. Though the lands there at that time were claimed – at least in part – by the neighboring Creek Indians, the Cherokees had little choice in the matter, even though it meant exchanging warfare with the Whites for warfare with the Creeks. At least the Creeks were far fewer in number and weapons.

In 1802, after the close of the Revolutionary War, the United States government and the state of Georgia finally reached an agreement for the removal of the remaining Indian nations – the Creeks and the Cherokees – from within the boundaries of the land being claimed by Georgia. In exchange for removal of the Indians, the state of Georgia in turn agreed to relinquish its claims upon the lands to the west, which ultimately became the states of Alabama and Mississippi as "Manifest Destiny" began unfolding in the young nation.

"State's Rights" Issue

The removal of the indigenous tribes in the Southeast however, proved to be a much more difficult task than those in charge of Georgia's state government had anticipated. As the issue evolved, the justices of the Supreme Court of the United States surprised the political leaders in Georgia by becoming "strange bed-fellows" with the Cherokees, ruling that Georgia was in fact forbidden from expelling the natives from their own lands.

During this same period throughout the South, the extreme and oppressive tax – known as the "*Tariff of Abominations*" – had been levied in 1828 by the federal government upon Southern goods which had been destined for more profitable sale in foreign markets instead of northern U.S. markets. This action had inflamed the already swiftly-growing issue of "*State's Rights*," – particularly in the South – which maintained that each state, by virtue of the **U.S. Constitution** and the "**Bill of Rights**," had the legal authority to "nullify" and/or overrule certain federal laws if those "laws" were deemed to be unfairly oppressive and illicit. This movement, which came to be known as "*the Nullification Crisis*," had quickly grown to such proportions that it had raised the real possibility of the secession of many Southern states thirty years prior to the actual U.S. Civil War.

Rolled up within the vortex of this "State's Rights" controversy was the issue of legal control by state governments such as Georgia over the territory of the indigenous Indian tribes within or adjoining those states. By the 1830s, the states' presumed right of control over indigenous peoples – including Georgia's presumed authority over the native Cherokee and Creek Indians and their territory contiguous to the state – had joined the Nullification Crisis as a dominant issue in national politics.

Georgia Initiatives

Not surprisingly, debate upon the institution of slavery was also an incendiary aspect of the "state's rights" issue. The conflict between Georgia and the federal government over the Indian removal issue carried much the same "state's rights" rhetoric that would later accompany the Southern arguments in support of slavery.

Following the unique establishment by the Cherokees of their impressive formal government in 1827 – modeled as it were after the American government – Georgia subsequently began combining the issues of Indian removal and "state's

Augustin Smith Clayton ultimately lost his judgeship for ruling that the state of Georgia could not constitutionally arrest a Cherokee for mining gold on the Indian's own land. Clayton later apologized to Cherokee Chief John Ross for his part in the Tassels case and other actions in his opposition of the Cherokees. (Painting courtesy of Hargrett Rare Books & Manuscripts Library, University of Georgia Libraries)

rights." It had no choice if it was to achieve the state's desired goal of the enlargement of Georgia's geographic mass and usurpation of the areas in which gold had been discovered in 1828.

Georgia's governmental leaders realized that the state must also move quickly in this matter, since it literally was being out-maneuvered societally and politically by the Cherokees who had finally realized that their only chance for survival in the Southeast was to assimilate with the White culture – a task which they were swiftly successfully achieving. This not only would allow the native Cherokees to retain ownership and control of their lands contiguous to Georgia, but also to

A newspaper advertisement at what then was the Georgia state capital in Milledgeville announces the lotteries being conducted for White ownership of the former lands of the Cherokees in north Georgia.

control the gold which existed in what then was Cherokee Indian Territory.

By an act of the state legislature on December 26, 1827, the Georgia General Assembly therefore expanded the legal jurisdictions of Carroll and DeKalb counties to include the Indian lands adjoining those counties. Two years later, the state also extended the legal boundaries of Gwinnett, Habersham, Hall and Rabun counties as well into the neighboring lands of the Cherokees.

In order to establish even greater and more powerful control, the new law, as written, further declared all legal actions and enactments of the Cherokee government to be null and void. In the fifteenth and final paragraph of this legislation, the state of Georgia also *banned any testimony by an Indian in a state court suit involving a White man, unless the White man resided in Indian territory*. This law, amazingly, remained officially on the books and "in force" until the advent and success of the Civil Rights movement in the United States in the 1960s.

By 1830, these acts and other issues had heightened tensions between

Georgia and Cherokee officials almost to the breaking point. Because gold had been discovered on Cherokee lands in 1828, hundreds of White miners had illicitly moved into the territory in a voracious search for the precious yellow metal.

In a quest to control the trespassers and the associated abuse, Georgia Governor George R. Gilmer wisely requested and was granted federal assistance in the form of troops which were used to arrest anyone of any race found "mining" on the Indian lands. Georgia residents, however, ultimately rebelled against this federal oppression, threatening the tenure of Gilmer, and compelling him later that same year to have the federal troops replaced with soldiers employed by the state of Georgia – the "Georgia Guard."

This diminishment in enforcement opened the door for gangs of outlaws to then overrun the Cherokee Territory, robbing, killing, burning-out, evicting and otherwise abusing the Cherokees mercilessly, particularly since Georgia law now prevented any Indian from legally acting as a witness or pressing suit against a White man in state court.

The Cherokee leadership at that time, which was actually far more "White" than "Indian" and advised by missionaries from the North scheming to control a quarter of Georgia's territory, fought back in the federal courts. And despite being successful in these legal endeavors, it, nevertheless, was a vain success as history has shown.

Cherokee Initiatives

Former Western Circuit Judge William H. Underwood and his partner, Thomas H. Harris, as well as William Y. Hansel and Samuel Rockwell, were hired by the Cherokee Nation to represent any Cherokees brought before a

Murder Site? – The actual site of the murder committed by Corn Tassels has been lost to history. Scholars and researchers for many years have believed the offense may have been committed at the Taloney / Mt. Carmel Indian Mission which was once located in the present-day mountain community of Blaine in present-day Pickens County. However, the missionaries at Carmel Mission who normally were very meticulous in their records-keeping did not record any details whatsoever of George Corn Tassels or his murder of Cornelius Dougherty, which, at best, is highly unusual. One of the last-remaining historic mission buildings at Carmel was photographed above shortly before the site fell into complete ruin. (Photo courtesy of Charles O. Walker)

Georgia court. These attorneys served as legal representatives for their Native American clients in dozens of court cases over several years. Though often suffering the threat of violence from Georgia citizens, these attorneys nevertheless persevered.

The Cherokees also hired former United States Attorney General William Wirt of Baltimore, Maryland, to represent their interests in Washington. As attorney-general, Wirt had twice offered the opinion that the Indian nations existed as independent nations beyond the authority of the states.

Wirt, Underwood, and the Cherokees searched earnestly for strong court cases to use to test the Georgia law before the United States Supreme Court,

but struggled in vain to find the right case to use to set precedent – that is, until the case of George Corn Tassels came to their attention.

Tassels had murdered a fellow Cherokee on Indian land in 1830. There was no question about that. It was not even denied by Tassels himself. Wirt learned at almost the last moment that Georgia authorities had arrested Tassels, but after studying the incident, he knew he had finally found the legal case for which he had long been searching. In January of 1831, the case for Tassels' defense became a vital part of the nationally-known *Cherokee Nation vs. the State of Georgia*.

Interestingly, the most obvious source today for primary source

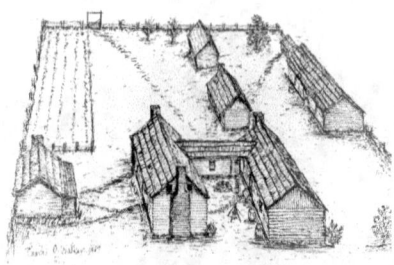

Taloney / Mt. Carmel Mission – The late Charles O. Walker of north Georgia's Pickens County sketched this recreation (based upon period descriptions of the site and several rare photographs) of historic Taloney / Mt. Carmel Indian Mission which once existed in the present-day community of Blaine. (Drawing courtesy of Rev. Charles Walker; reprinted with permission)

information on Tassels' case not surprisingly no longer exists. The Georgia State Supreme Court records for the year of 1830 in Hall and Gwinnett counties have disappeared completely. No official copy of any of those proceedings is known to exist today – not in the official records of the State of Georgia, nor the Georgia Department of Archives & History in Atlanta, nor within the University of Georgia's Library system (not even in the *Hargrett Rare Books and Manuscripts* section), nor even in the Congressional records. This, however, does not mean that no description of this incident has survived.

At some point in later years, legal scholars to their ironic and delighted surprise, discovered details of the crime reported in a story recorded by a Ms. Belle K. Abbott in 1889. Ms. Abbott was a local historian in Georgia who was also a correspondent for the Atlanta press, and according to her report, Tassels had murdered a fellow Cherokee in the small Indian community of Sanderstown (known in general today as

Talking Rock) in a neighborhood called "Taloney" in Pickens County, Georgia.

The Murder

According to Abbott's description of the murder carried in the *Georgia Journal* – a Milledgeville, Georgia newspaper of that era – there were a number of confusing sources of information on the incident. Also to their eventual dismay, they learned that the actual site of the murder had become a virtually-unsolvable mystery, and this "site location" was vitally important to the ability of the state of Georgia to *legitimately* establish legal jurisdiction in the matter.

According to Abbott's article, Letty Proctor who was present at her home in "Sanderstown," reportedly testified that Indians George Corn Tassels and Cornelius Dougherty were drunk at her home on the morning of July 15, 1830. Abbott, quoting Proctor, said the two men seemed amicable enough initially, although Tassels at some point suddenly announced matter-of-factly that he was "going to shoot" Dougherty, but Proctor said Dougherty merely took the statement as a joke.

Abbott wrote that Ms. Proctor went on to state that she *"felt safe in leaving the men for a moment"* while she was otherwise engaged, but that while she was absent, she heard a gunshot at approximately ten o'clock and rushed back into the house as a wounded Dougherty staggered out through the front doorway announcing that George had shot him in the right side.

Ms. Proctor further stated that she immediately sent for the nearest constable – Mark Castleberrry. An individual by the name of John Dougherty (relation to Cornelius is unknown) eventually arrived at Proctor's home and took care of the victim who nevertheless subsequently died two days later. *(In the 1830s, there quite often was very little that could be done to save an individual who had been wounded abdominally.)*

Continuing her article, Abbott related that John Dougherty later stated before Constable Castleberry that he had heard Tassels state – somewhat psychotically – that he had no grudge against Cornelius, but only wanted to guarantee that he and his friend from boyhood would "share the same grave." Castleberry later testified that George nevertheless had also stated that there had been a previous quarrel between the two of them over *"a woman."*

Yet another witness in the subsequent trial in this incident – a member of the Georgia Guard – later testified that Tassels spoke in English and admitted that he and Cornelius had been arguing. Tassels himself never denied commission of the murder, even openly admitting it.

Historian James C. Flanigan published yet another account of George Corn Tassels and his victim being involved in a dispute over a woman who later appeared in court to tearfully plead for "her lover." Whether or not the woman to whom he referred was Letty Proctor is unknown today.

Once again, however, the issue of most vital importance to attorneys Wirt, Underwood and the Cherokees was the *actual site* of the Cornelius Dougherty murder, and it has become wrapped in mystery and controversy. Reverend Isaac Proctor headed the "Taloney" or "Carmel Mission" at Talking Rock where Belle Abbott supposedly heard – more than 50 years later – that the murder had occurred, but crucially, no *record* of the murder at this site actually exists. The missionaries at Carmel – who normally were very meticulous

Inalienable Right? – William Wirt, as United States Attorney General, made some decisions which favored Cherokee Indian sovereignty, and others which did not. As attorney for the Cherokee Nation, however, he fought for George Corn Tassels and for the right of the Cherokees to keep their nation in Georgia. (Painting courtesy of Hargrett Rare Book and Manuscripts Library, University of Georgia Libraries)

records-keepers – did not record any details whatsoever of George Corn Tassels or his murder of Cornelius Dougherty in any of their writings, which, at best, is highly unusual. Interestingly, no record of a resident at Taloney named Letty Proctor has ever been discovered either.

Murder Site Mystery

That much being known, it is today considered quite possible that this incident actually occurred someplace other than Taloney. In the 1830s, at what was known as "Big Savannah" in the present-day adjoining county of Dawson, there actually existed a Cherokee community by the name of "Dougherty."

Tinder for the Flames of War? – U.S. President Andrew Jackson refused to enforce the decisions of the U.S. Supreme Court regarding the protection of the rights of the Cherokee Indians. In this manner, he was able to stave off the secessionist tendencies within the Southern states which were reaching a boiling point even as far back as the early 1830s. Twenty-five years later, the pressure could be contained no longer, helping to ignite the U.S. Civil War.

U.S. Supreme Court Chief Justice John Marshall argued in favor of the sovereign rights of the Cherokees regarding the state of Georgia in "Cherokee Nation vs. Georgia" (the George Corn Tassels case) and in "Worcester vs. Georgia." Marshall, according to some sources, did so to help President Andrew Jackson's efforts to stop state secessionism in the Nullification Crisis, and he reportedly did it in a manner which would spare the president from being forced to enforce federal laws in favor of the Indians. Other quarters maintain that following the court's decision regarding the rights of the Cherokees, President Jackson merely ignored the mandate which ruled in favor of the Native Americans. (Photo courtesy of Hargrett Rare Books & Manuscripts Library, University of Georgia Libraries)

The large household of James Dougherty, Sr., actually lived at this site.

The Dougherty family at Big Savannah quite probably was descended from a White man – likely pioneer Cornelius Dougherty – who lived among the Indians before Oglethorpe founded Georgia in 1733. Even more interesting is the fact that these Doughertys of Big Savannah were neighbors to a household headed by one John "Proctor."

Also living nearby in Big Savannah were Cherokee families that used their native names – translated into English – of which "Corn Tassels" could serve as an example. It is also a matter of historic record that George Corn Tassels told a guard that he would prefer to face trial at "Savannah" before the Cherokees.

Tassels subsequently appeared before Mark Castleberry of Hall County, who was the nearest constable, and who, incidentally, also lived much nearer to Big Savannah than to the far-off Carmel Mission at Taloney. A large extended family by the name of Castleberry lived in nearby Auraria, just a few miles away from Big Savannah. There is still a road and bridge in Auraria named "Castleberry" even today.

In late November of 1830, the

Tassels trial was finally held. Historian Flanigan wrote that a change of venue caused the trial to be moved to Lawrenceville in Gwinnett County, but no contemporary source supports that claim.

Attorney William H. Underwood served as defense counsel while Turner H. Trippe represented the State. On November 22, 1830, a Georgia court found Tassels "*Guilty*" of murder and sentenced him to death.

Judge Clayton not only delivered the jury's verdict, but, interestingly, also seized the opportunity for a long public discourse on the "*States' Rights*" issue, and the need for the removal of the Cherokees – perhaps to get it in the public record of the trial. In a later letter to Governor Gilmer, Clayton denied that he sought a confrontation with the federal government over "States' Rights," but his record indicates otherwise. *(As a side note, this also adds emphasis to the fact that the States' Rights issue definitely extended back at least as far as the 1830s.)*

Georgia newspapers subsequently reported that the Tassels' trial would likely go to the United States Supreme Court. On December 22, a *Writ of Error* arrived for Governor Gilmer from United States Chief Justice John Marshall. It was dated December 12. This document announced that the authority of Georgia in the case of Tassels and other matters in Wirt's petition would be heard before the high court.

Accordingly, Governor Gilmer suddenly found himself "*between a rock and a hard place.*" He had fought to avoid a federal challenge to the Georgia laws as he feared such action would dramatically favor the Cherokees. Wirt had a tremendous reputation not only in political power, but as a legal scholar, and no

Actual Murder Site? – Palmer Gristmill, built circa 1906, once existed beside the original bridge across the Etowah River (located approximately 100 yards north of the present-day State Road 53 Bridge) at Dougherty, Georgia, Dawson County. In the 1830s, this was a Cherokee town composed greatly of the extended family of Cherokee James Dougherty, Sr. It is believed by some researchers that the murder committed by George Corn Tassels may actually have occurred at this site instead of at Taloney Mission in Murray County.

doubt would prove very effective in defending the Cherokee cause.

The governor subsequently took the matter of the *Writ* before the Georgia State Legislature which was then in special session. According to one source, he arrived at the State House out of breath and in a panic, urging defiance of the high court.

The Georgia House and Senate both quickly passed a resolution ordering Sheriff Jacob Eberhart of Hall County to carry out the sentence immediately as handed down. Gilmer's letter – dated that same December 22, 1830 – which he sent to Eberhart with this resolution, traveled the 120 miles to Gainesville and reached the sheriff before December 24 – an amazing feat which likely could not be equaled even by today's plodding U.S.

Postal Service in motorized vehicles on modern highways.

Tassels's Execution

On a cold winter day, as sleet fell, George Corn Tassels rode in his coffin – no doubt shivering – to a scaffold in a large open field near present-day Cotton Avenue in Gainesville, Georgia. As with all public hangings, a substantial law enforcement contingent was present to make certain the sentence was carried out without interruption. Crowds of men, women, and even children clogged the roads to reach the site of the hanging which had become a substantial public event.

When Tassels and his guards reached the gallows, Eberhart ordered the prisoner to stand up. As is standard in such sentences, he tied the Cherokee's hands and pulled a cap over his face before securing the rope around his neck.

Though it is not known for certain today, Tassels was probably hung from the branch of a tree after having a wagon or cart pulled from beneath him. Whatever the circumstances, he was hung by the neck – for approximately 20 minutes – until he ceased movement.

Death by strangulation is an extremely traumatic manner of execution. Normally, the noose of a gallows is positioned to the side of the neck in order to snap the vertebra and spinal cord after the convicted has fallen suddenly through a trap door, killing the victim immediately. This method of execution, however, was not used on Tassels. He was simply strangled painfully slowly to death.

For a condemned person to hang for 20 minutes duration before death ensues would be excessively cruel, but on the opposite side of the coin, how much latitude did the condemned allow the individual whose life he ended? At best, it is an extremely paradoxical situation.

When his body ceased moving, doctors approached Tassels to examine him. They then pronounced him dead and the rope was cut to release his body.

Often repeated accounts of this incident maintain that hundreds of Cherokees silently witnessed this hanging. A correspondent to *The Athenian* newspaper of Athens, Georgia, however, reported eighteen to twenty Indians were present.

The Cherokees, interestingly, did not transport Tassels' body back to his home for interment, but rather buried him somewhat unceremoniously in a vacant area in the middle of what later became South Broad Street in Gainesville. Their reasoning for this lack of respect is unknown today, as is the actual site of Tassels' burial, since no historic marker or memorial has ever been erected to mark the sad spot.

Interestingly, some twenty years later, Tassels' body was exhumed. The reason for this exhumation is unknown today. Perhaps the burial site had come into general use as a travel route by that point, requiring a street or road to be laid out.

A traveler by the name of William Jasper Cotter, according to records, witnessed the exhumation of the body. In his writings, Cotter recorded that coagulated blood was still visible around Tassels' neck even after the 20-year point.

Tassels' remains were relocated to a new grave. The site of this reburial is unknown today, adding further to the long list of mysterious aspects of this entire incident.

Effect of the Execution

Tassels' execution ultimately had widespread implications. John Ross and the Cherokee leadership reported the hanging to the U.S. Congress, where their friends used it to adamantly denounce Georgia's actions in extending its authority over the Cherokees and executing an Indian in defiance of existing treaties. Nevertheless, from that point forward, the case that brought George Corn Tassels to his tragic demise – *State vs. George Corn Tassels* – became the primary court citation for state authority over Native Americans until 1831.

In the year following Tassels' death, the United States Supreme Court heard *Cherokee Nation vs. Georgia*. Wirt represented the Cherokees but the State of Georgia simply ignored the case and provided no representation.

The U.S. Supreme Court subsequently handed down a divided and somewhat confusing ruling. Though Wirt's petition had maintained that the Cherokees were a foreign nation within the confines of the United States, Chief Justice John Marshall and one other justice denied this standing, stating that as such, the Indians could not therefore file suit in the United States Supreme Court.

Interestingly, on the face of this decision, it would appear that one could conceivably therefore argue that the Cherokees' non-status as a foreign nation would in fact therefore positively grant them the ability to sue in the U.S. Supreme Court since one would logically deduce at that point that they therefore must in fact be U.S. citizens.

Despite the denial by Chief Justice John Marshal and his supporting justice, two other justices nevertheless agreed with Wirt's petition. The remaining two justices fell squarely in the middle of the argument, stating that the Cherokees were neither a domestic nor a foreign nation, but merely a conquered people without rights (a decision which a fair number of quarters would admit is a logical choice).

Four of the justices, however, did agree that Georgia had no authority over the Cherokee lands, laying the groundwork for yet another suit (which many Americans would also agree rings logically). In that case (*Worcester vs. State of Georgia, 1832*), concerning Judge Clayton's trials of White Northern missionaries arrested for resisting Georgia's laws, the Court ruled that the State of Georgia had no legal authority in the Cherokee lands, a verdict which at the very least established a precedent granting substantial power to the Cherokees in their quest to retain their homeland. Unfortunately, in the end, it had little effect.

Today, legend maintains that following this decision, U.S. President Andrew Jackson cynically stated that *"Marshall has made his decision. Now let him enforce it."* In all likelihood, Jackson never actually made such a statement, but his administration also nevertheless took no actions either to threaten or contest the Georgia laws, and, instead continued to encourage Indian removal to reservations in the West, a policy which Jackson strongly supported.

> *In the year following Tassels' death, the United States Supreme Court heard Cherokee Nation vs. Georgia.*

Federal soldiers enforced the final removals of the last organized Native American peoples in the southern and mid-western states east of the Mississippi River in the late 1830s. With no federal intervention in support of the Cherokees' sovereignty, (despite their success at the U.S. Supreme Court), their situation steadily declined.

So also followed the fortunes of other indigenous Native American societies. In 1833, the State of Georgia took control of and divided the lands of the Cherokee Nation into eleven new Georgia counties. State authorities completely ignored the existence of the Cherokee judicial system and the rulings of the United States Supreme Court.

Similar Cases

The same summer (1830) that Tassels had committed murder, the Cherokees' own court at Coosawattee tried Cherokee Indian James Graves after he boasted, while drunk, of murdering an unknown White man. The Cherokee court found Graves "*Not Guilty*" due to a lack of evidence, and therefore not liable, according to treaty, for his surrender to the federal Indian agent and the State of Georgia for re-trial.

The State of Georgia, nevertheless, took Graves into custody anyway, and re-tried him for the presumed murder in the newly-created county of Murray in northwest Georgia. This time, a White jury found Graves "*Guilty*."

Judge John W. Hooper postponed the execution of Graves in a vain hope for federal intervention. The Georgia State Legislature, however, again in defiance of the U.S. Supreme Court, passed yet another resolution ordering the execution proceedings to continue without delay. On November 21, 1834, Graves met the same fate as had Tassels.

In a similar set of circumstances, Cherokee John Hogg Smith was hanged in Walker County in 1834, supposedly for murdering two Indians in that vicinity.

Following his arrest for the murders of everyone in the James L. Bowman family at Salacoa, Georgia, in 1832, George Tooke (known to the Cherokees as "Une'ga-tehee" or "White Man Killer") escaped from the DeKalb County, Georgia jail. A White Cherokee County posse wounded and recaptured him in 1835 and a Cass (present-day Bartow) County jury found him "*Guilty*." He also was hanged. By then, an act of November 12, 1834, even provided state funds to counties for the prosecution and punishment of Cherokees.

Ironically, Georgia's advocates for "*State's Rights*" won such legal battles in the 1830s against Native Americans, only to literally "lose the war" at least in part for the same cause with Blacks in the U.S. Civil War.

As a result of the incendiary political climate of the 1830s, the details of George Corn Tassels' ordeal had begun to vanish even while he yet lived. They were literally buried beneath the overwhelming issues of "*State's Rights*" and Indian Removal politics.

Though his crime was murder for which Tassels did not deny his guilt, his trial nonetheless became an important lynch-pin in the quest of Native Americans for treatment as a sovereign nation within a nation – conquered or not. It would be many years in the future, however, before the rights of Native Americans in the United States – despite the fact they were a conquered people – would be legally established within U.S. courts. In the interim, there was much suffering and despair

Some Surprising Tales Occurred in This Jail

Built in 1906, the criminals it held and the incidents experienced therein were many and storied. This structure, now on the National Register of Historic Places, was the site of several escape attempts, and once held a number of notable outlaws.

A historic "old jail" on Main Street in Jasper, Georgia, is often assumed – erroneously – to be the county's first jail. Though it is indeed an important structure from the county's past history, it is not the oldest jail ever used by the town – not by a long shot. It, however, is indeed the one noted in the county's history as having experienced the most sensational incidents.

Prior to the 1900s, many north Georgia jails were composed of little more than a stout wooden box chained to a location on the town's dusty main street. These enclosures were crude, open to the weather, obviously absent fresh water or toilet facilities, and accessible by all manner of wildlife and vermin. Incarceration in such a lock-up was exceedingly undesirable, and criminals would do virtually anything to avoid them.

The first Pickens County jail was built in the 1850s. It was two stories tall and was indeed constructed of logs. It too was extremely inhospitable, and was burned during the chaos of the U.S. Civil War, quite likely by riff-raff who had

been detained inside it in months or years past. During the dark days of the late 1860s, a favored objective of the many outlaws frequenting the north Georgia region was the destruction – usually by burning – of all enclosures formerly used to detain prisoners.

As a modest improvement over the log box jail, the second Pickens County jail was made of rock and existed to the rear of the present-day courthouse. Pickens County, from its earliest days up to the 1970s, was largely inhabited by middle-to-lower-income mountain residents who had no interest whatsoever in the imposition of taxes to the level necessary to construct a jail which provided accommodations "hospitable" to criminals. It simply was not a priority.

As a result, the second "rock" jail – though constructed of more "weather-proof" materials, nevertheless still was absent running water and toilet facilities, and had very limited capability for heat in the cold winter months. As a result, it also was only a breath away from medieval quality.

This second jail, nevertheless, held

Hardly Escape-Proof – In some respects, the old Pickens County Jail resembles a medieval fortress, but it fell far short of that quality in actuality, suffering a number of escapes due to its bad design and poor construction. It is nevertheless listed today on the **National Register of Historic Places.**

a number of individuals sensationalized in early trials, including the notorious murderess Kate Southern, her husband, Bob, and their first child in 1877. *(Readers please see the associated article "The Strange 1877 Murder Case of Kate Southern" within this publication.)* After being abandoned for prison purposes it housed a portion of a sewing plant for a short while, and then was demolished in the 1960s. The large stones from this "old jail" now shore up the courthouse parking lot.

A "New" Jail

Much of the discourse among the local populace regarding the Pickens County jails in the past has focused upon the exceedingly crude construction and building materials used in those edifices. As explained above, the funds for higher quality structures of incarceration have never been a high priority for

Pickens taxpayers, and the low quality of these structures has been reflected in the numerous escapes and other problems associated with prisoners in Pickens.

The situation with the old stone jail eventually reached such a remarkably-low state of affairs that even the Pickens County grand juries began assailing it as *"unsanitary, unsafe, uncomfortable, and in a deplorable condition,"* but this nevertheless was not enough to spur its replacement until the spring of 1906.

The prime mover in building what was then "the new jail" was Dr. William B. Tate. He served as foreman on the final two grand juries to condemn the old rock jail as inferior and uninhabitable, and as a leader on a citizens' committee appointed to oversee construction of a new jail.

According to records, *J.W. Coluke and Company* were the 1906 jail's architects. *William Landrum and Son* were the construction contractors. The sophisticated marble work on the front of the jail was done by Lee W. Prather, a local stone mason, and the actual marble used in the construction was a product of the Delaware Quarry in Marble Hill – the first marble quarry in Georgia (originated circa 1836 by Henry Terry Fitsimmons).

Most old buildings have at least one love story and the 1906 Pickens County Jail is no different. When Luther Cartright of the *Pauley Jail Company* of St. Louis, Missouri, came to Jasper to install the heavy steel bars in the jail, he roomed at the *Lennings Hotel* (present-day *Woodbridge Inn*). He reportedly fell in love with and married the innkeeper's daughter.

When Cartright retired from the jail business, he and his wife had become so enamored with the Pickens County environs that they returned with their family to the area to live. At last check, descendants of this family still lived in the Pickens vicinity – a family that owes its beginnings to the jail. Luther Cartright also worked on the pink marble mansion in Tate in the 1920s, which happens to be the county's only other *National Register Historic Site*.

The Cartrights were not the only non-criminal family to be associated with the jail. The sheriffs (and later the deputies) and their families were required to live on the first floor of the jail and for that reason many of the county's more prominent families have spent more time in the jail than any criminal!

For some of the sheriffs this was a minor inconvenience; for others it was a severe drudgery. Indeed, according to former Pickens County Sheriff Billy Wofford, he and his family, by having to domicile in and tend to the jail, were more prisoners than the inmates, since the inmates eventually got to leave.

The first floor of the jail has but four rooms into which each sheriff had to squeeze what was sometimes their somewhat large families. For this and other reasons, it wasn't long before the brick and marble "new" jail on Main Street became an outmoded "old" jail itself. The "new conveniences" which were all modern in 1906, had ultimately become antiquated and outmoded once again.

For starters, the jail originally had no plumbing of any kind. Water from a well off the back porch had to be hauled inside the jail each day for the sheriff and his family and the inmates. This well also served the huge crowds that periodically gathered in Jasper for singing conventions.

Cooking in the jail was conducted on a wood-burning stove, although the jail did have a coal furnace in the basement. And an always odoriferous "outhouse" out back served as – well – the outhouse.

Conditions were worse for the prisoners. Until more recent times, the jail didn't even have any separate cells. The only cell door was the first floor door at the stairs leading to the second

And an always odoriferous "outhouse" out back served as – well – the outhouse.

floor where the prisoners lived in a general population. This obviously meant the sheriff and his family were constantly in close contact with – and potential danger of – the prisoners. It also meant the prisoners were able to freely associate with each other and casually plan whatever mischief or escape attempts of which they could conceive during their time of incarceration.

1923 Jail-Breaks

It was under these circumstances that a notable jail-break occurred in the 1920s. At 5:00 P.M. on May 23, 1923, Pickens County Sheriff D.P. Poole climbed the stairs to the cells on the second floor of the jail to bring his prisoners the usual bucket of fresh water for the evening.

One can understand how it might be somewhat easy over time for a sheriff, living right in the midst of the inmates under his supervision, to at least become casually-trusting, if not friendly, acquaintances with those inmates. A seasoned lawman such as Sheriff Poole however, should have known better than to fall prey to such a trap. On the day of the May 23 escape, he apparently misjudged the criminals under his supervision completely.

Among the "guests" on the second floor that day, was an individual by the name of Ralph King, accused of *"assault with intent to commit murder,"* and his accomplice, Fred Hill. The latter had escaped from this same jail hardly a month earlier via a route which surprisingly had been used by several previous prisoners. The bars in the windows of the cells apparently had not been sturdily installed, and Hill had found it quite simple to loosen and remove one of the bars, and then slide quietly down to the back porch roof.

On the day that Fred Hill escaped from the jail for the first time, he had been visited by his wife earlier that morning. For reasons unknown today, she had mentioned in passing to one of the guards that she would be staying with her parents, so the lawmen in later pursuit of the escaped Hill had a relatively good hunch where they might at least begin their search for the escapee.

Interestingly, despite being surprised by lawmen on the premises of his wife's parents' home, the determined Hill nevertheless eluded his captors once again as he lit out across a swamp. He was later apprehended some 50 or 60 miles away in Rome, Georgia, and had been back in jail only a week, when he and King decided to attack Sheriff Poole in order to escape once again.

Despite the background of these two men, Poole, for reasons unknown today, apparently did not consider them dangerous. He didn't have a sidearm, nor even a deputy as he ascended the stairs to tend to the prisoners for the night. Any attempt to accomplish a task of this nature in the absence of a back-up deputy is a serious lapse in judgement.

At the top of the stairs, the two men immediately jumped Poole. One of them had a brick which he had worked loose from the jail wall, and the other reportedly had a bottle. After being struck by the brick, Poole fell to the jail floor, temporarily stunned.

While the duo searched Poole for a weapon, the lawman recovered and began fighting back. With exhaustion near at hand, the two men finally decided flight was their best option, and they abandoned the determined sheriff.

The two prisoners turned to run down the stairs to Poole's living quarters on the first floor of the jail, but the sheriff was not about to give up that easily.

Never one to be conquered without a fight, he latched onto the two prisoners with all his might, apparently hoping to slow them down long enough for help to arrive.

By this time, Poole's wife had heard the commotion and obvious struggle taking place upstairs, and had run to the bottom of the stairs, screaming like a banshee. Though obviously in shock, she at least was raising enough of a ruckus to draw attention to the situation from outside the jail.

While the duo searched Poole for a weapon, the lawman recovered and began fighting back.

Champion to the Rescue

Jasper resident Oscar Champion lived next door to the jail at that time. Mrs. Poole's screams had been effective, for Champion had been alerted and had run onto the back porch of the jail. Realizing that a prisoner escape was in progress, he ran into the sheriff's living quarters and found Poole's pistol.

By this time, the two prisoners had finally reached the bottom of the stairs and were only inches away from freedom. King finally broke free and leapt from the jail porch, heading towards a cotton field (a site occupied today by the Jasper Elementary School) and freedom.

Oscar Champion had never fired a weapon at anyone before (or since) in his life. However, on this day, he closed his eyes, pointed the pistol at the escapee, and ordered the fleeing man to stop.

When the man failed to halt, Poole yelled at Champion to shoot. Oscar squeezed off a round from the big pistol

and the countryside around the normally peaceful mountain community resounded from the loud discharge.

According to Mr. Champion, despite the fact that King was running at an incredible clip across the cotton field, he almost fell backwards in his immediate effort to halt and raise his hands. He then marched quietly back to the jail as the sheriff subdued the other man.

This, however, was not the conclusion of this little tale. Things were just beginning to get interesting. . . .

The sheriff, as one might imagine, assumed the desperate attempts at freedom were at an end, and that he would simply return his two escapees to the lock-up with the rest of the prisoners on the second floor. By this time, however, the general population of remaining prisoners had been exposed to a semblance of a taste of freedom themselves, and were not so easily cowed back into submission.

Jail Unrest

According to reports, the detainees began raining a shower of bricks, soft drink bottles and disinfectant down upon anyone who attempted to reach them, refusing to allow the sheriff access even back into the facility. This speaks volumes to the insecure nature of this aging lock-up. Normally, no inmate should have any type of access whatsoever to any open window out through which a volume of objects might be rained down upon law enforcement officials.

By this point, Poole's patience was exhausted, and he responded to this revolt by firing another heavy round from the revolver into the air. The prisoners, however, still would not submit. Many of them had been fired upon previously in their "professional endeavors" – some of them many times. They responded with still more bottles and bricks. They also probably suspected that Poole, as a law enforcement officer, was not going to fire directly into them and risk the murder of already incarcerated inmates.

By this point, however, some fifty or sixty men, most of them armed, had gathered around the jail and one of them – Felix Allred – simply directed the prisoners to give up or die. It was just that simple. In those days, prison revolts and namby-pamby negotiated settlements simply were not part of the plan, nor were spineless apologists for criminal activity, nor socially-liberal lawyers tolerated.

In 1923, Pickens County was barely beyond frontier status, and frontier justice therefore sometimes still prevailed. The disgruntled prisoners, realizing they had little choice, finally succumbed, but remained restless and agitated nonetheless.

Ironically, the two escapees from

In 1923, Pickens County was barely beyond frontier status, and frontier justice therefore sometimes still prevailed.

that day were eventually found *"Not Guilty"* of the original charges for which they were being held, but were each sentenced to two years in prison for the attack on Sheriff Poole. So instead of a clean criminal record, they both became convicted felons with all the delights which go with that station in life.

Poole, by this time, had decided discretion was the better part of valor, and opted out of the law enforcement profession at the next election cycle. He had had enough. He simply chose not to seek re-election to his position, no doubt strongly encouraged to depart by his wife whose nerves undoubtedly were shot.

The late Oscar Champion subsequently decided to put some distance between himself and the jail as well, moving to nearby Tate, Georgia, and living to be over 100 years of age. Before he passed away, he would discuss the 1923 Pickens County jail-break and riot only if specifically asked, and even then a fair amount of coaxing was necessary.

There were a number of other escapes from the 1906 jail, a fact which did nothing to diminish the obvious need for a newer, more secure facility. One popular method of escape was through a second floor window above the back porch. With a cable attached to a mule team or truck, the bars and window could easily be ripped out and the inmate could then escape to the roof and from there to the ground. This, admittedly, required determined criminals for success to occur, but the mountains were full of them in those days.

Today, if one examines the roof of the old jail, he or she will see several sheets of metal which have been welded to the roof of the second floor of the jail to thwart further escape attempts.

Notorious Confinements

Despite its failures, the 1906 jail also capably served its purpose to some degree. It successfully confined a number of highly-notorious individuals who attracted state and even nation-wide attention over the years for their crimes.

In 1924, following his arrest for the murder of his brother, Hobert, and the attempted murder of his father, famed Pickens Policeman Lee Cape, Levi Cape was held in this jail. He ultimately was sentenced to *"Life"* in prison (paroled in 1934 for good behavior) for his vicious acts of violence.

Over the years, the elder Cape – who eventually recovered from his son's assault – arrested and was responsible for the incarceration of many area moonshiners in the old jail for the illicit production and sale of untaxed liquor. Eventually, one such case was the catalyst for Cape's horrendous highly-publicized 1927 murder.

On a sunny September 17 afternoon of that year, Lindsey Evans; his brother, Hoyt Evans; and C.L. Smith murdered Cape with a shotgun, then took his body to a remote site where they beheaded the lawman, fired numerous shotgun blasts at his face to obscure it, stripped his corpse naked, and then tossed it to the side of the road. Following their arrest, Hoyt Evans and Smith were incarcerated in the old jail.

During the subsequent trial for this crime, the testimony in the case was so gruesome that the presiding judge was forced to clear the courtroom of women and children. Hoyt Evans and C.L. Smith were both given *"Life"* sentences. Lindsey Evans, the actual triggerman and primary perpetrator in Cape's murder, was never captured. Following imprisonment, C.L. Smith escaped and was never recaptured.

Also confined within the jail's walls were the men convicted of the brutal 1948 murder of Jasper, Georgia cab driver Earl Holbert, which has gone down in the annals of Pickens crime history as one of the most unusual murders on record. Some of the details of that murder remain unresolved even today.

In order to conceal information regarding a highly-lucrative illicit north Georgia moonshine operation of which Holbert apparently was aware, the cab driver was lured to a remote north Pickens farmhouse near Talking Rock. There, Weldon Sullivan, a sawmill operator, and Bryan Tatum, a former dairy farmer, strangely and brutally beat Holbert to death with hammers, after which his body was tossed down an abandoned freshwater well at the site for concealment.

The 1906 Pickens County Jail building also boasts one of Georgia's few remaining gallows, an item not to be missed on any tour of the old building. Despite its intended purpose, however, no one was ever hanged at this site. Amazingly, when the gallows was installed, the trap was constructed backwards, rendering the device useless, so even if its use had been necessitated, the punishment would have required application elsewhere.

There have been at least two suicides in the jail, and at least one infant was born there to an inmate. (*The child-bearing inmate, incidentally, later returned for a tour of the old facility in which she was once incarcerated.)*

Over the ensuing years, the old jail continued to deteriorate despite the addition of a number of modern improvements such as electricity, plumbing, and extra cells. When the number of necessary bunks, mattresses, and other necessities became too few to service the inmates being housed in the facility, circumstances at the jail had reached the breaking point.

One individual, held for only a minor violation, remembered being imprisoned in the same room with a murderer and a rapist. Sheriff Wofford remembers instances when mischievous inmates plugged up the water drain upstairs in order to flood the sheriff's quarters below, just for amusement.

Plans for a new jail were discussed in 1960, and a 1965 grand jury called for the sale of the existing jail property to raise money for a new county prison. New construction however met with delay after delay as conditions at the jail continued to degenerate.

Jail Closure

By 1980, circumstances at the jail had reached an absolute impasse. The Atlanta newspapers eventually got wind of the deplorable circumstances and described the lock-up in a news story as *"the worst jail in Georgia."*

Finally, in the spring of 1980, two inmates filed a class-action lawsuit in federal court, claiming that confinement in the jail violated the 1st,

4th, 6th, 8th, and 14th amendments of the **U.S. Constitution**. The jail, subsequently, was ordered closed by the state. In 1982, the present Pickens County jail was opened near the county airport.

After the old 1906 jail was closed, it next became necessary to decide what to do with it. If the decision had been left to the former inmates, sheriffs, sheriffs' families, and many of the county's taxpayers, the structure undoubtedly would have been demolished.

Ms. Kathryn Downes, however, one of the founding members of the *Marble Valley* (Pickens County) *Historical Society*, was preservation – not demolition – minded. She managed to persuade two successive county commissioners to allow her to save the dilapidated but historic building.

Following the Historic Society's initiation of restoration efforts on the old jail, the building was nominated and ultimately accepted for placement on the **National Register of Historic Places**, and a historical marker was placed in front of the building. Others were obviously preservation-minded as well, because $10,000 in cash and $30,000 in labor and materials ultimately were donated to and expended upon the historic structure.

The entire building was subsequently permanently preserved for posterity. And much of the old jail has been maintained just as it was in the days in which it saw active service, a reminder of what life was like for the criminals of old Pickens County in days of yore.

> *By 1980, circumstances at the jail had reached an absolute impasse.*

Outlaws Versus "Revenoorers"

In the years following the U.S. Civil War, strange individuals in still-stranger garb, patrolled the mountainous region of what today is Pickens County. They have often been accused of many crimes throughout the years, due in particular to the disguises they used. The sole purpose in life of these vigilantes however – most all of whom were of Scots-Irish descent – was to rid the north Georgia area of U.S. Revenue agents who were denying these early American residents of the mountains the ability to produce and sell one of the few sources of income they enjoyed.

In 1889, some twenty odd men in the Sharptop Militia District of Pickens County, Georgia, gathered around a blazing fire in a secluded area back in the mountains. As far as they were concerned, they were simple soldiers in a common cause to protect a way of life to which they felt they were entitled. To others, however, they were little more than common criminals who functioned through violence and intimidation to achieve their goals. They dubbed themselves *"The Honest Man's Friend and Protector"* (HMF&P).

For the next two years, the HMF&P provided Pickens with a period of unwanted statewide notoriety. Though many of them were prominent citizens in the light of day, they were also desperate mountain residents who were devoted to the need to *"fight the revenue laws for the good of the country and ourselves."* They strongly opposed any effort of the United States government to deny them

what they felt was their God-given right to produce and sell untaxed liquor in order to survive in the harsh realities of the mountains they called "home."

Conversely, when the production and consumption of liquor was legal in the United States, federal officials demanded the government's "pound of flesh" from the production of any taxable product. It likewise sought to deny the production of same when the laws of the United States made production and sale of the product a criminal offense. In order to eliminate their tormentors, the HMF&P essentially declared guerilla war against the United States Army which were the enforcement arm of the federal government in this instance.

The HMF&P membership hid their identities with *"weird and terrifying black cloaks and hoods."* Due to the nature of their disguises, the vigilantes were often confused with the membership of the notorious Ku Klux Klan. In reality, they were an entirely separate and distinct organization dedicated to an entirely different mission in life.

The poor Scots-Irish of the Appalachian highlands owned virtually no slaves whatsoever, and even if they had enjoyed the latitude to do so, undoubtedly would have declined, having been so recently enslaved themselves by the English in the British Empire. It was for these reasons that so few mountaineers in north Georgia, Tennessee and North Carolina supported the Confederacy during the war years.

The HMF&P membership knew and occasionally associated with each other, but for the most part they avoided any possibility of identification through regular public association. They always gathered under the cover of darkness and were all sworn to the protection of each other, even if it meant perjuring themselves in court. They would help each other *"in bearing the business of life,"* and promised death to any member who divulged their secrets.

Members of HMF&P did not use their actual names in signing their by-laws, but instead, in a twist of ironic vengeance, assumed the names (and identities) of local law enforcement officials and others who testified against "moonshiners" for rewards (called "reporters"), in order to confuse their pursuers.

The members were deadly serious about their mission, and those who failed to appear when summoned for a meeting or task were fined fifty cents for each infraction (the approximate equivalent of $13.30 in 2024 dollars) which could amount to a substantial sum in the depressed north Georgia mountains of the 1880s. Members arriving drunk at a meeting – implying they were

untrustworthy – were tempered with the whip – or worse.

"Revenoors" & Night Riders

North Georgia history includes numerous instances of such groups. Vigilantes helped remove the Cherokees from the state in the 1830s. Before the Civil War, secret political societies such as the *"Know Nothings"* and related organizations also existed. Later, groups of men outraged over federal government tariffs, highly-unfair trade practices, and other matters banded together to fight for (and sometimes against) the Confederacy. And of course the well-known Ku Klux Klan (KKK) served as the forerunner for later secret societies after the war.

Although identified then and since with the KKK, the members of the HMF&P – as explained above – were not concerned with racial circumstances. Their one and only objective was the departure of the revenue agents – by any means necessary – who were depriving the mountaineers from their main source of income – untaxed mountain whiskey, better known as "moonshine."

During the first half of the 1860s, the Confederacy had prohibited the distillation (production) of alcoholic beverages, in order to conserve foodstuffs such as the corn used to make the liquor. After the war, the federal government continued this trend, imposing unnecessary "licenses" and taxes on the "luxury" and "vice" of alcohol.

This "luxury," however, was the only real source of income available to many small farmers in the mountains, since tillable land in that area was extremely limited, and rich river-bottom sediment capable of growing substantial crops was almost nonexistent. The federal excise taxes being imposed upon the liquor produced by the mountaineers actually exceeded the income produced by the liquor for the mountaineers – a circumstance fully intended by federal government officials. Their objective was to put "moonshiners" out of business by whatever means necessary.

From whence sprang this vendetta against the liquor being so ably produced by the mountain Scots-Irish one might ask? Interestingly, while it was "legal," all officially "legal" liquor was manufactured at a substantial profit by New England distillers. Also, during the U.S. Civil War years, federal military planners and strategists wished to make certain that no items of medicinal value might be produced by the South. And then, of course, there was the period of *"Prohibition,"* when Congress outlawed the production of alcoholic drink entirely.

Interestingly, despite all the federal law enforcement efforts in the eradication of untaxed liquor before and during Prohibition and following its repeal, some of the largest markets for the product were not in Southern cities, but rather Northern municipalities such as Chicago, Philadelphia and New York. And when buyers in these markets were unable to obtain the product legally, they were more than willing to produce it illegally.

Faced with the choice of losing their livelihoods or carrying on their occupations in secret by working "blockade stills," many mountain men in Pickens County and elsewhere chose the latter. They had little choice. Federal legislation and the enforcement of same literally forced them to become outlaws.

The United States Treasury responded with a system of payments or bounties to local citizens in the north Georgia mountains for "spying" on their moonshining neighbors. Persons later arrested were taken to Atlanta for trial, leaving their families with no alternative but the sale of family possessions for the payment of legal expenses. If convicted (and virtually all were convicted), a moonshiner would be sent to prison while his family struggled to survive on little more than charity.

The liquor production situation for the mountaineers/moonshiners therefore eventually became an extremely serious matter – even to the point of requiring them to die if necessary in order to defend their livelihood. Violence against the revenue agents – and the neighbors who served as their spies – became a common affair.

In neighboring Murray County in 1888, and almost immediately afterwards in Pickens, Gilmer, Whitfield, and Gordon counties, this resistance had reached the level of organized vigilantism. *(Readers please see "The Murder and Mutilation of Lawman Lee Cape" in the pages of this book.)* There is no doubt they were desperate individuals, but beyond their illegal moonshining endeavors, most of those involved in the practice and production were far from criminals. No record of previous illegal activity has ever come to light for any of the Pickens County HMF&P vigilantes.

Even the federal commissioner of Pickens in 1889 testified at one point that the Pickens County vigilantes – with whom he apparently was familiar – were men of good character. They reportedly included five former or current county officials, but the acts they eventually committed marked them as criminals for life.

A Burning Affair

On a Sunday night on November 10, 1889, the activities of the HMF&P

had reached a fever pitch in Pickens. The membership gathered one evening in the "Sea Field" to organize their first raid in the defense of their way of life. Activities such as these eventually became common in north Georgia during this period, as small, desperate but otherwise law-abiding farmers fought for what they considered to be their chief means of supporting their families and their way of life.

The following Tuesday, these men entered the house of another who, despite their warnings, was in Atlanta testifying against his moonshining brethren. After robbing the man's home of food, some of which they ate and the remainder of which they scattered down the road, the HMF&P burned the house, sparing only a stack of hay and a cow and a calf. The owner's family was not home at the time.

The situation was different on December 3, when the HMF&P came down Sharptop Mountain, passing around a bottle – in violation of the organization's bylaws – enroute to a rendezvous at a nearby church. From there, dressed in bizarre and terrifying disguises (their captain wore "blacking" on his face, a white moustache, purple coating on his chin, and an oil-skin coat), they walked to a house on Jones Mountain to pay a visit to another man testifying in Atlanta.

The wife and children of their intended victim were at home asleep when the HMF&P stormed the farm from two sides. The wife was awakened by the crashing invasion of her home and the noise of the burning stable. Running outside into the freezing cold night, she was met with gunfire, shouts and laughing. The house was burned next, while the frightened mother gathered her children in the cold night air.

The leader of the vigilantes reportedly mocked the baby's crying. Out of desperation, their defense of their way of life was taking on an abusive and desperate nature.

The HMF&Ps of Pickens County eventually burned the homes of at least three men who testified in Atlanta. Folklore and local legends have exaggerated the burnings of the group over the ensuing years to *"100 houses in the Marble Hill area."* No such devastation ever actually occurred. There weren't even "100 homes" in the Marble Hill area at that time to burn.

When the incidences of arson began on November 12, 1889, a posse of deputies were organized. Local lawmen and federal agents began a practice of rounding up the persons against whom testimony had been rendered in Atlanta. In the first instance of these arrests, the men were brought before the justice of the peace in the Sharptop District, but were strangely released. *(The agents were unaware that the JP himself was a fellow member of the HMF&P.)*

Feds Fight Back

Eventually, the increased federal law enforcement efforts overwhelmed the resources of the HMF&P. The federal posses – whose numbers were continuously increased – advanced their interruption of the activities of the night riders on a growing basis. Some of the vigilantes began fleeing to other states to assume new identities and lives. Other members remained, but were forced to post "lookouts" and patrols to avoid capture, a necessity which began draining their resources.

In one gun battle with a posse, one member of the HMF&P was seriously wounded. Other members were eventually captured, and to avoid prosecution and the loss of everything they owned, they eventually began informing on their comrades. By this point, their loyalty oaths apparently were valueless and forgotten.

In Pickens County, the activities of the HMF&P eventually were quelled after the close of the two-year stint. A copy of the bylaws of the organization – along with a black cloak and hood – was recovered from a hollow tree following the confession of one participant.

The leader of the Pickens vigilantes eventually was arrested with another member and confined in the Pickens County Jail in Jasper. Undeterred, a group of their friends assisted them in an escape during a storm on the night of February 13, 1890, but both men were soon recaptured. By that point, the "informers" far outnumbered the loyal members.

Nevertheless, the conviction of these "nightriders" proved to be much more difficult than the arrests. In May, 1890, seven men *"who a year ago were put down as staunch and respectable,"* were tried for *Arson*. Evidence and witnesses (principally HMF&P members who had turned state's evidence) could only be obtained for a single house-burning incident.

The ***Atlanta Journal*** reported that there *"was never such excitement over the trial of criminal cases in Georgia or the South. Hundreds of men and women thronged the courtroom and the town."*

Despite the lack of evidence and witnesses, the seven men charged with *Arson* ultimately were sentenced to life in prison. Following the close of the U.S. Civil War, and all the damage wrought by General William T. Sherman's infamous "March to the Sea," in which town after town was put to the torch,

Georgians had become significantly sensitized to the crime of *Arson*. As a result, though it was often difficult to obtain the proper evidence and witnesses for use against suspected arsonists, when those rightfully suspected of the heinous crime were finally convicted, they were often punished with a maximum sentence.

At the time of this trial, these seven men were reported as the largest single group sent to prison in the state's history. The convicted men ultimately were sent to work in the coal mines of northwest Georgia's Dade County, not too far removed from Pickens. Among them was the leader of the HMF&P and his son. He ultimately was killed and his son seriously wounded in the Coal City Mutiny of June 21, 1891.

Ironically, the son escaped from coal mines work camp on January 5, 1893, and returned to Pickens County long enough to inspire a number of stories. He subsequently moved to another region where it is assumed he changed his name and began life anew.

Ten other members of the HMF&P were tried in Atlanta for conspiracy before the Federal Circuit Court of May, 1891. Certain of a conviction, their lawyers were announcing plans for an appeal even before a verdict had been rendered by a jury. One can only imagine their surprise when a verdict of *"Not Guilty"* was handed down. Outraged at this eventuality, government prosecutors charged, tried, and convicted five of the defendants almost immediately for defrauding the federal government of alcoholic beverage taxes.

The persistence of federal officials eventually ended the HMF&P throughout north Georgia forever. Individual resistance to the revenue laws however, continues, even to this day

Legendary Lawman from Pickens:

The Shocking 1927 Murder Of Policeman Lee Cape

Since the Scots-Irish first arrived on the shores of America circa 1715, the production of corn liquor has been a staple custom brought from the old country. They produced this liquor from shore to shore, but more often than not, it has been best-known in the Blue Ridge and Appalachian Mountain Ranges of the Southeast. Since it has always been an illicit product, the sites of its production ("stills") could best be hidden in highland recesses. In conjunction with this un-taxed liquor or "moonshine," came law enforcement authorities dedicated to its eradication. The struggles to both produce and eliminate it have been long and bloody.

O ne of the most heinous crimes ever to occur in the history of north Georgia's fabled Pickens County undoubtedly would be the gruesome 1927 murder of County Policeman W. Lee Cape. On the afternoon of September 17 of that year, this highly-respected lawman was searching for illicit liquor production sites ("moonshine stills") in a remote area of Pickens, and in the process, lost not only his life, but also his head – literally.

Born in South Carolina on June 5, 1862, during the height of the U.S. Civil War, Lee Cape was orphaned at an early age, and therefore undoubtedly quickly learned to be self-sufficient and independent. By 1880 at the age of 18, he was living with his grandmother Cape in Pickens County, Georgia.

Early Lawman

It is unknown today just how or when Cape initially entered the law enforcement profession. He, nevertheless, must have begun this career at an early age, because even by 1890 at the age of 28, he had already garnered enough of a reputation for his prowess at arresting moonshiners for his name to be included on a list of law enforcement officials targeted for death by the Pickens County vigilantes known as "The Night Riders" *(Readers please see the "The Mysterious Night Riders of Pickens County" within the pages of this book.).*

The Night Riders were early American terrorists who raided and burned the homes of state and local lawmen in retribution for their enforcement of the liquor laws. Fortunately for Cape, the Night Riders were all apprehended and sent to prison before they were able to savage the young policeman from Pickens.

Lee Cape was active in the pursuit of all criminals, but he reportedly was one of the more active county policemen who ever pursued illicit liquor traffickers. He eventually was appointed as a deputy United States marshal for his prowess. As a result, he was a sharp thorn in the side of many mountaineers who depended upon the production of illegal liquor for income.

Despite the threats on his life and property, Lee Cape eventually advanced to the front lines of his profession. To put this in perspective, the famed gunfight behind the O.K. Corral in Tombstone, Arizona, which involved another deputy United States marshal – Virgil Earp – and his deputy, Wyatt Earp, had occurred a few years earlier in 1881.

By 1893, Lee Cape reportedly was apprehending and bringing in moonshiners almost daily, and by 1927, he had already spent more than forty years in the law enforcement profession. He was a highly-respected citizen of Pickens County as well as an effective policeman. Those who knew him agree he was determined in his efforts to enforce the laws against trafficking untaxed liquor in the mountains of north Georgia.

"On The Take?"

But therein lies one of the inescapable mysteries involving Cape. His livelihood and income at any point in his life could only be described as exceedingly modest. He was a county policeman in one of the poorest backwoods counties in Georgia, so some historians have wondered over the years just how was he

But therein lies one of the inescapable mysteries involving Cape.

able to afford a substantial and impressive (at least for that date and time in north Georgia) two-story home in Hinton, as well as other luxuries such as an automobile in the years which can only be described as "Depression Years" when no one else but bankers sported such objects of affluence?

Pro-Cape accounts (including those of the newspapers of that day and from interviews of persons who knew him well) steadfastly contend that Cape was guilty of nothing more than law enforcement, an effort for which he eventually paid the ultimate price. Other suspicions, however, maintain that he would have been a very natural target for bribes paid out by those producing untaxed liquor in quantity.

After he had reached a certain level of success in his professional pursuits, Lee Cape also was sometimes described as excessive and over-zealous in the performance of his duties. It was an over-confident laxness in the performance of his professional duties which ultimately exposed him to the dangers which took his life. In the final analysis, he simply became careless and fell victim to a wanton murderer.

But, was Lee Cape "on the take" in his policing of the untaxed liquor production in his region? One cannot help but wonder about that possibility today, when all the facts are considered, but absolutely nothing either before or after his death has ever even hinted at such dishonesty. No one ever even accused him of unethical – and certainly not illicit – behavior in the performance of his duties.

The system of enforcement at that time of the federal revenue laws involving untaxed liquor definitely did not help the situation. Revenue agents and deputy U.S. marshals such as Cape were not paid salaries for those law enforcement duties, but rather fees based upon the number of illegal distilleries or "stills" they captured and the number of arrests they made.

As a result of this system, the agents were often accused of making fraudulent arrests to pad their fees, and their incomes reportedly were often supplemented by bribes, and even by profiteering from the illegal sale of captured distilleries back to their former owners after the devices were in the custody of law enforcement officials. Such was the environment in which Lee Cape worked, and the reason for the suspicions which have been perpetuated to the present day.

The "Roaring Twenties" was a time of firearms, illegal liquor, and violence. In general, Chicago was – and remains today – an epicenter of crimes such as this, but in point of fact, the social ill was a nationwide phenomenon. Nevertheless, much of the illegal liquor was produced in remote mountain regions, and Pickens County was as active as any locale.

It was during these times that the counties added extra deputies and county police (such as Lee Cape) to ease public fears and to beef up rural enforcement efforts in what had become an American guerrilla war against those persons who made and transported the illegal liquor. And as a result of the infinite amount of money exchanging hands in the production and sale of this product, these law enforcement personnel just naturally became very obvious targets for bribes – which many times unfortunately were accepted.

Dedicated Lawman

Nevertheless, according to Pickens County records, Lee Cape gave absolutely no special treatment to anyone when the laws of the state of Georgia and the United States were involved – not even his own family. He is on record for having even arrested his own sons on occasion, so his diligence and devotion can for this reason be considered unquestionable.

Despite his dedicated law enforcement background, Lee Cape's sons ironically were the exact opposite. They frequently appeared in the Pickens County police and court records, and were collectively the subject of almost as much sensation as was Cape's untimely death. In 1924, Levi Cape, amazingly, was sentenced to life in prison *(he was nevertheless paroled in 1934)* for killing his brother, Hobert, and then leaving his father – Lee – for dead in Hinton where the family lived. The third son, Waldo, was killed in 1942 in Hinton, during a drunken brawl.

It can therefore only be considered amazing today, that despite his heroic efforts at the elimination of illegal alcohol in the Pickens County area, much of Lee Cape's family lost their lives in fatal activities involving the illicit substance. Their excessive consumption, associated violence, and the tragic losses these represented to the elder lawman from Pickens no doubt spurred on his devout pursuit of the eradication of illicit untaxed liquor from the mountains of Pickens.

Not only was the pursuit, arrest and jailing of moonshiners an extremely dangerous occupation, north Georgia in general from the 1870s through the

1930s was an extremely dangerous area to be practicing police work. Vicious cut-throat outlaws proliferated in this region, left over from the lawless days of the U.S. Civil War. Lee Cape, however, strangely never expressed any concern whatsoever, or gave any indication that he feared for his life. Whether Cape's bravado was sincere or foolhardy in unknown today. He frequently traveled unarmed, and his "deputies" in his raids, more often than not, were his unarmed wife or his young grandsons.

This "modus operandi" of Cape was somehow successfully practiced by the lawman for many years. Despite the extreme hazards and physical requirements of such an occupation, Cape always seemed up to the task. Even as a middle-aged man, he was known to be fleet of foot and raw-bone strong, able to easily out-run and take into custody most suspects who chose to challenge his authority.

To some, Cape was reckless; to others, he was simply relentless. Regardless of the circumstances, his skills were highly respected in his community and by law enforcement personnel at large. As late as 1922, he was described as having never harmed anyone in the pursuit of his duties. Even in the testimony in the trial of persons accused of his murder, including that of the men later convicted of the crime, Cape was described as well-liked and even as a friend of the very individuals he often arrested.

Cape's quick and flawless performance of his duties, however, was not without exceptions. His neighbor, Tom Evans, remembered that Cape was once given a rude awakening late in his career. According to accounts published at the time in the *Pickens County Progress*, at 11:00 A.M. on Friday, April 7, 1922, the lawman – with the aid of the county

Poor Policeman? – Pickens County Policeman Lee Cape was photographed here prior to his death. Though employed only as a county law enforcement officer with a modest salary during his life, Cape somehow was able to own not only one of the most impressive homes in Pickens County, but also an automobile during the years of the Great Depression when virtually no back-country county policeman anywhere was able to afford such a luxury. Cape, nevertheless, was never once accused of unethical or illegal activity, and was a highly respected law enforcement official in his community.

sheriff and other county policemen – had been working a road-block one evening, successfully arresting bootleggers at the Aiken Cemetery, three miles north of Jasper. The men had just arrested thirty-three-year-old Willie Pickett McFarland of the community of Keithsburg in Cherokee County when tragedy struck. McFarland's buggy had been obviously overloaded, and upon inspection, had revealed a load of contraband whiskey. When the bootlegger had attempted to escape, he and Cape became involved in a struggle. In the midst of the fight, a pistol which Cape had confiscated from another prisoner accidentally discharged, killing McFarland on the spot.

The victim was described as an honest, hard-working, peach-grower, with a wife and two children. His mistake, according to the paper, had been an attempt to supplement his pitiful income with proceeds from illegal whiskey trafficking. Lee Cape, as a result, was devastated. The news report of the incident clearly exonerated Cape, describing him as *"fearless, truthful, and always self-possessed,"* but that did nothing to assuage Cape's conscience. Tom Evans remembered that the lawman was "never the same" after the McFarland shooting.

Interestingly, McFarland's widow subsequently moved to Alabama, and through the relocation of her residence to that state, she somehow became eligible to sue Cape in federal court for the death of her husband and her loss of income. She ultimately won $1,273.00 of the $35,000.00 she sought in damages for what she described as Cape's "recklessness." Whether it was Pickens County or Lee Cape himself who became liable for the damages is unknown today.

Fatal Final Raid

Following the McFarland incident, Lee Cape nevertheless remained relentless in his pursuit of moonshiners and bootleggers. *(And to the surprise of some, there is a definite difference between these two somewhat similar professions. "Moonshiners" produce the illicit liquor. "Bootleggers" illegally distribute it.)* With his usual disdain of personal safety, he departed Hinton on what would be his last raid on September 17, 1927, at 7:30 A.M.

> *The boys carried a shotgun; Lee Cape carried his standard service revolver.*

On this final foray, Cape's open "Touring Car" for which his detractors have questioned his honesty was driven by his sixteen-year-old grandson, Surber Cape. The duo were accompanied by Surber's young friend, Will Evans *(Tom's brother).* The boys carried a shotgun; Lee Cape carried his standard service revolver.

According to later testimony, the group reached the top of nearby Henderson Mountain near the Cherokee County line approximately half an hour later. Lee Cape stepped out of the car and instructed the boys to search the western slope of the mountain while he patrolled due east. He instructed the boys to fire shots if anyone in the group discovered anything. They were to meet at a nearby house at 3:00 P.M. to sort out the details of their searches.

At 12:30, the boys discovered a large illegal distillery for the fermentation of beer and the production of untaxed liquor. They fired the shotgun as they had been instructed to do, but to their disappointment, the elder Cape did not respond. The boys then drove to the rendezvous point. An hour later, when Cape still had not appeared, the boys drove around the mountain searching for the lawman.

It was at this point that the true danger of the situation began to manifest itself. According to later court testimony, at approximately 3:30 P.M., the boys suddenly encountered three large men – Lindsey Evans, his brother Hoyt Evans, and C.L. Smith – all of whom were obviously angry and blocking the narrow road with their personal car. Lindsey Evans of course instantly recognized the car in which the boys were riding as Lee Cape's vehicle. No doubt seeing the weapons being carried by the boys, he also instantly suspected the moonshine detection nature of the boys' activities. In a rush, the men reportedly charged up to the boys yelling and cursing, enraged that they were assisting their grandfather in the detection of distilleries to destroy.

Surber, realizing he was in desperate danger, quickly attempted to shift his grandfather's car into reverse, but when the stubborn machine wouldn't comply, he had no other option but to jump quickly from the car and run, abandoning Will Evans to the mercy of the approaching men.

Enraged beyond description by this point, Lindsey Evans reportedly snatched young Will Evans (no relation to Lindsey or Hoyt Evans) by the hair of his head and attacked him with a knife, severely lascerating one of his fingers. The younger Evans broke free, however, and fled in terror.

Surber, who had successfully outrun the men, arrived shortly thereafter at the home of Dott Pharr, a local bailiff, and reported the attack. Pharr reached Cape's automobile just as the Evans brothers and Smith were fleeing, having stolen the boys' shotgun.

Preparations for Murder

The rage building within Lindsey Evans was becoming white-hot by this point. According to the courtroom testimony, the three men stopped at

The rage building within Lindsey Evans was becoming white-hot by this point.

Lindsey's home where he went quickly inside to retrieve his own shotgun. Under those circumstances, shotguns loaded with double-aught buckshot were considered far more effective weapons than single-shot weapons. Evans checked his weapon – clicking the hammer on both barrels before loading the scattergun – then climbed back into their car.

Meanwhile, Lee Cape was oblivious to the circumstances unfolding around him. He had not heard the boys' signal shot because he had left the mountain to explore nearby Salacoa Creek. At some point after 12:00 noon, he began to walk back towards the scheduled rendezvous with the boys – a walk which tragically would prove to be his last.

R. Seab Newborn later testified that he had seen the county policeman as he trudged down the road in pursuit of the boys, and that thirty minutes later, on the same road, he had seen the car and the three violent men who had accosted the boys. Newborn stated that *"twenty to thirty minutes later,"* he *"heard shots."*

On their initial encounter on the road, the three men reportedly passed Cape without attempting to harm him, but the vindictive terrible anger within Lindsey Evans was not to be denied, and he angrily instructed his brother to turn their vehicle around so that he could confront Cape. Hoyt Evans, however, continued on, apparently doing the best he could to avoid further problems.

Unbeknownst to Hoyt however, the spot he picked to

BUSTIN' UP THE "STILL" – Captured for posterity on film after the discovery of this illegal liquor production ("moonshine") site in the wilds of north Georgia, the perpetrators - or perhaps hired laborers – in this photo are in the detested process of destroying the distillery. Untold hours and extremely-scarce funds were invested by illicit liquor producers in the covert construction and maintenance of an illegal distillery site. Such operations provided desperately-needed income for poor mountain families during the *Depression Era* in the United States. Even after the repeal of *Prohibition* in the early 1930s, illicit (untaxed) liquor production continued and occasional sites of untaxed liquor production are still in operation even today, though on a much lesser scale. (Photo courtesy of the Georgia Department of Archives & History, Atlanta)

eventually park their vehicle (the Evans family home on old Goshen Road, one and one-half miles below the former site of the community of Talmadge) was the very spot which Cape had selected as a rendezvous site with his two young assistants. Lindsey Evans who apparently was mentally unbalanced at this point was later quoted in court as stating *"Me or old man Lee Cape one is going to die, when he comes out the road."*

As he hiked up the road that day, Lee Cape reached the men in the car and in his usual inquisitive manner, inquired as to the owner of the vehicle. Cape, familiar with the men and apparently suspecting something to be amiss, began pecting something to be amiss, began casually searching behind the vehicle's seats – undoubtedly for illegal liquor – which angered Lindsey Evans even further.

At this point, Evans reportedly loudly and angrily warned Cape that he would have to pay for any damages to the vehicle which he was absently searching – an act which would be illegal in present-day law enforcement procedure without specific permission or clear motivation due to visible illicit materials. Had he known of the danger afoot, Cape quite possibly would have reacted differently, but he had no reason to suspect the murderous circumstances which were slowly unfolding around him. His reply to Evans's angry threat reflected Cape's usual fearless (and some would say reckless) demeanor.

"Well that would be very easy done I guess," Cape very lackadaisically reportedly retorted. "You've been atryin' to run ablazin' around all the time; nobody ain't scared of you."

Grisly Details

Those words had hardly escaped Cape's mouth when Lindsey Evans exploded. Witnesses at the scene later testified that the enraged man quickly took out a shotgun *(specifically whose shotgun was never proven)* and fired three rounds point-blank into Cape, killing the famed lawman almost instantly with the first round. Cape fell onto the side of the roadway, stone-dead from multiple wounds.

Shocked beyond belief, Hoyt Evans reportedly roughly grabbed the weapon from his brother, and pleaded with him to stop, but knowing the worst had already been done. Eyewitnesses at the scene ran into the Evans home.

Lindsey Evans, nevertheless, was completely unrepentant, and even threatened to shoot his fleeing neighbors as well as his brother. Cape's bloody body was roughly stuffed into the trunk of the men's automobile and the two brothers then amazingly drove quickly away. The motive for the removal of Cape's body from the scene of the crime apparently was somehow associated with an intended concealment of the evidence of the men's crime.

Any hope of an unwitnessed disposal of the body, however, was virtually eliminated, for in their panic, the two men careened up the road from Fairmount to Adairsville at an incredible rate of speed. Their reckless driving and open touring cars *(The men drove two vehicles to dispose of the body; whether or not one of the vehicles was Cape's car is unknown.)* made later identification easy for the numerous individuals who testified against them.

Grisly and varying accounts of what next transpired have been circulated for years. According to courtroom testimony, Cape's corpse was mutilated in a twisted hope that this would in some manner render identification of the body – and therefore an association with the murderers – impossible *(For reasons unknown today, the fact that the crime had been committed in full view of several witnesses seemed to have been lost upon the Evans brothers.)*.

Whatever the circumstances, at what is still *(at the time of this writing)* a lonely dirt crossroads five miles south of Adairsville, the body of Lee Cape was unceremoniously dumped. Horrifyingly, Cape's head was then somehow severed from his body and mutilated by shotgun blasts which rendered the face unrecognizable. The head was then thrown

> *Cape fell onto the side of the roadway, stone-dead from multiple wounds.*

to the opposite side of the road from the lawman's torso. The body, strangely, was also stripped naked before being abandoned. Whether or not this was Lindsey Evan's twisted idea of final humiliation for Cape is unknown today.

News of the murder traveled swiftly. The following morning, when the brothers paused for a meal at a Fairmount roadhouse, a crowd gathered around their clearly-recognizable automobile searching for grisly signs of the murder. By that evening, a crowd of more than one hundred had gathered at the home of Lindsey Evans, hoping to cash in on the $500.00 reward already offered by the Pickens County Commissioner's office for information leading to the identification and capture of Cape's murderers.

Coincidentally, one of the first persons at the scene when Cape's body was accidentally discovered by T.R. (Rex) Sherman two days later was C.H. Peacock of Canton. Peacock had administered to Cape years earlier when the lawman had been wounded by his drunken son. Peacock had no trouble identifying the body then and later for the court as Cape's corpse.

After Cape's body had been removed from the scene of the dumping and prepared for proper burial, he was given a hero's funeral. It was attended by more persons than any previous funeral

The body, strangely, was also stripped naked before being abandoned.

in Pickens County history up to that date. The old lawman was laid out in an open casket (although his head was concealed). Distinguished marble magnate Sam Tate gave the eulogy.

Evading Capture

Not one, but two men subsequently were appointed to replace Cape in his law enforcement capacity as county policeman, but filling his shoes was no small feat. According to an editorial in the **Pickens County Progress** newspaper, doubts existed: *"Can Pickens County get another Lee Cape? Do you know any man that will lay out all night in the cold, sleet and rain that people might enjoy full protection? . . . At public gatherings, he was usually on hand, and when he came up, everybody knew there would be no disturbance, no matter how large the crowd. . . He didn't know the meaning of the word 'fear'."*

Over the years, numerous bizarre tales have been circulated regarding the motive for Cape's murder. The most likely explanation, however, and the one supported by the trial transcript, maintains that the killer was enraged because he mistakenly suspected Cape had discovered his moonshine still, and that he (the perpetrator) was about to be arrested for the production and possession of illegal untaxed liquor, a highly volatile issue among the poor residents in the mountains of north Georgia.

In a rage, perhaps enhanced by alcohol intoxication, the assailant committed an unpremeditated act of violence. During the trial for Cape's murder, no evidence was presented which in any way indicated any dislike whatsoever of the lawman by his killer, Lindsey Evans.

Surprisingly, despite being indicted for the horrifying murder, Lindsey Evans managed to avoid capture for the remainder of his life by the authorities. His whereabouts from that day forward were never known.

Twenty years after the murder, an individual held in a Texas jail was suspected of being Lindsey Evans. However, when representatives from the Pickens County Police arrived in Texas, they were unable to make a positive visual identification, and other criminal investigation tools such as fingerprinting, etc., were not in use in remote Pickens County in 1927. Lindsey Evans remained at large.

In Lindsey's absence, four other men were subsequently brought to trial for participation in the Cape murder. Despite being ably defended by Atlanta attorneys, C.L. "Seal" Smith and Hoyt Evans were convicted and given life sentences. Smith amazingly later escaped from prison and was himself never again seen. The other two defendants – Carter Wilson and Carter Jones – pleaded *"Guilty"* and were given twelve-month sentences each.

An illegal liquor still near the site of Cape's death is presumed to have been the

Though the murderer Lindsey Evans was never captured, he is suspected of having returned to Pickens late in life.

motive for his murder. The still was destroyed the day after his shooting.

The men convicted for Cape's murder were also found to be guilty of the possession and production of illegal liquor. Their sentences for these crimes were added to the sentence for Cape's murder.

Though the murderer Lindsey Evans was never captured, he is suspected of having returned to Pickens late in life. A Jasper, Georgia physician claimed to have administered to him in the 1950s, as the wanted man lay dying. Whether or not this was accurate is unknown today, but the physician obviously never informed any law enforcement authorities of the murderer's presence.

Little more than verbal accounts remain of the sites associated with Cape's murder today. The roads and communities associated with the murder have either been considerably changed, or have disappeared completely.

In Hinton, Lee Cape's prominent home still stands as of this writing. It has been nominated for inclusion on the *National Register of Historic Places*. Across the road, in Hinton Cemetery, Lee Cape's monument is easily recognizable. On his headstone, a final epitaph is chiseled: *"Through The Performance of His Duty in the Enforcement of Law He Sacrificed His Life."*

Lee Cape, no doubt, would have been proud.

Motive for Murder in the Mountains

Northern Pickens County, Georgia, in its earliest settlement days was a very rural, and, in many ways primitive place for family life. The struggles were many and customs, such as marital relationships, were often very loose. It was an environment ripe for violent behavior which could descend into the realm of murder. The unusual case involving the death of Narcissa Fowler had its roots in jealousy, mental illness, selfishness, extra-marital sexual relations, and just pure uncontrolled rage, but no one ever truly explained why Kate Southern murdered Narcissa Fowler.

In the last decades of the 19th century, the mountainous northeastern region of Pickens County carried a very unsavory reputation for immorality and flash violence, many times involving desperate individuals left over from the U.S. Civil War. On February 10, 1877, a sensationalized murder which involved two women – instead of men – and a vicious sex triangle, is still occasionally discussed by distant relatives of the principal characters and long-time natives of the area.

Over the years, criminals and violence-prone individuals have frequently been involved in horrendous deeds in Pickens. Legends and tales abound in the county where strange "goings-on" have occurred for 100 years or more.

In 1877, the murder trial of Kate Southern focused national attention upon the county, as if the area hadn't already attracted enough attention. Here was the home of the "house-burners" and "night-riders" of the 1860s, '70s, and '80s, who were involved in many illegal activities. And in 1884, Democrats in Jasper – the county seat – celebrated Grover Cleveland's presidential victory by exploding two anvils full of gunpowder, making a racket so loud that the concussion was heard and felt many miles away. In 1927, the gruesome murder and dismemberment of Pickens Policeman Lee Cape again rocked the state, and dominated the news in early September of that year. These are just a handful of the many unbelievably shocking events which have rocked this county over the years.

Lured To Death

Despite the ultimate criminal nature of the Kate Southern – Narcissa Fowler incident, it began innocently enough. It, however, was a caldron of unreleased anger and vengeful desires that had been threatening to boil over for many weeks.

John Hambrick lived in what was known as "the Lansdown," a wooded valley in northern Pickens County near the Gilmer County line. It normally would have been known as a peaceful, attractive valley which was named after the area's most prominent family. It has been an isolated region since the earliest pioneer days, and, surprisingly, is even more so today.

Hambrick had a wife and four daughters – all nearly grown. One frigid evening in February, 1877, he – for reasons unknown today – decided he wanted "to have a party." Whether his intentions were perfectly innocent and honorable, or whether they were intended as a "set-up" for a vicious fight between two jealous females is unknown today as well.

Events of the nature of this "party" were often strangely referred to as "a play" by area residents. Such an occasion sometimes included wild activities, but more often than not involved mere dancing, music (fiddling in this case), socialization, and other such mundane actions of a friendly gathering, just as do present-day parties.

Nevertheless, the simple fact that this event was instigated by Hambrick instead of a female member of the area can only be viewed as suspicious behavior today, particularly in view of the fact that his daughter, Kate, would later claim that it was *"the fust time I ever seed a reel (dance) run."* Perhaps he was concerned about the future of one or more of his unmarried daughters and their inability to find a husband in the deep woods of north Pickens, and wanted to take on a "Cupid" role. Perhaps his intentions were darker, rooted in the enjoyment of violence between two females. We'll never know.

Among the participants of this party or "play" was nineteen-year-old Catherine or "Kate" Hambrick Southern, who was John Hambrick's daughter and married to Robert Southern. Though she should have been locked in matrimonial bliss with her husband, Kate, to the contrary, was known to be "carrying on lewd behavior out in the cane swamp" with an individual by the name of "Woods." The details of this "lewd" behavior apparently had been observed by Narcissa "Sis" A.M. Fowler, who had been spreading gossip of the details around the community.

As a result of the exposure of her transgressions by "Sis," Kate had been white-hot angry and revenge-minded now for a number of weeks. She was the type person who carried a grudge to the bitter end, and who could only see a resolution through violence. An acquaintance, Rachel Bramlet, would later testify in court that she had heard Kate threaten, in July of 1876, to "cut Sis's haunch out" if her father did not sue Sis for slander.

Kate Southern, however, apparently was not the only one angry at the fact that a clandestine extra-marital sexual relationship had been exposed. Sis Fowler – who must not have been much of a "catch" – had caught her husband, Taylor S. Cowart, in an adulterous affair as well, and when she had attempted to divorce him on those grounds, he had held her roughly between his legs while he gave her backside a substantial beating. Then, before his angry wife could have divorce papers served upon him, he simply abandoned Sis.

As if this were not already a complex sexual triangle, Sis Fowler herself was no angel, having been the object of a great deal of affection and subsequent gossip herself in an affair with Kate's husband,

Robert Southern. Truth be told, it quite likely was this sexual dalliance between Sis and Robert which most angered Kate, since, though she was undoubtedly also angry at the exposure of her own affair, she was more angry at the possibility of the loss of her husband, Robert to Sis.

At noon on that Saturday, which was the day of the dance, Mary Mealer was at the Hambrick home. She also later testified against Kate, stating that she (Kate) had remarked – to no one in particular – that if Sis Fowler was at the party, she (Kate) was going to kill her. Other persons present, however, would later surprisingly testify that these comments never occurred. And round and round we go.

Deadly Party

From the evidence provided, one almost has to at least suspect that John Hambrick's motive for setting up the "play" was two-fold. On the one hand, he perhaps was seeking attention for his unmarried daughters who apparently were growing a little "long-in-tooth" in the marriage venue. And on the other hand, one has to suspect that he was certainly aware of the animosity between his daughter Kate and Sis Fowler, and perhaps was at least indirectly setting up a scenario in which these two participants would have a "show-down."

Meanwhile, if Kate's public threats had reached Sis Fowler, she did not ever express any fear or misgivings in the matter. She and Kate were about the same height (5 ft., 5 in. tall), but while Sis was very "stout and healthy," Kate was thin and sickly, weighing only 110 pounds, thirty pounds less than even her younger and shorter sister Amazilla Hambrick. However, what Sis Fowler very obviously did not factor into the situation was a fight with the whole Hambrick family

(which is what ultimately occurred) – and with a Kate Hambrick Southern who was *carrying a deadly weapon.*

According to later testimony, John Haynes, Kate's brother-in-law, set out for the party with a group of his friends. "Someone" (identity unknown today) suggested that Sis Fowler be pointedly invited, supposedly to insure that enough women were at the dance, and because she was known to be "a good hand" at dancing. Haynes had a mule-drawn wagon and was traveling around the backwoods picking up the party participants – which apparently was a common occurrence – and therefore stopped at Sis's house to invite her. Unaware of the site of the party, Sis climbed quickly aboard, having no idea of the deadly circumstances afoot.

It was not until Haynes pulled up at the Hambrick house that Sis reportedly realized that the "play" or dance was not going to be held at the Haynes's house, and that she would be entering an "enemy camp" if she chose to attend the event. At this point, Sis wisely expressed a reluctance to enter into the house, but Kate's parents, interestingly, warmly invited Sis and urged her to attend. Again, was there a plot afoot to set the two females against each other?

Sis ultimately made a disastrous choice by allowing Kate's parents to usher her into their death-trap home. It was a decision which would haunt her family for the remainder of their lives. A Pickens County prosecutor at the murder trial would later refer to the Hambricks as *"welcoming Sis with hospitable hands to a bloody grave."*

The dance reportedly went on for hours to the music of fiddler William Bramlet. Witnesses guessed that from a dozen to twenty people were eventually present in a room that was between 14 x 14 feet and 16 x 18 feet in size, so to say that the "party was packed" would be a decided understatement. As was customary at such events, a bottle of liquor – of the un-taxed variety – was provided by John Hambrick and passed around the room.

Space for actual dancing (square dancing) at this event was at a premium, because the two beds and other furniture normally in the room were amazingly still there. The only alternative would have been to drag them out into the woods, and the Hambricks weren't about to do that. With up to 20 individuals dancing and socializing in the close quarters of the room – and since it was late at night, with the only light provided by the fireplace and a small brass lamp on the mantle – visibility was very poor.

Kate was reported to be on one of the beds with her husband, Bob. It is not known if her extra-marital partner – Mr. Woods – was in attendance on this evening. She went outside and asked her father for the loan of his pocket knife to trim her nails and to cut some "tooth brushes" (black gum twigs used by the girls.) She left the house but came back a few minutes later, and the stage was set for disaster.

Cold-Blooded Murder

As midnight approached, Sis was dancing with an individual by the name of James Honea. He would later testify that she stumbled and then complained that for the third time that evening, Kate had tripped her.

Sis, at this point, reportedly loudly warned Kate not to trip her again. All of a sudden, the circumstances in the room reportedly went deathly quiet. The music strangely ceased, and all eyes turned to the two women. It was quite obvious that most of those present had

Bound for Alabamy – Kate and Bob Southern were photographed in 1908 in Alabama, to which they eventually moved following her release from prison. Constantly ill, Kate passed away in 1927 at the age of 68. She and her husband are buried together in Posey Mill, Alabama. Prior to her sensational murder trial, only three women were known to have been executed in Georgia: Alice Ryley, a poor Irish immigrant in 1735, Polly Barclay of Wilkes County in 1806, and Susan Eberhardt in 1873. After the Southern trial, Lena Baker was executed in 1945, and Kelly Gissendaner in 2015.

anticipated this fight from the outset, and now were waiting for the action to begin.

According to testimony, the silence in the room reigned for a minute or two. Kate then approached Sis and said something which only they could hear.

Sis then openly challenged her with the statement "Come ahead."

Kate replied "Oh yes, God damn you," and the fight was on.

The stocky and strong Sis quickly pulled Kate to the floor, yanking her hair while clubbing her over the head. She fully intended to give Kate a good old-fashioned country beating and was well on the way toward this objective. What she, (Sis) however, didn't immediately realize was that every time Kate was within reach, she (Kate) was throwing what appeared to be blows, but what in reality were stabs and slashes with the knife she had earlier strategically borrowed from . . . her father.

Never one to leave things to chance when her family was concerned, Amazilla, (Kate's sister), soon joined in the fight. She quickly grabbed Sis by the hair and beat her viciously over the head, providing a distraction to allow her sister Kate a chance to regain her feet. At that moment, Kate pulled herself up by Sis's shirt tails and started landing some stout "stabbing" blows herself.

Weak and sickly, Kate was tiring quickly, and needed any advantage she could obtain. She had been using the knife to the greatest avail possible, and Sis had now slowed. According to later testimony, she and Sis continued grappling near one of the beds, and then tumbled over into a dark corner, rolling out near the fireplace and finally to the door. Not one person moved to stop the fight. Everyone seemed to be immensely enjoying the "entertainment" which this "cat-fight" was providing.

After the two had rolled over near the door, the action strangely ceased when Sis suddenly just collapsed over on her side. Even in the poor light of the room, the bright red aura of blood reportedly could be clearly seen pouring out of Sis's breast.

Realizing something terrible had occurred, Honea reportedly attempted to pull Sis to her feet, but she merely collapsed once again into a heap onto the floor. The terrible knife wounds which Kate had been steadily applying to Sis had taken their toll. Sis, with her eyes staring blankly, was clearly beyond help and already into her death throes.

Honea, who apparently had been attracted to Sis, then stood in front of the door and loudly instructed everyone to remain where they were, since Sis clearly appeared to be dead and it was obvious a murder had occurred.

Kate, who by then was in an even more murderous rage, screamed at him to get out. When he refused to move, her husband, Bob, pulled out a revolver from beneath his coat and forced Honea – at gunpoint – to leave the cabin.

Due to the darkness within the confines of the poorly-lit room, no one could later testify to having actually seen Kate use the knife on Sis, but no one doubted what had occurred either. Since she had been holding and stabbing with an opened knife the entire fight, striking Sis whenever possible, Kate herself had also felt the bite of the knife blade, since it had been forced closed upon her fingers several times, cutting them severely, particularly on her right hand, where she had nearly severed her little finger.

Amazilla was heard to ask Kate if she was sorry for having killed Sis, to which Kate reportedly replied that she did what she wanted to do.

Murder Investigation

To say that the news of the murder "quickly reached law enforcement authorities" would be an exaggeration at best, but it quite probably did arrive in the wee hours of the morning. In those days, the swiftest mode of transportation in that locale was a mule-drawn wagon on a rough and narrow mountain trails. No one moved "quickly" under those primitive circumstances.

Kate and her family did not take flight following the commission of the crime – at least not immediately. They instead merely attempted to eliminate as much of the evidence as possible. Nevertheless, Kate, ever the braggart, openly and readily confirmed that she was "the 'man' who had 'killed' Sis Fowler." She demonstrated no shock at her actions whatsoever.

According to a traditional account recorded from Jasper resident Dallas Byess, when Sheriff John Lindsay finally arrived the next day to search the Hambrick house, both the Hambricks and Southerns were still absent-mindedly washing blood from their clothing. Though the lawmen wanted to question and sought Kate, they failed to find her, reportedly because she had hidden in the arch of the chimney.

Due to the fact that an indictment for murder was not immediately issued, the Hambrick family had ample time to prepare themselves for flight once they had eliminated as much of the evidence as possible. This, however, was ridiculous on the face of it since there were so many eye-witnesses to the crime.

Following a packing of their valuables and necessities for life elsewhere, Kate and her husband, Bob, made good in their flight for freedom. They would not be captured until well over a year after the crime had occurred, and might not have been captured at all had not their pursuers been led by one of the most famous lawmen in Georgia history – Walter Webster "Web" Finley. Despite their absence, the Hambricks and Southerns nevertheless were all indicted for murder at the next term of the Pickens County Superior Court.

Susan Petit, the nearest makeshift undertaker, was called ten to eleven hours after the murder to remove the body, preserve any further evidence, and then prepare the body for burial. Again, the only mode of transportation in the highlands of Pickens County in 1877 was a mule-drawn wagon or a mounted mule or horse on very poor mountain trails. It is actually surprising that Ms.

Petit arrived as swiftly as she did, since, as a female, she probably did not depart for the scene of the crime until after sun-up the following morning.

Petit reportedly took the corpse by wagon to Sis's father's home and dressed the deceased for burial later that same day. In Pickens County Superior Court, she would later serve as a coroner of sorts, a capacity in which she proved to be quite adept.

When called to testify in court, Petit stated that Sis was about twenty to twenty-five years of age; a very stout woman and larger than Kate. She explained that the body had not one, but a total of six knife wounds – one on the temple, one on the jaw, one under the collar bone, one below the breast, and two others in the chest.

Apparently unbeknownst to those in the room, Kate had been delivering wound after wound to the unfortunate Sis during their fight, and Ms. Petit made clear that any one of several of the wounds would have been fatal. Petit also explained that the wounds appeared to have been made by a knife that was very intentionally pushed straight into the chest cavity of the victim where it struck vital organs and arteries.

Petit described other evidence as well, being very thorough. Hair which Petit said she found in Sis's hands at the Hambrick house and at the Fowler house, appeared to be Kate's hair.

Since she assisted her in the fight, Amazilla, Kate's sister, was arrested and also tried. On May 31, 1877, she was sentenced to two years in prison for her part in the murder.

Flight From Justice

As explained above, Kate Southern and her family took flight in the hours following the murder. Alfred H.

Colquitt, having taken office on January 12 of 1877, offered a reward of $150.00 (the equivalent of roughly $3,000.00 in 2024 dollars) for the capture and arrest of the Southerns. Sis Fowler's family – who, considering the $250.00 reward which they also offered – apparently were reasonably wealthy for that time and place. In 1877, $250.00 was the equivalent of approximately $6,300.00 in 2024 dollars.

Despite the rewards, Kate and Robert Southern nevertheless remained at large for over a year. With the situation becoming hopeless, it was decided that more sophisticated help would be needed to locate the fugitives. Men like Walter "Web" Finley were called "mountain trackers," but "tracking," in the usual sense, had little to do with their actual work. In reality, they were among the nation's first true "detectives," and were considered to be among the best in the business.

These lawmen, sometimes working as sheriffs or deputies, and at other times as freelance posses, knew the mountain roads, pig trails, and Indian paths intimately. Aside from their pure tracking abilities, they also had countless mountain people from whom they knew how to creatively extract information. They knew "who" to ask for information; "what" to ask; and "what to believe and not believe," all of which were vitally important in the capture of a fugitive. With common sense, experience, and patience, they enjoyed an exceptionally high rate of success in criminal apprehensions.

Having been born in Gilmer County and lived in the north Georgia area all his life, Walter W. Finley was well-versed with the harsh mountain environment. He was an ex-sheriff of Fannin County, and had won fame and fortune by tracking down and bringing to justice notorious Jackson County murderer Sanford Pirkle in 1875 and Fannin County killer Ayers Jones in 1876. Once hired for the Southern case, he set the wheels of justice into motion, and his tenacity for success was a thing of legend.

In late January, 1878, after considerable research, patience, and dogged effort for almost a year, Finley finally learned the Southerns were living on a farm near Franklin, North Carolina. With two other men, the famed detective arrived at the farm only minutes after the Southerns, accompanied by Bob Southern's father and two brothers, had left in an ox-drawn wagon, headed in the opposite direction for northern Alabama.

Having closed the gap this far, and with his quarry almost in view, Finley and his men set out in hot pursuit. After riding most of the day and the following night without pause, the three men finally closed to within a few minutes of the fugitives at Murphy, North Carolina.

As a meticulous and learned professional, Finley left his party at a hotel, and personally scouted the Southerns' camp to determine their numbers, the weapons they carried, and the best mode of apprehension. He decided to make his move at 4:00 a.m. the following morning.

At dawn, despite the dark and a miserably-cold rain, the Southerns again broke camp just minutes in advance of the Finley posse. They either possessed incredibly good intuition, amazing luck, or simply unbelievable timing.

This time, however, Finley was able to close on his quarry. After riding hard to make up for lost time and sensing that he had almost reached the fleeing Southerns, he slowed his tired horse to a trot.

In that day and time, most of the

trails – there simply were no "roads" – almost literally were "holes cut through the thick trees and undergrowth. If one wished to "flee" on one of these trails, he or she generally had but two options. As a result, once Finley had reached his quarry, he calmly rode his mount up the trail past the perpetrators – all of whom were totally oblivious to the famed lawman's identity – in order to get men situated on both sides of the Southerns.

With his men properly stationed, the mountain detective then closed the noose, surrounding the fugitives from front and rear and quickly taking them prisoner before they could use their two long-guns, pistols, or knives. The Southerns clearly were well-armed and prepared to resist violently if allowed the opportunity. Walter Finley did not allow them that opportunity.

Once their arrest had been effected and the fugitives had been bound and trussed, Bob Southern's two brothers – James and Miles – and his father, William, were turned over to a local bailiff. In those days, a number of the mountain trails were "toll-roads," and it was a crime to skip these toll payments. Since the Southerns had passed through the toll-gate of the Western Carolina Turnpike without making the necessary payment, they were charged and held for the offence. Finley had taken this strategy due simply to the fact that he was interested only in the apprehension and return of Kate and Bob Southern, and by leaving his brothers and father in custody in North Carolina, the task would be much simpler.

Meanwhile, Finley and his men took the still trussed Bob, Kate, and their recently-born baby to a nearby house for breakfast. (*Note: It could never be claimed that the mountain folk – particularly the Southerns and Hambricks*

– were not fond of procreation. Before her trial was finished, Kate would produce yet another child while in the Pickens County Jail, and would ultimately have a total of at least 8 children.)

No sooner had everyone commenced to eat, however, than William Southern and his sons – having escaped from the bailiff – miraculously attempted to free Kate and Robert Southern by force from the famed mountain detective. According to a later account of the incident, Finley and his men, however, were far and away the better of the match-up. They ultimately disarmed their attackers, taking two more pistols and a knife from them and avoiding any injuries. Just under a week later, Bob, Kate, and their baby were in the Pickens County jail.

Old man Southern and his sons would later claim – to no avail – that they had persuaded Robert and Kate to surrender to the authorities and were on the way back to Jasper to collect the reward to give to Kate's mother when they were apprehended and arrested by Finley and his men.

Media Frenzy

The **Atlanta Constitution** did not report Narcissa Fowler's murder in any of the February, 1877, issues, although it could have reprinted the account carried in the **Marietta Journal** had its editors so chosen. The trial and conviction of Kate's sister, Amazilla, also went unnoticed and unreported by the **Constitution**. It is unknown today if this was due to poor reporting, a lack of interest, or merely ignorance of a story which was considered to be beyond the paper's sphere of coverage.

The first account whatsoever of the incident to appear in the **Constitution** was a reprint from the **Ellijay Courier** which described Finley's capture of the Southerns. A news editor at the *Constitution* apparently realized at last that somewhere in this tidbit of information, a story could actually be found (or made).

Almost a year to the day after the murder, the *Constitution* published a lengthy – and decidedly distorted – story of the whole affair. The article was run in the February 14th (*St. Valentine's Day*) issue.

Contrary to the facts of the incident, the *Constitution* story entitled *"The Fatal Dance"* added some twenty-five pounds to the skinny, sickly Kate Southern, describing her as *"one of the prettiest girls in the up-country."* The published article also converted the somewhat amateurish and simple fiddling at the Hambrick house into *"a ball."* Here, Kate caught husband Bob *"in a cotillion"* with Narcissa Fowler, now described as "a former girl friend." In a fit of jealous rage, Kate, according to the article, pulled out the knife and dramatically shouted *"You have danced enough!"* at which point she killed the very plump Narcissa with a single blow to the neck that cut all the way to the heart.

As an apparent hedge on the accuracy of their story, the *Constitution* editors printed the disclaimer that *"the tragedy was committed in the heart of Pickens County, beyond the reach of newspapers, and what we know of it is received through mere hearsay."*

Unfortunately, the version of the incident which was printed in the *Constitution*, faulty though it may have been, even in its description of the Pickens County geography and its ignorance of the more accurate coverage by the *Ellijay Courier* and the *Marietta Journal*, would be the version that the national press, both pro-Kate and anti-Kate,

would use to build their own upcoming feature stories on the incident.

Even the local tales of this murder would be based at least in part upon this romantic fiction. If the *Constitution* had failed to find the truth (and had not even looked very hard for it), it at least had apparently found a *money-making* story. For several issues, Kate Southern articles were featured, frequently on the front page.

On Trial For Murder

In Pickens County, however, officials were looking for the truth. Kate Southern, her husband Bob, her father John Hambrick, her mother Sarah, and brother-in-law John Haymes had all been indicted for the 1877 Narcissa Fowler murder, and were now all crowded by Sheriff Lindsay into Pickens County's small rock jail. *(Editor's Note: this historic facility was demolished in the 1960s, and is not the restored and now historic 1906 brick jail which is still standing as of this writing).*

On April 23, 1878, Kate Southern finally stood trial for her crime. Thirty-six extra jurors had been summoned to guarantee that an impartial judgement could be obtained.

The testimony of the witnesses in this case, in the trial of Amazilla, and in the trial of the rest of Kate's family, has survived. In none of this material did any witness ever suggest that Bob Southern even knew Narcissa Fowler, much less that he had danced or was having sex with her, contrary to the sensational stories being published in the *Atlanta Constitution*. So was the Bob Southern – Narcissa Fowler romantic union a complete fabrication? Maybe. Maybe not.

Kate's true motive for the murder was never actually determined. Only one witness suggested that the crime was a result of the gossip Narcissa had reportedly been spreading about Kate's dalliance with Mr. Woods. So what was her actual motive? For reasons unknown today, Kate Hambrick Southern quite possibly was simply immensely jealous of Narcissa Fowler. There simply is no other way to justify her deadly actions. Perhaps she saw the healthier Narcissa as a threat to her marriage to Bob Southern. The answer to this mystery will never be known.

The witnesses variously also explained how Narcissa had been provoked into what appeared to be a fair fight, not knowing that Kate had concealed a dangerous weapon. The prosecution tried to prove that the *"dance"* was *"a deliberate and willful conspiracy, that was planned by the Hambricks"* and their friends, to set up the circumstances for the fight and possibly even for the murder itself.

Opening and closing arguments were not recorded, but nothing in the *Ellijay Courier's* report of the trial supported the love triangle or jealousy motive ignited by sexual affairs as stated in the *Atlanta Constitution*. S.A. Darnell, J.C. Allen, and T.F. Greer represented the state, and the defense was composed of D.P. Lester, W.T. Day, Carey W. Styles, and W.H. Simmons.

Both sides would be credited with making strong cases. Seven arguments were heard, besides the opening argument. The testimony took up a day and a half; the arguments required much the same; and the jury took twenty-four hours to render a verdict of *"Guilty"* for Kate Southern, but *"With a Recommendation of Mercy, if Possible."*

Judge George N. Lester had seen his share of death on Civil War battlefields, but he announced that the verdict he was about to render – the only one that the law allowed him to make – was the saddest moment in his life. On Saturday, April 28, he told Kate to make peace with her God, and, while he openly wept, sentenced her *"to be hung by the neck until dead between the hours of 10:00 a.m. and 3:00 p.m. on Friday, June 21."*

Kate's lawyers announced that they would appeal the verdict for a new trial at the June term of the Pickens County Court. However, Judge Lester met with an accident that left him incapacitated and, on May 10, the June term of court was postponed until July.

This was bad news for Kate, but for the *Atlanta Constitution*, matters could not have taken a better turn. A photographer from Canton was hired to make photographs of Kate, her husband, and her baby. The photographs were copyrighted and then printed, not for publication in the *Constitution*, but for sale to the public at the *Constitution's* offices and to other newspapers. A discount was offered if all three photographs were ordered. The *Constitution* advised that *"the history of this remarkable case cannot be thoroughly understood until these pictures have been seen."*

Media Distortions

On May 3, 1878, the *Constitution* reported the trial and its outcome in *"A Woman's Sin,"* which was hardly more than a rehash of the earlier *"Fatal Dance."* Previous inaccuracies were actually expanded. The very plump Narcissa Fowler was now described as *"a beautiful young lady, one of those handsome country girls who, knowing her charms, delighted in making conquests of men."* The *"ball"* was now explained as being given to celebrate Kate's marriage to Bob Southern and described as attended by

Sentence Commutation – This artist's rendering shows: (top) Kate and her husband Robert. She became pregnant while imprisoned. Kate (bottom) holds her new-born infant, as the commutation of her death sentence is read to her.

"all the belles and beaus of the neighborhood."

Beyond the pronouncement of a death sentence, very little of the actual trial was mentioned in the **Constitution** rehash. The story did add Congressman H.P. Bell to the defense team, and Kate was described as holding her baby in her arms while the sentence was read. The paper even misspelled her name as *"Sothern,"* yet another error that surprisingly was continued in the later articles.

The **Atlanta Constitution** ended its coverage of the trial of Kate Southern by pointing out the censure that former Governor James M. Smith had received for not commuting the death sentence of Susan Eberhart and that the present *"Gov. Colquitt will have to be thoroughly convinced of the justice of the sentence before he will allow her to hang."*

As inaccurate as were the stories that appeared in the **Constitution**, even stranger was the *"Atlanta Special"* that appeared in the **Chicago Times** newspaper on May 12, 1878. The fatal dance

was described in that account as having happened during a public Christmas ball held in Jasper in December, 1876. The former Kate *"Hambright," "acknowledged belle of what is known as the mountain counties"* was described as recently married to Bob Southern, and *"better fitted for breaking hearts than for any practical business."*

The **Times** went on to state that after an angry confrontation with Bob's ex-girlfriend, Narcissa Cowart, in the *"dressing room,"* Kate, in this version, reportedly caught Narcissa and Bob dancing. The jealous wife then entered the dance floor and, after shouting *"You have danced enough!"* plunged a knife to the hilt into Narcissa's shoulder, severing an artery. Not finished, however, the paper then had Kate slashing Narcissa across the breast, cutting through the heart. Finally, with an effort worthy of *Jack the Ripper,* she, *"like an infuriated tigress, jumped upon the dead body, ripped open the abdomen, and would have literally hacked it to pieces, had not someone attracted her attention."*

Through such profound publicity, Kate Southern strangely became both a national sensation and a national pariah, and the **Atlanta Constitution** suddenly became the forum for a debate on whether she should or should not be hung, publishing letters and reprinting editorials about the sentence. These pieces, however, were merely expansions based upon the romantic fiction in the *"Fatal Dance"* and other stories published earlier in the **Constitution**, not upon the actual court case testimony or the local newspaper accounts.

The **New York Herald** published an editorial that cited the Southern case as an argument for exempting women from capital punishment, while the **New York Globe**, refusing to comment on the reported circumstances of the case, argued against *"any discrimination in hanging on false and sentimental grounds."* The **Constitution** claimed that of the numerous petitions and letters that the governor had received from Georgia and elsewhere concerning Kate Southern, no one had written urging that the death sentence be carried out.

Saviour For Kate?

As if all of the above did not constitute enough nonsense, in the midst of this ink war, Kate suddenly acquired an anonymous "white knight." Writing under the pseudonym of *"Mortimer Pitts,"* a lengthy letter in opposition to the hanging of any woman, and particularly under the circumstances reported for Kate Southern, strangely appeared on the front page of the **Constitution**. Pitts reported that Kate Southern's case would be heard by the Georgia State Supreme Court in August, and possibly retried before Judge Lester in Pickens County in September.

In his "analysis," Pitts maintained that the very earliest that Kate could be hanged would be in November. In the meantime, he argued that the people of Georgia would do all that they could to prevent such a disgrace from happening. Pitt's letter of course was met with outrage in some quarters and with abject relief and hope in others.

A few days later, another article penned by Pitts appeared in the **Constitution**. In a story headlined *"Mrs. Sothern's* (sic) *Neck,"* Pitts argued that women are instinctively unable to commit murder except under the influence of whiskey or while otherwise not in full control of their senses. In Kate's case, Pitts claimed that she had suffered three epileptic fits the Monday before the murder, and was sick from her pregnancy which,

"New South" Nonsense – Henry W. Grady was managing editor of the *Atlanta Constitution* in the 1880s. Though often admired for his "New South" mantra advocating that Southern states endure the yoke of oppression from federal troops after the Civil War no matter what the price, he was often ridiculed by some for this position in later years. Following the conclusion of the sensationalistic Kate Southern trial, it was learned that it was Grady, writing under the pseudonym of "Mortimer Pitts" in the **Constitution**, who strongly (and somewhat irrationally) sought mercy for the murderess Catherine Southern simply because she was a female who had been allowed to become pregnant while in prison. Such a merciful verdict ultimately became a reality when Southern's death sentence was commuted, despite her cold-blooded murder of her Pickens County neighbor Narcissa Fowler.

with the noise of the party and the provocations from the victim, left her unbalanced.

From the outset, Kate Southern's defense attorneys had refused to use the *Insanity* plea, and following Pitts' suggestion now of the pursuit of such a strategy, the legal authorities in some quarters were outraged. S.A. Darnell of Atlanta, one of the prosecutors in the case, maintained that Kate Southern had already been examined in the Pickens County Jail by physicians who were prepared to testify regarding a plea of *"Guilty By Reason Of Insanity"* due to epilepsy sickness. Darnell felt that the defense, having refused to plead insanity at the trial, should not be allowed to do so now. The defense attorneys subsequently withdrew the plea, opting instead to enter a simple plea of *"Not Guilty."*

After the *Insanity* plea was discarded, Mortimer Pitts began a complete whitewash of Kate's moral circumstances, describing her as *"an active church member"* and as a person who had *"never attended a dance prior to the one held on the night of the murder."* He explained that she only happened to be staying with her parents that evening because of her ill health.

Pitts also reported that Kate's attorneys had decided against any further appeals in court, and that they were going directly to the governor. He added that Kate Southern was again (somehow) pregnant, and that the baby would be due in October if Kate didn't hang in June.

In a postscript, Mortimer Pitts announced the impending arrival in Atlanta of Kate's attorney – Col. Carey W. Styles – who intended to see the governor on her behalf. It is the defense of Southern by Col. Styles which remains as one of the true mysteries of the trial. Styles was from extreme south Georgia, but was well-known throughout the state as a soldier, politician, and newspaperman. Among the twenty-two newspapers with which he was associated, was the *Atlanta Constitution*, which he had founded. Up to the time of Kate's trial, Styles had practiced no law whatsoever.

Gubernatorial Intervention

In the end, it was Governor Alfred Colquitt who "rescued" Kate. He com-

muted her death sentence on May 22, a full month before the execution was to have taken place, and the executive action was reported almost immediately in the **Marietta Journal** and the **Atlanta Constitution** newspapers that were distributed and read in Pickens County. Gov. Colquitt had made a tough decision, despite the pressure by the news media and letters from the public on Kate's behalf. Colquitt's term of office came near the end of what historian E. Merton Coulter characterized as *"the golden age of Georgia hangings."*

The governor later maintained that his decision was based upon additional written testimony by respected Pickens County citizens. . . testimony which had not been used in the trial. He also noted a petition signed by all of the jurors which stated that they would not have found Kate guilty had they known she would be sentenced to die. Gov. Colquitt ultimately even reduced the ultimate sentence to ten years in prison.

No lesser a journalist than Henry W. Grady of the **Constitution** covered this reprieve. The only known account of his article, *"Mrs. Sothern's Neck Feels Relieved,"* is located in Grady's scrapbook at the Woodruff Library of Emory University. This piece is the nearest the **Constitution** came to a balanced account of the murder of Narcissa Fowler.

Grady described the affidavits that Col. Styles presented to Gov. Colquitt in great detail, and then followed with a much briefer account of the county's case against the Hambricks. Three of the signed statements dealt with Narcissa's bad character, including one *"the details of which cannot be published."*

Interestingly, it was revealed that a deposition by Kate's husband Bob, claimed that his *relations with Narcissa were "criminal,"* and an affidavit by

Bob's father stated that Fowler *"frequently came to the fields when Bob was working and took him away, usually for all night."* Other statements implied that shortly after Bob and Kate were married, Narcissa and Bob *"stayed alone together late into the night after a corn shucking, a story that had reached Kate."* Several depositions claimed that Narcissa had indeed threatened Kate's character and life. So are we to now understand that Bob and Narcissa were in fact carrying on an extra-marital affair after all? The mystery deepens.

Under the circumstances, it appears that at the very least, Miss Fowler might possibly have been anything but the innocent party-goer which some had claimed her to be. The actual circumstances, however, will never be known.

Amazilla's Destiny

A short time later, the *Atlanta Constitution* reprinted an interview with Amazilla Hambrick, Kate's sister, from the *Sandersville Courier*. Amazilla had turned sixteen and seventeen while serving her sentence for helping Kate murder Narcissa Fowler. A note beside Amazilla's name in the convict registers at the Georgia Department of Archives and History reads: *"young and pretty; ought not to be sent to the penitentiary."*

At the time of Amazilla's conviction, Georgia did not have a prison for females, and sent female convicts to county work camps or leased them to private individuals and companies as laborers. Amazilla had been lucky enough to be sold to Colonel Jack T. Smith's work farm in Washington County.

While at the farm, Amazilla was required only to do light work as a domestic for Smith's wife. During this time, she also learned to read and write, and to cut and sew garments.

In her interview with the *Courier*,

Amazilla repeated the story that Narcissa had been trying to take Bob Southern back from Kate, and added that Narcissa's husband had in fact left her not because she had filed divorce papers against him, but rather because she was in fact having sex with Bob. Narcissa was even quoted by Amazilla as having said at the dance: *"I knew Bob before you did and have as good a right to him as you."* So should one conclude from this that there was in fact more at stake for Kate than the simple loss of her clean reputation? Was Narcissa in fact having sex with Bob Southern and in danger of luring him away from Kate? We'll never know the truth to that either.

Amazilla added that her sister Kate did not approve of dances, did not know that the dance was even being held until the visitors started to arrive, and had been persuaded to stay. She described her family as land-owners who all worked together in the fields. So are we to conclude from this that there was in fact no conspiracy afoot for Narcissa's murder and that Kate's parents' warm invitation to Narcissa was in fact absent an ulterior motive?

Amazilla also claimed that she had pulled both Kate and Narcissa apart and had only tried to stop the fight. In the end, Amazilla ironically had no interest in being pardoned, and even indicated that she hoped she could stay with the Smiths after her sentence expired in twelve months, so life "at the work camp" must have been pretty good for Amazilla.

As a result of Amazilla's account of the murder, one could definitely conclude that all the actual circumstances did not necessarily correspond with the courtroom testimony any more than did the stories in the *Constitution*. Regardless of the circumstances, Kate Southern was a cold-blooded murderess who quite possibly was indeed caught up in a love-triangle, whether it involved sex between all the parties concerned, or not.

Kate Joins Amazilla

On May 28, 1878, in a front-page announcement, the *Atlanta Constitution* informed its readership that Kate Southern would arrive in Atlanta en route to confinement at Col. Smith's prison farm in Washington County. She would be carried sixty miles in an open buggy to the railroad

In a story entitled *"The Woman In Black: A Greeting To The North Georgia Murderess,"* Henry W. Grady reported of her arrival and the near riot at the train station. A mob of the curious, *"probably the largest crowd ever assembled in Atlanta so late at night,"* pursued her to the women's saloon at the train station and appeared ready to storm the building. Men and boys climbed over each other at the windows to see her. Some of the crowd reportedly stood on top of the train cars to catch a glimpse of the lewd woman in black as she went by.

They undoubtedly didn't see much, however, because Kate wore a dark hat and black veil. Having earlier described her as robust and beautiful, the *Constitution* shortly began reversing its glowing description of her beauty, admitting tactfully that in reality, she *"was not particularly striking, being tall and slender and with rather delicate features."*

The *Columbus Enquirer* was less kind, writing *"Kate Southern is not even pretty"* but only *"passably good looking"* and *"very ignorant, can hardly read and write,"* and speaks with *"the twang of a north Georgia cracker."*

Just as with Amazilla, Captain J.W. Nelms, keeper of the state convicts, had secured a position of light duties for Kate. She would be cooking and washing for the prisoners at the same farm where Amazilla worked and would be allowed to be accompanied by her husband, Bob, and their children. He even arranged for Bob, amazingly, to be employed there as a guard. Ironically, Kate, Bob and Amazilla probably had never had it so good. This was undoubtedly the reason that Amazilla requested to remain in Captain Nelms' employ even after her sentence had been served.

An unknown individual from Atlanta donated Bob's train fare. Shortly thereafter, Kate Southern and her little family pulled out of Atlanta on the train for Sandersville.

At this juncture, the *Atlanta Constitution* apparently decided that public interest in the story was exhausted. No mention whatsoever was made in the *Constitution* of the trial in the April, 1879 term of Pickens County Court in which Bob Southern and the Hambricks were tried for their alleged part in the circumstances which led to the murder of Narcissa Fowler. A verdict of *"Not Guilty"* was ultimately rendered in this case.

The last Kate Southern story to appear in the *Constitution* was printed on the last page of the March 26, 1882 issue, and carried an account of her pardon by Governor Colquitt. In his executive minutes, the Governor cited petitions for Kate's release from all parts of the state and her ill health, a case of nervousness brought on by another pregnancy. *(Editor's Note: Kate Southern bore at least one and possibly two children during her stint at the prison farm, so by this point, she quite likely had at least four children in tow.)*

So ended what the *Constitution* proclaimed as *"one of the most noted cases ever in the courts in Georgia; one that created perhaps more interest and excitement than any ever known in the state."*

After Kate reached the prison farm, the **Macon Telegraph** obtained a copy of the testimony in her trial from the Governor's Office, and printed the entire text. The **Columbus Enquirer** then reprinted the same and added in an editorial that was copied by the **New York Times:** *"On reading this evidence one feels utterly disgusted with the amount of sentimental twaddle that has been expended on the case. We do not believe there is a single woman, no matter how warm and sympathetic her heart may be, who, after reading this sworn testimony, will sign a petition for Kate Southern's pardon."*

The Later Years

Some mysteries to the Kate Southern story remained for a number of years. The identity of the individual who wrote under the pseudonym of *"Mortimer Pitts"* and who helped to create the sensational account which made Kate Southern's plight a national issue, is now known to have been Henry W. Grady.

Years later, when Grady won worldwide fame as the champion of the *"New South"* twaddle, adamantly preaching that the South must learn to live under the yoke of the North, no matter the circumstances, he clearly had no actual concept of the suffering and agony being endured by Southerners following the U.S. Civil War.

There is no way to prove today that it was Grady who actually orchestrated the campaign which eventually saved the cold-blooded murderess Kate Southern from execution. Nevertheless, as Grady would often glibly respond when queried about such matters, *"Why be hampered by the facts? It could be so!"*

After the trial, the Southerns announced they would never again return to Pickens County to live, but eventually, they in fact did exactly that. The "sickly," epileptic Kate Southern lived to have a total of at least eight children. She had proven that she was at least talented at procreation. She raised her brood among neighbors who undoubtedly, in one way or another, revealed their mother's dark past to them all.

Kate must have known a great deal of unhappiness in the remainder of her life. At least two of her children died before the age of seven. One of her daughters reportedly discovered her father's pistol under his pillow, and was killed when the weapon discharged as Kate was trying to extricate it from her daughter's grasp.

In the final analysis, Kate Southern seemed never able to escape a legacy of violence and misfortune. Interestingly, one of her granddaughters remembered her as *"the best grandmother anyone could have."* It is sometimes amazing how forgiving a child can be.

Author's Postscript: According to records, Kate and Bob Southern were living in the Lansdown after 1900, raising a large brood of children almost in sight of Long Swamp Cemetery where Narcissa Fowler is buried. Two of their children are buried at Burnt Mountain Baptist Church Cemetery near Jasper. The Southerns eventually moved to Winston County, Alabama, where Kate died on February 15, 1927. Her grave can be viewed there today. Robert Southern died there on October 9, 1930.

(Grateful appreciation is expressed herewith to Robert S. "Bob" Davis, Jr., for considerable research and most details associated with this article.)

The Asa Prior Family:

Frontier Fighters
From Yesteryear

*If one rides through Polk County today, the name "Prior" can still occasionally be
seen on a street name and in property descriptions. The once-prominent family
was composed of hard-working, honest, and law-abiding citizens, and when a
criminal element threatened their lives and livelihood during the U.S. Civil War, the
perpetrators seriously misjudged their adversary.*

The area of northwest Georgia known today as "Polk County" was originally settled as a portion of Paulding County. It had abundant natural resources, one of which was (and continues to be) the rich farmland in what came to be known as "Cedar Valley," named after the many cedar trees which proliferate in the area. Following the Georgia land lottery of 1832, large numbers of adventurous and ambitious white settlers began moving into the area and taking over the former lands of the Cherokee Indians. One of the earliest settlers in this area was a family by the name of Prior.

The Priors were led by family patriarch Asa, and they enjoyed a natural inclination toward the accumulation of property and wealth. They prospered not only from farming, but also from the buying and selling of property.

Sometime around 1826, two scouts – Linton Walthall and Hampton Whatley – visited the Cedar Valley area along Cedar Creek. Both men envisioned a bright future for this fertile region in their later reports on the area.

Two years later in 1828, gold was discovered in a diagonal belt which passed through the Cherokee Indian Territory. That eventuality, coupled with the desires of the leaders of the state of Georgia to grow appreciably beyond the state's current boundaries, accelerated the push for the removal of the Cherokees.

After the state legislature created ten new counties from the Cherokee lands in 1832, land lotteries were conducted to distribute the land to new owners. Settlements began springing up and developing into towns such as Cedartown, with farms, shops, schools, churches, roads and post offices.

On December 29, 1835, U.S. government officials and about 500 Cherokee Indians claiming to represent their 16,000-member tribe, met at New Echota, the last capital of the Cherokees, once located in present-day northwest Georgia, and signed a treaty which ceded the Cherokee lands in the Southeast to

Prior Family – John T. Prior was photographed in 1899 in Cedartown, Georgia. Pictured with him are his mother Ann M. Prior (far right), and his daughter, Anna Lou Davis. (Photo courtesy of Polk Co. Historic Society)

the states of Georgia, Tennessee, North Carolina and South Carolina. The fate of the tribe's home in the southeastern United States had been sealed.

Walthall and Whatley established trading posts in the vicinity of the beautiful valley they had discovered. Walthall located his post above one of the largest springs in the territory – which became known for obvious reasons as "Big Spring" – and Whatley selected a spot near Tanyard Branch, a little creek south of the new village already beginning to take shape along a modest stream which became known as "Cedar Creek."[1]

The Asa Prior Family

Prior to the family's migration to Georgia's Morgan County near the town of Madison, the genealogy of the Prior family is unknown. As with so many other early pioneers to the state's realm in

the early years of an infant United States, the Priors were a portion of the great wave of settlers moving down the eastern seaboard of the country. Their goal was to skirt the barrier of the Blue Ridge Mountains by traveling down through Virginia and South Carolina and on into Georgia before turning westward. In Georgia, these early settlers would either purchase cheap land or continue westward via the Alabama Roads to travel to "Indian Territory" where they would claim free land. It was the truest definition of what came to be known as "Manifest Destiny."

The Prior family led by Asa apparently decided that east Georgia was more than far enough for them to travel to acquire land and build an estate. In Madison, Asa began offering his services as the town blacksmith ("smithy") and became a well-known member of the

Town Father – The third Polk County Courthouse on this site (l) and the Jail (r) were photographed in the early 1900s. In 1852, Asa Prior sold the city of Cedartown 19 acres – including this property – for development of the town. (Photo courtesy of Watson Dyer Collection)

community. He labored long and hard and invested wisely to create a modest base for his family which had grown prodigiously.

Throughout his long travels, Asa had been faithfully followed by his spouse Sarah, to whom he lovingly referred as "Sally." She struggled along with him, through good times and bad, washing his clothing, preparing his meals, keeping his house and bearing his children.

Asa loved Sarah dearly. She bore him 14 children in all over a 25-year span. Three of these children died in infancy and one had already married and begun his own life by 1832 when Asa and the remainder of his family moved to what then was still Cherokee Indian Territory in northwest Georgia.[2]

The specific reason for Asa's departure from the Madison area is unknown today, but he appears to have decided to "pull up stakes" rather abruptly and migrate to what at that time was a wild, unsettled area in Cherokee Indian Territory. Perhaps the sudden opportunity for substantial new property was too tempting for him to resist.

Whatever the circumstances, according to records, the *"blacksmith from Morgan County"* was among the very first pioneers in what would soon become known as "Paulding County," Georgia, arriving in 1832[3], while numerous native Cherokees still resided in the area. Following the final removal of the Cherokees to Arkansas and Oklahoma Territories in 1838, Asa's property was officially located for a short while in "Paulding County." Approximately twenty years later in 1851, the area comprising Asa's property would be included with portions of Paulding and adjoining Floyd counties to create the new county of "Polk."

The living conditions for Asa's family and other newcomers to what came to be known as "Cedar Valley" in Paulding undoubtedly were exceedingly primitive and exhausting for a number of years, despite of the availability of slaves for the heaviest labor. Though the hardy settlers were blessed with abundant game, timber, water, and rich soil resources in their new home, the land first had to be cleared, planted and maintained in order to create arable farmland. It was a long and arduous process, but Asa – and subsequently, his sons – were accustomed to long hours and hard manual labor.

When another Cedar Valley settler, W.O.B. Whatley, also arrived about 1832, his family lived in a crude log cabin as well for two years until he could construct their fine home. This same year, the burgeoning Georgia State Legislature created, in addition to Paulding, a total of nine other new counties from the former Cherokee lands, and subsequently conducted lotteries to encourage settlement of this new land. It may well have been one of these land lotteries which initially attracted Asa's attention.

It is not known today exactly *where* the Priors first lived in Cedar Valley, but in 1848, the family patriarch reportedly built a substantial structure in the center of "the up and coming" new community – soon to be called "Cedartown" – not far from "the Big Spring." The log house he built still stands as of this writing, but Asa Prior would not recognize it today.

A later owner of the home (following the departure Asa and most of his family from the area) named Mrs. J.W. Pickett contracted to have the house raised from its foundation with heavy jacks and rotated a full 90 degrees, all accomplished by lowering the house onto logs lubricated liberally with grease. Her intention was to turn the home so that it would face North College Street instead of fronting onto East Avenue. Her reason for the repositioning of the aged home is unknown today.

Following still more changes by later owners, the house was modernized with wood siding and otherwise altered substantially in appearance. It eventually was purchased for use as a mortuary called Gammage Funeral Home, and continues in that capacity today.

Just six years after his relocation to Cedar Valley, Asa suffered a grievous loss. His wife, Sarah, who was indescribably dear to the elder Prior and who had borne him so many children, passed away suddenly on January 2, 1838, at the age of 54. Though that is considered only to be "middle-aged" for humans in the 21st Century, it was nevertheless a modestly-advanced age in the early 1830s.

Sarah's mortal remains were buried in a spot somewhat apart from the town home. She was laid to rest in a little family cemetery a mile south of the center of town – possibly near the site of an earlier temporary home prior to construction of the Priors' finer home in downtown

Civil War Lawlessness – This 1864 illustration by W.D. Matthews for ***Harper's Weekly*** magazine depicts a vigilante raid on a Southern plantation during the lawless days of the U.S. Civil War. Records indicate circumstances in the north Georgia area – including in Cedartown – were this bad and much worse during these times.

Cedartown or the plantation on the outskirts.

Sarah's tombstone – undoubtedly the first in the little cemetery in which she rests for eternity – can still be seen today, but weather and the passage of time have virtually erased from the stone the date and touching epitaph which Asa ordered inscribed therein:

Sleep on my loving wife sleep
This world shall thy memory keep
But deeper on my heart is graven
The thought that we shall meet in heaven.[4]

Though the Prior family ultimately enjoyed many fruits from their labors, they also suffered many sorrows. Prior to the days when the U.S. Civil War would visit so much devastation and despair upon the family, it already suffered the loss of several children and a mother. Numerous other children in the family were born deaf and remained unable to communicate orally throughout their lives.

A total of five of the fourteen Prior children, in fact, were born deaf. Today, with advances in remedies for deafness

Cedartown Recovery – Though most of the town was burned in 1864 by Union forces during Gen. W. T. Sherman's engagements through Georgia, Cedartown was eventually able to rebound as shown in this circa 1899 photo. (Photo courtesy of Watson Dyer Collection)

and in speech therapies, such a disability is not quite as severe. In the 1840s, however, one can only imagine the angst of parents gently attempting to use some form of sound to attract the attention of newborns suspected of deafness in order to establish whether or not the child in fact was deaf. In pioneer days in the United States, any such child lacking the ability to hear and speak was extremely seriously handicapped.

The malady which created this disability in the Prior children is unknown today. Perhaps it was genetically-related, or a health issue of which the parents and/or medical services of that day were unaware. It remains yet another mystery associated in perpetuity with this pioneer family which ultimately endured so much familial pain.

Throughout his life, Asa Prior was deeply concerned with the care of his handicapped children. His *Last Will & Testament* is a tangible reminder of his angst. In this document, he provides a lifelong income for each of his deaf children, no doubt filled with pain and pity as he carefully identified them as *"deaf and dumb."* [5]

Prior Landmarks

Asa Prior appears to have been a charter member of Cedartown's Baptist church. In 1835, the Baptists rented a building located on a knoll above Tanyard Branch which served as both a church and school. *(This site may have coincided with the little cemetery where Asa's wife was buried.)*

In 1845, the church congregation made the decision to build a proper church after an attractive parcel near what later would become Main Street and West Avenue was donated for construction of the edifice. One acre for the site of the new church and graveyard was donated by Asa,[6] and the adjacent acre was contributed by William E. West.[7]

The church and graveyard once stood where the First National Bank of

Polk County stands (as of this writing in 2024) on West Avenue near Main Street. *(Author's Note: When workmen were preparing a parking lot for the bank, they reportedly discovered pioneer gravesites, and were forced to reconsider their plans for the project.)* A second church on a new site replaced the first in 1891, but today, both of the old churches have disappeared, being replaced by a handsome modern structure.[8]

Yet another landmark created by the Prior patriarch was his gristmill. Though empty and abandoned at the time of this writing in 2024, it has stood a short distance from downtown Cedartown since being built by Asa circa 1840. This landmark has enjoyed numerous reincarnations over the years – most often as a scenic and popular dining facility.

Though a single gristmill often was all that was needed for the grinding of corn into meal and grain into flour during pioneer times, there, interestingly, were at least four – and possibly even as many as six – other gristmills in the Cedar Valley area just a short wagon ride from Asa's mill.

These early mills were a staple and high necessity in pioneer American communities, but there normally was only one – or possibly no more than two such mills – for each locality. This was due to the fact that the large millstones for these enterprises were exceedingly difficult (since they were of such great weight) and expensive to obtain.

The type stone most suitable for making millstones is a siliceous rock called "burrstone" (or "buhrstone"), an open-textured, porous but tough, fine-grained sandstone, or a silicified, fossiliferous limestone, the likes of which usually had to be shipped from far destinations such as France and Germany.

The difficulty in obtaining such stones, let alone obtaining them without their being shattered in transit, coupled with the fact that there was only so much grain that needed to be ground in any given locality, meant that there invariably were no more than one or two gristmills in any given locality. The gristmills competition for grain clients in Asa's day must have been exceedingly keen indeed.

The fact that there already were several gristmills in the Cedar Valley area apparently did not discourage Asa Prior in the least. According to Charles K. Henderson's ***Polk County Persons And Things***, written by Henderson and first published in the ***Cedartown Standard*** newspaper starting on May 27, 1897, *"Greenwood, the Indian, owned the mill located at the junction of Big and Little Cedar,"* (later known as Judkin's Mill).[9] John Wilson had a mill at Hightower Falls in 1832, later owned and operated by Elias Dorsey Hightower. On upper Big Cedar Creek yet another mill was operated by George Watts. On Simpson Creek outside Rockmart, another pre-Civil War gristmill was in operation there at roughly the same time, as was yet another outside the tiny community in Polk which came to be known as "Aragon."

To build his gristmill on Cedar Creek, Prior reportedly hired Milton H. Hanie of Cave Spring about 1849. This structure, amazingly, somehow survived the U.S. Civil War, when most of the remainder of Cedartown was burned to the ground by Union troops. For almost 100 years, Cedartown residents took their corn to this facility to be ground into meal before electricity and modern conveniences rendered the gristmills obsolete.

Asa's mill later changed hands and became known as "Benedict Mill," and finally, in 1945, the little enterprise fell victim to progress, as were gristmills all over the country at this time. Advances in the industrial age ushered in a new era of modern electrically-powered facilities, and fresh meal and flour suddenly were offered in abundance in shops and grocery stores everywhere. Operations at Prior's old mill ground to a halt – no pun intended.

In 1960, the aged mill underwent a rejuvenation of sorts, when Robert L. Stevens and his wife, who had operated a restaurant in Cartersville, Georgia, purchased Prior's old mill and opened what they called *"The Old Mill Restaurant."* The site quickly became a popular dining spot, lasting for thirtyone years, before closing. Many families in the area had fond memories of many a happy Sunday afternoon dinner at this facility, while watching the water gushing down the millrace and the ducks searching for treats in the millpond.

During his days in Cedartown, Prior reportedly accumulated an amazing six thousand acres of land and 500 to 600 slaves. By the 1840s, he had a sizeable plantation approximately eight miles west of town.

Asa's son – Haden – lived in a fine home at that site, and managed the plantation for his father. Asa continued to maintain his residence in town.

When the Southern Railroad laid rails from Rome, Georgia, to Birmingham, Alabama, a railroad depot *"Prior Station"* was established on Prior plantation. A number of these former Prior establishments are commemorated for posterity in street and road names and city parks today.

Cedartown – Early Days

Much of the property in the central portion of what today is downtown Cedartown was once owned by Asa Prior.

Knowing that the town would need room to grow and prosper, and a reliable and abundant source of fresh water to supply to the citizenry, Asa sold 19 acres to the city of Cedartown for $1,200.00 in 1852. That amount was the equivalent of approximately $48,000.00 in 2024, and the sale not only included the very important 19 acres, but the rights and access to "the Big Spring" as well.[10]

A courthouse ultimately was built on this acreage. When completed, the large brick and granite structure housed offices on the first floor and a courtroom on the second. As detailed above, however, this structure and most of the rest of the town, were put to the torch by Kilpatrick's cavalry of Gen. William T. Sherman's army during the Civil War. It was therefore, rebuilt in 1869.[11]

Another courthouse was built 22 years later in 1891. Today, on the same site as the original courthouse in the 1852 town plan, the Polk County Courthouse built in 1954 now stands.

In the 1850s, prior to the Civil War, Cedartown increased in importance when it became the county seat of government. Polk County had recently been created (primarily by taking a portion of Paulding County), and needed a more centrallylocated seat of government. Van Wert, formerly the seat of Paulding, was now in Polk, but it was quite near the edge of the new county, and thus was unsuitable as the new county's government seat.

With the loss of its status as county seat, Van Wert withered and died. The courthouse, bank, saloons, hotels, and other structures disappeared from the landscape over the years. Some were burned by the same cavalry unit from Sherman's army. Today, virtually nothing remains of Van Wert except the old Methodist Church and its adjoining cemetery, a portion of the old jail, one or two historic homes, and a state historic marker.

Changing of the Guard

Despite his plantation and businesses, and the vigorous growth being experienced in the community he had helped found, Asa Prior surprisingly pulled up stakes in Georgia sometime around 1850. Did he envision trouble on the horizon for the South and move to the American West to escape it? We'll never know the answer to that either.

Whatever the reason, Asa abruptly moved to Sabine County, Texas, purchasing a whole new spread not too far from his son, Andrew, who had been earlier bitten by wanderlust, settling in nearby Rusk County.

Ever the stalwart, Asa's son, Haden, remained behind in Georgia to maintain the Prior plantation and land development businesses there. He almost certainly was one of the most prosperous planters in the area. It, unfortunately, was a reputation which later would prove fateful.

On October 13, 1853, Asa Prior had traveled back to Cedartown from Texas. Was he merely visiting old friends and family, or was he aware of his impending death and returned specifically to draw up his *Last Will & Testament* which was dated that day. In this document, he left instructions for the disposition of the Prior properties both in Cedartown and Texas, upon his death.

It is unknown today whether or not Asa was suffering from severe health problems at this juncture, but he quite likely was aware of some malady threatening his life. Whatever the circumstances, only a few months later, on July 2, 1854, the old smithy turned plantation owner and philanthropist who had

Historic Home – This structure in Cedartown – one of the oldest extant in Polk County – remains in excellent condition today, but its former owner – Asa Prior – almost certainly would not recognize it due to substantial alterations. (Photo courtesy of Gordon Sargent)

done so much to foster the growth and development of the city of Cedartown, Georgia, passed away. He was buried in far-away Sabine County, Texas.

The enterprises and investments of the Priors undoubtedly continued to flourish throughout the 1850s, but came to a screeching, grinding halt with the advent of the 1860s, and the onslaught of the horrors which divided the Northern and Southern states.

War Comes Southward

Asa had one son and one grandson who enlisted on the side of the Southern cause in the Civil War, joining the Confederate Army in 1862. William H.C. Prior went off in June with a Polk County company of troops. John left Rome on April 5th with 65 other cavalrymen in a Cave Spring company,[12] but was able to return home a few months later after he hired a substitute.[13]

John reportedly had "seen the handwriting on the wall" early-on. Even though the armies of the South won battle after battle up through and including the year 1863, and quite likely would have won the war entirely had not President Abraham Lincoln freed all the slaves, therein wrecking the economic system in the South, young John nevertheless was convinced there was no hope of the Confederacy winning the war, and thus did not strongly support the cause. One has to wonder if he was composed of the same metal as were his brothers. Regardless, it would not be long before he would be confronted with a war of his own – one which would sorely test his endurance.

As the Civil War drew to a close, affairs in Polk County were going from bad to worse.

As the Civil War drew to a close, affairs in Polk County were going from bad to worse. Sherman's troops had swept through the area on their devastating *"March to the Sea"* and had burned Cedartown and the adjacent Polk community of Van Wert to the ground. Outlaw raiders, many of whom were inveterate criminals, but also Confederate deserters and even Confederate "Home Guard" troops as well, laid waste to what little was left in the countryside.

Lawlessness prevailed during this period, mainly because virtually all law-abiding men – including law enforcement personnel – and even young boys barely old enough to carry a weapon, eventually were serving in the Confederate Army. And as the war progressed and the casualties mounted – including those of the personnel who would have returned home to reinstall law and order – so also did the lawlessness. It was a situation ripe for advanced criminal actions. Homes were looted and residents who did not readily hand over their valuables were persecuted, maimed, raped and murdered.[14]

Outlaws had so terrorized the citizenry earlier in the war that the state of Georgia organized what came to be known as "home guard" units which were militia companies intended to provide law and order in the trouble spots. More often than not, however, these units merely took advantage of the circumstances themselves to become lawless bandits. For the Cedartown district, however, Governor Joe Brown appointed a very capable and strictly law-abiding citizen – Haden Prior – to command that company.

Prior's standing in the community apparently out-shined what had been, at most, a lackluster support of the Confederate cause. By the closing days of the war, however, Haden reportedly had become outspoken and active in the revolt against the North. By then, of course, it was too late. A few months earlier, Union soldiers had burned his barns and warehouses and carried off whatever cattle and provisions had been available.

The Outlaw Plague

Out of pure desperation, Haden and several of his sons were inexorably drawn into the vortex of these events in the last years of the war. It was a preoccupation which eventually would cost Haden his life, erupting into one of the bloodiest vendettas in Polk County history.

Ghost Plantation – The former site of Asa Prior's (and later Haden Prior's) plantation, known as "Prior Station," leaves much to the imagination today. The only remaining vestige here of the Prior home or out-buildings, is the sadly-overgrown and abandoned Prior Family Cemetery (undergrowth, left) where Haden Prior and others of the family are buried. At one time, the property even included a railroad flag-stop. (Photo courtesy of Gordon Sargent)

The story of the events which follow was documented by a reporter in an 1897 Rome, Georgia newspaper following an interview with John Thomas Prior, Haden's son. Needless to say, the events precipitated by the feud are still told in old-timer circles in Cedartown to this day.

At some point in the mid1860s, word reportedly reached Haden and his militia that an outlaw group led by an individual named Jack Colquitt was raiding local farms in Cedar Valley. The local Home Guard militia, including Haden and his son, John, promptly set out to hunt the men down, per their instructions from the governor of Georgia.

After picking up the outlaws' trail, Haden and his Home Guard troops soon caught five of the raiders on the road between Cave Spring and Prior Station. One of the outlaws reined in his horse, quickly turned him around and made the mistake of trying to escape. John Prior drew a bead on the fleeing horseman and fired, knocking him out of the saddle with one shot. He was the first of six men John would ultimately kill in a personal quest against the Colquitt gang.

Following a successful first stage in eliminating the lawless riffraff from Polk County, the posse brought back the four men they had captured and lodged them in the Cedartown jail. Within a few weeks, however, all four surprisingly had been released. By that point, hoodlums and virtual criminals controlled the political and justice systems of the South, ignoring virtually all crimes committed against Southern citizenry.

Eight .44 Slugs

"A fellow named Phillips was very bitter," John Prior explained in later years to the Rome reporter. *"Colquitt's gang put out the word that they would kill my father for having them arrested, but he never took it seriously."*

Determined to arrest Colquitt and bring him to trial before he and his gang could carry out their threat or inflict more suffering upon innocent farmers, John and his brother, James (who was also a member of the Home Guard), set out to search for Colquitt one night. It is not known today why the Prior brothers decided to search for the renegade at night, or if in fact they were simply availing themselves of an opportunity of which they had learned.

Whatever the circumstances, the two men appeared at a Cedartown grocery store that night where they found the outlaw in a drunken stupor, lying on the store counter. Colquitt did not know it at the time, but he was spending his last moments in an earthly environment.

"When we aroused him," John later stated for the newspaper reporter, *"he was very quarrelsome and cursed loudly. We let him rave, but when he reached for his pistol to shoot us, ... I (put) a bullet through his heart."*

George Battey, in his seminal *A History of Rome and Floyd County*, added some details to John Prior's account. According to Battey, when the shooting began, both brothers in fact fired at Colquitt, putting a total of eight bullets into him.

It seems apparent from the description of the incident, that the brothers wanted to make certain Colquitt did not move from the spot – at least not without being carried out. John later told a friend, "I was so close when I fired my first shot that I saw smoke coming out of his mouth."

The killing of Jack Colquitt, however, did nothing to dampen what by then had become a bloodlust among his men, particularly regarding vengeance against Haden Prior. It was a scene very reminiscent of the circumstances which led up to the now famous gunfight behind the O.K. Corral in Tombstone, Arizona, some 16 years later.

Undeterred by their leader's demise, members of the Colquitt outlaws bided their time, waiting for just the right opportunity for revenge. It finally came on April 6, 1865.

As events in Cedartown were boiling over, the final curtain was coming down on the U.S. Civil War. On that Sunday, two army chieftains, one in blue and one in grey, met at a tiny town called Appomattox Court House for an epic surrender. The following Friday, an event at Ford's Theatre in Washington City (D.C.) would further stun a nation that was already reeling.

Haden Prior Murder

In the spring of 1865, Haden Prior was visiting a Mr. Hampton about two miles from his Prior Station home. Haden was accompanied by an adolescent Negro servant, and had every reason to believe he was perfectly safe on his home turf.

As Haden was leaving the Hampton residence, four of the Colquitt gang-members suddenly appeared and confronted him not a hundred feet from the front gate of the Hampton home. According to later accounts of this incident, Phillips, the leader of the party, exchanged a few words and then drew his pistol and, without hesitation, shot Haden through the heart, killing him instantly. He also killed the servant to eliminate any witnesses.

Around noontime, Haden's son, John, learned the shocking news of his father's violent murder. He immediately saddled up and rode out to the Hampton property where he learned the details of the crime.

John Prior has been described as "tough as nails" when necessary – about five feet and eleven inches in height, and thin and wiry. His slight stature was said to have been deceptive, for he reportedly had a muscular physique, and rawboned determination in any objective set before him.

The feature, however, which most impressed those who knew John, was his eyes. They were said to have been small, gray, and glittering like jewels. Stranger still, there reportedly was no white around the glassy gray iris. John Prior's eyes literally were hypnotic in appearance.

John once stated, *"I never center my eyes on anybody but a person I hate, because I know their effect on people. I never stare at anybody because it would frighten them."*

John Prior's anguish upon the discovery of his father's crumpled body can only be imagined today. It is known that following the recovery of his father's body and preparation for his burial, John Prior set his sights upon his tormentors. He wasted no time in recruiting employees and a few friends before beginning the hunt for his father's killers.

The members of the Colquitt group responsible for shooting Haden Prior in cold blood may not have known it at the time, but John Prior "was coming," and Hell was coming with him.

Deadly Pursuit

By sunup the next day, the trackers had found first one and then another home plundered by the bandits whose blood-lust seemed to be growing by the hour. John and his men, however, knew that they could be only a few hours behind the outlaws.

The trail led due-west into Alabama and the area of Piedmont. There, however, the trail grew cold.

As John Prior later recalled, *"We rode on rapidly across the Alabama line to Ladiga* (presentday Piedmont), *for which point we thought they would make, but we could learn nothing of them. Baffled, but never despairing, I rode three miles to Cross Plains, a point lower down. Here, I could find no clue."*

Returning to Ladiga, John remembered another road leading out of town. He questioned some young boys at a school on the road and fortunately received a good description of the men they were hunting. They were able, once again to pick up the trail, and rode north for several miles.

"It was between 11 or 12 o'clock when just beyond Coloma, Alabama, I rode up in front of the Widow Lane's house and saw two men sitting under some trees and three horses tied nearby. I remember the pink and white blossoms of the peach trees. The house, situated as it was at the foot of the Wiseman Mountains, made a most inviting place.

"The men, I think, saw me about the same time I saw them and both sides were somewhat surprised. One of them made a movement to reach for his gun. I jumped off my horse, cocked my double barrel shotgun, and fired before he raised his.

"One of them fell over riddled with buckshot, while the other ran around the house. I drew my pistol and ran after him, but just around the corner came upon his dead body where he fell."

The third man fired and fled into the woods. Prior quickly caught up with him and, unwilling to leave the situation to a decision by a "fixed jury," gunned him down on the spot. John Prior apparently was deadly with almost any type of firearm. Ironically, he later stated, *"They were not the murderers of my father, but doubtless belonged to the same gang."*

Prior Gristmill – Built in 1849, Prior Mill near downtown Cedartown continues to weather the years. In more recent times, it has enjoyed reincarnation as a popular restaurant on several different occasions. (Photo courtesy of Gordon Sargent)

Within twenty-four hours of his father's murder, John Prior had found and killed three of the gang. Together with the earlier shooting of Colquitt and the gang member who had tried to escape when threatened with arrest, the death toll had now reached five men. However, the actual killer of Haden Prior – Phillips – and his two henchmen who had been identified as Montgomery and Bishop, were still at large.

Four Horsemen of the Apocalypse

"I learned that Phillips, when not on a freebooting excursion, lived on a farm down in Haralson County," John continued in his interview with the newsman. *"It was early July that (I with) one of my brothers and two friends started out about nightfall for Phillips' home with the determination of killing him. We surrounded his home somewhere about 3 o'clock in the morning."*

Early the next morning, John cornered his quarry. Phillips had emerged from his house and walked to a nearby field to begin a day of plowing.

John Prior later explained it was an easy matter to get close enough to surprise Phillips. John said he rode to the top of the hill above Phillips, dismounted, then eased down to the edge of the field, concealing himself in the undergrowth. He then waited until Phillips plowed to the end of a row, and then, just as he was about to turn his horse, John said he stepped out of the woods and covered the man with his pistol.

"Phillips," he said, *"I want you."*

"Let me go to the house first to see my wife," Phillips reportedly pleaded. He had to have known by then what had happened to the other members of Colquitt's criminal group. He had to know that his final moments on this earth were upon him.

262

"No. I want you right now," Prior replied harshly.

"Well, let me unhitch my horse from the plow."

"All right. Go ahead, but be quick about it."

John could see the bandit's women and children in the distance running out of the house. They, no doubt, had seen members of John's party and also suspected the worst, running to Phillips to warn him. However, it was far too late for that.

"I knew that unless I killed him pretty quick, the women and children would all be crying around me very shortly," John later explained.

Probing for a confession, John asked, *"Phillips, who killed my father?"*

Phillips responded with the name of a man who John knew had no connection with the murder.

"I have the best evidence that you did the killing," John replied, and with that, Phillips reportedly fell on his knees and began to beg for his life.

"You needn't expect any mercy from me," John added. *"I'm going to kill you."*

Desperate and realizing that his end was near at hand, Phillips reportedly broke into a run. John merely took careful aim and, without compunction, shot him in the back.

Phillips fell on his side and then rolled over on his back. With the women and children watching a short distance away, John walked over and shot Phillips through the heart at close range.

After making certain that his quarry was too dead to even kick again, John re-mounted his horse and set out in search of Montgomery, another of his father's murderers. After killing six men, there were two more left to hunt down.

Just as had Phillips, Montgomery had also heard what had happened to his partners in crime, and he (Montgomery) was not going to hang around to give John Prior an easy target. He had fled the district, but it made no difference. John Prior was relentless. After following clues for a length of time, he finally discovered the man in Arkansas, but for reasons unknown today, he relented and spared his victim this time.

Perhaps John had seen enough killing. Maybe he just had compassion for Montgomery. The exact circumstances have been lost through the passage of time. Montgomery, nevertheless, died about five years later in Arkansas, so his days were shortly numbered anyway.

John Prior still was not finished though. There was one left – a man by the name of Bishop. John told the newspaperman that he tracked Bishop many, many miles, no doubt making his life miserable.

John Prior again was relentless. When he finally reached Bishop's location, he learned the man had died of natural causes. If I had to guess, I'd say the last two men on John Prior's list had died prematurely from sheer terror. Whatever the circumstances, the hunting and killing was over.

The manhunt and ultimate murders of men – without benefit of a legal trial by jury – may seem horrific to a reader in modern times. However, during the U.S. Civil War and its immediate aftermath, the southern United States was not only a lawless area, besieged by cutthroats and criminals of all makes and descriptions, it was also often controlled by federal officials who, unfortunately, had little interest in justice, and a great deal of interest in retribution against the already-dying South. It was a brutal and bloodthirsty time, when many men lived by the gun. Violence was a way of life.

There were also many "kangaroo courts" and opportunities for criminals to slip through the cracks, particularly with the legal system in the South controlled by federal officials with less-than-altruistic intentions. They were merely a continuation of the then-accepted abusive system of the mid- and late-1860s designed to punish the South for its transgressions. John Prior was not about to allow any such system to deny him the justice he and his family deserved.

Peace at Last

Following this series of horrendous events, John Thomas Prior enjoyed a surprisingly quiet and uneventful life. He was never charged with any crimes for the shootings and the men he had killed. It is quite possible that many residents of Polk County in fact wanted to honor him, instead of prosecute him.

Six months after John Prior's story appeared in the Rome, Georgia newspaper in 1897, his son, George Prior, married and moved away, settling in Roseburg, Oregon. John and his daughter later moved to Oregon as well to live with him in 1906.[15]

Two years later, John's daughter married, and around 1910, the proud old avenger posed for a photograph with his new granddaughter, Georgia M. Davis.[16] That same year, John T. Prior reached

> *John's cause of death was attributed to "the direct infirmities attendant to old age."*

the age of 70, and died peacefully at his daughter's home.

John's cause of death was attributed to *"the direct infirmities attendant to old age."*[17] He was buried in the old Masonic Cemetery, now Memorial Gardens in Roseburg, Oregon.

Back in Cedartown, Georgia, it wasn't too many years after the Civil War and the infamous murder of Haden Prior, that the once-pleasant residence of Prior Station was finally completely abandoned by the Priors. The final disposition of this property out of the Prior name is unknown today.

Through investments and good business acumen, the Priors possibly had become financially independent and simply were no longer in need of the property. Or perhaps it was in fact sold out of the family by the last Prior in the family to own it. Today, as a result of fires and poor records maintenance, there are few if any records which extend back beyond 1864. The courthouse fire set by Sherman's minions that year destroyed virtually all deeds, titles of ownership and sale records for the county.

Most of the remnants of the Polk County Prior family ultimately drifted off to the West, always west. Haden Prior and his mother and a few other deceased Priors, however, remained behind, sleeping the eternal sleep in gravesites in Polk.

Today, descendants of Asa Prior can still occasionally be found in Cedartown, but few with the Prior name. And as for Prior Station, all traces of the once-grand plantation have vanished.

In more recent years, a home and dairy occupied the site where the Prior plantation house once stood. The railway depot – Prior Station – and associated rail line near this site also disappeared years ago. Nothing remains today except the small overgrown Prior family cemetery surrounded by an iron fence – ironically with a gate facing westward – always westward.

The city built by a blacksmith, and protected by his sons and grandsons, still thrives today. And sometimes, when native sons of the community gather to reminisce about area folklore, the life and times of the Asa Prior family inevitably become a topic of conversation.

Acknowledgements

The generous sharing of Prior family materials by the following is gratefully acknowledged: Miss Matilda West, Cedartown; Mrs. Marjorie Brown, Longview, Texas; Mrs. George O. Marshall, Jr., Athens, Georgia; and Ms. Eileen Talburt, Douglas County Genealogy Society librarian, Roseburg, Oregon.

Endnotes

1/ Whatley, George Fields, "Cedartown's Big Spring," *Georgia Life*, Spring, 1978, p. 2021.

2/ Georgia DAR Book 8, 194950, *Bible Records Of Revolutionary Soldiers*. William H.C. Prior family Bible. Prior file in genealogical records at the Georgia Department of Archives & History, Atlanta, GA. In the various records, the spelling of the family name changed with Haden although the records appear to be consistent otherwise. Fourteen children with their birthdays are listed for Asa Prior.

3/ Floyd County Deed Record Book C, p. 6. Deed records of Paulding County go back only to 1848, but Floyd County records show Asa Prior was a resident of Paulding County who was buying and selling numerous lots in Floyd County. His earliest recorded transaction was November 8, 1832.

4/ Brown, Marjorie Maxwell, various Prior family materials.

5/ Prior, Asa, October 13, 1853, recorded last will and testament in Record of Wills, Book A, Polk County, Georgia, pp 2627.

6/ Paulding County Deeds, Record Book X, p. 579. It is interesting to note that the 1832 survey shows the road which would become Main Street, although it had several twists in it which have disappeared.

7/ Paulding County Deeds, Record Book X, p. 580. The surveyor noted that one fortyacre lot included Judge Witcher's yard and field and another 160 acres included Witcher's farm. By 1845, this farm was owned, at least in part, by William E. West.

8/ Johnson, Larry G., *A History Of The Polk County Missionary Baptist Association*, Nashville, TN, 1977, p. 98.

9/ Henderson, Charles K., *"Polk County Persons And Things,"* Chap. 11 from the series appearing in the *Cedartown Standard* starting on May 27, 1897. Henderson observed that the mudsills of Greenwood's mill could still be seen. The state survey of 1832 noted the Indian, Greenwood, and his mill on Lot 887 on "East Cedar Creek." This lot appears on a current Polk County map at the junction of Cedar Creek and Pumpkin Pile Creek.

10/ Polk County Deeds, Record Book A, p 191.

11/ Henderson, op. cit., Chap. 2.

12/ Kinney, Shirley Foster and James Paul Kinney, *Floyd County Confederates* (and surrounding counties), Vol. VIII, SFK Genealogy, Rome, Georgia, 1992, p. 215.

13/ Battey, George Magruder, Jr., *A History Of Rome And Floyd County, Vol. I*, Atlanta, 1922, p. 384385. It may have been no coincidence that the company commander was Capt. M.H. Hanie the same individual who had built the gristmill for Asa Prior.

14/ Battey, op. cit., pp. 205208.

15/ Marshall, Mrs. George O., Jr., Athens, Georgia.

16/ U.S. Census of 1910, Deer Creek District, Douglas County, Oregon.

17/ Obituary of John Thomas Prior, *Umpqua Valley News*, November 7, 1910, Roseburg, Oregon.

High Times & High Crimes At Polk County's Esom Hill

Since the earliest days in Polk County, the tiny community of Esom Hill was known as a place where a person could go to "get a drank of likker," and have some high old times. Some people say it still is today.

Since the earliest days of Polk County, its residents and travelers alike never hesitated to visit all sections of this historic area – that is, except for one spot. For reasons unknown today, the area known as "Esom Hill" was simply off-limits to everyone except the residents therein, their relatives and friends – and those individuals who patronized the township in order to obtain a quantity of untaxed liquor known in Southern parlance as "likker," or "moonshine."

And if a stranger comes poking around who falls outside the requirements for visitation, retribution has usually been quick to arrive. On one occasion, a neatly-dressed stranger from an out-of-town company was examining a lot upon which his firm had contracted to build a home for a local resident. Suddenly, from out of nowhere, a man with a shotgun walked up. "Get out of Esom Hill," he rasped at the builder. "You ain't got no bidness here." After a glance at the business end of the deadly weapon, the builder had to agree, and quickly departed.

Such has been the reputation for the little state line township in northwest Georgia's Polk County for almost three-quarters of a century as of this writing. It is an image fostered by a long record of illicit activities such as "moonshining," gambling, and even darker crimes like murder. And interestingly, it seemed the stronger the criminal element became in the township, the less visible became law enforcement.

Now if one queried one of the numerous residents of Esom Hill, he or she would respond that the country town is a friendly community which welcomes strangers with open arms. And he or she would add that the town's bad reputation is nothing more than defamation perpetuated by "outsiders." Just like many situations of this nature, the truth lies somewhere in the "grey area" in between.

Settlers in this westernmost edge of present-day Georgia, in what once was Cherokee Indian Territory, interestingly were among the *last* to arrive in Paulding County, Georgia, since it was reorganized as a part of Polk County in 1851. The beginnings of "infamous" Esom

Hill ironically occurred with the founding of the "very religious" Shiloh Baptist Church[1] in 1848 and the "very law-abiding" first post office[2] in 1850.

Due to its location away from the watchful eyes of law enforcement authorities and virtually astraddle the Georgia-Alabama state line, an unusual situation has existed for many years in Esom Hill which has allowed moonshiners (those producing the un-taxed illegal liquor) to proliferate. It is a circumstance which has also allowed the site to gravitate toward lawlessness. For many years now, local tellers of "tall tales" have maintained – tongue-in-cheek – how bootleggers escaped law enforcement officers by moving their liquor from one room in a building (in Georgia) to another room in the same building (which then would be in Alabama).

Another claim even maintains the first Esom Hill, "Georgia" post office was actually established in "Alabama" (1847) and then later moved to Georgia (1849) after the discrepancy was discovered.[3] This could possibly be explained by the fact that the first postmaster – Benjamin Wheeler – lived in Alabama and operated the post office there from his home or store. Today, no one really knows for certain, nor cares.

Esom Hill – just as do many Georgia townships – also boasts local Indian lore. Folklore there maintains the name of the little community originated with an old trading post once operated by an Indian named "Esom" or "Easom," possibly prior to the removal of the Cherokees from the territory. The "Hill" apparently was later added to the moniker, and no one knows today to what it originally referred – nor, once again, cares.

Another version of the origin of the town name claims it came from an early settler now buried in Shiloh Baptist

Bustin' Up the "Still" – Law enforcement officials destroy an illegal liquor (read "moonshine") distillery at Esom Hill, Polk County, circa 1928. Untaxed corn liquor was an extremely important "cash crop" to rural settlers of north Georgia, particularly in the poor mountain regions during the 1920s and '30s, when a terribly depressed economy left many families with no other income options. Esom Hill in northwest Georgia – just as Dawson and other counties in northeast Georgia – has a long-standing reputation as a center of moonshine production. (Photo courtesy of Mrs. Brenda Bentley)

Church cemetery beneath an unmarked fieldstone. Whatever the origin, the name and fame of Esom Hill aren't just "local." The reputation of this tiny community has spread far and wide over the years – always accompanied by its dark reputation.

A book entitled the *Georgia State Gazeteer*[4], published way back in 1881, lists Esom Hill as a community of 169 people with five general stores, three churches, a school and a saloon. The village also boasted a steam gin, a water-powered gin, and a sawmill. The year 1881 was the same year, interestingly, as the famous Old West gun-fight behind

Joseph Proctor Screven Brewster (1856-1913) – Brewster was one of the original pioneers of Esom Hill. He built the Brewster General Store in town in 1901.

the O.K. Corral between the Earps and Clantons, just to put things into perspective.

Early Commerce

Four years earlier in 1877, when Amos West founded his Cherokee Iron Company in Cedartown, Esom Hill must have shared in the prosperity as mining operations grew (supported by plentiful iron ore deposits in the area). Farming, of course, undoubtedly also figured prominently as a professional pursuit, but according to early records, there surprisingly were quite a few small businesses in the "up-and-coming" little burg as well, suggesting a very self-sufficient environment:

- W.P. West, postmaster
- J.P.S. Brewster, general store
- Rev. V.A. Brewster, Baptist pastor
- A.A. and J.W. Camp, sawmill

- Dukes and Pearson, blacksmith
- H.A. Edmonson, notary and J.P.
- Jeremiah "Jerry" Isbell, general store
- M.E. McCormack, tax collector and teacher
- J.S. Mercer, general store
- Nobles and Adkins, blacksmith
- T.J. West, general store
- W.P. West, general store
- West and Hackney, grist- and saw-mill
- C.M. Wheeler and son, saloon

Today, many of these original residents of Esom Hill rest in Shiloh Cemetery, and many of their descendants still live in the same community.

The general stores of Brewster and Isbell are still remembered particularly well – one in the village center and the other located three miles east at Akes Station. Brewster's original general store reportedly burned sometime around 1900, and he subsequently built a new store right across the street in 1901, a structure which, as of this writing, still functions today as the Esom Hill Trading Post.[5]

Jeremiah Isbell's country store was operated out of the front room of his home[6] and was still standing until a few years ago when it was demolished. The Brewsters and Isbells were among the original families to settle in Esom Hill.

At some point early in the conflict, Jeremiah Isbell who lived at that time in northwest Georgia's Floyd County joined the Confederate Army and served until the war's conclusion in 1865. When Gen. Robert E. Lee surrendered at Appomattox Courthouse in Virginia that year, Jeremiah departed the army and finally made it back home to Floyd County, only to find that his family had "refugeed" westward.[7]

In those terrible post-war days,

many families were forced to abandon their homes and businesses and migrate westward in order to seek a place to begin life anew and escape the devastated starving South.

Rome having been largely destroyed and occupied by Union troops at the war's conclusion, was not a hospitable environment for conducting business, so the Isbells left. They, however, had made it no further than "west Georgia," joining many other Georgia residents headed to Texas and other parts westward in search of new opportunities, when Jeremiah reportedly tracked them down.

In 1860, the Rev. Vann Allen Brewster left Haralson County to move to Esom Hill with his family.[8] His motivation for migration to Esom Hill is unknown today. Perhaps he saw the "handwriting on the wall" early-on.

The Brewster and Isbell children grew up together as nextdoor neighbors in Esom Hill. The families were formally linked in 1879 when a son and daughter married – Joseph Proctor Screven Brewster to Laura Jane Isbell. From this union came twelve children, contributing to the family of the proud grandfather, and making these two families among the largest and most prominent in the community.

Jerre Isbell boasted in his eighty-first year, "There are now living, and physically and mentally strong, not an idiot nor invalid nor a deformed one, in whose total reaches 198."[9]

The Brewster Mercantile Company became one of the first in the county to have electric power when Brewster installed a "Delco System" to generate power for lights in his store and in his home across the road.[10] The little generator charged a system of batteries during the day, and at night, when the generator shut down, the bank of batteries took

Jeremiah Marion Isbell (1829-1913) – The Isbell family was another of the original pioneers in Esom Hill.

over in the provision of electricity. The store carried everything from toothpicks to two-horse wagons to serve the farmers in the surrounding area.

A counter and post office boxes were located behind swinging doors at the back of the store.[11] The enterprising Joseph P.S. Brewster also served as postmaster. Later, his son, Fred, would become postmaster when he and brother Gordon succeeded their father in the operation of the store.[12]

Mail deliveries from the Esom Hill Post Office were carried over two mail routes. In 1928, when Jack Phillips began carrying the mail, he covered two routes (Routes 1 and 2) which apparently were combined into one route at about that time. According to Cora Belle Honea, Phillips drove a car to make his deliveries.

Prior to Phillips' tenure, Ben Griffith had driven Route 1 and Jim Woods

The Bailey family – These hardy early residents of Esom Hill were probably captured on film by an itinerant photographer circa 1919, and offer a glimpse of the violence which once prevailed in this community. Warren Bailey (behind his mother) later killed Robert Hackney in an argument in the family home (rear) and was later killed himself in another dispute. Also pictured are: Silas Clayton Bailey (seated), Minerva Owens Bailey (seated), and (standing l to r) Will Bailey, Dave Woodward, Warren Bailey, and Andrew Bailey. (Photo courtesy of Billy Bailey)

had done Route 2, both of them using a horse-drawn postal buggy. In the beginning, Phillips also reportedly drove a horse-and-buggy to deliver the mail, but when his first horse, Maude, grew too old and slow, he bought another faster horse which he named "Dammit." The frisky beast would often trot too fast, necessitating a "Whoa, Dammit!" much to the amusement of any bystanders."[13]

As a rural mail carrier, Jack Phillips provided some services totally unavailable today. In the making of his rounds, he could be persuaded to carry eggs from one farm to another, or a basket of fruit to a shut-in. This courier might even delay the swift completion of his appointed rounds by stopping to read – or even write – a letter for someone needing assistance.

Phillips reportedly once helped an elderly lady to order a corset and some batteries for her radio from the *Sears Roebuck* catalogue – even to the point of installing them when they were delivered (the batteries of course, not the corset).[14]

Moonshine & Murder

It was from this bucolic-sounding setting that the illicit activities of Esom Hill eventually evolved, and the community, in many instances, did nothing to diminish its reputation or discourage the activities – often even reveling in the infamy. At one point many years ago, alongside the approach road and next to the railroad crossing, the town name and population were even proudly and boldly inscribed across the face of a "decommissioned" moonshine still, much to the delight of many.[15]

The production of un-taxed whiskey ("moonshine") eventually grew into big business in the hills and hollows between Esom Hill and Borden Springs five miles to the west in Alabama. Brokers lined up orders for the spirituous liquid, distributing it freely in a wholesale operation. During **Prohibition** (1920 - 1933), huge trailer-trucks reportedly transported literally thousands of gallons of illegal whiskey from these hills northward to thirsty markets such as Chicago. Cars and small trucks could be fitted to handle loads of 100 to 150 gallons to make such deliveries. Before one knew it, moonshine had became big-business in Esom Hill.

When law enforcement officials stepped up arrests and crack-downs on the production of un-taxed whiskey in northwest Georgia in the 1950s, they, for obvious reasons, began their efforts at Esom Hill. One group drove out to the Treat Mountain area south of Esom Hill to search for distilleries ("stills"), parking their car alongside the road. While they were searching, their car mysteriously caught fire and burned to the axles. The insult so stung the officials that they opened a local office and dedicated it to the eradication of Polk County moonshining.[16]

Because it often involved so much money and represented the main source of income for so many rural citizens, any destruction or interruption of moonshine operations could – and often did – result in violent consequences. Just like the Hatfields and McCoys of old, disputes between neighbors at Esom Hill frequently got out of hand as well, and became a deadly conflict.

Of the many storied shootings at Esom Hill – and there have been quite a few of them – the day in April of 1933 that Warren Bailey fatally wounded Robert Hackney undoubtedly stands out prominently in the memories of some old-time residents.

According to the **Cedartown Standard** of that day[17], *"Deputy Sheriff Stone was called to the scene early Sunday night and found the body of (Robert) Hackney alone in the Bailey home. He had been shot through the body by a Winchester rifle and death was believed to have been instantaneous.*

"Investigation by Mr. Stone revealed that Hackney held a pistol in his right hand under his body and that the pistol had been recently fired twice. Alvin Bailey, son of Warren Bailey, claims to have been an eye witness to the affair and states that Hackney entered the home under the influence of liquor and shot at his father with the pistol and that the elder Bailey then grabbed the rifle and killed him. The rifle load indicated it had been fired one time."

The shooting apparently took place in the Bailey home. The "liquor" which Hackney had consumed was of course of the Esom Hill variety.

Warren Bailey ultimately was acquitted of the charge of murder by a grand jury. Three years later, however, in another notorious incident, he was

> *Brokers lined up orders for the spirituous liquid, distributing it freely in a wholesale operation.*

Griffith's Cash Store and Post Office – This establishment was photographed in June of 1934, and once stood where a U.S. Post Office was later constructed. (Photo courtesy of Kathleen Griffith)

killed by his nephew, Clayton Bailey[18] *"He who lives by the sword. . . ."* Well, you know how it goes.

"Bell Tree" Smith

There of course are many many legends which have been generated by the folks at Esom Hill, but one of the most notorious by far was that of *"Bell Tree"* Smith. *Bell Tree's* real name was Will Smith, and in his day, he was considered the king of the "shine bidness" in Esom Hill.

Will's legend undoubtedly was artificially expanded over the years to be much more than it actually was, but he nevertheless was the creator of quite a large amount of moonshine. Today, however, Will's son, William Smith and his family are quick to down-play the significance of his father's role in the proliferation of untaxed liquor in Esom. In fact, they maintain that much of the legend is simply that – a legend – and nothing more.

Despite the disclaimer, it is known

for a fact *Bell Tree* had a unique method of selling his corn liquor – a system which somehow seemed to protect him from detection by law enforcement officials.

It actually was very simple in design. On a lonely backroad near the Georgia-Alabama state line and not far from his still, Smith reportedly rigged a dinner-bell in a large oak tree, attaching a rope from the bell so that it could be rung by customers.

In order to gain a quantity of moonshine, a prospective buyer would simply travel to the large tree and set his empty jug and money by the tree. The buyer would make certain no one else was in the area, then give the rope a tug to ring the bell, and then leave the premises. When the bell rang again, the buyer would return to the old oak tree to find his jug filled with "shine" and the proper change left, all accomplished without any sign of a proprietor.

The tree under which all this activity took place was eventually dubbed – Yep. You guessed it. – the *"Bell Tree,"* and over the ensuing years, Will Smith earned his eventual widely-known moniker.

Although Esom Hill today proudly lays claim to the *Bell Tree* legend, the former site of the old oak was not even in Georgia. And today, there is really no way to confirm the former location of the tree because it died and rotted away years ago. By most accounts, however, it stood in Alabama near the Georgia line, in a hollow formed by a stream draining the south side of Flagpole Mountain north of Tecumseh, Alabama. When queried today, members of Will Smith's family strangely respond that they "do not recall" any ties the elder Smith might have had with Esom Hill, or even the location of the infamous old oak tree.[19]

Though many of the tales concerning *Bell Tree* Smith vary, one item is known for certain – that of his ultimate demise. On a warm Sunday in August of 1908, the legendary Smith became yet another Esom Hill crime statistic, when he was killed – according to police reports – by an individual named Will Chandler.[20]

According to the reported details of this incident, Smith had attended an all-day church singing in Borden Springs, Alabama. As had become the custom, the men had gradually separated from their womenfolk after eating lunch, and had drifted off to a field near the Borden Springs Post Office to partake of "libations" and tall tales.[21]

Bell Tree and Will Chandler – with Will's brother Joe Ben – ultimately began arguing over a payment for two yearling bulls. The conflict soon became heated. It has also been reported that Smith was attempting to stop the Chandler brothers from roughing up a young friend who happened to be present.

It was actually his role as a peace-maker which inevitably brought the life of *Bell Tree* Smith to a swift conclusion. He, somewhat surprisingly, was recognized as a community leader, and was accustomed to being called upon by neighbors to help keep the peace. Whether intentionally or otherwise, in those days, the sheriff normally took an hour to reach these parts, and many times he would arrive too late to help, so an intermediate "referee" was often needed.

On this fateful day, Smith stepped into the fracas and proceeded to subdue the attackers. As he left the fray and climbed into his buggy, a stone reportedly was thrown by one of the Chandlers. It apparently was a relatively large stone, because when it struck Smith, it stunned him, and before he could recover, Will Chandler reportedly shot him, killing him instantly. Instantaneous crimes just such as that are one of the hallmarks of moonshine "fellowship."

An unusual twist to this story occurred when Will Chandler was tried for the crime. He ultimately was convicted, but strangely was only sentenced to one year in the Alabama State Penitentiary. And before he served even a single day of his sentence, young Will received a sudden inexplicable pardon from none other than the governor of the state himself. One cannot help but wonder today about the identity of that governor, and what piece of evidence it was that Will Chandler dangled over his head in order to gain the gubernatorial pardon.

Today, William *Bell Tree* Smith lies buried in the Salem Baptist Church Cemetery in Bluffton, next to his father, Melton. A simple but eloquent inscription on Bell Tree's tombstone reads: *"A light from our household is gone. He was a kind and loving son and affectionate brother."*

Frank Lott Murder

One of the most infamous crimes ever associated with the Esom Hill area occurred more recently in 1974, with the murder of prominent Polk County Sheriff Frank Lott, Sr.

In the late 1960s and early 1970s, much of the illicit activity at Esom Hill had been interrupted by investigations and arrests carried out by Lott, when, as the newly-elected sheriff, he began cleaning up the county. As a result of his uncompromising efforts in law enforcement, Lott inevitably made his share of enemies in Esom Hill.

Though no direct link has ever been established between his murder and a "pay-back" from bootleggers at Esom Hill, much public speculation about just such a connection has surrounded the incident since the fateful day. Lott's son, however, disagrees.

"When Dad went in (to the Esom Hill area just prior to his election as sheriff), a lot of the bootleggers asked him, 'How are you going to be if you're elected?'" explained Frank Lott, Jr. "Dad told them, 'My advice to you is if you're doing something illegal, you need to find another line of work.'

"(As a result), a good many of them did change their line of work. Some of them didn't though, and in time, Dad caught them, but he was always straight-forward with them and I don't think they would have hurt him."

Frank, Jr., says that on the evening just prior to the murder, some of the family had gone with his father to Rome for dinner. Upon his return from any such

A vehicle fitting this description was later found burned around Esom Hill.

trip, Lott, Jr. says his dad always went by the jail at night to make certain everything was in order. On this particular night (June 23, 1974), Lott reportedly was making his check on the jail when a silent alarm indicated a burglary was in progress at Cedartown High School.

"There was a trustee at the jail that night," Lott, Jr. continued. "He had a drinking problem and was serving some weekend time. He went with Dad (to the burglary), and when they got to the school, Dad drove around (to the back) where they saw a man getting into a car.

"When Dad got out of his car, the (burglar) got out too. Dad asked him 'What's going on here?'

"Dad started approaching the (burglar) and got between the cars (where) the lights probably blinded him. The (burglar), while he was standing there, apparently had a gun in his hand, and he came up firing and hit Dad three times." The gunman, according to reports, then jumped into his car and sped away.

"(Later), the boy that was with Dad was put under hypnosis," Lott added. "He was certain about the (burglar's) car – a Ford *Torino*. A vehicle fitting this description was later found burned around Esom Hill."

The prime suspect in the crime was described as a white male with long hair and driving a car with an Alabama license plate. When asked if the individual was from Esom Hill, Frank Lott Jr. would only reply, "They thought he was a psychopath. After the murder, nobody would have anything to do with this suspect. Some of them at Esom Hill that had been friends with him didn't even want anything to do with him from that point forward. He later killed himself."

Hoyt Dingler retired from the Polk County Sheriff's Department following 30 years of service. He maintains that he and others in the department knew who committed the crime, but that there simply was never enough evidence to make a case against the suspect, described also by Dingler as an Alabama man.

Dingler also maintained that the murder was not a set-up – at least not as far as Sheriff Lott was concerned. "There's no way they could have known that Frank would have answered the call that night, because ordinarily, he wouldn't have," Dingler explained. "At night, it would have been the county police that answered a burglary alarm at the high school. And it was also a fenced-in area with only one gate out. A person is not going to fence himself in to commit a murder."

As a result of its netherworld activities, Esom Hill, according to Dingler, is pretty widely known. "I've been in other parts of the country, and when people want to know where I'm from, and when I reply Cedartown, Georgia, they often say they've never heard of Cedartown, but they've heard of Esom Hill."

Today, Esom Hill is like any other rural northwest Georgia crossroads community. Most folks are friendly and accommodating, and you'd be hard-pressed to find any visible sign of criminal activity. Despite this seemingly peaceful demeanor however, one can't help but sense that just below the surface in this crossroads fiefdom, the action is still bubbling in Esom Hill.

Endnotes

1/ Johnson, Larry G., *A History Of Polk County Georgia* (GA) Missionary Baptist Association, Curley, Nashville, 1977, p. 7.

2/ U.S. Post Offices, Polk (and Paulding) County, U.S. Records, Microfilm Drawer 281, Box 32, Surveyor General Dept., Georgia Department of Archives and History, Atlanta, GA.

3/ Stewart, Mrs. Frank Ross, Alabama's Cleburne County, Centre, AL, 1982, p. 68.

4/ *Georgia State Gazeteer* (sic) *& Business Directory*, 1881-'82, Atlanta.

5/ The date of construction was once inscribed in the concrete on the front step, but is no longer legible today.

6/ Hoyt Dingler interview, August 17, 1994.

7/ Jeremiah Isbell served in the U.S. Civil War with his eldest son. His father, Pendleton Isbell (1806-1973), also served, as did eight of his sons and three of his grandsons. All but one son and one grandson – who were killed – returned home safely.

8/ "A Pioneer Dead," *The Cedartown Standard*, October 28, 1897.

9/ NW Georgia Document Preservation Project, 1993. Microfilm SHC156, Brewster/Isbell Papers.

10/ Brewster, Phil, Sr., Cedartown, Georgia, video interview, August 7, 1988.

11/ Honea, Cora Belle, Cedartown, Georgia, letter to Dennis Holland, August 31, 1992.

12/ NW Georgia Document Preservation Project, Op. Cit.

13/ "Vacancy At Esom," *The Cedartown Standard*, c. June 29, 1971.

14/ IBID

15/ Hoyt Dingler interview, August 17, 1994

16/ Hoyt Dingler interview, August 17, 1994

17/ "Warren Bailey Is Held For Murder In Hackney Death," *The Cedartown Standard*, April 20, 1933.

18/ "Clay Bailey Is Held For Killing Of Warren Bailey," *The Cedartown Standard*, August 1, 1935.

19/ Smith, William E., Tecumseh, Alabama, interview on July 29, 1994.

20/ "'Bill' Smith Is Killed," *Cleburne News*, August 20, 1908.

21/ Charlie Collins, Muscadine, Alabama, letter, March 4, 1994, interview, March 7, 1994.

The Rollicking Brief Life of Gunman John H. Holliday

Though he has been recorded in history as a ruthless gunman in the Old West, all indications point to the fact that, to the contrary, John Henry "Doc" Holliday was a man of "true grit" who sought only to live out what he knew would be a brief life under his own terms. In the process, his experiences became extraordinary, and the stuff of legend.

The story of John Henry Holliday begins in Griffin, Georgia, where his father – Major Henry Burroughs Holliday – was a farmer, a prominent druggist, and the clerk of Spalding County Courthouse. With the advance of General William Tecumseh Sherman and his "dogs of war" into Georgia in 1864, Maj. Holliday was no fool. He could see the handwriting on the wall. He subsequently sold his Griffin holdings and moved with his family to Valdosta down in the extreme southeast corner of the state.

Maj. Holliday settled with his family in a community of about 1,500 people in what then was a virtual wilderness at the little crossroads community of Bemiss outside Valdosta. It was far from the Holliday family home in Griffin, Georgia, but it was a safe haven from the looming Federal siege of Atlanta and Sherman's advancing Union Army.

Maj. Holliday, a veteran of the Creek Indian wars, the Mexican War and the U.S. Civil War, had retired from military service due to declining health. By that time, he and his wife had already reared to manhood a young orphan

– Francisco Hidalgo – brought home by a compassionate Maj. Holliday in 1849 after the Mexican War.

In the largely unsettled south Georgia countryside, the elder Holliday became an entrepreneur, opening a plant nursery, planting vineyards and promoting the production of pecans, an undertaking which today has grown into a major agricultural industry stretching from Valdosta westward across the clay hills of southwest Georgia and on to the north of the state. Indeed, Georgia now produces more pecans than peaches. It, in fact, produces more pecans today than any other state in the Union.

Young John Henry Holliday, 12 years old when he arrived in Valdosta, was remembered by area residents as a nice-looking and slightly-built young man, with piercing blue eyes and blonde hair. Later biographies recorded his gracious manners as well as his unpredictable temperament. Valdostans, however, remembered only a well-mannered adolescent who dressed neatly and grew into a young man known for his ability on a dance floor amidst the musical talents of his McKey relatives.

The McKey Family

History correctly records that young John Henry was well-educated. He was schooled at the private Valdosta Institute which, as reported by Louis Pendleton in his *Echo of Drums*, stressed classics and taught *"advanced branches."* Headmaster Samuel McWhir Varnedoe established a challenging curriculum for his students, including Greek, Latin, French, advanced English, mathematics and history.

Following the end of the U.S. Civil War, the Holliday/McKey family clung to a semblance of affluence when most other Southern families and former prominent businessmen were relegated to abject poverty. The young Holliday's three McKey uncles – James, William and Thomas – had purchased a large tract of land in the lakes area along the Georgia-Florida border south of Valdosta in an area known as "Bellview."

The McKey property, dubbed "Banner Plantation," is said to have been a favorite haunt of John Henry, who reportedly spent much of his adolescent life hunting and fishing on the property. His favorite uncle, Tom, who was only 10 years older than John, often accompanied him.

Years later and a world away out West, John Henry assumed the alias Thomas "Mackey" (as the family surname was then spelled) for a short time, presumably because he had encountered legal problems or conflicts of another nature, and needed to disguise his true identity.

"I don't know why he did that," said Susan McKey Thomas, a relative from Valdosta, and author of *In Search of the Hollidays*, a seminal collective work on the family history. "He wasn't famous, really, until the O.K. Corral." Many

Dr. John Stiles Holliday was the uncle of John Henry "Doc" Holliday of western fame. This artist's rendering of John Stiles was created circa 1860. (Collection of Morgan DeLancey Magee)

historians would reply, however, that despite the fact that he hadn't yet been involved in the famous October 26, 1881 gunfight in Tombstone, Arizona Territory, John Henry was, nevertheless, becoming known as a testy gunfighter even by the time he reached Dodge City, and had already reportedly been involved in more than one serious altercation.

Whatever the case, back in south Georgia, what seems to have been an idyllic childhood for John Henry was shattered by tragedy in the form of the unexpected serious illness of his mother. Alice Jane McKey Holliday gradually lost her strength and endured a lingering and torturous state of health until September 16, 1866, when she finally passed away from the same illness – tuberculosis – which would later haunt and prematurely-destroy John Henry. The youngster, who had dearly loved his mother, reportedly was devastated.

Mattie ("Sister Melanie") Holliday, was John Henry Holliday's first cousin, and has been the object of much speculation involving his life down through history. Some historians have maintained that a love affair between the two ultimately sent him out West and her to a convent. (Susan McKey Thomas collection)

As if his mother's death was not bad enough, family stories maintain that John Henry was shaken even worse by the almost immediate remarriage of his father to another woman a mere three months after his mother's death. Maj. Holliday married Rachel Martin, 23, a young lady who was less than half his age and only nine years older than John Henry. In fairness, in that day and time, it was not customary for a young widower with children to wait around and "court" for another wife, but rather to somewhat quickly remarry the most opportune potential spouse.

Reconstruction Trauma

Other outside factors also impacted the Holliday family in Valdosta. Following the U.S. Civil War, the turbulent years of *Reconstruction* took a serious toll on the Holliday family's financial

fortunes. An abusive Federal occupation with its associated retributive and punitive legalities for anything "Southern" set the Holliday circumstances back even further.

Rachel Martin's family owned farmland which adjoined the Holliday property. Records indicate that the Martins purchased the Holliday tract, and that Maj. Holliday's father-in-law gave to his daughter a house in Valdosta at 405 Savannah Avenue. The Holliday family – including young John Henry – soon relocated to this new address.

Never one to take defeat easily, Maj. Holliday immediately began working to recover the family fortune. He opened several businesses, including a furniture store. The *1870 Census* lists him broadly as "general agent." Eventually, Thomas says, Holliday regained all of his former properties, but he never fully recovered financially.

Maj. Holliday also gained some acclaim in the political arena in his community. He served four terms as Valdosta's mayor.

While his father was beginning to prosper once again, the younger Holliday began pursuing the behavior for which he would become more widely known later in life. Local tradition maintains – incorrectly – that he eventually fled town after running afoul of Federal officials.

Young John Henry was in fact accused of being associated with – and indeed may even have been the mastermind of – a plot to destroy with explosives the then-Federally-operated Lowndes County Courthouse in Valdosta. In the *Reconstruction South*, the county courthouses often were seized by occupying Federal forces in order to set up a headquarters for a legal sanctioning body charged with the responsibility of

The impressive home built by Dr. John Stiles Holliday in Fayetteville, Georgia, still stands as of this writing (2024). It has been in existence at least since 1855, and quite possibly was built as early as 1846 when Dr. Holliday first purchased the property. Dr. John Stiles Holliday was the uncle of John Henry "Doc" Holliday of western fame and diagnosed the tuberculosis in his nephew circa 1873. It was at this home that young John Henry spent much time in his youth forming a bond with his cousin Mattie which ultimately had a profound impact upon both their lives.

doling out of punishments of "White" Southerners. However, though a subsequent newspaper account of the incident (in which John Henry supposedly was involved) lists the names of five participants who were accused of the crime, John Henry, was not one of those identified or even implicated in the crime.

Maj. Holliday was one of five men appointed by the Valdosta City Council to draw up a plan to deal with the unrest in the Lowndes County area during Reconstruction according to Ms. Thomas. One could surmise that John Henry's family connections could have protected him from prosecution in the courthouse incident, but any such conclusion, like so many others involving John Henry Holliday, would be pure conjecture at this late date.

Swimming Hole Incident

Ms. Thomas said young Holliday was also reportedly involved in "a shooting incident," which supposedly was prompted by his discovery of a group of Blacks in a riverside swimming spot he and his friends often frequented near the confluence of the Withlacoochee and Little rivers at the old settlement of Troupville. In reality, however, what modern America wished to conveniently convert into yet another "racial issue" perpetrated by a "racist" Southerner, actually amounted to little more than young Holliday defending himself after being attacked by the Blacks when he had demanded that they leave the property.

Once again, this "racial incident" occurred during the Reconstruction

The infant John Henry Holliday from a tinted daguerreotype, 1852. (from the collection of Karen Holliday Tanner).

years, when tensions were extremely high. At that time, many Blacks reveled in their new-found superior social status, often intentionally inflaming a situation by flaunting their ability to violate long-standing Southern social mores. Rather than calm the circumstances, Reconstruction-elected officials and federal authorities often fanned the flames of divisiveness with abusive penalties for trumped-up (and oftentimes completely false) charges against Southern Whites.

Ms. Thomas said the story involving John Henry was confirmed by Thomas McKey, John's uncle. In the late 1920s, Thomas says McKey related the incident involving John Henry to writer Stuart Lake who was working on what later would become a controversial book about Wyatt Earp.

"He told the story of (McKey and Holliday) going to a swimming hole which Whites had traditionally used as a spot for swimming and leisure activity, and that was when they discovered a large group of Blacks in the water," Ms.

Thomas related. "[John Henry] first ordered the trespassers out of the water, and after being abusively spurned and threatened, he then turned to retrieve his pistol." One of the Blacks, however, who was already armed and prepared threatened young John Henry at gunpoint, while forcing him to leave the premises.

According to still further false contentions, a Black "federal officer" was supposedly killed in the incident, but in the interview with writer Stuart Lake, Thomas McKey firmly denied anyone was wounded or injured in any way. Here again, the supposedly "murdered Black federal officer" was nothing more than a complete fabrication designed to paint Holliday as a racist in order to fan the flames of divisiveness in a conquered South.

Today, there is no microfilm available for the *Valdosta Times* newspaper published during the period in question, but McKey's assertion of John Henry's innocence is given some credence by the fact that there is no evidence whatsoever of any such incident in the records of the Lowndes County Superior Court for the years 1866 through 1873, and the occupying Federal authorities, as well as Reconstruction-elected officials (as explained above), were always quick to record the details and take advantage of any opportunity to negatively-portray and punish any White Southerner involved in any incident or even the slightest infraction which held a hint of a racial edge. This "swimming hole incident" is explored in more detail below.

On To Dental School

Despite the trouble John Henry may or may not have initiated as a teen, he went on to graduate from the Valdosta Institute in 1870. Later that year, he applied and was admitted to the

Pennsylvania College of Dental Surgery from which he was graduated during the 16th annual graduation ceremonies of March 1, 1872.

During his studies in Pennsylvania, John Henry occasionally returned to work his required "preceptership" with Valdosta dentist Lucian Frederick Frink. Ms. Thomas said there is some evidence that Holliday performed dental work in Valdosta in October of 1871, and it is believed he returned home for a brief visit after his graduation, but a short time later, he struck out for Atlanta to open a dental practice in that newly-rebuilt city which was just then recovering from the devastation it had suffered at the hands of Union Army Gen. W.T. Sherman.

Though he did not know it at the time, even as he left Valdosta, the newly anointed "Dr." Holliday was no doubt already a doomed man. Within a year, he would be diagnosed with tuberculosis, a disease for which there was no treatment until the mid-20th century. It was the same disease which had killed his mother.

This diagnosis was a fate which quite possibly soon sent John Henry to the drier climate of the West for health reasons, and, within the span of four more years, found him – depending upon who one wishes to believe – either becoming a cold-blooded killer, or a playfully subversive gambler who had a "very short fuse" when larger and much stronger individuals sought to bully him or physically take advantage of his slight stature. Ms. Thomas, in the sincere opinion of one who has sought the truth for so very long, places her famous cousin somewhere in the middle of these two extremes.

Historians and researchers today maintain that John Henry almost certainly had been infected with the

Henry Burroughs Holliday, John Henry's father, was photographed circa 1852, while the family yet lived in Griffin, Georgia, south of Atlanta. He would ultimately refugee southward to Valdosta, Georgia, to escape the oncoming Union Army juggernaut of Gen. William Tecumseh Sherman who was headed for Georgia in his infamous "March to the Sea."

tuberculosis bacterium years prior to the diagnosis of his disease. He might possibly have contracted it from a dental patient upon which he trained early in his college education. However, in reality, he more than likely contracted it from his mother, although Thomas says there obviously is no way to prove that today. Each day, his advancing illness robbed him of still more of his strength.

Interestingly, Francisco Hidalgo, the Mexican youth raised by the Hollidays is also known to have died of the dreaded disease as well in 1873, providing still more strong evidence that the seeds of Doc Holliday's eventual demise in a Colorado hotel in 1887 were sown long before that time, either in Griffin or in Valdosta.

Old Courthouse – Major Henry Holliday, Doc's father, was the first clerk of court in Georgia's Spalding County. The historic courthouse, which still stands in downtown Griffin as of this writing (2024), included an office for Holliday in the 1850s. (Photo by Jackie Kennedy)

Leaving Home Forever

Once he departed Valdosta, "Doc" Holliday apparently considered his break with Georgia to be permanent. There is no evidence that he ever returned to visit, even though there is evidence that he strongly yearned for a reconnection with his family.

A legend within the Holliday family maintains that Maj. Holliday arranged a meeting with his son while in New Orleans at a Confederate veterans' convention in 1885, and begged the ailing John Henry to come home to his family. Whether the meeting ever took place or not is yet another detail of John Henry's short life which is unverifiable today.

What can be said with certainty, however, is that if the estranged father and son had such a meeting, it was their last. Doc Holliday did not return to Georgia, and by 1885, he was so sick that he could barely manage to support himself in the gambling profession any

longer – and by that point, the "game" of gambling was no longer a game to John Henry. To the contrary, it was literally his sole profession. After he ceased practicing dentistry, gambling became his sole method of obtaining income, and when healthy, he was quite adept at it.

Though often merry – and sometimes even comical in nature – John Henry's otherwise testy nature caused him to be involved in more than one serious altercation shortly after his migration to the West. In a locale which thrived upon reputations, the legend of Doc Holliday as a gunman quickly became established, and any return to his home in Georgia where his family's reputation might be tarnished by his disreputable identity became impossible for the wandering former dentist to even consider.

During her research of John Henry Holliday, Susan Thomas did make one very interesting – and very unexpected – discovery. The orphan – Francisco Hidalgo – left behind a legacy of his own in neighboring Berrien County in the form of the "Edalgo" family, of which he was the progenitor.

After more than a century, that piece of information came as a complete and total surprise to the Edalgos who continue to live in this south Georgia county even as of this writing, and who previously had been unable to trace their ancestry beyond their local community.

Remnants In Valdosta

Today, the Holliday legacy is alive and well in Valdosta, even if the Major and Doc are long gone and the Holliday name itself has all but disappeared in the community.

Maj. Holliday, in addition to serving as mayor of the city, rose to additional

Fort Stephens – Though the full details of this site have been lost through the passage of time, this rare historic print reveals a portion of the troops at this Confederate training encampment near Griffin, Georgia, in the early 1860s. This facility was located one-half mile east of the railroad and two miles north of Griffin. It was the presence of this camp adjacent to his plantation and the looming threat of a Union Army invasion of Georgia, which caused Maj. Henry B. Holliday to move his family – including a young John Henry – to south Georgia. (Confederate Stamps, Old Letters, and History)

prominence in that town. He served as secretary of the Lowndes County Agricultural Society, secretary of the Confederate Veterans of Camp Troup, census enumerator, and superintendent of local elections. He even had a street named for him near the original site of the Holliday house off Savannah Avenue.

The Holliday house in Valdosta – John Henry's adolescent home – lives on as well as of this writing (2024). In the 1970s, the aged structure was purchased by Valdosta businessman Dick Davis and moved to a new location off U.S. Highway 41 South. A few years later, the home was given a new lease on life when it was purchased by a local couple and moved to one of the new subdivisions which sprawl far to the northwest of town.

After its relocation, the house was extensively renovated, although many of its original aspects were preserved and incorporated into the new additions to the structure. It was later purchased and occupied by Dr. David Johnson and his wife, Susan, at 2605 Pebblewood Drive in Valdosta. Its disposition beyond that status is unknown today.

Myths About His Georgia Life

Though much of his life has been documented for posterity, a number of gaps still exist in the collective record of his life and times. One would just naturally anticipate that a person as "celebrated" as is John Henry Holliday would have little unknown information in the story of his life – even with a man as secretive about his personal life as was he.

Holliday, however, seems to be an exception to the rule. He not only was

Card Shark – Sophie Walton was a female slave born in January of 1856 on a farm owned by the Walton family. Sophie enjoyed a higher status than the other slave children because she had been fathered by Mr. Walton. Several years after the end of the U.S. Civil War, Mr. Walton was no longer able to care for all of his slaves, and arranged for Sophie to go live at the home of Dr. John Stiles Holliday, John Henry's uncle, in Atlanta. Among her many skills, Sophie reportedly was somewhat adept with cards, and taught John some of the tricks of the trade in gamesmanship which he later put to good use as a professional gambler out west. Sophie was photographed here in 1895 in Atlanta.

very "close-mouthed" about his life and family, his family members – as a general rule – were very "close-mouthed" about him.

Many subsequent "historians" and researchers have speculated and offered supposition regarding these "unrecorded" and therefore unknown details, and therein lies much of the intrigue of this famed Old West figure from Georgia. When details of his life were unknown,

those recording those details for posterity simply "manufactured" information to suit their needs.

As a result, it has been an uphill grind at best to correct the record regarding John Henry's life, and this has been complicated by the fact that even today, many details about his life still are clouded in mystery.

The Swimming Hole Incident

Much has been made over the years of a presumed "incident" between John Henry Holliday and several Blacks at whom he supposedly directed gunfire in an argument over a favored "swimming hole" at some point in his youth. Just as with many circumstances which make a grand story if one is able to "reinvent" them into an event involving a racial component, this one also has been blown out of proportion if not completely misrepresented. It just naturally makes the story and character that much more controversial if "the race card" can be played.

First of all, much of the knowledge of this presumed "incident" was initially presented as fact by John Henry's Uncle Thomas McKey and his daughter, Mrs. Clyde McKey White and subsequently repeated by William Barclay "Bat" Masterson, Walter Noble Burns and others as "fact." While not denying that such an "incident" may, in fact, have actually occurred, the individuals making this contention either used faulty information, or were simply unreliable as sources – or both.

Mrs. White's *"Papa told me. . ."* account regarding Doc and the incident appears highly unlikely when examined in the light of day. "Papa" quite likely told his daughter many things, but that doesn't necessarily make them true, and Mrs. White simply was not present herself to witness "the swimming hole incident", so she could only repeat what she "thought" her father had stated scores of years earlier. This isn't exactly the concept upon which "factual information" is based.

And by the time "Bat" Masterson got around to repeating what was little more than a rumor from Mrs. White, he (Bat) was little more than a derelict alcoholic who had earlier disgraced himself in towns in the West such as Denver, Colorado, to the point of being permanently ejected and barred from those municipalities. Having retired to the New York City offices of the *Morning Telegraph* newspaper, Masterson had been forced to support himself with inflated "remembrances" of his days in the West and the famed gunmen with whom he had interacted. Many of these remembrances at best included conjecture and faulty information – particularly those involving John Henry Holliday.

In May of 1907, Masterson produced an article for publication in *Human Life* which introduced many readers to the presumed swimming hole incident involving Holliday. Masterson had little evidence other than the rumor-mill to support his contention about Holliday and a matter as serious as murder. *"The indiscriminate killing of some Negroes in the little Georgia village in which he lived was what first caused him* (Holliday) *to leave his home,"* Masterson wrote. *"The trouble came about in rather an unexpected manner one Sunday afternoon – unexpected so far, at least as the Negroes were concerned."*

The article Masterson penned for *Human Life* can only be described today as a critically unfair fabrication regarding Holliday which unjustly became a portion of the Georgian's permanent

Valdosta home – Maj. Henry Burroughs Holliday moved to Valdosta, Georgia, circa 1863, to escape the anticipated devastation of north Georgia by invading Union troops. Pictured here is the Holliday home in Valdosta, where a young John Henry spent his adolescence attending Valdosta Institute and hunting and fishing in the surrounding countryside.

record. Masterson's dislike for Holliday is well-documented, resulting mainly from a distaste for the Georgian's quick temper and periodic alcoholic rages. Masterson, in fact, had no proof whatsoever to back up many of his *Human Life* article statements.

In retrospect, this incident could have involved Blacks. It could also have, to the contrary, involved only Whites. Holliday's actions – if they occurred at all – could easily also have been justifiable, but it makes a much more dynamic story if it can be conveyed in a dramatic racial context.

First of all, this supposed racial incident which was published in Masterson's fourth installment of his *"Famous Gunfighters of the Western Frontier"* series supposedly occurred after the Holliday family had relocated to "Valdosta," Georgia, to escape the onslaught of Gen. William T. Sherman's troops through Georgia in the final year of the U.S. Civil War. Masterson, avoiding specifics for understandable reasons, stated

Valdosta Institute – This private school, provided young John Henry with an impressive education in the classics. The date of this photo is unknown, but it quite likely was taken circa 1870s, possibly even during the time-period in which this school was attended by John Henry.

it occurred *"near the little town in which Holliday was raised. . ."*

Repeating Masterson's unsubstantiated statements in 1927, Walter Noble Burns in his *Tombstone: An Iliad of the Southwest* was the first to specifically establish Valdosta and the Withlacoochee River in that vicinity as the site of the incident. The "respected writer," William Barclay Masterson, had stated that it occurred in *"the little town in which Holliday was raised,"* so Burns immediately reasoned that Masterson had to be referring to Valdosta/Lowndes County and the Withlacoochee River. But is this accurate?

Since there were no other swimming holes – as it were – which John Henry might have conveniently frequented in the vicinity of his home in Lowndes County except along the section of the Withlacoochee River flowing through his McKey uncles' property (which adjoined the Holliday property), and with the logistical requirements of physical travel being what they were in the 1870s, logic would dictate that a popular swimming spot frequented by the McKey and Holliday boys would not

have existed anywhere except upon the Withlacoochee where it flowed through the McKey property. The Holliday property had no swimming holes.

And from whence did the Blacks at which John Henry supposedly fired his weapon originate? Neither the McKeys nor the Hollidays owned slaves at this time in Georgia, since it was the post-Civil War era, and no Blacks have been documented as living upon the McKey or Holliday properties at this time. The combined acreage created a reasonably extensive tract of land with few if any neighbors in what then was basically still an unsettled wilderness in south Georgia. So from whence did the manufactured Blacks come? Where did they live? No one has the answer. More speculation.

The time-line for the occurrence of this incident is faulty as well. A pre-February, 1872 swimming hole shooting incident in Valdosta must be ruled out, since Holiday's uncles – William H. and Thomas S. McKey – *did not even purchase their Withlacoochee River acreage until February of 1872*. Also, John Henry was involved with his education at the Philadelphia College of Dental Surgery from 1870 to 1872 – much too far away from home to be involved in swimming hole trivialities.

Granted, from March through October of 1871, John Henry was fulfilling the requirements for his eight-month dental preceptorship (apprenticeship) with Valdosta dentist Lucian Frederick Frink, so he was in the area had he been inclined toward childish dalliances such as swimming hole hijinks at 20 years of age after he had begun his professional career. But again, this period of time preceded the time of ownership of the Withlacoochee property by the McKey family, and regardless if they had owned it or not, a trip all the way out to this property from Valdosta (where John Henry was apprenticing) is highly unlikely, since it was far from easily accessible from Valdosta at that time – even on horseback. On November 6, 1871, John Henry's classes in Philadelphia resumed and continued until graduation in March of 1872.

Following the conclusion of his educational training in Philadelphia, John Henry immediately began the pursuit of his young professional life. On April 3, 1872, the *Georgia State Dental Society* opened its fifth annual convention in Atlanta which John Henry almost certainly attended in order to establish important professional contacts and pursue opportunities for employment. Though no written account of his actual presence at this event has been discovered, he, as a young and ambitious medical professional would have been loathe to have missed this opportunity to pursue employment opportunities.

Lest we forget, the sole aim of John Henry Holliday at this time in his young life was the pursuit of the profession in which he had invested so much time, energy and money. By this point, he had no thoughts whatsoever of idle playtime in a swimming hole in the wilds of south Georgia, much less of foolhardy gunplay with trespassing Negroes.

And what of the public records – the newspapers and court documents – which would have recorded a shooting of this nature? No such incident is mentioned anywhere in the Lowndes County news media nor court records, and, again, this was at a time when federal authorities and occupying appointed officials were swift to record and punish any White Southerner involved in any incident of a racial nature. No such record

Penn College Grad – John Henry Holliday was photographed here shortly after his graduation from the Pennsylvania College of Dental Surgery in Philadelphia. Totally unaware of the fatal illness within his body at this time, he assumed a long – and no doubt prosperous – life lay before him. He lived a scant 15 years after this photo was taken, most of which was spent in Texas, New Mexico, Arizona Territory and Colorado Territory, suffering desperately from the ills of tuberculosis. He would die in Glenwood Springs, Colorado in 1887. (Photo by O.B. DeMorat)

nor account of punishment exists for John Henry or his family.

It also is quite possible that in 1872 or even in 1873, John Henry Holliday returned to his original boyhood home of Griffin, Georgia, to practice dentistry there for a short period of time after inheriting the "Iron Front Building," a substantial commercial structure in the town. His mother had left this property to her son in her Will, and John Henry quite possibly briefly maintained a dental practice therein.

Tubercular Condition – An infant John Henry Holliday was photographed with his mother, Alice Jane McKey Holliday circa 1852. Even as a small tyke, John Henry demonstrates an unsettling gaze. Both he and his mother – from whom he quite possibly contracted the fatal disease – would die from the tuberculin bacteria. A cure for the dreaded malady would not be discovered until almost 100 years later in 1943. (Craig Fouts Photo Collection)

On April 3, 1873, the *Georgia State Dental Society's* annual convention was held once again – this time in Columbus, Georgia. Dr. Arthur C. Ford was elected Society President, and he had already become significant in Holliday's life, providing him with his first opportunity for a professional dental practice through a partnership. The *Columbus Daily Sun* published a list of all dentists practicing in the state prior to August 24, 1872. Listed among the 143 dentists was *"Haliday, John H., Atlanta,"* where he practiced in concert with Dr. Ford.

At some point around 1873 or shortly thereafter, John Henry Holliday became acquainted with the gambling trade and the debauchery so prevalent in the vicinity of his early employment with Dr. Ford. At some point, drinking, gambling, and womanizing took over his life and his professional dental practice "took a back seat." He shortly became so dissolute that Dr. Ford apparently was compelled to sever his professional relationship with John Henry, sending Holliday's life spiraling out of control and ultimately converting him into a vagabond traveling the West for adventure.

The combination of all the above circumstances left, for all intents and purposes, no opportunity whatsoever for the aforementioned "swimming hole incident" – as described by Mrs. Clyde McKey White and mimicked by William Barclay Masterson and Walter Noble Burns – to have occurred in Valdosta at all. In point of fact, the most likely point at which something of this nature "might" have occurred would have been much earlier in Doc's life at the Holliday family home in Griffin (*not on the Withlacoochee in Valdosta*), where a younger John Henry spent the first twelve years of his life.

Actual Swimming Hole Site?

Born in Griffin in 1851, John Henry lived for the first two years of his life in a small home on that town's Tinsley Street. In October of 1853, Maj. Henry Burroughs Holliday purchased a plantation one and one-half miles north of Griffin where the young John Henry spent the following ten years of his life. As stated, this property would have been a much more likely locale for a "swimming hole incident." Even more telling, this property included a large natural spring (and associated popular swimming spot) at which a shooting incident quite easily could have occurred.

In March of 1862, Private Asbury H. Jackson (CSA infantry) sent a letter home to his mother from Griffin's Confederate Camp Stephens. Included in this letter was a finely-drawn map which intricately detailed Camp Stephens, a substantial military training facility for the Confederacy. Mrs. Jackson and her heirs somehow had retained possession of the map down through time until it eventually was discovered in a dusty file drawer by an individual named Mike Watson in 2002.

Without Pvt. Jackson's map, the specific location of Maj. Holliday's (and son John Henry's) home – which had been lost over the ensuing years – on his plantation might never have been known. Spalding County Deed Books A and B, provide a detailed description of the acreage included in the plantation, but no information whatsoever regarding the Holliday home itself.

Despite Pvt. Jackson's detailed map, the aforementioned plantation site – still wholly undeveloped right up to the 21st Century – had become completely obscured with the passage of years by dense undergrowth and forested expanses, causing any actual relocation of the former Holliday home to be extremely difficult. Even the ancient steel rails (which still exist as of this writing) from the historic *Macon & Western Railroad* had been completely hidden by all the heavy undergrowth of bushes, vines, scrub pines, and decayed vegetation. Nevertheless, after extensive research by *Doc Holliday Society* President Bill Dunn of Griffin and an associate, the foundation stones of the former Holliday home as well as the steel rails of the railroad were eventually uncovered and revealed.

Maj. Henry B. Holliday had initially purchased 147 acres in 1853 near Griffin situated north of the city proper and

Ford Dentistry – The structure which housed Muhlenbrink's Saloon on Alabama Street (photographed here circa 1980) still existed and was used for many years in the entertainment venue known as "Underground Atlanta." This site was a popular attraction of 1960s and '70s Atlanta before the inner city's crime necessitated its closure. Approximately 100 years earlier, in the summer of 1872, John Henry "Doc" Holliday, at the age of 21, had just graduated from dental school in Philadelphia, and was working in the Atlanta dental office of Dr. Arthur C. Ford on Alabama Street quite near to the site pictured here, adjacent to the old Atlanta rail yard.

along the east side of what today is the long-abandoned *Macon & Western Railroad* tracks right-of-way. Holliday subsequently sold 136 acres at this site to Confederate authorities for the creation of Confederate Camp Stephens and retained 11 acres for his home. He then purchased an additional 278 acres outside the bounds of Camp Stephens for a total of 289 acres in his plantation where he planted Sea Island cotton and corn. Henry Holliday's 289-acre plantation was then bounded on the west by the *Macon & Western Railroad*, and on the east by Camp Stephens.

"Holliday Creek" which rises from the large natural spring on Maj. Holliday's property, almost certainly was the site of the much-debated "swimming hole incident" – again, if it ever occurred

Doc's Atlanta Office" - Photographed either on a hazy or somewhat dusty day, Alabama Street in downtown Atlanta is pictured circa early 1920s. At the far end of the street, the Georgia Railroad freight depot topped with its distinctive cupola is visible. It was completed in 1869. This view, looking southeastward down Alabama, was taken from Whitehall (Peachtree) Street, and shows Alabama prior to construction of the concrete viaducts built in the late 1920s to bridge "railroad gulch" in downtown Atlanta. Newly-lettered "Dr." John Henry Holliday was a dental surgeon in the offices of Dr. Arthur C. Ford, whose practice was located on the southeast corner of the dark building (far right margin). Following construction of the viaducts system, the lower level of the structures to the right disappeared beneath the concrete overlays. Many of the lower levels of these buildings survived beneath the concrete as the structures above them were modernized. The street-view of the buildings on the right later became much of the infrastructure of the popular 1970s and '80s Atlanta attraction "Underground Atlanta," and still exist beneath the viaducts today.

at all – although it would, by virtue of the time-period, have involved a much younger John Henry Holliday who could not have been more than 12 years of age at the time.

According to Bat Masterson's 1907 *Human Life* article on the swimming hole incident, *"The Negro boys were informed that in the future, they would have to go further down the 'stream' to do their swimming, which they promptly refused to do, telling the Whites that if they didn't like existing conditions, that they would have to hunt up a new swimming hole."* Defiance of this nature from Black slaves in 1860s Confederate Georgia

– particularly as involved someone else's private property – would have been highly unlikely, which, again, makes the occurrence of this presumed incident suspect at best – but it, nevertheless, made a good story.

If this incident in fact did occur, there were a number of different scenarios which might have transpired. At the top of the list would have to be the possible altercation between John Henry Holliday and the aforementioned Blacks. The "swimming hole," however, was located on Holliday property, so if this did occur, young John Henry would have been well within his rights

A city policeman in the center of old Alabama Street (prior to construction of the immense concrete viaducts over "railroad gulch" in old downtown Atlanta in the late 1920s) stares balefully toward the cameraman. This photograph, taken in 1895, was approximately 20 years after John Henry Holliday was a dental surgeon in this neighborhood, and shows the old cobblestoned streets and a view up old Alabama Street toward the intersection with Pryor Street. "Doc" Holliday's dental practice was in the offices of Dr. Arthur C. Ford at the beginning of the next block (beyond Pryor) up the hill at the intersection with Whitehall (Peachtree) Street. This same cobblestone street and the lower level of these buildings can still be viewed today beneath the concrete viaducts in this vicinity which later became the popular 1970s and 1980s entertainment complex known as "Underground Atlanta." Doc Holliday lived and worked in this neighborhood for a couple of years prior to migrating to Texas and beyond where he earned lasting fame in the old West.

to order any trespassers from his father's property. And if said trespassers threatened the youngster, he would have been well within his rights even to fire warning shots to ward them off, particularly in Confederate Georgia.

Scenario number two would involve a group of Whites trespassing at the swimming hole who likewise refused to depart the Holliday property and who likewise were warded off with warning shots. There was at least one White family – that of William and Lucinda Bates – who lived on property directly across the railroad tracks from the Holliday tract who had male children of ages 17 and 19, as well as two other males of ages 12 and 14 in the household, all of whom would have been of the "bully" age at this time, and no doubt often patronizing the swimming hole. John Henry, once again, would have been well within his rights to demand their departure from the spot if this formed the basis of the scenario. It, however, would not include the racial component, so it no doubt would have gone with little mention beyond the actual occurrence of the incident.

And finally, if this incident ever occurred at all (because as detailed above, the original reference sources used by

Known in John Henry Holliday's day as "the Iron Front Building," this structure which still stands in downtown Griffin, Georgia, as of this writing (2024) was once partially owned by Doc Holliday. He inherited this building from his mother's estate upon her death, and briefly set up a dental practice here in the summer of 1872. It was at this approximate time that he quite likely learned of the tuberculosis he had contracted in his lungs. The prospect of a career in Georgia was soon dimmed for him by his disease, and he subsequently traveled to the western United States where he began life anew. (Photo by Jackie Kennedy)

those describing this presumed incident were, at best, highly suspect or nonexistent), it most certainly did not involve any deaths or injuries, since no mention is made of any such injuries or deaths in either the newspapers or court records of either Lowndes or Spalding counties or the towns of Valdosta or Griffin, and John Henry – if involved at all – almost certainly would have been more than justified in his actions in that day and time anyway.

Also as explained above, all of this would have been occurring with a John Henry Holliday who was not more than 12 years of age, since the Holliday family only resided in Griffin for the initial twelve years of John Henry's life, so he would have been barely more than a youngster at the time anyway, even though he quite likely would have been well-versed in the use of firearms by age 12.

All these things having been said, the "swimming hole incident" and its highly-publicized racial component quite likely did not occur at all, and even if it did, John Henry Holliday would have been well within his rights for being involved in such an incident, and little more than a youngster to boot. It would therefore appear that this presumed incident was, in all likelihood, nothing more than a sensationalized event wrapped in a non-existent racial component.

The Atlanta Dental Practice

Much of Atlanta's former White-hall Street is today named Peachtree Street (since it, in fairness, is basically the south end of that famed avenue). The building at the southeast corner of Alabama and Whitehall/Peachtree streets is not the one which once housed the dental offices of doctors Ford and Holliday, but it is the site at which John Henry "Doc" Holliday set up his first "recorded" dental practice in Georgia.

In Doc's day, Peachtree Street ended and Whitehall Street began at the east-west juncture of the *Macon & Western Railroad* at this site *(which interestingly is the same railroad which passed through his father's property at John Henry's boyhood home in Griffin, Georgia).* "Railroad Gulch" still exists at this site in Atlanta today, but it is partly covered over and virtually obscured on the east side by viaducts and bridges which hide much of the rail yard which was so visibly portrayed in the epic and major motion picture *Gone With the Wind.*

Unbeknownst to many, remnants of the former site of Holliday's practice were still extant in the former popular 1960s and '70s entertainment complex once known as *Underground Atlanta.* Cobblestoned portions of Alabama and Whitehall streets still exist there beneath the viaducts even today, as do the lower level/basement sections once comprising some of Atlanta's original commercial buildings.

In Doc's day (1870s), the Whitehall Street district formed the "Deadline" section of town "on the south side of the tracks." Saloons and bordellos proliferated there, and, in a short period of time, these came to be heavily patronized by John Henry. The legend of the "Doc Holliday" known in Western lore was born and bred in this neighborhood. Did his eventual debauched behavior in Atlanta begin after his discovery of the fatal disease he carried in his lungs? Possibly. Likely.

The *Hanleiter City Directory* for the year 1870 lists a total of twenty saloons and bars in Atlanta. Fourteen of the twenty are clustered in the blocks just south of the railroad on Alabama, Hunter (present-day Martin Luther King Street), Mitchell, Broad, and Whitehall Streets. The fourteen saloons are: ME. Kenny, T.F. Grady, Dan Fleck, G. Hentschel, N.M. Robinson, Steadman and Kreis, J.L. Griffin, H. Muhlenbrink, M.E. Maher, D. Wallace, Michael Haverty, Frantz Eddleman, John Gaven, and Jake Emmel. "Muhlenbrink's Saloon" was one of the storefronts which survived beneath the viaducts and which was later renovated and reused in the *Underground Atlanta* complex. This structure, quite possibly frequented by John Henry, likely still exists there even today.

In the years 1870 to 1874 (excluding 1873 for which there was no listing), a grand total of forty-six saloons operated south of Railroad Gulch. The bulk of Atlanta's non-Whitehall Street saloons listed in *Hanleiter's* were located in the mid-town district just north of the railroad.

The Dodge House – When John Henry arrived in Dodge City, Kansas, sometime around 1878, he took up residence in the Dodge House, a popular rooming facility in town. As with most Western burgs in those days of the old frontier, Dodge was a rough and tumble town full of cattle drovers and hard-nosed drifters, some of whom occasionally challenged Holliday until his reputation began preceding him.

The exact time that the dissolution from drinking, gambling, and womanizing took possession of John Henry's life is unknown today (yet another gap in his collective history), but it quite probably is fair to say it began with the severance of his professional partnership with Dr. Arthur C. Ford. At some point no more than a year after the initiation of their promising dental practice, Dr. Ford decided that he had erred in the assumption of a business relationship with his young protégé, sending John Henry Holliday adrift into the unknown.

After alcoholism took over his life, John Henry apparently pursued the lure of the gambling tables to an even greater extent, until his depravities had robbed him of any financial security he might have previously enjoyed. At this point, his inheritance of the Iron Front Building in Griffin from his late mother no doubt became a much-needed sudden windfall which allowed him to continue without a steady job.

As explained above, he apparently

Longbranch Saloon – The Longbranch in Dodge City was nowhere near as impressive as the descriptions passed down in folklore and created on the film sets of television westerns. In the actual structure (pictured), Doc, the Earp brothers, Bat Masterson, Bill Tilghman and many other notables from the history of the old West passed many hours drinking, gambling and carousing in this former Kansas cow-town. (Courtesy of Kansas State Historical Society, Topeka, Kansas)

made a brief attempt at resuming a professional dental career in Griffin, but it was short-lived. The incident or incidents which had culminated in the termination of his relationship with Dr. Ford apparently had poisoned any further hope for employment in Atlanta or environs. After, all, no one wished to go into partnership with a drunken ne'er-do-well, nor did patients wish to have their teeth pulled or cavities drilled out by such a dentist.

As a result, at some point, John Henry Holliday was forced to face the conclusion that Atlanta and Georgia held little to no further allure for him. Realizing that he needed to depart for a site where he might "begin anew," he set out for Texas, eventually winding up in Dallas.

Did this departure from Georgia coincide with his debauched behavior and the ruination of his professional

career opportunities in Georgia; or was it the result of a tortured romance with his cousin Martha Anne "Mattie" Holliday; or was it in fact the diagnosis of his contraction of the terrible incurable disease known as tuberculosis which spurred his travel westward? We'll never know, because he kept few if any letters or records on matters of this nature, and the reason or reasons for his relocation to the West became yet another gap in the collective record of the life of John Henry Holliday.

Cousin Mattie Holliday

Much has been made down through history of the reason or reasons for the departure of famed Western gunman John Henry "Doc" Holliday from Georgia. Was it due to a dissolution of his professional career as a result of an addiction to liquor and the gambling dens of Atlanta? Or was it due to a "swimming hole incident" in which he supposedly had maimed or killed one or more arrogant Negroes? Or was it due to a star-crossed romance with a cousin which sent her into a Convent for the remainder of her life and him into banishment from his home state of Georgia for the remainder of his life? Or was it due to the incurable disease which he knew would dramatically shorten his life? As explained above, the simple answer to this is: We'll never know.

Martha Anne "Mattie" Holliday, the daughter of John Henry's uncle – Robert K. Holliday – was Doc's soulmate and playmate in the early years of his life, and his confidant until the day he died on a cold winter day in Glenwood Springs, Colorado in 1887. She was the one to whom he told his secrets, and the one with whom he formed a bond which endured for the remainder of both of their lives.

How deep was this relationship? The blessed few inklings offered by John Henry during his lifetime revealed nothing more than an unbreakable bond strongly akin to – if not the actual condition of – deep and affectionate love.

John Henry talked of her sparingly to others during his lifetime, but from the scant comments he did make, it was clear that she was extremely important to his life and that he deeply regretted the fact that they had been separated for life.

Unbeknownst by many, John Henry and Mattie (or "Sister Melanie" as she became known after making a life-time commitment to a Convent) communicated often by letter. And Mattie saved all of these letters, right up until the time of John Henry's death, when she made the decision to burn them. She later deeply regretted destroying the letters, stating, *"Had the letters from John been*

Mary Katherine "Big Nose Kate" Harony, Doc's consort during much of his time in the West, was photographed here circa 1869. Though ultimately bereft of any beauty and maligned in her later years, she was not unattractive as an adolescent. (Boyer Collection, Sharlot Hall Museum Archives)

retained, the world would have known a much different man from that described in books and magazine articles."

So what happened? What caused Mattie to commit her life to a Catholic Convent and him to commit his life to that of an alcoholic gambler drifting across the Old West? We'll likely never know the answer to those questions either. Still more gaps in John Henry "Doc" Holliday's life history.

Actual Site of His Grave

Also contrary to popular myth and modern movie portrayals, Doc Holliday did not die in the Glenwood Springs "Sanitarium." There was no sanitarium in Glenwood Springs in 1887. Doc

Another view of the Dodge House, looking west down Front Street in Dodge City, Kansas. This photo was taken in 1874, just four years prior to Holliday's arrival in the town. (Courtesy of Kansas State Historical Society, Topeka)

Holliday died in his room in the Hotel Glenwood.

Mystery seems to have followed Doc right into the grave. The actual site of his burial is not known today. There is a Doc Holliday gravesite in Linwood Cemetery outside Glenwood Springs, but it is an acknowledged fact that many historians believe Doc Holliday is not buried there. Even the cemetery records state only that it is believed that he is *"buried somewhere in this cemetery."*

On the day of Doc's funeral, the weather reportedly was bitterly cold. Along with John Henry, one other recently-deceased gentleman was to be buried in Linwood Cemetery on the same day. On the day of the burials, the trail up to the cemetery was completely impassable, and, as a result, Doc and the other deceased individual reportedly were buried by the side of the road *"somewhere along the route up to the cemetery,"* the intention being that they would

be exhumed in the spring and re-buried within the actual cemetery.

The following spring, however, things changed a bit. The individual buried beside Doc apparently had family in the Glenwood Springs area who readily paid to have their loved one dug up and re-buried in Linwood. Doc, however, had no family in the area, and according to reports, no one was forthcoming to pay the fee to have him exhumed and re-buried. He, therefore, according to most reports, was left buried beside the road.

As the years passed, local residents came and went and died out, and the actual site of the grave of famed John Henry Holliday was simply lost to time. It was only in the mid- to late-20th century that local residents – realizing the historic and tourism-related value of Doc's burial site – began trying to re-locate his grave.

Despite considerable efforts toward

this attempted relocation, the positive identification of John Henry's gravesite has completely eluded researchers and historians. Today, the mortal remains of Dr. John Henry Holliday from Griffin and Valdosta, Georgia, possibly exist beneath someone's back porch or in someone's yard on the route up to Linwood Cemetery.

Other accounts, however, differ with the above scenario. According to one, Doc's remains were indeed later dug up and re-buried in Linwood Cemetery, where they exist today. Another account maintains that they were dug up, but were transported – via the new railroad in Glenwood Springs – back to Georgia in the late 1880s, where they were re-buried in an unmarked grave in Griffin, Doc's birthplace. If the remains in the unmarked grave in Griffin are excavated and examined via DNA analysis and for a tubercular condition, a connection to John Henry might be finally established. Time will tell.

In 1879, a few years after his arrival out West, Holliday had this full-length photograph taken while he was living in Prescott, Arizona. At the time, he was rooming with Richard E. Elliott, and John J. Gosper, the acting-governor of Arizona Territory. (Photo courtesy of Craig Fouts)

John Henry Holliday's Last Georgia Possession

Dallas, Deadwood, Dodge City, Tombstone.... The names evoke images of the wild, wild West and the now legendary world of Old West figures such as "Doc" Holliday. John Henry, however, had another world as well – a Southern world in Georgia where he once lived and worked, and of which remnants still exist today.

These sites include landmarks like the home of his uncle, Dr. John Stiles Holliday, in Fayetteville, Georgia, where the future gunman often visited with his cousin, Mattie; the former Holliday home in Griffin, Georgia, where he was born and lived the early portion of his life; the former Holliday home in

Valdosta, Georgia, to which his family refugeed in 1864, fleeing the on-coming juggernaut of Gen. William T. Sherman; and the Griffin, Georgia office building – known collectively as "the Iron Front Building" and "the Merritt Building" – where a young Dr. John H. Holliday reportedly once practiced dentistry a short time.

It is a matter of legal record that the Iron Front building on Griffin's historic Solomon Street was a portion of John Henry's inheritance from his mother, Alice Jane McKey Holliday. When Alice Jane died in 1867, the building was passed to thirteen-year-old John, with his father, Henry Burroughs Holliday, acting as his guardian over the property until he became "of age."

Montezuma Street Digs – Pictured is North Montezuma Street in Prescott in 1881. An 1879 Arizona Territory Census records Holliday's address as Montezuma Street where he, John J. Gosper, 39, and Richard E. Elliott, 45, were listed as rooming together. Elliott was known as a good friend of Virgil Earp, and Gosper, the acting governor of Arizona Territory. The boarding house pictured here, photographed in Prescott, is believed to have been the one in which Holliday, Gosper and Elliott roomed. (Sharlot Hall Museum Archives, Prescott, AZ)

A Family Rift

A short three months later, Henry Burroughs shocked the Holliday family by quickly remarrying. The unusually-quick remarriage caused a rift within the family, which, in turn, also surprisingly caused John Henry's relatives on his mother's side – the McKeys – to file suit against the Hollidays in an attempt to reclaim what they felt was "McKey property."

The suit was brought by John Henry's (Doc's) uncle, Tom McKey, and was tried in the Lowndes County courthouse in Valdosta. Ironically, this is the same uncle who Doc so admired, and whose name he later used as an alias to disguise his own identity while in Colorado. Even more surprising is the fact that the case, *McKey vs Holliday*, ultimately

proved to be at least a partially-successful suit, causing Alice Jane's estate to be divided equally between the McKey and Holliday families.

This unique settlement included the Merritt/Iron Front building in Griffin, of which ownership was likewise divided equally between the McKeys and John Henry. The legal solution had been to literally create a partition down through the middle of the building from roof to basement, with the eastern half being returned to McKey ownership, and the western half remaining as John Henry's legal inheritance. Though this suit and subsequent settlement obviously denied John Henry a substantial portion of his "legal" inheritance, history does not record his reaction to the decision or to his McKey relatives who prevailed in the case.

It is likewise unknown today just how John Henry's mother, Alice Jane, came to own such a substantial downtown Griffin property as the Merritt/Iron Front building. It presumably had been in the family for a number of years, with Alice Jane inheriting it following the death of another member of her family who had owned it.

Impressive Asset

Any way one looks at it, the Merritt/Iron Front was certainly a property worth fighting for. It was an impressive structure, two stories high with an iron infrastructure (and thus its name) beneath its fancy red brick façade. Both floors of the building had long multi-paned windows facing the street in Doc's day. They allowed the morning sunlight to stream into the rooms with their hardwood floors and pressed-tin trimmed ceilings.

At the rear of the main floor, a huge mechanical lift carried merchandise from the loading dock to the second floor sales offices. In Doc's day, the Iron Front was leased out as shop space to various businesses, and brought in good income in rents.

Henry Burroughs Holliday continued his guardianship of the property until his son reached the age of 21 in the summer of 1872, allowing him to legally take possession of his inheritance. At that time, John Henry had just graduated from dental school in Philadelphia, and was working in the Atlanta dental office of Dr. Arthur C. Ford on Alabama Street in the vicinity of old downtown Atlanta adjacent to what once was known as 'railroad gulch.'

With his own office building, John Henry enjoyed the unique distinction of being able to immediately open his own dental practice in his hometown, Griffin. It is therefore believed today that he in fact did return to Griffin and open a small practice there for a brief time.

John Henry registered his ownership of the Iron Front building in the Spalding County Deed Book in November of 1872. According to old-time Griffin residents, he also did a modest amount of remodeling to the building, adding an exterior iron staircase which rose from the alley beside the building up to the little second floor office where he set up his practice.

Validation of Doc's Griffin Practice?

According to researcher Gene Carlisle in his *Why Doc Holliday Left Georgia*, "It is possible that Doc Holliday – in 1872 or '73, returned to Griffin, Georgia, the city of his youth, and there practiced dentistry for a brief duration in an office in the Merritt Building (a.k.a. 'Iron Front Building') on Solomon Street. A

Original Edifices – Though the streets are paved today and new buildings have filled in spots where older structures had succumbed to neglect or one of the town's three major fires over the years, Allen (Main) Street in Tombstone is otherwise little-changed from the days of Doc Holliday and Wyatt Earp. A number of the original structures in this very historic former silver-mining town still stand. (Photo by Olin Jackson)

vivid account, penned by the late Griffinite, Judge L.P. Goodrich, has withstood the test of time and numerous assaults by diligent researchers who failed to strike it down. Judge Goodrich's account is excerpted as follows:

'One evening when I was a boy, my father looked up from the newspaper which he had been reading, and said, "Doc Holliday is dead." His tone indicated that he knew Doc Holliday, and that his death was a matter of regret. So I inquired who Doc Holliday was. I was informed that Doc was an old Griffin boy, the son of Major H.B. Holliday, who had lived in Griffin prior to the War Between the States.

'Major Holliday had moved to Valdosta when his son was a small boy, but Doc Holliday (had later) returned to Griffin after the war and practiced dentistry here in an office in the old Merritt Building where Dr. Hopkins now is. While in Griffin, Doc Holliday developed tuberculosis, and went to Arizona, where he became famous – not as an outlaw, but

Wyatt Berry Stapp Earp was born in 1848 and died in 1929. Doc Holliday saved Wyatt's life on at least one, and possibly two separate occasions, a fact that Wyatt never forgot. He and Doc, as a result, became life-long friends. They had parted in Tucson in 1879, when Wyatt – with several of his brothers – relocated to the booming silver-mining town of Tombstone. Doc, however, also soon departed Tucson as well for Tombstone where he and the Earps ultimately joined forces to defeat a group of semi-outlaws known as the Cow Boys.

as the relentless foe of the outlaws on that wild frontier. The description which my father gave of this singular person, whom he (obviously had known) intimately, established him in my imagination as a hero.'"

Sudden Departure

Dr. John Henry Holliday's shingle, however, didn't hang in Griffin very long. Just a few months later in January of 1873, he suddenly sold his half of the Merritt/Iron Front building, and by October of that year, records indicate he was practicing dentistry in faraway Dallas, Texas – the first stop "Doc" made in his countless western wanderings.

What was the motivation for John Henry to suddenly sell his hard-won inheritance and leave Georgia only a few months after opening his dental practice in Griffin? Some sources have argued it was the tuberculosis with which he had been diagnosed – supposedly by his uncle, Dr. John Stiles Holliday – earlier that year. Others claim it was a star-crossed romance with his cousin, Mattie Holliday (daughter of Capt. Robert Kennedy Holliday) from which Doc was running. Still others maintain there were various other motivations for his departure.

Whatever the circumstances, vestiges and memories of Doc Holliday remain strong in his Georgia homeland. And visitors to the little second-floor office in Griffin's Iron Front building constantly imagine what it was like in the days of yesteryear, when a fearless Old West gunfighter was a simple dentist in a sleepy Southern town.

Leaving the "Old South" for the "Old West"

Though he was a native son of the old South, John Henry Holliday earned lasting fame in the old West in the 1880s.

He was born August 14, 1851, in Georgia's Spalding County in the small town of Griffin. In 1864, with the advancing devastation being wrought by Gen. William T. Sherman's dogs of war as they burned their way through north Georgia during the U.S. Civil War, Maj. Henry Burroughs Holliday relocated his family to the relative safety of southeast Georgia's Lowndes County where 13-year-old John Henry spent the remainder of his formative years, attending the Valdosta Institute and, upon graduation, leaving Georgia to attend the Pennsylvania College of Dental Surgery in Philadelphia.

Following graduation from medical school and a return to Georgia for a short stint to practice dentistry in Atlanta, "Doc" began a vagabond journey to the West, never again to return to Georgia. He traveled to and took up temporary residence in many towns of the old West. Places such as Dallas, Fort Griffin and Jacksboro, Texas; Pueblo, Leadville, Glenwood Springs and Denver, Colorado; Cheyenne, Wyoming; Deadwood, South Dakota (He reportedly was there when his friend, James Butler Hickok, was murdered); Dodge City, Kansas; Las Vegas, New Mexico; Prescott, Tucson and Tombstone, Arizona; and numerous others all witnessed the comings and goings of the famous Georgian. No town held him or his interest more than two or three years.

Despite all these travels, it was the town of Tombstone, Arizona Territory which truly defined him. The years he spent in this fast-growing gold mining town in the desert – while he was still reasonably healthy – earned him the bulk of his lasting fame. And it was for these years that he is best remembered.

By the early 1990s – with the Hollywood releases of major motion pictures such as *Tombstone* (1993) starring Val Kilmer, Kurt Russell, and Sam Elliott – the name "Doc" Holliday had reached almost mythic proportions in the folklore of America, but it was not always so. After the initial newspaper coverage of the actual shoot-out behind the O.K. Corral in Tombstone in October of 1881, much of the fame of Wyatt Earp; his brothers James, Virgil, Morgan and Warren; and Doc Holliday, died out over the ensuing years. After the huge water pump at the Tombstone silver mines failed and the price of silver plummeted in the late 1880s, the town had withered and died, and the exploits of the Earps and Doc

Morgan Earp, younger brother of Wyatt, was born in 1851, the same year as Doc. The happy-go-lucky Morgan offered much more of a friendship to Holliday than did the dour Wyatt and Virgil, and the two spent considerable time in Tombstone drinking, carousing, and protecting each other in what was quickly becoming a very dangerous environment. Doc was particularly bereaved when Morgan was murdered in Campbell & Hatch Saloon in Tombstone in 1882. He ultimately sought vengeance – with Wyatt – upon Morgan's murderers. (Glenn G. Boyer Collection)

Holliday were almost completely forgotten for almost 75 years.

Old Tombstone Today

By the 1890s in Tombstone, most of the miners had departed Cochise County (which included Tombstone). Since the town was located in the middle of the desert, most people just boarded up their homes or stores and left on horseback, in buckboards, and covered wagons. Most of them also simply abandoned in Tombstone most of their possessions which wouldn't fit into a covered wagon.

The Bird Cage Theater – Though not built until December of 1881, this popular site of entertainment was patronized by most of the clientele of Tombstone, including Holliday and the Earps prior to their departure from the town. Today, the Bird Cage is one of numerous original structures still standing from the days of the Old West in Tombstone. After being boarded up and abandoned for 40+ years, this historic building was reopened as a tourist attraction in the 1960s, and still contains many of its original furnishings. (Photo by Olin Jackson)

Though Tombstone did get regular passenger train service on April 5, 1903, this was long after the good ol' days of the town had come and gone.

As a result, Tombstone – despite the damage caused by two major fires – remained for many years much as Holliday and the Earps had left it. There really wasn't any way to steal or even freely take substantial quantities of the relics left in Tombstone. Few were willing to chance it across the desert.

The now-quiet, dusty, and virtual ghost-town lay dormant in this manner for well over half a century – until the 1950s when American servicemen at nearby Fort Huachuca began taking weekend excursions to the historic site. It was also about this same time that several writers – following the success of a nationally-broadcast Western television series based upon the life of Wyatt Earp – realized the value in publishing the biographies of the old West icons from this vicinity.

Luckily, the handful of local townspeople who remained in Tombstone – which had quite literally receded into virtual ghost-town status by the 1950s – eventually realized they had a money-maker on their hands. They banded together and created a historic district out of the town, preserving it for future generations – and for the income it could generate.

A number of the very structures which the Earps, Doc Holliday, Buckskin Frank Leslie, William Barclay "Bat" Masterson, Ike Clanton, Johnny Ringo, Texas John Slaughter, the McLaury brothers, Turkey Creek Jack Johnson, Texas Jack Vermilion and a host of other famous and notorious figures of the old West had frequented, amazingly still stand even today in Tombstone.

Portions of the original O.K. Corral site have survived, though much of it was destroyed by the aforementioned fires. The original Wells-Fargo building also still exists, as does the billiard parlor (though re-built) in which Morgan Earp was murdered.

Though also heavily damaged by fire in 1882, the Crystal Palace Saloon was rebuilt that same year. It was here and in the Oriental Saloon which once existed across the street that Holliday, the Earps and most of the other aforementioned historic figures spent much time in the 1880s, gambling, drinking, fighting and carousing. The rebuilt Crystal Palace may still be visited today as well. Even the home once owned and inhabited by Virgil Earp on First Street still stands (as of this writing in 2024), as do the bank, and other structures.

The Birdcage Theatre is another of the original prominent relics from that day. Built in December of 1881, it was a popular place to enjoy bawdy women, gambling, theatrical productions, and other forms of adult entertainment in old Tombstone. It, amazingly, has been virtually completely preserved – with full original furnishings – from the days when it was frequented by all the above-described historic figures – a virtual museum of relics from the famed silver-mining town.

A Life In The West

John Henry Holliday was 21 in 1872, when he departed Georgia to begin his travels in the West. Interestingly, though doctors had advised that he had but a year or two left to live due to the tuberculosis in his lungs, he, in fact, lived for 15 more years, and in the interim, traveled throughout the last frontier in the continental United States, earning a well-deserved reputation as one of the deadliest gunmen walking the dusty streets of the old West.

Holliday has frequently been accused in print and folklore of being testy and irritable, but these likely were traits he acquired in his growing impatience with anyone unlucky enough to be perceived as wasting the Georgian's rapidly-diminishing time on this earth. It also didn't help matters that he liberally and regularly indulged in the "devil-water" of the West. In retrospect, who wouldn't have been short-tempered under these circumstances?

Holliday also was known to be very gracious to those who were courteous to him, and his honor was the most valuable asset he possessed. When bullied or persecuted as a result of his frail condition and appearance, Doc invariably proved to be a game opponent – and even seemed to welcome a good "knock-down, drag-out," even though he, more

Oriental Saloon – This corner site (above) was once occupied by the Oriental Saloon in which Wyatt Earp owned and operated a gambling concession in 1881, and in which Doc Holliday gambled and became embroiled in several gunfights that year. The Oriental was also the site of a vicious brawl between Holliday and saloon owner Milt Joyce in which Doc - always gamely-ready to defend himself despite his weakened condition - was beaten unconscious. In the street (left foreground), Tombstone Marshal Virgil Earp was shot and crippled for life in an assassination attempt on the evening of December 28, 1881, as he walked from the Oriental on his way to the Crystal Palace Saloon on the opposite side of the street. The Oriental Saloon was consumed by the Tombstone fire of 1882. (Photo by Olin Jackson)

often than not, suffered the brunt of any injuries in these affairs. For that reason, he ultimately became quite adept in the use of firearms and knives for self-defense.

Though he often used what was known as a "pocket holster" (actually a reinforced pocket in his coat for carrying the heavy revolvers which dominated as weapons of that day), Doc Holliday was one of the first gunmen to use the new-fangled "shoulder holster." His weapon of choice early in his western career was an 1851 Colt Navy

Golden Eagle Brewery – Originally built in 1879 as the Golden Eagle Brewery, this saloon was burned in the devastating 1882 Tombstone fire, but was immediately rebuilt that year in the same spot and renamed the Crystal Palace Saloon. This was one of John Henry Holliday's favorite haunts in Tombstone. (Photo by Olin Jackson)

revolver given to him by his uncle. Holliday later carried a nickel-plated .41 caliber Colt *Thunderer* which usually found refuge in his shoulder holster.

It has been documented in testimony from both Wyatt Earp and Bat Masterson that with these weapons, Doc Holliday was one of the deadliest shots that they both had ever known. His considerable reputation for adeptness with weapons eventually began preceding him wherever his travels took him, earning him respect from bullies much larger and stronger than he who normally would have quickly overpowered him.

Despite his ill-luck in the contraction of tuberculosis, John Henry Holliday lived what might otherwise be called a charmed life. Although he was involved in quite a few gunfights and other affrays during his days in the old West,

he managed to avoid death's door from these affairs, though he was wounded at least twice – once seriously. At the O.K. Corral gunfight in which he was credited with the death of at least one and possibly two of the opponents, a round from one of the McLaury revolvers grazed the pocket holster (in his coat) on his hip, causing him to suffer a bad bruise and a painful limp for several days, but little else. Few other prominent gunmen of the old West – Earp and Masterson interestingly being two exceptions – endured this life without being killed. Wyatt Earp, amazingly, was never even wounded.

All four of Wyatt's brothers were seriously wounded at some point in their lives, and two of them were killed in gunfire. His brother Morgan was assassinated in Tombstone in 1882, and Warren was murdered in 1900 in a bar-fight in Wilcox, Arizona, just a few miles away. (Even though no one was arrested or charged in the incident, nor any inquest ever held, one can safely claim Warren was "murdered," since he was unarmed at the time, and the .45 round fired at him was most intentional.)

James Butler "Wild Bill" Hickok was killed in Deadwood, South Dakota. Johnny Ringo and most of the Clantons and McLaurys were killed in and around Tombstone in the 1880s. William "Billy the Kid" Bonney was killed in New Mexico in 1881. Jesse James, Pat Garrett, Butch Cassidy and the Sundance Kid, Billy Claiborne and many others all also met with equally bloody deaths at about this same time. Doc, Wyatt, and Masterson, however, seemed almost invulnerable to bullets, despite their lifestyles.

A Friendship With Earp

Doc and Wyatt had become fast friends in Dodge City, Kansas, while

Crystal Palace Saloon – This view of Allen Street (looking west) in Tombstone was photographed in 1880. Despite being a silver-strike boomtown, the oppressive heat of Arizona forced the town's inhabitants to remain inside saloons, restaurants and other businesses as much as possible during the height of each day. This view, at the intersection of 5th and Allen streets, shows the Eagle Brewery (right) with the Crystal Palace Saloon occupying the lower level of the building. This saloon was a favorite of Holliday's, and he spent many hours here drinking and gambling. Though this structure was partially burned in the fire of 1882, it was quickly rebuilt.

Wyatt was a deputy city marshal there. Holliday reportedly came to Wyatt's rescue (possibly saving his life) on at least two separate occasions – once in Dodge, and once again later in Tombstone – and Wyatt never forgot it. Though they quarreled in 1882 and went their separate ways, the two men nevertheless remained close friends to the end.

Wyatt was quoted as saying he enjoyed Doc's company because the clever dentist *"makes me laugh."* Doc was indeed known to have quite a sense of humor, as well as a love of practical jokes. According to one documented account, on one occasion when a stranger rode into Tombstone wearing a fancy suit and derby hat, Doc reportedly followed him throughout the town, gleefully tinkling a miniature sterling silver hand-held dinner bell everywhere the man went

– much to the well-dressed gentleman's uncomfortable chagrin.

There is so much history in the little town of Tombstone, that one would be well-advised to spend at least a weekend in explorations there if ever a visit is made to this historic site. Above and beyond the commercial buildings and homes in the town associated with Holliday and the Earps, many other sites in that vicinity were often frequented by other individuals who later gained fame on the frontier.

The Earps had traveled to Tombstone specifically in search of gambling and gold mining opportunities. Holliday, too, made the arduous trip to this desert town which had not only become renowned for its gold and silver mines, but for the plethora of gambling opportunities as well. Indeed, he spent most of his years beyond his 21st birthday in

The interior of the Crystal Palace Saloon was photographed here in the 1880s. This photograph, no doubt, was taken by the town's venerable photographer, Camillus S. Fly, in whose rooming house Doc Holliday took up quarters several blocks away, during his stay in Tombstone.

search of the pleasures of life because, as a doctor, he was well aware of the premature aging and early death which accompanied the dreaded tuberculosis from which he suffered. He had watched in angst as his mother before him – whom he dearly loved – had suffered greatly from the same disease before finally succumbing to it.

Doc's adventures in Arizona Territory were many and varied. He was accompanied by his consort Katherine "Big-Nose Kate" Harony. The early days in Tombstone were a time of fun and delight for Holliday, but a criminal element composed of the Clantons, McLaurys, Johnny Ringo, and others eventually required the Earps – and thus also Doc – to take up arms against them.

Ultimately, in their last days in the Tombstone area in 1882, Doc, Wyatt Earp, Warren Earp, Texas Jack Vermillion, Turkey Creek Jack Johnson, Sherman McMasters, Dan Tipton, and

a handful of other close friends began what was known as *"the Vendetta Ride."* They in essence hunted down the outlaws who had assassinated one Earp (Morgan) and maimed another (Virgil) for life and who had been protected for years by a corrupt judicial system in Cochise County. Months later, after much of the outlaw element had been "eliminated" (by what has been described by some as "vigilante justice"), Doc, Wyatt, and Warren began an odyssey across the West in a search for further adventure and income opportunities.

Doc, with the remainder of the Vendetta cabal, drifted east to New Mexico Territory. At this point, the men reportedly separated. Turkey Creek Jack Johnson and Texas Jack Vermillion struck out on their own and faded into history. Eventually, Doc, Wyatt, Warren and Tipton drifted northward up to Colorado, to the gold and silver mining towns which offered a better refuge from the Arizona authorities, and an opportunity for income from the multitude of gambling endeavors always attendant to this industry.

John Henry traveled for a time with Wyatt and Warren before striking out on his own. The Earps – at least Wyatt – didn't mind camping out and sleeping upon the cold hard ground in the mountains of Colorado as they evaded Arizona law enforcement authorities, but John Henry Holliday was accustomed to a slightly more refined life, and his extreme illness reinforced this need for more hospitable circumstances. He therefore exchanged this "uncivil" existence of camping and/or otherwise "roughing it in the mountains" for the bright lights and comfortable gambling mecca of Denver. The Earps and Tipton spent the summer of 1882 in Gunnison, with Doc traveling down from Denver to visit them there for a brief time.

For the rest of their days, both Doc and Wyatt did little more than travel and enjoy life. Neither of them ever owned a home after leaving Tombstone (Doc never owned a home at all, preferring to live in hotels and rooming houses his entire adult life), and they both literally went wherever the wind blew them.

The Lonely Years

In the ensuing years, John Henry Holliday essentially traveled alone. He had abandoned his female consort – "Big Nose" Katherine Harony – but continued to frequent the mining towns where quick money and poorly-schooled gamblers often offered steady income. The locations of these gold and silver-strike meccas invariably involved the extremes of nature – either the horrendous heat of the desert, or the freezing cold of the 12,000-foot Rocky Mountains. Each new extreme took its toll on the stamina of Doc Holliday.

The Georgian also was extremely limited by this point in his options for income. He now had such a reputation as "a lunger" that he was completely unable to ply his original trade as a dentist. The gambling opportunities in gold and silver-mining towns had long ago become his sole source of income.... and it was a lonely preoccupation. Despite his adeptness at various modes of gambling, John Henry wasn't the only professional on the circuit, so the "pickings" weren't always so easy.

Traveling from town to town and saloon to saloon, Doc was able to maintain a reasonably steady income for several of the ensuing years, but with each new town, his physical appearance more and more became that of one who was weaker and weaker. This ultimately attracted a growing line-up of individuals suddenly willing to challenge the Georgian, hoping to earn the acclaim which would come with ending the life of the famed "Doc Holliday."

And not only was he meeting new challengers, the fact that his travels were predominantly confined to gold and silver mining towns meant that he inevitably began meeting old enemies from his Tombstone days as well.

Confrontations in Colorado

It was the wildlife and gold in the Rocky Mountains of the West which attracted the early miners and trappers as the last frontier in America was being settled in the late 19th century. Many of the later arrivals were the gamblers such as John Henry, and a large number of them traveled to Colorado because that's where gold and silver were being discovered in large quantities.

Despite the many things that are known about him today, Holliday is, in many ways, an enigma – a mysterious

Accurate Recreation – The now-famous shooting which actually occurred at the rear of the O.K. Corral in Tombstone, Arizona Territory, on October 26, 1881, is very realistically portrayed in this illustration by Mark Warren. All the participants appear very nearly in the spots at which they actually stood when the shooting occurred. This incident, more than any other, galvanized public attention upon not only the Earp brothers, but John Henry Holliday as well, earning them lasting fame in the annals of American history. Holliday appears in the street (center) holding the shotgun. (Illustration by Mark Warren)

individual. He traveled aimlessly throughout the West in the dying days of the old frontier. He left few writings of his experiences, so a great deal of his life and history are sheathed in mystery. Newspaper accounts of that time were notoriously inaccurate and sometimes virtually fictitious, and many of the letters he sent back home to family and friends were later destroyed or lost.

It is known, however, that once out West, Doc had no intention of returning to his Georgia home. Whether this was due to his gambling and widely-reported gunfights, or to his debilitating health, is unknown today.

Despite their beauty, the Rockies in Colorado must have been very taxing for Doc toward the latter portion of the 1880s. His tortured lungs had been seriously impaired by the tuberculosis bacterium eating away within him. He must have been constantly out of breath, often wondering if he was going to make it to the next day. Anyone who has been to the 10-, 11-, and 12,000-foot altitudes in these mountains has experienced this gasping need for oxygen. One can only imagine how it affected an individual as sick as was John Henry Holliday.

By this point, however, the die had been cast. There was little left for which he wished to live, and no way to make a living except the gambling trade. His terrible coughing fits had eliminated not only his pursuit of the dental profession for which he had been trained, but also were quickly thinning out the individuals who even wished to sit down with him for a game of cards.

He spent a substantial amount of time in Denver from 1882-1884. His last days, however, were spent in the mining towns of Leadville and Glenwood Springs, Colorado.

From Arizona To Colorado

On the way to Denver, Colorado, in the summer of 1882, Doc encountered several old acquaintances in Pueblo: Bat Masterson, Sam Osgood and an individual known only as "Texas George." According to later reports, the men planned to attend the horse races in Denver and checked into the Windsor Hotel on the northeast corner of Eighteenth and Larimer streets in that city.

The five-floor Windsor was a 300-room hotel – one of Denver's finest – and with its white marble floors, plush red carpeting and sixty-foot mahogany bar, it was just the type lavish establishment that the gambler from Georgia both admired and coveted. Again – the finer things in life always drew his attention.

One must find it at least mildly surprising that Masterson would stoop to socialize with Holliday at all, since it was widely-known that he detested him because of his oft-drunken and abrasive habits. One could also find Masterson's attitude toward Holliday ironic, since Masterson himself would soon be officially ejected from Denver and told never to return due to his own outrageous drunken behavior.

Unfortunately, Doc's penchant for trouble caught up with him once again in Denver. An individual by the name of Perry Mallen arrested Holliday on a warrantless and fraudulent murder charge associated with Doc's days in Arizona Territory. Mallen identified himself as an associate and envoy of Sheriff Johnny Behan of Cochise County in Arizona,

O.K. Corral Victims – This photograph, one of the most famous from the days of the Old West, almost certainly was taken by Camillus S. Fly, photographer for many years in Tombstone, Arizona Territory. Pictured here are the victims of the shoot-out near the O.K. Corral: Frank McLaury, Billy Clanton, and Tom McLaury. Two of these fatalities were attributed to Doc Holliday.

where Doc was in fact *"Wanted"* for his participation in the earlier-referenced *"Vendetta Ride."*

As a result, Mallen was able to have Doc jailed in Colorado, but the Georgian ultimately was rescued several weeks later by Bat Masterson, who, as a law enforcement official himself, indicated he was taking Doc into his custody for the return to Arizona. Masterson, to his credit, escorted Doc out of town and then set him free. Though he generally found Holliday detestable, he came to the tubercular gambler's assistance at the request of his friend Wyatt Earp, who had come to his (Bat's) aid on more than one occasion in the past.

Denver To Leadville

In a continued effort to escape his past, and to maintain his livelihood in gambling, Doc departed Denver and traveled by stage approximately 125 miles southwestward to the town of Leadville in Colorado. This community had been a mining boomtown since

Boot Hill – The victims of the October 26, 1881 O.K. Corral gunfight were buried in "Boot Hill" Cemetery just outside Tombstone. Frank McLaury, Tom McLaury and Billy Clanton all went to the hereafter as a result of the brief but fierce 30-second shoot-out. Footage filmed at this and other sites in Tombstone was used in the 1993 major motion picture "Tombstone," starring Kurt Russell, Val Kilmer, Michael Biehn, Sam Elliott, Dana Delany, Bill Paxton and others. (Photo by Olin Jackson)

1877 when a rich vein of silver and lead ores had been discovered. By the time Doc arrived in July of 1882, the mining of these metals had slowed, but there were still many gambling opportunities at the scores of saloons and bordellos yet remaining in this former boomtown.

One can only guess today at Holliday's perception of Leadville back in the 1880s. Did he enjoy the snow, or did he simply find it to be another shivering impediment to life? What was it like in the bleak shadows of the Rockies in a time when there was no indoor plumbing in most establishments, and no warm comfortable automobiles in which to travel about? Granted there were trains to the site. The *Denver & Rio Grande* had arrived in 1880, and the *Colorado Midland* arrived in 1887. Doc reportedly made use of them whenever possible, but more often than not, he either traveled

on horseback or within the freezing confines of a jarring stagecoach.

When he arrived in the high mountain town, Doc found employment as a faro dealer at Cyrus "Cy" Allen's Monarch Saloon which was located at 320 Harrison Avenue. *(This structure still exists today in this now sparsely-populated town.)* However, he didn't last long there. His illness had caused him to become heavily dependent upon alcohol by this time, and it affected his ability to perform his job. His employment at Allen's Saloon ended almost as quickly as it had begun.

According to reports, Holliday found new work nearby as a faro dealer in one of the clubrooms of Hyman's Saloon owned by Mannie Hyman. It was located at 316 Harrison Avenue next door to the Tabor Opera House *[both of which also are still in existence as of this*

Campbell & Hatch Assassination – On March 18, 1882 at 10:00 P.M. Saturday night, Morgan Earp was assassinated (shot in the back) while playing billiards in Campbell and Hatch Saloon (photographed here shortly after the shooting) on Allen Street near the intersection of 5th Street in Tombstone. At the time that he was shot, Morgan was standing with his back to the rear of the saloon. A gunman fired thru one of the panes in the rear door for the kill-shot. The bullet entered Morgan's right side, shattered his spine and vital organs, and emerged from his left side. Doc Holliday, who was good friends with Morgan, took the news of his death extremely hard, and vowed vengeance. He kept his word, helping Wyatt and Warren Earp hunt down the killers.

writing (2024) in downtown Leadville]. Doc apparently decided this was a good spot to put down some roots. He was able to obtain a room upstairs on the northwest corner of this building. *(At last check, this room was still being maintained as a historic memorial to the famous gambler.)*

Bleak Existence

Doc's tiny room – seven by fourteen feet to be specific– was his refuge in these years in Leadville. It gave him a beautiful – albeit no doubt extremely bleak to him – view of the snow-covered Rockies. When he wasn't sleeping, Doc almost always could be found in Hyman's saloon, dealing the faro games, or, across the street at John G. Morgan's Board of Trade Saloon *[present-day Silver Dollar Saloon which also still stands as of this writing (2024)]* where he often sat on the player's side of the table, playing stud poker.

According to reports, during the years 1882 to 1886, Doc occasionally visited most of the gambling houses along Harrison Street, plying his trade. However, by this time, his physical condition had severely debilitated his skills as a gambler, and his winnings had declined considerably. He also almost certainly had difficulty finding a table at which to play due to his bad cough. As a result,

"Texas Jack" Vermillion – A number of renowned figures from the Old West of the 1880s participated with Wyatt and Warren Earp and John Henry Holliday in what came to be known as "the Vendetta Ride," including "Turkey Creek" Jack Johnson, Sherman McMasters, and Dan Tipton. They pursued and eliminated a number of the "Cow Boy" outlaws of Arizona Territory in 1882. Vermillion was photographed here during his service as a Confederate soldier in the U.S. Civil War. Following the Vendetta Ride, Vermillion faded into history.

he was often short of money, and began leaning upon the goodwill of others to survive.

It seems almost pitiful to imagine Doc Holliday by this point in his life. He was very quickly succumbing to the tuberculosis ravaging his lungs and his health in general. He had always been slight in stature, but had been lightning quick with strong hands and arms, and usually capable of handling himself when confronted. His growing alcoholism, however, had affected his diet

– and thus his weight and strength. He had also lost most of his stamina due to the tuberculosis in his lungs and to two bouts of pneumonia with which he suffered during this period, not to mention the debilitation caused by the 12,000-foot altitude in which he now lived. In short, Doc Holliday was a pitiful sight by the mid-1880s.

When the whiskey – with which Doc was liberally self-medicating himself – ceased to offer a balm to the pain and destruction of his lungs, the once handsome dentist and gambler reportedly found another medication – laudanum. A local druggist who owned an apothecary at the corner of Sixth and Harrison streets, befriended Holliday and reportedly provided the drug to him.

His growing dependency on laudanum coupled with the severe bouts of pneumonia weakened Holliday even more. He was able to sustain himself with an occasional win at the card tables, but it was a meager existence at best.

Becoming A Target

As a result of his obviously weak physical state, the wolves began circling Holliday. He increasingly became a target for roughneck gamblers and predators in general who sought to earn a name for themselves by becoming the person who out-gunned or defeated the great Doc Holliday.

In his prime, Doc had usually needed only to identify himself to most belligerents – even vicious ones – in order to avoid a fight. However, by the time he reached Leadville, he was so obviously weak and debilitated that he had become an easy mark. Even worse, he was no longer able to use the threat of the use of weapons since he was a known gunman, and was routinely threatened with being jailed should he be searched and weapons be discovered. And Doc knew he wouldn't last long within the confines of the freezing cold jails.

At this point, Holliday basically no longer had any way to defend himself. Weak, debilitated and unarmed, he was now a huge target for bullies. More and more, the stronger ones pushed ever harder to humiliate and goad him into a confrontation or fistfight.

Though he was weak and disabled, Doc – to his credit – was never a coward, and he would not be bullied, regardless of the circumstances. For this reason, Leadville, Colorado, enjoys the unique distinction of being the site of John Henry Holliday's last gunfight.

Two of Doc's old Tombstone, Arizona, enemies – William "Billy" Allen and Johnny Tyler – unfortunately were living in Leadville at the time of Doc's residence there. According to Karen Holliday Tanner in *Doc Holliday: A Family Portrait*, Allen was a former Leadville policeman who had been a friend of Ike Clanton – Doc's old Tombstone nemesis. Allen had even served as a prosecution witness during the O.K. Corral shooting inquest and had testified against Doc.

"...he (Allen) had accompanied Reuben Coleman on the day of the gunfight in Tombstone," Ms. Tanner writes. *"They had walked down Allen Street through the O.K. Corral to the front of Camillus S. Fly's Gallery (behind Fly's Boarding House). It was believed by some, and certainly by Doc, that during the fracas, Allen had fired a number of shots aimed at both Holliday and the Earps from the passageway between Fly's buildings. After coming to Leadville, Allen had been a part-time policeman and had been hired as a bartender at the Monarch Saloon."*

John Henry Holliday as he appeared during the so-called "Vendetta Ride." Gone was the vitality of youth even though he was only in his thirties, age-wise. (Photo courtesy of the Colorado Historical Society)

Confronting Johnny Tyler

Ms. Tanner also explains how Johnny Tyler – after the Tombstone years – was dealing faro at the Casino Gambling Hall in Leadville. *"Tyler had not forgotten the humiliation he had suffered in 1880 when he was evicted from Tombstone's Oriental Saloon by Wyatt Earp with Doc looking on, laughing and taunting him,"* Ms. Tanner adds. *"Tyler harbored tremendous anger and resentment toward Doc and now prepared to vent it.*

"Johnny Tyler and Billy Allen plotted their vendetta. . . In August of 1884, Doc found himself in the unenviable position of owing Billy Allen five dollars. Allen, knowing of Doc's dire straits (financially), had willingly loaned the money, assuming that Doc would have difficulty repaying the debt. This would give Allen justification to goad the weak, sick Holliday into a gunfight. Doc had borrowed the money with the promise to repay it in

Gunnison, Colorado Hideaway – Following the "Vendetta Ride" many of the participants divided up and went their separate ways. John Holliday spent a few days with Wyatt, Warren and Dan Tipton in Gunnison, Colorado, to which they had traveled to elude the "law enforcement authorities" from Arizona in the summer of 1882 who had pursued them for their actions in what came to be known as "the Vendetta Ride" earlier that same year. Though the weather in Gunnison eventually turned frigid and unforgiving, the Earps and their party preferred camping out in these climes – at least before winter arrived – in order to put the odds in their favor against bounty hunters. Doc, however, in his ill condition, ultimately preferred the warmth, service, and finery of hotels, and soon departed unfavorable Gunnison for Denver. Virginia Avenue in Gunnison – virtually unchanged from the days of Doc and Wyatt – was photographed here circa 1890s. (Denver Public Library, Western History Department)

less than a week. Seven days later, he had to go to Billy and humbly explain that he had not been able to collect an outstanding debt and therefore did not have the money (to repay Allen)."

For a number of weeks in Leadville, Doc was continuously insulted and humiliated by Johnny Tyler and his cohorts. In an earlier day, they would not have dared to confront and challenge him in such a manner, but in 1884, Doc was only a shadow of his former persona, and his antagonists knew it. They relentlessly taunted him, threatening him with gunplay.

Contrary to Doc, his tormentors were able to carry weapons since they would rarely be stopped and searched by a city policeman. Doc, however, was regularly stopped and searched, so his firearms had to be left in his room, since, as

explained above, he was virtually destitute and could not afford to pay a fine for possession of a firearm nor survive in the cold dank jails of that day. He therefore was very careful not to violate the city ordinance concerning firearms.

"Words passed between him and Tyler and his cronies at Hyman's Bar, and several of them called him to 'pull his gun,'" a local Leadville newspaper reporter wrote at the time. *"He said he had none, and as he passed outside, he was called filthy names. . . Next day, he told this writer, with tears of rage coming to his eyes as he talked, that they were insulting and humiliating him because they knew he could not retaliate."*

Allen Eats Lead

Billy Allen, who had been waiting for his opportunity, finally issued Doc

Palace Theater, Denver – Of all the towns in the West to which he had traveled, Doc preferred Denver, Colorado. Its comfortable and modern hotels, gambling establishments and opportunities for entertainment suited his nature. He traveled back and forth to Denver while camping in Gunnison with the Earps, and living in nearby Leadville, and other localities offering gambling opportunities in gold- and silver-strike towns. When in Denver, Doc frequented the Palace Theater, as did Wyatt Earp and Bat Masterson. Masterson even managed it for a time.

an ultimatum: Pay the debt owed to him by noon of the following Tuesday or face the threat of severe violence.

"When Tuesday arrived, some of Doc's friends went to his room and told him that Allen was looking for him with a gun," Ms. Tanner continued. *". . . . On the stairway down into the saloon, Doc asked Mannie Hyman to get an officer for protection. He continued into the saloon but did not find Allen. He asked his friend and fellow boarder Frank Lomeister, who was working the day shift as bartender, to get Capt. Edmond Bradbury of the Leadville Police Department or Marshal Harvey Faucett, adding that he did not want to sit around for the afternoon unprotected."*

Though death's angels were closing in upon him, John Henry Holliday continued nevertheless to fight for life. According to reports of this famous

incident, he returned to his room where he remained in the tiny enclosure until approximately five o'clock in the afternoon. He knew he eventually would have to go back down to the saloon to work, and that when he did so, he would have to be prepared to defend himself.

Ironically, this was one of Doc's greatest fears. He had successfully faced far too many bullies and killers by this point to be unnerved by such circumstances. To the contrary, he feared simply being unable to "go out game." In this instance, however, he was approaching one of his finest hours.

Totally frustrated, Doc instructed one of his friends to take his (Doc's) Colt's .41 revolver down and hide it behind the bar so that it would be within reach if necessary. In that manner, he would not have to be in possession of the

Brutal Opponent – William J. "Billy" Allen was photographed circa 1895, in Carrollton, Missouri, approximately 11 years after being wounded by Holliday in Leadville. In this photo, to even the least discerning eye, Allen looked every bit the part of the bullying predator described in historic accounts. He had blithely assumed he would severely beat, if not kill, the sick and weakened Holliday in a confrontation in Leadville, Colorado, but he was seriously disappointed, and, in actuality, lucky to have survived the incident. By that point, other than his immortal soul, Holliday had absolutely nothing left to lose, and fully intended – if possible – to arrange a permanent meeting between Allen and his Maker. Though he survived, Allen never again confronted Holliday.

weapon (and thus vulnerable to being jailed), but the weapon would nevertheless be within easy reach if he needed it. He then went down to the saloon himself and sat near the end of the bar behind the cigar case where he could reach the weapon.

Though diminutive in comparison to some of his earlier confrontations, this was nevertheless a very dramatic setting, one more characteristic of those earlier days in places like Dodge City or Tombstone. According to reports of the incident, Billy Allen eventually did enter the saloon, and he had the audacity and temerity (yet also the misfortune) to have his hand in his pocket as if holding a weapon.

When Doc saw Allen's hand in his gun pocket, that posture created Doc's alibi to defend himself. Without hesitation – and in a flashback to the days when he had fearlessly defended himself against worthy opponents – Doc immediately snatched his handgun from beneath the counter and quickly fired a round at Allen. The bullet found its mark, striking the unfortunate victim in the fleshy part of his upper arm and severing an artery.

Though Allen was down, Doc was far from done. When his adversary fell to the floor in pain, Doc thundered yet another round at him. He meant to legally end this threat once and for all, because he knew if he did not, Allen would be back to try yet again. This second round struck the door sill, barely missing Allen's head. Even with his severe debilitation, Doc was still a deadly-accurate gunman when necessary.

Before he could get off another shot, however, Doc was grabbed from behind by Henry Kellerman who wrestled the gun away. This action almost certainly saved Billy Allen's miserable life, and also possibly saved Doc from being charged with first degree murder.

Doc, nevertheless, was subsequently arrested by the Leadville marshal and charged with *"Assault with intent to commit murder."* He was locked up in jail and his bail reportedly was set at $5,000.00 – both circumstances were exactly what the gambler had feared. In 1883, the sum of $5,000.00 was the equivalent of well over $150,000.00 in 2024 dollars. It might as well have been a million dollars.

Interestingly, in an earlier day and time, John Henry Holliday might possibly have raised that amount for bail, but by the time of his days in Leadville, the ex-dentist – as explained above – was living virtually hand-to-mouth. For that reason, $5,000.00 was an impossibly high bail for him to raise, and he must surely have thought he was going to be incarcerated in a freezing-cold and damp jail for months until his trial date arrived – if he lasted that long.

On Trial For Assault

Interestingly, though it has seldom been publicized, Doc – despite his oft-abrasive personality – seemed to consistently cultivate a coterie of close friends willing to help him when necessary. Two of these stepped forward immediately. John G. Morgan and Samuel Houston, co-owners of the Board of Trade Saloon *(which also still exists today in Leadville as of this writing in 2024)* arrived the next morning and immediately posted bail for Doc.

In the trial that followed, a number of eye-witnesses testified to the threats that had been issued at Doc by Allen, and the circumstances of the shooting that had followed. Doc took the stand on his own behalf and explained the details of the loan and the subsequent threats.

"I saw Allen coming in with his hand in his pocket, and I thought my life was as good to me as his was to him," Holliday explained in his courtroom testimony. *I fired the shot and he fell on the floor, and (I) fired the second shot; I knew that I would be a child in his hands if he got hold of me; I weigh 122 pounds; I think Allen weighs 170; I have had pneumonia three or four times. I don't think I would have been able to protect myself against him."*

The jury ultimately returned a

Final Gunfight – During the winter of 1883-84, Doc Holliday found work at Mannie Hyman's Saloon at 316 Harrison Avenue in Leadville. It was here on the afternoon of August 19, 1884, that he confronted the predator Billy Allen, wounding him severely with a Colt .41 revolver as Allen moved aggressively through the doorway of the saloon in pursuit of the sick Georgian. This was the final gunfight in which Doc Holliday was ever involved. (Courtesy of Denver Public Library)

verdict of *"Not Guilty"* in the case of *People vs John Henry Holliday*. Following this last gunfight, the curtain essentially came down on the public life of John Henry Holliday, ending his gun-fighting days forever. He was never again involved in a shooting incident. Probably due to the notoriety attached to this last gunfight, however, the wolves ceased circling him too.

Not too long after the trial, Doc, for good reason, no doubt felt the urge to move on to another town. He first took a short trip back to Denver one last time before returning briefly to Leadville.

Holliday had learned of a town called Glenwood Springs, Colorado,

Mannie Hyman's Saloon – This former Leadville saloon was photographed in 2001. In the early to mid-1880s, John Henry Holliday lived upstairs on the second floor of this building. The window of his former room is visible (above, left) at the corner. It was in the downstairs where the saloon once existed that he confronted his antagonist, Billy Allen, in his final gunfight. (Photo by Olin Jackson)

which had a variety of steamy sulfur water grottos outside town, and of the fact that some individuals had gone there for the treatment of various health problems. This town, no doubt, was doubly attractive, since it was not only known as a health resort, but also as a mining town too, with many saloons and other gaming establishments to provide Doc the possibility of renewed income. It was just the opportunity he sought at this point in his life.

Last Days

Today, Glenwood Springs isn't much larger than it was in Doc's day in 1887. *(It might even be smaller.)* The

warm springs are still active and frequented by many individuals interested in the presumed curative qualities of the waters.

In order to reach this town, Doc once again found himself on a cold and exceedingly uncomfortable stagecoach headed farther up into the Colorado Rockies. He made the trip from Leadville to Glenwood Springs in May of 1887. *[Note: The railroad (Denver & Rio Grande) did not reach Glenwood Springs until October 5, 1887, so it was unavailable as a travel medium for Doc's trip.]*

By 1887, Doc's appearance reportedly was that of an individual well-advanced in years, with silver hair and an emaciated stooped posture. According to a news article of that day, *"He walked down the street with a feeble tread and a downcast look. If he heard a (gun)shot, he raised his head with eager attention and glanced this way and that."* Even in 1887, Glenwood Springs obviously was still somewhat wild and unsettled.

He fully intended – and did – take advantage of the sulfur springs in a never-ending quest to stem the tide of the destructive bacteria in his lungs. Ironically, rather than curing Doc's ills, the acidic and acrid vapors caused even more damage to his already-ruined system. His cough quickly worsened, and his health declined even more rapidly.

Just as had been the case in both Denver and Leadville, Doc reportedly was admired and welcomed by a number of individuals, and quickly cultivated a coterie of friends in Glenwood Springs in the weeks immediately following his arrival. After reaching town and settling in, he attempted once again to ply his old trade at the gambling tables. By this point, however, he simply no longer had the stamina to participate. Gone was the vitality which had served him so well in

Kansas and Arizona and earlier in Colorado. With the departure of his strength also went his will to live. He no doubt knew his last days truly were upon him at this point.

His spirits understandably were low, and, according to Karen Holliday Tanner, Doc had written to his former consort – Mary Katherine "Big-Nose Kate" Harony in Globe, Arizona – telling her he was traveling to Glenwood Springs, and asking her to join him there. By this point, Doc must have known he was fast approaching the time when he would need someone to physically assist him with the rudimentary tasks of daily life. He no doubt knew of no one to call upon except Kate, and she, to her credit, responded admirably.

Doc and Kate had traveled many miles together earlier in their lives. They had enjoyed many adventures across the West in places like Las Vegas, New Mexico; Dodge City, Kansas; Tucson and Tombstone, Arizona. This bond no doubt held them together as Doc fought for life in the final months of his existence.

In Kate's Care

Many accounts today indicate Doc died alone and abandoned in the Hotel Glenwood in his last days. One recently-discovered (2004) and very credibly-documented record *(explained in detail in the following chapter)* however, indicates an entirely different scenario.

Whatever the circumstances, Doc took a room at the Hotel Glenwood on the northeast corner of Grand Avenue and Eighth Street in Glenwood Springs. This exceptional hotel had just recently been built (1886), and was among the finest in the West at that time. It offered among its amenities electric lights, both hot and cold running water in every room, and even flush-toilets. The water was pumped directly from the Grand (later renamed Colorado) River, since there was no water system in the town, with the sewage being returned directly into the river where it flowed downstream to the next town.

Most of the old saloons and gambling establishments in Glenwood Springs are gone today, replaced by more modern structures. The Hotel Glenwood burned to the ground on December 14, 1945, killing five people, and destroying forever the final home of John Henry Holliday.

Though the town fathers of Glenwood Springs seem to have paid limited heed toward historic preservation over the years, the community yet retains a scenic air, unique with its warm springs. The stark Rockies are still startlingly beautiful, but they must have been cold and forbidding to Doc in his dying days.

During the final 57 days of his life, John Henry Holliday reportedly rose from his bed at the Hotel Glenwood only twice. He and Kate reportedly relied upon the bellhop to serve them their meals so that Kate did not have to leave his bedside.

It is poignant to imagine Kate attending to him in these last hours. She easily could have ignored his request to join him in Colorado, knowing the task of caring for him during this time would not be pleasant. She reportedly never wavered from her duties however, and even used her meager savings to support them after Doc could no longer work. In her later years, she said she considered her relationship with Doc to be a marriage.

All the years of smoking, drinking, poor diet and poor care finally caught up with the famed gambler. Pneumonia and tuberculosis ultimately combined to do what many gunmen over the years had failed to accomplish. By the third week in October of 1887, Doc was delirious, and by Monday of November 7, he reportedly was unable to speak, so many researchers and writers maintain it is unlikely he ever uttered the now-famous last words, *"This is funny,"* which have become so noted in folklore. He died on November 8, 1887.

Kate's Last Days

Interestingly, Doc's consort for all those years in Arizona and Colorado – Mary Katherine Horony – reportedly gathered up Doc's belongings from his room after his death, and shipped them to Doc's one true love – his cousin, Sister Mary Melanie of the Order of the Sisters of Mercy – who had entered a convent to become a nun after Doc left Atlanta, Georgia for the West.

After she had disposed of Doc's worldly possessions, Kate then left the sadness in Glenwood Springs forever, but reportedly remained for a time at her brother's home nearby in the Crystal Valley region of Colorado.

On March 2, 1890, Kate married George M. Cummings in the mining town of Aspen, Colorado, a well-known ski resort today. The couple moved about the West before finally settling in Bisbee, Cochise County, Arizona, in 1895, just a few miles from Tombstone where Doc had gained so much fame in 1881-1882.

This marriage lasted approximately nine years before Kate left Mr. Cummings who was an alcoholic. *(Katherine Harony enjoyed little if any luck in her selection of men.)*

On June 2, 1900, Kate accepted employment as the housekeeper of John J. Howard of Dos Cabezas, Arizona. She remained in his employ until Howard's death in 1930.

On June 13, 1931, Kate wrote to Arizona Governor George W. Hunt requesting permission to live in the state-supported Arizona Pioneers Home in Prescott. Governor Hunt reportedly granted Kate's request.

For the last nine years of her life, Mary Katherine Cummings (nee Horony) – also known in history as "Big-Nose Kate" – lived out her final days in the town where, in 1880, she and Doc had spent time together just prior to his Tombstone days. She died on November 2, 1940, and was buried at the Pioneer Cemetery in Prescott.

Today, one can only imagine how John Henry Holliday felt in his last days, separated from his family and friends back in Georgia, as well as his surrogate family – the Earps – who, by that time, were scattered from Arizona to California. Thankfully, he did have Kate in his last days. She no doubt brought him comfort in his final hours.

It, nevertheless, seems a pity the last remains of one of the most famous and fabled of all the individuals of the old West, lie in an unknown and unmarked grave today, mysterious and yet respected even in death. Ironically, that's probably just the way Doc would have wanted it. His lonely wandering soul is finally at peace.

Retracing Doc's Footsteps In the Colorado Rockies

Today, many of Doc Holliday's former haunts on the frontier of the Old West in the 1880s surprisingly still exist, much as they did when he yet breathed the fresh Arizona and Colorado air.

Almost all serious researchers and historians know that John Henry Holliday was born in Griffin, Georgia, where he spent the first twelve years of his life,

Cut Down to Size – The front portion of the room occupied in 1884 by Mannie Hyman's Saloon was a gift shop at the time this photo was snapped almost 120 years later. It was in this room that John Henry Holliday worked and confronted Billy Allen. At that time, a bar existed along the wall to the right, and Holliday was positioned just behind it near the front window. After earlier threatening Holliday, Allen entered the doorway which at that time existed where the gift items framed in the big picture window (left center) exist in this photo. After being wounded by Holliday, Allen collapsed to the floor (foreground). (Photo by Olin Jackson)

and that he spent the remainder of his formative years at the family's Civil War-era home in Valdosta, Georgia, to which they relocated in 1864 to escape the ravages of Gen. William T. Sherman's Union Army.

Many people are also well aware of the drama surrounding Holliday's years in Tombstone, Arizona Territory, but his travels elsewhere in the West (and there were many of them) are muddled in the minds of most people.

An Arduous Journey

It is difficult to imagine what it must have been like for Holliday – sick as he was – to travel by stagecoach and on horseback to various towns of the West in the 1870s and 1880s. He traveled by train when possible, but since railroads in the West were somewhat limited at

that time, he took stagecoaches to most of his destinations and occasionally traveled by horseback in some of the more remote areas.

Doc visited Denver a number of times both early in his career out West and in the years just prior to his death simply because it was a more modern and civilized city than most any other west of the Arkansas River at that time. He supported himself by gambling, and Denver, as a result of its gold rush heritage, offered many saloons and gambling houses at which the former dentist could ply his trade.

By the time he returned to Denver in 1882, however, he was a *"Wanted"* man in Arizona for his involvement in what came to be known as *"the Vendetta Ride."* He had joined Wyatt and Warren Earp, Turkey Creek Jack Johnson,

Harrison Avenue (1880) – Photographed here shortly before the arrival of Doc Holliday in Leadville, Colorado, the dusty town is just beginning to experience a bit of upgraded development. Notice the concrete sidewalks which have recently been constructed. The street, however, remains a dirt conveyance, and much of the town's early rustic status is yet visible.

Texas Jack Vermilion, Sherman McMasters, Dan Tipton and several others in hunting down the outlaws – particularly those known as the *"Cow Boys"* who had been involved in the murder of Morgan Earp in Tombstone, Arizona, and the attempted assassination of Virgil Earp.

As a result, Denver no longer was able to offer John Henry the comfortable refuge he had enjoyed in the past. After being arrested there and very nearly extradited back to Arizona, he was literally forced to leave the town and to seek new horizons. He therefore moved on to other gold mining towns which also offered gambling opportunities.

Today, few if any of Doc's former haunts in Denver remain for the curious. Modern development has eliminated virtually all of the old hotels and saloons from yesteryear in this town.

Losing In Leadville

One needs only to travel the highlands of Colorado today in a comfortable automobile to understand just how uncomfortable it must have been riding in a freezing cold jarring stagecoach for hundreds of miles through the dangerous snow-covered Rocky Mountains of the 1880s. Warm comfortable restrooms at various locations and hot meals at safe comfortable restaurants were of course non-existent.

In the stage coach inns – known as "stands" – where the stage overnighted, male travelers slept several to a bed – oftentimes just to stay warm – and that is assuming there were beds, which many times there were not. And little horrors such as bed-bugs, body lice, ticks and other nuisances were commonly-accepted irritants.

Holliday, just as were most travelers of that day and time, was a resilient individual, and bore these types of inconveniences without complaint, but his illness coupled with the harshness of this trip took a toll upon his health.

According to records, the tubercular

Harrison Avenue (2001) – Photographed in modern times, this main thoroughfare – though now crowded with additional civic structures – still appears much as it did during the days of the Old West of the 1880s. Doc lived in a room above Hyman's Saloon at 316 Harrison, which still stands today approximately two-thirds of the way down this street on the left. (Photo by Olin Jackson)

dentist took a stage to the icy-cold altitudinous realm of Leadville in 1882, living there for four years (the most time he spent in any spot in the West).

Located at 10,152 feet above sea level, this Old West mining town is surrounded by Colorado's tallest peaks, and includes many historic aspects above and beyond the distinction of being one of Holliday's former residences. Entering the town on historic Harrison (or Main) Street, one enjoys almost the identical view as had Holliday over 100 years earlier.

The historic Tabor Opera House which still stands in town on Harrison hosted many famous entertainers and celebrities over the years, including boxer Jack Dempsey, author Oscar Wilde, magician Harry Houdini and even musician John Philip Sousa and his Marine Band.

The Tabor home at 116 E. 5th Street in town was built by H.A.W. "Haw" (Horace) Tabor sometime around 1877. Horace and his first wife, Augusta, lived in this residence until 1881. At that time, Horace moved to the nearby Windsor Hotel to be near his mistress "Baby Doe." The Tabor love triangle grew into a national scandal, ultimately ending in a divorce between Horace and Augusta, and a marriage between Horace and Baby Doe.

Unfortunately, Tabor, who was extremely wealthy, was heavily invested in silver. In 1893, after the repeal of the *Sherman Silver Act* which removed silver as the metal which "backed" currency issued in the United States, a silver panic ensued, sending silver prices plummeting. Tabor, who had owned the huge Tabor Grand Building and the opulent Tabor Opera House among other properties, began a long but steady slide toward insolvency. *(It is difficult*

323

Tabor Opera House (2001) – Located next door to the now-aged Hyman Saloon building where Holliday lived and worked, the Tabor, which opened in 1879, was said to be the grandest theater in its day between St. Louis and San Francisco. Wealthy businessman and silver magnate H.A.W. "Haw" Tabor built the monumental structure which seated 880 people within its once-luxurious interior. It hosted many notables during Leadville's heydays, including appearances by heavyweight boxing champion Jack Dempsey, author Oscar Wilde, famed magician Harry Houdini, and renowned musician John Philip Sousa and his Marine Band. Holliday, who thoroughly enjoyed theatrical productions and professional entertainment, no doubt visited this facility at least occasionally from 1882 to 1886. (Photo by Olin Jackson)

to understand how one can be as wealthy as he supposedly was, and still be over-extended financially to the degree that bankruptcy becomes inevitable by circumstances beyond one's control.)

In 1895, Horace Tabor, amazingly, finally did declare bankruptcy, and Baby Doe eventually began walking the streets of Leadville in rags. Also in 1895, Augusta Tabor died as a result of respiratory problems. She, interestingly, was a millionaire at her death. Horace had become a pauper.

In 1884, in the building next door to the Tabor Opera House, John Henry Holliday was involved in his last gunfight.

In the 1880s, Leadville was a gold and silver mining town of considerable repute. Holliday had turned to gambling – which had served him well in places like Dodge City, Kansas; Tombstone Arizona; and Denver, Colorado – as a profession. Leadville offered a continuation of the same gambling opportunities.

One could only imagine that Holliday, with his ruined lungs, must have struggled to an unbelievable degree. He is known to have contracted pneumonia several times while living in the town, but amazingly survived the illness each time.

In 1884, the population of Leadville was approximately 20,000 (not counting "soiled doves" as the towns literature proclaims). According to records, it had 92 saloons, 61 lawyers, numerous gambling houses and brothels, and 8 churches. A number of the same structures which existed in Holliday's time still exist today, and the entire town retains a somewhat "frontier" appearance.

As with Tombstone, Arizona, Leadville, Colorado – due to its somewhat isolated and inhospitable location – has changed little from the Old West days of Holliday. Modern development in the town has been limited. Some of the buildings from yesteryear have disappeared as a result of fire and general neglect, and occasionally, a new church or a new saloon – designed much the same as the old ones – has been built, but little else has changed. The area presumably is simply too unattractive, climate-wise to experience any significant increase in population.

To understand this, all one has to do is walk to a second or third floor room in a hotel in the town. Following this effort, a full four or five-minute recuperation will be required by almost anyone over 35 who has not lived in the area for a period of time and become accustomed to the paucity of oxygen.

Though some mining continues in Leadville today, the town now derives most of its income from tourism. Long gone are the fast times and fast money generated by the one-time mineral wealth of the area in the 1880s. Leadville, however, is very much worthwhile as a tourism destination.

The Delaware Hotel in town was built in 1886, and it may or may not have been patronized by John Henry Holliday. He left Leadville in 1887, spending the final months of his life in Glenwood Springs prior to his death there in November of that year. If he did not visit the Delaware, however, it would be one of the few buildings in town which escaped his attentions, for he was surprisingly active in the community during his residence there, moving from saloon to saloon to ply his trade.

The accommodations at the Delaware are acceptable, if somewhat Spartan. This is assuming one doesn't mind somewhat smallish rooms, and a shower which runs icy cold and scalding hot intermittently as one bathes.

According to this inn's interesting literature, one outlaw for which a documented use of its accommodations has been discovered is Butch Cassidy. Whether or not John Henry Holliday ever entered these premises is unknown.

Doc's Old Hotel

The old hotel/saloon (originally Mannie Hyman's Saloon) in which Doc lived and worked from 1882 to 1887 still stands at 316 Harrison Avenue. This saloon was also the site of Holliday's last gunfight in which he shot (and almost killed) Billy Allen in 1884.

In the 1880s, Mannie Hyman

Board of Trade Saloon (2001) – Opened originally as the Board of Trade saloon in 1879 in Leadville, the facility at 313 Harrison Avenue was known as the "Silver Dollar Saloon," a novelty and collectibles shop, when photographed here in 2001. From 1882 to 1886 however, when it was actually a saloon and gambling establishment, it was regularly patronized by Holliday during his off hours when he wasn't working across the street in Hyman's Saloon. The owners of the Board of Trade were the individuals who bailed Doc out of jail following the Billy Allen shooting in Leadville in 1884. (Photo by Olin Jackson)

rented nine rooms in this building to various individuals. Holliday's room included a view through the front window of the distant snow-covered peaks of the Rockies.

Although Doc was a faro dealer in Hyman's, he also regularly gambled himself in John G. Morgan's Board of Trade Saloon across the street, as well as in a number of other saloons and gambling establishments in town. The Board of Trade building, which also still stands (as of this writing in 2024), was called the Silver Dollar Saloon in recent years. Its owners – as it turned out – became an important source of bail money after Holliday's arrest for the Billy Allen shooting.

The Last Gunfight

In his day, John Henry Holliday developed a strong friendship with the Board of Trade's owners – John Morgan and Col. Samuel Houston – and it later proved to be a valuable association. When he was arrested for shooting Billy Allen, Holliday was destitute, and so sick he could no longer support himself as a gambler. As a result, he could not raise bail, and undoubtedly would have been forced to endure a long very cold incarceration in jail prior to his trial had not Morgan and Houston stepped forward.

Together, the two merchants quickly posted the $5,000 bail money and Holliday was released to return to his sick-bed until the day of his trial. He subsequently was justifiably acquitted of the charges against him.

Allen was an old enemy of Holliday's, dating back to the Tombstone days in 1881. In an amazing stroke of bad luck, the weakened Holliday had the misfortune to be in Leadville at the same time as did Allen, who was a friend of the Clantons, a family of outlaws who had opposed the Earps and Holliday during their days in Arizona.

Allen had also testified against Holliday at the *Inquest* following the

When he was arrested for shooting Billy Allen, Holliday was destitute, and so sick he could no longer support himself as a gambler.

shooting behind the O.K. Corral, and a number of individuals – including Doc himself – believed Allen had fired several shots at him during the Tombstone fracas. For this and other reasons, Allen and Holliday were anything but friends.

By the time Doc and Allen met again in Leadville, Holliday was much weaker and sicker, and Allen no doubt saw an opportunity to gain a reputation for himself as the individual who finally got the drop on the famed gunman.

As an indication of just how desperate Doc had become by this point, he had fallen into a trap set by Allen (who was feigning goodwill for Holliday) by borrowing $5.00 for a gambling stake. When he was unable to repay the loan at the appointed hour, Allen began publicly bullying and humiliating him.

Doc eventually received word that his tormentor was coming to pay him a final visit, and that if he did not come forth with the overdue $5.00, a physical beating at the very least would be forthcoming. In the end, however, it was Allen who ended up writhing upon the floor, with Doc escaping uninjured.

Newspaper Account of John Henry's Last Days

Though the actual circumstances of his last days on this earth have been debated for decades, a credible

Grand Avenue – This main thoroughfare in Glenwood Springs was photographed on June 18, 1898, a little over 10 years after Holliday's death. The gambler from Georgia strode down this street more than a few times. Visible on the right side of the street in the distance is the Hotel Glenwood in which he died.

recently-discovered newspaper article possibly describes the actual events, and debunks some previously-held notions.

Some writers and researchers have maintained that John Henry Holliday spent his last days alone in the Hotel Glenwood, slowly wasting away until death finally took him. Until recent times, no detailed first-hand account of Doc's last days was known to exist, but a recently-discovered newspaper article may prove otherwise.

Revelatory News Article

According to Karen Holliday Tanner, Doc summoned his long-time consort – Katherine "Big Nose Kate" Harony – when he realized his last days were upon him, and she subsequently traveled to his bedside, caring for him until he died. However, very little if any corroborating evidence of this or many of the other details of Holliday's presumed last

hours were known to exist – that is until a copy of the February 14, 1899 issue of the *Sulphur Headlight* of Sulphur, Oklahoma, was discovered.

The information in the article was detailed by an individual named Origen C. "Harelip Charlie" Smith, a bona fide ally of the Earps and Holliday during the volatile days in Tombstone, Arizona Territory, in 1880-1882. Smith was a business associate of Bob Winders in Tombstone, and had allied himself with the Earps in support of law and order in the frontier town. His days in that town are well-documented, and are a matter of public record today. He was respected as knowledgeable and trustworthy by associates in Tombstone, so there is little reason to doubt his claims.

By coincidence, Smith found himself traveling in the same stagecoach as Holliday to Glenwood Springs, Colorado, in 1887, and even living in the

Hotel Denver – The Leadville Bar in the Hotel Denver in Glenwood Springs no doubt experienced a crisis of identity at least occasionally. It was photographed here circa 1890s, and quite possibly was visited by Holliday prior to his demise in Glenwood Springs. (Courtesy of Frontier Historical Society)

same hotel there as Doc. According to the *Headlight* article, Smith was present during Holliday's dying days and was intimately familiar with the individuals present and the events surrounding the last hours of the celebrated Georgian.

Later, after moving back to Tombstone, Arizona, Smith, realizing the importance of the body of knowledge he carried with him regarding his Tombstone days and the years thereafter, began writing down his memoirs for posterity. He reportedly sought out an old friend – Lundsford Bryant Shockley – to collaborate with him on the memoirs. Though there is no specific reason to doubt Smith's veracity or the accuracy of his memory in describing Holliday's last hours, it of course is not impossible that portions of his recollections were imprecise.

In 1899, Shockley reportedly shared the portion of Smith's memoirs involving Doc Holliday's last days in Glenwood Springs with the publisher of the *Sulphur Headlight*. Why he chose to share Smith's work with this particular newspaper at this particular point in time is unknown today. He was living in the Indian Territory near Sulphur, Oklahoma, at the time, which provides a measure of explanation for his use of that town's newspaper. Whatever the circumstances, on February 14. 1899, the *Headlight* published the very interesting details of Doc's last days as drawn from Shockley's revelation of Smith's memoirs.

The article from the *Headlight* is re-published here in its entirety, exactly as written by Smith, with the exception of quotation marks and paragraph delineations for ease of reading. The article is very detailed, and includes considerable information which would have been exceedingly difficult to fabricate had not the writer actually been present as a witness at Holliday's death. The initial portion of the article was written from the editor's perspective, with the remainder from Smith's perspective. It reads as follows:

"The story comes to the **Headlight** from colleague Lundsford Shockley, resident of the Chickasaw Nations, Ardmore, Indian Territory. It is known that Mr. Shockley came to town by wagon early in the evening and boarded at the Hotel Sulphur Springs in preparation to meet the **Headlight** staff.

"It is apparent that connections to Mr. [Origen Charles] Smith came from Shockley's days with John Roberts of the [John] Slaughter crew, driving those vast Texas herds up to the San Pedro Valley. Shockley comments: 'We were encamped up in the Sierra Vistas in '81. On the first time out, many of the boys wanted to go to Tombstone and experience the town's pleasures. Tombstone was a mining camp built from the dust much like the old pueblo, Tucson, which offered a cowboy anything imaginable.'

"According to Charlie Smith, it was also a community built on politics; 'a common cause of much of the troubles there.'

"When upon reading the Harelip Smith papers, I might comment that the significance surrounds the death of John H. Holliday, known as Doc, on November 8, 1887, where Smith occupied a room across the hallway from him in the Hotel Glenwood, some twelve years ago. It is important to note that Origen Smith's recollections serve as a standard account of the dentist's last days in Glenwood Springs who wrote on his Sol Israel stationary on October 8, 1887, that Holliday was confined to his bed by the local physician who had told his [Doc's] mistress: 'I have done all that can be done. It is in John's hands now. And God's.'

"Origen Smith gives an account of Doc Holliday's arrival to the mountain resort on May 24, 1887 [as follows]:

"'The Concorde coach had slammed into the rocks along the narrow gauge of mountain road near Carbondale, which damaged the wheel at the rear of the coach which suddenly ended their journey until a mechanic could be brought in from several miles distant. The narrow gauge out of Leadville was hard on Holliday and its three passengers, but it was the best means of travel for the day.

"'The three passengers on the stage knew who Doc Holliday was, but I doubt they had heard of Origen Smith when I arrived on the Leadville laundry train with a group of miners who flooded Leadville when Hoarse Tabot [Horace "Haw" Tabor] discovered the "Matchbox" [Matchless] mine. We were packed in that coach like a can of sardines, fighting to get out.

"'I had boarded the coach heeled but concealed it inside my coat just as Doc had done that day when all hell broke loose down at Montgomery's [the O.K. Corral]. In Tombstone, I had served as vigilance messenger for Colonel Wm. Herring, a prominent Tombstone attorney who's [sic] office located at 534 Freemont, served as a meeting place for many of Wyatt Earp's backers. In 1882, I had been a messenger for Wyatt, joining his federal posse after the death of his brother by cowards.

"'Experience had taught me that a man like Holliday – who told me once that I should join the game – did not fear death. It was the living that he feared most. The fear of not going out game. Many times I had seen Doc cry tears from the agony the dreadful disease scourged him when the whiskey failed to do its work.

"'The trip from Leadville [to Glenwood Springs] was hard on Doc. The jolting from the narrow gauge would cause him to cough up pieces of lung and blood. It was about two o'clock when the stage reached the Hotel Glenwood. Kate said it was May 24th.

"'Doc was coughing from almost each breath and upon arrival, had to use his cane to support his weight. He was very frail in body when I saw him, and his hair was a silver gray. His face showed the lines of age and he looked sick in the eyes. His appearance resembled that of an older man, since pulling out of Hooker's Ranch [outside Tombstone, AT, where the Vendetta riders had been temporarily protected in 1882].

"'One might argue that Doc was content in his actions and that his daily consumption of whiskey came to be his only escape from his suffering. I was rightly taken with the general surroundings of Glenwood Springs upon reaching Eighth Avenue, holding my duffle and looking for the hotel.

"'Kate had told me Doc was boarding. All I wanted was to register and find a bathhouse. I had run into Kate in the lobby who had sent this young bellhop, whom Doc had nicknamed Kenny [Art Kendrick], on an errand.

"'The welcome feeling I experienced far exceeded that of Tombstone I soon discovered. The district was full of excitement when the train pulled into the station house. I recall most of all how many people were about on the streets.

"'There was a definite resemblance to Denver; the big blue sky and the "Rockies" that seem to surround the town, which I would soon see was a perfect view from Doc's hotel window.

"'The Denver and Rio Grande [which was completed into Glenwood Springs in 1887] was due to arrive the following day [October 5], and the town was full of anticipation of the arrival of the new iron horse. Banners swung across streets, and merchant signs from store front windows. Great expectations filled the streets.

"'I refrained from the moment and walked in the lobby of the Hotel Glenwood. The lobby was furnished with fine Victorian trimmings and elaborate knotted-Persian carpets, and reminded me of the Cosmopolitan and Grand hotels in Tombstone, and the White Club House Room in Denver.

"'There was this need to put down words on paper since leaving Hooker's Ranch in '82, but it was Kate's enduring patience and devotion to Doc that gave me my inspiration to [finally] tell the story.

"'There was a sense of fatalism in Kate's voice, yet talk of the springs which had brought Doc to Glenwood was the last hope the West had to offer a lunger like Doc. I suppose if there was a chance for Doc's health to improve, he would take up its resources in Glenwood Springs.

"'Writing this down is not to judge him for past actions, but to understand him. Doc's memory seemed to be unaffected at times, although he lost much of his lungs over the years out West since leaving his beloved Georgia. I know the whiskey came to be his only escape from the pain that came with the consumption, and his desperate longing for home.

"'There is no doubt that the short time Doc lived inside the Hotel Glenwood, [it] became his sanctuary. What transpired within the walls will leave a lasting impression. One that is etched in my memory.

"'Coming to Glenwood Springs with the miners in October, I found Doc delirious and dying. He had fallen to a pneumonia the local doctor said, and had not spoken a word in weeks. Kate was already there taken (sic) *care of him when I arrived. She said Doc had sent word to her in Globe from Leadville and told her he was leaving after a bit of excitement with Will Allen, and was taking a stage to Glenwood Springs, in Garfield County to see if the sulfur springs would ease his consumption.*

"Kate's devotion to Doc was not surprising, for she remained by his side till the end. Doc had tolerated my presence in Tombstone, though suggested I join the game after Morg's death, since Morg and I had a fondness to billiards at Robert Hatch's. Doc was still a young man though he began to deteriorate in Denver and became more advanced as his struggle for pain was no longer at his control. Doc was at the point of never leaving his bed again.

"I imagine Kate felt helpless not being able to ease his pain. Shortly after Doc arrived, he tryed [sic] dealing faro but no longer could keep up the long hours he was used to in Tombstone, for he tired easily. Walking from gambling house to gambling house became an exhausting event, and the treatments at the springs [never] seemed to have any effect.

"Kate was their means for support, for Doc could not work. I would help to bring in money by doing odd jobs around town, and doing mechanic work for a blacksmith shop.

"Since October, Doc hardly spoke and hardly sat up twice. Kate never wanted to be far from Doc. I consoled her and saw to it no harm came to Doc from the traffic coming and going inside the hotel. Doc had made many enemies in his life and perhaps [because of] the troubles Doc faced in Arizona and Colorado, she still sensed danger to him.

"A light snow had fallen early in the morning and Kate had to shut the window in Doc's room. His breathing had become shallow overnight and the color in his face

Hotel Glenwood – This accommodation at the corner of 8th Street and Grand Avenue was photographed circa 1887, the year of Holliday's death in a single room on the fifth floor. Holliday was removed from this room the day of his death and ultimately buried – at least for a year or two – at a site nearby which has been lost to history. The actual location of his grave today remains a matter of conjecture. (Photo courtesy of Frontier Historical Society)

had turned pale. It is important to know the last day as I was in the hotel room with Doc and Kate as he clinged [sic] to life.

"An era was ending Kate thought. I don't write about an era changing, but a man's life who was shaped around it. For Kate the day began to fall apart when I was told that she sent for the doctor and that I should return to Doc's room. It seemed strange for anyone besides Doc or Kate to summon me at once. I went, expecting the end had come.

"In the lobby I had a strange feeling. Instead of the heavy traffic, there was this stillness in the hotel lobby as I hurried up to Doc's room. Then the bellhop told me that Doc was sitting up. I felt relief for Kate. For a moment I thought Doc had cheated death one last time.

"Doc had been found that morning sitting up by the maid who had awoke [sic] Kate who had slept in Doc's chair that he liked sitting by the window in. The doctor was there when I got there. He was saying something to Kate, but his words didn't make her feel better.

Final Ride – Photographed sometime after 1898 during one of the periodic Strawberry Days parades in Glenwood Springs, this funeral coach from 1885 almost certainly transported Holliday's body from his last home in the Hotel Glenwood to the vicinity of Linwood Cemetery on November 8, 1887 where he reportedly was buried – at least temporarily. (Courtesy of Frontier Historical Society)

"'For the first time in weeks, the details and the sound of Dr. B.'s [possibly Dr. Baldwin] voice was [sic] clear. She knew the end was upon him. Knowing Doc, I figured he might pull out another winning hand. It was not meant to be. This would be his last game.

"'I did not know the complete story from the doctor who had been making house calls to Doc's room the past few weeks. Though I never doubted his opinion. In the final hour I knew one thing. Doc was about to cash in his chips.

"'There were several Glenwood residents in the room, Sarah Copper [Sarah Field Cooper] and Walter Devereaux, whom [sic] [had] shared a seat with Doc on the Concorde stage.

"'The doctor who had been sent for by Kenny stood over Doc pouring him a tumbler of whiskey, jotting down medical quotes [notes] in his notebook. During the final moments, when the end was approaching, Doc turned his head toward Kate and smiled. He turned up the tumbler with great fashion as he always had done in the past.

"'As the light began to fade from his eyes, he took his last breath, and I heard him say, "This is funny." Then his eyes stood still, and his body relaxed. Doc was lying on his bed, dead. I remember Kate saying in a distraught voice, "The end of Holliday." The room seemed as lifeless as he was.

"'He had opened his eyes once or twice that morning, but his gaze was clouded. When I saw him open his eyes at Kate, she leaned over him straining to hear something or read something from his eyes. Kate was trying to tell him something, though I doubt he heard her. The Colt, which he employed laid idle in the bureau, retired for all times. "Doc is at peace, Charlie. The worms won't get Doc today."

"'It is unthinkable, but during his time of dying, I realized the loss that Kate was feeling. In the beginning when I first met him in Tombstone, he had been a sporting man, usually staying among

Alexander Harony, brother to Kate ("Big Nose") Harony, lived with his family at Penny Hot Springs in the Crystal Valley region near Glenwood Springs, Colorado. Extant records place Kate Harony at this site shortly after Holliday's death. This photo of Alexander Harony's cabin during this approximate time-period includes a female who bears a striking resemblance to Kate. (Glenn G. Boyer Collection)

Wyatt's crowd, yet everyone who knew him was certain of his loyalty to friends.

"'Doc didn't have many friends, and he showed honor to the ones he did have. Those in the room were showing their respect for Doc. During the moment when he at last found peace, and the pain had left him, I knew he had found what he longed for. Doc had died a slow, lingering death.

"'It would surprise him to have escaped death so many times, to have died in a room in Glenwood Springs. At the end when Doc was gone, the doctor noted the time of death. "Nine fifty-five, November 8, 1887."

"'Preparations were made for a quick funeral, which would take place in a place called Linwood, a short distance by hack at two o'clock the same day. It would be a quiet procession, with the Reverend Rudolph officiating. His coffin would be elaborate with silver trimmings, donated by Glenwood's social class and friends he had made.

"'By 11 o'clock, the undertakers came to remove Doc's body from the hotel. It was the first time I had seen the physical scars the consumption had left on his body. The body was taken away. A black hearse rolled to a stop near the front entrance, and everybody came outside. Those who were standing on the boardwalk and those in the street tipped their hats to Kate as the hearse drove away.

"'Kate left Glenwood Springs after Doc's possessions were in order to be sent back to relatives in Georgia. It was a sad parting. I left November 10th, the day after Kate. Will stop by Leadville to see Bob I think.'"

It is interesting to note from the above article that several items which have been questioned over the years as to

Mary Katherine Harony Cummings (a.k.a. "Big-Nose Kate") was photographed here circa 1890. Gone was the limited beauty she had enjoyed as a young adult. She, nevertheless, was devoted to John Henry Holliday, and, according to at least one reputable newspaper account, cared for him lovingly in his last days as he lay dying in the Hotel Glenwood at Glenwood Springs, Colorado. (A.W. Bork and Glenn G. Boyer Collection)

their authenticity can now quite possibly be certified as being accurate.

- First of all, this article confirms that Kate Harony did in fact come to Doc's aid during his last days, staying with him and caring for him until the end.
- The article also gives a specific date (May 24, 1887) for Doc's arrival in Glenwood Springs. Prior to this article, it was known only that he had arrived in the spring of 1887.
- Also confirmed by the article is the fact that Art Kendrick ("Kenny") – who long claimed he was the bell-hop in the Hotel Glenwood during

Doc's last days and ran many errands for him – was also actually telling the truth about those experiences.

- Finally, one of the most enduring legends of the Old West is also put to bed with this article, since it seems to confirm – despite many claims to the contrary – that Doc did indeed quite possibly utter the famous words *"This is funny"* in a final moment of lucidity shortly before his death, acknowledging the humor in the fact that he was dying with his boots off.

Though Origen C. "Harelip Charley" Smith seems to be attempting to a great degree to weave in his own history with that of John Henry Holliday and the Earp faction with his memoirs, he does, nevertheless, provide and corroborate a number of previously-unknown valuable details regarding the history and legend of John Henry Holliday.

Buried in Colorado or Georgia?

Where Lie The Bones Of John Henry Holliday?

Many of the locations of the last remains of popular figures from the old West are known quite well today. Others, not so well. One of the most profound examples of mythic Old West icons with an unknown burial site today is John Henry Holliday. . . . but this mystery might actually be solvable.

Somewhat strangely, a lost burial site for the infamous – and sometimes even the famous – isn't that unusual. These men often were buried where they fell – and fairly quickly before putrefaction could set in. Their graves also invariably were very poorly marked for posterity – usually due to the little matter of "money for the burial." And more often than not, most of the grave markers were not permanent stone tombstones. Those usually came much later – if at all.

For instance, no one today knows the "exact" gravesite of William H. Bonney, alias "Billy the Kid" – though his is at least known generally. Not so, however for Butch Cassidy, nor "the Sundance Kid," nor "Curly Bill" Brocius, nor "Buckskin" Frank Leslie, nor "Turkey Creek" Jack Johnson, nor Warren Earp, and on and on, all of whose graves are a total mystery today. Strange? You be the judge.

Most of these men were intentionally mysterious in life, often identifying themselves by aliases, and secretively withholding almost all actual details about themselves and their familial background for their entire lives. So what's so unusual about that circumstance carrying over into death? John Henry Holliday himself occasionally used an alias when he was "on the run." He also played the facts of his life "very close to the vest" while he was alive, though the mystery about his actual gravesite is just a bit different.

John Henry Holliday's parents – Maj. Henry Burroughs Holliday and Alice Jane McKey – were from South Carolina, before moving to Georgia. They provided a good education for their son, but his primary interest was the great outdoors. Nothing interested young John Henry more than hunting, fishing and horseback riding in what then was still a rolling wilderness in the Georgia back-country. In time, he also became intensely interested in the use of firearms as did many young men of his day. Some of these became very adept in the use of weapons; some others not so much.

In 1861, Henry Burroughs Holliday accepted a presidential appointment from Jefferson Davis to serve as quartermaster in the 27th Georgia Infantry, Confederate States of America. After the Battle of Manassas, Henry Burroughs was promoted to the rank of major and fought in the Peninsula Campaign as well as in the deadly Battle of Malvern Hill.

In 1862, a short time after fighting at Malvern Hill, Major Holliday was forced by ill health – watery dysentery – to leave the army and return to his family in Griffin. He, no doubt, thought death for him was eminent at that time, as ultimately became the case for most individuals suffering from this malady. He, however, somehow managed to survive. Approximately 26 years later, he would suffer through the mortality of his famous son, John Henry.

A False Image

During his lifetime, John Henry was credited with the deaths of a number of men who were actually shot by other individuals.[1] The newspapers of that day – in the absence of factual information – often chose to simply fabricate the identity of those responsible for deaths, and once he had gained a bit of notoriety, John Henry Holliday suffered from this misidentification quite a bit. It just made for better reading, and, subsequently, better sales of the publications in which these defamatory statements were made.

With its usual artistic license, Hollywood also created a false image and persona for John Henry Holliday. In most instances, it portrayed him as a bloodthirsty and cold-blooded killer.

In reality, of the handful of actual shootings in which Holliday was involved, they occurred because much larger and stronger men who – due to

John Henry's much weaker and therefore vulnerable physical condition – tried to increase their own stature at his expense by attempting to either severely injure him, or kill him outright. These attackers, however, almost always misjudged their opponent when his name was Holliday.

Rather than resulting in John Henry's submission or serious injury or death, these attacks invariably ended in either a gun or a knife fight with Holliday virtually always gaining the upper hand. John Henry was weak and small in stature physically. There was no doubt about that. He, however, had been blessed with strong arms and hands, lightning-quick reflexes, and deadly accuracy with firearms, and he used all of his advantages – physical and mental – when attacked. And those who attacked him almost always regretted it – if they lived to rue that day.

Doc Holliday's life contradicts the myth of the man. He was not a ruthless individual, nor was he "blood-thirsty" in nature, nor necessarily evil. "When any of you fellows have been hunted from one end of the country to the other, as I have been, you'll understand what a bad man's reputation is built on," John Henry is reported to have once quipped.

Holliday pursued life under the only circumstances available to him. He sought to remain alive as long as his body would allow him, and along the way, unfortunately, his reputation from incidents in which he was forced to defend himself became twisted and tainted, and caused violence to follow him just as do fleas a dog. This myth of his preponderance or desire for violence, however, is just one of many which followed him into the grave.

Lost Burial Site

Inaccurate information seemed to plague Doc in death just as it had in real life. His obituary was printed in a variety of newspapers, but very few if any of them printed factual information about him or his death.

The local newspaper in Glenwood Springs, Colorado (where he died), stated that Doc was buried *"in Linwood Cemetery,"* Glenwood Springs, Colorado, at 4:00 p.m., November 8, 1887. However, the steep trail that led to the cemetery (which exists on a hilltop mesa) reportedly was impassable due to snow and ice on the day Holliday's mortal remains were to be interred.

According to records, Doc was therefore actually buried in a temporary grave someplace near the foot of the hill. When spring and warmer weather returned, even if a burial detail had been organized to dig up his body to re-bury it in the cemetery-proper, no such re-burial ever occurred. As the years passed, the grave of John Henry Holliday supposedly was simply forgotten, and eventually, no one knew the site of his grave at all – just as they still do not

> *According to records, Doc was therefore actually buried in a temporary grave someplace near the foot of the hill.*

today. Despite this fact, the signage in Linwood and the media accounts of his death and burial have consistently maintained that he is buried *"in Linwood Cemetery."*

The same Glenwood Springs newspaper which misstated the site of his burial also stated that many friends attended Holliday's funeral, but since he reportedly was buried the same day he died, this too is doubtful.[2] Also, adding insult to injury, both a monument and Holliday's headstone in Linwood Cemetery contained numerous mistakes for many years. It was almost as if his detractors were attempting to harass him even in death.

Tombstone, Arizona historian Ben Traywick seemed to state it best: *"It is difficult to see how so many mistakes could be made on a headstone without trying,"* he wrote.[3]

Despite the fact that a monument in Linwood Cemetery continues to proclaim that Holliday is buried *"somewhere in this cemetery,"* some historians today are convinced he was not.

One account maintains that following the spring thaw in 1888, a relative of Holliday's traveled to Glenwood Springs, retrieved the famous Georgian's body, and returned with it to that state where it was re-interred in Oak Hill Cemetery in Griffin, his boyhood home. Bill Dunn, a distant relative of Holliday's who headed up the *Doc Holliday Society* in Griffin, extensively researched the Holliday family for a number of years, and has an opinion of his own on this issue.

"There is no doubt in my mind why the people in Glenwood Springs don't know exactly where Doc is buried," Dunn said in an interview in 1999. "[It's because] *he isn't there. Doc is buried right here in his hometown of Griffin. He was*

Faulty Marker – This tombstone, though replaced in recent years, existed for over half a century in Linwood Cemetery outside Glenwood Springs, Colorado. It supposedly identifies Holliday's grave, but the actual site has never been determined. Ironically, not only did the headstone not identify the specific burial plot of the famed gunman, the engraving in the headstone contained numerous errors of fact about Holliday, including his birth site, birthday, and the medical school he attended. (Photo by Olin Jackson)

originally buried near Linwood Cemetery, but he is not there now. You just don't lose the grave of a man who held his celebrity status."

Buried In Georgia?

Some researchers believe that Doc's father, Maj. Henry B. Holliday (or his emissary) traveled to Glenwood Springs and claimed his son's remains. In retrospect, this is a definite possibility, since transportation of the coffin and remains could easily have been accomplished via the *Denver & Rio Grande Western (D&RGW)* railroad which had been completed to Glenwood Springs in 1887 – the year Holliday died and prior to his death. And back in Griffin, Georgia, the train depot was within a mile of Oak Hill Cemetery.

Dunn says he believes that if it was not Maj. Holliday who retrieved his son's remains, he quite possibly sent his nephew, Robert Alexander Holliday, to perform the task. Doc's consort out West – Mary Katherine Harony – recalled in a later interview that one of Doc's cousins visited him in Tombstone after the shootout at the O.K. Corral. Dunn says he believes this man was Robert.

Strangely coincidental – or maybe not – is the fact that the final resting place of Maj. Holliday himself is also unknown today. Considering the fact that Henry Burroughs Holliday was a wealthy landowner, a decorated veteran of three wars, and a four-time mayor of Valdosta, Georgia, it is highly unlikely that his final resting place would not have been both clearly marked and definitely known today – unless he intentionally made arrangements to be buried in a secret location for a particular reason.

Maj. Holliday outlived his son by several years. He died on February 22, 1893 in Valdosta. Despite many years of searches, the location of his grave has eluded researchers just as has that of his famous son.

Bill Dunn maintains that he has located a marked grave for every Holliday family member in Valdosta and Griffin – except for Maj. Holliday and his son, John Henry. Dunn says he

The two graves which Dunn says belong to Henry Burroughs and John Henry Holliday are located in the Thomas family plot at Oak Hill.

now believes without a doubt he has found the unmarked graves of both in Griffin's Oak Hill Cemetery.

The Plot Thickens

The two graves which Dunn says belong to Henry Burroughs and John Henry Holliday are located in the Thomas family plot at Oak Hill. The families were related through marriage, and enjoyed a very close relationship. Dunn says he believes the Thomas family may have agreed to an anonymous burial of the two men in their family plot to avoid vandalism of the graves.

"I believe they buried Doc in Oak Hill when he was brought back from Glenwood Springs, and Maj. Holliday was buried there when he died," Dunn remarks. "Why would a plot containing expensive marble markers of the Thomas family contain two concrete slab graves with no marking or identification whatsoever? Could it be that they wanted them to remain anonymous and their last remains protected from vandalism?"

Osgood Miller, an employee of *Clark Monument Company* for forty-six years, once made a statement which lends credence to Dunn's claim. He said he remembered the late Charlie McElroy – who was cemetery superintendent during the 1930s – telling him that Doc Holliday was buried in Oak Hill. Osgood said Charlie even pointed in the direction of the Thomas plot when he made the statement. Several years later, the late Griffin historian Laura Clark pointed out the same area as Doc's final resting place.

Wyatt Earp, who was probably the closest friend John Henry Holliday ever had, died in 1929. Ironically, after all the gunfights in which he was involved, Earp was never once wounded. He died in bed from what undoubtedly was prostate cancer (listed as "prostatitis" on his death certificate).

While he and Doc were both still alive, Earp was quoted as saying *"Doc Holliday is the nerviest, fastest, deadliest man with a six-gun I ever saw."* And in Denver, Colorado, when last the two met and he realized that his old friend was near death, Earp, with tears in his eyes, also told Holliday that *"You saved my life on two separate occasions. Isn't it strange that you must go first."*

One can only marvel today that the final resting place of such a celebrated figure of the old West is, for all intents and purposes, completely unknown, as is that of his father, Henry Burroughs Holliday.

Endnotes

1/ *John Henry by Ben T. Traywick*

2/ *Ibid*

3/ *Ibid*

Acquaintances & Opinions

What do we know today that can be confirmed as factual information regarding the "friendly" and "adversarial" acquaintances of John Henry Holliday? Well, according to Doc's first cousin, the "friends" comprise a short list, but then, she didn't seem to try very hard. Admittedly, however, the list of individuals who despised and wished ill of him certainly seems lengthier than that of those who loved or admired him.

For more than a century now, the gunfight behind the O.K. Corral in Arizona Territory in 1881 has carried the dubious distinction as "one of the most confusing 15 seconds in American history." Even more conflicting, however, are the various modern descriptions of the relationships John Henry Holliday had with his various acquaintances in the West.

Fanned by ceaseless rumors and the imaginations of the masses, as well as the countless erroneous articles and portrayals from the days of dime novels in the late 19th Century all the way up to the modern books and major motion pictures of the present-day, the confusing brushfire that supposedly represents "the real Doc Holliday" of Western lore continues to burn unabated.

Susan McKey Thomas is Holliday's first cousin once-removed. Perhaps it is appropriate that her educated, scrupulously studied opinions of Doc become, if not the last word, at least a part of the final sentence.

"Cousin Mattie" (Sister Mary Melanie)

It seems to go without saying, that any list of Doc's acquaintances with whom he had a positive or favorable relationship has to include cousin Martha Anne "Mattie" Holliday, daughter of Robert Kennedy Holliday of Fayetteville, Georgia. In his early life, John Henry had played and enjoyed secrets with Mattie that were shared with no one else. This relationship supposedly grew into much more than just friendship. It goes without saying that Mattie quite possibly had a much stronger bond with him than anyone else.

When the relationship turned from friendship to whatever it later became is anyone's guess today. Whatever the circumstances, when John Henry left his Georgia home, though it was claimed that he departed for dryer climes for health reasons, some have speculated that the departure also involved some type of unfortunate incident which had occurred between him and cousin Mattie.

At approximately the same point as Doc's relocation to the West, Mattie had suddenly entered a Catholic convent, taking her vows and remaining in that capacity for the remainder of her life. It is a matter of record that John Henry mourned the loss of his relationship with Mattie for the remainder of his life. Despite this fact, he and Mattie continued to communicate – quite often – by letter long after he had relocated. Very personal and engaging letters which no doubt revealed a side of John Henry unknown to the outside world.

When John Henry finally passed away due to the ravages of tuberculosis, Sister Mary Melanie reportedly burned the letters she had received from him, in order that they not fall into the hands of others and be misinterpreted after her death. For many years thereafter, as a result of the harsh and negative publicity which had grown up around John Henry's name before and after his death, Sister Mary stated openly that had she not burned the letters, the world would have known a much different John Henry Holliday than the one portrayed in the harsh and sensationalized Western mythology that had become so prominent and unattractive.

"Big Nose Kate"

Aside from the famous incident behind the O.K. Corral in Tombstone, Arizona Territory, on October 26, 1881, one of the few things about which most historians agree regarding Holliday was his intimate relationship with Mary Katherine Harony (Haroney) Cummings (a.k.a. "Big-Nose" Kate Elder), a prostitute who was known by at least seven different identities during her life. She appears to have been the gunfighter's only romantic interest of consequence after he left Georgia.

Though she passes no judgment on the Holliday-Harony/Cummings coupling, Ms. Thomas says with no reservation that no official marriage ever took place regarding the pair, in spite of the fact that many sources accept the marriage as fact and Harony/Cummings herself was vehement in her assertions that she was Doc's widow. She also maintains a long list of evidence to back up her assertion to the contrary.

"There are so many reasons not to believe he was ever married to Katie Elder," Ms. Thomas explained in an interview in 2001. *"When she told the story, she said they were married in Valdosta, supposedly on a visit in 1880, and she gave a date. Well, the marriages of that period are available on record, and there is no record of any marriage between Doc and Katie."*

Thomas's argument is augmented by the fact that Doc Holliday almost certainly never returned to Georgia after traveling to the West. Thomas maintained that most of what Doc's immediate family even knew of the prodigal son after he traveled to the West was gleaned from the *Valdosta Daily Times* newspaper.

Then there also is the family **Bible**.

*"I have an authentic copy of the records in the family **Bible**,"* Ms. Thomas continued. *"Now his father was a meticulous man, and in that **Bible** are entries of births, deaths – anything that pertained to the family. The major almost certainly would have entered the marriage – whether he approved of it or not – and he did not enter anything about such a marriage."*

Although Doc Holliday did not correspond with his Valdosta relatives, his correspondence with Mattie (Sister Mary Melanie) is a matter of record. There is a great probability that Sister Mary would have passed along the news of such a marriage – unless Doc specifically instructed her to the contrary, which of course is always possible.

According to Ms. Thomas, however, there is even more evidence of the absence of such a marriage. *"Katie told an interviewer about their relationship, and not only did she not know the names of Doc's family, but she got Doc's birth date wrong – by about 10 years."*

Further evidence rests in the fact that census records from 1880 show Doc Holliday residing in Prescott, Arizona, with two other men, one of whom was John Gosper, acting governor of Arizona Territory.

Regardless of the circumstances, Doc did enjoy a long and sometimes combative relationship with Mary Katherine Harony, traveling on many adventures with her. And when it came time to select someone with which to spend his last days as he lay dying in a Glenwood Springs, Colorado, hotel room, it was Mary Katherine Harony to whom he wrote. And it was she who responded and indeed traveled to the high Rockies to care for him until he passed. That's pretty darn close to a marriage.

The Earp Family

As far as Doc Holliday's relationship with the Earp family is concerned, it seems a little hazy too, which is not surprising under the circumstances. After an alliance with the Earps which lasted at least four years, Holliday parted ways with Wyatt in Albuquerque, New Mexico, in 1882. By that time, Morgan Earp – a very close friend of Doc's – had been assassinated in Tombstone, and brother Virgil Earp had also been shot in the back and relegated to a life as a cripple in Los Angeles, California.

"I can't really say if they parted as friends or as friendly enemies," Thomas added. *"I'm not certain, but from everything I can gather, my impression is that they just reached a parting of the ways. Sometimes friendships just reach a point where everything that can be said has been said, and people just go their separate ways. I really think that's probably what happened. Maybe there simply was no reason to continue their partnership after what happened* (in the Tombstone affrays and the Albuquerque incident).*"*

Thomas suggested the bond between Holliday and the Earps may well have been little more than a friendship of necessity in what then was virtually a lawless environment, making a parting of the ways less than surprising. Documents today indicate that Wyatt and Doc had a falling out over an innocent but perhaps unflattering comment Doc made concerning Wyatt's respect for Jewish traditions. (By that time, Wyatt's bond with his future common-law wife, Josephine Sara Marcus, a Jewess, was quite strong.)

And though he had an exceptionally-strong friendship with the fourth Earp brother – Morgan – it was cut short by an assassin's bullet in a Tombstone billiard parlor in 1881. According to reports, Morgan and John Henry truly were best friends, and Doc grieved deeply over the younger Earp's death.

His (Doc's) relationships with Virgil and Jim, however, were strictly business. The taciturn Virgil was "all business" in all his endeavors, and basically tolerated Doc due to his friendships with his brothers.

Bat Masterson

Ms. Thomas has a much more definite opinion about Bat Masterson, who, like the Earps, was allied with Holliday during the heady days of Dodge City, Kansas, where Masterson served as a city marshal.

"For some reason, Bat Masterson didn't like Doc," Thomas asserted. *"He seemed to like the Earps, but he definitely didn't like Doc."*

Ms. Thomas said she also blames much of the Holliday bad press on Masterson, who went on to write about the period known as the "Wild West" in respected publications such as the *New York Times*. After living in the West for many years, Masterson later moved back East to New York where he went to work as a writer for the *Times*. He ultimately died at his desk, a worn-out old man.

"Bat Masterson never wrote anything complimentary about Doc," Thomas added. *"He* (in fact) *made some very disparaging remarks about Doc."*

Though Ms. Thomas did her best to maintain a position as an impartial historian, she said she clearly saw Masterson as a self-serving opportunist eager to secure a place for himself as one of the "heroes" of the period when in fact, some sources describe Masterson's law enforcement skills as lax at best.

"Bat defended himself [in the newspaper] *and he had a big audience. Poor old Doc just died young and had no one to defend him,"* she sighed.

The Haters

Very high on the list of individuals who despised and would dearly have loved to have maimed or killed John Henry Holliday, have to be the Clantons and McLaurys of Tombstone fame (or infamy). Ike Clanton hated Holliday in particular due to the fact that

he (Holliday) constantly mocked and taunted him. Doc apparently was also very adept at taking Clanton's money in poker games, which didn't help matters.

This hate became particularly intense following the shoot-out behind the O.K. Corral in 1881, when Holliday was credited with at least one – and possibly two – of the kills made that day. It was a fight from which Ike Clanton had fled in an exceedingly cowardly fashion, running back into the corral and its buildings.

Following several particularly heated exchanges in the later courtroom testimony and open challenges made by Holliday against Ike in the streets of Tombstone, the hate grew incrementally. As a result, few people yearned more to see Holliday dead than Ike Clanton, his brothers, and the McLaury brothers.

In the Tombstone days, even though he was a small man in stature due to the tuberculosis ravaging his body, John Henry Holliday's amazing hand-speed and deadly accuracy with both a sidearm and knife were put on public display on more than one occasion. These were defense capabilities that Doc had honed to a fine finish in his earlier travels across the West. As a result, by the time he reached Tombstone, his reputation preceded him, and few dared to challenge him. Though their hate for him was intense, none of the McLaurys or Clantons were willing to publicly attack Holliday man to man.

Johnny Tyler, also of Tombstone renown, must be included among the intense haters of Holliday. In the days prior to his submission to the ravages of tuberculosis, Doc Holliday feared no man, and his unnecessary bravado often unfortunately got the better of him. In 1880, shortly after Wyatt Earp's arrival in that town, he forcefully ejected and permanently barred Tyler from the Oriental Saloon, and Holliday unnecessarily taunted Tyler as he laid in the dusty street. Tyler never forgot the incident, and years later in Leadville, Colorado, Doc no doubt regretted those actions when, in a weaker condition, he was hard-pressed to defend himself against the much-stronger revenge-minded Tyler.

Another on the haters list has to have been Billy Allen. He was one of the many "wolves" who began circling Holliday in his later years, waiting for an opportunity to make a name for themselves by being the one to snuff out the Georgian's life. Allen had testified against Holliday and the Earps at the inquest in Tombstone following the noted shootout, and, as fate would have it, also was present in Leadville when Doc – again disarmed and much weaker – took up quarters in that city.

While in Leadville, Allen's strategy had been to loan a then-penniless and desperate Holliday $5.00 when he was too weak to continue earning a living as a regular daily professional card dealer. When Doc was unable to repay the loan, Allen openly abused and publicly insulted him, threatening to give him a beating for failing in repayment. Holliday however – game to the end – was the one who ultimately left Allen bleeding from a gunshot wound on a barroom floor, earning still more hate for the former dentist.

The list goes on and on, but it's pointless to go further. Holliday was small and weak, and as such, he constantly was forced to use his talents with a handgun or other weapons to disabuse bullies of the notion that they could mistreat, insult, and/or harm him. Though this kept his challengers at bay in the early years, it actually did little other than make the list of haters longer and longer.

Movie Portrayals

As far as the movies about Doc Holliday are concerned, Ms. Thomas said she believed actor Val Kilmer – who researched Holliday extensively for his role in the 1993 major motion picture *Tombstone* – may have provided the most accurate portrayal of the man.

"It's obvious that Val thoroughly enjoyed the characterization," Thomas stated. *"Of course, some of what he portrayed was valid and some was not so valid. But it was obvious he had done his homework."*

Thomas said that in general, she regarded almost all the other movies about Holliday to be wildly inaccurate as well as simply poor cinema. She critiqued actor Dennis Quaid's take on Holliday in the 1994 movie *Wyatt Earp* as *"horrible, just horrible. . . an absolute waste of time."*

Another aspect of Holliday's life upon which history buffs disagree wildly is the circumstances of his death. Thomas said a letter, dated June 12, 1973, addressed to her, nailed down with probable finality that information. The letter quotes A.E. Axtell, city manager of Glenwood Springs, Colorado, where Holliday died on November 8, 1887, after spending two months in and out of consciousness at the Hotel Glenwood. Axtell tells of former Glenwood Springs Mayor Art Kendricks, who reportedly worked as a busboy at the hotel during the time of Holliday's death.

Last Hours

According to Axtell, Kendricks told of carrying bottles of whiskey to Holliday's room and each time being tipped a dime. Kendricks reportedly stated that when Holliday finally died, only the busboy and two others attended the funeral.

This seems to cement Ms. Thomas's argument against Mary Katherine Harony Cummings (a.k.a. Katie Elder), who claimed she was with Holliday for the last two months of his life. Still, many sources, and at least one credibly-published newspaper account [*Sulphur* (Oklahoma) *Headlight*, February 14, 1899] paint the situation in a different light, stating unequivocally that Kate was indeed present, attending to Holliday and spending what little savings she had to pay the hotel bill, and finally, after his death, gathering Holliday's belongings and shipping them home to his relatives in Georgia.

It is known that Kate was in northwestern Colorado at roughly the same time as Doc's death, since records have been passed down of time she spent in the Crystal Valley region of that state near what then was the mining town of Aspen. If she had been that near to Doc during his last days, it is difficult to imagine that she would not at least have paid him a final visit. Further, with her meager funds at that time, it is also unlikely she would have traveled to northwestern Colorado all the way from southern Arizona had her destination been of frivolous intent.

And what about the long-standing claim that at the end of his life, Doc regained consciousness just long enough to look at his bare feet and utter the words

> *Kendricks reportedly stated that when Holliday finally died, only the busboy and two others attended the funeral.*

"*This is funny*" then take one last breath and die? Ms. Thomas won't even wait for the question about that incident to be finished.

"*The man was in a coma!*" she exclaimed, when queried. "*Really, I don't think he regained consciousness for those few seconds just to say that.*" She clearly considered any such suggestion to be an abject absurdity.

Nevertheless, physicians will explain that invalids on their death-bed will often indeed re-gain consciousness in one final seemingly lucid moment, to perform some action or make some final statement. History is rife with such incidents. It would not have been unusual at all for John Henry Holliday to therefore have made such a statement in his final moments.

And this is exactly the type brief "lucid moment" described in the credible article in the *Sulphur Headlight* – which was never denied by anyone mentioned in the article – including Glenwood Springs Mayor Art Kendricks. And when one stops to think about it, that brief unique final statement which some – including the *Headlight* article – claim was made by John Henry Holliday is an awfully original-sounding statement for someone to have just manufactured out of thin air.

The Actual Gunfights of John Henry Holliday

The Georgia native was involved in numerous affrays in the Old West over the years, and didn't hesitate to defend himself – usually to great advantage. Nevertheless, many shootings attributed to Doc Holliday either never happened at all, or were simply done by other individuals.

In the instances in which John Henry was challenged, he was anything if defenseless. He carried with him almost constantly several deadly weapons, and didn't hesitate to use them – usually to great success. He was a "dead-shot" with a sidearm, having honed the skill during his youth and into his young adulthood.

He also learned to hide and quickly retrieve for use a small knife which he carried with him at all times. Anyone who chose to attempt to assault or bully John Henry Holliday – particularly in his early years out West – had made a serious mistake.

Over the years, as legends grew throughout the Old West, the reputations of many noted gunmen invariably exceeded the actual circumstances of their experiences quite significantly. John Henry "Doc" Holliday was no exception, being credited with many more shootings and deaths than the ones with which he was actually involved. . . but that did not in any way diminish the fact that he had successfully defended himself on numerous occasions.

According to Karen Holliday Tanner (***Doc Holliday: A Family Portrait***, University of Oklahoma Press, 1998) who has extensively researched the experiences of her famous forebear, Doc can be documented as having been involved in four affrays in which no fatalities occurred:

A gunfight with Charles Austin in Dallas, Texas; A gunfight with Henry Kahn in Breckenridge, Colorado; A gunfight with Milt Joyce in Tombstone,

Virgil Earp home – The domicile once occupied by Virgil and Allie Earp at 528 West "H" Street in Colton, California, is pictured. After being seriously wounded in Tombstone, Arizona Territory in 1881, Virgil departed that town forever when he was well enough to travel. It was in Colton that Virgil and Allie resided for a number of years while he served as marshal of that community and engaged in other business endeavors. Though permanently crippled in his left arm by the Tombstone assassination attempt in 1881, he nevertheless was still a dependable and effective law enforcement officer for a number of years.

Arizona; A gunfight with Billy Allen in Leadville, Colorado.

Though none of the above shootings involved any fatalities, all resulted in wounded participants – none with the name of Holliday.

Doc was indicted in the Austin case and found *"Not Guilty."*

In the Henry Kahn shooting, Doc was fined, but not charged.

In the shooting incident with Milt Joyce a charge of *"Assault with a Deadly Weapon with Intent to Kill"* was dismissed, and for the misdemeanor charge of *"Assault and Battery"* Doc paid a $20 fine.

In the Billy Allen shooting, Holliday, surprisingly, was charged with *"Assault with Intent to Commit Murder,"* a slightly more serious offense. He was jailed and his bail set at $5,000.00.

Newton Earp – Newton was the son of Nicholas Earp and his first wife, Abigail Storm. As such, he was a half-brother to James, Virgil, Wyatt, Morgan and Warren and sisters Martha, Adelia, Virginia and Mariah. Residing in numerous locales from Missouri to Nevada, Newton spent much of his later life in north California, but lived for a short time in San Bernardino. Despite his half-brother status to his famed male siblings, Newton was very close with his brothers his entire life.

In an earlier day, the gunman from Georgia might have raised a $5,000.00 bail, but by the time of his days in Leadville, the ex-dentist was a pauper, living virtually hand-to-mouth, and $5,000.00 was an impossibly high amount for him to post.

Despite his oft-abrasive personality, Holliday seemed to consistently cultivate a coterie of close friends willing to help him in times of need. Two of these – John G. Morgan and Samuel Houston, co-owners of the *Board of Trade Saloon* in Leadville, arrived the morning following his incarceration and posted his bail.

In the trial that followed, a number of eye-witnesses testified to the threats that had been issued at Doc by Allen, and the circumstances of the shooting that had followed. Doc took the stand on his own behalf and explained the details of the incident.

"I saw Allen coming in with his hand in his pocket, and I thought my life was as good to me as his was to him," Holliday explained in his courtroom testimony. *I fired the shot and he fell on the floor, and (I) fired the second shot; I knew that I would be a child in his hands if he got hold of me; I weigh 122 pounds; I think Allen weighs 170; I have had pneumonia three or four times. I don't think I would have been able to protect myself against him."*

The jury ultimately returned a verdict of *"Not Guilty"* in the case of *People vs John Henry Holliday*.

There were, however, two additional gunfight incidents which did result in the deaths of Holliday's opponents:

At Fort Griffin, Texas, Ed Bailey died at Doc's hand, as did Charlie White in Las Vegas, New Mexico. Despite these deaths, no charges were ever brought against Holliday in these two incidents, so they quite possibly were simply considered obvious cases of self-defense. Both quite likely were more examples of attempts at bullying in which Doc's attackers came to regret – in their final breaths – their actions.

As a result of her research, Ms. Tanner admits that it quite likely was Doc who ended the days of Old Man Clanton – the leader of the outlaw Clantons in Tombstone, Arizona Territory in the 1880s, but the details of that incident are sketchy since there were no "extant" witnesses.

It is a documented fact that Doc definitely fired the shot that killed Tom McLaury, and he delivered at least one of the three fatal shots which ended the life of Frank McLaury in the October

Scenic Ouray, CO – Located high in the Colorado Rockies, this quaint mountain town was yet another site of mining after gold was discovered here in 1875. Many renowned figures from the Old West have been documented as having passed through this tiny town. Wyatt and Warren Earp are known to have spent time here, as also undoubtedly did John Henry Holliday, although his presence has not been documented. The scenic quality of this site also drew Hollywood movie-makers in 1968 for the filming of scenes from the Academy Award-winning motion picture, *True Grit*, starring John Wayne, Robert Duvall, Glen Campbell, and Kim Darby. (Photo by Olin Jackson)

26, 1881 shooting near the O.K. Corral in Tombstone. In this famed incident which lasted all of 30 seconds, Ike Clanton, brother to the deceased Billy Clanton who died along with Tom and Frank McLaury, filed murder charges against Virgil, Wyatt and Morgan Earp and John Henry Holliday on October 30, 1881.

In an unusual preliminary hearing for the murder charges, Tombstone Justice of the Peace Wells Spicer heard testimony from a large number of witnesses during the next 30 days, and ultimately concluded there was no basis for a trial. Although he criticized Virgil Earp's use of Wyatt and Holliday as deputies, he concluded that no laws had been violated.

And finally, Doc may or may not have been involved in other killings during what later came to be known as *"the Vendetta Ride,"* when Wyatt and Warren Earp, Doc, Texas Jack Vermillion, Turkey Creek Jack Johnson, Dan Tipton, Sherman McMasters and others sought out the assassins of Morgan Earp and the individuals who attempted to kill Virgil Earp. These vigilante – but necessary – actions ended forever the days of the organized gang of outlaws which had frequented the Tombstone area in the 1870s and early 1880s.

So, if one adds up the obvious cases of record, John Henry Holliday can be credited with ending the lives of at least four men – and quite possibly more, since he was responsible for at least one of the three fatal wounds in Frank

McLaury, and he was involved in the Vendetta Ride which definitely resulted in other deaths of unspecified numbers.

Holliday can also be credited with wounding at least five other individuals. Collectively, in the known gunfights in which he was involved, approximately 10 individuals were either killed or wounded.

A Doc Holliday TimeLine In Georgia and the West (1851-1887)

1851: John Henry Holliday was born on August 21, in Griffin, Georgia, to Henry Burroughs Holliday and Alice Jane McKey Holliday.

1864: Major Henry B. Holliday sells all his property and moves his family from Griffin to Valdosta, Georgia, to escape the Union Army troops advancing upon Atlanta.

1866: Alice Jane McKey Holliday, Doc's mother, dies in September, a victim of tuberculosis. John Henry's father remarries a scant three months later, an act which has been described with some import, but which was not uncommon in the least in those days of male spouses with motherless children.

1870: Doc enrolls in the Pennsylvania School of Dental Surgery at Philadelphia.

1872: Doc graduates from dental college.

1873: Doc learns he has tuberculosis. Decides to move to the West, and travels to Dallas, Texas.

1874: Doc is arrested in Dallas for gambling. Moves to Denison, Texas.

1875: In a New Year's Day shooting, Doc is arrested and charged with *"Assault"* and *"Intent to Murder"* Charles Austin in Dallas. He was tried and acquitted. Following his acquittal, he left Dallas, traveled to Fort Griffin, Texas, where he was indicted yet again for gambling.

1876: Doc travels to Denver, Colorado, under the identity of "Tom McKey." He is involved in an altercation and knifes gambler Budd Ryan. Returns to Texas.

1877: Doc is arrested three more times in Dallas for gambling. He later meets Wyatt Earp for the first time at Shaughnessey's Saloon in Fort Griffin. Doc reportedly kills Ed Bailey in Fort Griffin, but no charges were ever lodged, so one must assume the incident was considered a clear-cut case of self-defense.

1878: Doc moves to Dodge City with "Big Nose" Kate Elder (a.k.a. Mary Katherine Harony) where he eventually saves Wyatt Earp's life during an altercation. He shortly travels to Trinidad, Colorado, and Las Vegas, New Mexico, ever the vagabond.

1879: Doc participates in what came to be known as the "Royal Gorge War" during the time of competing railroads being constructed across the United States. He opens a saloon in Las Vegas. May or may not have been involved in the shooting of Mike Gordon. He is indicted once again for running a gambling operation and carrying a deadly weapon. He decides to leave Las Vegas for Prescott, Arizona with the Earps.

1880: Doc returns to Las Vegas where he

shoots Charlie White; the wound, however, is only superficial. No charges were ever brought to bear. He is again arrested for carrying a deadly weapon. Returns to Prescott where he rooms with John J. Gosper, the acting-governor of Arizona Territory. He later moves to Tombstone where he is involved in an altercation with Johnny Tyler and a gunfight and brutal fist-fight with Milt Joyce where he is beaten senseless. He, nevertheless manages to shoot Joyce in both the hand and the foot. A charge of *"Assault With A Deadly Weapon With Intent To Kill"* was ultimately dismissed.

1881: Doc provides much-needed assistance to his friend Wyatt as the two defend the arrested "Johnny-Behind-The-Deuce" from a lynch-mob. Doc is accused and arrested for robbery and murder involving a stage coach robbery in Benson, Arizona Territory, but the outlandish charges – leveled by the outlaw Clanton faction – are dismissed upon examination of the circumstances. Doc is involved in what came to be known as the "Gunfight at the O.K. Corral" which ultimately brought both him and the Earps extreme fame. He was arrested for this shooting and acquitted in the Judge Spicer Hearing and Inquest.

1882: Doc joins Wyatt and Warren Earp, Turkey Creek Jack Johnson, Texas Jack Vermillion, Sherman McMasters, Dan Tipton, and possibly others in what came to be known as the "Vendetta Ride" in Arizona. He was present at the killings of Frank Stillwell, Florentino Cruz, and Curly Bill Brocius, but his actual participation in any of these shootings is unknown. Following these actions, he fled Arizona for New Mexico with the Earp Faction. In Albuquerque, New Mexico, he quarreled with Wyatt Earp during a heated discussion of Earp's latest conquest, Josephine Sarah Marcus. Doc separates from the Earp Faction and travels to Trinidad, New Mexico with Dan Tipton. He eventually leaves there and travels to Denver, Colorado, were he is arrested for extradition back to Arizona. Before the extradition can take place, Doc is rescued by Bat Masterson. He leaves Denver to travel to Gunnison, Salida, Pueblo, and Leadville, Colorado, then back to Denver.

1883-1886: Doc lives much of these three years in Leadville where he is involved in his last gunfight as he shoots Billy Allen in Hyman's Saloon. His arrest for the Billy Allen shooting ultimately goes to trial where he is once again acquitted. Doc travels back and forth to Denver several more times. During his final visit to the Colorado capital, he sees Wyatt Earp for the final time. By this point he is reaching destitution, and is arrested in Denver for vagrancy. Chastened, he returns to Leadville.

1887: Doc had seen enough of Leadville, and decides to move to Glenwood Springs, Colorado, where he finally dies of consumption ("galloping tuberculosis") on November 8, at the age of 36. He reportedly is buried someplace "near Linwood

Cemetery" in Glenwood Springs. The exact site of his final remains is a total mystery today.

The Final Disposition of His Old West Friends

Though his life was cut short by tuberculosis, John Henry Holliday's closest friends – the Earp family – lived considerably longer, with many of them ultimately expiring in California where they occupy numerous gravesites today.

Though the lives they lived were dangerous beyond description, the Earp brothers – many of whom were considered the best friends of John Henry Holliday – lived far beyond the death of the dentist from Georgia. But just as did Holliday, the Earps traveled far and wide in the old West in search of livelihood and adventure. Wyatt eventually even traveled as far as Nome, Alaska, where he lived for several years. Prior to that time and following their departure from Arizona Territory in 1882, James, Virgil, Wyatt and Warren and their common-law wives all resided for a number of years in California in the Colton/San Bernardino vicinity.

Colton Crossing outside Colton, California, was the site of one of the more notable "frog wars" in American railroad history. A frog war occurs when one private (and early) railroad company found itself in need of constructing its rail line across the tracks of another major rail line, particularly as the trans-continental rail lines were being constructed across the western continental United States. It was a situation which inevitably resulted in hostilities between the two competing railroads.

In the summer of 1882 (just a few months following the famed gunfight behind the O.K. Corral in Tombstone,

Arizona Territory), tensions reached their boiling point when construction of the tracks for the California Southern Railroad reached Colton, California. In an attempt to forcibly prevent the competing California Southern crews from completion of their line which intersected the tracks of the Southern Pacific (SP), a SP locomotive and gondola were parked on the tracks at the location of the planned crossing. In addition, the SP hired armed men, including the by-then well-known Virgil Earp of Tombstone fame, to guard the tracks. Competition for control of the major east-west routes of the rails was big and valuable business.

Before the growing potential for violence at the Colton crossing could get out of hand, Governor Robert Waterman ordered San Bernardino County Sheriff J.B. Burkhart to enforce a state court order for completion of Cal Southern's route. Waterman informed Earp of the court order, causing the former lawman to acquiesce and instruct the SP engineer to remove its locomotive where it was blocking the intersection. The crossing then was built, ending the Southern Pacific's monopoly in Southern California.

The Earps in California

Nicholas Earp, patriarch of the by-then famed Earp family had initially arrived in San Bernardino County, California, from their former home in Lamar, Missouri, on December 17, 1864. They remained in the vicinity, living on a small farm for approximately four years until 1868 when they inexplicably returned to Lamar.

Most of the early travels of the Earp family (and there were several) back and forth between California and Missouri were made via covered wagon, since there was no railroad or other

Pioneer Trace – Located on an ages-old travel route between what today are Arizona and Colorado, numerous noted figures from the Old West passed through Ouray, Colorado. A 1800s-era stagecoach trail which roughly parallels the modern highway along this route is periodically identified today by historic markers. (Photo by Olin Jackson)

mode of transportation from the eastern United States (or elsewhere) to California until 1869. These trips were made under extremely dangerous circumstances, since the western interior of the nation at that time was still an extremely wild and remote country largely controlled by hostile native Indians, and populated by millions of buffalo and other wildlife.

In 1877, Nicholas and family returned to San Bernardino, this time with youngest son **Warren** – who was twenty-three years of age at the time – in tow. Warren did not initially share the adventures of his older brothers in Kansas and Arizona, choosing instead to remain in the shadow of his parents in California during his early years.

As a result of his very aggressive personality, the family often referred to young Warren fondly as "the tiger." Unfortunately, this undesirable personality trait would gradually evolve into a bullying and very abusive personality trait which he imposed upon almost everyone with whom he came into contact, particularly if he (Warren) was under the influence of alcohol – which was often. It ultimately was largely responsible for ending his life prematurely.

According to the *San Bernardino Index* newspaper, *"Warren Earp of Colton, while intoxicated, entered the French restaurant on D Street and called for a supper. While his order was being prepared and before it was served, he became very noisy and tried to break the bottles in the caster. The night steward spoke to him politely and told him to keep quiet or else go out. At this Earp turned to and began to abuse the steward, raising up and striking him in the face at the same time. Earp struck the steward on the arm with a pickle jar, shattering the bottle and lacerating the waiter's arm and hand in a fearful manner. Officer Thomas was called in and placed Earp under arrest."*

Over the course of the next nine years – well into the 1880s – Warren reportedly was involved in at least three major bar fights at sites in San Bernardino County which were recorded as news items. In one incident, he shot off the right thumb of his antagonist – a man named Jones. In another, he faced off against two Mexicans, waging war against them with a wooden club with which he reportedly imposed serious injury upon one of the men.

All three participants in this wooden club melee were arrested, but as was often the case, father Nicholas was there to bail Warren out of jail that same night. That fatherly over-protection, it appears, was responsible to a great degree for Warren's dissent into unpredictable and socially-unacceptable behavior. He seldom, if ever, was required to pay a price for his transgressions.

The other Earp siblings – *James*, *Virgil*, *Wyatt* and *Morgan* – had departed from the family nest well prior to Nicholas's arrival in San Bernardino to pursue various other occupational opportunities – usually in law enforcement, saloon operation, or mining – in neighboring states. Though some of them would later temporarily take up residence in and around San Bernardino, none – save James and Morgan – would ultimately die and be buried in that vicinity.

In 1880, *Nicholas* and wife, *Virginia*, and *Warren* moved yet again, this time to nearby Colton where the elder Earp purchased a farm outside of town

which became the center of Earp operations for a number of years. He also purchased a saloon in Colton which he named the "Gem." Warren, as befitted his personality, became a bartender in this saloon for a period of time.

Since he had a legal background – having served earlier in Missouri as a judge – Nicholas was able to apply this knowledge to several occupations associated with the legal profession in the Colton and San Bernardino areas, including service as justice of the peace in Colton. As such, he interacted on a regular basis with the Colton populace for many years.

All of Nicholas's sons and their various wives lived on and off in Colton from the 1870s through the 1930s, until their deaths or migrations to other locales eliminated their Colton residence.

On October 26, 1881, Virgil, Wyatt, and Morgan were involved in the aforementioned famous and epic gunfight behind the O.K. Corral in Tombstone, Arizona Territory, which resulted in three deaths. Their lives were never the same from that point forward.

Final Days of the Earps

On March 18, 1882, in an attempt to eliminate what remained of the ever-vigilant and rigorous Earp law-enforcement cabal remaining in Tombstone, several members of the "Cow Boy" outlaw group assassinated *Morgan Earp* as he played billiards in Hatch's Saloon and narrowly missed placing a round in *Wyatt* as well as he sat watching the game.

James and his wife, "*Bessie*," accompanied Morgan's body back to Colton where he was buried in that town's *Slover Mountain Cemetery*. When, five years later, quarrying operations encroached upon Morgan's remains in *Slover*, he was relocated to nearby *Hermosa Garden Cemetery*.

Morgan's beautiful wife, **Louisa "Lou" Houston Earp** reportedly had actually left Morgan earlier in Tombstone and traveled to Colton to live after discovering that he had another consort in the Tombstone area. Louisa therefore never again saw Morgan alive after leaving Tombstone. She, also, unfortunately died prematurely in 1894 in Long Beach, California, at age 39. She was buried in *Evergreen Cemetery* in Los Angeles.

No doubt sensing his brothers' need for support in Tombstone in 1881 following the rising tensions there, **Warren** had relocated from Colton to Arizona during this period for a short time, but just as in Colton, his trouble-prone ways continued to follow him as he was involved in dangerous incident after incident. He, nevertheless, teamed up in Tombstone with brother Wyatt and his law enforcement associates to support them as the outlaw element became more determined than ever in their efforts to eliminate the Earp faction.

Later, in 1882, after ridding the southern Arizona Territory of many of the outlaws residing there, Wyatt and Warren, accompanied by **John Henry "Doc" Holliday**, **"Texas Jack" Vermillion**, **"Turkey Creek" Jack Johnson**, **Dan Tipton**, and one or two others departed that vicinity, traveling to New Mexico, Colorado, Idaho, California, and other

*In 1900, **Warren's** penchant for trouble finally caught up with him in a fatal manner, resulting in his shooting death in a saloon in Willcox following a drunken argument.*

locales in a constant search for adventure and sources of income.

Warren eventually returned to the Colton/San Bernardino environs to live a short while with brothers Virgil, James, and other members of his family, but he eventually tired of life in Colton (or else had worn-out his welcome there) and returned, surprisingly, to Arizona, where he was hired by a cattle business near Willcox. In one of the last photos taken of him, he is pictured (either in Tombstone or Colton) with James's wife, Bessie.

In 1900, **Warren's** penchant for trouble finally caught up with him in a fatal manner, resulting in his shooting death in a saloon in Willcox following a drunken argument. He and range boss **Johnny Boyette** had engaged in numerous violent confrontations in recent months, and had both become extremely hostile to the opposite party. Finally, following threats of violence by Earp, Boyette reportedly drew his revolver without provocation, and shot Warren in cold blood, killing him instantly.

Just as he had been in Colton, San Bernardino, and Tombstone, the youngest Earp was so roundly disliked in Willcox that no law enforcement authorities ever even attempted to arrest Boyette, nor were any charges filed against him nor even any investigation made of the shooting.

Warren Earp was buried in an unmarked grave in *Willcox Pioneer*

Warren and "Bessie" (circa 1883) – Nellie "Bessie" Bartlett Ketcham Earp was married to the eldest Earp brother, James. She was a modestly attractive female who had nevertheless lived a hard life, reflected in her no-nonsense uncompromising gaze. She is pictured here with the youngest Earp brother, Warren. Prior to (and possibly even after) meeting James, Bessie was a prostitute which was not uncommon in those days in the West. She died prematurely at the age of 47 in January of 1887 in Colton, and was buried in San Bernardino's Pioneer Memorial Cemetery. Warren was so roundly disliked by virtually all his acquaintances that when he was murdered in 1900 in Willcox, Arizona, he was hastily buried in an unmarked grave and forgotten. The specific site of his grave today is unknown.

Cemetery (no doubt to eliminate the possibility of a coroner's inquest to determine Boyette's guilt or innocence). It was recorded by a number of sources that Warren was clearly unarmed at the time of the shooting. The exact site of his grave was never marked, and though the cemetery in which his remains reside is known, the specific site of those remains is a complete mystery today. A similar fate had earlier befallen John

Henry Holliday in Glenwood Springs, Colorado.

Following the Tombstone misfortunes and his later crippling wounds from an attempt on his life in that town on December 28 of 1881, *U.S. Deputy Marshal Virgil Earp* had decided a change of venue was in order and he moved from Tombstone to Colton where he resided with wife, **Alvira "Allie" Packingham Sullivan**, at 528 West "H" Street. This home, now a historic site, still stands in Colton as of this writing (2023).

Despite his devastated left arm which hung useless by his side for the remainder of his life, Virgil nevertheless was still effective as a law enforcement officer. He opened a detective agency in Colton, and, in 1886, he was elected the town constable. When Colton was incorporated as a city, Virgil was elected as the first City Marshal on July 11, 1887. He was paid $75 a month and was re-elected to another term in 1888.

In later 1888, Virgil resigned as city marshal and he and Allie strangely left Colton for nearby San Bernardino. Five years later, in 1893, he and Allie moved yet again to the short-lived mining town of Vanderbilt, California, where he owned and operated *Earp's Hall*, a saloon, gambling hall, and meeting place used for public gatherings and even the town's weekly church services. His successes in the political arena in Vanderbilt, however, did not rise to the level of his previous electoral endeavors, since he lost the election for town constable in 1894.

In 1895, the San Bernardino City and County Directories carried the following listings: *San Bernardino Section: Earp, Warren – Capitalist. Earp, Virgil W. – Saloon Keeper. Colton Section: Earp, Nicholas P. – Book Agent.*

San Miguel Bank (1889) – The San Miguel Valley Bank building (2nd from right) in Telluride, Colorado, is pictured at about the same time as it was robbed by famed outlaw Robert LeRoy Parker (a.k.a. Butch Cassidy) on June 24, 1889. Cassidy reportedly was assisted by several accomplices in the robbery, and used the novel technique of "staged" fresh horses at various points along his getaway route in order to outrun his pursuers. His escape route was a well-traveled ancient trail down through the San Juan Mountains, and is the same as would have been used by many adventurers of that day, including John Henry Holliday and the Earp brothers circa 1882-1883.

In 1901, *Virgil* and *Wyatt* attempted to open a gambling hall in Colton, but the town fathers voted down the enterprise, much to the two brothers' disappointment. The two continued nevertheless with other business endeavors in the Colton/San Bernardino area for several years, as well as in a number of other states and locales.

In 1905, *Virgil's* hard life finally caught up with him when, at age 62, he came down with and died from pneumonia. As an inveterate cigar-smoker, his tobacco affinity had not aided his attempt at recovery from the pneumococcal bacteria with which his lungs were infected. Since his first wife and child lived in Portland, Oregon, Virgil's body was shipped there by rail for burial in that city's *Riverview Cemetery*.

In February of 1907 in Colton, *Nicholas Earp*, patriarch of the Earp family who had lived to the ripe old age of 94, finally succumbed to the rigors of life. As a veteran of the Black Hawk and Mexican American wars, Nicholas was entitled to free burial at a nearby military cemetery.

Nicholas's wife – *Virginia Anne Cooksey Earp* – died in San Bernardino and is buried in the *Pioneer Memorial Cemetery* in that town.

In January of 1926, *James Earp*, the oldest full brother who had survived the U.S. Civil War, as well as the troubles in Tombstone, Arizona, where he had been a barkeeper, died quietly in San Bernardino at age 84. He was buried in that city's *Mountain View Cemetery*.

James's beautiful wife, *Nellie*

"Bessie" Bartlett Ketcham Earp had died prematurely in January of 1887, in Colton, at the relatively young age of 47. She was buried in San Bernardino's *Pioneer Memorial Cemetery* as well, not far from her mother-in-law, Virginia Anne Cooksey Earp.

On December 18, 1928, at the advanced age of 91, *Newton Earp* passed away in Sacramento, California. Born in 1837 in Ohio County, Kentucky, Newton was the son of Nicholas Earp and his first wife, *Abigail Storm*. As such, he was a half-brother to James, Virgil, Wyatt, Morgan and Warren and sisters *Martha*, *Adelia*, *Virginia* and *Mariah*. Despite his half-brother status to his famed male siblings, Newton was very close with his brothers his entire life.

Following service in the Union Army during the U.S. Civil War, Newton had returned home and married *Jane "Jennie" Adam* in Marion County, Missouri, in 1865. The newlyweds then joined patriarch Nicholas and siblings in Southern California's San Bernardino. There, Newton worked as a saloon manager.

The elder brother later returned with his wife and children to the Midwest in 1868, first settling in Lamar, Missouri, where he became a farmer. Finding himself unsuited for that profession, Newton relocated with his wife and family to Kansas. Just as with all the other members of his later-renowned family, Newton was a wanderer.

Newton and Jennie ultimately became the parents of five children: *Effie May*, *Wyatt Clyde*, *Mary Elizabeth*, *Alice Abigail*, and *Virgil Edwin*. The couple obviously named their first-born son (born August 25, 1872) after his not-yet-famous uncle, Wyatt, and their second son (born April 19, 1880) after his equally not-yet-famous uncle, Virgil.

Following another relocation to California, Newton became a carpenter, building homes in northern California and northwestern Nevada. Newton's wife, Jennie, died on March 29, 1898, in Paradise Hill, Nevada (also known as "Paradise Valley").

Only his half-brother Wyatt and half-sister Adelia outlived Newton, with Wyatt dying approximately one month later on January 13, 1929. Newton is buried in Sacramento's *East Lawn Memorial Park* cemetery.

In 1929, despite all the many dangerous engagements and gunfights which he had survived in his life, *Wyatt Berry Stapp Earp* finally was himself felled, but not by an outlaw's or assassin's bullet. Prostate cancer took the famed lawman just short of his 81st birthday in Los Angeles, California. During his life he had been a buffalo hunter, lawman, gambling table manager, saloon keeper, miner, boxing referee, gambler, and brothel keeper, to name a few of his occupations.

Wyatt's famous last utterances as he passed away were *"Suppose. Suppose."* If they were understood by those in his presence at the time, the cryptic final words were never explained. Wyatt was cremated and his ashes were interred in Colma, a suburb of San Francisco, California, in a Jewish cemetery where wife, *Josephine*, was later buried alongside him.

Virgil Earp's common-law wife (who was actually his second spouse) – *Alvira* – died in November of 1947. She had weathered all the tough years with the Earps, including the shoot-outs in Tombstone and elsewhere, outliving her husband by 42 years. She was one of the last original Earps in Colton, and was buried with a number of the other Earp family members in Colton's *Mountain View Cemetery*.

Murder in the Mountains

The law enforcement domain of a rural mountain sheriff is, more often than not, a reasonably peaceful pursuit. The years immediately following the U.S. Civil War in north Georgia, however, were anything but peaceful. In fact, they were an exceedingly dangerous and deadly time for the entire Southeast. Ruthless crime and criminals were rampant. Union County Sheriff Charles L. Hill, had hardly been on the job six months before his life was quickly extinguished.

A pioneer Civil War-era cabin in Georgia's Towns County still stood right up until the 1980s in the peaceful valley through which Crane Stream still passes today. The aged structure had fallen into disuse and abandonment, and weather and the termites eventually did their work, causing the historic former domicile to collapse into a rotted heap. The property, which is only a few miles east of the Union County line, is now quiet, but in 1867, it was the site at which 27-year-old Union County Sheriff Charles L. Hill was murdered.

Charles' father and mother – Felix Walker and Elizabeth Hill – migrated with Charles and his sister, Ursula Elizabeth, from Snow Hill, North Carolina, to Mauney Road in the upper reaches of Union County to live. In addition to Felix, brothers Adam C. and Napoleon B. also lived in the area.

The exact date and even the reason for the family's relocation is unknown today. Perhaps they were similar to many Southerners of that day and time who had lost everything they owned through the tragedy and depredations of the U.S.

Civil War, and were refugees seeking a place where they might make a new start.

The 1860s, '70s, and '80s, were extremely dangerous times in the Southern states in America, particularly in the mountainous regions. The majority of the male members of families who resided in those areas – and, indeed throughout the Southeast – had either been killed or completely disabled during the war, as had most all members of the law enforcement community. In the absence of an armed male deterrence, criminals and opportunists of all make and measure frequented the remote mountain regions, especially in north Georgia, Tennessee, North Carolina, Alabama and South Carolina. It was an extremely dangerous time to be living.

Though they obviously were strangers to the north Georgia area, the Hill family apparently was out-going and friendly – at least to the degree that young Charles was able to become elected as Union County's new sheriff. The reason for Charles' pursuit of a law enforcement career in 1866, during such an unsettled time is yet another inexplicable detail. Perhaps some of his numerous Union County friends had encouraged him to stand for election to the dangerous job of sheriff of Union. Perhaps no one else wanted the task or was even available in this outlaw-infested area. As with many aspects involving Hill, the reason for his decision to take the job is yet another mystery today.

Due to the short nature of his life, Charles's law enforcement career obviously would be brief as well. He was elected in 1866, and his career would be ended less than a year later.

A Sheriff's Duty

One of the early tasks assigned to Sheriff Hill was that of serving a warrant on and making the arrest of an individual by the name of William Campbell. He set out to accomplish this task on May 14, 1867.

There is no known record today of the crime that Campbell had committed. Perhaps someplace deep within the Union County Sheriff's homicide archives – or maybe even the Towns County Sheriff's homicide records – an accounting of this incident may be gleaned. To date, however, such information and records have eluded the efforts of researchers. With the destructive nature of fires and the like which often pervaded early county courthouses, it is likely that no records for the perpetrator of the Sheriff Hill murder will ever be discovered.

Just as is the case in modern times, the arrest of any individual can easily be life-threatening, particularly as involves a hardened criminal. It is for this reason that law enforcement personnel in Hill's position almost always are accompanied by at least one deputy-sheriff for assistance and "back-up" in such circumstances. It is one thing to charge a man

with a crime. It is quite another entirely to get that individual restrained with handcuffs in order to transport him or her to a jail.

Aside from the fact that the 1860s were very unpredictable times as involved legal matters, they often were also very primitive times regarding the quality of the jail or "calaboose" in which an arrestee would be confined. Jails in the 1860s in rural mountainous areas many times were nothing more than a heavy wooden box constructed along a town's dusty road, open to the elements. No heat. No toilet. No protection from wildlife or any of the vermin of nature. It was not a pleasant experience by any stretch of the imagination in a town jail of the 1860s in the north Georgia mountains, and William Campbell almost certainly was fully aware of all of this.

To accomplish this arrest, Sheriff Hill would first be required to "locate" William Campbell, and the most logical place to begin this search was Campbell's mountain cabin. Since this domicile was actually physically located in Towns (not Union) County, it is unknown today why Hill was even making this arrest in the first place. Normally, this task would have fallen to the sheriff of Towns County. Hill, nevertheless, proceeded for the arrest.

The only explanation that might be offered for the unusual circumstance in which a Union County sheriff might venture to make an arrest on Towns County soil, is that Campbell perhaps had committed some offense in Union County for which cross-county pursuit was warranted. Nevertheless, even under those circumstances, this arrest should still have been the legal domain of the Town's County Sheriff's Office.

In those highly lawless times in mountainous north Georgia, areas of jurisdiction – particularly as involved county lines – were not always strictly known or observed. In 1867, Towns County was but eleven years old, having been created from portions of Rabun and Union counties in 1856. Under the circumstances, it would have been quite easy for the boundaries to have been blurred or misunderstood.

Prior to the formation of Towns County, Campbell's cabin would also in fact have actually been located on Union County soil. Perhaps Sheriff Hill was not even aware his quarry was located in a different county. Perhaps, under the circumstances, he just didn't care. In those days, outlaws were everywhere, and law enforcement in the Deep South was a tough and exceedingly dangerous business.

It unquestionably would have been very easy for Charles Leonidas Hill to have pursued a different criminal – or even no criminal at all – at that time, but that apparently was not Hill's method of operation. Whatever his reasoning for his determined pursuit of Campbell, Sheriff Hill was, without question, a dedicated law enforcement official to advance beyond the Union County line into Towns County if he was aware of the jurisdictional circumstances.

Abandonment of Caution

Perhaps Sheriff Hill's personality included a certain amount of bravado. His thoughts on this early summer day in 1867 as he departed the sheriff's office in Union County to arrest Campbell will now remain a mystery forever. Campbell's cabin was a two-story log structure that had been built at the base of a mountain a few yards from Crane Creek. If a settler had no fresh mountain spring or deep-water well from which to draw his drinking water in those days, a fresh mountain stream

was a worthy substitute, particularly in those days when other human inhabitation which might pollute such a stream was extremely limited.

According to Howard Nichols – who had inherited the farm from his father Adam Nichols – the Campbell cabin had a porch across the back which faced the mountain trail down which Sheriff Hill descended that fateful morning. The structure's two rooms were divided, with a shared chimney between them. Each room could be entered only by outside doors as was customary in many cabins at that time.

Nichols, who learned the story of the murder from his father, says Sheriff Hill had apparently not even used stealth to approach Campbell's cabin on the fateful day, having earlier alerted Campbell of his impending service of the warrant. As he neared Campbell's cabin, Hill reportedly bravely instructed his deputies to wait for him at the ridge-top while he proceeded *alone* down the mountain path to arrest Campbell. In retrospect, this was both foolish and amateurish.

Perhaps Hill felt that Campbell could be taken without resistance if he (Hill) went alone to persuade the law-breaker to give himself up. Campbell, however, apparently had no intention whatsoever of being arrested, and since he enjoyed the advantage of advance warning of Sheriff Hill's approach, he (Campbell) was fully armed and prepared to effect his resistance.

On Death's Doorstep

One has to remember that the 1860s were anything but calm, civilized, respectful days. To the contrary, these were the days when blood oaths and bloody deaths were virtually an everyday common occurrence. Most men were accustomed to a constant nature of preparedness for danger and conflict. They were steadfastly ready to defend themselves – with deadly force – if an attempt was made upon their lives, their freedoms, or their possessions.

When he became aware of Sheriff Hill's approach, William Campbell – according to details of the incident as described by Mr. Nichols – reportedly snatched up his pistol, opened the door to the cabin slightly, and clearly warned Hill not to approach any nearer. Campbell is said to have shouted that if Hill would only leave him alone, he would depart the area in the morning, and never again return to the north Georgia mountains. But if Hill insisted upon an arrest, Campbell warned that though it was not his desire to do so, he would shoot Hill if so forced.

Despite Campbell's clear-cut warning to Hill, the young sheriff nevertheless foolishly advanced upon the cabin. In retrospect, depending of course upon the crime which Campbell had committed, Sheriff Hill might have been wise to allow the man his requested latitude. Had he so done, the good sheriff might have lived out a much longer life. However, he would also have had some explaining to do to his deputies – possibly to the detriment of his law enforcement career.

In the absence of a crime or police report, the details of what actually transpired are not specifically known today, and virtually all aspects of this incident have been handed down by word of mouth. As with most law enforcement events of this nature in which the details were not carefully recorded at the time, several different versions of the story have survived. The first one is as follows:

After considering the circumstances with which he was confronted,

Sheriff Hill apparently misjudged his quarry, and kept walking down to the cabin porch. It is not known whether or not Hill had carried a weapon with him down to the cabin, but he evidently did not think Campbell would shoot him. Imagine his surprise when Campbell's weapon reportedly fired point-blank into his midsection.

Another version of this incident at this juncture, as told by Roy Mauney of Blairsville, great-nephew of Charles Hill, maintains that Campbell refused to come out of the cabin, forcing Sheriff Hill to take an axe from a nearby woodpile to break down the door. With his door being broken down, Campbell reportedly fired his pistol through a hole, striking Hill at point-blank range.

Whatever the circumstances, Campbell apparently did, one way or another, fire his pistol into Hill's abdomen, mortally wounding him. Campbell then made his escape from the area. In retrospect, Hill, to his misfortune, had used poor judgement and, accordingly, had paid a very stiff price for it.

Fatal Wound

Worse yet, though the wound in Sheriff Hill's abdomen would prove fatal, it was not instantly so. Abdominal wounds, unless they cause arterial blood loss, can take quite a bit of time to kill the victim. It is a slow, very painful and agonizing death. It is a death which could even cause the victim to take his or her own life just to end the pain.

Sheriff Hill's agonies were emphasized even more by the fact that after his men were able to reach him, they then had no choice but to transport him by wagon to his father's home in Union County. This trip which Hill was forced to undergo that morning, undoubtedly was made either in abject conscious agony, or in an almost-equally-painful state of semi-consciousness, travel being what it was in those days on the crude very bumpy mountain roads. And the amount of time that it took Hill's deputies to locate a wagon for such use is unknown today. Suffice it to say that all of the above created a scenario which was far worse than nightmarish for the slowly-dying Sheriff Charles Hill.

According to the Towns County indictment which was eventually handed down against Campbell for Hill's murder in the May term of court that year, Campbell had *"feloniously, willfully, and with malice aforethought"* taken *"a certain pistol of the value of $10.00"* and shot a *"leaden ball"* into the belly of Charles L. Hill, near the navel, giving Hill *"one mortal wound of the breadth of one inch and of the depth of ten inches, from which Hill languished and lingering did afterwards die."*

If he was conscious at the time, Hill must have known he was going to die, abdominal wounds being what they were in the 1860s. It is not known whether Hill's ultimate death finally came from blood loss, infection, or other complications, and it is not known whether any attempts were made by a surgeon or surgeons to remove the lead ball. In the 1860s, however, with a wound of that nature, which invariably punctured the bowel numerous times, there was very little that even a good surgeon was able to do, and an extremely painful lingering death was the only known inevitability.

It is interesting to note that the indictment of Campbell contains an obvious error, since it states that Hill was shot by Campbell on the 19th of May, and died after a period of lingering on May 17th. The inscription on Hill's tombstone indicates he died on May 17th, and it is likely that the date of the shooting as

stated in the indictment is simply an error. Hill most probably was shot on the 14th, since local folklore maintains that he clung agonizingly to life for three days after being wounded.

The perpetrator, meanwhile, fled north Georgia, making good his escape. In so doing, he abandoned his wife, children, home and farm forever, and undoubtedly many of his personal items as well, since he would be traveling "light" on a fast horse through the mountains. Campbell's ultimate destination and any other circumstances surrounding the remainder of his life remain a mystery today.

From that day forward, William Campbell vanished from the public record. Though Towns County indictments charged him with murder, robbery, assault and battery, the fugitive was never found, and therefore never stood trial on the charges.

Many years later – in the 1980s – a tiny clue to Campbell's ultimate circumstances appeared. According to Mr. Nichols, a woman who claimed to be Campbell's descendant, stopped by his old Union County farm in order to see the place where her ancestor had lived. It is unknown today just how this woman knew the location of Campbell's farm. She explained to Mr. Nichols that her family had no information on the ultimate resolution of Campbell and/or his family other than the fact that William Campbell himself had *"gone West."*

In the late 1860s following the devastation of the U.S. Civil War, multitudes of Georgia families "pulled up stakes" and traveled west on what was called "the Alabama Roads." They usually traveled no further than Texas or Oklahoma, at which locales they located ample free arable lands and a relatively stable place for a new home. If the migrants, by chance, had left family back in

Georgia, they occasionally would travel back east to retrieve them, particularly if the "family" was a wife and children, but this was rare, the difficulty of travel in that day being what it was.

Information in a Towns County deed indicates that in the October, 1882 term of court, William L. Sutton was appointed administrator of the estate of William Campbell, whom the deed lists as "deceased," empowering Sutton to sell the property. Since Campbell's family reportedly never learned of his whereabouts, he apparently was declared legally dead in order to allow the family to liquidate his assets.

Whether Campbell never returned because of his demise, or because he did not intend to stand trial for the murder of Sheriff Hill will never be known. In any case, Campbell either willingly or unwillingly made good on the promise he made to Hill before shooting the sheriff.

Hill Family Deaths

Due to the agonies that their son was forced to endure, the Hill family no doubt suffered right along with Charles as they nursed him in his last three days, hoping upon hope for his survival, but knowing the reality of the situation meant that death imminent. Charles's father, Felix, was 53 at the time, and his mother, Elizabeth, was 48, when they laid their young son to rest in Antioch Cemetery, five miles north of Blairsville, Georgia, near the Hill family's farm.

If Charles or his sister – young Ursula Elizabeth – were ever married or had children, there is no record of either circumstance. Nevertheless, the name "Hill" still survives in that section of Union County, and the cemetery markers attest to the fact that there have been not one, but several Charles Hills, any one of which quite likely was named

after the young sheriff who had no children of his own.

The loss of their young son and his promising law enforcement career was the second tragedy the Hill family suffered in the span of a decade. Young Ursula Elizabeth, born in 1842, had died on October 27, 1859, at the age of 17 years, one month and 21 days, according to her marker – less than eight years before Charles himself would join her in the cemetery. The cause of her demise is not known today, and her headstone holds no revelatory details.

Today, Antioch Cemetery includes the graves and headstones of Charles, his mother, father and sister. The inscriptions on their headstones all include short verses and the amount of time – counted to the day – that each lived, indicating perhaps that they valued and took note of each moment the deceased had spent among loved ones.

Though the verses upon their parents' headstones are now unreadable, one can still, with great difficulty, make out the inscriptions upon Charles's and Ursula Elizabeth's markers - inscriptions which would seem to indicate the family's feeling of ultimate triumph over death.

Charles's marker almost certainly was picked out by his parents, as were the words inscribed upon it. Interestingly, the inscription includes several misspelled words, which is somewhat unusual – but not unheard-of – for a headstone, particularly in the mountainous backwoods region of north Georgia. The inscription reads: *"God, my Redeemer, live* (sic) *and ever from the skies, look* (sic) *down and watches my dust till He shall bid it rise."*

They apparently were more cautious (or perhaps were more cautious with their selection of an engraver) with Ursula Elizabeth's headstone, for it carries no misspellings in the work, and reads: "*Companion, earth and worms shall but refine this flesh till my triumphant spirit comes to put it on afresh.*"

The stones of Charles's parents - Felix and Elizabeth - (though not identical) match each other's, but differ from the two matching stones of their children. Likely, by that time, readily available marker designs had changed, or perhaps they were selected to be different from the children's.

It is also interesting to note that the mother's stone is of a different style than the others in bearing the notation at the top: "*Sacred to the Memory of Elizabeth, wife of Felix Walker Hill.*"

Since Felix died August 24, 1883, at the age of 77 years and 17 days, Elizabeth, who died November 15, 1896, at the age of 85 years and 82 days, would have outlived Felix, and therefore would have been the one most likely to have chosen the headstones for them both. From the inscription on Elizabeth's marker, however, it would seem that perhaps some other family member chose the headstones, unless Felix and Elizabeth chose their own stones in advance of Felix's death, which is a distinct possibility.

Tragic Reminders

Besides the stories handed down from generation to generation, and the lonely gravestones in Antioch Cemetery, the only other lasting reminders of the fateful event are the doors of the old Campbell cabin and the old fireplace hearthstones which were preserved on the Nichols farm. The doors still serve

> *The old hearthstones, have, for years now, served as the entrance steps to the old home of Mr. Nichols's father.*

their function on the Nichols barn and storage shed. It is impossible to know which of the four is the door behind which Campbell stood as he fired the round into Hill's midsection. If the boards on these doors are the originals, they have been worn and weathered smooth in the past 150+ years. This circumstance would also indicate that no axe was ever used by Sheriff Hill on one of them in an attempt to gain entry into William Campbell's cabin.

The old hearthstones, have, for years now, served as the entrance steps to the old home of Mr. Nichols's father. Once upon a time, an ordinary man named William Campbell and his family warmed themselves and cooked their supper upon a fire made on these stones.

It is equally interesting to note that once, behind one of the now innocent-looking old doors, a desperate Campbell clutched a $10.00 pistol which he fired to fell an unsuspecting Sheriff Charles Hill.

It seems doubly tragic to think that on a summer day more than 150 years ago, when all life was budding anew against the back-drop of the beautiful Blue Ridge Mountains, a young sheriff made a terrible mistake in judgment which ended his life on earth forever.

When William Campbell pulled the trigger on that fateful day in May of 1867, he not only took the sheriff's life, but sealed his own fate as well. So far as is known, he never again saw his family, friends, or his snug little cabin in the beautiful north Georgia mountain valley.

A Pioneer Georgia Family Massacred in the Okefenokee

In the early days of settlement of what today is the United States of America, one of the most terrifying incidents one could experience was that of attack by angry Native Indians. Though the state of Georgia today is not normally associated with what came to be known as "the western frontier," our nation's vast unsettled region at one time actually began in Georgia, and some of the earliest Indian attacks occurred in that vicinity. The Wildes Massacre was just such an event.

At sunrise on the morning of July 22, 1838, the Maximilian Wildes family were suddenly awakened in their homestead just northwest of the Okefenokee Swamp in what today is south Georgia to find themselves in a horrible situation. They were surrounded and under attack by a group of hostile natives who were believed to be Seminoles later associated with what came to be known as the very deadly "Red Stick" Creek Indians.

Perhaps members of the Wildes family had previously experienced angry encounters with hostile Indians in the vicinity of their home and had become concerned. Legend persists today that they had spent the night previous to the attack on their home peering into the darkness outside their cabin, listening intently to unfamiliar and eerie sounds, sleeping little, and trying in vain to reassure themselves that the Seminoles they knew to be in the area would

perhaps simply steal their food and then leave. If these were the Wildes family's thoughts, they would soon prove to have been woefully misplaced, for the actual circumstances would shortly be infinitely worse.

History variously records Mrs. Wildes' given name as "Elizabeth" or "Mary," but tradition maintains that she was actually part Creek Indian – making her children part Creek as well. Many historians believe that this was at least a portion of the reason the Wildes had not fled with other frontier families into the safety of a U.S. Army fort not more than four miles distant when tensions in the area had intensified. If this was the case, it also was a woefully inadequate presumption on the part of the family.

Local historian Luther Thrift, a former resident of the Boggy Bay community near the site at which the Wildes were massacred, later maintained that family patriarch Maxey Wildes assumed – erroneous as he obviously was – that the Creeks would show mercy upon people of their own race. Thrift also stated that there was reliable information through surviving family members that the Wildes had actually made plans to retreat into the safety of the fort after breakfast of the very morning of the attack. If this was the case, then this tragic pioneer family was the epitome of the expression *"A day late and a dollar short."*

It is believed today that it quite possibly was Mrs. Wildes who first sensed the presence of the warriors skulking in the undergrowth around the perimeter of the Wildes cabin as she walked out the doorway early on that hot summer morning to prepare the family's breakfast over an open fire. Thrift stated that by most accounts, the position of her body indicated that she had been allowed just enough time to dash back inside the cabin and scream a warning to her husband before gathering their children (including her niece and nephew who had the misfortune to be spending the night with them) and dashing to a nearby hiding spot in the forest.

All of the Wildes family members apparently had clearly received prior instructions from their knowledgeable elders that in the event of an attack by the natives, the cabin would be a death-trap and that they must seek concealment in the undergrowth. Some of them actually reached this protective cover, but most did not.

Mrs. Wildes's screams were among her final acts on this earth. In a matter of moments, the male members of the family had rushed out to face a mob of vicious warriors. Maxey and his eldest son were able to get off quick shots from their muskets at the intruders, but it did little to slow the natives. The fact that they had hastily fired their inadequate weapons at the warriors confirms that the elder Wildes and his son had quickly determined that there was no hope except through bloodshed. The circumstances almost certainly had degenerated to that level of seriousness and horror in order for them to have resorted to that type of violence that quickly.

As they had been ably instructed many times, the children scattered like little partridges into the nearby undergrowth in order to have a chance for survival. Mrs. Wildes apparently had initially sought to join them, clutching her youngest child to her breast in her desperate bid for life.

Most of the survival efforts of the family, however, were simply wholly in vain. Maxey – along with three of his children – was quickly slaughtered by a Seminole with a war axe near the front doorstep. Mrs. Wildes, apparently hearing the bloody assault to her rear, paused – still clutching her small child – just long enough to be cut down herself as she turned to take in the unbelievable carnage so quickly building before her. She never even made it to the undergrowth.

In times of a flash attack such as this, the Native American war axe was an unbelievably deadly and effective weapon. It was also very equivalent to its name – a long-handled device with a sharp heavy stone on the end which was used to quickly and decisively crush the skulls and other bones of opposing forces. The Indians – who obviously had outnumbered the Wildes family members – were able to dash into the midst of the family, viciously strike with their axes and quickly overpower the opposition. It was the picture and definition of the word "massacre."

Two of Mrs. Wildes' sister's children – the previously-mentioned "niece and nephew" were also among those murdered in the rampage. All in all, it was a scene of inconceivable horror being visited upon the Wildes family, and would go down in the annals of American history as one of the more horrendous on record.

The Seminole warriors continued their devastating attack until all within their sight had ceased movement. Any still-struggling injured were dealt whatever final blows were necessary to render the victims into lifeless bloody messes. These Red Stick Creek warriors gained their identity and notoriety from the large war clubs which ultimately were blood-soaked from their conquests in battle.

Finally sated in their murderous rage, the Indians retreated. All around the Wildes cabin, the bodies of eight individuals lay scattered and broken, never again to draw the breath of life. It is assumed – though not known for certain today – that the warriors also took the provisions from the family's smokehouse before torching the Wildes's home.

This practice of "torching" was the very reason all family members were repeatedly instructed to rush quickly out of the cabin and seek concealment in the surrounding undergrowth in the case of an attack. The natives had clearly demonstrated in prior attacks on area families that the stout cabins were in fact no protection at all from the Indians in the event of an attack, because anyone remaining inside would simply be incinerated in a horrible death by fire.

Within hours, the shock of the surrounding settlers evolved to outright panic.

The worst fears of generations of White settlers in colonial America had come to pass for the Wildes family. The Okefenokee frontier – generally lawless and yet orderly in many ways – would not be the same for many years.

Survivors

Miraculously, four of the Wildes's sons – among those who had fled into the undergrowth – had managed to survive. Following the departure of the natives, the young boys traveled cautiously to a neighboring home which had not been targeted by the warriors. There, they related in angst and agony the details of the attack.

Within hours, the shock of the surrounding settlers evolved to outright panic. Despite some scattered clashes with the natives in years past, most of the settlers had settled into a tolerant and reasonably respectful – if uneasy – attitude toward the Seminoles.

The Georgia-Florida frontier in the vicinity of the Okefenokee had been a dangerous place for settlers for generations, and even prior to the coming of White settlers, the area had marked the contentious boundary for many Indian tribes for centuries – perhaps even for millennia, according to Dr. C.T. Trowell, former assistant professor of history at South Georgia College in Douglas, Georgia, and author of the 1992 treatise *Exploring The Okefenokee: Letters and Diaries from the Indian Wars, 1836-'42.*

Long before the largely Celtic settlers had arrived at the edge of the

Okefenokee, the once-powerful indigenous native groups of that vicinity had been decimated by disease and other maladies following their earlier contact with European explorers who carried diseases against which the natives had no immunity. These early explorers also enslaved as many of the natives as possible for manual labor. The impoverished and ragged remnants of these once-proud Indian cultures were left to be further impacted by the additional waves of settlers whose numbers no doubt seemed endless to the Indians.

The great Timucuan culture encountered by Ponce De Leon, whose dominance stretched from what today is central Florida to southern Georgia, reigned for over 2,000 years. They, nevertheless, had literally become extinct before any but the very first White settlers in Georgia reached the new land.

Into this void drifted the disaffected Creeks, Yuchis, Hitchitees, and vestiges of other tribes. It was they who had abandoned the Creek culture to evolve into what came to be known as the "Seminoles," many of whom later were assigned the moniker of *"Red Stick Creeks"* by conquering American forces.

The ranges of these Creek warriors and their families ultimately were expanded. While competing with their native brethren for space and hunting grounds, some members of the fragmented tribes began slipping through the adjoining Pinhook and Okefenokee swamps to raid the new White settlements and homesteads which were appearing in southern Georgia.

These early explorers also enslaved as many of the natives as possible for manual labor.

Such almost certainly was the case with the Wildes Massacre.

Despite their ability to live off the land, the Seminoles and Red Stick Creeks were suffering under desperate conditions of that day – sometimes to the point of starvation. A series of harsh winters coupled with the theft of their limited cattle stocks by bands of White rustlers had decimated their food supplies. It was a situation ripe for conflict.

The circumstances were worsened – if that was even possible – by the ages-old custom of the provision of "fire-water" (corn liquor), along with iron tools, cloth, and other items to the natives in return for manual services, sexual relations, and the scant products the poor females were able to produce domestically.

The situation ultimately degenerated to the point that the natives eventually produced no products of their own. Indeed, the archaeologists of today rarely discover artifacts in south Georgia which date later than 1650, but countless artifacts which date prior to that period and on into pre-history.

Atrocities of Horror

Though many accounts of the early history of our nation record only the atrocities of the Native Americans, there were in fact depredations on both sides. There were more than enough horrible actions from both sides.

The shock waves of the Wildes Massacre reverberated from the halls of the state capital at Milledgeville to the chambers in the national capitol at Washington City, right up to the desk of the president of the United States. Though all of these officials were shocked at the incident, it certainly was not the first time such an atrocity had occurred, nor would it be the last. However, it did mark a watershed moment in southeast Georgia history, and indelibly seared into the minds of south Georgians a story which quickly approached the ranks of legend.

The story of the Wildes Massacre might not have risen to the level of notoriety in enjoyed had not four of the Wildes children survived to relate the details of the terrible incident to the American public. What they described – and what the settlers at the scene of the incident later recorded – eclipsed a bloody 1836 U.S. military action against a group of Creeks believed to have raided the south Georgia settlement of Roanoke where a White settler was murdered near the mouth of Suwanoochee Creek in Ware (present-day Clinch) County.

Though the horrifying experiences of settlers in south Georgia during this time-period were laid almost exclusively at the feet of the Seminoles and their Creek brethren – particularly the Red Stick Creeks – much confusion and lawlessness was responsible for at least some of the depredations.

Indeed, John Wildes, 12 years of age at the time of the massacre, reportedly described to federal officers just after the attack that one of the warriors involved in the attack on his family fell over him as he cowered in a palmetto thicket during the murder of his family. To his abject astonishment, the youthful Wildes said he discovered the warrior was not an Indian, but rather a "White." A Lt. Darling reported that the boy explained the White attacker "asked him why he did not run." According to the report, young Wildes responded that he

told the White attacker that he would indeed flee if the man would allow him to do so – which he did.

This ironically was not an unusual situation, since it was not uncommon for Whites to "go Indian" during that period, accepting the ways of the natives and intermarrying with the females. At that point these renegade Whites dressed as Indians, learned and spoke the Indian language, and accompanied them to war when attacks were made.

Growing Confusion

The Wildes murders galvanized settlers' fears, and led to calls for action from local volunteers, as well as pleas for Georgia militia and federal troops. It also set in motion scores of communications between the Okefenokee frontier, the state capital at Milledgeville, and the federal government in Washington, all the while fanned by exaggerated or totally-false claims of further Seminole atrocities.

Nevertheless, it soon became more than apparent that the Wildes Massacre was anything but an aberration, exaggeration, or false claim. It shocked south Georgia settlers and initiated four long years of military action in the area.

Lt. Darling's letter concerning the murders, published in the *Niles National Register* of August, 1838, and reprinted in the *Jacksonville Journal*, provided a first-person account of the horrific incident:

"... *a man came full speed into the camp with the cry of 'Indians!' I asked where. He said about five miles off, that he had just removed a family who heard the report of guns and screams of people. We were in our saddles in a few minutes, and under full speed to the spot where the alarm originated; and O, God! Of all the scenes I have ever seen, or ever wish* (not) *to see, it presented itself to view.*

"On reaching the ground, a man, his wife, and four children of his own, and two of his own sister's had fallen by the Indians. Three children of the six were yet alive when we reached the spot; one about three years old had been shot through the abdomen and lay asleep on the dead mother; another about two rods from the mother.

"But oh, horrid to tell, I found a fine young lady of 18, shot in two places and dirked in another, with about 20 hogs around her (Hungry hogs are notorious for greedily consuming, when fed, the remains of humans.) *and she yet alive and had her senses perfectly. This was the most trying time I had ever seen. I gave her cold water, which she wished much. I remained with her as long as I could, till obliged to go in search of the Indians. We left a guard to protect them, and administer to them all that they could, but all expired in less than twenty minutes after we left. . ."*

Despite a considerable search, the Indian murderers of the Wildes family had vanished into the wilderness and were never found. The story of this incident would be repeated time and again in the ensuing four years, as troops conducted largely fruitless scours of the area in the wake of further attacks.

Various reports put the number of Seminoles in the Wildes Massacre as low as five, but some as high as 50. Subsequent estimates on the actual count of "Seminoles" in the group of attackers ranged from zero to more than 500.

Whatever the circumstances, the Wildes family was overcome very quickly, without any visible loss of life within the ranks of the Indians. The natives must therefore have struck very rapidly and with numbers sufficient to quickly overpower all of the Wildes family. Though several of the Wildes family members were able to discharge their weapons at their attackers, they apparently were completely ineffective due to the horrendous shock and horror of the experience.

For two years, rumor, insufficient and sometimes contradictory information, and a growing resentment of the federal officers by militia members combined to accomplish little. It certainly could not bring back the Wildes family.

What had exploded with the Wildes Massacre ended with a whimper. Seminole raids from the Okefenokee slowly tapered off into nothing, as the natives fled far into what today is known as central and southern Florida.

Farther down in that realm, the war continued for another decade as the Seminoles eventually took up residence in the protective confines of another great swamp – The Everglades – as the federal army at last recalled its exhausted troops in 1854.

Brig. Gen. Charles Floyd, the son of a wealthy Camden County plantation owner who had gained notoriety for his effective actions in removing the Cherokees from north Georgia, made a significant – but mainly frustrated effort – in searching out any remaining Seminoles and renegades.

Finally recalled to Washington, Floyd was insulted when he was passed over for a much-coveted military command. In retribution, he retreated back to his plantation where he eventually receded into failing health and death.

The Seminoles, pursued for years unsuccessfully by Floyd, his men, and others, eventually stabilized in the Everglades, where a remnant of the once-great Seminole Nation still thrives today, just as the remnant of the once-great Cherokee Nation thrives today at the Qualla Reservation in western Carolina

Last Days of the Confederacy
And Its Treasury Gold

During the dark closing days of the U.S. Civil War, casks of gold and silver coins comprising the Confederate Treasury and the assets of several Virginia banks – a glittering hoard worth untold millions of dollars today – were spirited across the Carolinas and northeast Georgia in a last-ditch effort to avoid their confiscation by Federal authorities. Portions of these funds ultimately simply disappeared into thin air in the confusion of a mass exodus.

On April 2, 1865, in the closing days of the U.S. Civil War, Confederate President Jefferson Davis and his Cabinet were finally forced to admit the obvious. Little hope remained for the Confederacy, and with Union troops kicking down the doors of Richmond, Virginia, Davis, accompanied by his Cabinet and most-trusted assistants, fled – via the nearby Danville railroad depot – the soon-to-be-burning city around 8:00 p.m. At approximately midnight of that same evening, the Confederate Treasury, as well as almost half a million dollars in gold and silver specie (coins) composing the assets of several of the banks of Virginia, were also being transported as quickly as possible on the same rail line.

By this point, the Southern populace and its starving, diseased, and ravaged armies had become the hallmark of a dying nation, and lawlessness erupted freely throughout the southland. Fleeing southward into Georgia, Davis hoped to avoid being arrested by Federal authorities and somehow make it to Texas where he planned to reestablish the Confederacy.

Davis's remaining Cabinet was composed of Secretary of War John C. Breckinridge, Secretary of State Judah P. Benjamin, Secretary of the Navy Stephen R. Mallory, and Acting Secretary of the Treasury John H. Reagan. Other cabinet members resigned and fled as the group later crossed into South Carolina.

Preserving the Treasury

The Confederate Treasury alone was comprised of a fabulous cache of silver and gold coins; silver and gold bullion; $600 to $700 million dollars-worth of Confederate treasury notes (dropping in value like cow flop by the hour); 16,000 to 18,000 pounds sterling in Liverpool, England, acceptances; a chest of silver jewelry donated by Confederate devotees; and more. The value of the gold and silver items (coinage, bullion and jewelry) being spirited southward was estimated at that time (1865) to be in the realm of $500,000.00 to $527,000.00, a treasure which would be worth well over $9,000,000.00 in 2024 dollars. Interestingly, those virtually worthless Confederate paper funds would also be quite valuable in today's collectors' market.

This assessment of the Confederate Treasury does not begin to consider the total actual worth of this breath-taking treasure trove, since the $500,000.00 (equivalent to $9,000,000.00 in 2024) provided almost unlimited purchasing power in 1865. If discovered today with provenance to this incident, the collectors' value of these extremely rare and historic coins would be astronomical.

Captain Micajah Clark, Confederate Acting Treasurer, maintained meticulous records (outlined below) of the entire dispersal of the Confederate Treasury, so in actuality, there is no mystery as to what ultimately became of these funds. Nevertheless, some portions of his accounting – just by virtue of the *size* of some of the individual dispersals, as well as the final disposition of those dispersals – have in fact caused those portions of the funds to fall into the realm of "mystery" today.

The monumental task of protection and transport of this immense treasure had fallen to Captain William Harwar Parker (CSN) and his 50 midshipmen guards. Though almost all of the men were less than 18 years of age (and some reportedly no more than 14 years old), those who had chosen this group for this task seemingly could not have made a better choice, particularly in view of all of the intelligence and non-stop vigilance necessary to avoid the thousands of Federal troops, bounty hunters, and general bushwhackers eager to gain control of this valuable cargo. Though largely forgotten today, the logistical criteria and expertise necessary to accomplish this feat of avoidance can only be acknowledged as one of the truly amazing achievements of either side during the entire war.

Prior to its ultimate dispersal to loyal supporters and staff, this gold and silver comprising the Treasury would undergo an amazing 33-day odyssey across South Carolina and Georgia zig-zagging back and forth across the Carolinas and northeast Georgia countryside in avoidance strategies. Due to the expert technique and unwavering dedication exercised by the Confederate Navy midshipmen, the Confederate Treasury was never close to being intercepted by Federal troops, despite their heavy presence in the vicinity.

According to historian and researcher Marshall P. Waters III, PhD, of Washington, Georgia, the train containing the Treasury (as well as the assets of the banks of Richmond, Virginia) was moved onto a railroad siding in Danville, Virginia, where it sat from April 3-6. During this pause in travel, treasury clerks wisely exchanged – with all comers – paper Confederate dollars for silver coins, offering the swiftly-depreciating Confederate paper at the rate of $70 to $1. The Confederate clerks and bankers were well aware that the value of the Confederate script was dropping steadily by the moment, and they hurried to convert the paper funds as quickly as possible.

"Near 6:00 p.m. on April 6, Captain Parker was ordered to move the Treasury (and banks of Virginia assets) by rail to Charlotte, North Carolina," Waters wrote, *"and to store these funds within the safe confines of the Mint there. Prior to departing the rail siding, the Confederate Treasury was counted for the first time by Senior Teller Walter Philbrook. It reportedly contained a total of $327,022.90."*[1]

From Danville, the treasure train continued to Greensboro, North Carolina. It was there that, according to records, approximately **$39,000.00 of the**

Treasury was paid out to Major General Joseph E. Johnston's (CSA) troops at the rate of $1.15 per soldier. This payment rate is obviously a very paltry sum in modern times, but in 1865, one dollar was the equivalent of approximately eighteen dollars in 2023. That amount also had much greater purchasing power in 1865 than in 2023, particularly for the ragged, penniless, and desperate troops comprising the Confederate forces at that time.

When Jefferson Davis and his entourage reached Sandersville, Georgia, on May 6, 1865, it apparently had become obvious that there would be no easy route to Texas. At that point, **$35,000.00 was removed from the Treasury** *"for later use by President Davis and his Cabinet"* **and sent to a destination in Florida "for future needs."**

The ultimate disposition of this $35,000.00 (equivalent to $619,500.00 in 2023 dollars) is unknown today. At no time did Davis ever have any of the Confederate Treasury in his personal possession, nor were any funds discovered with him or his entourage when he was later captured in Irwinville, Georgia on May 10, 1865. These funds therefore were either hidden in some secret spot and forgotten, or were taken and spent illicitly by "trusted officials."

Meanwhile, from Greensboro, the treasure train had proceeded to Charlotte, North Carolina, and from there to Chester, South Carolina, where any/all serviceable rail lines ended. At that point, the Treasury was *off-loaded* onto horse-drawn wagons which then proceeded toward Newberry, South Carolina upon exceedingly rough pioneer trails. Today, one cannot conceive of the virtual impossibility of securing healthy horses and the necessary wagons

at this late stage in the war, when virtually all equine-related stock had either been killed in battle or butchered for the starving Confederacy. This feat, accomplished over and over again by Parker and the Navy midshipmen, must truly be acknowledged as a small miracle.

Destination Quandary

At Newberry, the treasure was *again loaded* back into a railroad boxcar and transported to Abbeville, South Carolina, where it was then *off-loaded once again* onto horse-drawn wagons, with the parties then proceeding overland to Washington, Georgia. The wagon train crossed a pontoon bridge near the tiny burg of Vienna, South Carolina *(Author's Note: This site is today beneath the waters of Clark Hill Reservoir on the Savannah River)*, arriving at Washington on the afternoon of April 17.

According to Capt. Parker's personal memoirs of this event, the Confederate Treasury was at this point *unloaded yet again* from the wagons and transferred to *"a local house,"* described in more recent years as *"the Heard House"* on the public square in Washington. In point of fact, *"the Heard House"* is the descriptive name which was assigned "post-war" by writers and researchers to describe the home owned by Dr. J.J. Robertson, the lower floor of which served, strange as it may sound today, as the Bank of Georgia Branch in Washington.

When Parker learned here that troops commanded by Major General James H. Wilson (US) were approaching Macon, Georgia (to which Parker had originally planned to travel to deposit the Confederate Treasury), he altered his plans to travel instead to the Confederate Depository in Augusta, Georgia. This was just one of countless logistical nightmares he and his young charges encountered and somehow successfully navigated. Federal forces and other pursuing authorities had become so numerous across the South by this point that it shocked those fleeing their pursuit.

From Washington, the Treasury's circuitous route found it being *loaded yet again* into railroad boxcars for transport to Augusta where it arrived on April 18. Several days later, when Augusta itself was threatened by Federals troops, Parker, amazingly, decided he had no alternative but to *again load* the Treasury back onto still more railroad boxcars and convoy back to Davis and his Cabinet, since he (Parker) was out of options. Worse yet, at this point, the leader of the midshipmen had no firm idea of Davis's actual location.

Parker, nevertheless correctly guessed that Davis was moving south toward Abbeville to join his wife. In his pursuit of Davis, the intrepid Naval captain amazingly returned *yet again* to Washington by rail on April 23rd where he *re-loaded yet again* the Treasury back onto horse-drawn wagons, and set out *yet again* for Abbeville, South Carolina, on April 28. Upon his arrival at that destination on the afternoon of April 29, and being unable to locate President Davis or any members of his Cabinet, a no-doubt totally-frustrated Parker, uncertain of a further course of action at that point, apparently simply wisely decided to remain where he was until he might gather further intelligence on Davis's location. He ordered his men to *unload yet again* the Treasury from the wagons and store the immensely-valuable hoard of gold and silver coins in a warehouse on the town square.

Meanwhile, at 10:00 AM on May 2, Davis's entourage finally reached Abbeville. Confederate Navy Secretary Mallory accompanying Davis ordered Parker

Resourceful Leader – An engraved portrait of Lieutenant Commander William Harwar Parker (CSN). It was the intrepid Parker who, with 50 midshipmen guards, was charged with the physical task of transporting the Confederate Treasury from Richmond, Virginia, to a safe site for temporary storage. It was also Parker who ultimately refused to abandon the unwieldy gold and silver coins until they could be returned to the protection of Confederate Cabinet officers. (Photo courtesy of Mark Waters)

to transfer the Treasury to Acting Secretary of the Treasury, John H. Reagan – an order to which Parker no doubt happily and wearily – yet quickly - complied.

By Mallory's order, the corps of Navy midshipmen were also disbanded and instructed to proceed to their respective homes – their service done. These 50+ young men, most of whom were threadbare and shoeless by this point yet continuously loyal, devoted and dedicated to their mission, had walked from Chester to Newberry, South Carolina, then from Abbeville, South Carolina to Washington, Georgia, and back yet again from April 12 to April 29, none ever once shirking their duty of protection of the Confederate Treasury nor voicing any known

Mutinous Troops – Major Gen. John C. Breckinridge was forced to pay out a significant portion of the Confederate Treasury funds to a mutinous cavalry unit traveling with, and supposedly protecting Confederate President Jefferson Davis and the Treasury. (Photo courtesy of Mark Waters)

complaints despite their constantly-miserable circumstances.

The harrowing nature of the mission of Captain Parker and the Confederate Navy midshipmen cannot be over-emphasized. Aside from their responsibilities in guarding the golden treasure, they were also totally responsible for the logistical requirements involving the safe transport of the gold, a task at which they proved to be astoundingly adept. "It should be noted that the weight of $250,000.00 in silver dollars is approximately 9,555 pounds (4.78 tons)," historian Waters adds.

At 11:00 PM on May 2, President Davis and a small party set out from Abbeville toward Washington. Separately, Confederate Secretary of War Major General John C. Breckinridge also soon departed after having ordered that the Confederate Treasury be *loaded once again* onto horse-drawn wagons and accompanied by a contingent of Confederate cavalry troops.

On the evening of May 3-4, 1865, after having crossed the Savannah River, the cavalry troops who had been accompanying Davis and the Treasury cross-country finally began having reservations about their dedication to the task at hand. They knew this immensely-valuable horde of gold they were guarding could be intercepted and taken from them at any time by a significantly-larger army of Federal troops of which the numbers were growing daily. They also were hungry, sick, extremely poorly supplied, dressed in rags, penniless, and finally of the decision that they should be granted their "share" of the Confederate Treasury before they were overtaken by Federal troops. They, therefore, confronted Major Gen. Breckinridge (CSA) in whose charge the Treasury was traveling.

Treasury Dispersal

At this point, the Treasury had been reduced to approximately **$253,000.00** (as valued in 1865). Try as he might, Gen. Breckinridge ultimately was unable to stave-off the demands of the cavalry troopers and was forced to pay out approximately $26.00 to each man in the 4,000-man unit (some accounts maintain approximately $50.00 each to a 2,000-trooper unit), which came to a total of approximately $108,322.90.[2] After being reduced by this amount, the Confederate Treasury now held approximately **$144,700.00** in Confederate gold and silver – the equivalent of approximately $2.56 million in 2023 dollars.

The payout of these funds to the Confederate cavalry troops reportedly was made from the parlor window of the Mrs. David M. (Susan) Moss house in Lincoln County, Georgia (approximately 3 miles from the Savannah River). Amazingly, it would later be learned that the troops in this payout included some twenty First Ohio Cavalry under the command of Lieutenant Joseph A.O. Yeoman (USA) who were actually Union Army spies disguised as Confederate cavalry who had been secretly moving with President Davis and his escort party. *(Yeoman and his men later applied for and received a portion of the reward money for the capture of President Davis. However, the fact that Davis and his entourage were able to flee almost to the Florida state line prior to their capture speaks volumes as to the poor espionage talents of Yeoman's unit.)*

That night, Gen. Breckinridge wrote to Davis: *"Nothing can be done with the bulk of this command. It has been with difficulty that anything has been kept in shape. I am having the silver paid to the troops and will, in any event, save the gold and have it brought forward in the morning, when I hope Judge* (Treasury Secretary John) *Reagan will take it. Many of the men have thrown away their arms. Most of them have resolved to... make terms. A few hundred men will move on and may be depended upon for the object we spoke of yesterday (i.e., escaping to Mexico)."*

Jefferson Davis, meanwhile, traveling separately from the Confederate Treasury and its escort, arrived in Washington, Georgia, in the late morning of May 3. While there, he conducted his final Cabinet meeting and issued his final orders of the Confederate government in the Dr. J.J. Robertson home (a.k.a. the Heard house), which also housed the aforementioned Bank of Georgia branch building on the Washington,

Georgia, town square. Among other directives, Davis instructed Major Raphael Moses (CSA) to carry $40,000.00 to Augusta for distribution to returning Confederate soldiers.

According to researcher Waters, "Not long after Davis and his small group departed Washington, Georgia, the wagon train transporting the Confederate Treasury arrived at Brigadier General Basil Duke's camp about a mile NNE from the Washington Public Square. Here, beneath the shade of an elm tree, Captain Micajah Clark (CSA), now the Acting Treasurer, dispensed what remained in the Treasury to various Cabinet members, officers, soldiers, naval personnel and others in the service of the Confederate government."

Those paid included:

$150.00 ($50.00 each to S. Brittain, Jas. Miller, and J.B. Macmurdo of the First Auditor's Office;

$300.00 to Captain Given Campbell (CSA) for payment to Presidential Scouts at Abbeville;

$300.00 to Lieutenant Bradford (CSA) for payment to the marines at Abbeville;

$520.00 to Captain Joseph M. Brown (CSA), acting quartermaster, for services of the Quartermaster's Department; $806.00 to Quartermaster General Alexander Robert Lawton (CSA) for payment of five commissioned officers and 26 men under Brigadier General L. York's Louisiana Brigade;

$1,000.00 to Major General John Breckinridge for transport to the trans-Mississippi Department;

$1,500.00 to John F. Wheliss (Captain Parker's paymaster) for payment of the midshipmen and other Naval scouts at Abbeville (about twenty days' pay each);

$2,000.00 to General Braxton

Bragg for transport to the trans-Mississippi Department;

$3,500.00 to Acting Secretary of the Treasury John H. Reagan (taken by Federals at Irwinville);

$6,040.00 ($1,510.00 each to Colonels William Preston Johnston, Francis Richard Lubbock, Charles E. Thorburn, and John Taylor Wood;

$40,000.00 (transported to Augusta, Georgia) to Major and Chief of Commissary Raphael Moses (CSA) to help paroled soldiers and stragglers who were passing through that town. (Davis's last order.);

$86,000.00 in gold and bullion was made to Lieutenant Commander James A. Semple (CSN). This last dispersal – the final payment made by Acting Treasurer Clark – has been associated with deceit since the day it was made. Semple, who apparently was a highly-trusted officer, had been directed to transport these funds to Charleston or Savannah to be shipped to Bermuda, Nassau or Liverpool, where they were to be deposited into an account in the name of the Confederate government.

Semple, however, apparently chose to disobey that order, and instead gave **$27,000.00** to Edward M. Tidball and **$25,000.00** to William F. Howell (Varina Davis's brother). Both were naval purchasing agents under Semple. The logic for their entitlement to these funds is unknown today. The remaining **$34,000.00** apparently was simply kept by Semple for his own personal use;

And finally, there was **$2,584.00** for which there was no accounting whatsoever, but which may simply have been consumed by miscellaneous expenses encountered enroute to Washington. In that day and time, however, even excessive travel expenses would have been impossibly-pressed to consume $2,584.00

for travel from Richmond, Virginia, to Washington, Georgia.

As is obvious from the detailed accounting above, virtually none of the funds from the Confederate Treasury actually "disappeared." Nevertheless, there were some dispersals – for instance the $86,000.00 assigned to Lieutenant Commander James A. Semple and the $35,000.00 supposedly sent ahead to a destination in Florida for President Jefferson Davis – which remain a mystery today. In all likelihood, those funds were simply taken contrary to directive and intended purposes and personally utilized by the individuals to whom they were entrusted during the turmoil and confusion of the last days of the Confederacy.

Davis's Final Acts

Many Confederate government documents and items of former value were ordered by Davis and his Cabinet to be destroyed prior to their departure from Washington. Confederate bonds, paper funds, and other documents were burned in front of the courthouse on the town square by Major Raphael Moses (CSA). These acts were witnessed by the Secretary of War John C. Breckinridge and the Postmaster General John H. Reagan.

Though, as explained above, Davis's original destination had been Texas, the growing cordon of Union troops and Federal authorities had forced the Confederate president to alter his route and flee instead toward Florida. Even as he had departed Richmond, Davis knew Georgia – with its heavy infusion of and occupation by Union Army troops – would be difficult, if not impossible, to cross without being captured.

Davis's last official act as President of the Confederacy had been to appoint

Washington, GA Depot (circa 1900) – Photographed some thirty-five years after the close of the U.S. Civil War, the depot at Washington, Georgia, was still standing and active. It was into and out of this train station that millions of dollars in gold and silver coinage were shipped in a desperate bid to prevent the Confederate Treasury and the funds from six Richmond, Virginia banks from falling into the hands of bounty hunters and pursuing Federal officials. (Photo courtesy of Mark Waters)

Capt. M.H. Clark (CSA) as Acting Treasurer of the Confederacy. After he had realized how undependable the cavalry unit "protecting" him actually had become (and indeed, after they had essentially mutinied), Davis had ordered that the troopers be released to proceed as they saw fit. It was either that, or jeopardize the safety of the funds remaining in the Confederate Treasury at that time. *(Author's Note: It quite likely was due to this peril for the Treasury demonstrated by the cavalry troops that Davis and his Cabinet ultimately decided to disperse the funds completely.)*

History has demonstrated that in times of war and national disaster, the trustworthiness of formerly loyal assistants often "falls by the wayside," as demonstrated by the Treasury funds

with which several trusted aides obviously absconded in those dark days of 1865. Once those funds were divided among Davis's Cabinet officers and trusted assistants such as James Allen Semple, no further record or mention of them has ever been discovered.

Composed of gold and silver coins, the $86,000.00 taken by Semple would, as described above, have been exceedingly heavy, requiring at minimum some type of horse or mule-drawn wagon(s) for transport. In other words, it would not have been a simple matter to secretly spirit these funds away, yet that is exactly what seems to have occurred – unless these funds were somehow hidden and later secretly retrieved (or not) by the absconders.

Interestingly, even though the pre-

The three separate trips in which the Confederate Treasury was desperately transported back and forth between various cities and Washington, Georgia, are depicted on this map. (Map courtesy of Mark Waters)

viously-described $2,584.00 – for which there is no accounting in the final reckoning of the Confederate Treasury – would be mere "pocket-change" to many individuals today, the coins themselves – if discovered today – would, again, be an almost priceless treasure for the aforementioned reasons.

The ultimate destination of the $27,000.00 and $25,000.00 and $34,000.00 (totaling $86,000.00 entrusted to Semple) which had been ear-marked for the "new" Confederacy remain – as stated – a mystery today. Perhaps Semple remained honorable in his actions and the funds remain in a hidden cache even today. There also was no final accounting for the ultimate disposition of the 16,000 to 18,000 pounds Sterling in Liverpool, England acceptances. Just as with the many other mysteries surrounding the old Confederacy during the closing days of the U.S. Civil War, the truth regarding these outstanding funds may never be known.

Davis directed Breckinridge to take command of the five cavalry brigades which had been riding with the party. He (Davis) went off separately with an escort of about 350 horsemen. Of these 350, Davis quickly discharged all but about ten devoted volunteers. Breckinridge continued southward, amazingly evading Federal patrols, and managing to escape to Florida, Cuba, Great Britain and ultimately Canada.

Meanwhile, Jefferson Davis was not as successful in his evasive efforts. His wagon-train composed of the ten Confederate cavalrymen remaining as his protective escort, three of his military aides, and various servants, teamsters, and secretaries continued southward out of Washington on May 5. For security purposes, Davis traveled separately a short distance away from the group accompanying him.

The deposed Confederate President crossed the Oconee River below the Dublin Ferry, then proceeded to the southeastern edge of the town of Dublin. He never entered the community, but remained at a site in the area now bounded on the north by Madison Street, east by Decatur Street, south by the railroad, and west by South Franklin Street.

The wagon train accompanying Davis pulled into Dublin late Sunday morning. In those days, Dublin was a bare village which had practically become a ghost-town during the war. The group continued on, ultimately making it as far as Irwinville in south Georgia before being intercepted and captured.

Virginia Banks' Gold

The hoard of Confederate Treasury gold is often confused with the assets of six state banks in Richmond, Virginia – the Bank of Virginia, the Bank of Richmond, the Bank of the Commonwealth, the Exchange Bank, the Farmer's Bank, and the Trader's Bank – which traveled in the same general vicinity of the Confederate Treasury. U.S. Court of Claims documents indicate the assets from these banks were valued at that time at $450,000.00 in gold specie which had been quietly transported out of Richmond and on to Washington (Georgia) simultaneously with the Confederate Treasury funds in the closing days of the war and deposited into the vault of Washington's Bank of Georgia Branch.

When Jefferson Davis departed Washington, Georgia, on May 5, officials with the banks of Virginia – apparently concerned with the security of the banks' funds – surprisingly attempted to ship those assets *back to what then was the totally-insecure and Federally-occupied Richmond.* Under any other circumstances, such an action would have been sheer financial suicide for the banks' funds, but at the helm of this wheeling and dealing was an individual by the name of Judge William W. Crump, president of the Bank of Virginia and Assistant Treasurer of the Confederacy.

Since he had realized he would be unable to "hide the Virginia banks' funds" from Federal authorities, Crump had hit upon a new strategy, that being to return to Virginia where he intended to "come clean" with Federal Provost authorities and plead his case as an innocent "civilian." In so-doing, the ingenious banker hoped to officially sever any association of the $450,000.00 with the Confederacy, and have it certified for what it actually was – private property. Had his idea worked out as planned, it would indeed have been a crackerjack scheme. There is, however, an old saying: *"Man makes plans. God laughs."*

Much of what actually transpired in this incident has been obscured down through the years in folktales, rumor and half-truths. At least two separate and distinct explanations for the actual location of the ultimate initial theft of the gold from the banks of Virginia have persevered for well over 158 years now (as of 2023).

One account maintains the treasure was transported successfully to the vicinity of the old Chennault plantation once owned by John Chennault approximately 17 miles northeast of Washington, Georgia, where it was plundered and partially stolen by thieves. The two-story Georgian mansion (circa 1853) at this plantation – which is still in existence (as of this writing in 2023) and private-ly-owned today – was constructed atop a prominence overlooking the crossroads of what today are State Highways 44 and 79.

Another more logical and well-doc-umented account (herewith) maintains that the group transporting the Rich-mond banks' gold made it as far as the home of Mrs. David M. (Susan) Moss, three miles from the Savannah River and approximately one mile beyond the Chennault plantation. Both accounts maintain the wagons with their golden treasure circled up in a horse lot for the night.

No matter which account one chooses to believe, the treasure definitely traveled toward this destination on May 24, 1865. Present-day GA Highway 44 which winds by the plantation mansion was the main thoroughfare – albeit little more than a dusty trail – between Wash-ington, Georgia, and what remained of the once-thriving river-port town of Pe-tersburg during Civil War days. It car-ried a steady stream of paroled Confed-erates heading for Washington and its rail spur which would carry them home to all parts of Georgia and Alabama. To a man, these troops were ragged, starv-ing, destitute, war-weary, and absolute-ly desperate.

Accompanying this treasure (which, as described above, was being shipped back to Virginia) was a group of smartly-dressed bankers selected by the aforementioned Judge William Crump. These wealthy businessmen from Rich-mond knew their credibility was at stake should they fail to return the gold specie to the banks from whom it had originat-ed. The treasure convoy was escorted by a squad of Federal cavalrymen acquired by the resourceful Crump, all of whom were headed to a military pontoon bridge across the Savannah River to the Abbeville, South Carolina, rail-head.

The assets which these men escort-ed – hundreds of thousands of dollars in gold coins – were packaged in wooden casks and heavy crates loaded into wag-ons, and were, understandably, a substan-tial burden for the draft animals pulling the wagons. The Abbeville, South Caro-lina-bound group hoped to soon be leav-ing that town by rail to return to the for-mer Confederate capitol of Richmond and the banks whose funds they were guarding and transporting.

A general sense of unease pervasive among these riders stemmed from their realization of what they suspected was a growing threat on the horizon which they had noticed. A party of Confed-erate renegades who obviously had been tipped off to the treasure were shadow-ing the slow-plodding wagons which had departed Washington that morn-ing. The entourage had hoped to make it to the relative safety of the military pontoon bridge across the Savannah by nightfall, but their unusually-slow rate of travel had delayed them, and they ulti-mately were forced to stop short of their destination to camp for the evening.

According to long-time Wash-ington, Georgia resident and historian Waters, instead of overnighting at the Chennault plantation as has been re-ported in some quarters, the group al-most certainly stopped instead at what was known as the Moss house. "Bank officials present at the time of the rob-bery remembered the site being the yard of 'William Moss,'"[3] said Waters. "This was most likely the home of Mrs. Da-vid M. (Susan) Moss, approximately one mile down the road beyond the Chen-nault home toward the Savannah Riv-er. It, coincidentally, was the same site where Confederate Secretary of War

John C. Breckinridge had earlier paid out $108,322.90 (in silver specie) of the Confederate Treasury from the parlor window to mutinying Confederate cavalry troops on the evening of May 2nd-3rd.

"It is hard to believe that even after sundown," Waters continued, "(intelligent) bank officials could confuse the Chennault house – which is columned and two-storied – with the Susan Moss house (no longer in existence) which was a simple (one-story) farmhouse with a porch."

The question of whether the gold convoy overnighted at the Chennault plantation or at the Moss home has been a matter of conjecture for many years. Whatever the circumstances, owner John Chennault was known to be an amiable and welcoming host during these terrible times who did not deny hospitality to the poor and desperate travelers and war-weary troops streaming daily down the dusty road beside his home.[4] His kindnesses, coupled with his residence quite near to the robbery site, would later unfortunately earn him several days of torture and imprisonment at the hands of a mad-man.

The 11-man squad of Federal cavalrymen escorting the wagons containing the gold undoubtedly knew their journey was a perilous one. History does not record the name of the sergeant commanding these troops, but he no doubt had been watching the cloud of dust from the renegades following the wagons, and ruing the day he had been near enough to be assigned as an escort to the bankers.

When the men had departed Washington earlier that day, the town had been filled – just as it had been for weeks – with ex-Confederate soldiers, most of them Kentucky and Tennessee

Wilkes Co. Courthouse (1880) – The 1817 courthouse (demolished in 1904) on the Washington, Georgia town square was photographed here in 1880. Some fifteen years earlier in 1865, in one of his last official executive actions, Confederate President Jefferson Davis instructed Major Raphael Moses (CSA) to burn Confederate bonds, paper funds, and other documents in front of this courthouse on the town square. These acts were witnessed by the Confederate Secretary of War John C. Breckinridge and the Postmaster General John H. Reagan. (Photo courtesy of Mark Waters)

cavalrymen, all of whom were battle-toughened men who had suffered long and hard, and who knew how to fight viciously. Judging from the appearance of the bankers and the military escort accompanying the obviously heavily-laden wagons, it would have been a simple matter for lawless renegades to deduce that the cargo was a valuable commodity had they not already been tipped off to that fact back in Washington. They had not wasted any time in planning their assault of the gold treasure train.

Theft of the VA Gold

The sergeant in charge of these men no doubt knew they would be "easy pickings" if they were attacked by a substantial number of determined outlaws. He, however, apparently was just as determined not to be caught flat-footed. Near sundown, he ordered the teamsters to drive the wagons into a fenced horse-lot and to draw them into a circle.

As explained above, whether this horse-lot was located at the Chennault plantation or the Moss farmhouse remains a matter of conjecture today. These two sites, nevertheless, were within approximately one mile of each other, and research has indicated the robbery site almost certainly was the Moss farm.

The cavalrymen, teamsters and the junior tellers bivouacked with the wagons in a defensive posture. The Federal pickets guarding the gold wagons no doubt nervously watched the flickering fires of the renegades in the distance through the trees as the moon rose that night.

Evening ultimately passed into early-morning. Whether the pickets were careless in their vigil, or merely fell asleep on their watch is unknown today. Whatever the circumstances, in the early morning hours, the troopers and bank tellers were suddenly and shockingly awakened by a tremendous tumult of countless hoof-beats, insanely-sounding screams and shouts of men, all punctuated by gunshots. The Federal troopers – completely overwhelmed in an instant according to reports – were horrified, and simply broke and ran.

The mounted attackers – spectral images and shadowy figures in the pale moonlight – steadily assaulted the wagons, jumping upon them and tearing into the casks of gold and silver coins and scooping them out by the double-handfuls into sacks and saddlebags. Images on foot teemed around the wagons like wolves upon a feast – hacking and slashing at the casks and crates of treasure they had discovered to their great delight – all done with no opposition whatsoever.

Cursing and shouting, the men reportedly fought amongst themselves for the booty. They stripped the coins from the heavy containments, and loaded them as quickly as possible into whatever they could be conveyed by mounted horses, cackling and screaming insanely in their obvious amazement at the riches. In the process, hundreds of the gold coins reportedly were scattered haphazardly across the ground in the darkness.

According to later testimony, *"they waded ankle-deep in gold and silver, filling their haversacks and pockets as they went. They tied bags of gold and silver to their saddles."*[5] And then, just as quickly as they had appeared, the hoard of thieves were gone – hooting, laughing, and screaming maniacally as they dashed into the concealment of the thick forest, undergrowth and darkness.

Totally aghast, the remaining junior tellers and bankers could only watch as the renegades departed into the nearby timber. The riders spurred and whipped their mounts up the roads and across the fields toward the river and the creek fords. Their lathered horses galloped to the jingle of silver and gold coins, many of which continued to be sprinkled across the countryside as they were jostled and tossed from the loose containers.

Despite the diabolical nature of this incident, not a single drop of blood was spilled. The Iowan troopers and the teamsters who had been assigned to transport and protect the gold were nowhere to be found. They reportedly did not put up any resistance whatsoever, and basically fled in terror in the face of the sheer overwhelming number of maniacal raiders. Where and when they (the Iowans) stopped running history does not record.[6]

With the first rays of early dawn,

Bank of Georgia Branch – Often referred to as "the Heard Building" by "post-war" writers and researchers, this home was actually owned by Dr. J.J. Robertson. The lower floor of this structure served as – strange as it may sound today – a Bank of Georgia branch in Washington. It was into this bank that Judge William W. Crump deposited nearly half a million dollars in gold coin (as valued in 1865) comprising the funds of six banks of Virginia. This building was also the site of the final Cabinet meeting of Jefferson Davis and what remained of the Confederate government in 1865. The "new" Wilkes County Courthouse was constructed upon this site following the Robertson House's/Heard Building's demolition in 1904. (Photo courtesy of Mary Willis Library, Washington, GA)

the Virginia bankers took stock of their losses. The horse-lot and the surrounding yard literally glittered in the morning sunlight with stray silver dollars and five- and twenty-dollar gold pieces, as did the road and fields into the distance.[7]

According to records, the bankers amazingly managed to collect more than $40,000.00 (in face value) in odd coins lying scattered about on the ground. Ex-Confederate Brig. Gen. Porter Alexander would later recover approximately $70,000.00 from a portion of the thieves who resided in the nearby Danburg community, bringing the total initial recovery to $110,000.00.

A later accounting would also determine that, in their rush to plunder,

the thieves had left behind an additional amount of the treasure untouched in the cases and casks in the wagons, and these funds would ultimately make it back to the banks in Richmond. This amount, however, was still far short of the original $450,000.00 treasure originally spirited out of Richmond in the evacuation.

Origin of the VA Gold

So. . . How did the $450,000.00 in gold and silver coins from the Virginia banks come to be crated up in wagons which ultimately were robbed and pillaged at a quiet Georgia backwater near Petersburg on the Savannah River? Why was it there? Who stole it?

The answers are rooted in the

Jefferson Davis – The Confederate president conducted the last meeting of the government of the Confederacy in Washington, Georgia. The Treasury had followed close behind Davis to Washington. These funds ultimately were taken to an isolated location outside the town and divided among Davis's Cabinet members, Army assistants, and other trusted advisors and staff. The group then disbanded and departed Washington, seeking to escape pursuing Union troops and bounty hunters. (Illustration courtesy of GA Dept. of Archives & History, Atlanta)

twilight days of the Confederate government. Strapped for cash and desperate for funds to revitalize a dying war effort, the Confederacy had turned to the private sector. On March 14, 1865, the Virginia State Legislature had authorized a loan of $300,000.00 in hard money to the Confederate leadership if it could somehow be properly collateralized – bankers as they are, being somewhat sticky about such matters. In order to accomplish this, the state of Virginia borrowed the funds in a loan which was to be secured by two million pounds of cotton held in various local warehouses.

With the collateral and loan approved, the banks which handled the state of Virginia's finances began scrambling to scrape up the necessary hard money (read: gold and silver specie) from smaller banks and private holdings. At the helm of this wheeling and dealing was the aforementioned Judge William W. Crump. Shrewd and competent, Crump made easy work of a hard job, but the ever-shifting winds of war soon made him regret his assumption of this task.[8]

By this point in the war, Richmond, Virginia, was under siege by the Union Army. *"It is just a matter of time,"* wrote Gen. Robert E. Lee (CSA) depressingly to Jefferson Davis.[9] Despite still-high hopes in some quarters as March waned, a gloomy reality soon began settling over the Confederate capital. With the city's fall imminent, the Confederate Congress had adjourned and fled – without finally authorizing surety (the two million pounds of cotton) for Virginia's loan.

As a result of all of the above, the deal for the collateral and hard cash for the Confederacy suddenly collapsed, leaving the Virginia bankers totally flustered – but flush with an amazing amount of hard currency they had collected from the state's banks. What were they to do? They were now suddenly in possession of hundreds of thousands of dollars in gold and silver, with their enemy – the Union Army – poised to sweep into their city at any moment, at which point the funds would be confiscated.

Crump knew the Confederate Treasury Department had plans to remove the *government's* specie and bullion reserves southward, so he made similar arrangements to spirit the Virginia banks' funds out via the same pack-train. It was either that, or sit idly by as Federal officials rode in and took the gold and silver as spoils of war, and he wasn't about to allow that to happen.

As Richmond was gradually being burned and looted, Crump and his hand-picked cadre of bankers gathered their new-found wealth – a sum amounting to approximately $450,000.00 – and smuggled it through the bedlam, loading it into the same railroad boxcar into which the Confederate Treasury funds had been loaded. How ironic that the very funds the Rebel government had so desperately needed a few months earlier were now traveling in concert on the same train with that government's Treasury, yet the gold was now essentially useless as the Confederacy collapsed around them.

Near midnight, the treasure train filled with the Confederate Treasury's and Virginia banks' funds creaked out of the dying city. Dawn would find a Union flag flying over the former capitol as the remnants of the Rebel government sought an escape southward through Georgia.

The Midshipmen

As previously explained, this train moving across southern Virginia with all this Confederate Treasury gold traveled under the authority and protection of the officers and midshipmen of the Confederate Naval Academy. Lieutenant William H. Parker, superintendent of the Confederate Naval Academy, ten officers of his faculty, and fifty of his midshipmen – cadets ranging in age from seventeen down to fourteen – had been assigned the task of arranging the logistics and protection for the funds.

These young guards probably never inspired Judge Crump with much confidence, but Parker's fledglings proved to be more than up to the task, providing the most reliable protection the banks' funds would ever have. They never wavered in their commitment or reliability.

Parker pushed his command steadily southward, staying well ahead of the Federal cavalry sweeps out to net the fleeing Jefferson Davis who was moving his refugee government along the same route. When the rail lines ran out in Chester, South Carolina, Parker and his staff switched the treasure to horse-drawn wagons and continued southward, utilizing whatever backroads were available for concealment. Davis and his advisors had also earlier transferred to horses but had taken a separate alternate route.

The lieutenant quickened his pace as rumors of what – and how much – he was carrying became more widely known. In order to make escape as difficult as possible for Davis and his Cabinet, U.S. President Andrew Johnson and federal authorities had been widely circulating information which announced the huge value of the Confederate Treasury accompanying Davis, and the fact that any captors of the Rebel president would be rewarded with a share of the gold.

"One hundred thousand dollars Reward in Gold will be paid to any person or persons who will apprehend and deliver JEFFERSON DAVIS to any of the military authorities of the United States," Johnson announced. *"Several millions of specie reported to be with him will become the property of the captors..."*

The farther south Davis and the Confederate Treasury traveled, the taller grew the tales in the telling of the golden hoard. This made Parker and his staff's task of successful transport of the Treasury doubly difficult, because he gradually had to fear not only the pursuing

Warthen Store (1913) – This structure may or may not have been in existence when Confederate President Jefferson Davis paused in Warthen on May 5, 1865, to purchase supplies as he fled federal forces who were in hot pursuit. (Photo courtesy of GA Dept of Archives & History, Atlanta, GA)

Federal troops, but the growing number of desperate renegades as well. He nevertheless remained confident – as he later noted in his memoirs – that if attacked by anyone, that *"we could give a good accounting of ourselves."*

Davis and his entourage, meanwhile, had traveled across South Carolina toward Georgia. He initially was destined for Texas. The Treasury was destined for the protection of a secure lock-up in Macon, Georgia, but Parker altered this route after learning that Federal troops were headed toward that objective. As an alternate destination, he chose the Confederate Depository in Augusta, Georgia, to secure the Treasury. Due to the ever-changing nature of the Federal drag-net in pursuit of Davis, however, the plans changed almost daily.

Crump, his bankers and the bank funds, accompanied by Parker and his Confederate Naval Academy midshipmen, reached Augusta on April 18. Upon arrival, Parker received instructions to disband his command, but realizing the desperate nature of the circumstances (since Augusta was also under imminent threat by that point from Union troops), he made the decision to disobey orders for the first time in his life, refusing to abandon his duty to guard the Treasury. This was just too much gold to leave unguarded.

Why the Confederate government cabinet officials believed they could simply dump the Confederate Treasury in Augusta and then somehow later retrieve it unopposed from Texas is unknown today. Suffice it to say that confusion reigned supreme in those dark days. Whatever the circumstances, Parker wasn't having any of the disbandment orders.

In the final analysis, after foregoing both Macon and Augusta (since both were about to be occupied by Union troops) as safe harbor for the Treasury, Parker, as detailed above, decided he had no choice but to retrace his route back northward in the hope of tracking down Davis and turning the Treasury over to his staff. As for Crump and the Virginia banks' treasure, he decided to remain – at least for the immediate future – in Augusta. This, however, would soon change as well.

Hiding the Gold

It wasn't long before Crump also reconsidered the plan of remaining in Augusta. He had discovered that officers of no less than twelve Tennessee banks were already hiding over $500,000.00 in specie in Augusta, and that they feared Federal officials already had them targeted. Crump immediately decided that Augusta therefore was far too dangerous for temporary concealment of the Virginia banks' $450,000.00 in gold. With his options becoming more limited by the hour, Crump found himself retracing his route with the funds back to Washington.

Avoiding the railroads this time, Crump and the bankers moved their trove once again through the back country, arriving in Washington on May 3. The small, remote town of 2,200 residents was the political and commercial center of a fairly wealthy farming district – but, unknown at the time to Crump, it also was a Union Army target.

The community itself had been little touched by the war. General William T. Sherman or the bummers who followed in his wake hadn't quite reached out that far.

The converging roads and the Georgia Railroad spur line made Washington a natural way-station for anyone bound for someplace else in an attempt to escape the war. In the full flower of spring and absent the destruction of the war, the hamlet offered memories of happier times to many of the war-weary Confederates passing through it.

Given his desperate situation, Crump can almost be excused for misjudging Washington's presumed virtues. Almost. If, however, he had carefully and systematically weighed the little town's assets and liabilities with his usual shrewd banker's eye, he almost certainly would not have found it to be so comforting a haven.

To begin with, Robert Toombs, the former Confederate Secretary of State, Brigadier General and all-around secessionist firebrand had been nursing his bruised ego in Washington – his hometown – for over two years. And Confederate Vice-President Alexander H. Stephens – though not fleeing arrest – was also ensconced in his home only nineteen miles away in Crawfordville. Both were top Federal targets of arrest.

Had he adequately sized-up the situation, Judge Crump would have figured both men as the liabilities for safety they represented. What's more, he ought easily to have reckoned that Washington's transportation hub circumstances would likely draw President Jefferson Davis through that vicinity as well, and virtually anyone should have deduced that Davis would have Federal hounds hot upon his trail.

As it happened, only a few hours after Crump and his party had stored their banks' gold in the Washington branch of the Bank of Georgia, Davis and what remained of his government rolled into town. Judge Crump requested a meeting with Davis to discuss his dilemma, but the president of the dying Confederacy had enough problems as it was. He had no interest whatsoever in taking on new ones from Crump, and therefore declined to meet with the banker.

Since the assassination of Lincoln, the Federal dragnet for Davis had been steadily tightening, and he knew he would have to lighten his load if he were to have any hope at all of escaping his pursuers. He had thus ordered what remained of the Confederate Treasury – which had caught up with him in Washington – to be divided among his Cabinet officers, trusted assistants and military attaches who then all rode off in different directions, planning to regroup in Texas.[10]

Federal Protection

Crump and his associate bankers now knew that Washington would shortly be overrun with Federals searching for Davis. And even before Davis had departed, Crump had learned still more disturbing news. Some of Davis's escort had mutinied and demanded part of the Treasury in payment of back wages. Now the whole countryside in Wilkes County and beyond was aware of the treasure-trove in town.[11] It was quickly becoming obvious to Crump that his problems were about to become too great to overcome.

On May 6, 1865, Federal cavalry entered Washington, Georgia, and seized any property with even a whiff of the Confederate government about it. The $450,000.00 in gold sitting in the Washington branch of the Bank of Georgia smelled fairly to high Heaven of the Confederacy.

On the advice of his host, Judge Garnett Andrews, Crump had decided to try his new strategy – that being to return to Virginia and plead his case that

the banks' funds were "private" funds, unassociated with the Confederacy. As explained above, had this idea borne fruit, it would have been ingenious, but instead, it resulted in disaster – at least on a partial scale.

On May 18, two more bank officers fresh from Virginia and the meeting with the Federal provost authorities reached Washington. They carried instructions from Judge Crump and official Federal *"Letters of Transit"* signed by Major General Marsena R. Patrick, the Federal Army's Provost Marshal General.

Against the longest of odds, Crump had actually seemingly accomplished his objective. The bankers would not only be allowed to transfer the specie back to Richmond to its rightful owners, they would be given a Federal military escort to guarantee safe delivery! What could have been better? Crump no doubt was feeling much more confident at this point, but, unknown to him, dark clouds were continuing to gather upon the horizon.

Happy to have their money back nevertheless, and eager to set off for Virginia, the bankers in Washington set out almost immediately. Though the mode of transport is uncertain, they quite likely had obtained mule or horse-drawn wagons – since all that weight could not be simply transported upon the backs of their horses – and at mid-morning on May 24, they embarked for the railhead at Abbeville, South Carolina, their problems seemingly diminishing by the hour.[12]

However, if the bankers had hoped to steal away unnoticed, their hopes had been in vain. Gold has a way of diminishing any possibility of secrecy almost from the get-go. It is extremely difficult to hide its existence, particularly if

Gold Coins Scattered – This artist's depiction of a Southern plantation mansion of the 1860s is quite similar to the mansion at Chenault Plantation outside Washington, Georgia. It was near this plantation that the robbery of the casks of gold and silver coins from the banks of Virginia occurred in 1865. (Engraving courtesy of GA Dept. of Archives & History, Atlanta, GA)

more than one person is involved with it. And that brings us full-circle, back to the Confederate renegades' attack and theft of the gold near Petersburg at a tiny burg known ironically as "Graball," Georgia.

Years after the gold had been looted that night by the former Confederate soldiers, Lewis Shepard, a Tennessean from Vaughn's brigade, recalled (without owning up to any involvement in the incident himself) what happened after word of the gold had spread:

"... Some of the officers and men of Vaughan's brigade became appraised that a train of specie was being carried North under Federal guard, and they jumped to the conclusion that it was the property of the Confederate government which the Federals had captured. They concluded that their .... hard service for the Confederacy entitled them to a share of this gold and silver provided they could ... (succeed) in securing it from the Federal guard. .. They organized an expedition with the view of capturing this money and followed the (wagon)-train until a favorable opportunity of attack presented itself...."[13]

Partial Gold Recovery

In the early afternoon of May 25, following the theft of the Virginia banks' gold, Brigadier General Edward Porter Alexander and a band of paroled Confederates cantered toward the site of the gold theft which, as explained above, was almost certainly the Moss home. Just as all the returning Confederate veterans, these men also were ragged, starving and destitute. Nevertheless, they, just as Gen. Alexander, were – for the most part – also very good and honorable men.

Following the trauma of the assault

and robbery of the gold, Alexander – due no doubt to his uncompromising honor – had either been recruited by the bankers, or had volunteered outright to help recover the stolen gold and silver. The brilliant 30-year-old engineer who had risen through the ranks to Confederate general, had returned to Washington barely three weeks earlier from the very painful surrender at Appomattox Courthouse in Virginia.

Alexander's remarkable knowledge and astute management of the artillery for Longstreet's Corps had made him one of the Confederacy's most respected soldiers, and a near-legend around his hometown. More importantly, his reputation for integrity and bravery was beyond reproach. If there was one man in the community who might carry weight with any raiders remaining in the area, it was Alexander.

The young general had gathered six members of his former Irwin Artillery company and had pushed on immediately for the site of the robbery, adding eight more recruits to his band as they passed through the Danburg community. Also along was Judge William M. Reese, a local magistrate, to provide any necessary warrants and official sanction if Alexander was required to make arrests and take back the loot by force. Reese, as a Confederate magistrate appointee, ironically had no legal authority any longer to issue any warrants or to be involved in any other legalities since the Confederate surrender, but he accompanied the group nonetheless.

More importantly, his reputation for integrity and bravery was beyond reproach.

"We came upon a party of guerrillas who had about $80,000.00 of the money in charge," Alexander recalled in an 1881 interview. "They said they did not know it was private property; believing it to belong to the Confederacy, they thought they were as much entitled to it as anyone else... but being convinced that it was private property, they were willing to surrender it."[14]

The fact that these desperate renegades were eventually willing to part company with $70,000.00 of their ill-gotten gains is amazing in itself, and a testament not only to the respect Alexander engendered among his neighbors, but also to the honor of the men who returned the gold. Men had regularly killed and been killed for far less money during good times prior to the 1860s, and this theft recovery was being attempted during some of the darkest most desperate days to date in the United States.

The initial confrontation between Alexander's men and the renegades took place with guns drawn, but luckily, no shooting occurred. Alexander could see other raiders gathering and watching from the shadows, and he shortly became certain there were too many others he could not see. He wanted the money, but not at the risk of serious injury or death of a number of his men. He was ready for an end to the conflict pervading the South.

Since he was badly out-numbered, Alexander soon came to the conclusion that any of the stolen gold which was not voluntarily surrendered would not be pursued. He simply had not anticipated the sheer number of outlaws with which he now was confronted. For the same reason, he knew it would be imprudent – if not downright foolhardy – to attempt to make any arrests for the theft. Besides, money or no money, Alexander had little taste for arresting Confederates – even guerrillas – who would ultimately face Federal martial law.

When he had collected all of the gold and silver that the men were willing to surrender, Alexander returned to Washington to report to Crump. After turning over the recovered gold, ex-Confederate Brigadier General Edward Porter Alexander returned to his ancestral home in Washington which still stands as of this writing (2024) on what today is Alexander Drive.

All told, the bankers had now – according to U.S. Court of Claims official records – recovered approximately $110,000.00 of the stolen funds. They also retained possession to a substantial amount of the funds in the casks and cases in the wagons which the thieves had never touched. Though this was far short of the original $450,000.00, Crump undoubtedly didn't feel quite as bad. Had he been able to see a bit into the future, however, he, no doubt, would have been crestfallen.

A Damned Yankee

Brigadier General Edward A. Wild was that sort of "damned Yankee" whose very name Southerners for three generations after the war couldn't hear uttered without feeling compelled to spit. A rabid abolitionist from Massachusetts,

Wild held a deep, burning hatred for all White Southerners, slave-holders or not.

He had lost an arm at the battle of South Mountain in Maryland, and the wound had fostered an addiction to laudanum (opium) that twisted Wild's already demented mind and constantly stoked the fires of his hatred to a white-hot heat. Wherever he served, Wild cut a swath of wanton destruction and cruelty against prisoners and civilians alike.

In Virginia in 1864, several random hangings of Confederate prisoners, with Wild personally acting as hangman, prompted his then commanding officer, Major General Benjamin F. Butler to write Secretary of War Stanton: *"I wish Wild were elsewhere. He has no common sense."*[15] The mild, almost passing nature of this criticism can only be interpreted as a ridiculously weak effort at a rebuke of an individual on the edge of madness who should, at the very least, have been relieved of his command (which eventually did occur).

Wild had come to Washington, Georgia, to investigate several lynchings, but when he learned of the looted treasure train, the lynchings suddenly were forgotten. He became fixated upon the massive gold cache and the capture of the raiders involved in its theft. The local population quickly began to experience Wild's cruel hand.

The twisted brigadier general began by arresting the Virginia bankers and confiscating their recently-recovered $110,000.00 in gold and silver, despite their legitimate and official *"Letters of Transit"* which had earlier

> *"I wish Wild were elsewhere. He has no common sense."*

Insane Abolitionist – Brigadier General Edward A. Wild was a Union Army officer from Massachusetts who held a deep, burning hatred for all White Southerners – slave-holders or not. He had lost an arm at Gettysburg, and the wound fostered an addiction to laudanum (opium) that exacerbated the descent of his already deeply-disturbed mental state into an obsession with the infliction of pain upon others. He used numerous methods of extreme torture on various residents who lived in the vicinity of the Moss home and Chenault plantation in an attempt to extract information about the stolen assets of the banks of Virginia. Though suffering from all manner of pain, the individuals whom Wild tortured knew absolutely nothing about the stolen assets. (Photo courtesy of Mark Waters)

been issued by Union Provost Marshal General Marsena R. Patrick. In his uncontrolled lust for violence, Wild filled the county jail and several temporary jails with suspects.[16]

It was out of these circumstances that one of the numerous mysteries involving the Richmond banks' gold originated. It is unknown today why the portion of the gold and silver coins left behind untouched in the wagons by the thieves (approximately $159,929.90 according to records) was returned to the

possession of the Richmond banks, and yet the $40,000.00 recovered from the thieves' droppings on the ground and the $70,000.00 recovered by Brig. Gen. Alexander were confiscated by Federal officials, but that apparently is what occurred. History does not record the exact circumstances of these two separate caches of funds, or the specific logistics involved in their apparent separate journeys.

For several weeks, the insane Gen. Wild and his men ravaged the countryside in Wilkes County in an effort to root out any of the stolen funds remaining in the hands of any renegades or guerrillas. When his efforts bore no fruit, he was emboldened to more brutal actions and cruelty.[17]

In mid-July, a former slave once owned by John Chennault made her way to Wild's headquarters, possibly seeking some type of vengeance against her former owner. She accused Chennault not only of taking part in the raid conducted by the thieves, but also of hiding a great deal of the loot himself. With the woman, Angelina, in tow as a guide, Wild led a detail to the Chennault plantation where he intended to initiate a painful interrogation.

Brutal Torture

When they arrived at the plantation, Wild's men opened accounts by killing the Chennault children's dog, shooting and stabbing the animal to death in front of the children. The men, laughing and jeering, ignored the desperate pleas from the weeping and distraught children as the poor animal was cruelly tortured and dispatched.

For his part, Wild arrested John Chennault and his brother, Dionysius, as well as John's 16-year-old son, Frank, and set about meticulously torturing the three in order to extract confessions and/or any information concerning the location of any hidden loot. The "prisoners" were taken to a nearby wood-lot, where the first punishments were meted out.

"They tied their hands behind them and then hung them up by their thumbs with their feet off the ground," explained Mary Ann Chennault Shumate in a later interview who was seventeen at the time of Wild's tortures. *"My brother and father said the pain was so great that after the first time they begged the Yankees to shoot them dead rather than suffer so a second time. . . . Their hands were so black and swollen that it was a long time before they could use them again."*[18]

According to later reports, the torture being administered by Wild and his men continued throughout the day and into the night. When torturing the Chennault family proved futile (since they were innocent and knew absolutely nothing about the stolen gold), Wild turned to torturing John Chennault's body servant, Tom, who ironically was Angelina's son (causing her, no doubt, to greatly regret her earlier false accusations).

Meanwhile, back inside the plantation house, more of Wild's men and Angelina heaped abuse upon the other Chennaults. *"Some of the soldiers came into the house cursing and abusing Ma and the children,"* Mary Ann Chennault Shumate continued. *"They took Ma and me and Aunt Deasy* [Ardesia (Mrs. Dionysius Chennault)] *and shut us up in a room and forced us to strip off our clothes while Angelina came in and searched us."*[19]

A number of the former Chennault slaves managed to spirit the younger children away to the neighbors or to their own cabins. In the end, all that Wild could seize were the Chennault women's few pieces of jewelry and $150.00 in coin the Chennault brothers had accumulated.

All six Chennaults – John, Dionysius, their wives, Mary Ann and Frank – ultimately were hauled to Washington and illegally imprisoned for no reason whatsoever. Amazingly, as cruel as were Wild's torturous tactics, they were nowhere near as criminal as the abuses in other quarters where rape, assault, theft, arson, and beatings were standard fare across north Georgia and Alabama in particular where lawlessness reigned.

The Chennaults remained in prison for several days while Judge Garnett Andrews of Washington traveled to Augusta to plead their case before Wild's superior, Major General John B. Steedman. Andrews, much respected in Washington though he had remained a staunch Unionist, was perhaps the only person in a position to offer the Chennaults any hope. He returned to Washington with Col. E.I. Drayton of Steedman's staff.

"Colonel Drayton behaved very gentlemanly and sent us back home, just as soon as he could finish investigating the case," Mary Shumate added. Drayton also returned the Chennaults' money and jewelry as well and freed the rest of Wild's prisoners, including the Virginia bankers, but unfortunately for Crump and the bankers, their gold apparently was too much of a temptation and Drayton refused to return it.[20]

Interestingly, though Wild was not present to witness it, his torture of the Chennaults ironically may actually have yielded the results he sought. *"A good many others* (who did have portions of the stolen gold and silver coins) *when they saw how things were going, they got uneasy and gave up their shares,"* Shumate said, *"and so the Yankees got a good deal of it back."*[21]

Thankfully, those remaining in Wilkes County were spared any further cruelties by the obviously unbalanced Brigadier General Wild. After learning of the extent of the attrocities meted by the mad general and his troops to innocent civilians, Major Gen. Steedman instructed that Wild be arrested at Augusta on July 31. He was sent to Washington, D.C. for formal inquiry shortly thereafter, subsequently removed from command by General Ulysses S. Grant, and mustered out of service on January 15, 1866.[22]

"Federal" Theft of Gold

Under orders from President Andrew Johnson, Maj. General Steedman transferred to Augusta, Georgia, the earlier-recovered $110,000.00 gold and silver funds from the banks of Richmond. It shortly thereafter was transferred from Augusta to United States Treasury officials in Washington, D.C. As a result of Judge Crump's agreement with Provost Marshal General Patrick (USA), the Virginia banks petitioned President Johnson and the Secretary of the Treasury to have these funds returned. Following a full investigation, Johnson, the Secretary of the Treasury, and the U.S. Attorney General all collectively held forth in March of 1867 that the specie was indeed private property and that the banks were entitled to have it returned.[23]

Secretary of War Stanton, however – as many powerful Federal officials continue practicing to this very day – had his own agenda, and simply refused to obey official law. He called upon his "Radical Republican" allies in Congress to alter the mandate handed down by Johnson, the Treasury and the attorney general, and on March 22, 1867, the U.S. House passed a resolution claiming the Virginia bankers' funds for the U.S. Treasury.

The U.S. Senate proved equally cooperative with Stanton, passing an identical resolution the following day. In both instances, the margin of votes clearly indicated to President Johnson that he would lose a fight to sustain a veto if he pressed the issue, so he signed the bill into law.[24]

The seizure of the Virginia bankers' specie fit a pattern Stanton had vigorously mandated in the war's waning days. On May 14, 1865, he had cabled Major General James H. Wilson (US) at Macon, Georgia, instructing him to move at once against Augusta and confiscate the assets of the various Tennessee banks known to be on deposit in that town.

After that, any funds to which a Unionist Tennessean could establish claim were returned to that individual, but those funds of any other Southern residents or commercial businesses were simply deposited into the U.S. Treasury. This pattern was played out all over the old Confederacy. It was inarguably outright theft, and served to emphasize the hypocrisy of politics, but the funds were considered "spoils of war," and there simply was no way to fight it.[25]

It was for this and many other reasons that the deep wounds of the U.S. Civil War were so painfully slow in healing, causing unimaginably cruel suffering felt in many quarters until the 1890s. Outrageous taxation on Southern properties and the denial of legally-elected representatives in the U.S. Congress, caused untold numbers of families to lose all they owned, creating beggars by the thousands.

The legal fight over the funds from the Virginia banks didn't end with the acts of Congress. Lawsuits ground on for twenty-six years as first the banks, and then their receivers, brought claim after claim for the return of the funds. Finally, on June 22, 1893 – almost 30 years after their theft by the Federal government – the suits were settled when the U.S. Court of Claims ruled that the receivers of the Bank of Virginia were entitled to recover a grand total of $16,987.88.[26]

In the end, though a large portion of the Virginia banks' gold assets were permanently confiscated by the U.S. Federal government as "spoils of war," and another large portion was stolen by thieves, some of the gold – as described above – nevertheless did make it back to Richmond intact. These funds, as explained below, amounted to "approximately" $159,929.90. So how much of this tremendous treasure is still actually a mystery today?

A Legend for the Ages

Almost from the moment the din of the shouting raiders and their pounding horses' hooves died away, the tales of "lost treasure" began growing thick as the cotton which once graced the fields and vales of the Wilkes County countryside. So, . . . How much of the gold and silver specie from the banks of Virginia funds – which originally totaled approximately $450,000.00 – was actually lost to and never recovered from the thieves who attacked the wagon-train that fateful night? That information is sketchy at best today, but an approximation, according to researcher/historian Marshall Waters is as follows:

"IF $450,000.00 was the total original amount being transported by the bankers when they fled Richmond – and this figure might not be totally accurate," says Waters – "the Wilkes County thieves who attacked the treasure train that night definitely did NOT leave with the entire $450,000.00 (or whatever the exact sum may have been).

"According to the Virginia bankers'

Courageous Leader – Brig. Gen. Edward Porter Alexander, a native of Wilkes County and noted artillerist with Confederate Gen. James Longstreet's army, was instrumental in the recovery of a portion of the tens of thousands of dollars in gold coins from the banks of Richmond which had been stolen by thieves. (Photo courtesy of Mark Waters)

records of the incident (as explained above)," Waters continues, "approximately $40,000.00-worth of the coins were left scattered upon the ground at the robbery site. Records at the U.S. Court of Claims also indicate that $159,929.90 was later taken to the railhead at Abbeville then on to Richmond, so one must assume that those were the funds which were never even removed from the wagons that night by the bandits.

"Then there was Brig. Gen. Porter Alexander and his men who recovered approximately $70,000 from the thieves from the Danburg area who had participated in the robbery then returned their stolen funds. This $70,000.00, coupled with the approximately $40,000.00 picked up on the ground, totaled a little over $110,000.00 which was returned to the Bank of Georgia Branch in Washington (and later confiscated by the U.S. government).

"**If** one assumes the $159,929.90 supposedly taken to Abbeville, plus the

This pontoon ferry on the Oconee River was photographed circa 1914. It was via a conveyance just such as this forty-nine years earlier on May 6, 1865, at Ball's Ferry a short distance away, that Confederate President Jefferson Davis and several men in his escort crossed the Oconee, then proceeded to the southeastern edge of the town of Dublin, Georgia. (Photo courtesy of GA Dept. of Archives & History, Atlanta)

approximately $110,000.00 supposedly returned to the Bank of Georgia Branch in Washington (and later confiscated by Federal officials) are true and reasonably accurate figures, then this sum total is approximately $269,929.90," Waters adds. "And **if** $450,000.00 was the accurate amount originally in transit with the Virginia bankers, it then follows that there was approximately $180,000.00 taken by the thieves in Wilkes County that night for which there has never been any accounting whatsoever."

It, interestingly, is this $180,000.00 portion which left the most enduring legacy in the folklore of the Washington, Georgia, area with its now-renowned legend of the "lost gold of the Confederacy." Years later, right up to the present-day, local folklore continues to attribute the wealth of a local landowner or businessman in Washington or the near vicinity to *"that gold stolen back during the war."*[27]

Modern discoveries have added to the folklore. Young boys seining a creek for fish in recent years discovered several gold "Double-Eagles" in the creek waters – much to their delight. Were these lost by one of the wagons crossing the creek on that fateful evening, or were they among the hundreds of coins which tinkled from the filled saddlebags and haversacks upon the galloping horses as they fled the robbery that night?

Today, the now-historic (and legendary) Chennault mansion can still be seen by driving northeast out of Washington on GA 44, or by turning south onto GA 79 off GA 72 twelve miles east of Elberton. The mansion was recently restored and is privately owned as of this writing (2024). It is important to emphasize herewith that although some of the incident – particularly some of the tortures administered by Brigadier Gen. Wild (US) and his men – occurred at this plantation, research has indicated the actual theft of the banks of Richmond gold quite probably took place approximately one mile away at the Moss farmhouse.

Are there still coins sprinkled in the fields, or in the streams and upon the hillsides from that night so long ago – or perhaps even hidden away in a cave somewhere in the Wilkes County vicinity? Only one way to find out, but you better ask permission before you go traipsing illegally across private property in that area. The insane ghost of old Brig. Gen. Eddie Wild just might still be in the area!

(Grateful appreciation is expressed herewith to researchers Marshall P. Waters III, Ray Chandler and Robert S. Davis, Jr., who provided details regarding various segments of the mystery of the Confederate Treasury gold and the theft of the banks of Virginia gold near Chennault Plantation in Georgia's Wilkes County.)

Footnotes:

1/ Clark, Captain Micajah H. (CSA), *"The Last Days of the Confederate Treasury and What Became of the Specie," Southern Historical Society Papers* (1881), Vol. 9, No. 1, Page 545, reprinted, Broadfoot Publishing Company, Morningside Bookshop, Dayton, OH (1990)

2/ Parker, William Harwar, *Recollections of a Naval Officer, 1841-1865, p 379,* Charles Scribners' Sons, New York (1883)

3/ Davis, Robert Scott, *"The Georgia Odyssey of the Confederate Gold," Georgia Historical Quarterly,* Vol. LXXXVI, p 575, No. 4, Winter, (2002)

4/ Ashmore, Otis, *"The Story of the Virginia Bank Funds," Georgia Historical Quarterly,* p 179, (December, 1918), Ashmore cites letter from Mary Ann Chennault Shumate.

5/ Davis, Burke, *The Long Surrender,* p 185, Vintage Books, New York (1985)

6/ The Iowans presumably made their way back to the 22nd Iowa Infantry Regiment, which was enroute to Augusta at the time. However, a search of the official records turns up no report filed by Captain Abraham referring to the incident or the fate of the detail.

7/ Ibid, Davis, Burke, p 185

8/ Ibid, Ashmore, Otis, p 190

9/ Ibid, Davis, Burke, p 17

10/ Hanna, A.J., *Flight into Oblivion,* pp 88-93, Indiana University Press (1959), and Ibid, Davis, Burke, *The Long Surrender,* pp 123, 129-130.

11/ Ibid, Davis, Burke, pp 114-115.

12/ Ibid, p 184

13/ Willingham, Jr., Robert M., *No Jubilee: The Story of Confederate Wilkes County,* p 197, Wilkes Publishing Co., Washington, GA (1976)

14/ Ibid, Ashmore, Otis, pp 174-175

15/ Nolan, Dick, *The Damndest Yankee: Benjamin Franklin Butler,* pp 242-243, Presidio Press (1991)

16/ Andrews, Eliza Francis, *The War-time Journal of a Georgia Girl, 1864-1865,* Ardivan Press, Macon, Georgia, (1908); reprinted (1960)

17/ Ibid, Davis, Burke, pp 186-187

18/ Ibid, Ashmore, Otis, pp 180-181and Andrews, Eliza Francis, *The War-Time Journal of a Georgia Girl, 1864-1865,* Ardivan Press, Macon, Georgia (1908); reprinted (1960)

19/ Ibid, Ashmore, Otis, p 181

20/ Ibid, Ashmore, Otis, p 182

21/ Ibid, p 183

22/ Casstevens, Frances H., *Edward A. Wild and the African Brigade in the Civil War,* p 231, McFarland & Company, Inc., Jefferson, NC, (2003)

23/ Ibid, Ashmore, Otis, pp 186-188

24/ Ibid, pp 190-197

25/ *Official Records of the War of Rebellion, Series I, Volume 49, Part II* (Correspondence), p 799. General Wilson acknowledges cable from Stanton and discusses its contents.

26/ Ashmore, pp 196-197

27/ Ashmore, p 172

Supplemental Bibliographical References

1/ Amerson, Anne Dismukes, **Dahlonega, Georgia: Site of America's First Major Gold Rush** (2013), Chestatee Publications, Dahlonega, GA

2/ Andrews, Eliza Francis, **The War-Time Journal of a Georgia Girl, 1864-1865** (1908), Ardivan Press, Macon, GA

3/ Aycock, Roger, **Stand Watie Strong Leader in Times of War & Peace**, (1971), **Rome News-Tribune**

4/ Bartow County Genealogical Society, **Bartow County Heritage Book** (1995)

5/ Battey, George Magruder, **A History of Rome and Floyd County** (1922), Cherokee Publishing Company,

6/ Boyd, Kenneth W., **The Historical Markers of North Georgia** (1993), Cherokee Publishing Company, Atlanta, GA

7/ Cain, Andrew, **History of Lumpkin County, 1832-1932** (1979), The Reprint Company Publishers, Marietta, GA

8/ Casstevens, Frances H., **Edward A. Wild and the African Brigade in the Civil War** (2003), McFarland & Company, Inc., Jefferson, NC

9/ Clark, Captain Micajah H. (CSA), "The Last Days of the Confederate Treasury and What Became of the Specie" (1881), Southern Historical Society Papers, Volume 9, No. 1, Page 545, Broadfoot Publishing Company, Dayton, OH

10/ Coulter, E. Merton, **Auraria: The Story of a Georgia Gold Mining Town** (1956), UGA Press

11/ Cunningham, Frank, **General Stand Watie's Confederate Indians** (1998), University of Oklahoma Press, Norman, OK

12/ Dabney, Joseph E., **Mountain Spirits** (1974), Bright Mountain Books

13/ Davis, Burke, **The Long Surrender** (1985), Vintage Books, New York

14/ Davis, Donald E., **The Land of Ridge and Valley, A Photographic History of the Northwest Georgia Mountains**, (2000), Arcadia Publishing

15/ Davis, Robert Scott, Jr., "The Georgia Odyssey of the Confederate Gold" (2002), **Georgia Historical Quarterly, Vol. LXXXVI, p. 575, No. 4, Winter, 2002**

16/ Dickens, Jr., Roy, **Cherokee Pre-History** (1976), University of Tennessee Press, Knoxville, TN

17/ Dillman, Caroline M., **Days Gone By: Alpharetta and Georgia** (1992), Chattahoochee Press

18/ Dorsey, James E., **The History of Hall County, Georgia** (1991), Magnolia Press, Gainesville, GA

19/ Ehle, John, **The Trail of Tears** (1988), Anchor Books

20/ Farmer, William C., **Facets of Fannin: A History of Fannin County, Georgia** (1989), Curtis Media Corp.

21/ Foster, Jr., W.A., **Paulding County: Its People and Places** (1983), W.H. Wolfe Associates, Alpharetta, GA

22/ Franks, Kenny A., **Stand Watie and the Agony of the Cherokee Nation** (1979), Memphis State University Press, Memphis TN

23/ Furnas, J.C., **The Americans: A Social History of the United States, 1587-1914** (1969), G.P. Putnam's Sons, New York

24/ Garrett, Franklin and Rice, Bradley,

Atlanta Historic Society, *Atlanta History, A Journal of the South* (1980), Atlanta GA

25/ Glover, V., James Bolan; McIntyre, Joe; and Rebecca Nash Paden, *Marietta 1833-2000*, (1999), Arcadia Publishing, Mt. Pleasant, SC

26/ Gordon County Bicentennial Committee, *A Historical Tour of Gordon County Celebrating 1976* (1976) America's Bicentennial Year

27/ Hanna, A.J., *Flight into Oblivion* (1959), Indiana University Press, Bloomington, IN

28/ Head, Sylvia Gailey, *The Neighborhood Mint* (1986), Gold Rush Gallery

29/ Henderson, Charles K., *Polk County Persons and Things* (1897)

30/ Hicks, John D., *The Federal Union (Second Edition), A History of the United States to 1865* (1952), Houghton Mifflin Company / The Riverside Press Cambridge

31/ Jackson, III, Ralph Olin, *A North Georgia Journal of History, Vol. 1* (1989), Legacy Communications, Inc., Roswell, GA

32/ Jackson, III, Ralph Olin, *A North Georgia Journal of History, Vol. 2* (1991), Legacy Communications, Inc., Roswell, GA

33/ Jackson, III, Ralph Olin, *A North Georgia Journal of History, Vol. 3* (1995), Legacy Communications, Inc., Roswell, GA

34/ Jackson, III, Ralph Olin, *A North Georgia Journal of History, Vol. 4* (1999), Legacy Communications, Inc., Roswell, GA

35/ Jackson, III, Ralph Olin, *Moonshine, Murder & Mayhem in Georgia* (2003), Legacy Communications, Inc., Roswell, GA

36/ Jackson, III, Ralph Olin, *Mystery & History in Georgia, Volune I* (2023), Whippoorwill Publications, LLC, Roswell, Georgia.

37/ Jackson, III, Ralph Olin, *Tales of the Rails In Georgia* (2004), Legacy Communications, Inc., Roswell, GA

38/ Johnson, Larry G., *A History of the Polk County Missionary Baptist Association* (1977), Nashville, TN

39/ Kinney, Shirley Foster and James Paul, *Floyd County Confederates, Vol. VIII* (1992), SFK Genealogy, Rome, GA

40/ O'Kelley, Harold E., *Dahlonega's Blue Ridge Rangers in the Civil War* (1992), Georgia Printing Company

41/ Kloeppel, James E., *Georgia Snapshots* (1994), Adele Enterprises

42/ Kollock, John, *These Gentle Hills* (1976), Copple House Books

43/ Lesberg, Sandy, *A Picture of Crime*, (1976), Haddington House, pp 109-110

44/ *Lumpkin County Federal Census of 1834* (1834), United States Federal Government, Lumpkin County, Georgia

45/ Lyle, Katie Lecher, *Scalded to Death by the Steam* (1988), Algonquin Books

46/ McLoughlin, William G., *Cherokees and Missionaries, 1788-1839* (1984), Yale University Press, New Haven, CT

47/ McRay, Sybil, *A Pictorial History of Hall County* (1985), Taylor Publishing

48/ McRay, Sybil and James Dorsey, *Windows of Memory, The Hall County That Was* (1989) Chestatee Regional Library, Gainesville, GA

49/ Mooney, James, *Myths of the Cherokees and Sacred Formulas of the Cherokees* (1982), Charles & Randy Elder Booksellers

50/ Nolan, Dick, *The Damndest Yankee: Benjamin Franklin Butler* (1991), Presidio Press

51/ Parker, William Harwar, *Recollections of a Naval Officer, 1841-1865* (1883), Charles Scribners' Sons, New York

52/ Paulding County, *Paulding County Deeds Record Book X, p. 579-580*

53/ Reeve, Jewell B., *Climb The Hills of Gordon* (1979), Southern Historical Press, Easley, SC

54/ Sargent, Gordon, *The Heritage of Polk County, 1851-2000* (2000), Polk County Heritage Committee, Cedartown, GA

55/ Shadburn, Don L., *Cherokee Planters in Georgia, 1832-1838*, (1989), W. H. Wolfe Associates, Roswell, GA

56/ Shadburn, Don L., *Pioneer History of Forsyth County, Forsyth County Heritage Series, Vol. 1* (1981), W.H. Wolfe Associates, Roswell, GA

57/ Sherman, Gen. William T., *The Capture of Atlanta and the March to the Sea* (2007), Dover Publications, Inc., Mineola, New York

58/ Stanley, Lawrence L., *A Little History of Gilmer County* (1975)

59/ Tate, Luke, *History of Pickens County* (1987), The Reprint Company Publishers

60/ U.S. Post Offices, Polk (and Paulding) County, *U.S. Records, Microfilm Drawer 281, Box 32, Surveyor General Department*, Georgia Department of Archives & History, Atlanta, GA

61/ Whatley, George Fields, *"Cedartown's Big Spring"* (1978), *Georgia Life Magazine*, Spring, 1978

62/ Webb, J.A., *History of New Holland, GA* (1985)

63/ Wells II, Ridley, *Old Enough To Die* (1996), Hillsboro Press, Franklin, Tennessee

64/ Whitfield-Murray County Historical Society, *Murray County's Indian Heritage* (1987), W.H. Wolfe Associates

65/ Williams, David, *Georgia Gold Rush* (1993), University of South Carolina Press

66/ Williams, Harry T.; Current, Richard N.; and Freidel, Frank; *A History of the United States to 1876* (1959), Alfred A. Knopf, New York

67/ Willingham, Jr., Robert M., *No Jubilee: The Story of Confederate Wilkes County* (1976), Wilkes Publishing Company, Washington, GA

Name Index

A

Abbott, Belle K. 204, 205
Accardo, Tony 45
Adonis, Joe 45, 46, 55
Alderman, William "Ice Pick Willie" 45
Alexander, Arthur 72, 76
Alexander, Brig. Gen. Porter 383, 389-392, 395
Allen, Cyrus "Cy" 310
Allen, J.C. 243
Allen, William "Billy" 313, 314, 316-318, 321, 325, 326, 343, 345, 346, 349
Allred, Felix 216
Allred, Lemuel J. 122
Anderson, Benjamin F. "Doc" 168, 170, 171
Anderson, Benjamin Harrison 174
Anderson, Charles Martin 174
Anderson, Dave 108
Anderson, Donald 13, 14, 15, 17
Anderson, George (alias "Bill Miner") 139-151, 178-181
Anderson, Capt. George Whitfield "Whit" 100-108
Anderson, Grover 61
Anderson, Henry 168, 170, 171
Anderson, Henry Franklin 174
Anderson, Isaac 168
Anderson, Jimmy 101
Anderson, John 168
Anderson, Margaret 168
Anderson, Mary Georgia Ann 173
Anderson, Mary "Mollie" Rebecca Dilbeck 170, 172, 173, 176
Anderson, Mattie 174
Anderson, Maud Josephine 174
Anderson, Robert E. 108
Anderson, Rueben 100

Anderson, Susannah 101, 108
Anderson, Thomas Abraham 168, 173, 176, 177
Anderson, Thomas Jefferson "Jeff" 168-177
Anderson, Viola 174
Anderson, William Arthur "Clint" 174, 175
Anderson, William H. 168
Anderson, William M. 168
Anderson, William Martin 101, 102
Anderson, Woodrow 60-62
Andrews, Judge Garnett 388, 393
Andrews, James J. 172
Archer, Russell 13
Ash, Wallace 5, 6
Ash, William 5, 6
Ash women 6
Austin, Charles 345, 348
Axtell, A.E. 343

B

Bailey, Alvin 271
Bailey, Andrew 270
Bailey, Billy 270
Bailey, Clayton 272
Bailey, Ed 346, 348
Bailey, Minerva Owens 270
Bailey, Silas Clayton 270
Bailey, Warren 270, 271
Bailey, Will 270
Baker, Lena 237
Bandy, Mrs. B.J. 98, 99
Barclay, Polly 237
Barker, Harrison 123
Barnes, Ransom 85
Barrett, E.W. 79, 80
Barrow, Clyde 11
Bates, Lucinda 291
Bates, William 291

Battey, George Magruder 83, 260
Battey, Dr. Henry 79, 81
Bearden, Jackson 111
Beauregard, Gen. P.G.T. 105
Behan, Sheriff John 309
Bell, H.P. 244
Bell, Joe 198
Bell, Sarah ("Sallie") Carolina 129
Benjamin, Confed. Sec. of State Judah P. 370
Berry, M.A. 117
Biehn, Michael 310
Bingham, J.F. 111
Bird, Georgia 22
Blackburn, Lewis 92, 93
Blacker, U.S. Deputy Marshal Charles B. 116-123
Bolding, W.R. 66
Bonney, William "Billy the Kid" 304, 335
Booth, Howard T. 162
Borden, Lizzie 29
Boudinot, Elias 31, 126, 129, 130
Bowman, James L. 210
Box, Dr. J. Brent 135, 136
Boyette, Johnny 353
Bradford, Lt. (CSA) 375
Bragg, Gen. Braxton (CSA) 375, 376
Bramlet, Rachel 235
Bramlet, William 236
Brannon, John Jr. 85
Brannon, William R. 84, 85, 87, 88
Breckinridge, Confed. Sec. of War John C. 370, 374, 375, 376, 378, 381
Brewster, Fred 269
Brewster, Joseph Proctor Screven 268, 269
Brewster, Rev. V.A. 268, 269

Topic Index

www.ingramcontent.com/pod-product-compliance
Lightning Source LLC
Chambersburg PA
CBHW060852120626
46553CB00001B/55